INFORMATION TECHNOLOGY PROJECT MANAGEMENT

FIFTH EDITION

Providing Measurable Organizational Value

Jack T. Marchewka

WILEY

The fifth edition is dedicated to Beth, Bill, Tim, Kellie Ann, and Matt.

VICE PRESIDENT AND EXECUTIVE PUBLISHER   *Don Fowley*
EXECUTIVE EDITOR   *Beth Lang Golub*
EDITORIAL ASSISTANT   *Jayne Ziemba*
SPONSORING EDITOR   *Mary O'Sullivan*
PROJECT EDITOR   *Ellen Keohane*
MARKETING MANAGER   *Margaret Barrett*
MARKETING ASSISTANT   *Elisa Wong*
SENIOR PRODUCT DESIGNER   *Lydia Cheng*
ASSOCIATE EDITOR   *Christina Volpe*
ASSOCIATE PRODUCTION MANAGER   *Joyce Poh*
PRODUCTION EDITOR   *Wanqian Ye*
INTERIOR DESIGN   *Kristine Carney*
COVER DESIGNER   *Wendy Lai*

This book was set in 10/12 Times Roman by Laserwords Private Limited.

Founded in 1807, John Wiley & Sons, Inc. has been a valued source of knowledge and understanding for more than 200 years, helping people around the world meet their needs and fulfill their aspirations. Our company is built on a foundation of principles that include responsibility to the communities we serve and where we live and work. In 2008, we launched a Corporate Citizenship Initiative, a global effort to address the environmental, social, economic, and ethical challenges we face in our business. Among the issues we are addressing are carbon impact, paper specifications and procurement, ethical conduct within our business and among our vendors, and community and charitable support. For more information, please visit our website: www.wiley.com/go/citizenship.

Evaluation copies are provided to qualified academics and professionals for review purposes only, for use in their courses during the next academic year. These copies are licensed and may not be sold or transferred to a third party. Upon completion of the review period, please return the evaluation copy to Wiley. Return instructions and a free of charge return mailing label are available at www.wiley.com/go/returnlabel. If you have chosen to adopt this textbook for use in your course, please accept this book as your complimentary desk copy. Outside of the United States, please contact your local sales representative.

Library of Congress Cataloging-in-Publication Data

Marchewka, Jack T.
    Information technology project management : providing measurable organizational value /
    Jack T. Marchewka. – Fifth edition.
        pages cm
    Includes bibliographical references and index.
    ISBN 978-1-118-91101-3 (paperback)
  1. Project management. 2. Information technology–Management. 3. Microsoft Project.
  4. Project management–Computer programs. I. Title.
    HD69.P75M367 2015
    004.068'4–dc23
                                2014031899

Printed in the United States of America

V10005041_110518

CONTENTS

PREFACE   xiii

ABOUT THE AUTHOR   xviii

CHAPTER 1   **The Nature of Information Technology Projects**   1

Introduction   1
What Is a Project?   2
Project Attributes   2
What Is Project Management?   4
Projects, Programs, and Portfolios   4
Project Management and Information Technology   5
The State of IT Project Management   7
Why Many Projects Fail   8
Improving the Likelihood of Success   10
The Purpose of this Book   12
Chapter Summary   12
Review Questions   13
Husky Air—Pilot Angels   14
Husky Air Assignment   15
The Martial Arts Academy—School Management System   16
Quick Thinking—Involving the User   19
Quick Thinking—FAA Nextgen Air-Traffic
   Control Project   20
Case Studies   20
Bibliography   23

CHAPTER 2   **Project Methodologies and Processes**   24

Introduction   24
The Project Life Cycle   25
The Project Management Body of Knowledge (PMBOK®)   27
Project Management Knowledge Areas   27
Project Processes   28
Project Management Process Groups   29

PRINCE2® 31
    PRINCE2® Processes 31
    PRINCE2® Themes 32
    PRINCE2® Principles 33
The Systems Development Life Cycle (SDLC) 34
    The PLC and the SDLC 35
    Implementing the SDLC 35
    Waterfall 36
    Agile Systems Development 38
    What Is Agile? 38
    Some Commonly Used Agile Methods 40
    Waterfall versus Agile? 41
Learning Cycles and Lessons Learned 42
Chapter Summary 46
Review Questions 48
Husky Air—Pilot Angels Assignment 50
Martial Arts Academy (MAA) Assignment 51
Quick Thinking—Learning from Failure 53
Quick Thinking—Doing Agile or Being Agile? 54
Case Studies 55
Bibliography 58

CHAPTER 3 Measurable Organizational Value and the Business Case 59

Introduction 59
Measurable Organizational Value (MOV) 60
    The MOV and Project Objectives 61
    Developing the MOV 62
The Business Case 67
    What Is a Business Case? 67
    Developing the Business Case 68
Project Selection and Approval 76
    The IT Project Selection Process 76
    The Project Selection Decision 76
Chapter Summary 77
Review Questions 77
Husky Air Assignment—Pilot Angels 78
*The Martial Arts Academy (MAA)—School Management
   System* 80
Quick Thinking—Measuring the Immeasurable 83
Quick Thinking—The Elevator Pitch 83
Case Studies 84
Bibliography 89

CHAPTER 4   Project Planning: The Project Infrastructure   91

Introduction   91

Project Governance   92

The Project Team   94

   The Project Manager   94

   The Project Team   95

The Organization and Project Planning   96

   The Functional Organization   96

   The Project Organization   99

   The Matrix Organization   100

Procuring External Project Resources   101

   Procurement Planning   102

   Contracts Between Sellers and Buyers   103

The Project Environment   105

The Project Charter   105

   What Should Be in a Project Charter?   106

   Project Identification   106

   Project Stakeholders   107

   Project Description   107

   Measurable Organizational Value (MOV)   107

   Project Scope   107

   Project Schedule   107

   Project Budget   108

   Quality Standards   108

   Resources   108

   Assumptions and Risks   108

   Project Administration   108

   Acceptance and Approval   109

   References   109

   Terminology   109

Chapter Summary   110

Review Questions   111

Husky Air Assignment—Pilot Angels   112

*The Martial Arts Academy (MAA)—School Management
   System*   113

Quick Thinking—The Project Sponsor   114

Quick Thinking—Projects as Social Networks   114

Case Studies   115

Bibliography   119

CHAPTER 5   Project Planning: Scope and the Work Breakdown Structure 120

Introduction 120

The Triple Constraint 121

Defining and Managing Project Scope 122

Plan Scope Management 123

Collect Requirements 123

Define Scope 123

The Scope Boundary 123

The Statement of Work (SOW) 124

The Scope Statement 124

Project-Oriented Scope 125

Product-Oriented Scope 125

Validate Scope 128

Control Scope 128

Scope Change Control Procedures 129

The Work Breakdown Structure (WBS) 130

Work Packages 131

Deliverables and Milestones 131

Developing the WBS 132

Project Estimation 134

Guesstimating 134

Delphi Technique 134

Time Boxing 135

Top-Down Estimating 135

Bottom-Up Estimating 136

Poker Planning 136

Chapter Summary 138

Review Questions 139

Husky Air Assignment—Pilot Angels 140

The Martial Arts Academy (MAA)—School Management System 141

Quick Thinking—Sinking a Project 142

Quick Thinking—More People = More Problems 143

Quick Thinking—Politics and Estimates 143

Case Studies 144

Bibliography 147

CHAPTER 6   Project Planning: The Schedule and Budget 149

Introduction 149

Developing the Project Schedule 151

Gantt Charts   **151**
Project Network Diagrams   **153**
Critical Chain Project Management (CCPM)   **157**

Project Management Software Tools   **159**
Developing the Project Budget   **161**
The Baseline Plan   **163**
The Kick-Off Meeting   **164**

Chapter Summary   **164**
Review Questions   **166**
Husky Air Assignment—Pilot Angels   **166**
*The Martial Arts Academy (MAA)—School Management
    System*   **167**
Quick Thinking—Planning versus the Plan   **168**
Quick Thinking—The Map is Not the Territory   **168**
Case Studies   **169**
Bibliography   **172**

CHAPTER 7   Managing Project Risk   173

Introduction   **173**
Create a Risk Plan   **176**
Identify Risks   **176**
A Project Risk Identification Framework   **176**
Applying the Project Risk Identification Framework   **178**
Other Tools and Techniques   **179**
Analyze Risk   **182**
Qualitative Approaches   **183**
Quantitative Approaches   **186**
Discrete Probability Distributions   **186**
Continuous Probability Distributions   **186**
Develop Risk Strategies   **191**
Monitor and Control Risk   **193**
Respond and Evaluate Response to Risk   **193**

Chapter Summary   **194**
Review Questions   **196**
Husky Air Assignment—Pilot Angels   **197**
*The Martial Arts Academy (MAA)—School Management
    System*   **197**
Quick Thinking—Send in the Reserves   **198**
Quick Thinking—Risky Management   **199**
Case Studies   **200**
Bibliography   **204**

CHAPTER 8   **Managing Project Stakeholders and Communication 205**

Introduction 205
Stakeholder Analysis 206
  The Informal Organization 206
  Stakeholders 206
  Stakeholder Analysis 206
Monitoring and Controlling the Project 207
The Project Communications Plan 209
Project Metrics 211
  Burn-Down Chart 213
  Earned Value 213
  Analyzing Current Performance 216
  Forecasting Project Performance 218
Reporting Performance and Progress 222
Information Distribution 222
Chapter Summary 223
Review Questions 224
Husky Air Assignment—Pilot Angels 225
*The Martial Arts Academy (MAA)—School Management
  System 227*
Quick Thinking—Projects as Social Networks 228
Quick Thinking—Communication and Mentoring 229
Case Studies 230
Bibliography 233

CHAPTER 9   **Managing Project Quality 234**

Introduction 234
Quality Philosophies 237
  Craftsmanship 237
  Scientific Management 238
  The Total Quality Management (TQM) Gurus 238
Process Capability and Maturity 240
The Project Quality Management Plan 242
  Quality Philosophies and Principles 242
  Quality Standards, Processes, and Metrics 244
  Quality Assurance 245
  Quality Control 247
  Continuous Improvement: Learn, Mature, and Improve 251
Chapter Summary 251
Review Questions 252
Husky Air Assignment—Pilot Angels 253
*The Martial Arts Academy (MAA)—School Management
  System 253*

Quick Thinking—Why Do We Accept Low-Quality Software? **254**
Quick Thinking—OPM3® **254**
Case Studies **255**
Bibliography **259**

CHAPTER 10   **Leading the Project Team 260**

Introduction **260**
Project Leadership **261**
    Some Modern Approaches to Leadership **261**
    Leadership Styles **263**
    Emotional Intelligence **264**
Ethics and Leadership **265**
    Ethical Leadership **266**
    Some Common Ethical Dilemmas in Projects **268**
    Making Sound Ethical Decisions **269**
Teams and Leadership **270**
Multicultural Projects **272**
    The Challenges of International Projects **272**
    Understanding Diversity **273**
Chapter Summary **274**
Review Questions **275**
Husky Air—Pilot Angels **275**
*The Martial Arts Academy (MAA)—School Management
   System* **276**
Quick Thinking—Leadership and Listening **277**
Quick Thinking—Sitting Ducks **277**
Case Studies **278**
Bibliography **281**

CHAPTER 11   **Managing Organizational Change, Resistance, and
Conflict 282**

Introduction **282**
The Nature of Change **284**
    Change Has an Impact **284**
    Change Is a Process **285**
    Change Can Be Emotional **286**
The Change Management Plan **287**
    Assess Willingness, Readiness, and Ability to Change **287**
    Develop or Adopt a Strategy for Change **289**
    Rational-Empirical Approach **289**
    Normative-Reeducation Approach **290**
    Power-Coercive Approach **290**
    Environmental-Adaptive Approach **291**

Implement the Change Management Plan and Track Progress   291
Evaluate Experience and Develop Lessons Learned   292
Dealing with Resistance and Conflict   292
Resistance   292
Conflict   293
Chapter Summary   295
Review Questions   295
Husky Air Assignment—Pilot Angels   297
*The Martial Arts Academy (MAA)—School Management
System   298*
Quick Thinking—It's Not Easy Going Green   299
Quick Thinking—Cross-Functional and Multicultural Teams   299
Case Studies   300
Bibliography   305

CHAPTER 12   Project Completion   306

Introduction   306
Product Release or System Implementation   307
Direct Cutover   307
Parallel   308
Phased   308
Project Closure   310
Project Sponsor Acceptance   312
The Final Project Report   312
The Final Meeting and Presentation   313
Administrative Closure   313
Project Evaluation   314
Individual Performance Review   314
Project Close-Out (Postmortem) Review   315
Project Audit   316
Evaluating Project Success—The MOV   316
Chapter Summary   317
Review Questions   318
Husky Air Assignment—Pilot Angels   319
*The Martial Arts Academy (MAA)—School Management
System   319*
Quick Thinking—Killing a Project   320
Quick Thinking—The Post-Implementation Audit   320
Case Studies   321
Bibliography   324

**APPENDIX: An Introduction to Function Point Analysis (Available online at
www.wiley.com/college/marchewka)**

INDEX   325

PREFACE

Welcome to *Information Technology Project Management—Providing Measurable Organizational Value (5th Edition)*. This book was written to help you learn the processes, tools, techniques, and areas of knowledge needed to successfully manage information technology (IT) projects.

The idea of project management has been around for a long time. In fact, it was around before the great pyramids of Egypt were created. Today, project management has emerged as its own field, supported by a body of knowledge and research. Although still relatively new, the fields of management information systems (MIS) and software engineering have their own bodies of knowledge that include various tools, techniques, and methods supported by a continually growing base of research.

Unfortunately, the track record for IT projects has not been as successful as one might expect, although the situation appears to be improving. One reason for this improvement has been a greater focus on a project management approach to support the activities required to develop and deliver a product, service, or information system. Just as building a system is more than sitting down in front of a computer and writing code, project management is more than just creating fancy charts or diagrams using one of the more popular project management software packages.

We can, however, build a system that is a technical success but an organizational failure. Information systems—the products of IT projects—are planned organizational change. Information technology is an enabler for new products, services, and processes that can change existing relationships between an organization and its customers or suppliers, as well as among the people within the organization.

This change can represent a threat to many groups. Therefore, people may not always be receptive to a new IT solution regardless of how well it was built or whether cutting edge technology, tools, and techniques are used. On the other hand, people in an organization may rightfully resist an information system that does not function properly or meet their envisioned needs. Therefore, we must take an approach that does not consider the technical side over the organizational side or vice versa. Attention to both the technical and organizational sides of IT projects must be balanced in order to deliver a successful project.

APPROACH

In writing this book, I have tried to create a balance between concept and application. Many project management books tend to cover a broad set of topics with little practical application. Others tend to focus on the tools and techniques, but fall short in showing how everything ties together.

This book was written with the student in mind. Many years ago—more than I would care to admit—when I was a student, one of my instructors said that the problem with many textbooks was that they were written by professors for other professors. That statement stuck with me over the years. When I first began writing this text, I wanted to be sure that it was written with the student in mind.

Learning and understanding how to apply new concepts, tools, and techniques can be challenging enough without being made more complex by obscure writing. As you will find out, learning concepts is relatively easy when compared to putting them into good practice. This book is intended for both undergraduate and graduate students. While it has no specific prerequisites, you should have at least an introductory class in information systems or programming under your belt. You should find that the concepts of IT project management will complement courses in systems analysis and design.

Those of you who are undergraduates will not be thrust into the role of a project manager immediately after graduation. My goal is to help prepare you for the next several progressions of your career. For example, your first assignment may be to work on a project as a programmer or analyst.

The knowledge that you will gain from this text will give you a good idea of how your work fits into the big picture so that you can be a more valuable project team member.

More challenging and interesting assignments and opportunities for advancement will follow as you continue to gain more knowledge and experience. Eventually, this may lead to a leadership role where your knowledge and experience will be put to the optimal test.

On the other hand, you may have already acquired some experience and now find yourself in the role of a project manager. This text will provide you not only with the big picture but also with a foundation for applying directly the tools, processes, and methods to support the management and delivery of a successful IT project.

Most students who read this book will never have been on a real project. I have written this book based on a flexible methodology that attempts to bridge the questions: How do I get started? What do I do next? How do we know when we're finished? This methodology provides a structure for understanding how projects are initiated, conceptualized, planned, carried out, terminated, and evaluated. This methodology will take you through the different phases of the project life cycle and introduce the concepts and tools that are appropriate for each specific phase or stage of the project. In addition, you will find the methodology and central theme of this text is that projects should provide measurable value to organizations.

The text provides an integrated approach to project management. It incorporates the ten areas outlined in the Project Management Institute's Project Management Body of Knowledge (PMBOK®), as well as many of the themes and principles outlined in the PRINCE2® project methodology. The concepts associated with information systems management and software engineering when integrated with PMBOK® provide an important base of knowledge that builds a foundation for IT project management. This integration helps to distinguish IT projects from other types of projects such as construction or engineering.

The text also integrates a knowledge management approach. The area of knowledge management is an area of growing interest and development. Knowledge management is a systematic process for acquiring, creating, synthesizing, sharing, and using information, insights, and experiences to create business value. Here, the concept of learning cycles provides a unique approach for defining and creating new knowledge in terms of lessons learned. These lessons learned can be stored in a repository and made available throughout the organization. Best practices can be developed from the lessons learned and integrated or made a part of an organization's project methodology. Over time, the generic methodology may evolve and become a valuable asset to an organization as it becomes aligned with the organization's culture and business. In turn, this evolving process will provide the organization with increased capability and maturity that, hopefully, will increase the likelihood of successful projects.

CHAPTER OVERVIEWS

The material in each chapter provides a logical flow in terms of the phases and processes required to plan and manage a project. The text begins with an introduction to project management and why IT projects are organizational investments. Once a decision to approve and fund a project is made, the project must be planned at a detailed level to determine the schedule and budget. The planning and subsequent execution of the project's plan are supported by the project management and information technology bodies of knowledge.

- *Chapter 1: The Nature of Information Technology Projects* provides an introduction to what a project is and why projects must be viewed as organizational investments that must align with a chosen business strategy. In addition, this chapter discusses how the disciplines of information technology and project management have evolved together and have led to how we manage projects today.

- *Chapter 2: Project Methodologies and Processes* introduces the concepts of lifecycles, methodologies, and processes for managing and developing the project's product, service, or system. Overviews of the knowledge areas and processes associated with Project Management Body of Knowledge (PMBOK®), as well as the core principles, processes, and themes of the PRINCE2® methodology are provided. This chapter also describes the waterfall method and two common Agile approaches for developing the project's product or system. In addition, the concept of Learning Cycles is introduced and can be used throughout the end of chapter case assignments.

- *Chapter 3: Measurable Organizational Value and the Business Case* focuses on the processes, tools, and deliverables to conceptualize and start a project. Conceptualizing a project begins by developing a clear goal defined as the project's **measurable organizational value** (MOV). The MOV provides a clear understanding of the project's purpose and is the foundation for writing the business case. In addition to learning how to prepare a business case, students are provided with an understanding of how projects are often selected among other competing projects.

- *Chapter 4: Project Planning: The Project Infrastructure* focuses on defining the infrastructure required to support and plan the project. This includes governance of the project, selection of the project team, the acquisition of internal and external resources, and procurement contracts that are summarized in the next project deliverable called the project charter.

- *Chapter 5: Project Planning: Scope and the Work Breakdown Structure* describes the relationship among scope, schedule, and budget. It introduces a set of processes and tools for defining and managing the project and product deliverables. Students also learn how to develop a work breakdown structure (WBS) and several methods for estimating the work to be completed.

- *Chapter 6: Project Planning: The Schedule and Budget* introduces several project management tools, including Gantt charts, activity on the node (AON), critical path analysis, program evaluation and review technique (PERT), and precedence diagramming, that aid in the development of the project schedule. A budget can then be developed based upon the activities defined in the WBS and the resources defined in the project infrastructure in order to develop the baseline project plan. In addition, the concept of critical chain project management (CCPM) is discussed.

- *Chapter 7: Managing Project Risk* describes the concept of risk management and introduces a framework for defining and understanding the integrative nature of risks associated with a project. Several qualitative and quantitative approaches and tools are introduced for analyzing and assessing risks so that appropriate risk strategies can be formulated.

- *Chapter 8: Managing Project Stakeholders and Communication* focuses on understanding the informal organization by developing a stakeholder analysis. This analysis provides the basis for creating a communication plan for reporting the project's progress to various project stakeholders. This chapter also introduces the concept of earned value and several common project metrics to monitor and control the project.

- *Chapter 9: Managing Project Quality* describes planning for quality, quality assurance, and quality control in order to improve the project's products and supporting processes continuously. This chapter also introduces several founders of the quality movement, as well as their philosophies that form an underlying basis for the project's quality plan. In addition, the quality management system called the capability maturity model and verification and validation activities are discussed.

- *Chapter 10: Leading the Project Team* focuses on project leadership and two important related components—ethics and development of the project team. This chapter also discusses some common ethical dilemmas that may be encountered on projects and a process is introduced for making sound ethical decisions. Moreover, several challenges and issues associated with managing multicultural projects are discussed as more organizations attempt to diversify their workforce or conduct business across the globe.

- *Chapter 11: Managing Organizational Change, Resistance, and Conflict* describes the nature and impact of change associated with the delivery of a new product or system on the people within an organization. Several organizational change theories are introduced so that a change management plan can be formulated and executed in order to ease the transition from the current system to the system that will be implemented.
- *Chapter 12: Project Completion* focuses on three important areas necessary for project completion: project implementation, closure, and evaluation
- *Appendix: An Introduction to Function Point Analysis* provides a more detailed discussion on counting function points and is provided online at www.wiley.com/college/marchewka.

WHAT'S NEW IN THE FIFTH EDITION

- The new edition has been updated to reflect changes from the latest version of *A Guide to the Project Management Body of Knowledge (PMBOK Guide)*, 2013.
- CHAPTER 2 PROJECT METHODOLOGIES AND PROCESSES was completely re-written.
- CHAPTER 8: MANAGING PROJECT STAKEHOLDERS AND COMMUNICATION combines two chapters from the previous edition.
- The author has also added an overview of PRINCE2® Methodology.
- The discussion of an Agile approach to product/system development has been expanded.
- Integration of learning cycles has been added to end-of-chapter assignments.
- The discussion (including examples) of measurable organizational value (MOV) has been expanded.
- Content on project governance and its role in project management has been added to the text.
- CHAPTER 4: PROJECT PLANNING: THE PROJECT INFRASTRUCTURE now integrates procurement contracts.
- There is an expanded discussion on the relationship among scope, schedule, and budget—the triple constraint.
- A relatively new Agile estimation technique called Poker Planning has been added to the text.
- Content throughout the book has been streamlined and reorganized so that it is now 12 chapters instead of 14.

ORGANIZATION AND SUPPORT

Instructor Resources (go to www.wiley.com/college/marchewka)

Instructor's Manual
This manual contains detailed solutions to questions in the textbook.

Test Bank
Test your students' comprehension with this digital collection of true/false, multiple-choice, short answer, and essay questions.

Lecture Presentation Slides
These PowerPoint™ presentations contain a combination of key concepts allowing instructors to illustrate important topics with images and figures from the textbook.

Husky Air Case Sample Solutions

Solutions are provided to this integrated case study that provides students with the opportunity to work as a project team and apply the concepts presented in each chapter.

Student Resources

Microsoft Project Tutorials

The author has provided a set of online-only Microsoft Project tutorials at www.wiley.com/go/ marchewka/msprojecttutorial. Using these tutorials, students can learn some basic skills that will help them create a work breakdown structure using Microsoft Project.

Project Management Software

Students can download a 60-day trial of Microsoft Project Professional 2013 from the following web-site: http://www.microsoft.com/en-us/evalcenter/evaluate-project-professional-2013. Note that Microsoft has changed its policy and no longer offers the 120-day trial previously available.

Another option now available to education institutions adopting this Wiley title is a free introductory 3-year membership for DreamSpark Premium. DreamSpark Premium is designed to provide the easiest and most inexpensive way for academic departments to make the latest Microsoft software available in labs, classrooms, and on student's and instructor's PCs. Microsoft Project software is available through this Wiley and Microsoft publishing partnership, free of charge with the adoption of any qualified Wiley title. Each copy of Microsoft Project is the full version of the software, with no time limitation, and can be used indefinitely for educational purposes. Contact your Wiley sales representative for details. For more information about the DreamSpark Premium program, contact drmspkna@Microsoft.com.

ACKNOWLEDGMENTS

I would like to thank Beth Lang Golub, Ellen Keohane, Sangeetha Parthasarathy, and Mary O'Sullivan for all their help in writing this 5th edition. Also, I would like to thank the following reviewers for their valuable insight, comments, and suggestions.

Rajeev Agrawal, North Carolina A&T State University

David Bantz, University of Southern Maine

Phyllis Chasser, Nova Southeastern University

Barbara Cullis, University of Delaware

Robert Fredericks, Drexel University

Valarie Griep, University of Minnesota

Mark Kwandrans, State University of New York at Buffalo

Paul Licker, Oakland University

Miriam Masullo, University of Maryland University College

Toru Sakaguchi, Northern Kentucky University

Jeanne Sawyer, San Jose State University

Patricia Shamamy, Lawrence Technological University

Gerhard Steinke, Seattle Pacific University

Jeremy St. John, Texas A&M University Commerce

ABOUT THE AUTHOR

Jack T. Marchewka is a professor of Management Information Systems at Northern Illinois University. He received his Ph.D. from Georgia State University's department of Computer Information Systems and was a former faculty member at Kennesaw State University. Prior to entering academia, Dr. Marchewka was a vice president of MIS for a healthcare company in Atlanta, Georgia.

Dr. Marchewka has taught a number of courses at both the undergraduate and graduate levels and has been a guest lecturer at the Rotterdam School of Management at Erasmus University in the Netherlands and the University of Bordeaux in France. His current research primarily focuses on IT project management, and his articles have appeared in such journals as *Information Resources Management Journal, Information Technology and People, Journal of International Technology and Information Management, Communications of the IIMA,* and *Information Management.*

He is currently a board member and fellow of the International Information Management Association, where he has served as program chair, conference chair, and past president.

Dr. Marchewka was also editor of the *Communications of the IIMA.*

Jack Marchewka is also a black belt in Kajukenbo and an instrument-rated commercial pilot who enjoys his family, karate, fishing, playing guitar, good BBQ, riding his motorcycle, and a good laugh.

The Nature of Information Technology Projects

CHAPTER OBJECTIVES

Chapter 1 provides an overview of information technology project management (ITPM). After studying this chapter, you should be able to:

- Understand why information technology (IT) projects are organizational investments.
- Understand why projects are planned organizational change and why they must align with an organization's business strategy.
- Define what a project is and describe the attributes of a project.
- Define the discipline called project management.
- Understand the relationship among project portfolios, programs, and projects.
- Understand how the disciplines of information technology and project management have evolved together and have led to how we manage projects today.
- Understand the current state of IT project management.
- Understand why some projects fail and how to improve the likelihood of success.

INTRODUCTION

Information technology (IT) projects are organizational investments. When an organization builds or implements a new IT-based product, service, or solution, it commits time, money, and resources to the project with an expectation of receiving something of value in return. Just as an investor considers the expected return and risk of a financial opportunity, an organization must weigh the expected costs, benefits, and risks of a project in order to make an effective business decision. It is up to the project manager and project team to deliver that value to the organization.

Projects play an important role in organizations and can have a major impact. Business strategy supports the vision and mission of an organization's current or desired markets, products, and services. While an organization must have an effective business strategy to be successful, projects are the planned organizational changes or means for achieving a chosen strategy. More specifically, IT projects enable the integration of technology in new products, services, or processes that can change existing relationships between an organization and its customers or suppliers, as well as among the people within the organization. An IT-based product, service, or solution can be a technical success if it functions properly, but it can also be an organizational failure if it fails to meet the needs and expectations of the customer, client, or user group.

WHAT IS A PROJECT?

The Project Management Institute (PMI) is an organization that was founded in 1969 and has grown to become the leading nonprofit professional association in the area of project management. In addition, PMI establishes many project management standards and provides seminars, educational programs, and professional certifications that are recognized globally. It also maintains the *Guide to the Project Management Body of Knowledge* (PMBOK© Guide) that provides commonly used definitions for a **project** and a **project manager** (1).

> *A project is a temporary endeavor undertaken to create a unique product, service, or result. (p. 3)*

> *A project manager is the person assigned by the performing organization to lead the team that is responsible for achieving the project objectives. (p. 16)*

Project Attributes

Projects can be large or small, short or long in duration, or relatively cheap or expensive; however, all projects share some common attributes.

- *Time Frame*—Because a project is a temporary endeavor, it must have a definite beginning and end. Some projects must begin on a specific date, and the date of its completion must be estimated. On the other hand, some projects have an immovable date that defines when the project must be completed. In this case, it becomes necessary to work backwards to determine a date when the project should start. Regardless, a project ends when all the promised work is completed and the organization's expectations are met, or it can be terminated prematurely when the work or expectations cannot be met. While a project is temporary, the product, service, or system created by the project can have either a brief or lasting impact.

- *Purpose*—Projects are undertaken to accomplish something. A project must also create something unique. This could be a new product, service, system, or an enhancement to an existing product, service, or system. For IT projects, this could include engineering or building a custom solution or integrating and implementing an existing third party's product or system. Regardless, a project must have a clear goal that defines the value of the project to the organization. This is important for setting expectations, defining the work to be done, setting direction for the project team, and developing a schedule and budget. A clear (and measurable) project goal can be used after the project is completed to evaluate its overall success.

- *Ownership*—A project can have many *stakeholders* that include people, groups, or other organizations that have a vested interest in the project's success or failure. In many cases, the product, service, or system will be developed for stakeholders other than those involved directly with the project team. Projects undertaken within an organization support internal customers such as a high-level manager, often called a *sponsor*, a business unit, or a group of users, while external projects developed by third parties such as consultants or other IT-service providers support external customers, often called *clients*. At the completion of most projects, ownership of the product, service, or system is transferred from the project team to the customer, client, or user group.

- *Resources*—All projects require resources. Resources include time, money, people, facilities, and technology. Although resources provide a means for achieving the project's goal and completing the work, they can be a constraint as most organizational resources are limited. Subsequently, project resources must be managed and controlled to ensure a project achieves its anticipated organizational value to its internal or external customers.

- *Project Roles*—All projects require people with skill sets that include both technical and nontechnical (soft) skills. The technical skills required will be determined largely by the product, service, or system that is to be built or implemented. On the other hand, nontechnical or soft skills can be just as important to the success of the project. These skills focus more on interpersonal skills such as the ability to communicate not only with fellow team members, but also with users, customers, or the client. Based on the project and skills required, a project may include the following roles:
    - *Project Manager or Leader*—The project manager or team leader is responsible for ensuring that all the project management processes and processes associated with the creation of the product, service, or system are in place and carried out efficiently and effectively.
    - *Project Sponsor*—The project sponsor may be the client, customer, or high-level executive who plays the role of champion for the project by providing resources, making project-related decisions, giving direction, and publicly supporting the project when needed.
    - *Subject Matter Experts (SME)*—A subject matter expert may be a user or a person who has specific knowledge, expertise, or insight in a specific functional area needed to support the project. For example, if the organization wishes to develop a system to support tax decisions, having a tax expert either as part of the project team or available to the team to share his or her expertise can be more productive than having the technical people trying to learn tax accounting.
    - *Technical Experts (TE)*—Technical expertise is needed when engineering or building a product, service, or system. Technical experts may include database analysts, network specialists, engineers, programmers, graphic artists, and so forth.
- *Risks and Assumptions*—All projects include an element of risk, and some projects entail more risk than others. Risk can arise from many sources, both internal and external to the project. For example, **internal risks** may arise from the way the project work is estimated to cost or the time to be completed. Another internal risk could be a key member of the project team leaving in the middle of the project to take another job. **External risks**, on the other hand, could arise from dependencies on other contractors, project teams, or suppliers. **Assumptions** are different forms of risk that are introduced to the project as a result of forecasts or predictions. They are what we use to estimate schedule and budget. For example, a project manager may need to hire a programmer. While estimating the project's budget, the project manager may make an assumption that this programmer's salary will be $75,000 a year. If this assumption is too low and the programmer is hired for more than $75,000 a year, then the project's budget will be higher than what the project manager estimated and the project may run the risk of being over budget.
- *Interdependent Tasks*—The work to deliver a product, service, or system requires many interdependent tasks or activities. For example, a network cannot be installed until a server and other hardware is delivered, or important requirements cannot be incorporated into the design of a product or an application (app) unless a key customer or user is interviewed. Often the delay of one task can affect other subsequent, dependent tasks. As a result, the project's schedule may slip, and the project will not meet its planned deadline. In addition, projects can be characterized by **progressive elaboration** whereby the details of a project become clearer as more information becomes available. For example, the features and functionality of a new smartphone app may be defined at a high or an abstract level early on in the project but become defined in much greater detail later on as the project team and user/customer work more closely together during the design phase.
- *Organizational Change*—New products, services, or systems are planned organizational change. Change must be understood and managed because a project can alter how people

work or how they related to one another. Because not everyone likes or is in favor of change, the potential for resistance and conflict exists. This is where a new IT-based product or solution could end up being a technical success but an organizational failure. Subsequently, the potential value of the project may not be fully realized.

- *Organizational Environment*—Projects operate in an environment larger than the project itself. Organizations choose or select projects for a number of reasons, and the projects chosen can impact the organization (1). It is especially important for the project manager and team to understand the organization's culture, environment, politics, and structure. These organizational variables influence the selection, funding, and support of a project. The project team must understand the organizational variables and the political climate within the organization so that potential issues that could impede the project can be recognized and handled appropriately.

WHAT IS PROJECT MANAGEMENT?

A project is undertaken to create something new or unique, as well as to enhance an existing product, service, or system. The *Guide to the Project Management Body of Knowledge* (PMBOK© Guide) defines project management as (1).

> *Project management is the application of knowledge, skills, tools, and techniques to project activities to meet project requirements. (p. 5)*

Projects, Programs, and Portfolios

Organizations often fund more than one project at any given time. Some projects may be in the beginning stages, while others are somewhere in the middle or close to completion. Similar to the idea of a financial investment portfolio, organizations should have a **project portfolio** comprised of a collection of diverse projects. Just as a wise investor should not invest too heavily in any given financial instrument like a particular stock or fund, organizations should seek to balance their project portfolio with respect to risk, experience, and technology so that the project portfolio is balanced (2). In short, an organization may not want to take on too many large, risky projects. On the other hand, an organization may not want to have a portfolio of low-risk projects using soon-to-be obsolete technologies that cater only to a single business unit. A portfolio of projects should be managed collectively so as to align with the organization's strategy and overall plan to achieve competitive advantage.

Some projects within the portfolio may be independent and not directly related to one another. Conversely, some projects are managed as a **program** where the projects' activities are coordinated so that the benefits of the program are greater than the sum benefits of the individual projects (1). Therefore, projects that are part of a program have a common outcome or capability. While a project may not be part of a program, a program will include more than one project. For example, an organization may approve a project to move its existing data center to a new building. On its own, this could be an individual project. However, if the project to move the data center is part of a strategic plan to integrate a new supply chain system and customer support system, then a single project that includes moving the data center and development of two systems may be too risky. Instead of planning and managing the data center move, supply chain system, and customer support system as one large project, it may be wiser and saner to coordinate this collectively as a program of three interdependent projects. Each project would have its own project manager, team, budget, schedule, and so forth with a shared governance structure in place for resolving issues and conflicts and to ensure that each project aligns with the overall success of the program (1).

Project Management and Information Technology

Modern-day project management is often credited to the U.S. Navy's Polaris missile project undertaken in the early 1950s to deter potential Soviet nuclear aggression. The Polaris project was strategically important, complex, and risky, so the Navy needed to ensure it was managed well from concept through deployment. This new approach included a set of tools to manage projects and was viewed by many as a success. As a result, other organizations in various industries began to adopt this new approach as way to define, manage, and execute work with the hope of achieving similar success.

Today, project management is viewed as a discipline that addresses a wide variety of organizational opportunities and challenges. However, the field of project management has in many ways evolved in parallel with the field of information technology. According to Richard Nolan, the use of the computer in business from 1960 to 2000 has gone through a series of three dominant eras: the electronic data processing (EDP) era, the micro era, and the network era (3).

The *EDP era* began in the early 1960s and was characterized by the purchase of the first centralized mainframe or a minicomputer by large organizations. The IT projects during this era focused generally on automating various organizational transactions such as general accounting tasks, inventory management, and production scheduling. The manager of this technology resource was often called the data processing (DP) manager and usually reported to the head accounting or a financial manager. The goal of using technology was to improve efficiency and reduce costs by automating many of the manual or clerical tasks performed by people. The use of computer technology was similar to the ways that farmers or engineers applied steam engine technology to mechanize agriculture. The process remained relatively unchanged, while the means for realizing the process became more efficient. Subsequently, IT projects during this era were generally structured, so a structured, formalized approach similar to the one used on the Polaris project was effective. Because the requirements of a business process such as payroll were fairly stable, changing the requirements was not a major issue and large multiyear projects were common. Unfortunately, in many cases these legacy systems created information silos, as projects supported specific business functions that often employed different technology platforms, programming languages, and standards for data.

In the early 1980s, the IBM personal computer (PC) and its subsequent clones signaled the beginning of the *micro era*. However, the transition or integration from a centralized computer to the PC did not happen immediately or without conflict. The often uncontrolled proliferation of the PC in many organizations challenged the centralized control of many management information system (MIS) managers. For example, the first PCs cost less than $5,000, and many functional department managers had the authority to bypass the MIS manager and purchase these machines directly for their department. This often led to the rise of user-developed, independent systems that replicated data throughout the organization. Security, data integrity, maintenance, training, support, standards, and the sharing of data became a rightful concern. The organization often had an IT resource that was split between a centralized computer and a collection of decentralized user-managed PCs. The organization needed to regain control of its IT resource while using IT strategically.

Many organizations created a new position called the chief information officer (CIO) to expand the role of IT within the organization. While the DP manager often reported to the head accounting or financial manager, the CIO often reported to the chief executive officer (CEO). Therefore, IT increasingly became viewed as more than just a tool for automating low-level transactions and more of a tool for supporting the knowledge worker. Shoshana Zuboff (4) coined the term "*infomate*" to describe the role of computers in this era.

The computer no longer remained under the direct control of the IT function and its spread throughout the various levels of the organization made IT ubiquitous. IT projects had to take more of an organizational view so that policies, standards, and controls become a part of all systems in order for existing mainframe or minicomputer applications to coexist or integrate with a growing surge of PCs. Moreover, a project manager and team could no longer rely on stable business processes, requirements, or technology that would allow for longer project schedules; otherwise, they would face the risk of implementing an obsolete IT solution. Shorter project horizons that crossed functional lines became the norm, while software development methodologies attempted to shorten the development life cycle.

Meanwhile, in the late 1960s and early 1970s, a defense project called ARPANET allowed university researchers and scientists to share information with one another even in the event of a nuclear war. By the mid-1980s, this network of computers became known as the Internet and led to the *network era* that began around 1995. In the network era, IT projects focused primarily on the challenge of creating an IT infrastructure to support many business partners, strategic alliances, vendors, and customers. This started a digital convergence or the integration of data, voice, graphics, and video that allowed for innovative ways to deliver new products and services to customers worldwide. While micro-era projects tended to focus on an organization's internal network, the network era extended this network externally. Network-era projects not only faced the challenge of coordination and control, but also how to support a dynamic business strategy and new organizational structures. The IT project team needed to understand new and evolving technologies as well as the organization and its competitive environment. As witnessed by the rise and fall of many dot com businesses in the late 1990s, the benefits and risks of managing IT projects were much higher than in the first two eras. Project schedules and the time to develop IT solutions had to be shortened as many projects had to be completed in a few weeks or a few months.

However, the combination of a global network infrastructure and lowering of political barriers in the late 1990s and early 2000s led to a rise of *globalization*. Countries like India and China became connected to North America and Europe. According to Thomas L. Friedman, the world has become flatter so that it is possible for people and organizations to work with almost anyone in any place and at any time (5). Many organizations outsourced and offshored business processes, projects, and even entire business units. As a result of globalization, projects began to cross time zones as well as organizational and cultural boundaries. Instead of working and meeting at the same time and place, a virtual team with project members working in different places and time zones became common. Instead of relying on stable requirements, new project management approaches and development methodologies acknowledged that many product and system requirements cannot be defined upfront and, once defined, often change.

Today, IT projects support a wide range of organizational activities that range from maintaining existing (legacy) systems to developing innovative ideas that take advantage of emerging technologies like 3-D printing or cloud and mobile computing. IT projects can be relatively straightforward like upgrading a network or developing a simple web site, while large, expensive, and risky enterprise applications like ERP (enterprise resource planning) and CRM (customer relationship management) can support core business processes and activities throughout the organization. Moreover, social media and big data analytics are increasingly redefining the customer relationship and enhancing the customer experience. A number of companies hope that alternative reality or how people use technology in their everyday lives will become integrated into consumer products such as smartphones, smart watches, and smart glasses.

What does this mean for you? As a project manager or member of a project team you will be involved in projects that are more dynamic, more geographically dispersed, and more ethnically or culturally diverse than ever before. The risk and rewards will be greater than in the past. Therefore, a solid set of technical, nontechnical, and project management skills founded upon past experience and adapted to this new, dynamic environment will be needed to successfully manage IT projects.

In both economic good times and bad times, senior management will make a certain level of funding available for IT projects. The budgeted amount will depend on such things as the overall financial strength of the organization, the economy, the competitors' actions within the industry, and the organization's strategic plan. Regardless whether an organization's budget for IT projects shrinks or grows, the resources available for any given period will be relatively fixed. Quite often the total funding requests for proposed projects will be greater than the available budget. As a result, any project that receives funding will do so at the expense of another project. The competition for funding IT projects proposed by the various business units or departments within an organization will be especially keen when the budget is tight. Projects that do not receive any funding will either have to wait or fall by the wayside. Therefore, the decision to fund a specific project will always be an important management decision because it will have a major impact on the organization's performance.

The decision to fund or invest in an IT project should be based on the value that the completed project will provide the organization. Otherwise, what is the point of spending all that time, effort, and money? Although senior management must make the difficult decision as to which IT projects receive funding and which ones do not, others must plan and carry out the project work. Which situation is worse: successfully building and implementing a new product, service, or system that provides little or no value to the organization, or failing to roll out or implement a new product, service, or system that could have provided value to the organization but was developed or managed poorly? It's probably a moot point: In either situation everyone with a direct or an indirect interest in the project's success loses.

THE STATE OF IT PROJECT MANAGEMENT

Although IT is becoming more reliable, faster, and less expensive, the costs, complexity, and risks of managing IT projects continues to be a challenge for many organizations. There is no shortage of stories in the trade magazines about failed IT projects. Very often, these failures end up in lawsuits that cost people and organizations vast amounts of money, as well as damaged careers and estranged relationships (6).

Some recent examples of IT project failures include the cancelation of an ERP project that cost the U.S. Air Force more than $1 billion. The project was called the *Expeditionary Combat Support System* and was envisioned to replace more than 200 legacy systems. Although the project started in 2005, it was scrapped in 2012 after spiraling costs and the inability to create "any significant military capability." Only about 25 percent of the original features and functionality were developed, and an additional $1.1 billion would be needed to complete the project by 2020 (6).

In 2008, the beverage distributor Major Brands decided to replace a number of its 20-year-old application systems with a software package developed and sold by Epicor. According to the lawsuit, a contract was signed in September 2009 whereby Major Brands paid $500,000 to Epicor for software licenses and support with about $670,000 for implementation. Although Epicor assured Major Brands that its software system would be a good fit and that it would be up and running by the middle of 2011, issues associated with training, installation, and performance arose very early in the project. Major Brands spent an additional $100,000 to upgrade its servers, but the application system continued to perform well below acceptable performance targets. Epicor informed Major Brands that it would need to make major changes and upgrades to the existing software that would extend the project's schedule significantly. Although the suit was settled in April 2012, the terms of settlement were not disclosed (6).

Many people heard about the problems associated with the Healthcare.gov web site that was scheduled to launch October 1, 2013 to help many Americans purchase health insurance as part of the Affordable Care Act. While the project was in planning and development for three years after the initial law was passed, only about 30 percent of the users were able to sign up for health care (7). After a frenzied "tech surge" to fix the "glitches," the system was still experiencing problems by the end of December 2013. Although the contractor for the web site was initially awarded $93 million for the project, the final cost is estimated between $300 million and $500 million (8).

Unfortunately, the stories behind these three examples are nothing new. The truth is that the overall success rate for many large governmental and nongovernmental projects throughout the world is low (9). In fact, a great deal of research suggests that IT projects have and will continue to fail and experience challenges.

In 1995, the Standish Group drew attention to what many called the *software crisis* when it published a survey of 365 IT managers conducted in 1994. The study was called **CHAOS** and reported that only 16 percent of the application development projects were successful in terms of being completed on time and within budget. Moreover, about 31 percent of the projects were canceled before completion, while 53 percent were completed but over budget, over schedule, and did not meet original specifications. The average cost overrun for a medium-size company surveyed was about 182 percent of the original estimate, while the average schedule overrun was about 202 percent. That is, the results of the survey suggested that a medium-size project estimated to cost about $1 million and take a year to develop actually cost about $1.8 million, took just over two years to complete, and only included about 65 percent of the envisioned features and functions. Many took this to mean that IT project management was in a state of crisis, especially since 48 percent of the IT managers surveyed believed that there were more failures at the time than five or ten years earlier (10).

The original CHAOS study has been updated every two years and provides a valuable and interesting long-term, global study of IT project success and failure. The latest study in 2013 reports that 39 percent of the IT projects were classified as *successful*, while 43 percent were classified as *challenged*, and 18 percent as *failed* (11). Project success is defined as a project being completed on time, within budget, and including all of the features or requirements envisioned. A challenged project is defined as a project that is late, over budget, and having fewer features and functionality than envisioned, while a failed project is a project that was canceled before completion.

A poor success rate has been supported by other studies. For example, a 2007 study of 800 senior IT managers from the United Kingdom, United States, France, Germany, India, Japan, and Singapore conducted by Tata Consultancy Services reports dire results similar to the CHAOS Studies (12):

- 62 percent of the IT projects failed to meet their schedules
- 49 percent experienced budget overruns
- 47 percent experienced higher than expected maintenance costs
- 41 percent failed to deliver the expected business value and return on investment (ROI)

In addition, a 2012 study by McKinsey reports that, on average, a large IT project runs 45 percent over budget, 7 percent over the scheduled deadline, and delivers 56 percent less value than expected. Even more dire, is the statistic that 17 percent of IT projects perform so poorly that they threaten the very existence of the organization (13).

Why Many Projects Fail

One reason for the reported high failure rates in the various studies may be how "success" and "failure" are defined. For example, Robert Glass (14) asks, How should a project be classified if it is "functionally brilliant" but is over budget and over schedule by 10 percent? According to the CHAOS definition, this would be considered a failure, while in reality, it could be a success for the organization. However, no matter what value a project is envisioned to bring to an organization, a project that continues to surpass its budget and schedule will eventually exceed any potential or real value it can pass on to the organization.

All studies have strengths and weaknesses. More research over time and broader samples will allow us to better understand the state of IT project management. While we will never be able to achieve a 100 percent success rate for all projects, we should strive to understand why certain projects are successful and others are not. While some people may argue that the success rate for IT projects is getting better, there is still ample room for improvement.

The number of reasons why projects fail is pretty much unlimited. Generally, a project does not fail because of one single reason, but because of a whole host of problems, issues, and challenges that build upon one another. However, as illustrated in Figure 1.1, most reasons for project failure can be grouped into four categories: people, processes, technology, and organizational.

- *People*—People are the stakeholders of a project, and stakeholders can have varied roles and interest in the project's success or failure. The support of top management or a high-level executive consistently ranks as one of the most important criteria for project success (1). The support of upper management is critical in terms of acquiring and maintaining financial backing for the project. Visible support by senior management is also important in terms of emotional support

People	Processes	Technology	Organization
• Lack of Top Management Support • Ineffective User Involvement • Lack of Skills • Lack of Experience • Poor Communication • Poorly Defined Roles and Responsibilities • Lack of Accountability • Unrealistic Expectations • Conflicting Stakeholder Goals • Poor Decisions	• Poorly Defined Goals & Objectives • Poor Planning • Lack of Controls • Poorly Defined Requirements • Changing Requirements • Inadequate Testing • Project Management & Product Development Processes Nonexistent or Not Followed • Poor Execution	• Obsolete • Unproven • Incompatible	• Lack of Direction • Changing Priorities • Lack of Funding • Competition for Funding • Organizational Politics • Bureaucracy • Lack of Oversight • Poor Change Management

Figure 1.1 Examples of Why Projects Fail

and negotiation or resolution of organizational conflicts. Users can be thought of as the project's customer. Users are important project stakeholders that should be involved in important decisions because they may have vital knowledge of the business and processes not possessed by the more technical people. Working closely together, the users and developers can better understand the business opportunities and limitations of the technology. Ineffective user involvement can lead to missed opportunities, unrealistic expectations, or a lack of buy-in. Other people-related issues that contribute to project failure include poor communication, as well as not having the right people on the project team with respect to skills, experience, or decision-making ability. Often conflicts arise if stakeholders have competing goals or interests or if roles, responsibilities, and accountability are not well-defined.

■ *Processes*—This includes having a set of project management and product development processes. Project management processes define the project's goal and objectives and help to develop and carry out a realistic project plan. Product processes focus on the new product, process, or system to be designed, built, tested, and implemented. Processes that are not defined or followed can lead to poor quality in terms of a solution not providing the expected value or not meeting schedule, budget, or quality objectives. Often, requirements that are not properly defined lead to additional work or a product, process, or system that stakeholders did not ask for or do not need. In short, the project is poorly executed.

■ *Technology*—Only 3 percent of IT project failures can be attributed to technical challenges (15). However, projects run the risk of failure if a technology is obsolete, unproven, or incompatible with developing the project's product, process, or system. Choosing the right technology means having the right tool for the job and that the product, process, or system is not hindered by a technology that is not scalable, integrative, maintainable, or supported in the future.

■ *Organization*—Organizational issues can lead to project failure as well. A lack of clear direction in terms of strategy can allow an organization to fund the wrong project or overlook a potential winner. In a dynamic environment, changing requirements in terms of laws, the competition, or customer demands may create a moving target for the project's product, service, or system as the organization's priorities change. Funding can impact a project if business units within the organization compete for limited funds or if the organization suffers a financial downturn. Management can create its own problems because of a lack of oversight or through a bureaucracy of overly complex and unwavering rules and policies. Moreover, not having an organizational plan to prepare the stakeholders for the project's planned organizational change can lead to missed deadlines due to conflicts and resistance from stakeholders.

Improving the Likelihood of Success

How can we improve the chances for IT project success and avoid repeating past mistakes? Here are four approaches that will be focal points throughout this text.

- *A Value-Driven Approach*—Plain and simple: IT projects must provide value to the organization. Many people and organizations define project success in terms of the project being completed on time and within budget. While schedule and budget are important, they are not sufficient definitions of project success. For example, if an organization sets a mandate that a particular customer relationship management (CRM) package must be up and running within eight months and cost no more than $1 million to implement, would the project be considered unsuccessful if it required an extra day and an extra dollar to complete? You may think this is trivial, but at exactly what point, in terms of schedule or budget, does the project become unsuccessful? We can also turn things around and ask whether finishing a project early and under budget necessarily makes the project successful. Of course, any organization would like to spend less money and have its system delivered early, but what if the system does not perform as expected? More specifically, what value will the organization receive by spending six months and $1 million on this particular project? If IT projects are investments, what measurable value will it receive to offset the time, money, and opportunity cost of purchasing and implementing the CRM system? This value could come in terms of better customer service, more efficient business processes, lower costs, or expanded market share. Therefore, success should not be measured in terms of schedule or budget, but in terms of value. This will put less pressure on project stakeholders to set unrealistic schedules and budget, since the value of the project will be the true measure of success.

- *A Socio-Technical Approach*—In the past, organizations have attempted to improve the chances of IT project success by focusing on the tools, techniques, and methodologies of IT development. A purely technical approach, however, focuses attention on the technology. We can easily end up developing an application that no one asked for or needs. Applications to support electronic commerce, supply chain management, and integration require that at least equal attention be paid to the organizational side. The days of being good order takers are over. We can no longer be content with defining a set of user requirements, disappearing for several months, and then knocking on the user's door when it is time to deliver the new system. IT professionals must understand the business and be actively creative in applying the technology in ways that bring value to the organization. Similarly, the clients must become stakeholders in the project. This means actively seeking and encouraging their participation, involvement, and vision. The successful application of technology and the achievement of the project's goal must be an equal responsibility of the developers and users.

- *A Project-Management Approach*—One suggestion of the CHAOS studies has been the need for better project management. But, isn't building an information system a project? Haven't organizations used project management in the past? And aren't they using project management now? While many organizations have applied the principles and tools of project management to IT projects, many more—even today—build systems on an ad hoc basis. Success or failure of an IT project depends largely on who is, or is not, part of the project team. Applying project management principles and tools across the entire organization, however, should be part of a methodology—the step-by-step activities, processes, tools, quality standards, controls, and deliverables that are defined for the entire project. As a result, project success does not depend primarily on the team, but more on the set of mature, capable processes and infrastructure in place. A common set of tools and controls also provides a common language across projects and the ability to compare projects throughout the organization.

In addition, other reasons for project management to support IT projects include:

- *Resources*—When developing or purchasing an information system, all IT projects are capital projects that require cash and other organizational resources. Projects must be estimated accurately, and cost and schedules must be controlled effectively. Without the proper tools, techniques, methods, and controls in place, the project will drain or divert resources away from other projects and areas of the organization. Eventually, these uncontrolled costs could impact the financial stability of the organization.

- *Expectations*—Today, organizational clients expect IT professionals to deliver quality products and services in a professional manner. Timely status updates and communication, as well as sound project management practices are required.

- *Competition*—Internal and external competition has never been greater. An internal IT department's services can easily be outsourced if the quality or cost of providing IT services can be bettered outside the organization. Today, competition among consultants is increasing as they compete for business and talent.

- *Efficiency and effectiveness*—Peter Drucker, the well-known management guru, defined *efficiency* as doing the thing right and *effectiveness* as doing the right thing. Many companies report that project management allows for shorter development time, lower costs, and higher quality. Just using project management tools, however, does not guarantee success. Project management must become accepted and supported by all levels within the organization, and continued commitment in terms of training, compensation, career paths, and organizational infrastructure must be in place. This support will allow the organization to do the right things and to do them right.

- *A Knowledge-Management Approach*—A socio-technical approach and a commitment to project management principles and practices are important for success. However, excellence in project management for an individual or an organization takes time and experience. Knowledge management is a systematic process for acquiring, creating, synthesizing, sharing, and using information, insights, and experiences to transform ideas into business value. Although many organizations today have knowledge management initiatives under way, and spending on knowledge management systems is expected to increase, many others believe that knowledge management is just a fad or a buzzword.

What about learning from experience? Experience can be a great teacher. These experiences and the knowledge gained from these experiences, however, are often fragmented throughout the organization. Chances are that if you encounter what appears to be a unique problem or situation, someone else in your organization has already dealt with that problem, or one very similar. Wouldn't it be great to just ask that person what she or he did? What the outcome was? And, would that person do it again the same way? Unfortunately, that person could be on the other side of the world or down the hall—and you may not even know.

Knowledge and experience, in the form of lessons learned, can be documented and made available through applications accessible today, such blogs, wikis, and shared repositories like Microsoft's SharePoint©. Lessons learned that document reasons for success and failure can be valuable assets if maintained and used properly. A person who gains experience is said to be more mature. Similarly, an organization that learns from its experiences can be more mature in its processes by taking those lessons learned and creating best practices—simply, doing things in the most efficient and effective manner. In terms of managing projects, managing knowledge in the form of lessons learned can help an organization develop best practices that allow all of the project teams within the organization to do the right thing and then to do it the right way.

THE PURPOSE OF THIS BOOK

The goal of this book is to help you learn how to plan and manage information technology projects. We will focus on a number of different theories and concepts, but the main emphasis will be on applying the methods, tools, techniques, and processes for planning and managing a project from start to finish. If you are a project manager (or will be one soon), this book will help you to understand and apply project management principles in order to better manage your IT project. If you are just starting out in the field, this book will help you to understand the big picture of what a project is all about. This knowledge will help you to become a better team member and prepare you for the next several progressions in your career.

Many of the principles of project management can be applied to just about any project, but IT projects are unique in several ways. Throughout the text, we will discuss what makes IT projects different from other types of projects and how the principles and methods of system development can be integrated to define the IT project management discipline. Although many of the concepts for developing an information system will be integrated throughout, this is not a systems analysis and design text. More specifically, we will not delve too deeply into the systems analysis and design techniques that are used during systems development. We will leave that for other books and classes.

The remainder of this book provides a foundation for understanding project planning processes, methods, and tools. We begin by understanding the nature of IT projects and then will follow the project life cycle from project initiation through implementation and closure. Throughout the book you will be introduced to a number of project management knowledge areas and related software engineering concepts. While the goal of this book is not to prepare you for a professional certification in project management, it will provide a solid base to help you in your career and later on should you choose to become a certified project manager.

CHAPTER SUMMARY

- Information technology (IT) projects are organizational investments. When an organization builds or implements a new IT-based product, service, or solution, it commits time, money, and resources to the project with an expectation of receiving something of value in return.

- Organizations must have an effective business strategy to be successful, and projects are the planned organizational changes or means for achieving a chosen strategy.

- A *project* is a temporary endeavor undertaken to create a unique product, service, or result.

- A *project manager* is the person assigned by the performing organization to lead the team that is responsible for achieving the project objectives.

- All projects share some common attributes:
  - Time Frame
  - Purpose
  - Ownership
  - Resources
  - Project Roles

  - Project Manager or Leader
  - Project Sponsor
  - Subject Matter Expert(s) (SME)
  - Technical Expert(s) (TE)
- Risks and Assumptions
- Interdependent Tasks
- Organizational Change
- Organizational Environment

- *Project management* is the application of knowledge, skills, tools, and techniques to project activities to meet project requirements.

- Similar to the idea of a financial investment portfolio, many organizations have a **project portfolio** comprised of a collection of diverse projects.

- Some projects within the portfolio may be independent and not directly related to one another. However, some projects are managed as a **program** where the projects' activities are coordinated so that the benefits of the program are greater than the sum benefits of the individual projects.

- Modern-day project management is often credited to the U.S. Navy's Polaris missile project undertaken in the early 1950s to deter potential Soviet nuclear aggression. This new approach included a set of tools to manage projects and was viewed by many as a success. As a result, other organizations in various industries began to adopt this new approach as way to define, manage, and execute work with the hope of achieving similar success.

- The *EDP era* began in the early 1960s and was characterized by the purchase of the first centralized mainframe or a minicomputer by large organizations. The IT projects during this era focused generally on automating various organizational transactions such as general accounting tasks, inventory management, and production scheduling. IT projects during this era were generally structured, so a structured, formalized approach similar to the one used on the Polaris project was effective. Because the requirements of a business process like payroll were fairly stable, changing requirements was not a major issue and large multiyear projects were common.

- In the early 1980s, the IBM personal computer (PC) and its subsequent clones signaled the beginning of the *micro era*. The often uncontrolled proliferation of the PC in many organizations challenged the centralized control of many MIS managers. The project manager and team could no longer rely on stable business processes, requirements, or technology that would allow for longer project schedules; otherwise, they would face the risk of implementing an obsolete IT solution. Shorter project horizons that crossed functional lines became the norm, while software development methodologies attempted to shorten the development life cycle.

- A network of computers that formed the Internet led to the *network era* that began around 1995. IT projects focused primarily on the challenge of creating an IT infrastructure to support many business partners, strategic alliances, vendors, and customers. Project schedules and the time to develop IT solutions had to be shortened as many projects had to be completed in a few weeks or a few months.

- The combination of a global network infrastructure and lowering of political barriers in the late 1990s and early 2000s led to a rise of *globalization* as countries like India and China became connected to North America and Europe. Projects began to cross time zones as well as organizational and cultural boundaries. New project management approaches and development methodologies acknowledged that many product and system requirements cannot be defined upfront and, once defined, often change.

- Today, IT projects support a wide range of organizational activities that range from maintaining existing (legacy) systems to developing innovative ideas that take advantage of emerging technologies.

- The overall success rate for many large governmental and nongovernmental projects is low.

- Although the reasons why projects can fail is pretty much limitless, most reasons for project failure can be grouped into four categories:
  - People
  - Processes
  - Technology
  - Organizational

- The approaches for improving the likelihood of IT project success include:
  - A Value-Driven Approach
  - A Socio-Technical Approach
  - A Project-Management Approach
  - A Knowledge-Management Approach

REVIEW QUESTIONS

1. Why are projects organizational investments?
2. How do projects support business strategy?
3. What is a project?
4. What is the definition of a project manager?
5. What are the attributes of a project?
6. Why do projects have a time frame?
7. Why do projects need a purpose?
8. What is a stakeholder?
9. Give some examples of resources that may be required for an IT project?

10. What is the role of a project manager or leader?
11. What is the role of a project sponsor?
12. Why does a project need subject matter experts (SMEs)?
13. What types of technical experts (TEs) might an IT project need?
14. What is a risk? Provide an example of a project risk.
15. What is an assumption? Provide an example of an assumption.
16. What is meant by project tasks being interdependent? Provide an example of two interdependent tasks.
17. What is progressive elaboration?
18. Why would an IT project be considered a planned organizational change?
19. Why should the project manager and team understand the organization's culture, environment, politics, and structure?
20. What is project management?
21. What is a project portfolio?
22. Why should organizations manage their projects as a portfolio?
23. What is a program?
24. What is the purpose of managing a program?
25. Describe the EDP era. How were IT projects managed during this era?
26. Describe the micro era. What challenges did the micro era present?
27. Describe the network era. What challenges did the network era present?

28. What is globalization? What challenges did/does globalization present?
29. What are some challenges that project managers and teams face when managing IT projects today?
30. What seems to be the current state of IT project management?
31. What are the four categories for project failure? Give an example of each.
32. How might people influence the potential failure of a project?
33. How might processes influence the potential failure of a project?
34. How might technology influence the potential failure of a project?
35. How might an organization influence the potential failure of a project?
36. How does a value-driven approach to managing projects improve the likelihood of project success?
37. How does a socio-technical approach to managing projects improve the likelihood of project success?
38. How does a project-management approach to managing projects improve the likelihood of project success?
39. How does a knowledge-management approach to managing projects improve the likelihood of project success?
40. Why does the sharing of experiences in the form or lessons learned lead to best practices for managing and developing new products, processes, or systems?

HUSKY AIR—PILOT ANGELS

Background

Husky Air opened for business in January 2008 when L. T. Scully and several other investors pooled their life savings and secured a rather large loan from a Chicago bank.

Located at DeKalb Taylor Municipal Airport (DKB) in DeKalb, Illinois, Husky Air is a fixed base operator (FBO) facility that offers a full range of services to the growing demands for business and private aviation. Currently, the company has 23 employees composed of pilots, mechanics, and office staff.

As a FBO, Husky Air provides:

- Business jet, propjet, helicopter, and propeller aircraft charter
- Refueling

- Airframe, engine, propeller, and avionics maintenance
- Aircraft rental
- Flight instruction
- Pilot supplies

Although FBOs at other airports offer similar services, Husky Air has been receiving increased attention throughout the Midwest for its charter service, maintenance, and flight instruction.

Pilot Angels

In addition, Husky Air coordinates a charitable service called Pilot Angels. Working with hospitals, health-care agencies, and organ banks, Husky Air matches volunteer private pilots, willing to donate their time and aircraft, with needy people whose health-care problems require them to travel to receive diagnostic or treatment services. In addition, Pilot Angels also provides transportation for donor organs, supplies, and medical personnel. All flights are free of charge, and the costs are paid for by the volunteer pilots who use their own aircraft.

The pilots who volunteer for the Pilot Angels program need no medical training and offer no medical assistance. The planes do not carry any medical equipment and do not have to accommodate any stretchers. Patients, however, must be medically stable and able to enter and exit the aircraft with little or no assistance. The Pilot Angels passengers typically travel to or from a hospital or clinic for diagnosis, surgery, or some other treatment. Travel companions, such as a relative, friend, or nurse, are common.

Currently, a pool of pilot volunteers is kept in a file folder. If a hospital or person with a medical or financial hardship contacts Husky Air, the name of the traveler, the destination, dates/times, and the number of travel companions are requested. Because of limited weight restrictions in small aircraft, the weights of the passengers and their luggage are needed as well.

After the initial information is provided, Husky Air contacts the volunteer pilots to determine their availability. Although a volunteer pilot may be willing and available for a Pilot Angels flight, the plane may not have the range or weight-carrying requirements. This may be an inefficient use of time since many pilots may have to be contacted until a pilot and suitable plane can be found.

The Project Description

Husky Air would like to have a computer-based system to keep track of all its Pilot Angels volunteers. Basic information about the pilots may include their name, address, phone number, and so forth, as well as their total hours, certifications, and ratings. Moreover, specific information about a volunteer's aircraft would be useful. Such information should include the type of plane, aircraft identification number (called the N number), whether single or multi-engine, and its capacity for carrying passengers and cargo. Some pilots own more than one plane.

Husky Air also wants to know more about the people, hospitals, clinics, and organ banks that request the Pilot Angels service. In addition, they also would like basic information about the patients, their passengers, and specific needs to help match volunteers with the request for transport. Finally, Husky Air wants a list of all the Pilot Angels flights in order to recognize specific volunteers for their contributions. This would include:

- The pilot who flew the flight
- The passengers onboard
- The plane that was used
- The total time of the flight
- The distance and destination of the flight
- The date and time of the flight
- The total fuel used

HUSKY AIR ASSIGNMENT

The Team Charter

Congratulations! You have been hired as a consultant to work with a new client called Husky Air. The objective of your first assignment is to organize teams for completing the various Husky Air assignments. Your instructor will either assign you to a team or allow you to select your team.

Please provide a professional-looking document that includes the following:

- *Team Name*—You should come up with a name for your team to give yourselves an identity. This could be the name of your consulting firm.
- *Team Members*—Please list the names of your team members and their phone numbers and

email addresses. This will provide means for contacting each team member later on.

- *Skills and Knowledge Inventory*—List the specific knowledge and/or skills each team member can contribute to the project. This may include specific technical knowledge, communication skills, or leadership skills.
- *Roles and Responsibilities*—Based upon your team's skills inventory, define roles and responsibilities for each member of your team. Leadership roles can be defined for the entire project or can be shared or even rotated.
- *Agreed Upon Meeting Times*—You and your team should compare schedules so that you can

agree on times your group can meet to work on the case assignments. This may help you to discover any conflicts and reevaluate whether you should be a team.

- *Agreed Upon Meeting Location*—Also, decide where you will meet. This help you discover any issues beforehand if team members have to commute.

- *Team Communication*—Decide how the members of your team will communicate and share information. Will you meet face to face? Or will you take advantage of a software collaboration tool or other available technology to help reduce the dependency on same place/same time meetings. Where will documents be stored? Be specific as to what resources or technology your team will need to work effectively.

- *Team Rules and Expectations*—You probably have some experience working on a team before. As a team, share some of those experiences and discuss whether those experiences were positive or negative. Based upon your discussion define a:
  - *Team goal*—What do you want to achieve as a team? For example, this could be a specific grade for the course or minimum grade for the case assignments you will turn in over the semester.

- *Set of team values*—You may want to start by developing a list of values that you and your team members feel are important. Based on that list, develop a statement or itemized list that summarizes those values.

- *A code of ethics*—A project team has a responsibility to itself and to its client or sponsor. Based on your team values, create a statement or itemized list that summarizes a code of ethics to guide your team's ethical behavior.

- *Set of rules and expectations*—What are the rules for being on the team? For example, how will the team make decisions? How will the team resolve conflicts? What happens if someone misses a meeting? Two meetings? Three? How will the team deal with someone who does not contribute equally? Each member of your team should agree to these rules. Do not take this lightly. You may also want to discuss and document how the team may change its charter if needed later on.

- *Signatures*—Each member of your team should sign the team charter. This will indicate that each member has read, but more importantly understands, and agrees to the rules and expectations of the team.

THE MARTIAL ARTS ACADEMY—SCHOOL MANAGEMENT SYSTEM

Background

Grandmaster Taylor has practiced and taught martial arts for more than 30 years. Two months ago he decided to sell his business, the Martial Arts Academy, and retire with his wife to Tennessee so that he could spend more time enjoying life and pursuing one of his other passions—golf. Before leaving for a warmer climate, Grandmaster Taylor sold the Martial Arts Academy to two of his black-belt instructors, Geoff and Julie.

Currently, the Martial Arts Academy has 35 students of various ranks, ranging from white belts (beginners) to advanced black belts. Each student pays to take a specific number of adult or children classes per week and then can attend any of the classes that are scheduled Monday through Saturday. Classes are led by a black-belt instructor and are 60 minutes long. Based on an individual's progress, students can schedule a day and time to test for

their next higher rank, or belt, after filling out a testing form, paying a testing fee, and getting permission from one of the black-belt instructors. Kids' classes are for children ages 6 to 12, while adult classes include people from all walks of life who are 13 years of age or older. The student base is primarily male with about 30 percent females.

Each student signs a contract that also includes personal information such as name, address, phone number, birth date, etc. The contract also includes a liability waiver.

This information is kept in a file folder in a filing cabinet next to the main desk near the front entrance.

As mentioned, students prepay in advance for a specific number of classes a week. Discounts are given for the number of classes a student signs up for a week and the number of months.

Number of Classes a Week	Number of Months	Cost
1		$120
2	3	$240
3		$360
1		$228
2	6	$432
3		$612

The system is paper-based and simple. Each student has a 3 × 6-inch class card that is kept alphabetically by last name in a file box. When attending a class, students will take their card from the file box and place it in a tray near the entrance of the dojo or workout area. After each class, one of the black-belt instructors takes all of the cards from the tray and writes his or her initials in a blank space that corresponds to the date the student took a particular class. If a student completes eight classes, the instructors will circle their initials and place a paper clip on the card to indicate that the student received eight hours of instruction.

The circled initials and paper clip provide a simple way to help gauge a student's progress. At the beginning of each class, an instructor will check the cards to determine if any students have earned a "stripe" on their belt for completing eight hours of class instruction. Students who earn a stripe are called to the front of the class where they are congratulated. The instructor places a piece of black plastic tape around the end of the student's belt. The number of black stripes on a belt allows the instructors to gauge a student's progress. In addition to learning and demonstrating knowledge of specific curriculum requirements, 36 class hours (i.e., four stripes) is the minimum number of hours students are required to have before they can test for their next rank or belt. Although this system is simple and effective, it is not perfect. Once in a while an instructor may not circle his or her initials and place a paper clip on the card after a student completes eight classes. Sometimes, the paper clip falls off the card. Eventually, this is corrected by another instructor or when the student brings this to the attention of one of the higher belts.

When students are ready to test for their next rank, they fill out and submit a testing form along with a $20.00 testing fee. Then, one of the black-belt instructors reviews the form and signs it if he or she feels that the student is ready to be tested. Once approved, students are scheduled to test for their next rank or belt. The progression of belts begins with white belt progressing through orange, yellow, green, blue, purple, brown, and black ranks.

Running the Business

Just about everyone who enrolls at the Martial Arts Academy aspires to become a black belt. However, this

Name: Kim Jones   Current Rank: Green Belt

Date Last Tested: 12/01

	1	2	3	4	5	6	7	8	9	10	11	12	13	14	15	16	17	18	19	20	21	22	23	24	25	26	27	28	29	30	31
Jan		T/J			S/M				P/L				T/J			T/J				P/L					T/J					P/L (circled)	
Feb			S/M		P/L				P/L		T/J						T/J					S/M			T/J						
March		T/J (circled)																													
April																															
May																															
June																															
July																															
Aug																															
Sept																															
Oct																															
Nov																															
Dec																															

journey requires a great deal of personal commitment, dedication, and hard work. Although many black belts received their rank within four or five years, the amount of time invested is no guarantee anyone will receive this advanced rank. In fact, perhaps 1 out of 100 students who enroll at the Martial Arts Academy will eventually earn a black belt. Geoff and Julie do not want to compromise the high standards set by Grandmaster Taylor by promoting students who are not ready or who do not deserve to be promoted to the next higher rank. Many of the students and instructors who train together consider themselves to be like a second family.

Since Geoff and Julie took over the Martial Arts Academy, their number-one priority has been to stay in business by retaining their current base of students while attracting new students. However, they understand the reality of student turnover. They also realize that much of their competition is not from other martial arts schools, but other outside interests. For example, kids and teenagers tend to drop out because of their involvement in other sports such as soccer, baseball, or swimming. Adults and many teenagers often find difficulty maintaining a regular training schedule because of work, family, school, or other personal commitments and responsibilities. There are two other martial arts schools in the area and one martial arts club at the local university. The classes at the Martial Arts Academy are priced competitively.

The Martial Arts Academy also has a small shop where students can purchase school uniforms and shirts, sparring gear, patches, and, with an instructor's permission, various martial arts weapons. This retail component has been viewed more as a convenience for the students since people have a greater selection and perhaps better pricing from the larger martial arts stores or online retailers.

The Need for a School Management System

Geoff and Julie believe an information system offers an opportunity to help them manage the day-to-day operations more efficiently and effectively. However, their knowledge of technology is limited to using their smartphones, surfing the Web, using email, and keeping up with friends and several of MAA students on a popular social networking site. Geoff feels that the MAA needs to hire someone to build a custom application system, but neither he nor Julie has the knowledge and skills to develop and maintain their own system. On the other hand, Julie has researched several school management software systems designed specifically for martial arts schools. Some of these software packages

can be purchased and installed on a workstation, while others are subscription-based and hosted by a third party through the Web.

Geoff and Julie are willing to spend the time, money, and resources for this project only if they believe that MAA will receive a reasonable return on this investment. Julie has mentioned that she doesn't want to buy a computer system and pay consultants "to just automate the existing file card system." Moreover, Geoff has stated plainly that anything you recommend must pay for itself and provide tangible benefits; otherwise, he will be reluctant to change from the paper-based system.

Deliverable: The Team Charter

Geoff and Julie have asked you and your team to come up with a viable solution to help them manage their business. Over the course of the semester, you will play the role of consultants who have been hired by the Martial Arts Academy. Each case assignment will take you through various situations that might happen on a real project. You will plan, organize, and manage your project through the entire project life cycle. However, before you can begin the project, you will need to organize your team by creating a team charter. The purpose of a team charter set expectations and rules of governance to guide your team.

Please provide a professional-looking document that includes the following:

- *Team Name*—You should come up with a name for your team to give yourselves an identity. This could be the name of your consulting firm.

- *Team Members*—Please list the names of your team members and their phone numbers and email addresses. This will provide means for contacting each team member later on.

- *Skills and Knowledge Inventory*—List the specific knowledge and/or skills each team member can contribute to the project. This may include specific technical knowledge, communication skills, or leadership skills.

- *Roles and Responsibilities*—Based on your team's skills inventory, define roles and responsibilities for each member of your team. Leadership roles can be defined for the entire project or can be shared or even rotated.

- *Agreed Upon Meeting Times*—You and your team should compare schedules so that you can agree on times your group can meet to work on the case assignments. This may help you to discover any conflicts and reevaluate whether you should be a team.

- *Agreed Upon Meeting Location*—Also, decide where you will meet. This help you discover any issues beforehand if team members have to commute.

- *Team Communication*—Decide how the members of your team will communicate and share information. Will you meet face to face? Or will you take advantage of a software collaboration tool or other available technology to help reduce the dependency on same place/same time meetings. Where will documents be stored? Be specific as to what resources or technology your team will need to work effectively.

- *Team Rules and Expectations*—You probably have some experience working on a team before. As a team, share some of those experiences and discuss whether those experiences were positive or negative. Based on your discussion define a:
  - *Team goal*—What do you want to achieve as a team? For example, this could be a specific grade for the course or minimum grade for the case assignments you will turn in over the semester.
  - *Set of team values*—You may want to start by developing a list of values that you and your team members feel are important. Based on that list, develop a statement or itemized list that summarizes those values.

- *A code of ethics*—A project team has a responsibility to itself and its client or sponsor. Based on your team values, create a statement or itemized list that summarizes a code of ethics to guide your team's ethical behavior.

- *Set of rules and expectations*—What are the rules for being on the team? For example, how will the team make decisions? How will the team resolve conflicts? What happens if someone misses a meeting? Two meetings? Three? How will the team deal with someone who does not contribute equally? Each member of your team should agree to these rules. Do not take this lightly. You may also want to discuss and document how the team may change its charter if needed later on.

- *Signatures*—Each member of your team should sign the team charter. This will indicate that each member has read, but more importantly understands, and agrees to the rules and expectations of the team.

QUICK THINKING—INVOLVING THE USER

Users can be your best friend or your worst enemy. Projects can be viewed as a social network where users and developers must work together to share knowledge, ideas, and information. The CHAOS studies suggest that user involvement is one of the leading factors for project success, while lack of user involvement is a leading factor for project failure. Therefore, it is critical to correctly identify the appropriate user or user group because the right users will provide vital information and feedback. Conversely, the wrong users can lead the developers down the wrong path by not specifying requirements accurately or completely. It is important to develop a good rapport and relationship with the user and user groups so that they feel involved and understand their roles and responsibilities as members of the project team. Good communication and feedback can also help achieve consensus and harmony regarding the project's direction even though projects can be more of an autocracy than a democracy. Projects sometimes need someone to play the role of an evangelist who believes strongly in the goal or value of the project and can help to gain the support of the rest of the user community and upper management.

1. What are some key factors or characteristics you should consider when attempting to identify the correct user or user group to be part of a project team?

2. What are some potential conflicts between users and developers? As a project manager, what steps could you take to minimize or avoid these conflicts to ensure that the user or user group is involved?

SOURCE: *The CHAOS Manifesto: The Laws of CHAOS and the CHAOS 100 Best PM Practices*. The Standish Group. 2010.

QUICK THINKING—FAA NEXTGEN AIR-TRAFFIC CONTROL PROJECT

The current air-traffic control systems in the United States are at least 20 years behind the current technologies and without an upgrade the United States is at risk of falling behind the rest of the world. The NextGen project is attempting to change U.S. air travel from a ground-based, analog system to a satellite-based system using global positioning system (GPS) technology by 2018. The new system would automate many parts of ground and air-traffic control, enable real-time GPS maps of air and ground traffic, incorporate weather monitoring to reroute planes, and allow planes to fly closer together without a loss of safety. The NexGen system is the largest project undertaken by the Federal Aviation Administration (FAA), but a report from the General Accountability Office (GAO) has determined that the original cost of $40 billion will quadruple to $160 billion if the FAA maintains its plans for requiring extensive electronic systems to be installed on every aircraft. The GAO also reported that the FAA has not established clear performance goals and metrics for NextGen whereby the "FAA could pursue and implement capabilities that fail to produce the desired results." Witnesses before a House of Representatives subcommittee called into question the

FAA's handling of the project and raised concerns that the project would be able to be completed on schedule. A few months later, another report publicized that the FAA failed to develop the necessary skill sets to make NextGen work and that more planning was needed. A third report by the GAO found that the FAA failed to have adequate performance metrics in place to monitor and manage the project. In order to control the ballooning costs of the project, the GAO reports that the FAA will have to develop NextGen with "lower levels of capabilities, whose cost estimates remain in the $40 billion range.

1. Using Figure 1.1 as a guide, what are some of the warning signs that this project may have problems or fail?

2. In your opinion, what could be done to improve the likelihood of success?

SOURCES:

Hoover, J. N. "FAA NextGen Air Traffic Control Costs Could Quadruple." *InformationWeek*. 12/3/2010.

Cary, S. "The FAA's $40 Billion Adventure." *The Wall Street Journal*. 08/19/2013.

 # CASE STUDIES

Project Ocean—The Troubled Water Billing System

The city of Philadelphia entered into an agreement with Oracle Corporation to replace its antiquated, custom-built, 30-year-old water billing system that fails to collect all the revenue it should. After three years and spending $18 million on "Project Ocean," the project was two years behind schedule and at almost twice the cost originally envisioned. Moreover, the new billing system still had not been deployed to support its 500,000 customers.

Philadelphia Chief Information Officer (CIO) Dianah Neff cited technical complexity, administrator turnover, and Oracle's inexperience building such a system as the reasons for Project Ocean's problems. Alan Butkovitz, the City Controller, said that his office is currently reviewing what happened with Oracle, but that it is too soon to speculate as to what went wrong with Project Ocean. An official at Oracle has said that

Oracle would deliver on its promise to complete the project and that implementation is "still in progress, and Oracle believes that the work performed to date conforms with the current agreement."

Project Ocean is currently on hold until the Mayor's Office of Information Services (MOIS) and other city officials can reach an agreement with Oracle to put Project Ocean back on track. Neff stated that she believes a workable solution can be delivered within 18 months to protect the city's investment.

Former City Water Commissioner Kumar Kishinchand was a vocal critic of Project Ocean since before leaving the commission after 12 years. Kishinchand believes that Project Ocean was doomed from the start. "One reason is that they picked a company that had never done a water billing system. Oracle had only done viable customer service systems with a small portion for billing purposes. Municipal billing systems tend to be tremendously complex. The off-the-shelf components of such systems have to be heavily modified, a complex and time-consuming effort."

Kishinchand also believes that the project managers did not have much to lose if Project Ocean failed because the city's Finance Department was in charge of the project—not the Water Department, which is the main operator and user of the system. He believes that Neff and the MOIS were interested in building empires because the water billing system takes in more than $300 million in revenues a year. Kinshinchand also accused city officials of "putting all of their eggs in one basket [Oracle], without consulting the Water Department."

In rebuttal, Neff contends that MOIS chose the Oracle Enterprise Resources Planning E-Business suite for a number of city uses that include human resources and that the Finance Department made the decision to make water billing the first application. MOIS was then brought in to implement the system once the decision was made. As Neff contends, "it [the water billing system] was a big system, very complicated with very unique features. Hindsight is 20/20 and ERP is difficult anyway."

In addition, the system was designed to be run by a number of city departments, but there was constant turnover among executive sponsors. Neff contemplated: "Continuity was a problem, and we could have had better-defined business processes. Problems came up between the contractor and business people. As we put it, it was a project that 'washed ashore' for IT to handle."

About 12 months ago, MOIS was assigned to review the work completed on Project Ocean so far. This led to a work stoppage and the suspension of several consultants, Oracle employees, and a private contractor who had been indicted by a federal grand jury in Connecticut on unrelated charges that she had paid a state senator to help her win consulting contracts.

While negotiations between the city of Philadelphia and Oracle continue, Neff is preparing to start a new job as a consultant in another city. After five years as CIO, Neff maintains that her impending departure is unrelated to Project Ocean.

1. Do you believe that the trouble with Philadelphia's water billing system is a technical problem or a people problem? Why?

2. What factors contributed to the problems associated with Project Ocean?

3. Compare the different views the city's MOIS and Oracle may have when negotiating a new agreement that will continue that project.

4. Can this project be saved? If so, what should the new agreement include? If not, can Philadelphia and Oracle come to an agreement that satisfies both parties? Or would this end up being a "win/lose" situation?

SOURCES:

Hamblen, M. "Philly CIO: Troubled Water Billing System Can Still Work." *Computerworld*. August 10, 2006.

Hamblen, M. "Philadelphia Flushes Oracle Out of Water Bill Project." *IT World Canada*. January 14, 2007.

Hamblen, M. "Oracle Goes Down the Drain in City's Water Bill Project." *Computeworld UK*. January 15, 2007.

The FBI's Virtual Case File

After the tragic events of September 11, 2001, the Federal Bureau of Investigation (FBI) recognized the need to modernize its largely paper-based system for gathering intelligence. After years of developing information systems without an overarching organizational view, the agency found itself with an "improvised" IT infrastructure with more than 50 independent application systems written in different programming languages and running on disparate platforms. The result was a shortfall of knowledge management that became even more apparent after September 11. The FBI concluded that it was losing intelligence as fast as it could gather it.

Robert Chiaradio, an agent in charge of the field office in Tampa, Florida, was requested by FBI Director Robert Mueller to help push a three-part modernization project called Trilogy that was started by former Director Louis Freeh. The project centered on upgrading the agency's desktops and servers, Web-enabling a number of the most important investigative database systems, and, most importantly, an automated case file system.

As the new CIO, Chiaradio was in charge of the entire IT operation for the Bureau, and one of four officials who reported to Mueller. Recognizing that there was no time to waste, Mueller instructed that the year schedule for the project had to be put into overdrive so that the Trilogy project could completed "as soon as technically possible." After a meeting at 6:00 AM on October 1, 2001, Chiaradio quickly developed the concept for the Virtual Case File system.

The Virtual Case File was envisioned to help FBI agents efficiently share data about cases in progress, especially terrorist investigations. The system would also enable agents anywhere in the United State to quickly search various documents and allow them to connect possible leads from different sources. In addition, the Virtual Case File would include a case management system, an evidence management system, and a records management system. The intention was to eliminate the need for FBI employees to scan hard-copy documents into computer files. A custom-developed system was needed because no existing commercial software packages were available that meet the agency's needs when the project began in 2001. Development of the Trilogy Project was contracted to Science Applications International Corp. (SAIC) in San Diego, California and was to be completed by late 2003.

After 18 months, Robert Chiaradio left the FBI to take a new position as managing director of homeland security at BearingPoint Inc. in McLean, Virginia. By the end of 2004, SAIC had delivered only about 10 percent of what the FBI had envisioned and didn't include many of the enhancements that were recommended by a second contractor.

In January 2005, the FBI was faced with trying to salvage the $170 million project and appease a growing number of critics who believed that the four-year-old project was a waste of taxpayer money. Moreover, Robert Mueller confided to reporters that while the Virtual Case File project has not been scrapped, the FBI had asked another contractor to look for commercial or government off-the-shelf software packages that could be used instead.

The project's lack of progress drew public criticism from Senator Patrick Leahy (D-Vt.), who said "the FBI's long-anticipated Virtual Case File has been a train wreck in slow motion, at a cost of $170 million to American taxpayers and an unknown cost to public safety." To the contrary, Duane Andrews, SAIC's chief operating officer, said "The FBI modernization effort involved a massive technological and cultural change, agency wide. To add to that complexity, in the time that SAIC has been working on the Trilogy project, the FBI has had four different CIOs and 14 different managers. Establishing and setting system requirements in this environment has been incredibly challenging."

One FBI official remarked that this experience has led to a number of lessons learned in contract management, and this particular contract has led the agency to change its IT contracting practices and develop an IT roadmap. The official also added, "It's definitely not fair to say we haven't gotten anyplace. We haven't gotten the overarching program we wanted, but we're going to take these lessons and move forward with it."

In March 2005, the FBI officially terminated the Virtual Case File and announced that it would develop a new case management system called Sentinel. This announcement was made by Robert Mueller during his testimony before a subcommittee of the U.S. House Appropriations Committee. Mueller said "I am disappointed that we did not come through with Virtual Case File." However, he added that he sees the decision to cancel the project as an opportunity to use off-the-shelf software to create a more up-to-date system that will allow FBI agents to share information about cases more easily.

An FBI official who wished to remain anonymous said that agency will begin to evaluate software packages next month in order to develop a more firm direction. In addition, the FBI will be conducting a test of SAIC's most recent version of the system. Although the system developed by SAIC does not meet the agency's requirements, "we needed to evaluate what they had given us as far as user capability and usability" was concerned.

Interestingly, Jared Adams, a spokesman for SAIC, contends that the FBI hasn't formally killed the Virtual Case File project. Ongoing tests are proof that a final decision has not yet been made. He added, "When the tests are done at the end of March, I think then a decision will be made."

Robert Mueller stated that the new case management system will be implemented in four phases and should take about 39 months to complete. He was unwilling, however, to estimate how much the new system will cost.

The House Appropriations Committee said that it would open a formal investigation as to why the project failed.

1. A *Computerworld* article by Paul Glen lists a number of ways to detect disaster projects. Discuss how the following may apply to the FBI's failed Virtual Case File.

    a. **No real plan**—No baseline to work from, so no one really knows that a project is late.

    b. **Excessive optimism**—Many times there's a perpetual optimism that just because a project is behind there's no reason why things can't get caught up.

    c. **Fear of admission**—When a project is in trouble, no one wants to go to senior management and admit it, because that may be uncomfortable. And maybe things will get better.

    d. **Poor team morale**—Although this may not be a leading cause of project failure, it may be a leading indicator.

    e. **Poorly understood team roles**—People may not be clear as to what their role should be or how they should be interacting with others.

f. Absent sponsors—If sponsors can't be bothered with investing time in the project upfront, chances are they won't like what they get in the end.

g. Not enough methodology—If the project team doesn't have a common and well understood approach to completing the work, it is likely to have trouble doing so.

h. Too much methodology—A methodology is a tool for completing the work, but not a guarantee that everything will go smoothly. A team can become overburdened with a methodology where the means become more important than the ends, or become a process to further political goals.

i. Meager management—An inexperienced or unskilled manager can doom a project to failure.

j. Lacking leadership—Good leadership may be difficult to define, but we often know it when we see it. A project must have good leadership to succeed.

k. Inadequate technical skills—While not the most common cause for project failure, it can happen if we assign people without the requisite skills, or training to projects, or when we assign people because they are available at the time.

l. Too many meetings—Project team members who spend an inordinate amount of time in meetings may be trying to make up for inadequate planning. Because they may not have thought things out in advance, they are forced to coordinate on the fly.

SOURCES:

Verton, D. "FBI Has Made Major Progress, Former IT Chief Says." *Computerworld*. April 18, 2004.

Gross, G. "FBI Trying to Salvage $170 million Software Package: Its Virtual Case File Project Is under Fire for Not Working as Planned." *Computerworld*. January 14, 2005.

Rosencrance, L. "FBI Scuttles $170 million System for Managing Investigations." *Computerworld*. March 14, 2005.

Hayes, F. "FBI on the Move." *Computerworld*. May 30, 2005.

Glen, P. "Opinion: Detecting Disaster Projects." *Computerworld*. February 6, 2006.

BIBLIOGRAPHY

1. Project Management Institute (PMI). *A Guide to the Project Management Body of Knowledge (PMBOK Guide)*. Newton Square, PA: PMI Publishing, 2013.

2. Marchewka, J. T. and M. M. Keil. "A Portfolio Theory Approach for Selecting and Managing IT Projects." *Information Management Resources Journal*, 1995, Vol. 8, 5–14.

3. Nolan, R. L. *Information Technology Management from 1960-2000*. June 7. Boston, MA: Harvard Business School Publishing, 2001. Vols. 301-147. 9-301-147.

4. Zuboff, S. *In the Age of the Smart Machine: The Future of Work and Power*. New York: Basic Books, 1988.

5. Friedman, T. L. *The World Is Flat: A Brief History of the Twenty-first Century*. New York: Picador, 2007.

6. Kanaracus, C. "The Scariest Software Project Horror Stories of 2012." *Computerworld*. 2012. Accessed from www.computerworld.com.

7. ———. "The Worst IT Project Disasters of 2013." *Computerworld*. 2013. Accessed from www.computerworld.com.

8. Ditmore, J. "Why Do Big IT Projects Fail So Often?" *Information Week*. 2013. Accessed from www.informationweek.com.

9. Thibodeau, P. "Healthcare.gov Website 'Didn't Have a Chance in Hell'." *Computerworld*. 2013. Accessed from www.computerworld.com.

10. Standish Group. *CHAOS*. West Yarmouth, MA: The Standish Group, 1995.

11. ———. *The Chaos Manifesto 2013*. Boston, MA: The Standish Group, 2013.

12. Krigsman, Michael. "Tata Consultancy: New IT Failure Sstats and COO Interview." *ZDNET*. December 12, 2007. Accessed from www.zdnet.com

13. Bloch, Michael, Sven Blumberg and Jurgen Laartz. "Delivering Large-Scale IT Projects On Time, On Budget, and On Value" (2012). Accessed from www.mckinsey.com.

14. Glass, Robert L. "IT Failure Rates—70% or 10-15%?" *IEEE Software*, Vol. May/June 2005, 109–112.

15. Gulla, Joseph. "Seven Reasons IT Projects Fail." *IBM Systems Magazine*. 2012. Accessed from www.ibmsystemsmag.com.

2

Project Methodologies and Processes

CHAPTER OBJECTIVES

Chapter 2 introduces the concepts of lifecycles, methodologies, and processes for managing and developing the project's product, service, or system. After studying this chapter, you should be able to:

- Define what a methodology is and the role it serves.
- Describe the Project Life Cycle (PLC).
- Describe the Project Management Body of Knowledge (PMBOK®) and be familiar with its knowledge areas and process groups.
- Describe PRINCE2® and be familiar with its core principles, processes, and themes.
- Describe the Systems Development Life Cycle (SDLC).
- Describe the Waterfall method for developing the project's product or system.
- Describe the Agile approach for developing the project's product or system as well as two commonly used approaches called eXtreme Programming (XP) and Scrum.
- Describe and apply the concept of Learning Cycles and lessons learned.

INTRODUCTION

In this chapter, you will learn about several widely used project methodologies. In the sciences, the *scientific method* outlines a series of steps and techniques for testing hypotheses when we want to study some natural phenomenon. Similarly, **project methodologies** provide a systematic way to plan, manage, and execute the work to be completed by prescribing phases, processes, tools, and techniques to be followed.

Think of a methodology as a template or a game plan for initiating, planning, and developing a product or information system. While all projects are unique in terms of the product or system to be developed or delivered, the processes for managing the project or development can be quite similar across different projects. Therefore, methodologies focus on the commonality among projects so that a standardized approach can be used and adapted as needed without having to "reinvent the wheel" for every project.

Project methodologies must be flexible in order to be useful. Moreover, methodologies should evolve over time to include best practices derived from experience or lessons learned from past projects. Over time, the methodology will better fit the organization in terms of the types of projects it takes on, its organizational culture, and the skills of its employees. As an organization's experience with a particular methodology increases, its capability becomes more predictable. Completing projects more successfully will better support an organization's business strategy and will hopefully lead to competitive advantage.

A project methodology also provides a common language among the project stakeholders and allows management to compare projects more objectively because each project's planned and actual progress can be reported the same way. Ideally, this allows management to make better informed and more objective decisions with respect to which projects get funded and whether that funding should continue. In summary, following a project methodology has the following advantages (1):

- A project team can focus on the product or system without having to debate how the work is to be done.

- Stakeholders understand their role, and these roles can be applied to future projects.

- Experiences can be documented in terms of lessons learned and integrated into the methodology as best practices. Hopefully, previous successes can be repeated.

- Past, present, and future projects can be compared with confidence in terms of planning and progress reporting.

- Valuable time can be saved because approaches, tools, techniques, and templates can be reused across projects.

- As you will learn in later chapters, following a methodology provides a useful template for planning the project work and associated tasks.

In addition, you will also learn about the Project Life Cycle (PLC) and the Systems Development Life Cycle (SDLC). The PLC is a collection of logical stages or phases that map the life of a project from its beginning to end. A life cycle is defined within a particular methodology (2). You will learn about the **Project Management Body of Knowledge** (PMBOK®) and **PRojects IN Controlled Environments** (PRINCE2®)—two popular and widely used project management methodologies.

The SDLC, on the other hand, is a software development life cycle that focuses on the development and delivery of the project's product or information system solution. In this chapter, you will learn about two widely known and used approaches for product and systems development—Waterfall and Agile. While Waterfall provides a more structured approach, Agile has been gaining popularity as a flexible approach to developing systems in a dynamic environment. Each approach has its own strengths and weaknesses, and choosing the right approach for the right project is an important project management decision. In addition, you will be introduced to eXtreme Programming (XP) and Scrum—two widely known and used approaches to Agile. In later chapters, you will learn how to implement both Waterfall and Agile when developing an overall project plan.

Lastly, you will be introduced to Learning Cycles. Learning Cycles provide a tool for the project stakeholders to challenge assumptions, increase team learning, and document lessons learned.

THE PROJECT LIFE CYCLE

Just like living things, projects have life cycles. They are born, grow, peak, decline, and then end (3). Although project life cycles may differ depending on the industry or project, all project life cycles will have a beginning, middle, and an end (4).

Regardless whether a project is large or small, projects are organized into sequential phases to make the project more manageable and to reduce risk. **Phase exits**, **stage gates**, or **kill points** are the phase-end reviews that allow the organization to evaluate the project's performance and to take immediate action to correct any problems or even cancel the project. **Fast tracking**, or starting the next phase before the current phase is complete, can sometimes reduce the project's schedule, but the overlapping of phases can be risky and should only be done when the risk is deemed acceptable.

Figure 2.1 provides a generic life cycle that describes the common phases or stages shared by most projects. Regardless whether you are building a house, designing a new consumer product, developing a web site, or launching a spacecraft to Mars, each project could be managed using the same project life cycle.

- *Define Project Goal*—All projects have a beginning. Although a project is initiated when some-one comes up with a new idea for perhaps a new product, service, or system, the first step

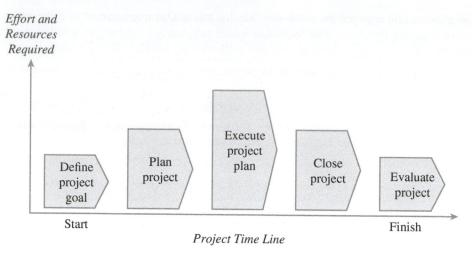

Figure 2.1 A Generic Project Life Cycle

in beginning a project should be to define the project's goal. The project's goal should make explicit the project's envisioned business value because projects are organizational investments that require time and resources and involve risk. A well-defined goal will set stakeholders' expectations and drive the other phases of the project. The project goal should also answer the question: How will we know if this project is successful given the time, money, and resources invested? Once the project's goal has been clearly defined, it must be agreed upon by the project stakeholders before the project can begin the planning phase.

- *Plan Project*—The project's goal provides direction for planning the project; otherwise, it would be like driving a car without a destination in mind. A project plan defines:

  - *Project Objectives*—A project's objectives include scope (the project work), schedule, budget, and quality. Objectives support the project's goal by defining what work needs to be completed, when it needs to be completed, how much it will cost to complete, and whether the work is acceptable to specific stakeholders.

  - *Resources*—Resources are needed to complete the project work and include such things as people, facilities, and technology.

  - *Controls*—A great deal of managing a project includes ensuring that the project goal and objectives are being met and resources are used efficiently and effectively. In addition, risk, change, and communication among the project stakeholders must be proactively managed throughout the project.

- *Execute Project Plan*—Approval of the project plan is required before moving to the execution phase. While the *plan project* phase outlines the anticipated or planned progress of the project, the *execute project plan* phase concentrates on the design, development, and delivery of the project's product, service, or system. Moreover, the controls defined in the planning phase now allow the project stakeholders to compare the project's planned progress with the actual progress in terms of the work being completed on time, within budget, and within quality standards so as to achieve the business value envisioned. At the end of this phase, the team implements or delivers a completed product, service, or information system to the organization.

- *Close and Evaluate Project*—A project should have a definite end. The last phases ensure that all of the work is completed as agreed to by the team, the sponsor, or other stakeholders. However, the project and the project team should be evaluated during a postmortem review to determine whether the project's goal defined in the initial phase was achieved. In addition, any best practices based on experiences and lessons learned should be documented and made available to future projects.

In addition, most projects seem to share the following characteristics:

- The effort, in terms of cost and staffing levels, is low at the start of the project, but then increases as the project work is being done, and then decreases at the end as the project is completed.
- Risk and uncertainty are the highest at the start of a project.
- For many projects, the ability for stakeholders to influence the product's features or functionality is highest at the beginning of the project. The cost of changing the product's features or functionality and correcting errors becomes more expensive as the project progresses.

THE PROJECT MANAGEMENT BODY OF KNOWLEDGE (PMBOK®)

The PMBOK® Guide is a document available from the Project Management Institute (PMI®)—an international, nonprofit, professional organization with more than 700,000 members worldwide. The original document was published in 1987, and subsequent updated versions provide a basis for identifying and describing the generally accepted principles and practices of project management. However, as the PMBOK® Guide is quick to point out, "generally accepted" does not mean these principles and practices work the same way on each and every project. It does mean that many people over time believe that these principles and practices are useful and have value. Determining what is appropriate is the responsibility of the team and comes from experience.

PMI® provides a certification in project management through the Project Management Professional (PMP®) certification exam. To pass, you must demonstrate a level of understanding and knowledge about project management, satisfy education and experience requirements, and agree to and adhere to a professional code of ethics.

Project Management Knowledge Areas

The PMBOK® Guide defines ten knowledge areas for understanding project management. These ten knowledge areas are illustrated in Figure 2.2 and will be covered in more detail in later chapters.

- *Project integration management*—Integration focuses on coordinating the project plan's development, execution, and control of changes.
- *Project scope management*—A project's scope is the work to be completed by the project team. This may include specific requirements, features, functionality, or standards for the product or system to be delivered, or it could include project-related deliverables like the project's schedule and budget. Scope management provides assurance that the project's work is defined accurately and completely and that it is completed as planned. In addition, scope management includes ways to ensure that proper scope change procedures are in place.
- *Project time management*—Time management is important for developing, monitoring, and managing the project's schedule. It includes identifying the project's phases and activities and then estimating, sequencing, and assigning resources for each activity to ensure that the project's scope and objectives are met.
- *Project cost management*—Cost management assures that the project's budget is developed and completed as approved.
- *Project quality management*—Quality management focuses on planning, developing, and managing a quality environment that allows the project to meet stakeholder needs or expectations.
- *Project human resource management*—People are the most important resource on a project. Human resource management focuses on creating and developing the project team as well as understanding and responding appropriately to the behavioral side of project management.

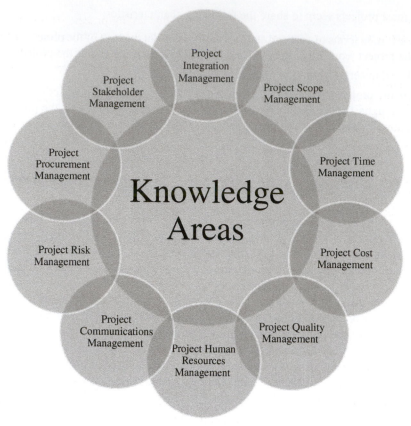

Figure 2.2 PMBOK® Knowledge Areas

- *Project communications management*—Communication management entails communicating timely and accurate information about the project to the project's stakeholders.
- *Project risk management*—All projects face a certain amount of risk. Project risk management is concerned with identifying and responding appropriately to risks that can impact the project.
- *Project procurement management*—Projects often require resources (people, hardware, software, etc.) that are outside the organization. Procurement management makes certain that these resources are acquired properly.
- *Project stakeholder management*—Stakeholders are people and include individuals, organizations, or business units that have a vested interest in the success (or failure) of a project. Stakeholder management focuses on identifying project stakeholders to better understand their expectations or interests, and then developing appropriate strategies for communication and managing potential conflicts.

PROJECT PROCESSES

The PMBOK® Guide defines a **process** as "a set of interrelated actions and activities performed to achieve a pre-specified product, result, or service" (37). In other words, a process is something you do to achieve a result. It may involve some kind of input as well as directions, tools, or techniques to change the input to the desired output or result. For example, if you wanted to bake a cake, you would need specific inputs, including ingredients (such as flour, eggs, etc.), tools (oven, mixing bowls, mixer, etc.), and directions (a recipe). This whole process could be subdivided into subprocesses, such as a mixing process, baking process, measuring process, and decorating process. If this was the first time you baked a cake, you might follow the recipe directions to the letter in terms of mixing the ingredients and baking time. However, with experience, you may experiment with the ingredients to produce a cake that is more to your liking and learn when the cake should come out of the oven—a little early or when it needs just another minute or two.

Processes are an integral component of projects. They support all of the activities necessary to plan, create, and manage all of the project activities. Project management processes are different from the PLC phases, because they are actions or tasks to initiate, plan, execute, monitor and control, and close a project as well as interact with the project management knowledge areas. In Chapter 3, for example, you will be introduced to a project management process for developing a business case and another for developing the project's goal. If you were a caterer hired to bake a wedding cake, project management processes would be needed to define, plan, estimate the cost, and deliver a cake that meets your customer's expectations, budget, and needs while being profitable or at least cost-effective for you.

On the other hand, product-oriented processes are tasks or activities to create the project's product. For an IT project, this would be all of the processes required to design, build, test, document, and implement an application system. Just like baking a cake, product-oriented processes require specific domain knowledge, tools, and techniques to complete the work. Otherwise, this could result in a poor cake or an information system that is a technical failure.

An emphasis or sole focus on project management processes does not provide an ability to develop a quality product, regardless whether it is a cake or an information system. However, focusing on the product-oriented processes may not provide the management controls to ensure that the delivered cake or information system meets the expectations or needs of the intended customer or user. There must be a balance between project management processes and product-oriented processes in order to deliver a successful project. As one's experience grows, processes may not have to be applied the same way on all projects. The situation at hand will dictate the appropriateness of how each process should be applied.

Project Management Process Groups

The PMBOK® Guide outlines five process groups. As illustrated in Figure 2.3, the process groups overlap within and between the phases of the project as the output of one process group within a phase becomes the input for a process group in the next phase.

- *Initiating*—The *initiating process* group signals the beginning of the project or a phase. For example, an organization may initiate a project by requiring the development of a business case as part of its project methodology. During this phase, a set of project management processes would define how the project and the first phase of the methodology should be initiated. The approval of the business case would then provide an authorization to start another set of processes to begin the second phase of the project methodology. Although all of the phases of the project should have some type of initiating process, the first phase of the project would be the most important.

- *Planning*—The *planning process* group supports planning of the entire project and each individual phase. Supporting project management processes may include scope planning, activity planning, resource planning, cost estimating, schedule estimating, and procurement planning. The *planning process* should be in line with the size and complexity of the project—that is, larger, more complex projects may require a greater planning effort than smaller, less complex projects. Planning processes are most important during the second phase of the project methodology when planning the project is emphasized. However, *planning processes* can be important for each phase whereby objectives and activities may need to be defined or refined as new information becomes available. In addition, planning is often an iterative process. A project manager may develop a project plan, but senior management or the client may not approve the scope,

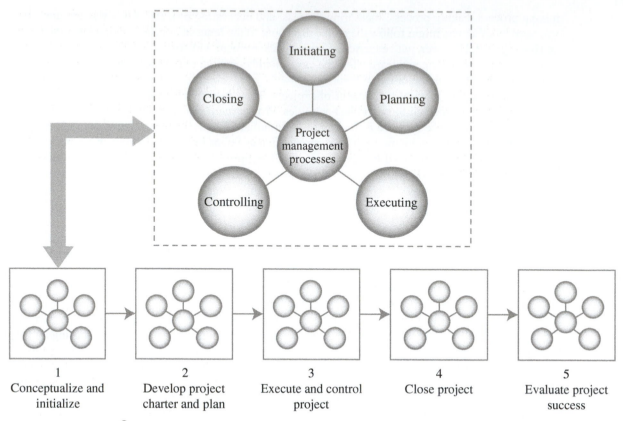

Figure 2.3 PMBOK® Project Management Process Groups

budget, or schedule. Or circumstances may arise that warrant changes to the project plan. This could happen as the result of a competitor's actions or legislation (external), or even changes to the project team or sponsor (internal).

- *Executing*—Once a project phase has been approved and planned, the *executing process* group focuses on integrating people and resources to carry out the planned activities of the project plan or phase. During the *execute and control* phase, the SDLC and associated project methodology play an important role in developing the product or system. For example, software engineering processes, tools, and methods for developing and/or implementing an application system become critical for delivering the project's end result. Project management processes such as quality assurance, risk management, and team development play an important supporting role. Although executing processes are part of every project phase, the majority of executing processes will occur during the *execute and control* phase of the project life cycle.

- *Monitoring and Controlling*—The *monitoring and controlling* process group allows for managing and measuring progress toward the project's goal and scope, schedule, budget, and quality objectives. These processes also allow the project manager and team to keep an eye on project variances between actual and planned results so that appropriate corrective actions can be taken when necessary. Supporting project management processes include scope control, change control, schedule control, budget control, quality control, and a communications plan. The emphasis of monitoring and controlling processes will occur during the execution and control phase of the IT project methodology.

- *Closing*—The *closing* process group provides a set of processes for formally accepting the project's product, service, or system so that the project or phase can be brought to an orderly close. The project manager or team must verify that all project work has been satisfactorily completed before the project sponsor accepts a phase's or the project's end product. Closure of a project may include processes for contract closure and administrative closure. Contract closure ensures that all of the deliverables and agreed upon terms of the project have been completed and delivered so that the project can end. It allows resources to be reassigned and settlement or payment of any account. Administrative closure, on the other hand, involves documenting and archiving all project documents. It also includes processes for evaluating the project in terms of whether it achieved its goal. Lessons learned should be documented and made available to other teams. Although each phase must include closing processes, the major emphasis on closing processes will occur during the *close project* and *evaluate project success* phases of the project methodology.

PRINCE2®

PRojects IN Controlled Environments (PRINCE2®) is a nonproprietary project management methodology that was developed originally for government projects in the United Kingdom. Today, PRINCE2® has been adopted worldwide by more than 20,000 public and private organizations (1).

The aim of PRINCE2® is to ensure that projects are well-thought out in the beginning, well-managed throughout, and organized until the end (5). Similar to the PMBOK® Guide, PRINCE2® follows the PLC and provides stakeholders with a common language and approach to managing projects of all sizes and types. It focuses on managing and controlling costs, schedules, quality, risk, as well as the project work or activities in order to achieve the value or benefits envisioned. In addition, there is a large number of training opportunities for people and organizations interested in gaining more knowledge of PRINCE2® or who want to become PRINCE2® certified.

Under PRINCE2®, a **Project Board** is created and is accountable and responsible for managing, monitoring, and controlling the project activities to ensure that the project achieves the value envisioned in the business case. The Project Board may have up to eight people and includes three important roles: a **customer**, a **senior user**, and a **senior supplier**. The customer can be a customer, client, or executive sponsor who represents the business interests of the organization. Furthermore, the senior user represents the interests of the users or stakeholders who will use the project's product in order to bring the expected value or benefits to the organization. The senior supplier represents the suppliers or specialists who provide the skills or resources needed to deliver the project's product. In addition to providing direction, the Project Board makes important decisions such as change requests and whether the project should continue. The Project Board is accountable for the project's success or failure. The project manager, on the other hand, oversees the day-to-day project activities and reports the project's progress and any issues directly to the Project Board.

As shown in Figure 2.4, the PRINCE2® methodology is comprised of seven processes, seven themes, and seven principles based on established project management best practices. As an organization gains experience with the methodology, knowledge gained from lessons learned can be useful to future projects. In this section, we will cover the basic concepts associated with PRINCE2®.

PRINCE2® Processes

The PRINCE2® includes seven processes that define how the project work is to be completed, by whom, and the targeted result (5). These processes outline sets of activities throughout the project's life cycle.

- *Start Project*—The first process should be relatively short and focused on developing a project brief or document that provides business justification for the project. The Project Board is created and determines whether the project should be commissioned to continue to the next stage. This is more of a basic fact-finding stage, where the organization attempts to determine whether the project is doable and worth doing without spending a great deal of time and money.

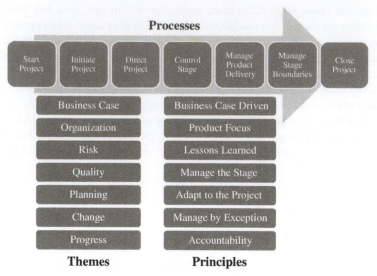

Figure 2.4 THE PRINCE2® Methodology

- *Initiate Project*—The main focus of this process is to develop the project brief into a more detailed business case, which is a key document that lays a foundation for all important project decisions. In addition, the project manager documents performance targets for benefits, costs, schedule, quality, scope, and risk in an overall project plan.

- *Direct Project*—The Project Board's overall activities are defined so that it can direct the project successfully throughout each stage up through the project's closure.

- *Control Stage*—During this process, the project manager's day-to-day activities are defined as well as how the project tasks will be controlled and monitored.

- *Manage Product Delivery*—The project manager plans each stage as a set of work packages to be delivered. A **work package** includes such things as the products to delivered, the people authorized to do the work, constraints, tolerances, as well as the resources and time line for completing the work. This process ensures that the work packages are developed, delivered, and approved as planned.

- *Manage Stage Boundaries*—This includes the information or reporting mechanisms the project manager will give to the Project Board in order to review the status of the project and to determine whether continued business justification for the project exists.

- *Close Project*—This ensures that the project is completed in a controlled manner if the project work is completed as planned or if it is no longer viable. More specifically, activities are defined for the acceptance of the project, as well as for the project manager to archive documents and release project resources.

PRINCE2® Themes

Themes act as guidelines to ensure that the project processes help the project achieve its goal (6).

- *Business Case*—Although the business case is an important PRINCE2® process, its importance is also underscored as a theme that asks the questions, "Why should this project be funded?" and "Why should this project continue to be funded?" It is a key document that not only justifies the initiation of a project, but also ensures that the project can deliver its intended value.

- *Organization*—The organization theme attempts to answer the question, "Who is involved with the project?" Under this theme, roles, responsibilities, and accountabilities are defined.

- *Risk*—All projects entail elements of risk, and the risk theme attempts to manage uncertainty by answering the question, "What if ....?" The approach to managing risk under PRINCE2® includes identifying, assessing, and managing risk systematically and proactively.

- *Quality*—The quality theme attempts to ensure that the project is not only completed on time and within budget, but that it also is completed within standards so that the product fits its intended use or purpose.

- *Planning*—The planning theme provides clear communication by attempting to answer the questions, "Who does what?" and "When will it get done?" Plans also provide control for the delivery of the project's product and to determine whether the cost, time, quality, risk, work performance targets are achievable by providing a reference point to measure progress against.

- *Change*—Often changes are required to the project's plans and target objectives. Requests for changes can come from any of the project stakeholders, so a systematic way to document, manage, and decide whether proposed changes are necessary is warranted. Subsequently, the change theme attempts to manage and control changes to the project as they occur.

- *Progress*—Metrics provide a means to measure a project's achievement and forecast whether the project's progress is going according to the approved plan. The progress theme attempts to answer the questions, "Where is the project now?" and "Where will it end up?"

PRINCE2® Principles

Similar to the PMBOK® Guide, PRINCE2® Principles have been proven over time and provide a foundation for sound project management practices in terms of providing a universal guidance for all projects (1). To be a PRINCE2® project, all seven of the following principles must be followed:

- *Business Case Driven*—The business case is a key document that is developed at the beginning of the project and must be continually justified throughout. Therefore, it is a key driver for starting the project and for continued funding of the project.

- *Product Focus*—Projects are not just a series of activities or tasks, but rather are undertaken to produce a product. PRINCE2® projects emphasize the design and delivery of a quality product.

- *Lessons Learned*—PRINCE2® is based on proven best practices. Therefore, documented experiences in terms of lessons learned are an important component for the PRINCE2® methodology that are sought throughout the life of the project.

- *Manage the Stage*—At each stage of the project, the Project Board reviews the project's progress in comparison to the business case. Each stage is planned, monitored, and controlled.

- *Adapt to the Project*—The PRINCE2® methodology can be tailored to projects large or small. The methodology can be scaled to the size of the project and should be flexible in terms of the risks and environment unique to the project.

- *Manage by Exception*—Tolerances are defined and used to empower project stakeholders by allowing them to make decisions without having to ask for approval from the next higher level of authority.

- *Accountability*—PRINCE2® projects should have clear roles and responsibilities. Stakeholders need to know their role as well as everyone else's. The Project Board includes executive sponsorship that defines the project's objectives and ensures that the project remains viable. In addition, internal or external suppliers provide resources, skills, or the knowledge to deliver the project's products, while users represent those stakeholders who will benefit from the delivery of the final product.

THE SYSTEMS DEVELOPMENT LIFE CYCLE (SDLC)

Although projects follow a project life cycle, the development of new products, services, or information systems follow a product life cycle. The most common product life cycle in IT is the Systems Development Life Cycle (SDLC), which represents the sequential phases or stages a product or information system follows throughout its useful life. The SDLC establishes a logical order, or sequence, in which the system development activities occur and indicates whether to proceed from one system development activity to the next (7). Although there are variations of the SDLC, the life cycle depicted in Figure 2.5 includes the generally accepted activities and phases associated with systems development. Keep in mind that these concepts are generally covered in great detail in system analysis and design books and courses. For some, this may be a quick review, while for others it will provide a general background for understanding how IT project management and information system development activities support one another. Planning, analysis, design, implementation, and maintenance and support are the five basic phases in the systems development life cycle.

- *Planning*—The *planning phase* involves identifying and responding to a problem or opportunity and incorporates the project management and system development processes and activities. Here a formal planning process ensures that the goal, scope, budget, schedule, technology, and system development processes, methods, and tools are in place.

- *Analysis*—The *analysis phase* attempts to delve into the problem or opportunity more fully. For example, the project team may document the current system to develop an "*as is*" model to understand the system currently in place. In general, systems analysts will meet with various stakeholders (users, managers, customers, etc.) to learn more about the problem or opportunity. This work is done to identify and document any problems or bottlenecks associated with the current system. Here the specific needs and requirements for the new system are identified and documented.

- *Design*—During the *design phase*, the project team uses the requirements and "*to be*" logical models as input for designing the architecture to support the new information system.

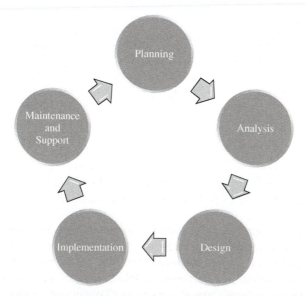

Figure 2.5 The Systems Development Life Cycle (SDLC)

This architecture includes designing the network, hardware configuration, databases, user interface, and application programs.

- *Implementation—Implementation* includes the development or construction of the system, testing, and installation. In addition, training, support, and documentation must be in place.

- *Maintenance and Support—*Although maintenance and support may not be a true phase of the current project, it is still an important consideration. Once the system has been implemented, it is said to be in production. Changes to the system, in the form of maintenance and enhancements, are often requested to fix any discovered errors (i.e., bugs) within the system, to add any features that were not incorporated into the original design, or to adjust to a changing business environment. Support, in terms of a call center or help desk, may also be in place to help users on an as-needed basis.

Eventually, the system becomes part of the organizational infrastructure and becomes known as a legacy system. At this point, the system becomes very similar to a car. Let's say you buy a brand new car. Over time, the car becomes less and less new, and parts have to be replaced as they wear out. Although a system does not wear out like a car, changes to the system are required as the organization changes. For example, a payroll system may have to be changed to reflect changes in the tax laws, or an electronic commerce site may have to be altered to reflect a new line of products that the company wishes to introduce. As the owner of an older or classic car, you may find yourself replacing part after part until you make the decision to trade in the old junker for something newer and more reliable. Similarly, an organization may find itself spending more and more on maintaining a legacy system. Eventually, the organization will decide that it is time to replace this older system with a newer one that will be more reliable, require less maintenance, and better meets its needs. Subsequently, a new life cycle begins at the start of a new project.

The PLC and the SDLC

The project life cycle (PLC) focuses on the phases, processes, tools, knowledge, and skills for managing a project, while the systems development life cycle (SDLC) focuses on creating and implementing the project's product—the information system. It bears worth mentioning again that how a project team chooses to implement the SDLC will directly affect how the project is planned in terms of phases, tasks, estimates, and resources assigned.

As illustrated in Figure 2.6, the SDLC is part of the PLC because many of the development activities occur during the *execution* phase of the PLC. The last two phases of the PLC, *close project* and *evaluate project success*, occur after the delivery of the product or information system.

The integration of project management and systems development activities is one important component that distinguishes IT projects from other types of projects.

Implementing the SDLC

As mentioned previously, product-oriented processes are needed to define and create a product, service, or information system. These processes will define how the systems development life cycle (SDLC) will be implemented. Subsequently, this will define all of the subphases and deliverables associated with the *execute and control* project management life cycle phase.

There are a number of ways to implement the SDLC. The chosen method or approach depends on the size and complexity of the project as well as the experience and skills of the project team. A particular method will not only define the software processes and tools needed, but will also be a critical factor for developing the project plan in terms of defining project phases, deliverables, tasks, and resources that will be used to estimate the project's schedule and budget. Today, an IT project will follow a structured development approach like Waterfall or an iterative development approach called Agile.

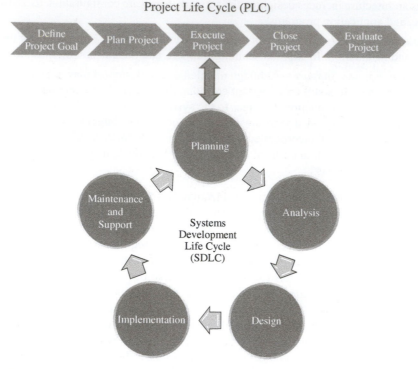

Figure 2.6 The Project Life Cycle (PLC) and the Systems Development Life Cycle (SDLC)

Waterfall

A structured approach to systems development has been around since the 1960s and 1970s, when large mainframe applications were developed. Winston Royce, a computer scientist, is attributed with proposing a model called "Waterfall" when he published a paper called "Managing the Development of Large Software Systems" in 1970 (8). Waterfall is a metaphor for a cascading of activities from one phase to the next where one phase is completed before the next phase is started.

The Waterfall model in Figure 2.7 stresses a sequential and logical flow of software development activities. For example, design activities or tasks begin only after the requirements are defined completely. Subsequently, the building or coding activities will not start until the design phase is complete. Although there is some iteration where the developers can go back to a previous stage, it is not always easy or desirable. One characteristic of the Waterfall model is that a great deal of time and effort is spent in the early phases getting the requirements and design correct because it is more expensive to add a missing requirement in the later phases of the project.

An advantage of the Waterfall model is that it allows us to plan each phase in detail so that the project schedule and budget can be computed by summing the time and cost estimates for all the tasks defined in each phase. In theory, the project will be completed on time and within budget if each phase is completed according to our estimates.

This approach is still used today, especially for large government systems and by companies that develop shrink-wrap or commercial software packages. A structured approach is suitable when developing large, more complex systems where one assumes, or at least hopes, that the requirements defined in the early phases do not change very much over the remainder of the project. In addition, because it will provide a solid structure that can minimize wasted effort, the Waterfall model may work well when the project team is inexperienced or less technically competent (7).

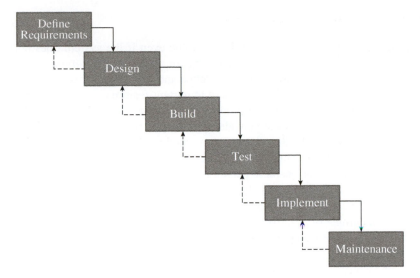

Figure 2.7 The Waterfall Model

Interestingly, although Winston Royce is credited for the Waterfall method, many people must not have read the whole paper because Royce did not called it "Waterfall" and even explained that such an approach was inherently risky. Instead, he proposed a more iterative approach to developing systems, but Waterfall gained popularity because its logical and systematic process appeals to many people.

Critics of the structured approach to systems development argue that it takes too long to develop systems and that this approach does not embrace the idea that changing requirements are inevitable. Inexperienced developers often have the false belief that if they ask the users what they want, they will be rewarded with a set of clear, accurate, and complete requirements. In truth, most users do not know or are unable to articulate their needs early on in the project. And if they do, those requirements will most likely change later on. In addition, users tend to be involved at three main points during a Waterfall project: 1) when they are needed to define the requirements (i.e., features and functionality) of the software, 2) when users ask for changes to the requirements, and 3) at the end of the project when the software is delivered. Many times this has resulted in strained relationships between users and developers. Users may not have articulated everything they want, and developers become resistant to making any changes later on. Adding new requirements or changing software that has already been written adds to the schedule and cost of the project. As a result, a new system may be delivered that does not meet the users' needs. On the other hand, changing software once it's been written can extend the project schedule and subsequently increase the cost of the project significantly.

Another issue is that the potential value of the project can only be attained at the end of the project when the system with all its defined requirements is delivered. For many projects, this could be months or years. On the other hand, let's say that a development team is building a new software system that has ten required features and is expected to cost $100,000. If the organization runs out of funds halfway through the project, then the software is incomplete and probably unusable because most or all of the code has not been written and tested. The organization receives absolutely no value from its investment even though it spent half of its budgeted funds.

Part of the problem is that not all requirements are created equally. Some requirements are important and are considered "must haves," while other lesser important requirements could be considered "would likes." Like many people, you probably use only a handful of the features available in your word processing or spreadsheet software. Each one of these features was a requirement when the software was designed and developed, but unfortunately, much of the available functionality can be considered "hardly or never used" features that we (or our organizations) paid for when the software was purchased.

Agile Systems Development

If Agile is said to have a theory, then it's to deliver value even if the system does not include all of the defined requirements. This is done by condensing the SDLC into an *iteration*, or *sprint*, where the users and developers work closely together to define and prioritize, for example, the three or four most important ("must have") features. Once these important features are defined, they are designed, coded, tested, documented so that a usable product or software system is usually delivered within a few weeks. Additional features and even new ideas can be part of future iterations, or sprints. Even if the organization runs out of funds after the first or second sprint where perhaps only five out of ten requirements are delivered, the organization still receives value from a working software system.

Unlike Waterfall, the user or business person is involved throughout the entire product/software development process. Instead of resisting changing requirements, Agile makes it much easier and less expensive to incorporate changes. Subsequently, the organization should get exactly what it needs.

Over the years, a number of iterative approaches to systems development have been proposed. The central theme focuses on shortening the SDLC and embracing the idea that requirements are difficult to define and will change. Iterative methods tend to emphasize working software to measure progress and rely heavily on face-to-face communication. Subsequently, a different approach to project planning will be needed.

WHAT IS AGILE?   The term *Agile* today is an umbrella term that includes a number of approaches, methods, or ways to develop products or systems. In 1986, Hirotaka Takeuchi and Ikujiro Nonaka published a paper in the *Harvard Business Review* called "The New New Product Development Game," and proposed a more holistic approach to developing new products (9). The authors suggest that how organizations create new products needs to change because quality and low cost is not enough to remain competitive. Organizations must also focus on speed and flexibility. Instead of relying on a relay approach that focuses on a sequential process, organizations should rely on self-organizing teams that approach product development like a scrum in a rugby match that moves the ball down the field as a unit.

Although Takeuchi and Nonaka's idea focused on developing new consumer products, a number of IT experts saw this as a new way to develop software. While a structured approach fit many engineering projects like the construction of buildings or early computer applications, it was clearly no longer the only way to build systems in a modern world. Not only had the technology changed, but the way people and organizations used technology changed as well. Systems had to be built in weeks, instead of months or years.

In 2001, seventeen IT experts gathered for a conference in Snowbird, Utah to discuss new ways to develop software. From this gathering, the group came up with the **Agile Manifesto** and twelve principles to describe how teams can transition to Agile (10). Interestingly, while the Agile Manifesto was written with the development of software in mind, these ideas have spread back to other industries focused on product development (11).

The Agile Manifesto is presented in Figure 2.8 and expresses the core beliefs and values behind Agile:

- *Individuals and Interactions over Processes and Tools*—As stated in the manifesto, it's not that processes and tools are not important, it's that people and interactions are more important. Often in the past, developers were held to strict plans and processes from which they seldom deviated. A command and control structure ensured processes were followed even if they didn't exactly fit or make sense for a particular project. Sometimes it's easier to follow the process rather than come up with an innovative solution. Under Agile, the development team is given autonomy to choose the best way to do the work for a given project. This requires multidisciplinary teams that are motivated, self-organizing, and able to communicate effectively. Innovation, problem

Manifesto for Agile Software Development

We are uncovering better ways of developing
software by doing it and helping others do it.
Through this work we have come to value:

Individuals and interactions over processes and tools
Working software over comprehensive documentation
Customer collaboration over contract negotiation
Responding to change over following a plan

That is, while there is value in the items on
the right, we value the items on the left more.

Kent Beck	James Grenning	Robert C. Martin
Mike Beedle	Jim Highsmith	Steve Mellor
Arie van Bennekum	Andrew Hunt	Ken Schwaber
Alistair Cockburn	Ron Jeffries	Jeff Sutherland
Ward Cunningham	Jon Kern	Dave Thomas
Martin Fowler	Brian Marick	

Figure 2.8 The Agile Manifesto. © 2001, the above authors. This declaration may be freely copied in any form, but only in its entirety through this notice. SOURCE: http://agilemanifesto.org

solving, and teamwork can hopefully lead to more creative products and solutions. In short, instead of the project team conforming to the processes and tools, the project team could customize the processes and tools to conform to the work the project team needs to do (11).

- *Working Software over Comprehensive Documentation*—As described above, if a project has ten requirements and five of the highest ranked requirements are designed, tested, and documented as a working product, then you could say the project is 50 percent complete. Under past approaches, early analysis and design phases emphasized the definition of requirements and the modeling of the current and future processes, data, and so forth as documents. While designs on paper or mockup prototypes for presentations can be useful, documents are not a finished product or system. Only working (and tested) software brings value to people and organizations. Moreover, project team members are often required to document the work they complete as a way to track the progress of the project. This is often viewed as excessive or needless documentation that consumes valuable time that could have been used more productively. Under Agile, documentation is only useful if it aids directly in the development of a working product or system.

- *Customer Collaboration over Contract Negotiation*—A subtle but important change from previous approaches to developing software is that products are developed for customers. While the term "user" still applies as in "people who use the product or system," practitioners of Agile tend to use the richer term "customer" instead. Therefore, a customer could be a user, or an important stakeholder internal or external to the organization. The customer is supreme, and Agile emphasizes collaboration to ensure that the customers get exactly what they need. A structured approach often tries to lock in users to requirements they cannot define or articulate fully early in the project. These requirements can be viewed as a contract for the design of software features that are subsequently coded, tested, and documented. Changes or additions become more costly, and any potential collaboration between users and developers can become adversarial as each side negotiates for or against proposed changes. Under Agile, all team members work together as partners who solve problems, learn, modify, and build the right product together (11).

- *Responding to Change over Following a Plan*—Under a more structured approach to software development, change is viewed as something that must be managed and controlled; otherwise, the project spins out of control. Therefore, it's important to get it right, so a great deal of time is spent creating a detailed plan. If the plan doesn't work, it's because someone didn't spend enough time planning or the plan needed more detail. The plan becomes so important that egos can drive the team to blindly follow a plan. Under Agile, resistance to change is viewed as futile so why fight it? Instead, change can be viewed as an opportunity to improve the product or system because new knowledge or insight can lead to new ideas and new innovations or stop the team from travelling down the wrong path before it's too late.

In addition, twelve principles were defined by the authors of the Agile Manifesto. These principles are summarized in Figure 2.9 and provide a set of guidelines for people and organizations that want to follow the values and beliefs outlined in the Agile Manifesto. If a team wants to say it is "being Agile," it must be true to the manifesto and follow these twelve principles.

The principles can be summarized into four themes or categories (11):

- *Customer*—Again, Agile takes a strong customer focus, and the customer could be internal (e.g., the user) or external to the organization. The product or system must be developed with the customer in mind; therefore, the customer and developers must communicate and interact effectively in order to work together collaboratively. The team should be collocated for daily face-to-face communication.

- *Product*—Only working software brings value, but it must be delivered in the shortest time practical. Although it is important to give customers what they want, it is also important to keep things simple and deliver only the most important features or functionality. Change is not the enemy. It is an opportunity.

- *Project Team*—An Agile team should include business people and technical people who are motivated, self-organizing, and mutually accountable. A team should be given the support and resources it needs and then trusted to get the job done. People who work long hours may burn out, get tired, become less motivated, and tend to make more mistakes. Therefore, the team should be able to work at a pace that is constant and sustainable.

- *Performance*—The team should have the authority to make adjustments when needed. In addition, a product is complete only when it is designed, tested, documented, and working.

SOME COMMONLY USED AGILE METHODS   In this section, you will be introduced to a few common Agile methods used today. The purpose here is to give you a general overview. Specific processes for implementing Agile will be defined in more detail in a later chapter when you learn about an important project management tool called the Work Breakdown Structure (WBS).

Today, a number of methods that conform to the Agile Manifesto and principles are available. Two of the most popular and commonly used choices are **eXtreme programming (XP)** and **Scrum**. However, organizations sometimes combine Agile methodologies successfully, so the line between them can become blurred (10).

XP was introduced by Kent Beck in the mid-1990s. Under XP, the system is transferred to the users in a series of versions called releases. A release may be developed using several iterations that are developed and tested within a few weeks or months. Each release is a working system that includes only one or several functions that are part of the full system specifications. XP includes a number of activities where the user requirements are first documented as a **user story**. The user stories are then documented

1. The main goal is to satisfy the customer by delivering valuable products constantly and quickly.

2. Since Agile processes are founded on changing requirements, change at any time during the project can be good for the customer and should be welcome.

3. Working products or software should be delivered as soon as practically possible (weeks or months).

4. Developers and business people should work together daily.

5. Provide support to motivated people and then trust them to finish the job.

6. Face-to-face communication is the best way to communicate (Colocation).

7. Progress is measured by a product that works.

8. People should be able to work at a pace that is constant and sustainable.

9. Focus on technical excellence and agility through good design.

10. Keep it simple.

11. A self-organizing team creates the best products.

12. The team should reflect on its performance often and then make adjustments as necessary.

Figure 2.9 The Principles of Agile
SOURCE: Beck, Kent, et al. (2001). "Principles Behind the Agile Manifesto"

using an object-oriented model called a **class diagram**. A set of acceptance tests is then developed for each user story. Releases that pass the acceptance tests are then considered complete. Small teams of developers often work in a common room where workstations are positioned in the middle and a workspace for each team member is provided around the perimeter. In addition, XP often incorporates team programming, where two programmers work together on the same workstation. Developers often are prohibited from working more than 40 hours a week in order to avoid burnout and the mistakes that often occur because of fatigue (10).

As you may have guessed, Scrum is a metaphor likened to a scrum in the game of rugby. As an Agile method, Scrum was developed from a collaborative effort between Ken Schwaber and Jeff Sutherland in the early 1990s. Under Scrum, there are three important roles: **Scrum master**, **product owner**, and the **development team**. The Scrum master is similar to the project manager, while the product owner represents the business side and ensures that the most important features are included in the product. The development team is responsible for delivering a quality product or system.

Requirements or features are defined by the product owner and time estimates for each feature is estimated by the project team. The product owner then prioritizes the features that become the **product backlog**, which is subsequently divided into iterations called a **sprint**. Each sprint generally takes a few weeks, and a completed product is delivered. Additional features and functionality are planned for the next sprint until all of the features in the product backlog are delivered. Each day, the Scrum master, product owner, and development team have a short, stand-up meeting called the **daily Scrum** during which information and the project's progress are shared.

WATERFALL VERSUS AGILE? No doubt there are those who advocate strongly for one approach or the other. Often people discount an established approach when a new one arrives and is heralded as being better. Keep an open mind and consider a few things. First, many projects have been successful and many have failed following Waterfall. Second, many projects have been successful and many have failed following Agile.

There are times when Waterfall will be the right choice, just as there will be times when the project should follow Agile. The old saying to choose the right tool for the job is appropriate. It also depends on the skills and ability of the project team. It would be a disaster for a project manager to announce to his or her team to stop "doing things the old way" and "start doing Agile." On the other hand, it's important to know what you're doing. Many project teams have started out "doing Agile," but didn't follow it fully or reverted back to what they're used to when faced with a stressful challenge.

The short answer is that no approach works in all situations. However, it is important that you learn and understand a number of different ways to approach a project. Then, choose or customize an approach from a set of methods, tools, and processes that conforms to the project at hand.

LEARNING CYCLES AND LESSONS LEARNED

Learning cycle theory was originally proposed by John Dewey in 1938 and used to describe how people learn (12). Learning cycles are a useful tool that can be used throughout the project life cycle regardless whether the project team follows Waterfall or Agile. More specifically, learning cycles provide a way to resolve ambiguous situations through the repeated pattern of thinking through a problem (13). Figure 2.10 illustrates a team learning cycle.

John Redding suggests that a team learning cycle has four phases (14):

1. *Understand and frame the problem*—It is important that a project team not accept the issues and challenges presented to them at face value. Assumptions must be surfaced and tested because the problem or issue as it is originally framed may not be the real problem after all. Thus, the project team must get to the root of the problem. At the beginning of a project, the team members' understanding may be quite general, or they may feel that they really do not understand the challenge assigned to them. Unfortunately, few people are willing to admit that they do not have all the answers or that their understanding of the team's challenge is limited. On the other

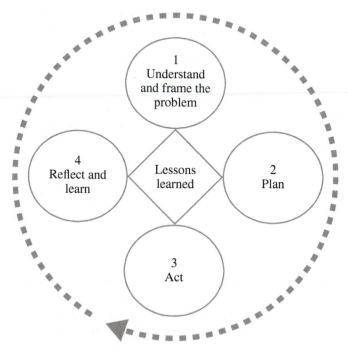

Figure 2.10 A Learning Cycle
SOURCE: Adapted from *The Radical Team Handbook*. John Redding, Jossey-Bass 2000. Reprinted by permission of John Wiley & Sons, Inc.

hand, other members of the team may approach the project with a high degree of certainty—that is, they may act as though they know what the solution is and, therefore, the team just needs to work out the details of how to go about implementing the solution. Opinions are often accepted without question and can result in erroneous assumptions that lead the project team in the wrong direction or keep the team from getting at the real problem. Moreover, there is often pressure for the team to take immediate action so that the project can be completed on time and within budget. In either case, the team runs the risk of not getting to the root of the problem and may propose solutions that have minimal impact on the organization.

For example, project team members may meet with a project sponsor who tells them that the company has an inventory problem. More specifically, the company has too much inventory on hand, and the cost to warehouse this inventory is becoming too exorbitant. After touring the warehouse, the project team can see that the company's product takes up just about all the available floor space and is stacked to the ceiling. The project sponsor tells team members that an information system would increase efficiency and therefore provide a solution for reducing inventory. Without questioning the problem (and solution) as it was handed to them, the team members may focus on solving the project just as it was handed to them.

Therefore, the project team must come to understand two things: Preconceived solutions are likely to produce run-of-the-mill results, and teams should encourage open humility. In other words, it is all right for team members to recognize and admit that they do not have all the answers, especially at the beginning of a project. As a result, team members may feel more comfortable admitting they have more questions than answers and the potential for preconceived ideas leading to mediocre solutions is reduced.

2. *Plan*—To help teams understand and reframe the problem, teams should create a shared understanding of the problem or opportunity. This understanding includes defining what team members are trying to accomplish and how they are going to go about it.

    The team can brainstorm what it knows (the facts), what it thinks it knows (assumptions), and what it doesn't know (questions to be answered). Early in the project, a team may have more questions and assumptions than facts. That is to be expected because the team may not fully understand the problem or challenge. Assumptions are ideas, issues, or concepts that must be tested (e.g., "The users will never agree to this," or "Senior management will never spend the money"). Often, a person can make an assumption sound like a fact, especially if she or he says it with enough conviction or authority. Therefore, it is every team member's responsibility to separate the facts (proof, evidence, or reality) from assumptions (theories, opinions, or guesses). On the other hand, if the team identifies (or admits) things it does not know, these can be classified as questions to be answered.

    Figure 2.11 shows an example of a team learning record. After meeting with the sponsor and touring the warehouse, the team may list the facts, assumptions, and questions to be answered. The first column lists all the facts or evidence from the tour of the warehouse. The second column attempts to separate the sponsor's opinion from fact so the team does not fall into the trap of solving the wrong problem or just a symptom of the problem. The third column provides an opportunity to admit that no one has all the answers at this time, but answers can be found.

3. *Act*—Once the project team identifies what it knows, what it thinks it knows, and what it needs to find out, it can create a plan of action. Team members can volunteer or be assigned to specific tasks that require testing assumptions or learning answers to questions. Documenting who does what by when also provides a tool for accountability. An example of a plan of action is illustrated in Figure 2.12.

    The key to team learning is carrying out the actions defined in the team's action plan. Team members can work on their own or together to test out assumptions, try out hunches, experiment, or gather and analyze data. The purpose of these actions should be to generate

What we know (Facts)	What we think we know (Assumptions)	What we don't know (Questions to be Answered)
Company has too much inventory on hand	It may be an efficiency problem	Why are inventory levels so high?
Cost of maintaining current inventory is becoming prohibitive	Management believes a new information system will improve efficiency and therefore lower inventory levels	What are the current levels of inventory?
Inventory turnover needs to be increased		What is the desired level of inventory?

Figure 2.11 An Example of a Team Learning Record
SOURCE: Adapted from *The Radical Team Handbook*. John Redding, Jossey-Bass 2000. Reprinted by permission of John Wiley & Sons, Inc.

Who?	Does What?	By When?
Shedelle and Steve	Interview sales team to understand past, current, and future trends for the company's product	Tuesday
Myra	Provide a detailed count of the current physical inventory on hand	Thursday
Corean	Research potential inventory management system commercial packages	Thursday
Steve	Research average inventory levels for the industry	Wednesday

Figure 2.12 An Example of an Action Plan
SOURCE: Adapted from *The Radical Team Handbook*. John Redding, Jossey-Bass 2000. Reprinted by permission of John Wiley & Sons, Inc.

knowledge and test assumptions, not to complete a series of tasks like a to-do list. Thus, the purpose of these actions is to confirm or disconfirm assumptions and learn answers to questions the team does not know. Redding suggests that what teams do outside of meetings is just as important as the meeting itself because only by acting do teams have the opportunity to learn.

4. *Reflect and learn*—After the team has had a chance to carry out the action items in the action-learning plan, the team should meet to share its findings and reflect upon what everyone has learned. To be effective, this reflection must take place in an environment of openness,

honesty, and trust. Once the team has a chance to meet and reflect on the information it has acquired, the team can document what it has learned.

Redding suggests that the team answer the following questions:

- What do we know now that we didn't know before?
- Have we encountered any surprises? Have we gained any new insights? If so, what were they?
- What previous assumptions have been supported or refuted by what we have learned so far?
- How does the team feel the project is progressing at this point?
- How effective has the team been so far?

Following our example, the team may find out that the real reason why inventory levels are so high is because the company's product is obsolete or no longer in style. If the team had followed blindly the sponsor's recommendation that an information system would reduce inventory levels through efficiency, only modest improvements would have resulted. Remember: Many times the problem may be the way the problem is handed to you.

The team learning cycles and lessons learned can be documented and shared with other project teams. However, the completion of a team's lessons learned marks the ending of one learning cycle and the beginning of another. Based on the learning that has transpired, the team can focus once again on understanding and reframing the problem and then repeat the plan, act, reflect and learn phases again. Figure 2.13 illustrates this concept.

As shown in Figure 2.13, an entire project can be viewed as a series of learning cycles. An initial team meeting can examine the original problem or challenge assigned to the team. During that meeting, the team can develop an initial action plan. Between meetings, the members of the team can then carry out their assigned tasks for testing assumptions or gathering information.

At the next meeting, the team can reflect on what it has learned, document the lessons learned, and then start the beginning of a new cycle. Each cycle should be used to challenge the framing of the problem and create new opportunities for learning.

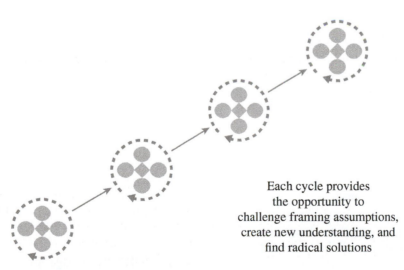

Each cycle provides
the opportunity to
challenge framing assumptions,
create new understanding, and
find radical solutions

Figure 2.13 Learning Cycles over the Project Life Cycle
SOURCE: Adapted from *The Radical Team Handbook*. John Redding, Jossey-Bass 2000. Reprinted by permission of John Wiley & Sons, Inc.

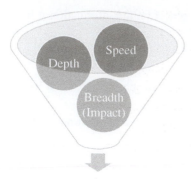

Team Learning

Figure 2.14 Team Learning

Teams do not always begin and end learning cycles at each meeting. Some learning cycles may take longer, and some can be accomplished in a shorter time if face-to-face meetings are not needed. Redding suggests, however, that three dimensions can be used to assess team learning: speed, depth, and breadth.

- *Speed*—First, a team should follow a learning cycle approach rather than a traditional, linear approach. Second, speed refers to the number of learning cycles completed. Therefore, the opportunity to learn can be increased if a team can complete more cycles in a given amount of time.

- *Depth*—Just increasing the number of learning cycles does not guarantee that teams will increase their learning. Subsequently, depth of learning refers to the degree to which a team can deepen its understanding of the project from cycle to cycle. This learning includes challenging the framing of the problem and various assumptions. In short, depth focuses on how well the team is able to dig below the surface in order to get to the root of the problem. Redding suggests that a team can measure depth by asking the question: "Was the team's conception of the project at the end any different from what it was in the beginning?" (p. 47).

- *Breadth*—The breadth of learning refers to the impact the project has on the organization. It also focuses on whether the learning that has taken place within the team stays within the team or is shared and used throughout the organization. If a team can uncover complex relationships, it can develop a solution that impacts the whole organization. For example, what originally was thought to be an inventory problem could very well cross several functional or departmental boundaries (Figure 2.14).

CHAPTER SUMMARY

- A project methodology provides a systematic way to plan, manage, and execute the work. It prescribes the phases, processes, tools, and techniques to be used.

- Project methodologies should be flexible and evolve over time from experience to better fit the organization and the project team. They provide a common language and provide a useful template for planning the project.

- A project life cycle (PLC) divides a project into phases that make the project more manageable and that are common to most projects.

- A PLC can be divided into five phases: define project goal, plan project, execute project plan, close project, and evaluate project.

- The define project goal phase signals the beginning of a project and attempts to define the business value the project will bring to the organization.

- The plan project phase focuses on defining the scope, schedule, budget, and quality objectives

as well as defining the resources and controls that are needed.

- The execute project plan phase starts when the organization approves the project plan and focuses on delivering the project's product, service, or system.

- The close and evaluate project phases provide an end to the project and ensure that the project work is completed as agreed upon. They also involve evaluating the project team and project goal to define lessons learned and to determine the project's true value to the organization.

- The Project Management Body of Knowledge (PMBOK®) is a project management methodology that includes ten knowledge areas and five process groups. It implements the PLC and provides generally accepted principles and practices for project management.

  - PMBOK® Knowledge Areas
    - *Project Integration Management*
    - *Project Scope Management*

- *Project Time Management*
- *Project Cost Management*
- *Project Quality Management*
- *Project Human Resources Management*
- *Project Communications Management*
- *Project Risk Management*
- *Project Procurement Management*
- *Project Stakeholder Management*
- PMBOK® PROCESS GROUPS
  - *Initiating*
  - *Planning*
  - *Executing*
  - *Monitoring and Controlling*
  - *Closing*
- **PR**ojects **IN** **C**ontrolled **E**nvironments (PRINCE2®) is a project management methodology developed by the British government and used in many organizations today. It implements the PLC and provides a generally accepted way to manage projects.
- Under PRINCE2®, a Project Board of representatives from the customer, senior user, and senior supplier oversees and is accountable for the project's success. PRINCE2® includes seven processes, seven themes, and seven principles:
  - PRINCE2® Processes
    - *Start Project*
    - *Initiate Project*
    - *Direct Project*
    - *Control Stage*
    - *Manage Product Delivery*
    - *Manage Stage Boundaries*
    - *Close Project*
  - PRINCE2® Themes
  - *Business Case*
  - *Organization*
  - *Risk*
  - *Quality*
  - *Planning*
  - *Change*
  - *Close Project*
  - PRINCE2® Principles

- *Business Case Driven*
- *Product Focus*
- *Lessons Learned*
- *Manage the Stage*
- *Adapt to the Project*
- *Manage by Exception*
- *Accountability*

- The Systems Develop Life Cycle (SDLC) is a product life cycle that provides a logical sequence for developing software.
- The phases of the SDLC include: planning, analysis, design, implementation, and maintenance and support.
- The planning phase focuses on identifying and responding to a problem or opportunity by developing a plan.
- The analysis phase addresses the problem or opportunity whereby an "as is" model is developed of the current business processes or system.
- The design phase defines the requirements for the new system and includes design of the "to be" business processes and system.
- The implementation phases focuses on the development or construction of the new product, service, or system as well as testing, documentation, delivery.
- The maintenance and support phase may not be a true phase in terms of planning the project, but it should be an important consideration once the product, service, or system is implemented.
- For IT projects, the SDLC is part of the *execute project* phase of the PLC.
- The Waterfall approach and Agile are two common approaches for carrying out the SDLC.
- The Waterfall approach provides a logical, systematic, and structured approach to developing software. Its phases include: define requirements, design, build, test, implement, and maintenance.
- An advantage of Waterfall is it allows for planning the development of a product, service, or system in detail.
- Disadvantages of Waterfall include trying to define the requirements at an early stage of the project and then hoping they don't change once they are coded and tested as these changes

become more expensive to implement. Often people have a difficult time articulating their requirements.

- Agile is an umbrella term that defines a number of approaches, methods, or ways to develop products or systems. Where change is often discouraged under Waterfall, change is welcome under Agile as an opportunity to deliver a better product or system.

- To be an Agile project, a project must adhere to the Agile Manifesto and to the twelve Agile principles.

- eXtreme Programming (XP) is a popular Agile method where a product or system is transferred to a customer in a series of releases within a few weeks or months. Each release is a working system that includes a number of user stories that are designed, build, documented, and tested. Often two programmers work together on the same workstation. Working more than 40 hours in a week is discouraged in order to prevent burnout and mistakes as a result of fatigue.

- Scrum is not an acronym, but is a metaphor from the game of rugby where the ball is moved down the field by a team working as a unit. It provides a holistic approach to product/software development that includes a Scrum master, product owner, and the development team. The product owner defines the most important requirements in a product backlog, which is divided into a series of iterations called sprints. A sprint lasts only a few weeks so that a finished working product is delivered. A daily Scrum meeting provides a valuable face-to-face communications tool where participants stand during the meeting.

- Learning cycles can be used throughout the PLC and provide a useful tool for team learning and lessons learned regardless whether a team follows Waterfall or Agile.

- The process for using learning cycles is to (1) understand and frame the problem, (2) plan, (3) act, and (4) reflect and learn. The conclusion of a learning cycle and the beginning of the next is marked by the documentation of lessons learned.

- A team's learning can be assessed using three dimensions: (1) speed or the number of learning cycles, (2) depth or the degree to which the team deepened its understanding of project, and (3) breadth or the impact of the team's proposed solution.

REVIEW QUESTIONS

1. What is a project methodology?
2. What are the advantages of using a methodology?
3. Describe the project life cycle (PLC).
4. What are phase exits, stage gates, and kill points? What purpose do they serve?
5. What is fast tracking? When should fast tracking be used? When would fast tracking not be appropriate?
6. Describe the "Define Project Goal" phase of the project life cycle.
7. Describe the "Plan Project" phase of the project life cycle.
8. Describe the "Execute Project Plan" phase of the project life cycle.
9. Describe the "Close and Evaluate" phases of the project life cycle.
10. Although the Guide to the Project Management Body of Knowledge (PMBOK® Guide) describes the generally accepted principles and practices of project management, why wouldn't these principles and practices work for every project?
11. What is Project Integration Management?
12. What is Project Scope Management?
13. What is Project Time Management?
14. What is Project Cost Management?
15. What is Project Quality Management?
16. What is Project Human Resources Management?
17. What is Project Communications Management?
18. What is Project Risk Management?
19. What is Project Procurement Management?
20. What is Project Stakeholder Management?
21. What is a process? Why are processes important in project management?
22. Describe the Initiating Process.
23. Describe the Planning Process.
24. Describe the Executing Process.

25. Describe the Monitoring and Controlling Process.

26. Describe the Closing Process.

27. What is the aim of PRINCE2®?

28. What is a Project Board? What is its role in a PRINCE2® project?

29. Define the roles of Customer, Senior User, and Senior Supplier in a PRINCE2® project.

30. What is the purpose the Start Project Process in a PRINCE2® project?

31. What is the purpose the Initiate Project Process in a PRINCE2® project?

32. What is the purpose the Direct Project Process in a PRINCE2® project?

33. What is the purpose the Control Stage Process in a PRINCE2® project?

34. What is the purpose the Manage Project Delivery Process in a PRINCE2® project?

35. What is the purpose the Manage Stage Boundaries Process in a PRINCE2® project?

36. What is the purpose the Close Project Process in a PRINCE2® project?

37. Describe the Business Case theme in a PRINCE2® project.

38. Describe the Organization theme in a PRINCE2® project.

39. Describe the Risk theme in a PRINCE2® project.

40. Describe the Quality theme in a PRINCE2® project.

41. Describe the Planning theme in a PRINCE2® project.

42. Describe the Change theme in a PRINCE2® project.

43. Describe the Progress theme in a PRINCE2® project.

44. Describe the Business Case Driven principle in a PRINCE2® project.

45. Describe the Product Focus principle in a PRINCE2® project.

46. Describe the Lessons Learned principle in a PRINCE2® project.

47. Describe the Manage the Stage principle in a PRINCE2® project.

48. Describe the Adapt to Project principle in a PRINCE2® project.

49. Describe the Manage by Exception principle in a PRINCE2® project.

50. Describe the Accountability principle in a PRINCE2® project.

51. What is the Systems Development Life Cycle (SDLC)?

52. Describe the Planning phase of the SDLC.

53. Describe the Analysis phase of the SDLC.

54. Describe the Design phase of the SDLC.

55. Describe the Maintenance and Support phase of the SDLC.

56. What is the relationship between the Project Life Cycle (PLC) and the Systems Development Life Cycle (SDLC)?

57. Describe the Waterfall method.

58. What are some advantages of using Waterfall?

59. What are some disadvantages of using Waterfall?

60. What is Agile?

61. What is the Agile Manifesto?

62. Why do Agile practitioners value individuals and interactions more than processes and tools?

63. Why do Agile practitioners value working software more than comprehensive documentation?

64. Why do Agile practitioners value customer collaboration more than contract negotiation?

65. Why do Agile practitioners value responding to change more than following a plan?

66. Why might practitioners of Waterfall and Agile view change differently?

67. What roles do the customers play in an Agile project?

68. Why is working software an important Agile focus?

69. Describe the attributes of an Agile project team.

70. When is a product or system considered complete under Agile?

71. Describe eXtreme Programming (XP).

72. Why is XP considered an Agile method?

73. Describe Scrum.

74. Why is Scrum considered an Agile method?

75. Describe the concept of a learning cycle.

76. Why do you think many teams accept the project problem or opportunity at face value and never question the way the problem or opportunity was framed?

77. What purpose does creating lessons learned at the end of a learning cycle provide?

HUSKY AIR—PILOT ANGELS ASSIGNMENT

Getting Started with Learning Cycles

For many people, the beginning of a project can feel like walking in heavy fog with little sense of direction. Sometimes it takes time for the project team to figure out where it's going and how it's going to get there. And once the team sets off in a direction, adjustments have to be made to make sure everyone stays on course.

Just like a compass, a map, or a GPS can help you navigate to your intended destination, learning cycles provide a useful tool that can guide you and your team throughout the project. You can use them regardless of what project management methodology you follow or whether you use Waterfall or Agile for product development.

Learning cycles also give structure to your team meetings and provide direction and accountability for when you and your team work outside a regularly scheduled meeting. Team meetings provide an opportunity to share information, challenge assumptions, and develop a plan of action that details each member's responsibilities (and accountability) for the next meeting where the learning cycle is repeated. Hopefully, this will make the team experience more efficient and effective as all members know their own responsibilities, as well as the responsibilities of each member of the group.

What to do:

1. It might be a good idea to reread the section on Learning Cycles in this chapter so that you become more familiar with what they are and how they work. A learning cycle is pretty straightforward, so you should feel very comfortable with the process once you've had a chance to work through one or two.

2. Learning cycles work best when the team meets face-to-face. Find a quiet place where the whole team can meet and work together. Ideally, this would be a comfortable room with a whiteboard or a poster chart that everyone can see, but just having a computer screen or even a piece of paper would work fine. You could even use a bunch of sticky notes on a wall or board. Just have some way to write ideas down for the group to see.

3. Assign roles to the group. From experience, you need only two roles: An organizer and a scribe. The *organizer* organizes the meeting by writing down the team's ideas and then puts them up for the group to see. The *scribe* documents the ideas and final action plan because the ideas and so forth that the organizer writes down may not be permanently available. A copy should be made available to the whole team. Roles can be rotated or assigned based on whether someone likes or is good at a particular role.

4. Go back and reread the background information for the Husky Air case at the end of Chapter 1. This is the background information that was given to you when you developed your team charter. Based on the background information, write a short summary of the problem, challenge, or opportunity. This should be just a paragraph with no more than a few sentences.

5. Using the following table as a guide, have the organizer write down the team's thoughts as to what you know (facts), what you think you know (assumptions), and what you don't know (things to find out or questions to be answered). Both the organizer and scribe should feel free to participate actively in this brainstorming discussion. Be sure to challenge any assumptions or opinions before concluding they are facts. Remember, learning cycles work best when everyone admits humility (i.e., we don't have all the answers) and there is openness to everyone's ideas.

What we know (facts)	What we think we know (assumptions)	What we don't know (questions to be answered)

Team Learning Record

6. Chances are you will write down very few facts at this time. You probably will have a few more assumptions, and a larger list of things that you don't know. That is common for many teams beginning the project (Remember the analogy of trying to find your bearings in a fog?). At this point, you and your team should not try to have

a specific number of items for each category. It's more important to be honest and open instead of trying to come up with a perfect solution. The process can be a bit messy as ideas can move from one category to another, so the scribe should document the finished product rather than the process (that's the organizer's job).

7. Once you and your team finish brainstorming the facts, assumptions, and questions, your next step is to develop an action plan to assign responsibilities to each team member. The responsibilities can be assigned individually or to two members who can work on a particular assignment together. Avoid giving the same assignment to more than two members to work on together unless there is good reason. It's probably easiest to start by first listing what has to be done. This should be based on the assumptions and questions to be answered that you just brainstormed. Hint: If someone suggests that a fact has to be checked, then it's really not a fact—it's an assumption. The organizer should organize the actions to be taken. Each team member should then volunteer or be assigned to the task, activity, or action. You are not trying to plan the whole project. You are just planning what has to be done before your next team meeting, which should be scheduled within a few days or a week. At your next meeting, each member should have completed his or her assigned tasks, share information or what was learned, and then the team starts the whole learning cycle process over with another Team Learning Record and Action Plan.

Who?	Does what?	By when?

Action Plan

8. The team should review the Action Plan before committing to it. Is the Action Plan doable in a few days? Are the assignments fair and balanced among the team members? Once you have agreement, you have team commitment and accountability. All members of the team know what the team expects from them, and what they expect from other members of the group.

9. The scribe should document the Team Learning Record and Action Plan and make it available to everyone on the team.

What to turn in:

Turn in a professional-looking document that includes the following:

1. The project name, project team name, and the names of your project team.

2. The brief summary of the challenge, problem, or opportunity statement that your team developed in this assignment.

3. Document the Team Learning Record and the Action Plan. You may not have had a chance to complete all of the tasks or assignments, so just include the Action Plan you developed during this Learning Cycle.

MARTIAL ARTS ACADEMY (MAA) ASSIGNMENT

Getting Started with Learning Cycles

For many people, the beginning of a project can feel like walking in heavy fog with little sense of direction. Sometimes it takes time for the project team to figure out where it's going and how it's going to get there. And once the team sets off in a direction, adjustments have to be made to make sure everyone stays on course.

Just like a compass, a map, or a GPS can help you navigate to your intended destination, learning cycles provide a useful tool that can guide you and your team throughout the project. You can use them regardless of what project management methodology you follow or whether you use Waterfall or Agile for product development.

Learning cycles also give structure to your team meetings and provide direction and accountability for when you and your team work outside a regularly scheduled meeting. Team meetings provide an opportunity to share information, challenge assumptions, and develop a plan of action that details each member's responsibilities (and accountability) for the next meeting where the learning cycle is repeated. Hopefully, this will make the team experience more efficient and effective as all members know their own responsibilities as well as the responsibilities of each member of the group.

What to do:

1. It might be a good idea to reread the section on Learning Cycles in this chapter so that you become more familiar with what they are and how they work. A learning cycle is pretty straightforward, so you should feel very comfortable with the process once you've had a chance to work through one or two.

2. Learning cycles work best when the team meets face-to-face. Find a quiet place where the whole team can meet and work together. Ideally, this would be a comfortable room with a whiteboard or a poster chart that everyone can see, but just having a computer screen or even a piece of paper would work fine. You could even use a bunch of sticky notes on a wall or board. Just have some way to write ideas down for the group to see.

3. Assign roles to the group. From experience, you need only two roles: An organizer and a scribe. The *organizer* organizes the meeting by writing down the team's ideas and puts them up for the group to see. The *scribe* documents the ideas and final action plan because the ideas and so forth that the organizer writes down may not be permanently available. A copy should be made available to the whole team. Roles can be rotated or assigned based on whether someone likes or is good at a particular role.

4. Go back and reread the background information for the Martial Arts Academy case at the end of Chapter 1. This is the background information that was given to you when you developed your team charter. Based on the background information, write a short summary of the problem, challenge, or opportunity. This should be just a paragraph with no more than a few sentences.

5. Using the following table as a guide, have the organizer write down the team's thoughts as to what you know (facts), what you think you know (assumptions), and what you don't know (things to find out or questions to be answered). Both the organizer and scribe should feel free to participate actively in this brainstorming discussion. Be sure to challenge any assumptions or opinions before concluding they are facts. Remember, learning cycles work best when everyone admits

humility (i.e., we don't have all the answers) and there is openness to everyone's ideas.

What we know (facts)	What we think we know (assumptions)	What we don't know (questions to be answered)

Team Learning Record

6. Chances are you will write down very few facts at this time. You probably will have a few more assumptions, and a larger list of things that you don't know. That is common for many teams beginning the project (Remember the analogy of trying to find your bearings in a fog?). At this point, you and your team should not try to have a specific number of items for each category. It's more important to be honest and open instead of trying to come up with a perfect solution. The process can be a bit messy as ideas can move from one category to another, so the scribe should document the finished product rather than the process (that's the organizer's job).

7. Once you and your team finish brainstorming the facts, assumptions, and questions, your next step is to develop an action plan to assign responsibilities to each team member. The responsibilities can be assigned individually or to two members who can work on a particular assignment together. Avoid giving the same assignment to more than two members to work on together unless there is good reason. It's probably easiest to start by first listing what has to be done. This should be based on the assumptions and questions to be answered that you just brainstormed. Hint: If someone suggests that a fact has to be checked, then it's really not a fact—it's an assumption. The organizer should organize the actions to be taken. Each team member should then volunteer or be assigned to the task, activity, or action. You are not trying to plan the whole project. You are just planning what has to be done before your next team meeting, which should be scheduled within a few days or a week. At your next meeting, each member should have completed his or her assigned tasks, share information that was learned, and then the team starts the whole learning cycle process again with another Team Learning Record and Action Plan.

Who?	Does what?	By when?

Action Plan

8. The team should review the Action Plan before committing to it. Is the Action Plan doable in a few days? Are the assignments fair and balanced among the team members? Once you have agreement, you have team commitment and accountability. All members of the team know what the team expects from them, and what they expect from other members of the group.

9. The scribe should document the Team Learning Record and Action Plan and make it available to everyone on the team.

What to turn in:

Turn in a professional-looking document that includes the following:

1. The project name, project team name, and the names of your project team.

2. The brief summary of the challenge, problem, or opportunity statement that your team developed in this assignment.

3. Document the Team Learning Record and the Action Plan. You may not have had a chance to complete all of the tasks or assignments, so just include the Action Plan you developed during this learning cycle.

QUICK THINKING—LEARNING FROM FAILURE

Michael Hugos says that he often learns more from failure than success. He concedes, *"When I succeed, it just confirms what I already know—I'm a genius. When I fail, I have an opportunity to learn, if I can bring myself to take an objective look at what happened. This is hard, but then making the same mistakes over again is even harder. So failure can be a great opportunity to learn."*

Hugos also provides some lessons learned from what he calls "one of the greatest learning experiences in his career" when he was a development leader on a systems development project that turned into a multimillion-dollar disaster. Since then, he has delivered many new systems successfully, and much of that success is due to the lessons he learned from the failure of this project. The following is a summary of what happened and some of the lessons learned from his experiences on that project.

- Although the project started out with great fanfare and enthusiasm, there were no clearly defined goals or objectives. The basic idea behind the system was to empower the sales force to grow revenues by $1 billion. *Lesson: Be wary when projects start out with wild enthusiasm and unclear goals. This can lead to the "bandwagon effect," where intelligent people do dumb things.*

- The first six months of the project was spent investigating technology and dreaming up ideas.

The development team put together a slide show and a short demonstration of some of the technology. Senior management liked what it saw and approved major funding for the project. *Lesson: Getting lots of ideas and money can commit a team to unrealistic expectations. A better approach maybe to focus on only a few realistic ideas that cost less money.*

- Four teams were working together on the project. One team was responsible for programming and hardware selection, while the other three worked on design specifications. Although all four teams were supposed to work together, the design teams began to duplicate each other's work. No single person was in charge of the entire project. Team members became confused, tempers flared, and feelings were hurt. *Lesson: Teams should have clear and defined assignments. The project leader should resolve disputes to keep the projection track.*

- After six months and hundreds of pages of specifications, the design was still incomplete, but pressure mounted to start programming. Regardless, the design was handed over to the programming team who were overwhelmed by the volume and complexity of the specifications. *Lesson: Spending more time designing a system will result in greater complexity. It may be better to design and build smaller components of the system in short, iterative steps.*

- To cope with the pressure, the programmers began to change the specifications and cut out features they didn't understand. In addition, new hardware and software releases kept coming out, so the programmers rewrote many of the programs to take advantage of the new technology releases. It took about a year to program and reprogram the system. *Lesson: System specifications must be clear and complete. Developers should stick to them and not redesign the system while building it. New features can be added in future releases.*

- Beta testing resulted in a slow system that crashed often. *Lesson: After almost two years and such high expectations, the performance of the tests seriously damaged the credibility of the project.*

- Support for the system began to fade as the programmers scrambled to fix the bugs. Senior management began to question the constantly increasing budget and cancelled the project—writing off millions of dollars. *Lesson: Dividing a large project into smaller subsystems or projects is better than trying to deliver one large system in a few years. Smaller systems are easier to debug and can show a return to the organization more quickly.*

1. Should a project team wait until the end of a project to document its lessons learned?

2. How can lessons learned be documented and made available to other project teams?

SOURCE: Michael Hugos, "Lessons Learned from a Major Project Failure," *Computerworld*. August 21, 2006.

QUICK THINKING—DOING AGILE OR BEING AGILE?

Many people believe Agile is the future. After all, Agile promises projects that are delivered on time, within budget, high quality, and satisfy the customer. In fact, success stories of IT projects has inspired Agile to be used on nontechnical projects like the development of NPR radio programs, managing churches, planning weddings, as well as running a household and raising children.

Lajos Moczar has a great deal of experience with Agile, but cautions, "I've concluded that agile has not only failed like other fad methodologies before it but, in fact, is making things worse in IT." He believes that Agile has three major flaws:

1. The continuous delivery of valuable software can lead to developers being more concerned with delivery over quality. Subsequently, this leads to an ever-increasing backlog of defects. This can increase the stress and workload of the developers who may burnout instead of working at a constant and sustainable pace. Moreover, the users or customers will become increasingly dissatisfied with a poor-quality product.

2. Another Agile principle is to respond to change over following a plan, where developers and the customers define and redefine requirements. These changes can be large or small, but many people don't make this distinction because Agile is predicated on supporting changes. As a result, many large and more costly changes are not made until late in the project. The only way to handle these major requests is to add more iterations, which can increase the project's schedule and budget, as well as the potential for more defects.

3. The third flaw arises from empowering self-organizing teams. This can lead to an "immature utopian myth" as there is still a need for responsible project management. The project team must have the right people with the right political motivations.

In addition, David Tabor suggests that distance and time can create problems for Agile projects. Agile requires close collaboration between users and developers to increase communication and to establish a strong and trusting relationship. Physical distance can create an impediment even if the project team is on different floors of the same building, but this becomes even more pronounced if the team members are in different geographical locations or when national boundaries are crossed.

While Agile projects are founded on speed and responsiveness, time, in terms of delaying the start of the project by just a few weeks, can pose significant issues or problems. If requirements were defined, they may have an expiration date because budgets and planned sprints may become quickly obsolete. As David Tabor explains, "To use a bad analogy, agile is fresh vegetables that are better for you—but they don't have the shelf life of the canned stuff."

1. Come up with a good example of how Agile could be used on a nontechnical project. What advantages would Agile have over a more structured approach like Waterfall?

2. As a project manager, how could you ensure that your developers and customers were "being Agile" rather than just attempting to "do Agile?"

SOURCES:

Johnson, P. "NPR Adopts Agile-like Method for Program Development." *Computerworld*. August 14, 2012.

Moczar, L. "Why Agile Isn't Working: Bringing Common Sense to Agile Principles." *CIO*. June 4, 2013.

Phelps, A. "Agile, Social, Cheap: The New Way NPR is Trying to Make Radio." *Nieman Journalism Lab*. April 27, 2012.

Sutherland, A. C., J. Sutherland, and C. Hegarty. "Scrum in Church." 2009 Agile Conference, Chicago, IL. August, 2009.

Tabor, D. "Time and Distance Enemies of Agile Project Management." *CIO*. July 11, 2013.

CASE STUDIES

Do Certifications Matter?

Many people and organizations value the Project Management Professional (PMP)® certification because it requires both project management knowledge and experience. According to the Project Management Institute (PMI), who administers and oversees the PMP certification, this recognition can provide increased marketability to employers and a salary up to 10 percent more than noncredentialed colleagues and peers.

The requirements for the PMP are a four-year degree (bachelor's or the global equivalent) and at least three years of project management experience. This should include 4,500 hours leading and directing projects and 35 hours of project management education. On the other hand, a person could have a secondary diploma (high school or the global equivalent) with at least five years of project management experience with 7,500 hours leading and directing projects and 35 hours of project management education.

In addition to real-world project management experience, PMP certification also requires passing a four-hour, 200-question examination that covers the Project Management Body of Knowledge (PMBOK)® knowledge areas and processes. The exam is challenging and comprehensive.

The fact that you cannot take the exam without substantial and demonstrated experience makes the PMP an often sought-after credential. Many advertisements for project managers require or prefer this certification. For example, IBM's Project Management Center of Excellence and the IBM Global Business Services' Project Management Competency oversees project manager development programs. More than 14,000 of IBM's 300,000 employees have attained the PMP certification, and the number is growing because clients want project managers with a PMP certification on their projects. Many clients associate certification with strong project management knowledge and may not consider a noncertified project manager.

Another reason PMP certified project managers are in demand is the perception that someone who has devoted thousands of hours to preparing the exam has the ability to keep a project on track. But the real question is whether having a certified project manager increases the likelihood of project success?

Two separate studies have linked certification with project performance. The first study, conducted by Price-Waterhouse Coopers (PWC) found that "higher-performing projects are significantly more likely to be staffed with certified project managers and 80 percent of projects classified as high-performing use a certified project manager." The second study was conducted by PMI in 2008 and is called the Pulse of the Profession. This study reports "that having project managers without PMP certification results in a lower percent of projects coming in on time and on budget—especially when less than 10 percent of the project managers in the company are PMPs."

However, many people are unconvinced by the findings of these two studies. It is difficult to prove that certification has a positive impact on projects because there are too many variables that can influence the outcome of a project, such as funding, resource management, end-user buy-in, and executive support. An effective project manager has the ability to deliver projects that meet stakeholder expectation on time and on budget, but the best project managers are also good leaders and communicators.

A growing number of noncertified project managers are concerned about the growing importance of the PMP certification. They believe that organizations that require the certification are making nonvalid assumptions regarding the capability of a project manager.

Although many critics downplay the importance of a certification, most professionals characterize the process for earning a PMP as rigorous, requiring a great deal of preparation and experience. Even though a certification does not automatically make one project manager better than another, it can still benefit someone personally and professionally. In a competitive job market, certifications can sometimes make a difference.

1. What are the pros and cons with earning a PMP certification?

2. If you were a project manager, would you consider getting a project management certificate? Why or why not? (If you have one, what were your reasons for becoming certified? How has it helped you in your career?)

SOURCES:
Fichtner, C. "How to Prepare for the PMP Exam Part 1: Assess Your Eligibility. *CIO*. October 19, 2010.
Levinson, M. "Six Attributes of Successful Project Managers." *CIO*. September 3, 2008.
Levinson, M. "Why Project Management Certifications Matter. *CIO*. January 20, 2010.
Levinson, M. "Inside Project Managers' Paychecks: PMI Salary Survey Results." *CIO*. April 22, 2010.
Perkins, B. "Opinion: Certifications Are No Longer Optional." *Computerworld*. March 8, 2010.
PMP Salary Survey–6th edition, 2009.

Waterfall or Agile?

The traditional "Waterfall" method of systems development has been the longest standing development methodology. Promoted as a "rigorous system methodology" (RSM) by the U.S. Department of Defense (DoD) in the 1950s, it emphasizes the concept of developing software in a series of phases that include planning, requirements specification, design, development, testing, and implementation. This highly structured method helped manage large government projects that often included a large number of vendors who worked on a various activities so that important components would not be missed. For example, one vendor may be responsible for defining and documenting the requirements, while another writes the code, and another tests the software.

Many public and private organizations throughout the world looked at the DoD as a leader in software development and adopted the Waterfall method as the standard. The Waterfall method puts the project manager squarely in charge of the project, and, therefore, the success or failure of the project will rest often on his or her shoulders. This approach tends to appeal to managers and organizations who value control of the project. Moreover, this common-sense approach appeals to individuals who believe that successful software development requires logical management practices.

On the other hand, the Waterfall method has been criticized for engaging the user or domain subject matter expert primarily in the early phases (i.e., requirements specification) and for creating voluminous paperwork. Changes to work and decisions made in the early stages can be costly and therefore less likely to be made unless absolutely critical.

For example, Scott Berinato describes two software projects that failed largely due to the inherent risks of the Waterfall method. Federal Express launched a large supply chain portal that would link order information and inventory with all parcel companies and their customers. After four years and $15 million, funding for the project came to a halt. After a few months, the director and chief architect resigned. This was soon followed by most of the development team, and FedEx was out of the portal business before the software was completed.

A major reason the project failed was because sales executives rejected the idea that the company's portal would be open to its competition even though the developers believed it was crucial to the system's success. The sales executives demanded that the developers change the system so it could be only used internally. Unfortunately, this was similar to a supply chain system FedEx already had in place. The original idea may have been too radical and having the users from the business side express their concern that FedEx would be managing a portal that supported packages from DHL or UPS should have been discovered before $15 million was wasted.

More recently, the Agile development method has been viewed as a liberator to the problems associated with the old or traditional methods of software development. The two most common approaches, eXtreme Programming (XP) and Scrum, emphasize adaptability especially when the organization does not know the exact requirements of the end product or when those requirements are expected to change.

Agile attempts to divide application development into a smaller or modularized component called an iteration or sprint. Each piece focuses on a specific set of requirements or features defined and prioritized by the user or customer. An iteration is completed within a few weeks and entails functionality that is designed, developed, documented, and tested so that even a partial application can be used.

Proponents of Agile argue that this method can reduce development costs, improve quality, reduce schedules, and ensure that users get exactly what they need. Moreover, many organizations are looking for a quick return on investment instead of waiting years for the product, service, or system to be completed. Because Agile-developed systems are delivered in iterations or sprints, the user or customer can begin to use at least a portion of the system right away instead of waiting for the entire application.

The cornerstone of Agile is face-to-face communication. Unlike the Waterfall model where communication tends to rely on written documentation, Agile methods support daily meetings where everyone meets while standing and close working relationships, like paired programming (i.e., where two developers work together on the same computer), are utilized. Moreover, Agile places a heavy emphasis on involving everyone. Both the developers and customer collaborate during the entire development process with the hope that the developers will have a clearer understand of what the customer needs and the customer will have a chance to interact with the product early on. This process is very different from documenting specifications or requirements then handing them off to someone else to code.

The Agile environment requires a different working environment. First, all team members must trust one another, so no one can withhold information, resources, or bad news from the other members. In addition, team members must be willing to compromise. Completing an iteration or sprint on time may mean giving up features or functionality that are nice to have but not absolutely necessary. This often means that not every decision will be popular, but the organization must trust the team's decisions. This is significantly different from the ideology associated with the Waterfall method where the manager or organization is in control and makes the important decisions. Many organizations' culture of command and control may make it difficult to accept an Agile approach. In addition, the Agile environment must encourage communication among team members. Aside from having a common area for meetings or working together, the team members should have similar working hours (often no more than 40 hours per week), and be available to the other team members as needed.

However, Agile is not a silver bullet because it will not work on every project. For example, often times a large application system cannot be broken down into smaller pieces and requires a large team of developers. As John Mueller explains, "If you're creating a heart monitor application for a major hospital, you don't want to create just the part that monitors the heart and deploy it without the parts that send out alerts when a patient's heart fails. In this case, you must create the entire application and test it as a whole before deployment, or else you'll end up with a lot of dead patients (and lawsuits). Agile programming techniques aren't a good solution in this case, because the system quickly breaks down when too many people are involved."

Agile techniques may not be appropriate when project teams work in different geographical locations. In such cases, communication is less efficient and can quickly bog down, even though various communication technologies such as instant messaging or video conference can help.

1. You are a project manager in charge of a large government project to replace an aging air-traffic control system. Would you choose Waterfall or Agile as your application development method? Support your decision.

2. You are a project manager in charge of developing a new game that will be sold as an application that can be run on a popular smartphone. Would you choose Waterfall or Agile as your application development method? Support your decision.

SOURCES:
Austin, R. D. "CMM versus Agile: Methodology Wars in Software Development." *Harvard Business School*, 607084-P.
Berinato, S. "Agile Development Can Avert Disaster." *CIO Magazine*. July 1, 2001.
Mueller, J. P. "Agile Programming Definition and Solutions." *CIO Magazine*. March 28, 2007.

BIBLIOGRAPHY

1. Barker, S. *Brilliant PRINCE2: What You Really Need To Know About PRINCE2*. Harlow, England: Pearson, 2009.
2. The Project Management Institute (PMI). *A Guide to the Project Management Body of Knowledge (PMBOK Guide)*. Newton Square, PA: PMI Publishing, 2013.
3. Meredith, J. R. and S. J. Mantel. *Project Management: A Managerial Approach*. New York: John Wiley & Sons, 2000.
4. Watts, A. *Project Management*. Press Books .com, 2013. http://bccampus.pressbooks.com/projectmanagement/.
5. Webb, A. *PRINCE2 for Beginners - Introduction to PRINCE2 Project Management Concepts*. Unknown: Andy Webb, 2013.
6. Munck, K. *i2eye with PRINCE2 Part 1 of 2*. Unknown: i2eyebooks.com, 2013.
7. McConnell, S. *Rapid Development: Taming Wild Software Schedules*. Redmond, WA: Microsoft Press, 1996.
8. Royce, W. "Managing the Development of Large Software Systems." *Proceedings of IEEE WESCON*. 26 Vols. August. 1–9 (1970).
9. Takeuchi, H. and I. Nonaka, "The New New Product Development Game." *Harvard Business Review*. Vols. 2–11 (January–February 1986).
10. Holcombe, M. *Running an Agile Software Development Project*. Hoboken, NJ: John Wiley & Sons, 2008.
11. Layton, M. *Agile Project Management*. Hoboken, NJ: John Wiley & Sons, 2012.
12. Kolb, D. *Experiential Learning*. Upper Saddle, New Jersey: Prentice Hall, 1984.
13. Dewey, J. *Logic: The Theory of Inquiry*. New York: Holt, Rinehart, and Winston, 1938.
14. Redding, J. C. *The Radical Team Handbook*. San Francisco, CA Jossey-Bass, 2000.

3

Measurable Organizational Value and the Business Case

CHAPTER OBJECTIVES

Chapter 3 describes how to conceptualize and start a project. Conceptualizing a project begins by developing a clear goal defined as the project's **measurable organizational value** (MOV). The MOV provides a clear understanding of the project's purpose and is the foundation for writing the business case. After studying this chapter, you should be able to:

- Describe and develop a project's MOV.
- Understand the purpose of a business case.
- Prepare a business case.
- Distinguish between financial and scoring models.
- Understand how projects are selected.

INTRODUCTION

If projects are organizational investments, then management needs to make an important decision as to which projects should be funded. Most organizations have limited resources, and a particular project may have to compete with other projects within the organization for those scarce resources. As a result, only a limited number of projects can and should be selected and funded to make up the organization's project portfolio. A project having a clear and measurable goal that brings value to the organization will have a greater likelihood of being selected.

The first phase of the project life cycle (PLC), and the start of a project, begins with conceptualizing the purpose or goal of the project and is defined as the project's **measurable organizational value**, or **MOV**. Once defined and agreed upon, the MOV becomes a driving force for the project as it sets direction and lays the groundwork for planning and design of the product or system and many project-related decisions. As you will see in later chapters, having a clear project goal aids in defining the project's scope or work as well as the requirements or features and functionality of the product or system. At the end of the project, the MOV provides a way to evaluate whether the project was a success.

Developing a clear, concise MOV that is accepted by the project stakeholders is then documented in the **business case**. A business case not only documents the MOV but also provides details of several project alternatives or options that are analyzed and compared. Alternatives may include the option to maintain the status quo, build a new product or system, or purchase a software package from a third-party vendor. For each alternative, the feasibility, costs, benefits, and risks are analyzed and compared so that a recommendation can be made with confidence to choose the best alternative. If an alternative is approved, the project manager and team are authorized to move to the next phase of the project where detailed planning begins; otherwise, the project opportunity is abandoned. The time and resources spent developing a business case depends on the nature of the project. For example, a large, complex, and costly project may require more time and resources than a smaller, less mission-critical project because the stakes are higher. Regardless, every organization considering a project should follow a similar process before continuing to the next phase where detailed plans define the scope, schedule, budget, and quality objectives.

MEASURABLE ORGANIZATIONAL VALUE (MOV)

The first step for starting a project should be to define the project's goal or measurable organizational value (MOV). In short, a project begins by defining its measure of success (1). To provide real value to an organization, a project must align with and support the organization's vision, mission, and strategy. For example, a top-down approach begins with an organization's vision and mission statements. A **vision statement** articulates and inspires purpose, while a **mission statement** clarifies what the organization does, who they do it for, and how or why they do it.

Based on the vision and mission statements, management devises an organization strategy. For example, Michael Porter's competitive forces model proposes that a company may want to enact a strategy that prevents its customers from leaving or switching to a competitor (2, 3). Therefore, the organization may want to develop a tight linkage with its customers to make them less inclined to leave. In turn, an organization may consider a business analytics project as a way to better understand its customers and to make recommendations based on known preferences. This project could provide a tactical implementation of the organizational strategy that aligns with the organization's vision and mission.

On the other hand, projects can start from the bottom up or, more specifically, be proposed by an individual, committee, or business unit within the organization. As illustrated in Figure 3.1, the MOV still needs to align with and support the organization's strategy and overall vision and mission in order to provide value to the organization.

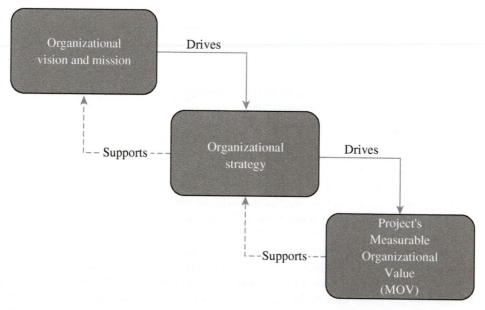

Figure 3.1 Project Alignment

The MOV and Project Objectives

As the name implies, the MOV must:

- *Be measurable*—Measurement provides a clear definition of success for all of the project's stakeholders. For example, consider the statement: *Our project will be successful if we install a database management system to improve our customer service to world-class levels*. Installing a database management system is an activity or a task that may need to be done. While important, the installation of the technology does not guarantee real value to the organization. Moreover, while "world-class" sounds inviting, it is difficult to define and impossible to know if ever achieved. Instead, consider the statement: *Our project will be successful if 95 percent of our customers receive a shipping confirmation within two hours after placing an order*. The second statement defines the project's purpose and allows the organization to evaluate whether 95 percent of its customers are receiving a shipping confirmation within two hours after placing an order.

- *Provide value*—Time and resources should not be devoted to a project unless it can bring value to the organization. For example, value could be in the form of better customer service if the organization can send a shipping confirmation to 95 percent of its customers within two hours after placing an order. Remember, technology is a means to an end and should not be part of a project's MOV. Technology is an enabler; that is, technology enables organizations to do things like reducing the time to send out a shipping confirmation. Value comes from delivery of the project's product, service, or system that achieves or meets the MOV and not from a particular vendor's software package or from a particular programming language.

- *Be agreed upon*—A clear and agreed upon MOV sets expectations for the project's stakeholders. The MOV must be doable and worth doing. Continuing with the previous example, the project's MOV may not be realistic if management sets a target that 100 percent of the customers must receive a shipping confirmation within two nanoseconds of placing an order. The project team may be set on a path of failure if it cannot deliver on this expectation. On the other hand, not much value may be achieved if a performance target is set too low and achieved easily. Perhaps two minutes or even twenty minutes might be a better performance target for sending out a shipping confirmation. In any case, stakeholders must agree upon an MOV that is both realistic and of value to the organization.

- *Be verifiable*—If the MOV acts as a measure of success, then it must be verified at the end of the project. This does not always mean that the MOV will be met immediately at the end of the project when the product, service, or system is delivered. Often there will be a time period of perhaps a week, a month, or even a year before the full value of the MOV is achieved; however, the organization should evaluate the MOV in order to know whether it received the value it envisioned for the time, money, and resources invested in the project.

So, why do we call the project's goal the MOV? Why not just call it a goal? The reason is that many people use the terms goal and objectives interchangeably while others say they are different. Project methodologies provide a common language for stakeholders in order to mitigate confusion and miscommunication. Therefore, calling the project's goal the MOV offers a clear meaning that the purpose of a project is to provide organizational value that is measurable. A project should have only one MOV but multiple project objectives are possible.

As shown in Figure 3.2, project objectives support the MOV. More specifically, project objectives include scope (the project work to be completed), schedule (time), budget (money), and quality (conformance or fitness for use). The difference is that a project's MOV becomes a measure of success, while objectives are important, but not necessarily sufficient conditions for success. For example, a project can be completed on time, within budget, and be defect-free but still it may not be of any use or value

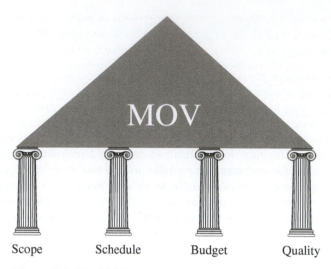

Figure 3.2 The MOV and Project Objectives

to the organization. On the other hand, a project that is late and over budget can still be considered a success if the benefits of the MOV outweigh the costs associated with the project being late or over budget. The only true measure of project success is the value defined in the MOV.

However, project objectives are important and must be managed and controlled because at some point a project that is way over schedule and budget will result in a situation where the cost of the project outweighs the benefits. At this point, the decision to discontinue funding and abandon the project is a sound management decision.

Developing the MOV

Before outlining a process for developing the MOV, let's begin with a good example. Back in the 1960s a U.S. president named John F. Kennedy made the statement:

> *"Our goal is to land a man on the moon and return him safely by the end of the decade."*

This simple yet powerful statement mobilized an entire nation and fueled the space race between the United States and then the Soviet Union. What is interesting about this statement is how clear, concise, and measurable the goal becomes:

- A human being is to land on the moon—not an unmanned spacecraft or even a spacecraft with a chimpanzee.
- The idea wasn't to get an astronaut on the moon and leave him there, or to make it just part of the way back. The astronaut had to make the whole trip and arrive back safely.
- This all had to be accomplished before 1970.

What is equally interesting is that Kennedy never told anyone *how* to do this. That was NASA's job, not his. The goal was to beat the Soviets to the moon, and this project's MOV defined this explicitly.

So, how do we go about developing an MOV? There are six basic steps. The project manager and team should not be responsible for defining the project's MOV. Instead, it is their responsibility to lead and facilitate the process by working closely with the customer, client, sponsor, or relevant stakeholders. This could be done over one or several one-on-one meetings or stakeholder group conferences.

Let's use an example of a nonprofit organization whose mission is to increase public awareness about healthy living. You meet with the director of the organization to develop an MOV for a potential project. Although there are many ways to increase awareness to promote healthy living, such as creating a web site, using social media, or renting a billboard, it is important not to come up with a preconceived solution until after the MOV is defined. Alternatives such as these will be detailed, analyzed, and compared in the business case. If a best alternative exists, then management would make the decision to fund the next stage or phase of the project where a detailed plan is created.

1. *Identify the desired area of impact*—A project can have an impact on an organization in many different ways. Figure 3.3 provides some potential areas of impact and a few examples for each area (4). Again, your responsibility is to lead this process and begin by asking the client, customer, sponsor, or group of stakeholders: *"Is the desired impact of the project strategic, customer, financial, operational, or social?"* Be advised that the worst possible answer is *"All the above"* or *"Yes, I want it to have an impact in all of those areas"* because a project needs to have a clear focus. Another way to gain a clearer picture would be to have the customer or stakeholders prioritize the four areas from most important to least important. The purpose here is to create a dialog to better understand why the project is being considered, as well as the role and impact it will have on the organization. Don't be surprised if this turns into a lively and spirited discussion among stakeholders as previously accepted wisdom is challenged. The key is to gain valuable insight by asking the question, *"Why do the project?"*

   Using the example of our nonprofit, after much discussion, it is agreed that increasing awareness for healthy living falls most closely under the ***social*** category as the organization wants to educate people so that they live longer and healthier lives.

2. *Identify the desired value of the project*—Once the desired area of impact is identified, the next step involves determining the desired value the project can bring to the organization. In simplest terms, you can ask the customer or stakeholders the following questions:

   - *Will the project help the organization do something* **better***? (For example, improve quality? Increase effectiveness?)*

   - *Will the project help the organization do something* **faster***? (For example, increase speed? Increase effectiveness? Reduce cycle times?)*

   - *Will the project help the organization do something* **cheaper***? (For example, reduce costs?)*

   - *Will the project help the organization* **do more** *of something that it's currently doing? (For example, increase market share? Increase growth? Increase sales? Increase safety?)*

   As depicted in Figure 3.4, the key words to identifying value from a project are *better, faster, cheaper*, and *do more*. The first three—*better, faster*, and *cheaper*—focus on quality,

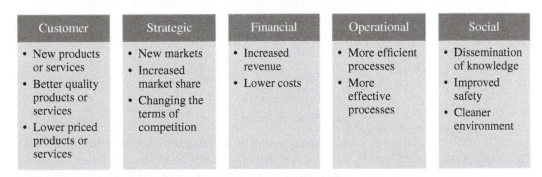

Customer	Strategic	Financial	Operational	Social
• New products or services • Better quality products or services • Lower priced products or services	• New markets • Increased market share • Changing the terms of competition	• Increased revenue • Lower costs	• More efficient processes • More effective processes	• Dissemination of knowledge • Improved safety • Cleaner environment

Figure 3.3 Potential Areas of Project Impact and Examples

effectiveness, and efficiency, while *doing more* of something focuses on growth. For example, if an organization has identified *financial* as its desired area of impact, it may want to reduce costs of a particular process or service. Therefore, value to this organization would be in the form of doing something *cheaper*. On the other hand, another organization may be faced with high inventory costs as a result of having too much inventory in its warehouse. The value that a project would bring to this organization would not be from growth; it does not want to do more of what it is currently doing. The value comes from doing something better (e.g., improved quality to reduce waste or rework), faster (e.g., fewer manufacturing bottlenecks or reduced cycle times), or even cheaper (e.g., lower overhead costs).

While the question in the first step focuses on why an organization wants to take on the project, this second step focuses on the question *"how will this project help us achieve what we want to achieve as an organization?"* At this point, the project manager and client should identify one or two value areas to emphasize. If all four of the value areas appear important, it is a good idea to rank them in order of importance. Keep in mind, however, that not having a clear idea of the desired impact or value of the project may well mean that the problem or opportunity is not clearly understood. The project team may end up treating the symptoms rather than the real problem.

Following our example, the nonprofit wants to increase awareness. Therefore, the director would like to *"do more"* of something it is doing already.

3. *Develop an appropriate metric*—Once there is agreement as to the value the project will bring to the organization, the next step is to develop a metric, or set of metrics, that:

   ■ provides the project team with a performance target or directive

   ■ sets expectations among all stakeholders, and

   ■ affords a means for evaluating whether the project is a success later on.

In general, tangible benefits to the organization are easier to measure than intangible ones; however, this can be done with some creativity. For example, knowing whether profits increased should be fairly straightforward, but customer satisfaction may require surveys or interviews. Often, evaluation requires benchmarking so that a before and after comparison can be made.

To develop a metric, the project manager and customer, sponsor, or other stakeholders should agree on a specific target or range. When not obvious, the target metric should indicate whether an increase or decrease from the organization's current state is desired. The metrics may be expressed as *money*, *percentages*, or *numbers*. For example, an organization that wishes to increase profits may state this as a 20 percent increase or an increase of $1 million from the last month, quarter, or fiscal year. On the other hand, an organization that would like to grow its customer base may set a goal of 100 new customers. Therefore, the metrics to support the MOV may be one or a combination of the following:

■ **Money** (in dollars, euros, yuan, etc.)	(increase or decrease)
■ **Percentage** (%)	(increase or decrease)
■ **Numeric value**	(increase or decrease)

Figure 3.4 Project Value

The nonprofit organization in our example would like to increase awareness for healthy living. There are a number of relevant metrics that could be used. The question is how can the director determine whether this project is a success? Keep in mind that the organization will make a relatively significant investment by the time the project is completed.

For example, would a web application be successful when the web site is finished and anyone with an Internet connection can view the site? It is important to have a working web site, but that alone will not make up for the investment and subsequent maintenance and support for keeping the site up and running. What about using a hit counter so that the director can tell how many times the web site was visited? Having traffic to a web site is also important, but awareness may not be increased just because people visit the web site.

After continued discussion with the director, she believes a good measure for awareness is the number of subscribers to a weekly newsletter produced by her organization. Therefore, she says that the project would be successful if 250 new subscribers sign up for the newsletter. The performance targets must be set by the customer, sponsor, or stakeholders empowered to make the decision. Keep in mind that your job is to guide the process and make sure that the MOV is realistic, that is, will you and the project team be able to deliver what is expected?

4. *Set a time frame for achieving the MOV*—Once you have agreement on the target metrics that will provide the desired impact to the organization, the next step is to agree on a specific time frame. For example, a company may focus on increasing profits or reducing costs, but the question is: *When will these results be achieved?* Keep in mind that the scheduled completion of the project is not the same thing as the agreed upon time frame for achieving the MOV. Scope, schedule, budget, and quality are project objectives. Moreover, these project objectives are defined in detail later on when we develop the project plan, so trying to guess what these objectives are at this point in the project can create false expectations. Rarely will the installation of an information system or delivery of a product or service provide the desired or expected value right away. The project manager and sponsor should also agree on how and when the project's MOV will be evaluated.

Continuing with our example, let's assume that the director believes that it is realistic to expect 250 new subscribers within 6 months after the project is completed.

5. *Verify the MOV and get agreement from the project stakeholders*—The next step in developing the MOV is to ensure that it is accurate and realistic. In short, will the successful completion of this project provide the intended value to the organization? And is the MOV realistic? The development of the MOV requires a close working relationship between the project manager and the sponsor. The project manager's responsibility is to guide the process, while the sponsor must identify the value and target metrics. This joint responsibility may not always be easy, especially when several sponsors or individuals need to agree on what will make a project successful or what exactly will bring value to the organization. Still, it is better to spend the time discussing and getting consensus now rather than during the later phases of the project. While the project manager is responsible for guiding the process, he or she needs to be confident that the MOV can be achieved. Being challenged is one thing; agreeing to an unrealistic MOV is another. The latter can be detrimental to your career, the project team, and everyone's morale.

After a soliciting feedback from several subordinates and two board members, the director confirms that 250 new subscribers will provide value to the nonprofit organization. You also believe that achieving this target is feasible.

6. *Summarize the MOV in a clear, concise statement or table*—Once the impact and value to the organization are verified and agreed upon by all the project stakeholders, the MOV should be summarized in a single statement or table. Summarizing the MOV provides an important chance to get final agreement and verification, provides a simple and clear directive for the project team, and sets explicit expectations for all project stakeholders. The most straight-forward way to summarize the MOV is in a statement form by completing the following statement:

This project will be successful if _____.

For example, the project's MOV to increase awareness for healthy living may be:

MOV: *Increase awareness for healthy living by having 250 new subscribers sign up for a weekly newsletter within 6 months.*

Table 3.1 provides some examples of MOV statements.

However, if the MOV includes a growth component, a table format may provide a better alternative than the single statement format. Continuing with the example, let's say that the director would like to have the 250 new newsletter subscribers 6 months after the project is completed. However, there is no reason why different targets cannot be set for different time periods. For example, what if the director would like to see the number of subscribers continue to increase for the next two years? Perhaps 250 new subscribers would be fine for the first six months, but another 350 could sign up by the end of the year as word spreads and more and more people know about the newsletter. Therefore, the director may establish a performance target of 1,850 new subscribers within two years. The MOV should be flexible to accommodate the expectations and needs of the project sponsor. Always adapt it to fit the needs of the customer or project stakeholders. Table 3.2 provides an example of the MOV in a table format.

It is worth emphasizing again that the MOV does not include any explicit statements about technology. More specifically, the MOV should never mention that a particular relational database vendor's product will be used or that the system will be programmed in a particular language. It is up to the project team to figure out how to build the product or system and determine what technology will be employed to achieve the project goal. At this point in the project, we are concerned with the organization—not with the technology!

In the past, purely technical approaches were often applied to organizational problems. A system would be built, but did it really support or have a significant, positive impact on the organization? Judging from the CHAOS studies discussed in a previous chapter, IT projects have not lived up to management's expectations. In short, the technical people may understand and be very good at working with the technology, but achieving this MOV will also require an organizational approach and commitment. Figure 3.5 shows a process for developing an MOV for increasing awareness related to healthy living.

Table 3.1 Examples of MOV Statements

Area of Impact	The project will be successful if …
Customer	Within 3 months 65 percent of our customers will visit our restaurant at least once a week.
Strategic	We will develop and manufacture a new router that sells for $50 less than our competitor's model by April 1 of next year.
Financial	Sales growth of our smartphone app increases from 3 percent to 6 percent by the end of next quarter.
Operational	Our inventory turnover ratio improves 15 percent by the end of our fiscal year.
Social	The number of accidents in our plant is reduced to zero next year.

Table 3.2 Example of MOV Table Format

Time Period	MOV
6 months	250 new healthy living newsletter subscribers
1 year	600 new healthy living newsletter subscribers
2 years	1,000 new healthy living newsletter subscribers

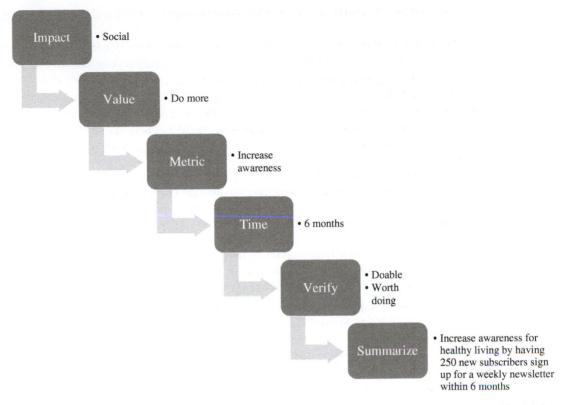

Figure 3.5 Summary of the Process for Developing the MOV to Increase Awareness for Healthy Living

THE BUSINESS CASE

What Is a Business Case?

Although organizations have increasingly turned to information technology to improve effectiveness and levels of efficiency, many projects have been undertaken without a thorough understanding of their full costs and risks. As a result, numerous projects have failed to return benefits that compensate adequately for the time and resources invested.

A business case provides the first deliverable in the project life cycle and is a major theme in the PRINCE2® methodology that was discussed in a previous chapter. It provides an analysis of the organizational value, feasibility, costs, benefits, and risks of several proposed alternatives or options. However, a business case is *not* a budget or the project plan. A business case must provide senior management with all the information needed to make an informed decision as to whether the project should receive funding in order to continue on to the next phase (5). In the next phase, the project will be planned in much greater detail where another go/no decision is made before the plan is executed or carried out.

For larger projects, a business case may be a large, formal document. Less formality may be suitable for smaller projects; however, the process of thinking through why a particular project is being taken on and how it might bring value to an organization is still worthwhile.

Because assumptions and new information are sometimes used to make subjective judgments, a business case must also document the methods and rationale used for quantifying the costs and benefits. Different people who work independently to develop a business case can use the same information, tools, and methods, but still come up with different recommendations. Therefore, it is imperative that decision makers who read the business case know and understand how it was developed and how various alternatives were evaluated.

One can also think of a business case as an investment proposal or a legal case. Like an attorney, the business case developer has a large degree of latitude to structure arguments, select or ignore evidence, and deliver the final presentation. The outcome depends largely on the ability to use compelling facts and logic in order to influence an individual or group with decision-making authority. Thus, a good business case should be

- Thorough in detailing all possible impacts, costs, and benefits.
- Clear and logical in comparing the cost/benefit impact of each alternative.
- Objective through including all pertinent information.
- Systematic in terms of summarizing the findings (6).

Developing the Business Case

Step 1: Define Measurable Organizational Value (MOV)—The most important step in developing the business case is to define the project's MOV. The process for developing the MOV was described in the previous section and should be established before or as the first step in developing the business case.

Step 2: Form a Cross-Functional Business Case Team—At this point, the project manager and project team may or may not be chosen. Some organizations may want to have the project manager and team in place at the earliest stages of the project and involved with the development of the business case. However, it is entirely possible that the team that develops the business case will be different from the project team responsible for carrying out the project only after the business case is approved. It really depends on the situation. Regardless, no one person should be solely responsible for the business case. If possible, development of a business case should include many of the stakeholders affected by the project or involved in its delivery. This should include managers, business specialists, and users who understand the business, as well as specialists who understand the opportunities, limitations, and risks associated with the technology. In general, there are several advantages for having a cross-functional team develop the business case (3):

- *Credibility*—Access to people from various organizational areas or departments can provide critical expertise and information that may not be readily accessible to others outside that particular area. Moreover, these individuals can provide different points of view and provide a check for important items that one person may overlook. It is important to get the right people involved who will ask the right questions (7).

- *Alignment with organizational goals*—Higher level managers can help connect the business case with the organization's long-term strategic plan and mission. This alignment may be beneficial in understanding and presenting how the expected business value of the project will support the overall goals and mission of the organization. Moreover, it may facilitate prioritizing, legitimizing, and assigning value of the project to the organization's strategic business objectives. In other words, the business case should outline how the successful completion of the proposed project will help the organization achieve its overall mission and strategy.

- *Access to the real costs*—The members of the business case team with certain expertise or access to important information can help build more realistic estimates with respect to salaries, overhead, accounting and reporting practices, training requirements, union rules and regulations, and laws.

In addition, the team that develops the business case can play a crucial role when dealing with various areas or departments within the organizational boundary. The advantages include:

- *Ownership*—A cross-functional team can spread a sense of ownership for the business case. A project that includes other areas from the outset has a better chance of reducing the political problems associated with territorial domains.

- *Agreement*—If you develop a business case in isolation, it is very likely that you will have to defend your assumptions and subjective judgments in a competitive or political setting. However, if a cross-functional team develops the business case, any critics may be more apt to argue the results rather than the data and methods used.

- *Bridge building*—The business case team may serve as an effective tool for handling critics of the business case. One tactic may be to include critics on the team or to at least allow recognition and consideration for their positions. This may lead to fewer surprises and attacks later on.

Step 3: Identify Alternatives—Because no single solution generally exists for most organizational problems, it is imperative to identify several alternatives before dealing directly with a given business opportunity. The alternatives, or options, identified in the business case should be strategies for achieving the MOV.

It is also important that the alternatives listed include a wide range of potential solutions that even includes maintaining the status quo. Doing nothing is always an option. In some situations, maintaining the status quo may even be the best alternative. However, the business case can provide a compelling reason for the organization to change and should delve into the realistic costs of maintaining the current product, processes, or system over time. This may include such things as increased maintenance costs of hardware and software as well as the possibility for more frequent system failures and downtime.

On the other hand, other options may provide the best solution. These options should consider a spectrum of choices that include:

- Changing the existing business processes without investing in IT.

- Adopting or adapting an application developed by a different area or department within the organization.

- Reengineering the existing system.

- Purchasing an off-the-shelf application package from a software vendor.

- Custom building a new application using internal resources or outsourcing the development to another company.

It is important to be open to and objective about all viable options.

Step 4: Define Feasibility and Assess Risk—Each option, or alternative, must be analyzed in terms of its feasibility and potential risk. **Feasibility** should focus on whether a particular alternative is *doable* and *worth doing*. **Risk**, on the other hand, focuses on *what can go wrong* or *what must go right*. Analyzing the feasibility and risk of each alternative at this point may act as a screening process for ruling out any alternatives that are not worth pursuing. Feasibility may be viewed in terms of:

- *Economic feasibility*—Although a cost/benefit analysis will be conducted to look at the alternatives in greater depth, some alternatives may be too costly or simply not provide the benefits envisioned in the problem statement. At this point, an organization may evaluate an alternative in terms of whether funds and resources exist to support the project. For example, although you may be in a market for a new car, the reality of your limited income rules out the fancy sports car. Conducting an economic feasibility should serve as a reality check for each option or alternative.

- *Technical feasibility*—Technical feasibility focuses on the existing technical infrastructure needed to support an IT solution. Will the current infrastructure support the alternative? Will new technology be needed? Will it be available? Does the current staff have the skills and experience to support the proposed solution? If outsourcing, does the vendor or company have the skills and experience to develop and implement the application?

- *Organizational feasibility*—Organizational feasibility considers the impact on the organization. It focuses mainly on how people within the organization will adapt to this planned organizational change. How will people and the way they do their jobs be impacted?

Will they accept this change willingly? Will business be disrupted while the proposed solution is implemented?

- *Other feasibilities*—Depending on the situation and the organization, a business case may include other issues, such as legal and ethical feasibility.

Risk should focus on:

- *Identification*—What can go wrong? What must go right?
- *Assessment*—What is the impact of each risk?
- *Response*—How can the organization avoid or minimize the risk?

Step 5: Define Total Cost of Ownership—The decision to invest in an IT project must take into account all of the costs associated with the application system. **Total cost of ownership (TCO)** is a concept that has gained widespread attention and generally refers to the total cost of acquiring, developing, maintaining, and supporting the product or application system over its useful life. TCO includes such costs as:

- *Direct or up-front costs*—Initial purchase price of all hardware, software, and telecommunications equipment, all development or installation costs, outside consultant fees, etc.
- *Ongoing costs*—Support, salaries, training, upgrades, supplies, maintenance, etc.
- *Indirect costs*—Initial loss of productivity, time lost by users when the system is down, the cost of auditing equipment (i.e., finding out who has what and where), quality assurance, and postimplementation reviews.

It is important to note that TCO goes beyond the original purchase or development costs. In fact, the TCO is really an organized list of all possible cost impacts. When preparing the business case, it is also important to document all data sources, assumptions, and methods for determining the various costs.

Step 6: Define Total Benefits of Ownership—Similarly, the **Total benefits of ownership (TBO)** must include all of the direct, ongoing, and indirect benefits associated with each proposed alternative. The TBO should address the benefits of an alternative over the course of its useful life. Benefits can arise from:

- *Increasing high-value work*—For example, a salesperson may spend less time on paperwork and more time calling on customers.
- *Improving accuracy and efficiency*—For example, reducing errors, duplication, or the number of steps in a process.
- *Improving decision making*—For example, providing timely and accurate information.
- *Improving customer service*—For example, new products or services, faster or more reliable service, convenience, and so on.

Tangible benefits are relatively easy to identify and quantify. They will usually arise from direct cost savings or avoided costs. On the other hand, intangible benefits may be easy to identify, but they are certainly more difficult to quantify. It is important to try and quantify all the benefits identified. One way to quantify intangible benefits is to link them directly to tangible benefits that can be linked to efficiency gains. For example, a corporate telephone directory on an intranet not only improves communication, but can cut paper, printing, and labor costs associated with creating and distributing a paper-based telephone directory.

Step 7: Analyze Alternatives—Once costs and benefits have been identified, it is important that all alternatives be compared with each other consistently. Understanding the financial and numeric tools and techniques required by financial people and senior management is critical, even for the technically savvy. Being able to communicate effectively using their terms and tools increases one's credibility and the chances of getting projects approved and funded. There are several ways to analyze the proposed alternatives. The most common are financial models and scoring models.

Financial models focus on either profitability and/or cash flows. Cash flow models focus on the net cash, may be positive or negative, and are calculated by subtracting the cash outflows from the cash inflows. In general, one could view the benefits associated with a particular alternative as a source of cash inflow and the costs as the source of outflows. Using a tool such as an electronic spreadsheet application, one could conduct a sensitivity analysis to view how changes in the initial investment or net cash flows would impact the risk of a particular project alternative.

The most commonly used cash flow models include **payback, breakeven, return on investment, and net present value**.

Payback—The payback method determines how long it will take to recover the initial investment. For example, if a company spends $100,000 developing and implementing an application system and then receives a net cash return of $20,000 a year, the payback period for that investment would be:

$$\text{Payback Period} = \text{Initial Investment} / \text{Net Cash Flow}$$
$$= \$100,000 / \$20,000$$
$$= 5 \text{ years}$$

Although the payback period is fairly straightforward to calculate and understand, it does not consider the time value of money or cash flows beyond the payback period. Still, the payback period is useful for highlighting the risk of a particular investment because a riskier investment will have a longer payback period than a less risky investment. Depending on the situation and the organization's policy, net cash flow may be either before tax or after tax.

Breakeven—Similar to the payback method, the breakeven method attempts to determine the point at which a project would begin to recoup its original investment. This method is useful if a certain number of transactions allow the original investment to be recovered. For example, let's say that you would like to create a web site to sell golf putters that you manufacture. If you spent $100,000 to create the site, how many golf putters would you have to sell to break even if you sell each putter for $30? To determine this point, you have to look at the cost of selling a putter. These costs may include the following:

Materials (putter head, shaft, grip, etc.)	$9.00
Labor (0.5 hours at $15.00/hr)	$7.50
Overhead (rent, insurance, utilities, taxes, etc.)	$8.50
Total	$25.00

If you sell a golf putter for $30 and it costs $25 to make it, you have a profit margin of $5. The breakeven point is computed as follows:

$$\text{Breakeven Point} = \text{Initial Investment} / \text{Net Profit Margin}$$
$$= \$100,000 / \$5$$
$$= 20,000 \text{ units}$$

Therefore, you would have to sell 20,000 putters over your web site to break even. Like the payback period method, the breakeven method is generally easy to compute and can provide a measure of risk. In general, riskier project alternatives will have a higher breakeven point than less risky project alternatives.

Return on Investment (ROI)—In a strict financial sense, ROI is an indicator of a company's financial performance. From a project management point of view, ROI provides a measure of the value expected or received from a particular alternative or project. It is calculated by dividing the net income, or return, of a project alternative by its total cost. So, if a project alternative, for example, is expected to cost $100,000 but provides $115,000 in expected benefits, its ROI would be:

$$\text{Project ROI} = \frac{\text{Total Expected Benefits} - \text{Total Expected Costs}}{\text{Total Expected Costs}}$$
$$= \frac{\$115,000 - \$100,000}{\$100,000}$$
$$= 15\%$$

The above formula shows the expected ROI for a project alternative; a completed project's ROI would use the actual costs and benefits derived and can be compared to its expected ROI to provide a comparison at the end of the project. The usefulness of a project's ROI depends on two important assumptions. First, there must be the ability to define accurately the total costs and benefits expected or realized. Second, the returns must arise as a direct result of the initial investment. For example, if you purchased a lottery ticket for $1 and won $1 million, you can determine the ROI directly because the $1 million return can be related to the $1 lottery ticket you purchased. Even though the chances of winning a lottery are pretty slim, the ROI calculated as ($1,000,000 − $1) ÷ $1 = 99,999,900 percent would be quite acceptable for most people. In complex business situations, however, ROI analysis may be difficult because intervening variables and conditions may have an indirect influence.

Regardless, with ROI one can see the relationship between a project's costs and benefits. A project's ROI will increase as the benefits increase and/or the expected costs decrease. When comparing two or more projects or alternatives, those with the higher ROI would be the most desirable (all other things being equal). Many organizations even have a required ROI, whereby no project or alternative may be considered unless a certain ROI value can be achieved. The idea is that it is not worth investing time and resources in a project that does not provide a certain level of value to the organization and its shareholders.

Net Present Value (NPV)—NPV focuses on the time value of money. For example, if you borrow $20 today, you may have to agree to pay back the original $20 plus another $2 at the end of the month. Someone may also be willing to give you either $18 today or $20 at the end of the month. If you could take the $18 and invest it, ending up with $20 at the end of the month, you might feel indifferent as to whether you collected $18 today or $20 at the end of the month. The point here is that there is a cost associated with time when it comes to money.

It is going to take time and resources (i.e., costs) before any particular project or alternative is completed and provides the returns we originally envisioned. NPV takes this into account by discounting streams of cash flows a particular alternative or project returns in the future so that we can determine if investing the time, money, and resources is worth the wait. Very simply put, only a project or alternative with a positive NPV should be considered. Let's say that one alternative is an application system that is expected to cost $200,000 and will be completed in the current year (Year 0). In addition, over the following four years the project's benefits will provide inflows of cash, while the costs to build, maintain, and support this application will require outflows of cash. The expected cash flows for the next five years may look something like:

	Year 0	Year 1	Year 2	Year 3	Year 4
Total Cash Inflows	$0	$150,000	$200,000	$250,000	$300,000
Total Cash Outflows	$200,000	$85,000	$125,000	$150,000	$200,000
Net Cash Flow	($200,000)	$65,000	$75,000	$100,000	$100,000

To discount the net cash flows, a **discount rate** is required. This rate is sometimes called a **cutoff rate**, or **hurdle rate**, because it basically defines the organization's required rate of return. In short, the discount rate is the minimum return a company would expect from a project if the company were to make an equivalent investment in an opportunity of similar risk. This discount rate is usually set by management. The NPV is calculated using the formula:

$$\text{NPV} = -I_O + \sum \left(\frac{\text{Net Cash Flow}}{(1+r)^t} \right)$$

Where:

I = total cost (or investment) in the project

r = discount rate

t = time period

Therefore, if we use a discount rate of 8 percent, we can discount the net cash flow for each period and add them up to determine the NPV.

Time Period	Calculation	Discounted Cash Flow
Year 0	($200,000)	($200,000)
Year 1	$65,000 \div (1+.08)^1$	$60,185
Year 2	$75,000 \div (1+.08)^2$	$64,300
Year 3	$100,000 \div (1+.08)^3$	$79,383
Year 4	$100,000 \div (1+.08)^4$	$73,503
Net Present Value (NPV)		**$77,371**

This alternative would be acceptable because a NPV of $77,371 is positive. One can compare the NPV for different alternatives and projects. In general, the project or alternative with a higher NPV would be more desirable. Remember, increasing the discount rate will decrease the NPV.

Scoring models provide a method for comparing alternatives or projects based on a weighted score. Scoring models also allow for quantifying intangible benefits or for different alternatives using multiple criteria. Using percentage weights, one can assign values of importance to the different criteria. The weights must sum to 100 percent, and when multiplied by a score assigned to each criterion they allow a composite score that is the weighted average. For example, one could compare several alternatives using the following formula:

$$\text{Total Score} = \sum_{i=1}^{n} w_i c_i$$

Where:

w_i = criterion weight

c_i = criterion score

$0 \leq w_i \leq 1$

Table 3.3 compares three project alternatives using this system. The scoring model in Table 3.3 highlights several important ideas:

- *The scoring model can combine both qualitative and quantitative criterion*—Whether one assigns more weight to tangible or intangible criteria depends on the philosophy of management or the client.

- *Weights and scores can be subjective*—This method of scoring is a two-edged sword. People use their judgment, or gut feelings, in assigning weights and scores, but may not necessarily have the same judgments. As a result, getting agreement among individuals may be difficult. One suggestion is to have different individuals assign weights and scores to the different criteria and then average these individual responses to create a composite score. Even if people don't agree, at least they have an opportunity to express their opinions. Another suggestion would be to use a relative score whenever possible. For example, let's say that the NPVs for the three alternatives were as follows:

Alternative	A	B	C
NPV	$200	$400	$1,000

Since Alternative C has the highest NPV, we can determine a relative score (on a basis of 0 to 10) for each alternative as follows:

Alternative	NPV	Calculation	Relative Score
A	$1,000	($1,000 ÷ $1,000) × 10	**10**
B	$400	($400 ÷ $1,000) × 10	*4*
C	$200	($200 ÷ $1,000) × 10	**2**

The scores used in this example range from 0 to 10; but there is nothing sacred about this range. One could use a scale of 0 to 100. Consistency rather than any particular scale is the key. Some things to keep in mind:

- *Financial models can be biased toward the short run*—Although financial models are important and should be considered, they focus solely on the periods used in discounting cash flows. Scoring models go beyond this limitation because they allow for multiple criteria (8).

Table 3.3 Comparison of Project Alternatives

Criterion		Weight	Alternative A	Alternative B	Alternative C
Financial	ROI	15%	2	4	10
	Payback	10%	3	5	10
	NPV	15%	2	4	10
Strategic	Alignment with strategic objectives	10%	3	5	8
	Increased market share	10%	2	5	8
Organizational	Likelihood of achieving project's MOV	10%	2	6	9
	Availability of skilled team members	5%	5	5	4
Project	Cost	5%	4	6	7
	Time to develop	5%	5	7	6
	Risk	5%	3	5	5
Customer	Customer satisfaction	10%	2	4	9
Total Score		**100%**	**2.65**	**4.85**	**8.50**

Note: Risk scores have a reverse scale—that is, higher scores for risk imply lower levels of risk.

- *Some criteria can be reverse-scored*—In our example, higher scores for certain criteria make sense. For instance, higher financial performance measures inherently have higher scores. However, a criterion such as risk can be reverse-scored with lower risk alternatives having higher scores. If you reverse-score any criterion, it is beneficial to note these assumptions conspicuously for the reader.

- *Past experience may help create a more realistic business case*—As mentioned before, many of the weights and scores are subjective. Instead of relying on guesswork, past experience with past projects can provide guidelines and a reference for ensuring that the selection models are relevant and realistic. Although the business situation, technology, and data will change over time, the process or method of preparing a business case and analyzing alternatives will remain much the same. Learning from past experience can improve the process and product associated with business cases and thus improves the likelihood of a project being approved and funded.

Step 8: Propose and Support the Recommendation—Once the alternatives have been identified and analyzed, the last step is to recommend one of the options. It is important to remember that a proposed recommendation must be supported. If the analysis was done diligently, this recommendation should be a relatively easy task. The business case should be formalized in a professional-looking report. Remember that the quality and accuracy of your work will be a reflection on you and your organization. A potential client or project sponsor may not give you a second chance. Figure 3.6 provides a template for developing a business case.

The following provides a suggested outline for developing and writing a business case:

Cover Page

- Title and subtitle
- Author and address
- Date

Executive Summary

- Brief description of the problem or opportunity
- Brief description of organization's goal and strategy
- Brief description of project's MOV and how it ties to the organizational goal and strategy
- Brief description of each option or alternative analyzed
- Brief explanation of which alternative is being recommended and why

Introduction

- Background
- Current situation
- Description of the problem or opportunity
- Project's measurable organizational value

- How achieving the project's MOV will support the organization's goal and strategy
- Objectives of writing this business case

Alternatives

- Description of alternative 1 (Base Case)
- Description of alternative 2 ...
- Description of alternative N

Analysis of Alternatives

- Methodology of how alternatives will be analyzed
  - Data collection methods
  - Metrics used and explanation why they are relevant
- Presentation of results that compares each alternative
  - Metrics
  - Sensitivity analysis
  - Risks
  - Assumptions
- Proposed recommendation

Figure 3.6 Business Case Template

PROJECT SELECTION AND APPROVAL

The objective of the business case is to obtain approval and funding for a proposed alternative. However, a proposed project may have to compete against several others.

The criteria for selecting a **project portfolio,** a set of projects that an organization may fund, are very similar to the analysis and subsequent selection of the proposed project alternatives. Similar to portfolio theory in finance, an organization may wish to select a portfolio of projects that have varying levels of risk, technological complexity, size, and strategic intent (9, 10). A project portfolio mainly composed of projects with low risk or those that do not attempt to take advantage of new technology may lead to stagnation. The organization may not move ahead strategically and the employees may fail to grow professionally due to lack of challenge. On the other hand, an organization that focuses too heavily on risky projects employing cutting-edge technology may end up in a precarious position if the projects experience serious problems and failures. Learning from mistakes can be useful, unless the same mistakes are repeated over and over. Thus, an organization should attempt to balance its project portfolio with projects that have varying degrees of risk, cutting-edge technologies, and structure.

Unfortunately, as Harold Kerzner (11) points out, "What a company wants to do is not always what it can do" (p. 20). Kerzner contends that companies generally have a number of projects that they would like to undertake, but because of limited resources, they must prioritize and fund projects selectively. Depending on the demand for experienced professionals, or the state of the economy, it is not always feasible to hire new employees or to have them trained in time.

The IT Project Selection Process

Although each organization's selection process is different, this section describes the general process for selecting and funding a given project. The selection process determines which projects will be funded in a given period. This period can be for a quarter, year, or a time frame determined by the organization. In order to weed out projects that have little chance of being approved, many organizations use an initial screening process in which business cases submitted for review are compared with a set of organizational standards that outline minimum requirements.

Projects that meet the minimum requirements are then forwarded to a decision-making committee of senior managers who have the authority to approve and provide the resources needed to support the project. For example, under PRINCE2®, this responsibility falls under the project board. On rare occasions an individual might make such decisions, but most organizations prefer to use committees. The committee may compare several competing projects based on the costs, benefits, and risks to projects currently under development and to those already implemented. Projects selected should then be assigned to a project manager who selects the project team and then develops a project charter and detailed plan.

The Project Selection Decision

Even though each project proposal should be evaluated in terms of its value to the organization, it is important to reiterate that projects should not be undertaken for technology's sake. The decision to approve a project requires that a number of conditions be met:

- The project must align with the organization's values, vision, mission, and strategies.
- The project must provide measurable organizational value that can be verified at the completion of the project.

CHAPTER SUMMARY

- The first phase of a project begins with conceptualizing the project's goal and overall measure of success called the measurable organizational value or MOV.
- The MOV must:
  - Be measurable
  - Provide value
  - Be agreed upon
  - Be verifiable
- Project objectives include scope, schedule, budget, and quality. They are important but not necessarily sufficient conditions for project success.
- A project can be late and over budget but still be considered successful if it delivers value to the organization. Similarly, a project can be completed early, be under budget, and be defect-free but still be considered a failure if it does not provide any value to the organization.
- The process for developing a project's MOV includes:
  - Identify the desired area of impact
    - Customer
    - Strategic
    - Financial
    - Operational
    - Social
  - Identify the desired value of the project
    - Better
    - Faster
    - Cheaper
    - Do More
  - Develop an appropriate metric or performance target
    - Money
    - Percentage
    - Numeric Value
  - Set a time frame for achieving the MOV
  - Verify the MOV and get agreement from the project stakeholders
  - Summarize the MOV in a clear, concise statement or table
- A business case is a document that documents the project's MOV and provides an analysis of the feasibility, costs, benefits, and risks of several options or alternatives for achieving the MOV.
- The steps or process for developing the business case include:
  - Define the project's MOV
  - Form a cross-functional team to develop the business case
  - Identify several options or alternatives
  - Define feasibility and assess risk
  - Define the total cost of ownership (TCO)
  - Define the total benefits of ownership (TBO)
  - Analyze the alternatives
  - Propose and support a recommendation
- The objective of the business case is to obtain approval and funding for the planning phase of the project.
- Although each organization may have a different process for selecting a project, the decision to select a project should consider how the project aligns with the organization's values, vision, mission, and strategies.

REVIEW QUESTIONS

1. What is a business case?
2. Why should a project begin with developing an MOV?
3. Why should a project align with an organization's strategy, vision, and mission?
4. Why must the MOV be measurable?
5. Why is it important that the MOV provide value to the organization?
6. Why must stakeholders agree on the project's MOV?

7. Who must verify whether the project's MOV is doable and worth doing?

8. Would the following be considered a good example of a project's MOV? "Develop a tablet-based application in Java that makes our company a lot of money."

9. Would the following be considered a good example of a project's MOV? "Raise $300 for a local homeless shelter by December 1 of this year."

10. What are project objectives?

11. Why are project objectives important but not necessarily sufficient conditions for project success?

12. Can a project meet its scope, schedule, budget, and quality objectives and still be considered unsuccessful? Why or why not?

13. Can a project not meet its scope, schedule, budget, and quality objectives and still be considered successful? Why or why not?

14. Is the time frame for achieving the project's MOV always the same as the scheduled delivery of the project's product, service, or system?

15. What is the purpose of developing a business case for a project?

16. Will the team developing a business case always be the project team that will work on the delivery of the project's product, service, or system? Why or why not?

17. What are some advantages of having a cross-functional team develop the business case?

18. Why should maintaining the current product, processes, or system (i.e., the status quo) be considered a possible option or alternative in the business case?

19. What is economic feasibility?

20. What is technical feasibility?

21. What is organizational feasibility?

22. What is total cost of ownership?

23. What is total benefits of ownership?

24. Give an example of an intangible benefit?

25. What is the payback method? Why would someone be interested in doing a payback analysis for a project?

26. What is breakeven analysis? Why would someone be interested in doing a breakeven analysis for a project?

27. What is return on investment (ROI) analysis? Why would someone be interested in determining a project's ROI?

28. What advantage does net present value (NPV) have over the payback and breakeven methods?

29. A project alternative's NPV is calculated to be $1,000. All things being equal, should you recommend this alternative for approval and funding?

30. What advantage does a scoring model have when comparing project alternatives?

31. What criteria should an organization use when selecting a project for approval and funding?

■ HUSKY AIR ASSIGNMENT—PILOT ANGELS

The Business Case

A business case should be the first project deliverable. It provides an analysis of the business value, several alternatives for achieving the project's MOV, the feasibility of the alternatives, and their costs, benefits, and risks. The business case is *not* a budget or the project plan; however, it does provide all the information necessary for senior management to make a decision whether a specific project should be undertaken.

The following is a suggested outline for developing your business case. Because this is a fictitious case, you will not be able to meet with your client. Subsequently, you will have to make a number of assumptions about the case and your project. Feel free to do so—just be sure that you document these assumptions in your business case.

This would also be a good chance for you and your team to do another learning cycle. Read through this assignment first and then meet as a team to develop a Project Team Record and an Action Plan. This will help to improve team learning and to assign responsibilities to complete the assignment.

Please provide a professional-looking document that includes the following:

1. **Project name**—You came up with a name for your project team when you developed your team charter. Now you need to name your project.

2. **Project team**—At this point, you should have your project team in place. Be sure to identify your team by its name and list all team members.

3. **Project description**—Provide a brief description of the project. A project description should be written so that anyone unfamiliar with the project can read and understand what the project is about.

Include a brief description of the organization and the problem or opportunity that led to initiating the project.

4. **Measurable organizational value (MOV)**—The MOV is the goal of the project and is used to define the value that your project will bring to your client. It will also be used to evaluate whether your project was a success later on. In reality, you would work very closely with your client in developing the MOV. Your responsibility would be to lead the process, while the client would commit to specific areas of impact, metrics, and time frames. Once the MOV is defined, it becomes the responsibility of all the project stakeholders to agree whether the MOV is realistic and achievable. For the purposes of this assignment, you will have to come up an MOV on your own. You are free to be creative, but please strive to make the MOV realistic. For our purposes, learning how to develop an MOV is an important process. Use the following steps to define your project's MOV:

   a. **Identify the desired area of impact**—At this point, what areas do you think are the most important to your client, Husky Air? Based on Figure 3.3, rank the following areas in terms of their importance:

      ■ Strategic

      ■ Customer

      ■ Financial

      ■ Operational

      ■ Social

   b. **Identify the desired value of the project**—Value to an organization can come from doing something better, faster, or less expensively (i.e., cheaper). On the other hand, it can come from growth by doing more of something that the organization is currently doing (e.g., increase market share). The next step in developing an MOV is to identify the project's potential value to the organization. In general, an IT project should focus on delivering one or two of the following types of value.

      ■ **Better?** Does Husky Air want to do something better? For example, is improving quality important to your client?

      ■ **Faster?** Does Husky Air want to do something faster? For example, does your client want to increase speed, efficiency, or reduce cycle times?

      ■ **Cheaper?** Does Husky Air want to reduce costs? For example, is cutting costs important to your client?

      ■ **Do More?** Does Husky Air want to do more of something? For example, does your client want to continue the growth of something that it is currently doing?

   c. **Develop an appropriate metric**—Once you have identified the desired area of impact and value to the organization, the next step is to develop a metric that sets a target and expectation for all of the project stakeholders. For example, if an organization desires to do more of something that is strategic to the organization (i.e., increase market share of a particular product or service), then the organization's management may feel that a project will bring value to the organization if it can grow its current market share from 10 to 25 percent. On the other hand, a bank may be able to process a loan request within 10 days. By developing and implementing a proposed information system, the bank's management may believe that it can reduce the cycle time of processing a loan to 24 hours or less. This would allow the company to do something faster operationally. Therefore, it is important to come up with a quantitative target. This target should be expressed as a metric in terms of an increase or decrease of money (dollars, euros, etc.), percentage, or a specific numeric value.

   d. **Set a time frame for achieving the MOV**—Once you have identified the area of impact, value to the organization, and an appropriate metric, you need to set a time frame for achieving the MOV. Keep in mind that this time frame may not coincide with the scheduled completion of the project work. For example, reducing the time to process a loan within 24 hours may be achievable once the system is implemented, but instant growth of market share from 10 to 25 percent may take a few months. Setting the time frame for achieving the MOV can be determined by asking the question: When do we want to achieve this target metric?

  e. **Summarize the MOV in a clear, concise statement or table**—Once the area of impact, value, metrics, and time frame are agreed on, the MOV should be summarized so that it can be clearly communicated to all of the project stakeholders. The MOV can be summarized in a statement by completing the statement: "This project will be successful if…" On the other hand, a table format may be more appropriate for summarizing the MOV if it has a growth component over two or more time periods. Keep in mind that the MOV should tell everyone *what* the project will achieve, not *how* it will be achieved. The MOV should focus on the organization not on the technology that will be used to build or support the information system.

5. **A comparison of alternatives**—To keep things simple, you may consider only three alternatives for your client: maintain the status quo (i.e., do nothing), purchase a software package, or build a custom system. Using the Internet or library, determine whether any software packages currently exist that you think may support Husky Air's requirements. If more than one exists, then select one that you feel may be the best option for your client. Compare each of the alternatives based on the following criteria:

  a. **Total cost of ownership (TCO)**—This can be only a rough estimate at this time. Later, you will develop a detailed project schedule and budget that can be compared to your ballpark estimate. Currently, Husky Air has a manual, paper-based system. If Husky Air purchases a software package or builds a system, it will need one desktop computer. Determine any other hardware and software that the company may need. This will require

a reasonable amount of research using the Internet, library, or company catalogs to estimate the cost of the hardware and software and to support your initial estimate. Keep in mind that total cost of ownership should include:

  - All direct or upfront costs
  - Indirect costs
  - Ongoing support and maintenance costs

  b. **Total benefits of ownership (TBO)**—Total benefits of ownership should include all of the direct, indirect, and ongoing benefits for each proposed alternative. It should focus on:

  - Increasing high-value work
  - Improving accuracy and efficiency
  - Improved decision making
  - Improving customer service

6. **A recommendation**—At this point, you may have more questions than answers and feel that you are being forced to make many assumptions. This is common for many real project teams and consultants at this stage of the project. You'll gain confidence from experience, doing good research, and paying attention to the details. Now, you are ready to make a recommendation to your client and support it. Given the limited amount of information and time, you should still be confident that your recommendation provides the best value to the organization and that the benefits outweigh the costs. Be sure that you not only recommend one of the three alternatives, but that you also provide support based on your analysis to back it up. The client will make a decision whether to continue to the next phase of the project. If the project continues, a detailed schedule and budget will provide a clearer picture of the project's true costs, and another decision whether to fund and support the project in the next phase will be made.

THE MARTIAL ARTS ACADEMY (MAA)—SCHOOL MANAGEMENT SYSTEM

A business case should be the first project deliverable. It provides an analysis of the business value, several alternatives for achieving the project's MOV, the feasibility of the alternatives, and their costs, benefits, and risks. The business case is not a budget or the project plan; however, it does provide all the information necessary for your client to make a decision whether a specific project should be undertaken.

The following is a suggested outline for developing your business case. Because this is a fictitious case, you will not be able to meet with your client. Subsequently, you will have to make a number of assumptions about the case and your project. Feel free to do so—just be sure that you document these assumptions in your business case.

This would also be a good chance for you and your team to do another learning cycle. Read through this assignment first and then meet as a team to develop a Project Team Record and an Action Plan. This will help to improve team learning and to assign responsibilities to complete the assignment.

Please provide a professional-looking document that includes the following:

1. **Project name**—You came up with a name for your project team when you developed your team charter. Now you need to name your project.

2. **Project team**—At this point, you should have your project team in place. Be sure to identify your team by its name and list all team members.

3. **Project description**—Provide a brief description of the project. A project description should be written so that anyone unfamiliar with the project can read and understand what the project is about. Include a brief description of the organization and the problem or opportunity that led to initiating the project.

4. **Measurable organizational value (MOV)**—The MOV is the goal of the project and is used to define the value that your project will bring to your client. It will also be used to evaluate whether your project was a success later on. In reality, you would work very closely with your client in developing the MOV. Your responsibility would be to lead the process, while the client would commit to specific areas of impact, metrics, and time frames. Once the MOV is defined, it becomes the responsibility of all the project stakeholders to agree whether the MOV is realistic and achievable. For the purposes of this assignment, you will have to come up an MOV on your own. You are free to be creative, but please strive to make the MOV realistic. For our purposes, learning how to develop an MOV is an important process. Use the following steps to define your project's MOV:

   a. **Identify the desired area of impact**—At this point, what areas do you think are the most important to your client, MAA? Based on Figure 3.3, rank the following areas in terms of their importance:
      - Strategic
      - Customer
      - Financial
      - Operational
      - Social

   b. **Identify the desired value of the project**—Value to an organization can come from doing something better, faster, or less expensively (i.e., cheaper). On the other hand, it can come from growth by doing more of something that the organization is currently doing (e.g., increase market share). The next step in developing an MOV is to identify the project's potential value to the organization. In general, an IT project should focus on delivering one or two of the following types of value.
      - *Better?* Does MAA want to do something better? For example, is improving quality important to your client?
      - *Faster?* Does MAA want to do something faster? For example, does your client want to increase speed, efficiency, or reduce cycle times?
      - *Cheaper?* Does MAA want to reduce costs? For example, is cutting costs important to your client?
      - *Do More?* Does MAA want to do more of something? For example, does your client want to continue the growth of something that it is currently doing?

   c. **Develop an appropriate metric**—Once you have identified the desired area of impact and value to the organization, the next step is to develop a metric that sets a target and expectation for all of the project stakeholders. For example, if an organization desires to do more of something that is strategic to the organization (i.e., increase market share of a particular product or service), then the organization's management may feel that a project will bring value to the organization if it can grow its current market share from 10 to 25 percent. On the other hand, a bank may be able to process a loan request within 10 days. By developing and implementing a proposed information system, the bank's management may believe that it can reduce the cycle time of processing a loan to 24 hours or less. This would allow the company to do something faster operationally. Therefore, it is important to come up with a quantitative target. This target should be expressed as a metric in terms of an increase or decrease of money (dollars, euros, etc.), percentage, or a specific numeric value.

d. **Set a time frame for achieving the MOV**— Once you have identified the area of impact, value to the organization, and an appropriate metric, you need to set a time frame for achieving the MOV. Keep in mind that this time frame may not coincide with the scheduled completion of the project work. For example, reducing the time to process a loan within 24 hours may be achievable once the system is implemented, but instant growth of market share from 10 to 25 percent may take a few months. Setting the time frame for achieving the MOV can be determined by asking the question: When do we want to achieve this target metric?

e. **Summarize the MOV in a clear, concise statement or table**—Once the area of impact, value, metrics, and time frame are agreed on, the MOV should be summarized so that it can be clearly communicated to all of the project stakeholders. The MOV can be summarized in a statement by completing the statement: "This project will be successful if..." On the other hand, a table format may be more appropriate for summarizing the MOV if it has a growth component over two or more time periods. Keep in mind that the MOV should tell everyone *what* the project will achieve, not *how* it will be achieved. The MOV should focus on the organization not on the technology that will be used to build or support the information system.

5. **A comparison of alternatives**—To keep things simple, you may consider only three alternatives for your client: maintain the status quo (i.e., do nothing), purchase a software package, or build a custom system. Using the Internet or library, determine whether any software packages currently exist that you think may support MAA's requirements. If more than one exists, then select one that you feel may be the best option for your client. Compare each of the alternatives based on the following criteria:

a. **Total cost of ownership (TCO)**—This can be only a rough estimate at this time. Later, you will develop a detailed project schedule and budget that can be compared to your ballpark estimate. Currently, MAA has a manual, paper-based system. If MAA purchases a software package or builds a system, it will need one desktop computer. Determine any other hardware and software that the company may need. This will require a reasonable amount of research using the Internet, library, or company catalogs to estimate the cost of the hardware and software and to support your initial estimate. Keep in mind that total cost of ownership should include:

   - All direct or upfront costs
   - Indirect costs
   - Ongoing support and maintenance costs

b. **Total benefits of ownership (TBO)**— Total benefits of ownership should include all of the direct, indirect, and ongoing benefits for each proposed alternative. It should focus on:

   - Increasing high-value work
   - Improving accuracy and efficiency
   - Improved decision making
   - Improving customer service

6. **A recommendation**—At this point, you may have more questions than answers and feel that you are being forced to make many assumptions. This is common for many real project teams and consultants at this stage of the project. You'll gain confidence from experience, doing good research, and paying attention to the details. Now, you are ready to make a recommendation to your client and support it. Given the limited amount of information and time, you should still be confident that your recommendation provides the best value to the organization and that the benefits outweigh the costs. Be sure that you not only recommend one of the three alternatives, but that you provide support based on your analysis to back it up. The client will make a decision whether to continue to the next phase of the project. If the project continues, a detailed schedule and budget will provide a clearer picture of the project's true costs, and another decision whether to fund and support the project in the next phase will be made.

QUICK THINKING—MEASURING THE IMMEASURABLE

According to Douglas Hubbard, the *IT value measure problem* is common in many companies today. Often business managers hear their IT departments say that the value of IT can't be measured because the benefits of IT are too intangible. Moreover, IT investments are fundamentally different from other types of investments. For example, accounting departments don't have to justify their budgets, and IT is just as basic to the business as accounting.

So, the logic is that the IT budget should likewise be exempt from justification. While this position may be popular among some executives because it gets them off the hook, Hubbard believes that many business managers are no longer buying it. Unlike most accounting departments, IT's budget is often large and growing. Given that many IT departments have had a few high-profile failures, business managers have the right to question the value of their organization's IT investments. On the other hand, many believe that only pseudo measurements are possible and that many of the benefits of IT are intangible and therefore immeasurable. Hubbard believes that the value of IT is measurable. He challenges the attendees of his seminars to come up with the most difficult or even impossible IT measurement problems they can think of.

No matter how difficult it seemed at first, no suggested intangible has taken more than 20 minutes to solve.

Hubbard believes that "immeasurability" is an illusion caused by the concept or intangible thing to be measured and the techniques or methods of measurement available not being well understood. For example, an organization may wish to measure something like employee empowerment, customer relationships, or strategic alignment. Organizations may consider these things as being intangibles because they don't fully grasp what they mean. Hubbard contends that specific, unambiguous measures can underlie these ambiguous concepts. Often, it is a lack of understanding that keeps us from developing a meaningful measure. Hubbard suggests that no matter how difficult a measurement problem seems, the first step requires changing your initial assumption that something is an immeasurable intangible and instead assume that it is tangible and therefore measurable.

1. The intangible concept of "user friendliness" is an often used and widely cited requirement for many information systems. Come up with some measurements that could be used to represent the concept of user friendliness.

SOURCE: Douglas Hubbard, "Everything is Measurable," *CIO Magazine*, May 23, 2007.

QUICK THINKING—THE ELEVATOR PITCH

Just about every IT project starts off as a written proposal or business case that was sold to a high-level executive. A poorly written proposal rarely results in a funded project. To make your project compelling, Alan Horowitz suggests that you first presell your proposal by having conversations with senior executives to gauge their reactions and listen to their concerns. Preselling also helps to create a strong partnership with the business units involved. Credibility and a business focus are key ingredients for selling the proposal.

A proposal should be tied to the organization's mission and management's current hot buttons. Unfortunately, IT often takes a narrow view. For example, a new

system may save an employee 30 minutes a day, but a successful proposal should go beyond that and explain how it can impact the rest of the organization, such as manufacturing or human resources. People prefer things be summarized, and most people focus on the executive summary—a short summary that explains why you are asking for the money, what you will do with it, and how it will benefit the organization.

An "elevator pitch" (a.k.a. elevator speech) can be a useful technique for preselling an idea and sharpening presentation skills. As the name implies, you need to state your case or sell an idea to someone in the time it takes to ride in an elevator from the ground to the top floor.

1. Prepare an elevator pitch to the director of human resources as if you were riding from the lobby to the 35th floor (say, 60 seconds) to presell a project proposal. The proposed project will be an addition to the company's current web site and will allow potential candidates to view and apply for available jobs online. Feel free to make assumptions, but unrealistic assumptions will not pass the scrutiny of an astute executive.

SOURCE: Horowitz, A. "The IT Business Case: It's Not War and Peace." *Computerworld*. March 29, 2004.

 ## CASE STUDIES

Data Mining to Prevent Terrorism

Data mining is becoming an important IT tool for the intelligence community. It combines statistical models, powerful processors, and artificial intelligence to find valuable information that can be buried in large amounts of data. Retailers have relied on data mining to understand and predict the purchasing habits of customers, while credit card companies have relied on data mining to detect fraud. After September 11, 2001, the U.S. government concluded that data mining could be a valuable tool for preventing future terrorist attacks.

There are two basic types of data mining: subject-based and pattern-based. A subject-based data mining application could be used to retrieve data that could help an agency analyst follow a particular lead. Pattern-based, or link analysis, can be used to look for suspicious behaviors through nonobvious associations or relationships between seemingly unconnected people or activities. For example, a pattern-based data mining analysis could identify two terrorists who use the same credit card to book a flight or who share the same phone number.

Pressure to prevent another catastrophic terrorist attack has led to a proliferation of data mining projects. A 2004 report by the General Accountability Office (GAO) reported that federal agencies were engaged in or planning almost 200 data mining projects. It comes as no surprise that agency heads have been approving data mining projects almost as fast as they are conceived because few people want to be on the opposing side if a terrorist plot could have been foiled. However, several media outlets have reported top secret programs that collect and look for patterns in phone records, emails, and other personal information. Although many government officials and politicians defend this as being critical to the war on terror, a growing number of people have expressed concerns for ensuring privacy.

A number of experts are questioning whether an IT strategy with no clear goals and unlimited scope, budget, and schedule will best serve its end. Given the government's poor track record for IT projects, many people are concerned that projects could drag on for years, and good projects could be overlooked because some bad projects may have serious privacy and civil liberties issues.

IT projects, no matter how vital, tend to experience serious problems when controls are nonexistent or drop to the wayside when organizations face a crisis. This is a problem that all organizations face, and this can lead to overly ambitious projects, an unwillingness to change the original vision, and overlooking signs when something is not working.

Moreover, some experts believe that the government's eagerness to apply IT to antiterrorism could backfire and disrupt the crime-fighting process if users view the system as an obstacle for getting their work done. They will rebel or simply not use it.

Few people are looking at these data mining projects from a value perspective. In short, few, if any, business cases have been developed to determine whether the government will receive any return on its investment—just a rationalization that a project would be worth the investment if it could catch just one terrorist.

However, a number of projects have been canceled. For example, Congress pulled the plug on a project to create a large database that would include everything and anything that could identify a terrorist. Moreover, after 9/11 the government decided to replace the Computer Assisted Passenger Pre-Screening System (CAPPS), which focused on passenger information (names, credit card numbers, and addresses) collected by the airlines, with CAPPS II, which would also include information purchased from data brokers such as ChoicePoint and LexisNexis. In 2003, a controversy was created when Northwest Airlines and JetBlue gave passenger information to the Transportation Security Administration (TSA) in order to test the new system.

Outcries from critics that privacy safeguards were virtually nonexistent led to Congress withholding funds for CAPPS II until a study completed by the GAO could determine how the TSA could protect people's privacy. After spending more than $100 million on CAPPS II, the

TSA cancelled the project and proposed a new system called Secure Flight. This new system was very similar to its predecessor, CAPPS II, in that both systems would combine passenger information with purchased information from commercial databases.

A group of data mining and privacy experts made up the Secure Flight Working Group and were asked to review the project. After nine months they submitted a confidential report that became available on the Internet within a week. The report was highly critical and suggests that the TSA did not articulate any specific goals for Secure Flight. Moreover, it also reported little support for whether screening passengers for aviation security is realistic or feasible.

Some believe CAPPS II and Secure Flight show how a poor understanding of what the systems must achieve can damage antiterrorist efforts. While a data mining system could be developed to search through phone records or credit card transactions and identify terrorists with 99 percent accuracy, it still would not be of much use to investigators. More specifically, if 300 million Americans make just 10 phone calls or other identifiable transactions per day, that would produce more than 1 trillion pieces of data each year that the government would have to mine. Even with a 99 percent accuracy rate, that would produce a billion false positives a year, or about 27 million a day. This would still mean missing transactions that would be made by terrorists. It may come as no surprise that while hundreds of FBI agents were looking into thousands of data mining leads each month, just about all of them turned out to be dead ends.

Despite the failures of CAPPS II, there is still a belief that data mining can be an effective tool against terrorism. One antiterrorism data mining system that has been deemed successful is a link analysis system that has been used by investigators at Guantanamo Bay to determine which detainees were likely terrorists. The Army's Criminal Investigative Task Force (CITF) used a commercially available tool and reliable data about detainees such as where they were captured, who they associated with, and other details about their relationships and behaviors to construct a chart of all the detainees. Using a system called Proximity—a system developed by the University of Massachusetts—the CITF was able to calculate a probability that a given detainee was a terrorist or just a person in the wrong place at the wrong time.

The Guantanamo system was viewed as having a high accuracy rate because it had a limited scope and reliable data that was gathered by human investigators. It was a specific application used to solve a specific problem. Link analysis projects are useful only if they have a narrow scope. According to Ben Worthen, "If you're just looking at the ocean, you'll find a lot of fish that look different. Are they terrorists or just some species you don't know about? If the government searched for only the activities mentioned above—emails, checks and plane tickets—without the added insight that one of the network's members was a terrorist, investigators would be more likely to uncover a high school reunion than a terrorist plot."[1]

1. Why should the government consider developing a business case for antiterrorist data mining projects?
2. Could instituting IT governance save taxpayers money, improve the likelihood of success, and ensure privacy or civil liberties?
3. Develop an MOV for a link analysis data mining application that could be used to identify a terrorist traveling on an airline within the United States. Use the process for developing an MOV that was outlined in this chapter.

SOURCES:

Worthen, B. "IT Strategy: IT Versus Terror." *CIO Magazine*. August 1, 2006.[1]

Vance. A. and E. Swartz. "IT a Key Component of New Airport Safety Recommendations." *Computerworld*. October 7, 2001.

Vijayan, J. "Passport Records Breach Highlighted by Targets' Prominence." *Computerworld*. March 21, 2008.

Vijayan, J. "DHS Must Assess Privacy Risk Before Using Data Mining Tool, GAO Says." *Computerworld*. March 22, 2007.

Wal-Mart's RFID Supply Chain

Wal-Mart of Bentonville, Arkansas announced its vision for an RFID-enabled transparent supply chain. The company decreed that its suppliers would be required to have a system in place for attaching radio frequency identification tags to a portion of its products destined for Wal-Mart stores. Unfortunately, as the deadline grew closer, many of the company's suppliers knew that they were not going to be able to meet that deadline.

Unfortunately, some of Walmart's suppliers stuck RFID tags on just enough pallets to satisfy Wal-Mart's mandate and were not confident that the tags would even work. It was estimated that approximately 30 percent of Wal-Mart's suppliers will integrate RFID fully, while the rest will follow the practice of "slap and ship" as just described. As a result, the efficiencies Wal-Mart envisioned for the RFID supply chain may not be realized any time soon.

In addition, the mandate by Wal-Mart has become a moving target. Originally, only Wal-Mart's top suppliers were required to put RFID tags on all products shipped to specific distribution centers in Texas. Wal-Mart now wants its suppliers to attach tags to only 65 percent of their products. Several suppliers have confided that the percentage of their products shipped with RFID tags would be much lower—about 10 percent. The method of slap and ship will involve only a small percentage of products shipped to Texas, minimal data integration, and leave the supply chain blind to the movement of product. Not surprisingly, Wal-Mart is not pleased with the slap and ship approach many of its suppliers are taking. Critics believe that RFID standards are incomplete and that the technology isn't fully developed. Other companies are struggling with the cost of implementing RFID.

The failure of the deadline for RFID could mean more bad press for the retail giant when it could use some positive publicity. Wal-Mart's reputation has received bad press in the past because of allegations of unfair wage practices, hiring illegal immigrants, and discriminating against female employees. Many believe that Wal-Mart made a critical mistake when it imposed a top-down mandate on its suppliers before the technology and business needs matured to the point where RFID technology made good sense for Wal-Mart and its suppliers and customers.

MIT's Auto-ID Center began to look at how RFID technology could help organizations track and manage products using embedded sensors. The center proposed an electronic product code (EPC) that replaces bar codes by utilizing radio frequencies to identify computer chips placed in tags. In a controlled environment, RFID works quite well. Although tags can vary in size and shape, they can be affixed to cases and pallets as stickers or labels, or like thin plastic wrist bands. Each tag contains a small antenna and a chip with a unique string of numbers to identify each product. Active tags contain a battery, while the more common passive tags acquire their energy from a reader and are less expensive. Readers are antenna devices that identify the tags as they pass by. The tag transmits its digital electronic product code to the reader and then to a computer system.

The promise of RFID is to help reduce the number of products that are misplaced or misdirected in a supply chain. Supporters of RFID contend that millions of dollars can be saved by increasing supply chain efficiencies. An RFID system can reduce the likelihood of picking the wrong inventory item and having to manually count inventory. It can also mean finding products more easily in a warehouse.

Before the year 2000, the price of RFID tags was about $1 to $2 apiece. Recently, the cost became as low as 25 cents, depending on the volume of the purchase. However, many suppliers contend that the price of an RFID tag must be even lower before they make economic sense.

Assuming a cost of 30 cents per tag, a supplier that ships 15 million items to Wal-Mart per year would spend about $4.5 million in RFID tags. Adding to the problem is Wal-Mart's one-size-fits all strategy, where there is no difference between such consumer products as razor blades, tires, or computers. Each pallet will require an RFID tag when shipped. While large ticket items like flat screen TVs and lawn mowers make RFID cost effective, using an RFID tag for relatively smaller, less expensive items like razor blades can be prohibitive.

Another problem with RFID is that no standard for the technology currently exists. Not all tags and readers are compatible. As a result, Wal-Mart may need more than one reader in its warehouses to read different tags. Moreover, the radio waves that are the foundation for the technology have not lived up to expectation in several pilots. One RFID technology provider wasn't getting a good read rate so its engineer kept increasing the power and adding more antennas. The read rate still never got higher than 50 percent and one reader kept drowning out another reader. Radio frequency also tends to act abnormally when it's near certain elements like liquids, metals, or porous objects. Many believe that the next generation of tags, which will supposedly be available in two years, will overcome many of these problems. Unfortunately, no one is sure how much they will cost.

Some of Wal-Mart's suppliers need to consider some unpleasant alternatives. If they wait for RFID to mature, they can lower the costs of developing an RFID system that meets Wal-Mart's demands. However, by waiting they may jeopardize their relationship with Wal-Mart and open the door for their competitors to slip into their place. As a result, some are complying with the mandate via slap and ship.

1. How would having a clear MOV and business case help Wal-Mart and its suppliers decide whether an RFID supply chain makes good sense for everyone?

SOURCES:

Wailgum, T. "Tag, You're Late." *CIO Magazine*. November 15, 2004.

Vijayan, J and B. Brewin. "Wal-Mart to Deploy Radio ID Tags for Supply Tracking." *Computerworld*. June 12, 2003.

Gaudin, S. "Some Suppliers Gain from Failed Wal-Mart RFID Edict." *Computerworld*. April 28, 2008.

Sliwa, C. "RFID Tag Prices Must Fall Fast for Users to Reap Rewards, Exec Say." *Computerworld*. April 18, 2005.

Making a Case for Microsoft's SharePoint®

Increasingly more and more organizations are attempting to make information more accessible and shareable among employees. While earlier versions introduced by Microsoft included SP 2001, SP 2003, and SP 2007, that latest version of SharePoint® offers a number of new features and functionality over previous editions. Although Microsoft Office® sales have been declining, SharePoint® sales have been increasing. More specifically, Microsoft reported that SharePoint® sales have seen 20 percent growth and revenues topping $1.3 billion. In addition, Microsoft claims it has shipped over 85 million seat licenses to approximately 17,000 customers since SP 2001. As Alan Pelz-Sharpe points out, "If there was ever any lingering doubt that SharePoint® was having an impact on the market, these numbers put that argument to rest."

The popularity of SharePoint® is that it makes it easier for people to work together. The latest version of SharePoint®, for example, allows individuals to set up their own web sites to share information, manage documents, and publish reports. According to Microsoft's web site, SharePoint® provides the following capabilities:

- *Sites*—allows for a single infrastructure to support all of an organization's web sites. People can share documents, manage projects, and publish information.

- *Communities*—provides enterprise collaboration tools found on the most popular social networking sites. Users can locate key contacts and information, join groups, and create wikis.

- *Composites*—supports the use of tools and components that allow individuals to build business applications without having to write code.

- *Content*—supports content management with features like document types, retention policies, and automatic content sorting that works seamlessly with Microsoft Office.

- *Search*—allows users to search for information and documents based on a combination of relevance, refinement, and social cues.

- *Insights*—gives people access to information stored in the organization's databases, reports, and business applications.

Large companies like Sony Electronics (a division of Sony Corporation) use SharePoint® to take advantage of its improved search, social networking, and document sharing features. The improved search capabilities of SharePoint® provide results by document type, author, or within a specific time period that can narrow thousands of documents down to a relevant dozen. In addition, the new search features provide results for search terms such as a company expert's profile.

With the hiring of younger workers and the popularity of social media sites, Sony wanted to encourage the use of My Sites to allow for a more progressive work style. This reduces many problems when employees have to work in different parts of the world by increasing social connections through online chats, wikis, and posts to discussion boards. The use of SharePoint® has allowed Sony to communicate more effectively and efficiently by curbing the reliance on sending emails back and forth.

On the other hand, small and midsize businesses have been adopting SharePoint® technology. For example, the Greater St. Louis Area Council of the Boy Scouts of America serves close to 60,000 kids and 15,000 adult volunteers with only 80 staff and an IT department of one. Although it considers other options like an open source tool, its SharePoint® web site allows scout leaders in 15 different regions to coordinate activities and update their own blogs. A SharePoint® web site enabled a culture shift toward collaborative content development and provides administrative controls that allow only authorized people to access troop activities and scouts' personal information as well as controls that ensure that blog posts meet certain organizational standards.

However, SharePoint® will allow the Council to have broader capabilities, which will come in the next phase of the project. Aside from enterprise content management, the next step will be to include the ability to use mobile phones to make online reservations or to check out equipment to go camping or rock climbing.

Russ Edelman of Corridor Consulting believes that the true costs of deploying and supporting SharePoint® are not well understood. Moreover, he contends that many executives believe that SharePoint® is a "shrink-wrapped" product that can be easily installed and configured within days. Edelman believes that it cannot, and provides a breakdown of the true costs that need to be considered when deploying SharePoint® or with rolling out any new software solution:

Expected Costs:
- *Product Licenses*—Microsoft, for example, offers different licensing options for SharePoint®, and these options can vary considerably. Even though some versions are free, the version selected should depend on the functionality required, the number of instances the server software will need to run, and the number of users.

- *Microsoft SQL Server® Licenses*—The cost of SharePoint® does not include the cost of Microsoft SQL Server®, a database management system (DBMS) that is required to store the SharePoint® content and metadata. In some instances, organizations may be already running SQL Server®, but an additional SQL Server® database may be needed, depending upon scalability, redundancy, and performance. Pricing will depend upon the configuration and the type of licensing agreement.

- *Windows Server Software*—SharePoint® also requires Windows Server®, which can be on physical or virtual machines. Again, pricing will depend upon the configuration and type of licensing agreement.

- *Virus Protection and Backup*—An organization's information must be secure. Virus and backup protection can be purchased from Microsoft or another third party, but the price of these products can vary and can be user- or server-based or both.

- *Hardware and Infrastructure*—This includes the actual computers needed to support a SharePoint® environment. Certain computers may be servers for SharePoint® or SQL Server® databases, as well as the necessary network hardware and workstations.

- *IT Staff*—In general, IT staff will be required to support the SharePoint® environment. If the SharePoint® users build their own basic applications, then the cost of support will be lower. However, if the organization plans to build more sophisticated business applications, then the cost will increase significantly because more staff, such as developers and quality assurance testers, will be required. Depending on the size and complexity of the projects, project managers, business analysts, and help desk staff may be needed as well.

- *Third-Party Products*—SharePoint® is not perfect and may not solve every problem directly. Therefore, third-party vendors may provide specific products to fill such gaps. This may include tools for image capture or workflow enhancements, and the price of such products varies widely.

- *Consulting Costs*—Organizations that wish to implement SharePoint® may not have all of the requisite skills or knowledge, and, as a result, may need to hire consultants to configure SharePoint® or to integrate third-party products.

- *Quality Assurance*—Testing must go beyond out-of-the-box functionality and include testing of any custom development and the integration of third-party products. As a general rule, organizations should allocate 5 to 10 percent of their SharePoint® project's budget to quality assurance.

In addition, Edelman outlines a number of unexpected costs in order to gain a true cost of ownership picture:

Unexpected Costs:

- *Governance*—Although one of SharePoint's® strengths is its simplicity and ease of use, a drawback is that it can be used inconsistently. Therefore, design and governance standards and policies need to be developed and implemented throughout the organization.

- *Change Management*—Users will have to change the way they manage and share information once SharePoint® is deployed. People often resist change, so a change management plan is highly recommended. This could be as simple as a formal communication, such as an email or newsletter, or a highly visible campaign to promote the proper use of SharePoint®.

- *Training*—All users will require some training, which can be performed by internal staff or outside consultants.

- *Community Participation*—The SharePoint® community of users has been described as collegial and growing. For example, a number of SharePoint® conferences are being hosted around the world, so user travel may have to be factored into the true cost of SharePoint®.

Although there a number of costs associated with a SharePoint® (or any other IT solution) project, it is important to develop a business case to determine if the benefits really outweigh the costs. Russ Edelman provides a framework for understanding the specific challenges of building a business case for SharePoint®. He believes that although SharePoint® deployments can lead to process improvements, it's not always easy to quantify the value of those improvements. Edelman suggests that the benefits for any software solution should include three core areas: The hard savings, the soft savings, and risk mitigation.

Hard Savings—A well-framed model of the true costs of a SharePoint® project is the first step of developing a good business case. Without it, a business case will fail to pass the "sniff test" by most financial analysts. The first step for any business case is the cost savings that will result. For example, an organization may deploy SharePoint® for imaging-based solutions. Here, the hard savings would focus on how the organization would save money by eliminating or reducing physical storage and retrieval cost or shipping costs if documents no longer have to be mailed or shipped to other locations. In addition, SharePoint® may allow an organization to eliminate other systems the organization may be using. This would result in a hard savings on support, maintenance, or software licenses.

Soft Savings—A business case should also include the soft savings—that is, the less tangible benefits that the software solution provides. This may include efficiency improvements, such as the amount of time a person or group will save as a result of using SharePoint® or any other system to replace a manual business process or retrieve stored documents. These efficiency claims can be backed up by using time and motion studies that track how long it takes a person to perform a specific task before and after the software is implemented. This may include, for example, the closure of a case from five days to one day.

Risk Mitigation—The third element should include a description of how using the product will mitigate certain risks. For example, SharePoint® can provide a redundant repository for storing electronic copies of original documents. If disaster recovery and business continuity are important concerns for an organization, then a portion of the system's costs could be amortized over the time a catastrophe may be likely. Moreover, since SharePoint® is used by many organizations worldwide, deploying SharePoint® can reduce the IT staffing risk since a pool of talented people who can support it exists.

The main point your business case wants to make is that the organization will be doing more for less. In addition, the key capabilities and the benefits those capabilities will provide are important to justify the costs of the investment. For example, global nonprofit Conservation International was able to show how SharePoint®'s functionality reduced the time and cost of implementing a web site.

1. Suppose you are a consultant working with a client who is interested in deploying SharePoint® in her organization. During a meeting, she tells you that she's heard about a free open source software system that has similar features and functionality to SharePoint®. She suggests that this option would be the best choice because it is free. Discuss why this may or may not be the best option.

2. An organization is considering purchasing an enterprise software package to track and manage potential leads for its salespeople. Which of the costs described in the case apply? Describe one hard savings, one soft savings, and one risk that could be mitigated by deploying this new system.

SOURCES:
Microsoft: http://sharepoint.microsoft.com/en-us/product/capabilities/Pages/default.aspx#.
Edelman, R. "How to Determine the True Cost of Microsoft SharePoint." *CIO Magazine*. June 30, 2009.
Edelman, R. "How to Build a Business Case for SharePoint." *CIO Magazine*. October 19, 2009.
McDougall, P. "Microsoft Unveils SharePoint 2010." *InformationWeek*. October 20, 2009.
McDougall, P. "Microsoft SharePoint Sales to Hit $1 Billion in 2008." *InformationWeek*. March 3, 2008.
Pelz-Sharpe, A. "Measuring Microsoft SharePoint Growth." *InformationWeek*. August 3, 2007.
O'Neill, S. "SharePoint 2010: Three Ways Sony is Using It." *CIO Magazine*. May 28, 2010.
Schneider, I. "Is Microsoft SharePoint 2010 Right for SMBs?" *InformationWeek*. November 27, 2010.

BIBLIOGRAPHY

1. Billows, D. *Project and Program Management: People, Budgets, and Software*. Denver, CO: The Hampton Group, Inc., 1996.
2. Porter, M. *Competitive Strategy*. New York: Free Press, 1980.
3. ———. *Competitive Advantage*. New York: Free Press, 1985.
4. Cummings, E. M. "Enterprise Value Award Judgement Call." *Computerworld*. February 2000.

5. Remenyi, D. and M. Sherwood-Smith. *IT Investment: Making a Business Case*. Woburn, MA: Routledge, 1999.

6. Schmidt, M. J. *The Business Case Guide, 2nd Edition*. Boston, MA: Solution Matrix Ltd., 2002.

7. Keen, J. "Intangible Benefits Can Play a Key Role in Business Case." *CIO Magazine*. September 1, 2003.

8. Meredith, J. R. and S. J. Mantel Jr. *Project Management: A Managerial Approach*. New York: John Wiley & Sons, 2000.

9. McFarlan, W. F. "Portfolio Approach to Information Systems." *Harvard Business Review*. September–October, 1981.

10. Marchewka, J. T. and M. Keil. "A Portfolio Theory Approach for Selecting and Managing IT Projects." *Information Resources Management Journal* Vol. 8 (1995): 5–14.

11. Kerzner, H. *Applied Project Management: Best Practices on Implementation*. New York: John Wiley & Sons, 2000.

C H A P T E R

4

Project Planning:
The Project Infrastructure

CHAPTER OBJECTIVES

Chapter 4 focuses on developing and defining the project infrastructure. After studying this chapter, you should be able to:

- Describe the planning phase of the project life cycle (PLC).
- Define the project's infrastructure.
- Describe project governance and its role.
- Understand the roles of the project manager and how the project team is selected.
- Understand how a project acquires both internal and external resources.
- Understand and describe the project environment.
- Describe the three general categories for procurement-type contracts.
- Develop a project charter and understand its relationship to the project plan.

INTRODUCTION

A project is undertaken for a specific purpose, and that purpose must be to create tangible value to the organization. The business case documents the MOV and several project alternatives or options that are researched, analyzed, and compared in terms of the costs and benefits as well as economic, organizational, and technical feasibility. The basic question when beginning a project should be: what is the value of this project to the organization? Making the right decision is critical. Abandoning a project that will provide little or no value to an organization at the earliest stage will save a great deal of time, money, frustration, and possibly careers. On the other hand, failure to launch a project that has a great deal of potential value is an opportunity lost.

After reviewing the business case, the customer, client, or a committee then makes a go/no go decision as to whether the project opportunity should continue to the next phase of the project life cycle (PLC). This provides closure to the first phase of the PLC, and, if approved, the project moves on to the next phase where a detailed project plan is developed. As you will see, defining the project's MOV not only sets expectations for the value the project must provide to the organization, it also provides direction for planning the project. A good project plan will define in detail the scope, schedule, and budget objectives that can support the project's MOV.

The **planning phase** generally requires more time, effort, and resources than was invested in developing the business case. This entails a subtle yet important transition from a strategic mindset to a more tactical one that integrates a number of subplans to identify, coordinate, authorize, manage,

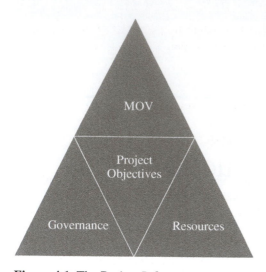

Figure 4.1 The Project Infrastructure

and control the project work. At this stage of the project, an attempt is made to answer the following questions:

- *What work needs to be done?*
- *Who will do this work?*
- *What resources will be needed to do the work?*
- *When will they do the work?*
- *How long will it take?*
- *How much will it cost?*
- *Does the time, money, and resources invested support the project's MOV?*

Unfortunately, the knowledge, tools, methods, and processes required for developing a project plan cannot be presented in a single chapter. Therefore, we will begin with defining the project's infrastructure. This **infrastructure** is documented in the project charter and identifies the project's governance structure and all of the project resources.

As depicted in Figure 4.1, the project's governance structure and resources provide a foundation for defining the project's scope, schedule, budget, and quality objectives needed to support and achieve the project's MOV.

A **project governance** structure provides a framework to guide all of the project decisions. This often includes the formation of a governance committee that represents the different interests of the project stakeholders. This group is responsible and accountable for ensuring that the project aligns with the organization's strategy and meets its intended MOV as documented in the business case. A project governance committee also establishes stakeholder roles, monitors progress, and ensures that the project has adequate funding and resources. It also defines authority as to what decisions can be made by the project manager and those that must be escalated to a higher level such as the governing committee or board.

Projects also require resources in terms of people, technology, and facilities. Some project resources will be acquired solely within the organization, while some projects will have to rely on external sources either in part or entirely. Together, knowing the type, cost, and availability of project resources and work to be completed provides a foundation for estimating the project's schedule and budget. This will be covered in more detail over the next three chapters where you will learn how to develop a detailed project plan that defines the project's scope, schedule, and budget. At the end of the planning phase, the organization once again makes a go/no go decision as to whether the project should continue to the execution phase where the project plan is carried out.

The project's MOV, infrastructure, and project objectives are documented in the **project charter**. If approved, the project charter serves as an agreement among the project stakeholders. For projects that require outside resources or are outsourced to externally, say between a consultant and a client, a legal contract is required to formalize the rendering of services and payment.

PROJECT GOVERNANCE

The word *governance* comes from the Latin word *gubernare* which means "*to steer,*" and provides a framework for ethical decision making by setting transparent boundaries that define stakeholder's roles, responsibilities, and accountabilities (1). Many organizations create an **organizational governance** structure to set strategic direction and to guide performance (2). For publicly traded companies in the United States, having a governance structure in place is a legal requirement. More specifically, the Sarbanes-Oxley Act of 2002 was enacted to ensure the accuracy of financial statements. The law was established as a result of several large financial scandals that devastated investor confidence and led to the plummet of stock prices. As a result of the billions of dollars in losses to investors, the law requires added independence of outside auditors, increased oversight by the board of directors, and stiff penalties for fraudulent activity. Organizational governance attempts to provide a set of values, methods, and processes to (1):

- Set organizational strategy and objectives
- Provide resources (people, processes, tools, and technology) to achieve the organizational strategy and objectives
- Monitor and control activities to ensure that the organizational resources are used efficiently and effectively

However, projects also require a set of "checks and balances" that work along with an organizational governance structure to ensure that the right decisions are made (3). This may include accepting and funding the project to move from one stage of the PLC to the next, changes to product design, supporting an increase in budget, choosing the project manager, or acceptance of the project's final product, service, or system. While organizational structures are designed to support the day-to-day operations of the firm, projects have different structural needs because a project operates in a more dynamic environment that must balance the interests of different stakeholders (4).

Figure 4.2 illustrates some important concepts associated with project governance. A Project governance framework provides the project manager and team with structure, processes, and decision-making models and tools for managing the project and ensuring its success. It includes a framework for making project decisions, defines roles, responsibilities, and accountabilities for the success of the project, and determines the effectiveness of the project manager. It also involves stakeholders as well as documented policies, procedures, standards, responsibilities, and authorities.

Therefore, **project governance** provides a framework to ensure that a project aligns with a chosen business strategy while ensuring that the time, money, and resources provide real value to the organization. It also is an important component of the project's infrastructure that defines accountability and responsibility. Project governance must define the following:

- *Structure*—The governance of a project requires structure. Many organizations have created a **project management office (PMO)**, which is a group or department within the organization that oversees all of the project management standards, methods, and policies based on, for example, either PMBOK® or PRINCE2®. However, often a **steering committee** is formed to represent the interests of different stakeholders. As discussed in Chapter 2, a project following the PRINCE2 methodology engages a committee called the project board. The **project board** can include a number of stakeholders, but roles of the customer, senior user, and senior supplier

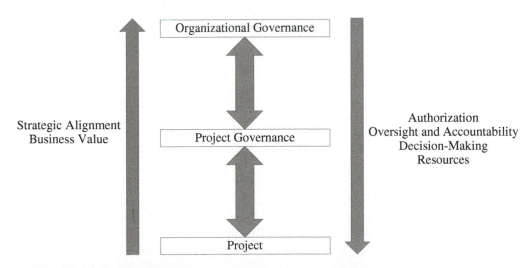

Figure 4.2 Project Governance

must be represented. Membership should be determined largely by the nature of the project. Depending on the circumstance, the governance committee may oversee a single project or the entire project portfolio.

- *Authorization*—Project stakeholders must have a clear understanding of their authority. For example, who will authorize the acceptance of project deliverables or give approval for the project to continue to the next phase? The aim is not to create an oppressive bureaucracy, but to empower people to make certain decisions while having a clearly communicated process for escalating issues or problems to a higher level of authority when appropriate.

- *Oversight and Accountability*—If the project stakeholders know their own role and responsibilities, as well as everyone else's, then people can be held accountable. A communication system must be in place that allows for the governing board to monitor and evaluate the project's progress. Because projects provide a means of implementing an organizational strategy, project governance must ensure that the project aligns with a chosen organizational strategy and provides value.

- *Decision Making*—With clearly defined roles and responsibilities, a reporting system must be in place so that project stakeholders can assess the current status of the project and forecast projected outcomes. An effective system of communication also allows stakeholders to take corrective actions or to know when to escalate an issue, problem, or risk to a higher level of authority.

- *Resources*—A good project governance framework ensures that the project has adequate resources. This includes choosing the right project manager and the right team for the project and then ensuring that they are supported with adequate resources. If an organization cannot supply these resources internally, it may have to go to external sources.

THE PROJECT TEAM

Project resources require people, technology, and facilities to complete the project work. In short, this component of the project infrastructure details everything that will be needed to carry out the project. Moreover, the resources must not only be in place, but also must be taken into account when developing the scope, schedule, budget, and quality objectives. For example, knowing who will be on the project team and what technology, facilities, and so forth will be available can be useful when estimating the amount of time a particular task or set of activities will require. It makes sense that a highly skilled and experienced team member with adequate resources should require less time to complete a specific task than an inexperienced person with inadequate resources. On the other hand, while skilled and experienced people may be more efficient, the cost associated with the skilled resource may be higher. While the project manager and team may or may not contribute to the development of the business case, it is critical that they be chosen at the beginning of the planning stage.

Projects require various resources; but people are the most valuable resource and have the greatest influence on the project's outcome. It is estimated that the human resource of a systems development project will consume up to 80 percent of its budget (5). It is important, then, that the project manager and project team members be chosen wisely.

The Project Manager

One of the most critical decisions is the selection of the project manager or team leader. The project manager must play many roles. First, the project manager must play a managerial role that focuses on planning, organizing, and controlling. The project manager, for example, is responsible for developing the project plan, organizing the project resources, and then overseeing execution of the plan. The project manager must also perform many administrative functions, including performance reviews, project tracking and reporting, and other general day-to-day responsibilities.

Although this work sounds fairly simple and straightforward, even the best thought-out plans do not always go the way we expect. As a result, the project manager must know when to stay the course, when to adapt or change the project plan by expediting certain activities or acting as a problem solver, and when to escalate a problem, issue, or decision to the governance committee.

The success of the project, of course, depends not only on the project team, but also on the contributions and support of all project stakeholders as well. Therefore, the project manager must build and nurture the relationships among the various stakeholders, including the governance committee. To do this effectively, the project manager must play a strong leadership role. While the managerial role focuses on planning, organizing, and controlling, leadership centers on getting people motivated and then headed down the right path toward a common goal.

Choosing a project manager for a project is analogous to hiring an employee. It is important to look at his or her background, knowledge, skill sets, and overall strengths and weaknesses. Some attributes of a successful project manager include:

- *The ability to communicate with people*—A project manager must have strong communication skills. A project manager need not be a great motivational speaker, but should have the ability to connect with people, share a common vision, and get everyone to respond or head in the right direction.

- *The ability to deal with people*—Aside from being a good communicator, a project manager must have the soft skills for dealing with people, their egos, and their agendas. The project manager must be a good listener, hearing what people say and understanding what they mean. This skill allows the project manager to get below the surface of issues when people are not being completely honest or open without being annoying or alienating them. A project manager must also have a sense of humor. Often, project managers and project teams are expected to perform during stressful situations, and a sense of humor can make these situations more manageable. Although a project manager does not have to be everyone's best friend, people should feel that the project manager is approachable and easy to talk to. In addition, the project manager must be willing to share knowledge and skills with others and be willing to help individuals develop to their fullest potential.

- *The ability to create and sustain relationships*—A good project manager must be able to build bridges instead of walls. Acting as a peacemaker or negotiator among the project client or sponsor, the governance committee, the project team, suppliers, vendors, subcontractors, and so forth may be necessary. In addition, the project manager should be a good salesperson. An effective project manager must continually sell the value of the project to all of the stakeholders and influence others over whom he or she has no direct authority.

- *The ability to organize*—A project manager must be good at organizing—developing the project plan, acquiring resources, and creating an effective project environment. The project manager must also know and understand both the details and the big picture, which requires a familiarity with the details of the project plan and also an understanding of how contingencies may impact the plan.

The Project Team

Another critical task of a project manager is selecting and staffing the project. In general, the size or nature of the project will determine the size and required skills of the project team. Staffing involves recruiting and assigning people to the project team. Selecting the right mix of people, with both technical and nontechnical skills, is a decision that can influence the outcome of the project. Although a project manager should strive to acquire the brightest and the best, project team members should be chosen based on the following skills:

- *Technology skills*—Depending on the nature of the project, members with specific technology skill sets—engineers, programmers, systems analysts, network specialists, and so forth—will be required.

- *Business/organization knowledge*—Although technology skills are important, it is also important to have people or access to people with domain knowledge. These skills include knowledge or expertise within a specific domain (e.g., compensation planning) as well as knowledge of a particular organization or industry (e.g., health care) to augment the technical skill requirements.

- *Interpersonal skills*—The ability to communicate with other team members and other stakeholders is an important skill for team members. It is important not only for the team members to understand one another, but also for the project team to understand the project sponsor's needs. Due to the nature of many projects, other desirable characteristics should include creativity, a tolerance for ambiguity, acceptance of diversity, flexibility in adapting to different roles, and the capacity to take calculated risks.

THE ORGANIZATION AND PROJECT PLANNING

The acquisition of internal resources of a project is influenced largely by the organization's structure. In general, an organization's structure is created to manage the input, processing, and output of resources. For example, departments or units may be based on the specialized skills needed to manage a particular resource; that is, accounting and finance manages the money resources, personnel manages the human resources, and information systems manages the information resource. As a result, many organizations adopt a structure based on function, while other organizations adopt a structure based on the products they sell geographically or by customer. An organization's structure must support a particular strategy, so it makes sense that no one structure will fit every organization. Therefore, there are different organizational structures and ways to efficiently and effectively manage not only the organizational resources but also the work and processes involved.

Projects are part of an organization and can be thought of as micro-organizations that require resources, processes, and structure. Moreover, these resources, processes, and structures are determined largely by the organizational structure of the supporting or parent organization, which may determine or influence the availability of resources, reporting relationships, and project roles and responsibilities. Therefore, it is important to understand how the project interfaces with the host or parent organization and how the project itself will be organized. In this section, we will focus on three formal structures that tie projects explicitly to the organization. Each structure provides distinct opportunities and challenges, and choosing and implementing the correct structure can have a major impact on both the project and the organization.

An organization's structure reveals the formal groupings and specializations or activities. Generally, these groupings and activities are documented in an organizational chart to clarify the lines of authority, communication, and reporting relationships. Although an organization's formal structure does not tell us about the informal lines of communication among its employees, it does provide us with an indication of how a project will interface with the parent or supporting organization. In other words, the formal organizational structure will determine how resources are allocated, who has authority over those resources, and who is really in charge of the project.

Figure 4.3 illustrates the three most common structures—the **functional**, **matrix**, and **project organization**. Keep in mind that these organizations are not exhaustive—they represent a continuum of approaches that may evolve over time or as the result of a unique situation. An organization may choose to combine these forms any number of ways to create a hybrid organization such as a **functional matrix** or **project-based matrix**.

THE FUNCTIONAL ORGANIZATION   The functional organizational structure may be thought of as the more traditional organizational form. This particular structure is based on organizing resources to perform specialized tasks or activities in order to attain the goals of the organization. As Figure 4.3

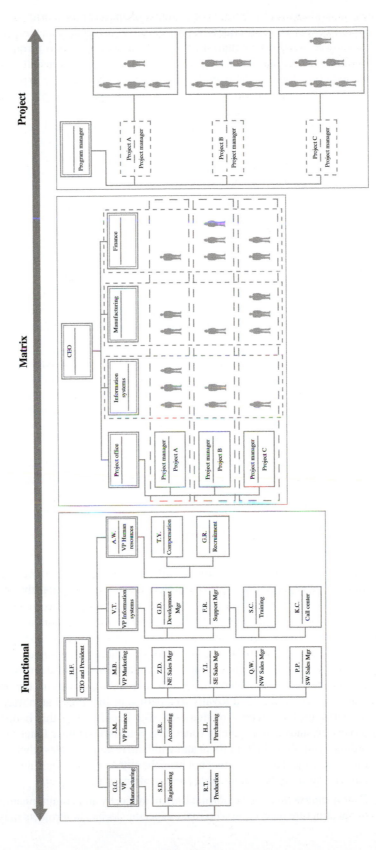

Figure 4.3 The Organization and Project Resources

illustrates, individuals and subunits (i.e., groups of individuals) perform similar functions and have similar areas of expertise. Subsequently, projects are managed within the existing functional hierarchy.

Projects in a functional organization are typically coordinated through customary channels and housed within a particular function. For example, a project to install a new machine would be a self-contained project within the manufacturing function because the expertise required for the project would reside within the manufacturing subunit. The project manager would most likely be a senior manufacturing manager, and the project team would be made up of individuals from the engineering and production areas. As a result, the manufacturing subunit would be responsible for managing the project and for supplying and coordinating all of the resources dedicated to the project.

However, a project may cross functional boundaries. In the case of an information technology project, the knowledge and expertise to design and develop an application may reside in the information systems subunit, while the domain or functional knowledge resides in one of the functional subunits. As a result, the project team may consist of individuals from two or more functional areas. There are three main issues that must be resolved at the outset of a project: Who will be responsible for the project work? What resources will each subunit provide? And who will make up the governing committee?

There are a number of advantages for projects sponsored by organizations with functional structures. These include:

- *Increased flexibility*—Subject matter experts and other resources can be assigned to the project as needed. In addition, an individual can be part of the project team on a full-time or part-time basis. Once the project is completed, the project team members can return to their respective functional units.

- *Breadth and depth of knowledge and experience*—Individuals from a particular subunit can bring a wealth of knowledge, expertise, and experience to the project. This knowledge can be expanded even further as a result of their experiences with the project. As a result, the project experience may lead to greater opportunities for career advancement within the subunit. If the project crosses functional areas, an opportunity exists for these individuals to learn from each other so that a less parochial solution can be developed.

- *Less duplication*—Coordination of resources and activities can lead to less duplication of resources across projects since specialization of skills and resources are housed within a functional area. The project also tends to be more focused because a primary functional area is responsible for and ultimately takes ownership of the project.

There are, however, several disadvantages associated with projects sponsored by organizations with functional structures. These include:

- *Determining authority and responsibility*—As was mentioned previously, determining who has authority and responsibility for a project must be resolved at the outset, especially when the project involves more than one functional area. For example, in an IT project, will the project manager be from the IS department or from the functional area? A project manager from the IS area may have knowledge and expertise with respect to the technology, but lack critical knowledge about the business. On the other hand, a project manager from the functional area may understand the business, but lack an understanding of the technology. Furthermore, there is a chance that the project manager will have an insular view of the project—that is, the project manager's allegiance and loyalty to a particular functional area may lead her or him to focus primarily on the interests of that area. The likelihood of this happening increases when the project expands across several functional boundaries. Other functional areas may begin to ask if there is anything in it for them and withhold resources unless their needs and expectations are met. The project manager may not have the authority for acquiring and providing the resources, but will certainly be accountable for the failure of the project.

- *Poor response time*—The normal lines of authority and communication delineated by the functional structure determine who makes specific decisions. Projects may take longer if important decisions have to pass through several layers of management and across several functional areas. Unfortunately, what's important to you may not be important to me if a particular functional unit has a dominant role or interest in a project. Due to the potential for parochial interests, problem resolution may break down because of finger pointing or placing blame for the problem rather than focusing on problem resolution.

- *Poor integration*—The culture of the organization may encourage functional areas to insulate themselves from the rest of the organization as a way to avoid many of these parochial issues. However, this can result in two problems. First, the individuals in a functional area may act in their own best interests instead of taking a holistic or an organizational view of the project. Second, the functional area may attempt to become self-sufficient by acquiring knowledge, expertise, and technology outside of its normal area of specialization. While specialization of skills and resources can reduce duplication of activities and resources, the functional structure can also increase this duplication. It may lead to an organization of warring tribes as functional areas compete for resources and blur lines of responsibility.

THE PROJECT ORGANIZATION   At the other end of the spectrum from the functional organization is the project organization (see Figure 4.3). Sometimes referred to as the pure project organization, this organizational structure supports projects as the dominant form of business. Typically, a project organization will support multiple projects at one time and integrate project management tools and techniques throughout the organization. Each project is treated as a separate and relatively independent unit within the organization. In general, a group or unit called the **project management office (PMO)** is responsible for assigning the project manager to the project, as well as overseeing the project methodology and project reporting requirements and ensuring that the project remains viable and on track. The project manager has sole authority over and responsibility for the project and its resources, while the parent or supporting organization provides governance controls. Both the project manager and the project team are typically assigned to a particular project on a full-time basis.

There are advantages and disadvantages associated with projects supported by the project organization. Advantages include:

- *Clear authority and responsibility*—Unlike the projects in a functional organization, the project manager here is fully in charge. Although he or she must provide progress reports and is ultimately responsible to someone who has authority over all the projects (e.g., a program manager and/or governance committee), the project manager has full authority over and responsibility for the assigned project. Moreover, a clear **unity of command** is created because each member of the project team reports directly to the project manager. This structure may allow the project team to better concentrate on the project.

- *Improved communication*—A clear line of authority results in more effective and efficient communication. In addition, lines of communication are shortened because the project manager is able to bypass the normal channels of distribution associated with the functional organizational structure. This structure thus results in more efficient communication and fewer communication problems.

- *High level of integration*—Since communication across the organization is increased, the potential for a higher level of cross integration across the organization exists. For example, the project team may include experts with technical skills or knowledge of the business. Fewer conflicts over resources arise because each project has resources dedicated solely to it.

Projects supported by project organization structures face several disadvantages. These disadvantages include:

- *Project isolation*—Because each project may be thought of as a self-contained unit, there is the potential for each project to become isolated from other projects in the organization. Unless a project management office or program manager oversees each project, inconsistencies in policies and project management approaches may occur across projects. In addition, project managers and project teams may have little opportunity to share ideas and experiences with other project managers and project teams, thus hindering learning throughout the organization.

- *Duplication of effort*—While the potential for conflicts over resources is reduced, various projects may require resources that are duplicated on other projects. Project managers may try to stockpile the best people and other resources that could be shared with other projects. Each project must then support the salaries of people who are part of the dedicated project team but whose services are not needed at all times. There is then the problem of what to do with these people when the project is completed and they have not been assigned to another project. Many consulting firms, for example, refer to people who are between projects as being on *the beach* or *on the bench*. While awaiting the next assignment, consultants are often sent to training in order to make the most of their idle time.

- *Projectitis*—Projectitis sometimes occurs when the project manager and project team develop a strong attachment to the project and to each other. As a result, these individuals may have a difficult time letting go, and the project begins to take on a life of its own with no real end in sight (6). The program manager or project office must ensure that proper controls are in place to reduce the likelihood of this happening.

THE MATRIX ORGANIZATION   The third type of organizational form is the matrix structure. The matrix organization is a combination of the vertical functional structure and the horizontal project structure (see Figure 4.3). As a result, the matrix organization provides many of the opportunities and challenges associated with the functional and project organizations.

The main feature of the matrix organization is the ability to integrate areas and resources throughout an organization. Moreover, people with specialized skills can be assigned to the project either on a part-time or on a more permanent basis. Unfortunately, **unity of command** is violated since each project team member will have more than one boss, leading to the possibility of confusion, frustration, conflict, and mixed loyalties. The functional manager will be responsible for providing many of the people and other resources to the project, while the project manager is responsible for coordinating these resources. In short, the project manager coordinates all of the project activities for the functional areas, while the functional areas provide the wherewithal to carry out those activities.

There are several advantages and disadvantages for projects supported by a matrix organization. The advantages include:

- *High level of integration*—The cross-functional nature of the matrix structure allows for the access and sharing of skilled people and resources from across the organization, and people within the organization can be assigned to more than one project. This ability to share can result in less duplication of resources and activities.

- *Improved communication*—Due to the high level of integration, communication channels are more efficient and effective. As a result, problems and issues can be addressed by the project manager and functional managers, and decisions can be made more quickly than in a functional organization.

- *Increased project focus*—Because a project under the matrix organization has improved communication channels and access to a repository of resources and skilled expertise, the project team can focus on the activities of the project. This ability to focus should increase the likelihood of projects being completed on time and meeting the needs of the organization better.

On the other hand, there are several disadvantages for projects supported by the matrix organization. These include:

- *Higher potential for conflict*—Because power is distributed, project team members may wonder who their boss is. They may receive conflicting orders, especially if the project and functional area managers have different goals or are fighting over scarce resources. In general, power may depend on which manager has the fewest direct reports to the chief executive office. The project manager may be required to be a skillful mediator and negotiator in order to keep the project on track.

- *Poorer response time*—Because the concept of unity of command is violated in a matrix structure, there can be confusion, mixed loyalties, and various distributions of power. Communication can become bogged down, and decisions may require agreement from individuals who are in conflict with each other. As a result, the project may stall and the project team may begin to experience low morale, little motivation, and the pressure to pick sides.

PROCURING EXTERNAL PROJECT RESOURCES

The project manager may acquire resources internally and/or externally. Internal projects are dependent largely upon the supporting or parent organization where resources can be determined or influenced by the availability of resources, reporting relationships, and organizational structure. Very often a project manager may have to recruit people who are currently in between projects or who will be soon rolling off an existing project. Moreover, a project manager may have to negotiate with other managers for specific resources such as individuals with specific skills or areas of expertise. Therefore, the timing of when a particular individual can begin work on the project is a significant factor that can impact the project's schedule. If internal resources are not available, the project manager may have to acquire the needed resources externally.

In addition, projects often require resources that must be acquired externally from sellers such as vendors or suppliers. This may include technology such as hardware and software for systems development or office automation tools to support the project team. Other items, such as office supplies or the printing of support and training manuals, are often acquired from outside sources as well.

Physical items are not the only things a project may acquire from external sources. Often services and components of the project's scope are subcontracted to another firm. More specifically, the project's scope can be broken up into a number of subprojects. This idea is not new, since construction contractors often subcontract specific components of a building to other subcontractors, such as framers, electricians, or plumbers. Today, however, the term "subcontracting" has been often substituted with the term "outsourcing." Outsourcing has become a strategic initiative for many organizations worldwide. It also has become a hot and controversial topic, especially when organizations look to fulfill their outsourcing needs overseas. The decision to go outside of the project team for products and services depends on several factors. First, the project manager and team may want to consider what products or services are available in the marketplace as well as the associated cost, quality, terms, and conditions.

Keep in mind that the project team can be both a buyer and a seller of products and services. A buyer could be a client or a customer, while a seller could be a consultant, contractor, vendor, supplier, or a subcontractor. For example, an organization may enter into a contract by outsourcing a specific project to a consulting firm. In this case, the organization would be the buyer of the consulting firm's (i.e., seller's) services. In turn, the consulting firm can also be a buyer of products (i.e., computers, software, paperclips) and services that could in turn be outsourced or subcontracted to other firms who specialize in a particular service (e.g., programming, system testing, printing of user manuals).

Today, outsourcing has expanded to include **business process outsourcing** in which an organization turns over processes such as accounting, information technology, research and development, and human resources management to another organization that specializes in that process (7). In recent years, a great deal of attention has been given to the outsourcing of jobs overseas. This type of outsourcing, or **offshoring**, allows an organization to take advantage of labor arbitrage (i.e., cheap labor) by procuring a product or service from a supplier that operates in another country.

Outsourcing can be an organization-level decision or a project-level decision. Just as an organization can pursue outsourcing as a strategic approach, so too can a project manager and team. Today, organizations and project teams have the opportunity to follow different approaches to outsourcing. This idea is illustrated in Figure 4.4, which shows that a continuum of outsourcing relationships can exist. For example, a project could follow a full-insourcing approach in which all products and services would

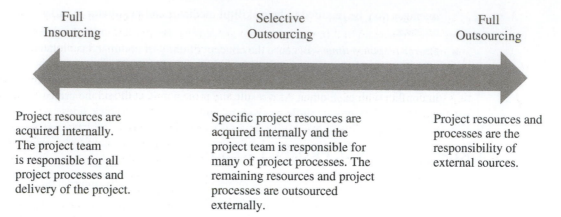

Full Insourcing	Selective Outsourcing	Full Outsourcing
Project resources are acquired internally. The project team is responsible for all project processes and delivery of the project.	Specific project resources are acquired internally and the project team is responsible for many of project processes. The remaining resources and project processes are outsourced externally.	Project resources and processes are the responsibility of external sources.

Figure 4.4 The Project Outsourcing Model

be acquired internally. This would also mean that the project team is responsible for all the project's processes and scope. On the other hand, a full-outsourcing approach would be followed if an organization or project acquires all products or services from external sources. However, the best approach for organizations and projects probably would be selective outsourcing. More specifically, selective outsourcing provides greater flexibility to choose which project processes or deliverables should be outsourced and which should be kept internal. Although low cost is one advantage for outsourcing, or offshoring, the main objective should be to increase flexibility and quality (8).

Often the decision whether to purchase or outsource specific project needs is similar to a "make or buy" decision that compares the total direct and indirect costs of "making" a particular product or performing a particular service internally to the total direct and indirect costs of "buying" or contracting externally. The same qualitative and quantitative tools for comparing various alternatives that were used to develop the business case can be used to make this decision. However, this decision can be viewed from a risk management perspective where risk is transferred to the seller. In many respects, this may be a good idea if the seller has a particular expertise or more experience than the project team. Unfortunately, when you transfer control over to someone else, you may lose your control over the project schedule and budget if the external party cannot meet its promised obligations.

Procurement Planning

Projects generally require resources, products, or services that must be purchased or acquired externally. This begins by determining which project needs can be fulfilled internally by the project team and which can best be met externally. Moreover, the project manager and team must not only decide *what* project needs can be met internally or externally, but also *how, when, how many*, and *where* these products and services will be acquired.

Depending on the needs of the project, the project manager and team may develop a **request for proposal (RFP)**, which will be used to solicit bids, quotes, or proposals from prospective sellers. These documents are generally structured by the buyer so that a common means and set of measures can be used to compare and evaluate the responses from the different sellers. The complexity or rigor of these documents can be high when dealing with a government agency or if the product or service to be acquired is highly regulated.

This also includes the development of criteria for evaluating bids, proposals, and so forth after they are received from the sellers. While price might be one important factor, sellers or contractors may be chosen based on their experience, expertise, and understanding of the seller's needs, management approach, financial strength, technical capability, or references from previous clients or customers.

The next step is for the buyer to obtain a reasonable number of high-quality, competitive proposals. To achieve this objective, a buyer organization may hold a conference with bidders, contractors, vendors, and so on. These preliminary meetings allow the sellers to have a better understanding of what products or services are needed and how to go about submitting the procurement document. Many times the governing policies and procedures for the buyer's organization entail a lengthy and public process to solicit bids from a number of prospective sellers. This may include advertising in newspapers, trade journals, or even the Internet to let other parties know that requests for proposals, bids, or quotations are being sought. Alternatively, in many cases, the buyer may contact the seller directly for a bid, quotation, or request.

The proposal developed by the seller generally includes the price of the requested product or service as well as a description of the seller's ability and willingness to provide what was requested. Depending on the nature of the product or service requested, this could entail something as simple as a phone call or a lengthy, complex, and formal written document and a formal presentation to the buyer.

Once the bids, proposals, or quotations are received, the buying organization begins the process of analyzing, evaluating, and selecting a seller. The criteria developed in the plan purchases and acquisition process are used as a basis. Again, price or cost may be an important consideration, but other factors should be considered because a decision on price or cost alone may prove moot if the seller is unable to provide a quality product or service in a timely manner.

Contracts Between Sellers and Buyers

Once a seller is selected, the buyer may enter into contract negotiations so that a mutual agreement can be reached. A **contract** is a document signed by the buyer and seller that defines the terms and conditions of the buyer–seller relationship. It serves as a legally binding agreement that obligates the seller to provide specific products, services, or even results, while obligating the buyer to provide specific monetary or other consideration. A contract defines the terms and conditions or such things as responsibilities and authorities, technical and project management approaches, proprietary rights, financing, schedule, payments, quality requirements, and price, as well as remedies and process for revisions to the contract. Depending on the nature of the relationship, a contract can be simple or complex, informal or formal. For example, a purchase order would be an example of a simple contract, while an outsourcing agreement between two firms would require a more lengthy and detailed document.

Organizational policies and procedures usually govern how these relationships are created and who is authorized to enter into and manage these various agreements. Today, many projects also involve multiple contracts and subcontracts with many buyer and seller relationships that must be managed actively throughout the entire project life cycle.

Given that you may be the buyer or seller of procurement services, it is important that you understand types of contracts that exist and that one may be more appropriate for a given situation. There are three general categories for procurement-type contracts (2):

1. *Fixed-price or lump-sum contracts*—A total or fixed price is negotiated or set as the final price for a specific product or service. For example, an organization may decide to outsource the development of an application system to a consulting firm. Based on the project's scope, the consulting firm will develop an estimated schedule and budget. Both firms may then negotiate a final cost of the project. On the other hand, the cost of a particular product or service may be fixed with little or no opportunity for negotiation. For example, let's say that a project team member requests a new laptop computer. Although policy and procedures vary greatly among organizations, usually some process is in place for acquiring products or services and involves requests, authorizations, and purchase orders. This process could be simple and straightforward or an inefficient, bureaucratic mess. Fixed-price or lump-sum contracts may include incentives for meeting certain objects or penalties if those objectives are not met.

2. *Cost-reimbursable contracts*—For these types of contracts a payment or reimbursement is made to the seller to cover the seller's actual costs. These costs include direct costs (e.g., direct labor, materials) and indirect costs (e.g., administrative salaries, rent, utilities,

insurance). However, an additional fee is added to the total direct and indirect costs as a profit to the seller. Cost-reimbursable contracts can also include incentives for meeting specific objectives or penalties if specific objectives are not met. In general, there are three types of cost-reimbursable projects:

- *Cost-plus-fee (CPF) or cost-plus-percentage-of-cost (CPPC)*—The seller is paid for the costs incurred in performing the work as well as a fee based on an agreed-upon percentage of the costs. For example, let's say that you take your car to a mechanic for a tune-up. The mechanic might say that the cost of the tune-up will include parts and labor plus a 20 percent fee. So, if the mechanic charges $50 an hour to cover direct and indirect costs, works 2 hours on your car, and uses $100 worth of parts, the cost of parts and labor would be $200 (i.e., 2 × $50 + $100). Your bill would be $240 after the 20 percent fee is added on. Unless the mechanic is someone you can trust, you might want to take precautions, such as getting an estimate in writing before the repair work begins; otherwise, an unscrupulous mechanic could increase the fee (i.e., profit) by driving up the costs of labor and/or parts.

- *Cost-plus-fixed-fee (CPFF)*—In this case, the seller is reimbursed for the total direct and indirect costs of performing the work, but receives a fixed amount. This fixed amount does not change unless the scope changes. For example, you may take your car to your friend who says that he will work on your car. In this case, the arrangement may be that you pay for all the parts needed for the tune-up, but your friend will do the work for $20 as a favor. If your car needs $100 in parts, then the cost of having your friend work on your car will be $120. However, if you can find the same parts for $80 at an automotive superstore, then the cost of having your car tuned up will be $100, since your friend will receive $20 for his time regardless of the cost for the parts.

- *Cost-plus-incentive-fee (CPIF)*—Under this type of contract, the seller is reimbursed for the costs incurred in doing the work and receives a predetermined fee plus an incentive bonus for meeting certain objectives. In this case, let's say that while your friend is working on your car, you receive a call from another friend who offers you two free tickets to a concert that starts in a couple of hours. You might offer the extra ticket as an incentive to complete the repairs in an hour or less so that you can take your car to the concert and make it in time for the start of the show.

3. *Time and materials (T&M) contracts*—A T&M contract is a hybrid of cost-reimbursable and fixed-price contracts. Under a T&M contract, the buyer pays the seller for both the time and materials required to complete the work. In this case, it resembles a cost reimbursable contract because it is open-ended, and the full cost of the project is not predetermined before the work begins. However, a T&M contract can resemble a fixed-price arrangement if unit rates are set. For example, let's say that you want to have your house painted. A painting contractor may tell you that the cost of painting your house will be $20 an hour plus the cost of paint. If a gallon of paint costs $10, the cost of painting your house will depend on how many gallons of paint are used and how long it takes. If one person works on your house for 20 hours and uses 5 gallons of paint, then the cost for the painter's time and the materials used will be $450.

Once the contract is signed, the buyer and the seller enter into a relationship in which both parties must fulfill their contractual obligations. This ensures that both parties are performing in accordance to the terms of the contract. Closure of the contract can result when the buyer and seller mutually agree that the obligations of the contract have been fulfilled. The seller may give the buyer a formal notice that all deliverables specified in the contract have been provided, and the buyer may provide the seller with a notice that the deliverables have been received and are acceptable. On the other hand, early termination of the project may occur when one party is unable to fulfill its rights and responsibilities. Based on the terms and conditions outlined in the contract, the other party may have the right to terminate the contract or seek punitive damages.

THE PROJECT ENVIRONMENT

The project manager is responsible for many things. In addition to acquiring resources, the project manager must also focus on the project environment. The **project environment** includes not only the physical space where the team will work, but also the project culture. More specifically, the project environment includes:

- *A place to call home*—It may seem obvious, but a project team must have adequate space to work and meet. If the project team is internal to the organization, a work area may already be available. However, consultants often are found camped out in a conference room or even the organization's cafeteria because no other space is available. Therefore, the project manager should make sure that the team has a place to call home and a place to meet as a team for the duration of the project. For an Agile project, this may require a central work space where the project team can communicate effectively and work collectively.

- *Technology*—In addition to having an adequate work area, the team will also need adequate technology support. Support may include a personal computer and appropriate software, Internet access, electronic mail, and a telephone. In addition, many teams today are geographically dispersed. Technology provides a means for teams to collaborate when they cannot meet at the same time in the same place. Collaboration tools, such as video conferencing, online meeting tools, and so forth, not only can improve communication, but can also increase the speed of the team's learning cycles by allowing the team to store and share minutes of team meetings, action plans, and lessons learned.

- *Office supplies*—Aside from technology resources, the team will need various office supplies, such as paper, pens, pencils, staplers, and so forth.

- *Culture*—Each organization has its own culture, but a project team should have its own culture as well. Culture reflects the values and norms of the team. One way of establishing a culture is for the project team develop a team charter early on in the project. The team charter allows the team to agree on a set of values and expectations that will help define the project team culture. This charter includes:
  - What is expected from each member?
  - What role will each team member play?
  - How will conflicts be resolved?

THE PROJECT CHARTER

The **project charter** serves as an agreement and as a communication tool for all of the project stakeholders. The project charter documents the project's MOV and describes the infrastructure needed to support the project. In addition, the project charter summarizes many of the details found in the project plan. A well-written project charter should provide a consolidated source of information about the project and reduce the likelihood of confusion and misunderstanding. More specifically, the purpose of the project charter is to:

- *Document the project's MOV*—Although the project's MOV was included in the business case, it is important that the MOV be clearly defined and agreed upon before developing or executing the project plan. At this point, the MOV must be cast in stone. Once agreed upon, the MOV for a project should not change. As you will see, the MOV drives the project planning process and is fundamental for all project-related decisions.

- *Define the project infrastructure*—The project charter defines all of the people, resources, technology, methods, project management processes, and knowledge areas that are required to support the project. In short, the project charter will detail everything needed to carry out the project. Moreover, this infrastructure must not only be in place, but must also be taken into account when developing the project plan. For example, knowing who will be on the project team and what resources will be available to them can help the project manager estimate the amount of time a particular task or set of activities will require. It makes sense that a highly skilled and experienced team member with adequate resources should require less time to complete a certain task than an inexperienced person with inadequate resources. Keep in mind, however, that you can introduce risk to your project plan if you develop your estimates based on the abilities of your best people. If one of these individuals should leave sometime during the project, you may have to replace him or her with someone less skilled or less experienced. As a result, you will either have to revise your estimates or face the possibility of the project exceeding its deadline.

- *Summarize the details of the project plan*—The project charter should summarize the scope, schedule, budget, quality objectives, deliverables, and milestones of the project. It should serve as an important communication tool that provides a consolidated source of information about the project that can be referenced throughout the project life cycle.

- *Define the project's governance structure*—The project charter should not only identify the project sponsor, project manager, and project team, but should also specify when and how they will be involved throughout the project life cycle. In addition, the project charter should specify the lines of reporting, who will be responsible for specific decisions, and how problems, issues, or risk should be escalated to an appropriate decision maker. In addition, changes to the project's scope, schedule, and budget will undoubtedly be required over the course of the project. But, the project manager can lose control and the project team can lose its focus if these changes are not managed properly. Therefore, the project charter should outline a process for requesting and responding to proposed changes

- *Show explicit commitment to the project*—In addition to defining the roles and responsibilities of the various stakeholders, the project charter should detail the resources to be provided by the organization and specify clearly who will take ownership of the project's product once the project is completed. Any contractual agreement should also detail the terms of all the parties involved. Approval of the project charter gives the project team the formal authority to begin work on the project.

In general, the project charter and project plan should be developed together—the details of the project plan need to be summarized in the project charter, and the infrastructure outlined in the project charter will influence the estimates used in developing the project plan. It is the responsibility of the project manager to ensure that the project charter and plan are developed, agreed upon, and approved. Like the business case, the project charter and plan should be developed with both the project team and the project sponsor or governance committee to ensure that the project will support the organization and that the project's MOV remains realistic and achievable.

What Should Be in a Project Charter?

Although the formality and depth of developing a project charter will most likely depend on the size and complexity of the project, the fundamental project management and the product-development processes and areas should be addressed and included for all projects. This section presents an overview of the typical areas that may go into a project charter; however, organizations and project managers should adapt the project charter based on best practices, experience, and the project itself.

PROJECT IDENTIFICATION   It is common for all projects to have a unique name or a way to identify them. It is especially necessary if an organization has several projects underway at once. Naming a project can also give the project team and stakeholders a sense of identity and ownership. Often organizations will use some type of acronym for the project's name. For example, instead of naming a project something as mundane as the Flight Reservation System in 1965, American Airlines named its system Semi-Automated Business Research Environment (SABRE). Today, SABRE has become a well-recognized product that connects travel agents and online customers with all of the major airlines, car rental companies, hotels, railways, and cruise lines.

PROJECT STAKEHOLDERS   It is important that the project charter specifically name the project sponsor and the project manager, as well as the members of the governance committee. This reduces the likelihood of confusion when determining who will take ownership of the project's product and who will be the leader of the project. In addition, the project team should be named along with team members' titles or roles in the project, their phone numbers, and email addresses. This section should describe who will be involved in the project, how they will be involved, and when they will be involved. Formal reporting relationships can be specified and may be useful on larger projects. In addition, including telephone numbers and email addresses can provide a handy directory for getting in touch with the various participants.

PROJECT DESCRIPTION   The project charter should be a single source of information. Therefore, it may be useful to include a description of the project to help someone unfamiliar with the project understand not only the details, but the larger picture as well. This may include a brief overview or background of the project as to the problem or opportunity that became a catalyst for the project and the reason or purpose for taking on the project. It may also be useful to include the vision of the organization or project and how it aligns with the organization's goal and strategy. Much of this section could summarize the total benefits expected from the project that were described in the business case. It is important that the project description focus on the business and not the technology.

MEASURABLE ORGANIZATIONAL VALUE (MOV)   The MOV should be clear, concise, agreed on, and made explicit to all of the project stakeholders. Therefore, the project's MOV should be highlighted and easily identifiable in the project charter.

PROJECT SCOPE   The project's scope is the work to be completed. A specific section of the project charter should clarify not only what will be produced or delivered by the project team, but also what will not be part of the project's scope. This distinction is important for two reasons. First, it provides the foundation for developing the project plan's schedule and cost estimates. Changes to the project's scope will impact the project's schedule and budget; that is, if resources are fixed, expanding the amount of work you have to complete will take more time and money. Therefore, the creation of additional work for the project team will extend the project's schedule and invariably increase the cost of the project. Formal procedures must be in place to control and manage the project's scope. Second, it is important for the project manager to manage the expectations of the project sponsor and the project team. By making the project's scope explicit as to what is and what is not to be delivered, the likelihood of confusion and misunderstanding is reduced.

At this point, a first attempt is made to define the project's scope and is based on information provided by the project sponsor. Only enough detail is needed to plan the project so that estimates for the project schedule and budget can be defined. This may include a high-level view of the project and product deliverables and the criteria for their acceptance by the project sponsor. Detailed system requirements will be specified later during the execution phase of the project when the SDLC is carried out.

PROJECT SCHEDULE   Although the details of the project's schedule will be in the project plan, it is important to summarize the detail of the plan with respect to the expected start and completion dates. In addition, expected dates for major deliverables, milestones, and phases should be highlighted and summarized at a very high level.

PROJECT BUDGET   A section of the project charter should highlight the total cost of the project. The total cost of the project should be summarized directly from the project plan.

QUALITY STANDARDS   Although a quality management plan should be in place to support the project, a section that identifies any known or required quality standards should be made explicit in the project charter. For example, an application system's reports may have to meet a government agency's requirements.

RESOURCES   Because the project charter acts as an agreement or contract, it may be useful to specify the resources required and who is responsible for providing those resources. Resources may include people, technology, or facilities to support the project team. It would be somewhat awkward for a team of consultants to arrive at the client's organization and find that the only space available for them to work is a corner table in the company cafeteria! Therefore, explicitly outlining the resources needed and who is responsible for what can reduce the likelihood for confusion or misunderstanding.

ASSUMPTIONS AND RISKS   Any risks or assumptions should be documented in the project charter. Assumptions may include things that must go right, such as a particular team member being available for the project, or specific criteria used in developing the project plan estimates. Risks, on the other hand, may be thought of as anything that can go wrong or things that may impact the success of the project. Although a risk management plan should be in place to support the project team, the project charter should summarize the following potential impacts:

- *Key situations or events that could significantly impact the project's scope, schedule, or budget*—These risks, their likelihood, and the strategy to overcome or minimize their impact should be detailed in the project's risk plan.

- *Any known constraints that may be imposed by the organization or project environment*—Known constraints may include such things as imposed deadlines, budgets, or required technology tools or platforms.

- *Dependencies on other projects internal or external to the organization*—In most cases, an IT project is one of several being undertaken by an organization. Subsequently, dependencies between projects may exist, especially if different application systems or technology platforms must be integrated. It may also be important to describe the project's role in relation to other projects.

- *Impacts on different areas of the organization*—As discussed earlier, projects operate in a broader environment than the project itself. As a result, the development and implementation of a new product, service, or system will have an impact on the organization. It is important to describe how the project will impact the organization in terms of disruption, downtime, or loss of productivity.

- *Any outstanding issues*—It is important to highlight any outstanding issues that need further resolution. These may be issues identified by the project sponsor, the project manager, or the project team that must be addressed and agreed upon at some point during the project. They may include such things as resources to be provided or decisions regarding the features or functionality of the system.

PROJECT ADMINISTRATION   Project administration focuses on the knowledge areas, processes, and controls that will support the project. These are actually separate subplans or strategies that make up the project management plan. Administration may include:

- A *communication plan* that outlines how the project's status or progress will be reported to various stakeholders. This plan also includes a process for reporting and resolving significant issues or problems as they arise.

- A *scope management plan* that describes how changes to the project's scope will be submitted, logged, and reviewed.

- A *quality management plan* that details how quality planning, assurance, and control will be supported throughout the project life cycle. In addition, a plan for testing the information system will be included.

- A *change management and implementation plan* that will specify how the project's product will be integrated into the organizational environment.

- A *human resources plan* for staff acquisition and team development.

ACCEPTANCE AND APPROVAL Because the project charter serves as an agreement or contract between the project sponsor and project team, it may be necessary to have key stakeholders sign off on the project charter. By signing the document, the project stakeholder shows formal acceptance of the project and, therefore, gives the project manager and team the authority to carry out the project plan.

REFERENCES In developing the project charter and plan, the project manager may use a number of references. It is important to document these references in order to add credibility to the project charter and plan as well as to provide a basis for supporting certain processes, practices, or estimates.

TERMINOLOGY Many projects use certain terms or acronyms that may be unfamiliar to many people. Therefore, to reduce complexity and confusion, it may be useful to include a glossary giving the meaning of terms and acronyms, allowing all the project's stakeholders to use a common language. Figure 4.5 provides a template for a project charter. Feel free to adapt this template as needed.

Project Name or Identification

Project Stakeholders
- Names
- Titles or roles
- Phone numbers
- E-mail addresses

Project Description
- Background
- Description of the challenge or opportunity
- Overview of the desired impact

Measurable Organizational Value (MOV)
- Statement or table format

Project Scope
- What will be included in the scope of this project
- What will be considered outside the scope of this project

Project Schedule Summary
- Project start date
- Project end date
- Timeline of project phases and milestones
- Project reviews and review dates

Project Budget Summary
- Total project budget
- Budget broken down by phase

Quality Issues
- Specific quality requirements

Resources Required
- People

- Technology
- Facilities
- Other
- Resources to be provided
  - Resource
  - Name of resource provider
  - Date to be provided

Assumptions and Risks
- Assumptions used to develop estimates
- Key risks, probability of occurrence, and impact
- Constraints
- Dependencies on other projects or areas within or outside the organization
- Assessment project's impact on the organization
- Outstanding issues

Project Administration
- Communications plan
- Scope management plan
- Quality management plan
- Change management plan
- Human resources plan
- Implementation and project closure plan

Acceptance and Approval
- Names, signatures, and dates for approval

References

Terminology or Glossary

Appendices (as required)

Figure 4.5 A Project Charter Template

CHAPTER SUMMARY

- The first stage of the project life cycle (PLC) focuses on conceptualizing and initiating a project by defining the project's measurable organizational value (MOV). The customer, client, or committee then makes a go/no go decision as to whether the project opportunity should continue to the next phase of the project life cycle (PLC). This provides closure to the first phase of the PLC, and, if approved, the project moves on to the next phase where a detailed project plan is developed.

- The **planning phase** generally requires more time, effort, and resources than was invested in developing the business case. This entails a subtle yet important transition from a strategic mindset to a more tactical one that integrates a number of subplans to identify, coordinate, authorize, manage, and control the project work.

- The project's **infrastructure** is documented in the project charter and identifies the project's governance structure and all of the project resources.

- **Project governance** provides a framework to ensure that a project aligns with a chosen business strategy while ensuring that the time, money, and resources provide real value to the organization.

- Many organizations have created a **project management office** (**PMO**), which is a group or department within the organization that oversees all of the project management standards, methods, and policies. This may also include forming a **governance committee** to represents the interests of different stakeholders. Membership should be determined largely by the nature of the project, and the governance committee may oversee a single project or the entire project portfolio.

- One of the most important project decisions is the selection of the project manager or team leader. The project manager is responsible for developing the project plan, organizing the project resources, and then overseeing execution of the plan.

- Staffing involves recruiting and assigning people to the project team. Selecting the right mix of people, with both technical and nontechnical skills, is a decision that can influence the outcome of the project.

- How internal resources of a project are acquired is influenced largely by the organization's structure. Moreover, these resources, processes, and structures are determined largely by the organizational structure of the supporting or parent organization, which may determine or influence the availability of resources, reporting relationships, and project roles and responsibilities.

- The three most common structures are the **functional, matrix, and project-based organization.**

- The project manager may acquire resources internally and/or externally. Internal projects are largely dependent upon the supporting or parent organization where resources can be determined or influenced by the availability of resources, reporting relationships, and organizational structure. Therefore, how the project itself will be organized and supported depends on how the project interfaces with the host or parent organization.

- A project can be both a buyer and a seller of products and services. A buyer could be a client or a customer, while a seller could be a consultant, contractor, vendor, supplier, or a subcontractor.

- Outsourcing can be an organization-level decision or a project-level decision. Just as an organization can pursue outsourcing as a strategic approach, so too can a project manager and team. Today, organizations and project teams have the opportunity to follow different approaches to outsourcing.

- A project could follow a full-insourcing approach in which all products and services would be acquired internally. This would also mean that the project team is responsible for all the project's processes and scope. On the other hand, a full-outsourcing approach would be followed if an organization or project acquires all products or services from external sources. However, the best approach for organizations and projects probably would be selective outsourcing. More specifically, selective outsourcing provides greater flexibility to choose which project processes or deliverables should be out-sourced and which should be kept internal.

- Projects generally require resources, products, or services that must be purchased or acquired externally. This begins by determining which project needs can be fulfilled internally by the project team and which can best be met externally. Moreover, the project manager and team must not only decide *what* project needs can be met internally or externally, but also *how, when, how many*, and *where* these products and services will be acquired.

- The project manager and team may develop a **request for proposal (RFP)**, which will be used to solicit bids, quotes, or proposals from prospective sellers.

- The next step is for the buyer to obtain a reasonable number of high-quality, competitive proposals.

- Once the bids, proposals, or quotations are received, the buying organization begins the process of analyzing, evaluating, and selecting a seller.

- Once a seller is selected, the buyer may enter into contract negotiations so that a mutual agreement can be reached. A **contract** is a document signed by the buyer and seller that defines the terms and conditions of the buyer–seller relationship. It serves as a legally binding agreement that obligates the seller to provide specific

products, services, or even results, while obligating the buyer to provide specific monetary or other consideration.

- There are three general categories for procurement-type contracts:
  - Fixed-price or lump sum contracts
  - Cost-reimbursable contracts
    - Cost-plus-fee (CPC) or Cost-plus-percentage-of-cost (CPPC)
    - Cost-plus-fixed-fee (CPFF)
    - Cost-plus-incentive-fee (CPIF)
  - Time and materials (T&M) contract

- The **project environment** includes not only the physical space where the team will work, but also the project culture.

- The **project charter** serves as an agreement and as a communication tool for all of the project stakeholders. The project charter documents the project's MOV and describes the infrastructure needed to support the project. In addition, the project charter summarizes many of the details found in the project plan.

- In general, the project charter and project plan should be developed together—the details of the project plan need to be summarized in the project charter, and the infrastructure outlined in the project charter will influence the estimates used in developing the project plan.

REVIEW QUESTIONS

1. What is a project's infrastructure?
2. What is the purpose of organizational governance?
3. What is project governance? What is its purpose?
4. What is a project management office (PMO)? What purpose does it serve?
5. What is the purpose of a project governance committee? Who should be on this committee?
6. Why is it important that a project governance framework define stakeholders' authority?
7. Why is it important that a project governance committee have oversight over a project?
8. Describe some common responsibilities of a project manager.
9. What are some important attributes of a good project manager?
10. What types of skills or knowledge should a project manager consider when selecting a project team member?
11. Why are projects dependent on the host or sponsoring organization?
12. Describe the functional organization. How does the functional organization influence the selection of a project manager and access to resources?
13. What are some advantages and disadvantages of projects hosted by a functional organization?
14. Describe the project-based organization. How does the project-based organization influence the selection of a project manager and access to resources?
15. What are some advantages and disadvantages of projects hosted by a project-based organization?

16. Describe the matrix organization. How does a project hosted by a matrix organization influence the selection of a project manager and access to resources?

17. What are some advantages and disadvantages of projects hosted by a matrix organization?

18. What is outsourcing?

19. What is business process outsourcing?

20. What is offshoring or offshore outsourcing?

21. What is meant by full insourcing?

22. What is meant by full outsourcing?

23. What is meant by selective outsourcing? Why might selective outsourcing be a better approach than full insourcing or full outsourcing?

24. What is the purpose of a contract?

25. Describe how a fixed-price or lump-sum contract works. Give an example.

26. What are the three types of cost-reimbursable contracts?

27. Describe how a cost-plus-fee or cost-plus-percentage-of-cost contract works. Give an example.

28. Describe how a cost-plus-fixed-fee contract works. Give an example.

29. Describe how a cost-plus-incentive-fee contract works. Give an example.

30. What is the project environment? Why must a project manager ensure that a proper project environment is in place?

31. What is the purpose of a project charter?

32. Why can a project charter serve as an agreement or a contract?

33. Why is a project charter a useful communication tool?

34. Why should the project charter and project plan be developed together?

35. How does the project charter support the project plan?

36. How does the project plan support the project charter?

HUSKY AIR ASSIGNMENT—PILOT ANGELS

Defining the Project Infrastructure

Husky Air's management has decided that building a custom information system will provide the most value to its organization. Your team has been asked to continue with the project and develop this system.

The first step before planning the details of the project's schedule and budget requires that you define an infrastructure for your project. The infrastructure is the foundation for the project charter. Knowing what resources you need or are available and their associated cost will directly influence your schedule and budget estimates. This will entail defining the stakeholders of the project and the resources that will be required.

This would also be a good chance for you and your team to do another learning cycle. Read through this assignment first and then meet as a team to develop a Project Team Record and an Action Plan. This will help to improve team learning and to assign responsibilities to complete the assignment.

Please provide a professional-looking document that includes the following:

1. **The project name, project team name, and the names of the members of your project team.**

2. **A brief project description.**

3. **The project's MOV.** (This should be revised or refined if necessary.)

4. **A list of the resources needed to complete the project**—This should include:

   a. **People (and their roles)**—Your team is responsible for planning the project. However, the project may need additional individuals with both technical and nontechnical expertise to develop the system.

   b. **Technology**—In the previous assignment, you estimated the hardware, network, and software needs for a system to support your client. You will also need various hardware, network, software, and telecommunication resources to support the project team.

   c. **Facilities**—Husky Air has limited space. The project team will have to do most of its project and development work at a different site.

   d. **Other**—For example, travel, training, and so on.

5. **An estimate for the cost of each resource**—Use the Internet, trade journals, or any other sources. For example, if you need to hire a

programmer, then you could use job postings or salary surveys as a basis for an annual base salary or hourly wage. The people who work on the project (including you and your team) will be paid a base salary or hourly wage plus benefits. Therefore, the cost of any people on your team will be a base salary (the person's gross income) plus an addition 25 percent paid out in benefits. Be sure to include a reference for all the sources you use.

6. **Since you will be paid for your work with Husky Air, decide which contract makes the most sense for you and your client.** Be sure to support your recommendation.

a. Fixed price or lump sum
b. Cost-reimbursable
  i. Cost-plus-fee or cost-plus-percentage-of-cost
  ii. Cost-plus-fixed-fee
  iii. Cost-plus-incentive-fee
c. Time and materials

7. **This would also be a good opportunity to revisit the team charter you created in your first assignment.** As a team, decide if anything has changed or needs to be updated.

THE MARTIAL ARTS ACADEMY (MAA)—SCHOOL MANAGEMENT SYSTEM

Defining the Project Infrastructure

Geoff and Julie have decided that building a custom information system will provide the most value to their school. Your team has been asked to continue with the project and develop this system.

The first step before planning the details of the project's schedule and budget requires that you define an infrastructure for your project. The infrastructure is the foundation for the project charter. Knowing what resources you need or are available and their associated cost will directly influence your schedule and budget estimates. This will entail defining the stakeholders of the project and the resources that will be required.

This would also be a good opportunity for you and your team to do another learning cycle. Read through this assignment first and then meet as a team to develop a Project Team Record and an Action Plan. This will help to improve team learning and to assign responsibilities to complete the assignment.

Please provide a professional-looking document that includes the following:

1. **The project name, project team name, and the names of the members of your project team.**
2. **A brief project description.**
3. **The project's MOV.** (This should be revised or refined if necessary.)
4. **A list of the resources needed to complete the project.** This should include:
    a. **People (and their roles)**—Your team is responsible for planning the project. However, the project may need additional individuals with both technical and nontechnical expertise to develop the system.
    b. **Technology**—In the previous assignment, you estimated the hardware, network, and software needs for a system to support your client. You will also need various hardware, network, software, and telecommunication resources to support the project team.
    c. **Facilities**—Husky Air has limited space. The project team will have to do most of its project and development work at a different site.
    d. **Other**—For example, travel, training, and so on.
5. **An estimate for the cost of each resource**—Use the Internet, trade journals, newspaper advertisements, or any other sources. For example, if you need to hire a programmer, then you could use job postings or salary surveys as a basis for an annual base salary or hourly wage. The people who work on the project (including you and your team) will be paid a base salary or hourly wage plus benefits. Therefore, the cost of any people on your team will be a base salary (the person's gross income) plus an addition 25 percent paid out in benefits. Be sure to include a reference for all the sources you use.
6. **Since you will be paid for your work with MAA, decide which contract makes the most sense for you and your client**. Be sure to support your recommendation.

a. Fixed price or lump sum

b. Cost-reimbursable

   i. Cost-plus-fee or cost-plus-percentage-of-cost

   ii. Cost-plus-fixed-fee

   iii. Cost-plus-incentive-fee

c. Time and materials

7. **This would also be a good opportunity to revisit the team charter you created in your first assignment.** As a team, decide if anything has changed or needs to be updated.

QUICK THINKING—THE PROJECT SPONSOR

A project sponsor should be an executive or manager with financial authority, political clout, and a personal commitment to the project. An effective sponsor is critical to the success of an IT project. Although no formal job description exists for a project sponsor, most agree that the project sponsor must provide leadership and direction as well as political protection and problem-resolution skills.

The project sponsor "champions" by:

- Empowering the project manager
- Ensuring sustained "buy in" from other project stakeholders
- Clearing political and organizational roadblocks
- Ensuring the availability of resources
- Reviewing the project's progress
- Approving plans, schedules, budgets, and deliverables
- Ensuring that the project's goal is realized

However, a project manager has very little control over the sponsorship of the project. Often when a project experiences problems, there's a good chance the sponsor is to blame.

1. Why is a good project sponsor or champion so important to the success of a project?

2. How could a project manager or team handle a situation where the project sponsor leaves the organization to take a job with another company?

3. How should a project manager handle a project sponsor who is either incompetent or loses interest in the project and withdraws?

SOURCES:

Perkins, B. "Executive Sponsors: What They Really Do." *Computerworld*. September 12, 2005.

Melymuka, K. "Project Management: Surviving the Sponsor Exit." *Computerworld*. February 16, 2004.

Melymuka, K. "Firing Your Project Sponsor." *Computerworld*. February 23, 2004.

QUICK THINKING—PROJECTS AS SOCIAL NETWORKS

Simply storing and disseminating information will not encourage individuals assigned to a project to share ideas or become involved as a team. A project social network is an influential mapping of people and ideas.

Managing a project is more than just a set of project plans, tools, and assignment to activities. It's also about people. An effective project manager understands that people assigned to a project enter with a set of self-interests and expectations, so it is important to know what makes them tick. For example, a newbie might try to overachieve and impress, while a more seasoned veteran may believe that he or she has seen it all, and a

negative neutron may find all kinds of reasons why nothing will work. As a result, a social network is created as each person shows and communicates a strong set of self-interests that, in turn, inform and influence the people they work with. Command-and-control techniques or a one-size-fits-all approach will not get people to work together. The project manager must understand the signals each person is sending out and how interests and events can be aligned to create a basis for a successful project.

The available resource pool is an important input for acquiring a project team. Unfortunately, many project managers don't consider fully a person's previous experience, interests, and characteristics when negotiating for or assigning people to a project team. Project managers should not just staff a project, but should also staff the social network in their favor.

In addition to getting the right people, the project manager adds to the social network by creating a sense of belonging that goes beyond a celebratory project kick-off. This may include thanking people for being part of the project or by bringing them into the loop by asking them what they think about the project charter, scope, or plan.

The project manager can create an environment where people want to belong to the project. By meeting with each person individually, the project manager can get a realistic sense of each person's involvement and commitment.

The project manager should craft a shared vision that is a collection of the expectations and interests of each of the team members. A constancy of purpose should tie everyone together and make everyone feel as though they've been heard. However, one of the most important criteria for creating a social network is a candid, approachable, and likeable project manager.

1. Why are project social networks important?
2. What other aspects should a project manager consider when developing a social network for the project?
3. Why is it important that a project team believe that the project manager is managing a project and not their work?

SOURCES:

Nagarajan, S. "The Project Social Network." *Project@Works*. November 29, 2007.

Roberstson, S. "Project Sociology: Identifying and Involving Stakeholders." *Technology Transfer*. September 2002. Accessed from www.technologytransfer.eu.

 # CASE STUDIES

Choosing the Right Team

Kellie was a novice attending her first meeting with other project managers to pick people for their upcoming projects. She felt like the other project managers stepped all over her when she ended up with all the "leftovers." She vowed that she would never let that happen again when her project didn't go all that well.

The next time, Kellie thought she was better prepared. Before the meeting, she approached the top-skilled people and sold them on the project so their managers agreed to let them work on her project. According to Kellie, "I got exactly who I wanted. But the project was still a nightmare."

Kellie picked her team for their technical skills and ended up with a team of prima donnas who couldn't work together. Kellie learned a few things over the years. First, a great project team requires more than just great technical skills. It takes the right mix of "soft" skills, personalities, and attitudes to make a team gel.

Unfortunately, many project managers fall back on some of the most common questions used in interviews to help select people for their projects. Some of them can be downright dumb. Examples include:

- "Where do you see yourself in five years?" Few organizations can guarantee you a job for five years so a career path is even more difficult to predict. You can always answer that you hope to be "happy and productive working in a job you love for a company that values your talents."

- "What would you do if I gave you a giraffe (or insert here: some other ridiculous object)?" Sometimes interviewers ask this ridiculous question to new graduates because they think it's cute and because it's supposed to test how they think.

- "What are your weaknesses?" The stock answer to this question is "I'm a perfectionist" even though you're really thinking that it's putting up with people who ask dumb questions.

This is just an example of some of the questions people ask. The objective of an interview is not to make the candidate squirm or to be a psychology exam. Some interview questions can be illegal if they deal with age, family responsibilities, and lifestyle. Some examples include:

- Can you work overtime, evenings, and weekends?
- What child care arrangements have you made?
- How old are you?
- Where were you born?
- What is your marital status?

- Are you living with anyone?
- Do you plan on having more children?
- What are your religious beliefs?
- Have you ever filed a lawsuit against an employer?

So, what questions should you ask to help you make the right decision? Questions should help make the right decision and give some insight as to how well someone will perform on the project. This requires being specific, since a decision to hire or bring someone on the project team can be very difficult to undo.

- Ask for real examples of what the person has accomplished. Resumes will tell you something about people, but you really need to find out what they can do. Looking at someone's work is a good method for understanding a person's capabilities. Ask people to provide you with a sample of their work.

- Use the review of their work as a guide to prepare specific questions. In a follow-up interview, you can ask candidates to take you through how they developed the sample of the work they left with you. You can ask them to critique it first by asking them what they liked and then didn't like about it. Ask them how they made certain choices and then ask your prepared questions concerning what else you'd like to know about their work.

- Give them a deliverable like a program, database design, or project plan to critique. A few days before, forward a good, but not great, deliverable, to the candidate. This could be something that has a few things that could be improved. Ask questions regarding what works or doesn't work. What could be improved? Or what would they have done differently?

- Scenarios and case studies can be used as an interview exercise. Real project situations that someone could reasonably expect to encounter can be a useful interview too. Examples could include handling a change request, or a risk that needs to be addressed, or dealing with conflicts. It is important to give the candidate enough time to think about a response and to have a specific response in mind.

- Have candidates meet with the team members they will work with. This can provide an invaluable sense of how the candidate might interact with the project team. The team members should have some specific questions in mind when talking with the candidate, and you should have questions in mind when talking with the team afterwards.

The focus should be on how the candidate and team interact—not on the skills. These suggestions will not guarantee that you always will pick the perfect team; however, they may help get a better sense of who you will be dealing with and how they may react in certain situations. As Mark Mullaly points out, "Sure, you can just ask someone what their strengths and weaknesses are. For my money, though, it's far more valuable to get them to show you."

1. Suppose you are the project manager for a small project that will be based in Chicago. At this point, you have four other project team members on board. All you need to do is hire a C++ programmer. Later today you will be interviewing Mary, who recently graduated from a large university nearby. Develop an interview plan that includes an itinerary and set of interview questions. Mary is scheduled to arrive at 10 am and will be available until 4 pm.

Sources:

Melymuka, K. "How to Pick a Project Team." *Computerworld.* April 12, 2004.

Mullaly, M. "Deadly Questions for the Killer Candidate." *Gnatthead.com.* August 11, 2005.

Ryan, L. "Stupid Interview Questions." *Business Week.* September 21, 2005.

Krannich, R. L. "38 Illegal, Sensitive, and Stupid Interview Questions … and How to Respond." *Washingtonpost.com.* April 11, 2003.

Service Level Agreements for Internal and External Projects

Service level agreements (SLAs) have been around since the 1960s when IT departments used them to assess technical services like the uptime of a data center. However, the SLA has evolved not only to guarantee IT services, such as email or specific software applications, but now are an important component for gauging the performance of projects and outside service providers.

According to Lynn Greiner and Lauren Gibbons Paul, "A service level agreement (SLA) is simply a document describing the level of service expected by a customer from a supplier, laying out the metrics by which that service is measured, and the remedies or penalties, if any, should the agreed-upon levels not be achieved." Moreover, SLAs can be between an organization and its external suppliers as well as between two departments within an organization.

For example, an IT department or web hosting company may pledge that a web site will be available for what is commonly called "five-nines," or 99.999 percent during a year. That would work out to be about 5.26 minutes of downtime during the year. Therefore, the SLA must document clearly all of the agreed-upon contract services, expected metrics, and responsibilities into a single document. Both parties should have the same understanding of the requirements so that neither side can claim ignorance.

Many service providers will have a standard set of documents outlining pricing for different levels of service. On the other hand, pricing and services can be negotiated or as part of a request for proposal (RFP). However, all important contracts should include an SLA and be reviewed by legal counsel to ensure the SLA does not slant in favor of one party over another. This is especially important if the SLA includes penalties for breach of service or bonuses for rewarding excellent service. In many cases, an SLA will include (or not include) a clause for indemnification whereby a provider will have to pay the customer for any litigation costs resulting from a breach of contract.

Subsequently, metrics are an important component of an SLA that can be made available on a web portal or by a third-party organization hired to monitor a vendor's performance and supplement the information that vendor provides. However, Greiner and Paul caution, "Many items can be monitored as part of an SLA, but the scheme should be kept as simple as possible to avoid confusion and excessive cost on either side. In choosing metrics, examine your operations and decide what is most important. The more complex the monitoring (and associated remedy) scheme, the less likely it is to be effective, since no one will have the time to properly analyze the data." In short, metrics and measurement should motivate the right behavior.

In addition, Greiner and Paul outline several types of metrics that should be used to monitor an SLA:

- **Availability of service**—The amount of time a service will be available (e.g., 99.999 percent).
- **Quality standards**—This could include defect rates like the number of incomplete backups or missed deadlines as well as coding errors.

- **Security**—The number of security breaches or the number of antivirus updates.

SLAs can serve as an internal contract, especially if the IT department is viewed as a business within a business in the organization. These internal contracts are not legal documents designed to hold up in court. An internal SLA should document an agreement between the internal customer (i.e., users) and the supplier (IT department) to hold people accountable for their end of the deal.

For example, Dean Meyer contends, "[internal] contracting is not a waste of time, not a bureaucratic ritual. The minutes spent working out a mutual understanding of both the customer's and the suppliers accountabilities at the beginning of the project can save hours of confusion, lost productivity, and stress later. Furthermore, contracts are the basis for holding staff accountable for results. They are not wish-lists; they're firm commitments. IT staff must never to agree to a contract unless they know they can deliver results."

Meyer believes that SLAs are essential if IT is going to be managed like a business. More specifically, SLAs should be contracted each year for such services as email, and an SLA can be developed for each project deliverable. Meyer also outlines several components that should be included in an SLA:

- Name of the customer
- Name of the supplier
- Name of the project
- Detailed description of the product or service to be provided
- Start date of the contract
- End date of the project or the renewal date of the SLA
- The price and terms of payment
- A complete list of the customer's accountabilities

Today, many organizations are turning to outside providers for IT services. One service that has been growing in importance is cloud computing. Kevin Fogarty states, "Cloud computing is a computing model, not a technology. In this model of computing, all the servers, networks, applications, and other elements related to data centers are made available to IT and end users via the Internet, in a way that allows IT to buy only the type and amount of computing services that they need. The cloud model differs from traditional outsourcers in that customers don't hand over their IT resources to be managed. Instead, they plug into the 'cloud' for infrastructure services, platform (operating system) services, or software services (such as SaaS apps), treating the 'cloud' much as they would an internal data center or computer providing the same functions."

Cloud computing is becoming increasingly common with web-based email services from Google or Yahoo, customer relationship management applications like Salesforce.com, instant messaging and voice-over-IP from Skype or Vonage, as well as backup services from companies like Carbonite or MozyHome. As Fogarty explains, "The arguments for cloud computing are simple: get sophisticated data-center services on demand, in only the amount you need and can pay for, at the service levels you set with the vendor, with capabilities you can add or subtract at will."

There are three basic types of cloud computing:

- **Infrastructure as a Service**—Designed to replace or augment an entire data center by providing grid, clusters, or virtualized servers, networks, storage, and systems software.

- **Platform as a Service**—Allows users to run existing software applications or develop new ones on virtualized servers without having to maintain operating systems or hardware or worrying about load balancing or computing capacity.

- **Software as a Service**—SaaS is the most common type of cloud computing and provides sophisticated applications through a web browser instead of being installed locally on a personal computer. Examples include email from Google or Yahoo, as well as instant messaging from AOL or VoIP from Skype or Vonage.

Unfortunately, an organization gives up control of its data and the performance of its applications when a third party is responsible for the computer infrastructure. Customers can end up having their data locked into proprietary formats or even have their data compromised. While groups like the Cloud Security Alliance and the Open Cloud Consortium are attempting to develop standards for interoperability management, data migration, and security, many experts agree that rigorous standards will not be widely accepted for a few more years.

While cloud computing continues to grow, Patrick Thibodeau contends that many customers are becoming increasingly frustrated. As Thibodeau explains, " ... cloud customers—and some vendors as well—are increasingly grousing about the lack of data handling and security standards. Some note that there aren't even rules that would require cloud vendors to disclose where their clients' data is stored- even if it's housed in countries not bound by U.S. data security laws."

According to Jon Brodkin, a cloud vendor's SLA generally guarantees at least 99 percent uptime, but how that is calculated and enforced can vary widely from one vendor to the next. For example, Amazon EC2 promises to make "reasonable efforts" to provide 99.95 percent uptime. However, this metric is calculated on an annual basis so service could fall below the targeted level for a week or a month but still be within the guaranteed service level for the year. The customer's business could be affected adversely without any service credit or penalty to Amazon. It also depends on who monitors the service. GoGrid promises 100 percent uptime, but whether individual servers deliver as promised is only known on GoGrid's network monitoring system.

Recently, Carbonite, a Boston-based company that backs up computer data using cloud computing, filed a lawsuit against a storage vendor called Promise Technology for "significant data loss" due to repeated failures of Promise hardware. Stephen Lawson reported that Carbonite paid more than $3 million for Promise VTrak Raid products, but the Promise equipment failed to monitor multiple computer hard drives to ensure that they were working properly. As a result, this caused "substantial damage" to Carbonite's business and reputation because the backups of more than 7,500 customers were lost.

Carbonite also contends that Promise did not solve any of these problems despite a 3-year limited warranty on its products. Promise believes that the suit is without merit, and the company statement explained, "Our investigation indicates that our products were neither implemented nor managed using industry best practices."

As an online backup service provider, Carbonite's ability to store data is vital to all of its customers. Regardless of how the lawsuit turns out, the real losers may be the 7,500 customers who lost both their data and their trust.

1. What role does having a service level agreement (SLA) play for supporting internal projects and IT services?

2. What role does having an SLA play for supporting external projects with consultants or third-party service providers.

3. Suppose you have been tasked with overseeing a service level agreement with another company that can provide backup services to the 500 PC users of your company. Use the Internet or other

resources to research and come up with a set of metrics that could be used to assess service availability, quality standards, and security to be part of an SLA.

SOURCES:

CIO. "SLAs: A CIO Guide to Success." *CIO Magazine*. November 15, 1988.

Greiner, L. and P. Gibbons. "SLA Definitions and Solutions." *CIO Magazine*. August 8, 2007.

Meyer, D. N. "Service Level Agreements." *CIO Magazine*. June 27, 2005.

Fogarty, K. "Cloud Computing Definitions and Solutions." *CIO Magazine*. September 10, 2009.

Thobodeau, P. "As Cloud Computing Grows, Customer Frustration Mounts." *Computerworld*. April 19, 2010.

Golden, B. "Cloud SLA: Another Point of View." *CIO Magazine*. November 16, 2009.

Brodkin, J. "FAQ: Cloud Computing, Demystified." *Networkworld*. May 18, 2009.

Lawson, S. "Backup Provider Carbonite Loses Data, Sues Vendor." *Computerworld*. March 23, 2009.

BIBLIOGRAPHY

1. Muller, R. *Project Governance*. Burlington, VT: Gower Publishing Company, 2009.

2. Project Management Institute (PMI). *A Guide to the Project Management Body of Knowledge (PMBOK Guide)*. Newton Square, PA: PMI Publishing, 2013.

3. Renz, P. S. *Project Governance: Implementing Corporate Governance and Business Ethics in Nonprofit Organizations*. New York: Physica-Verlag: A Springer Company, 2007.

4. Garland, R. *Project Governance: A Practical Guide to Effective Project Decision Making*. London: Kogan Page, 2009.

5. McLeod, G. and D. Smith. *Managing Information Technology Projects*. Danvers, MA: Boyd & Fraser Publishing Company, 1996.

6. Meredith, J. R. and S. J. Mantel, Jr. *Project Management: A Managerial Approach*. New York: John Wiley & Sons, 2000.

7. Brown, D. and S. Wilson. *The Black Book of Outsourcing: How to Manage the Changes, Challenges, and Opportunities*. Hoboken, NJ: John Wiley & Sons, 2005.

8. Lacity, M. C., L. P. Willcocks and D. F. Feeny. "IT Outsourcing: Maximize Flexibility and Control." *Harvard Business Review* 84–93 (May–June 1995).

5

Project Planning: Scope and the Work Breakdown Structure

CHAPTER OBJECTIVES

Chapter 5 introduces the next step for developing the project plan. After studying this chapter, you should be able to:

- Understand and describe the relationship among scope, schedule, and budget.
- Understand the processes and apply several tools for defining and managing the scope of a project.
- Understand the difference between project scope (i.e., project deliverables) and product scope (i.e., features and functionality of the product or system).
- Develop a work breakdown structure (WBS).
- Differentiate between a deliverable and a milestone.
- Describe and apply several project estimation methods.

INTRODUCTION

This chapter focuses on defining and managing the work that must be accomplished by the project team. The term **scope** is used to define the work boundaries and deliverables of the project so what needs to get done, gets done—and only what needs to get done, gets done. In other words, any work assigned to the project team comes at a cost in terms of time and budget. Therefore, all of the work or scope undertaken by the project team should focus on achieving the MOV; otherwise, inessential work simply consumes precious resources needlessly. Moreover, it is important to define not only what *is* part of the project work, but also what *is not* part of the project work (1).

Defining and understanding what you have to do is an important first step to determine how you're going to do the work that has to be done. How the work or scope is to be accomplished entails the use of a project management tool called the **work breakdown structure (WBS)**. It provides a hierarchical structure that acts as a bridge, or link, between the project's scope and the detailed project plan that will be created using a project management software package.

Today, most project management software packages are relatively inexpensive and rich in features. It is almost unthinkable that anyone would plan and manage a project without such a tool. Project success, however, will not be determined by one's familiarity with a project management software package or the ability to produce nice looking reports and graphs. It is the thought process before using the tool that counts. Thinking carefully through the activities and their estimated durations first will make the use of a project management software package much more effective. You can still create nice looking reports and graphs, but you'll have more confidence in what those reports and graphs say.

Once the project activities are defined, the next step is to forecast, or estimate, how long each activity will take. Although a number of estimation methods and techniques are introduced here, estimation is not an exact science. It is dependent upon a number of variables—the complexity of the activity, the resources (i.e., people) assigned to complete the activity, and the tools and environment to support those individuals working on the activity (technology, facilities, etc.). This is where having a well-defined project infrastructure is a valuable asset.

Moreover, confidence in estimates will be lower early in the planning stage. However, as we learn and uncover new information from our involvement in the project, our understanding of the project will increase as well. Although estimates may have to be revised periodically, we should gain more confidence in the updated schedule and budget. Even though no single estimation method will provide 100 percent accuracy all of the time, using one or a combination of methods is preferable to guessing. The last step, determining the overall project schedule and budget, will be covered in the next chapter.

THE TRIPLE CONSTRAINT

Projects require time, money, people, and technology. Resources provide the means for achieving a project's MOV and also act as a constraint. For example, the project's **scope**, or work to be accomplished, is determined directly by the project's MOV—that is, if we know what we have to accomplish, we can then figure out how to accomplish it. If the customer or project sponsor asks that an additional feature be added to the product or system, however, this request will undoubtedly require additional resources in terms of more work on the part of the project team. The use of a project resource has an associated cost that must be included in the overall cost of the project. The general rule is: *A resource has a cost associated with it. Therefore, you should account for the use of that resource; otherwise, you will never know the true cost of the project.*

In the past, computer technology was relatively more expensive than the labor needed to develop a system. Today, the labor to build a product or system is relatively more expensive than the technology. As salaries increase, the cost of projects will become even more expensive. Therefore, if team members must do additional work, their time and the costs associated with the time spent doing unscheduled work must be added to the project's schedule and budget.

This relationship is called the **triple constraint** and is illustrated in Figure 5.1. Often, a project plan will go through a number of iterations that attempt to derive a set of project objectives—scope, schedule, and budget—that are realistic and that have a high probability to achieve the project's MOV. Once the MOV and the scope, schedule, and budget objectives are agreed upon by the client, customer, governing committee, and the project manager, the project could be thought of being "in balance" or "in harmony" because the stakeholders' expectations are clear. The client, customer, or governing committee knows what value to expect from the project, what work will be done, how long it will take, and how much the project will cost. In turn, the project manager and project team have the same expectations and know what they must deliver.

So how does a project become imbalanced? The right side of Figure 5.1 shows what happens when the project's scope increases after the stakeholders agree to the scope, schedule, and budget objectives. Scope can increase for any number of reasons. For example, important product requirements or features might need to be added because the customer or user was not able to articulate his or her needs early on in the project or because customers are buying a competitor's new product that has features customers want but are not in the product.

Sometimes an important stakeholder, such as a customer or senior manager, will ask to add to the scope with no thought to the increase of the project team's workload. Often times, project managers may comply with the request either because they want to please the customer or because they feel pressured. If the project team cannot deliver the additional work with the same schedule and budget objectives, then the project is late or over budget and everyone is unhappy. The customer's expectations were not met, and the project team probably felt the stress of trying to achieve project objectives that it had very

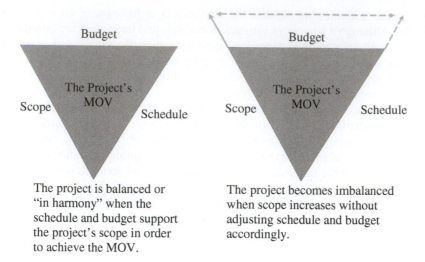

The project is balanced or "in harmony" when the schedule and budget support the project's scope in order to achieve the MOV.

The project becomes imbalanced when scope increases without adjusting schedule and budget accordingly.

Figure 5.1 The Triple Constraint: The Relationship Among Scope, Schedule, and Budget

little chance of attaining. Another time-honored project management tradition is to take shortcuts like reducing the time scheduled for testing. This may save some schedule and budget objectives, but the quality of the final product may be so impaired that the project falls short of its MOV. Again, no one is happy with the project because the project lost its "balance" or "harmony."

Another game often played is the for the project manager to inflate the estimates in anticipation that scope will increase or that schedule and/or budget will be reduced. Once the customer or sponsor knows that the estimates are inflated, he or she will ask for even more changes and so the game continues. It is important to understand playing this game serves no one's best interests. Estimates must be realistic and should not become a negotiation among project stakeholders.

The triple constraint should serve as a conceptual reminder whenever making a decision that affects the project's MOV, scope, schedule, or budget. In other words, the project manager must protect the scope, schedule, and budget objectives once they are agreed upon. As illustrated on the right side of Figure 5.1, if scope increases, then the schedule and budget of a project must increase accordingly. Things can become a bit tricky if the schedule and budget objectives change. While no one would ever tell a project manager to increase schedule or budget for no reason, cuts to the budget and schedule are quite common. The only way to reduce budget is to reduce the number of resources or to replace an expensive resource with a cheaper resource. For example, a project manager could replace a seasoned engineer with an intern and save a great deal of money, but this can have a discernible effect on the schedule and quality because the intern may require much more time to complete inferior work. On the other hand, the schedule can be reduced by running some tasks concurrently instead of sequentially. However, this may lead to project team members attempting to do more than one thing at a time. While multitasking may look fine on the computer screen, it can lead to shortcuts that compromise the project.

DEFINING AND MANAGING PROJECT SCOPE

A project's **scope** defines all the work, activities, and deliverables that the project team must provide in order for the project to achieve its MOV. It is an important step in developing the project plan since one must know what work must be done before an estimate can be made of how long it will take and how much it will cost. The PMBOK Guide® provides a valuable set of processes to manage project scope. These processes are summarized in Figure 5.2.

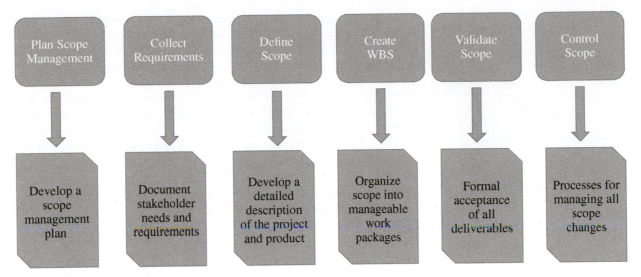

Figure 5.2 Scope Management Processes

Plan Scope Management

Scope planning begins when the project is formally accepted and funds are committed to developing the project charter and plan by the project sponsor, client, or governing committee. A **project scope management plan** defines and documents how the project and product scope will be defined, verified, and changed if necessary.

Collect Requirements

Collecting requirements focuses on engaging customers or users in order to define their needs. In essence, this entails planning how the project team will work with the customer, client, or users to define the scope of the project. Some common methods include:

- Interviews
- Workshops
- Brainstorming sessions
- Focus groups
- Surveys
- Observing people while they work

Define Scope

In general, defining the project's scope starts at a very high level and becomes more and more detailed. At this point, the project manager and team attempt to gain enough information about the project and product to develop a detailed plan. Specific, detailed product or system features and functionality will be defined using Waterfall or Agile when the project executes the systems development life cycle (SDLC).

THE SCOPE BOUNDARY Defining the scope boundary is the first step to establishing what is, and what is not, part of the project work to be completed by the project team. Think of the scope boundary

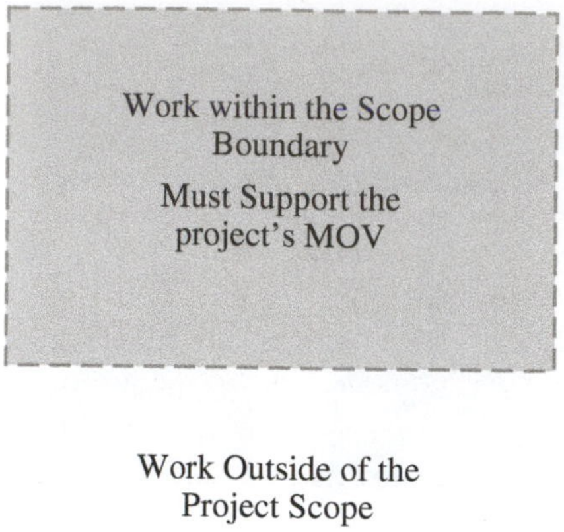

Work within the Scope Boundary

Must Support the project's MOV

Work Outside of the Project Scope

Figure 5.3 Scope Boundary

as a fence designed to keep certain things in and other things out. As Figure 5.3 illustrates, any work within the scope boundary should include only the work or activities that support the project's MOV. This work is what we want to capture and keep within our fence. On the other hand, a project team can spend a great deal of time doing work and activities that will not help the project achieve its MOV. As a result, the project will consume time and resources with very little return. Therefore, the scope boundary must protect the scope from these activities once it is set and agreed upon by the project stakeholders. Having a clear and agreed-upon definition of the project MOV is critical for defining and managing the scope boundary.

THE STATEMENT OF WORK (SOW)   A statement of work (SOW) is a narrative description of the product, service, or system. For internal projects, the SOW should tie together the business need with the specific requirements or expectation of the project. For projects that will rely on external sources, an organization or project manager may create a SOW that includes specifications, quantities, quality standards, or performance requirements that can be sent to prospective bidders. For external projects, the SOW is included in a document that may be called a **request for proposal (RFP)**, **request for information (RFI)**, or **request for bid (RFB)**.

THE SCOPE STATEMENT   Another way to define the scope boundary is to create a more detailed **scope statement** that documents the project sponsor's needs and expectations. This can be based on the preliminary scope statement developed in the project charter. For example, let's say a consulting firm is hired to develop a web-based application for a bank. After developing and presenting a business case to the client, the consultants have been given the authority to develop the project charter and plan. Although the business case provides a great deal of relevant information, several meetings and interviews with key stakeholders in the bank will still be required. Based on these meetings and interviews, the following scope statement is defined.

Scope Statement

1. *Develop a proactive strategy that identifies the processes, products, and services to be delivered via the WWW.*

2. *Develop an application that supports all of the processes, products, and services identified in this strategy.*

3. *Integrate the application system with the bank's existing enterprise resource planning system.*

It is just as important to clarify what work is not to be included, that is, what work is outside the scope of the project. Often the scope of a project is defined through interviews, meetings, or brainstorming sessions. Stakeholders often suggest ideas that are interesting, but not feasible or appropriate for the current project.

Let's say that in our example a certain bank vice president pushed for a customer relationship management (CRM) and a business analytics component to be included in the project. The bank's president, however, has decided that the time and effort to add these components cannot be justified because launching the web site in eight months is vital to the bank's competitive strategy. Let's also assume that conducting an assessment of the client's current technology infrastructure is an important piece of our project methodology. However, because the bank would like to control some of the costs of this project, it is agreed that the bank's IT department will conduct that study. The results of this study will then be documented and provided to the consultants.

In this case, it is critical that both parties define explicitly what is and what is not part of the project scope. Individuals from both organizations may believe that specific project work (i.e., the assessment study), system features, or functionality (i.e., CRM and data mining) will be part of this project. These beliefs may result in misunderstandings that lead to false expectations or needless work. To manage these expectations, it is useful to list explicitly what is *not* part of the project's scope.

Out of Scope for This Project

1. *Technology and organizational assessment of the current environment*
2. *Customer resource management and data mining components*

Developing a scope statement is a useful first step for defining the scope of the project and for setting a boundary. A project's scope, however, should also be defined in terms of the deliverables that the team must provide. A **deliverable** is a tangible and verifiable work product. These deliverables can be divided into *project-oriented deliverables* and *product-oriented deliverables*. This separation gives the team a clearer definition of the work to be accomplished and improves the likelihood of accurately assigning resources and estimating the time and cost of completing the work. Moreover, a clear definition of the project's deliverables sets unambiguous expectations and agreement among all of the project stakeholders. This will provide the important details needed to create the work breakdown structure.

PROJECT-ORIENTED SCOPE   Project-oriented deliverables, or scope, support the project management processes that are defined by the project life cycle (PLC) and the chosen project methodology. Project scope includes such things as the business case, project charter, and project plan and defines the work products of the various PLC phases. Project-oriented deliverables may also include specific deliverables such as a current systems study, requirements definition, and the documented design of the information system. These are deliverables supported by the systems development life cycle (SDLC) component of the overall methodology.

Project-oriented deliverables require time and resources and, therefore, must be part of the overall project schedule and budget. Their role is to ensure that the project processes are being completed so that the product or system achieves the project's MOV and objectives. Project-oriented deliverables also provide tangible evidence of the project's progress (or lack of progress). Finally, they allow the project manager to set a baseline for performance and quality control because they usually require some form of approval before work on the next project phase or deliverable begins.

A useful tool to define the project-oriented deliverables is to create a **deliverable structure chart** **(DSC)**. Figure 5.4 provides an example of a DSC that maps all of the project deliverables of the project life cycle (PLC) and systems development life cycle (SDLC) phases. The purpose of the DSC is to define all of the project-oriented deliverables to be provided by the project team. Each deliverable should have a clear purpose and each phase should produce at least one deliverable.

PRODUCT-ORIENTED SCOPE   **Product scope**, therefore, focuses on identifying the features and functionality of the product or system to be developed. A useful tool for refining the scope boundary and defining what the system must do is a modeling tool called the **use case diagram**, which has been

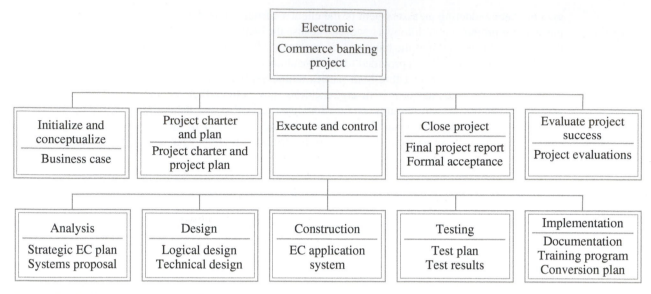

Figure 5.4 Deliverable Structure Chart

used in the object-oriented world as part of the Unified Modeling Language (UML). While introduced as a tool for software development, a use case diagram can provide a high-level model for defining, verifying, and reaching agreement upon the product scope (2).

The use case diagram is a relatively simple diagram in terms of symbols and syntax, but it is a powerful tool for identifying the main functions or features of the system and the different users/customers or external systems that interact with the system. At this early stage of the project, the use case can provide a high-level diagram that can be further refined and detailed during requirements analysis later in the project.

Actors are people (users, customers, managers, etc.) or external systems (i.e., the bank's ERP system) that interact, or *use*, the system. Think of actors in terms of roles (e.g., customer) instead of as specific individuals (e.g., Tom Smith). A **use case**, on the other hand, depicts the major functions the system must perform for an actor or actors. When developing a use case diagram, actors are identified using stick figures, while use cases are defined and represented using ovals. Figure 5.5 provides an example of a use case diagram for the bank example.

As you can see in Figure 5.5, the use case diagram provides a simple yet effective overview of the functions and interactions between the use cases and the actors. The box separating the use cases from the actors defines the scope boundary. Use cases inside the boundary are considered within the scope of the project, while anything outside of the boundary is considered outside the scope of the project. Listing the actors provides an opportunity to identify various stakeholders and can be useful for understanding the needs of the organization as a whole. It can be useful not only for addressing competing needs among various stakeholders, but also for identifying security issues (3).

The development of a use case diagram is an iterative process that can be developed using any of the aforementioned methods for collecting requirements such as interviews, workshops, brainstorming sessions, or focus groups.

The use case diagram used to define the product scope can also be used to refine the level of detail and functionality later on in the project. Following our example, the use case diagram in Figure 5.5 identifies the customer actor as using the system to transfer payments. However, a scenario or set of scenarios could be developed during the analysis and design phases of our project to determine how a

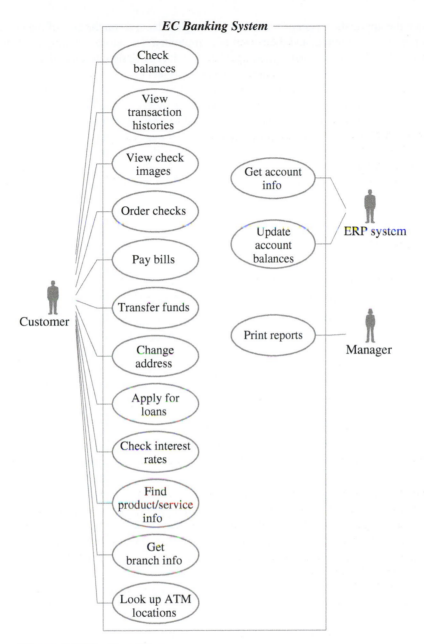

Figure 5.5 Use Case Diagram

customer would transfer funds successfully, while another scenario might focus on what happens when customers have insufficient funds in their account. This level of detail is more suited to the phases of the SDLC rather than the scope definition where we are trying to develop the project charter and plan. At this point, it is more important to identify that the system must allow a customer to transfer funds than to identify how the funds may be transferred.

But what is the appropriate level of detail for defining the product scope? Knowing the right level of detail is more an art than a science. The right level allows the project manager to estimate the time it will take to produce the application system accurately. This often depends on the size of the application, the number of features incorporated, and their level of complexity. Therefore, the quality of the estimates will be greatly influenced by our understanding of the product or system to be delivered.

The time and resources committed to developing the project charter and plan may limit the amount of time and energy we can devote to defining the details of the product or system. Therefore, the objective during this planning stage of the project should be to secure enough detail about the product or system to allow us to estimate the time and effort needed to produce this deliverable. During the analysis and design phases, we can commit more time and resources to increasing our understanding and to documenting the level of detail needed to build and deliver the product or system. Keep in mind that at this point we are planning the project. The project charter and plan must be approved before actual work on the product or system begins. Moreover, many of the features and functionality we define at this stage of the project can change later on.

VALIDATE SCOPE

Once the project's scope has been defined, it must be verified, validated, and formally accepted by the project sponsor and other appropriate stakeholders. This process should include:

- *Verification of the MOV*—At this point in the project, the MOV must be clearly defined and agreed upon. Failure to define and agree on the MOV could result in scope changes later in the project, which can lead to added work impacting the project's schedule and budget.

- *Documentation of all deliverables*—Are the deliverables tangible and verifiable? Do they support the project's MOV?

- *Specification of quality standards*—Are controls in place to ensure that the work was not only completed but completed to meet specific standards?

- *Identification of milestones*—Are milestones defined for each deliverable? Milestones are significant events that mark the acceptance of a deliverable and give the project manager and team the approval to begin working on the next deliverable. In short, milestones tell us that a deliverable was not only completed but also reviewed and accepted.

- *Review and acceptance*—Are both sides clear in their expectations? The project's scope must be reviewed and accepted by the project stakeholders. The project sponsor must formally accept the boundary, product to be produced, and the project-related deliverables. The project team must be clear on what it must deliver. In both cases, expectations must be realistic and agreed upon.

CONTROL SCOPE

Controlling scope is concerned with managing actual changes to the project's scope as and when they occur to ensure that any changes to the project's scope will be beneficial. In short, it is about understanding and managing the triple constraint. The most important benefit of scope change control procedures is that they keep the project manager in control of the project. More specifically, they allow the project manager to manage and control the project's schedule and budget. Scope control procedures also allow the project team to stay focused and on track because the team does not have to perform unnecessary work. Scope control is also concerned with:

- *Scope grope*—Scope grope is a metaphor that describes a project team's inability to define the project's scope. This situation is common early in a project when the project team and sponsor have trouble understanding what the project is supposed to accomplish. Scope grope can be minimized by having a clearly defined MOV and by following or applying the processes, concepts, and tools described in this chapter.

- *Scope creep*—Scope creep refers to increasing featurism, adding small yet time- and resource-consuming features to the system once the scope of the project has been approved. For example, a project sponsor may try to add various bells and whistles to the project scope. Yet, scope creep does not always come from the project sponsor side. The project team itself may come across interesting or novel ideas as the project work progresses. Its enthusiasm for adding these ideas can divert its attention or add features and functions to the product or system that the project sponsor did not ask for and does not need. Scope creep must be identified and controlled throughout the project because it will lengthen the project schedule and, in turn, lead to cost overruns.

- *Scope leap*—If scope creep is caused by increasing featurism, scope leap suggests a fundamental and significant change in the project scope. For example, the original scope for the bank's project was to provide new products and services to its customers. Scope creep may be adding a new feature, such as a new product or service, not originally defined in the project's scope. Scope leap, on the other hand, is an impetus to change the project so that the electronic commerce system would allow the bank to obtain additional funding in the open market. Adding this activity would dramatically change the entire scope and focus of the project. Scope leap can occur as a result of changes in the environment, the business, and the competitive makeup of the industry. Scope leap entails changing the MOV and, therefore, requires that the organization rethink the value of the current project. If this change is critical, the organization may be better off pulling the plug on the current project and starting over by conceptualizing and initiating a new project.

SCOPE CHANGE CONTROL PROCEDURES   A scope change procedure should be in place before the actual work on the project commences. It can be part of, or at least referenced in, the project charter so that it is communicated to all project stakeholders. This procedure should allow for the identification and handling of all requested changes to the project's scope. Scope change requests can be made, and each request's impact on the project can be assessed. Then, a decision whether to accept or reject the scope change can be made. A process for controlling scope changes is the first line of defense for protecting the project's triple constraint.

A scope change procedure may include a scope change request form. An example of a scope change request form is illustrated in Figure 5.6. Regardless of the format for a scope change request form, it should contain some basic information. First, the description of the change request should be clearly defined so that the project manager and governance committee understand fully the nature and reason for the scope change. Second, the scope change should be justified to separate the "would likes" from the "must haves." In addition, several alternatives may be listed to assess the impact on scope, schedule, resources, and cost. Often a trade-off or compromise will be suitable if the impact of the scope change is too great. The key decision makers (e.g., the project sponsor, customer, governance committee, etc.) must understand and approve these changes because the baseline project plan will have to be adjusted accordingly. Alternatives may include reducing functionality in other areas of the project, extending the project deadline, or adding more resources in terms of staff, overtime, or technology.

However, nothing can be more frustrating than making a request and then not hearing anything. Too often requests fall through the cracks, leading to credibility concerns and accusations that the project manager or project team is not being responsive to the client's needs. Therefore, a scope change control procedure should be logged with the intention that each request will be reviewed and acted upon. As seen in Figure 5.7, an example of a change request log includes information as to who has the authority to make the scope change decision and when a response can be expected.

Scope change request form

Requestor name: _____   Request date: _____

Request title: _____   Request number: _____

Request description:

Justification:

Possible alternatives:

Impacts	Alternative 1	Alternative 2	Alternative 3
Scope			
Schedule			
Resources required			
Cost			

Recommendation:

Authorized by   Date

_____   _____

Figure 5.6 Scope Change Request Form

Request Number	Request Title	Date of Request	Requested by	Priority (L, M, H)	Authority to Approve Request	Expected Response Date	Scope Change Approved? (Y/N)

Figure 5.7 Scope Change Request Log

THE WORK BREAKDOWN STRUCTURE (WBS)

Once the project's scope is defined, the next step is to define the activities or tasks the project team must undertake to fulfill the scope deliverable requirements. The **work breakdown structure (WBS)** is a useful tool for developing the project plan and links the project's scope to the schedule and budget. The WBS provides a framework for developing a tactical plan to structure the project work.

The total scope of the project is divided and subdivided into specific deliverables that can be more easily managed. This includes both product- and project-oriented deliverables. In short, the WBS provides an outline for all of the work the project team will perform.

WORK PACKAGES   The WBS decomposes, or subdivides, the project into smaller components and more manageable units of work called **work packages**. Work packages provide a logical basis for defining the project activities and assigning resources to those activities so that all the project work is identified (4). A work package makes it possible to develop a project plan, schedule, and budget and then later to monitor the project's progress.

As illustrated in Figure 5.8, a work package may be viewed as a hierarchy that starts with the project itself. The project is then decomposed into phases, with each phase having one or more deliverable as defined in the deliverable structure chart (DSC). More specifically, each phase should provide at least one specific deliverable—that is, a tangible and verifiable piece of work. Subsequently, activities or tasks are identified in order to produce the project's deliverables.

DELIVERABLES AND MILESTONES   One departure from most traditional views of a WBS is the inclusion of milestones. A **milestone** is a significant event or achievement that provides evidence that a deliverable has been completed or that a phase is formally over.

Deliverables and milestones are closely related, but they are not the same thing. Recall that deliverables can include such things as presentations or reports, plans, prototypes, and the final application system. A milestone, on the other hand, must focus on an achievement. For example, a deliverable may be a prototype of the user interface, but the milestone would be a stakeholder's formal acceptance of the user interface. Only the formal acceptance or approval of the user interface by the project sponsor would allow the project team to move on to the next phase of the project.

In theory, if a project team succeeds in meeting all of its scheduled milestones, then the project should finish as planned. Milestones also provide several other advantages. First, milestones can keep the project team focused. It is much easier to concentrate your attention and efforts on a series of smaller, short-term deliverables than on a single, much larger deliverable scheduled for completion well into the future. On the other hand, if milestones are realistic, they can motivate a project team if their attainment is viewed as a success. If meeting a milestone signifies an important event, then the team should take pleasure in these successes before gearing up for the next milestone.

Milestones also reduce the risk associated with a project. The passing of a milestone, especially a phase milestone, should provide an opportunity to review the progress of the project. Additional resources should be committed at the successful completion of each milestone, while appropriate plans and steps should be taken if the project cannot meet its milestones.

Milestones can also be used to reduce risk by acting as **cruxes** or proof of concepts. Many times a significant risk associated with projects is the dependency on new technology or unique applications of the technology. A crux can be the testing of an idea, concept, or technology that is critical to the project's

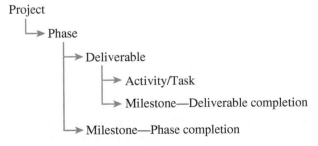

Figure 5.8 Work Package

success. For example, suppose that an organization is building a data warehouse using a particular vendor's relational database product for the first time. A crux for this project may be the collection of data from several different legacy systems, cleansing this data, and then making it available in the relational database management system.

The team may ensure that this can be accomplished using only a small amount of test data. Once the project team solves this problem on a smaller scale, it has proof that the concept or technique for importing the data from several legacy systems into the data warehouse can be done successfully. This breakthrough can allow the team to incorporate what it has learned on a much larger scale. Subsequently, solving this crux is a milestone that would encourage the organization to invest more time and resources to complete the project.

Milestones can also provide a mechanism for quality control. Continuing with our example, just providing the users with an interface does not guarantee that it will be acceptable to them. Therefore, the completion of the user's interface deliverable should end only with the user's acceptance; otherwise, the team will be forced to make revisions. In short, the deliverable must not only be done, but must also be done right.

DEVELOPING THE WBS   Developing the WBS may require several versions until everyone is comfortable and confident that all of the work activities have been included. It is also a good idea to involve those who will be doing the work—after all, they probably know what has to be done better than anyone else.

The WBS can be quite involved, depending on the nature and size of the project. To illustrate the steps involved, let's continue with our web-based banking project example. We created a DSC (Figure 5.4) to define the scope of the project, but to make things easier to follow, let's focus on only one portion of the project—creating a document called the test results report. As you can see in Figure 5.4, there are two deliverables—the test plan and the test results report—to be completed and delivered during the testing phase of the project.

The DSC defines the phases and deliverables for our project. Now, we can subdivide the project work into lower levels of detail, or components, that represent a verifiable product, service, or result. After a team meeting, let's say that we have identified and discussed several activities that we need to do in order to produce the test results document:

1. Review the test plan with the client so that key stakeholders are clear as to what we will be testing, how we will conduct the tests, and when the tests will be carried out. This review may be done as a courtesy or because we need specific support from the client's organization and, therefore, must inform the client when that support will be required.

2. After we have informed the client that we will test the system, we basically carry out the tests outlined in the test plan.

3. Once we have collected the test results, we need to analyze them.

4. After we analyze the results, we will need to summarize them in the form of a report and presentation to the client.

5. If all goes well, the client will approve or sign off on the test results. Then, we can move on to the implementation phase of our project. If all does not go well, we need to address and fix any problems. Keep in mind that the test phase is not complete just because we have developed a test plan and created a test report. The client will sign off on the test results only if the system meets certain predetermined quality standards.

On the right side of Figure 5.9 is an example of a WBS with the details shown for only the testing phase of the project. As you can see, the WBS implements the concept of a work package for the project, phase, deliverable, task/activity, and milestones. This particular WBS follows an outline format with a commonly used decimal numbering system that allows for continuing levels of detail. If a software

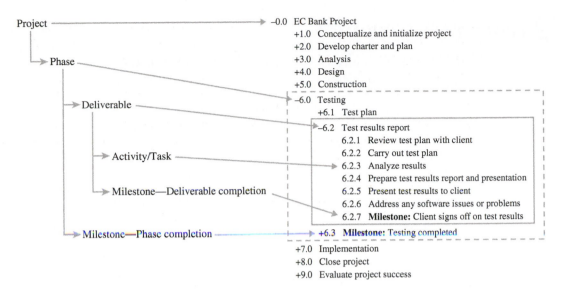

Figure 5.9 Work Package and Work Breakdown Structure

package is used to create the WBS, signs in front of each item can either hide or show the details. For example, clicking on "−6.2 Test Results Report" would roll up the details of this work package into "+6.2 Test Results Report." Similarly, clicking on any item with a "+" in front of it would expand that item to show the details associated with it.

The skills to develop a useful WBS generally evolve over time with practice and experience. Everyone, experienced or not, should keep in mind the following points when developing a WBS.

- *The WBS Should Support the Project's MOV*—The WBS should include only tasks or activities that allow for the delivery of the project's deliverables. Before continuing with the development of the project plan, the project team should ensure that the WBS allows for the delivery of all the project's deliverables as defined in the project's scope. In turn, this will ensure that the project is more likely to achieve its MOV.

- *The WBS Should Be Deliverable Oriented*—Remember, the focus of a project should be to produce something, not merely on completing a specified number of activities.

- *The Level of Detail Should Support Planning and Control*—The WBS provides a bridge between the project's scope and project plan—that is, the schedule and budget. Therefore, the level of detail should support not only the development of the project plan but also allow the project manager and project team to monitor and compare the project's actual progress to the original plan's schedule and budget. The two most common errors when developing a WBS are too little or too much detail. Too little detail may result in a project plan that overlooks and omits important activities and tasks. This will lead to an overly optimistic schedule and budget. On the other hand, the WBS should not be a to-do list of one-hour tasks.

- *Developing the WBS Should Involve the People Who Will Be Doing the Work*—One way to ensure that the WBS has the appropriate level of detail is to ensure that the people who do the work are involved in its development. A person who has experience and expertise in a particular area probably has a better feel for what activities need to be performed in order to produce a particular project deliverable. Although the project manager is responsible for ensuring that a realistic WBS is developed, the people who must carry out the activities and tasks may be more committed to the plan if they are involved in its development.

PROJECT ESTIMATION

Once the project deliverables and activities have been defined, the next step in developing the project schedule and budget is to estimate each activity's duration. One of the most crucial—and difficult—activities in project management is estimating the time it will take to complete a particular task. Since a resource generally performs a particular task, a cost associated with that particular resource must be allocated as part of the time it takes to complete that task. The time estimated to complete a particular task will have a direct bearing on the project's budget as well. As T. Capers Jones points out:

> The seeds of major software disasters are usually sown in the first three months of commencing the software project. Hasty scheduling, irrational commitments, unprofessional estimating techniques, and carelessness of the project management function are the factors that tend to introduce terminal problems. Once a project blindly lurches forward toward an impossible delivery date, the rest of the disaster will occur almost inevitably. ((5) p. 120)

In this section, we will review several estimation techniques—guesstimating, Delphi, time boxing, top-down, bottom-up, and poker planning.

GUESSTIMATING   Estimation by guessing or just picking numbers out of the air is not the best way to derive a project's schedule and budget. Unfortunately, many inexperienced project managers tend to **guesstimate**, or guess at the estimates, because it is quick and easy. For example, we might guesstimate that testing will take two weeks. Why two weeks? Why not three weeks? Or ten weeks? Because we are picking numbers out of thin air, the confidence in these estimates will be quite low. You might as well pick numbers out of a hat. The problem is that guessing at the estimates is based on feelings rather than on hard evidence.

However, many times a project manager is put on the spot and asked to provide a ballpark figure. Be careful when quoting a time frame or cost off the record, because whatever estimates you come up with often become on the record.

People are often overly optimistic and, therefore, their guesstimates are overly optimistic. Underestimating can result in long hours, reduced quality, and unmet client expectations. If you ever find yourself being pressured to guesstimate, your first impulse should be to stall until you have enough information to make a confident estimate. You may not, however, have that luxury, so the best approach is to provide some kind of confidence interval. For example, if you think something will probably take three months and cost $30,000, provide a confidence interval of three to six months with a cost of $30,000 to $60,000. Then, quickly offer to do a little more research to develop a more confident estimate. Notice that even though three months and $30,000 may be the most likely estimate, an estimate of two to six months was not made. Why? Because people tend to be optimists, and the most likely case of finishing in three months is probably an optimistic case.

DELPHI TECHNIQUE   The **Delphi technique** involves multiple experts who arrive at a consensus on a particular subject or issue. Although the Delphi technique is generally used for group decision making, it can be a useful tool for estimating when time and money warrant the extra effort (6).

To estimate using the Delphi technique, several experts need to be recruited to estimate the same item. Based on information supplied, each expert makes an estimate and then all the results are compared. If the estimates are reasonably close, they can be averaged and used as an estimate. Otherwise, the estimates are distributed back to the experts, who discuss the differences and then make another estimate.

In general, these rounds are anonymous and several rounds may take place until a consensus is reached. Not surprisingly, using the Delphi technique can take longer and cost more than most estimation methods, but it can be very effective and provide reasonable assurance when the stakes are high and the margin for error is low.

TIME BOXING   **Time boxing** is often used on Agile projects whereby a *box* of time is allocated for a sprint; however, this technique can also be used for a specific activity or task or for any component of the WBS. This allocation is based more on a requirement than just on guesswork. For example, a project team may have two (and only two) weeks to build a prototype during a sprint. At the end of the two weeks, work on the prototype stops, regardless of whether the prototype is 100 percent complete. Used effectively, time boxing can help focus the project team's effort on an important and critical task.

TOP-DOWN ESTIMATING   **Top-down estimating** involves estimating the schedule and/or cost of the entire project in terms of how long it *should* take or how much it *should* cost. Top-down estimating is a very common occurrence that often results from a mandate made by upper management (e.g., Thou shalt complete the project within six months and spend no more than $500,000!).

Often the schedule and/or cost estimate is a product of some strategic plan or because someone *thinks* it should take a certain amount of time or cost a particular amount. On the other hand, top-down estimating could be a reaction to the business environment. For example, the project may have to be completed within six months as a result of a competitor's actions or to win the business of a customer (i.e., the customer needs this in six months).

Once the target objectives, in terms of schedule or budget, are identified it is up to the project manager to allocate percentages to the various project life cycle phases and associated tasks or activities. Data from past projects can be very useful in applying percentages and ensuring that the estimates are reasonable. It is important to keep in mind that top-down estimating works well when the target objectives are reasonable, realistic, and achievable.

When made by people independent from the project team, however, these targets are often overly optimistic or overly aggressive. These unrealistic targets often lead to what Ed Yourdon calls a *death march* project:

> I define a death march project as one whose "project parameters" exceed the norm by at least 50 percent. This doesn't correspond to the "military" definition, and it would be a travesty to compare even the worst software project with the Bataan death march during the Second World War, or the "trail of tears" death march imposed upon Native Americans in the late 1700s. Instead, I use the term as a metaphor, to suggest a "forced march" imposed upon relatively innocent victims, the outcome of which is usually a high casualty rate. ((7) p. 2)

Project parameters include the schedule, staff, budget or other resources as well as the functionality, features, performance requirements, or other aspects of the project. A "death march" project means one or more of the following constraints has been imposed (7):

- The project schedule has been compressed to less than 50 percent of its original estimate.
- The staff originally assigned or required to complete the project has been reduced to less than 50 percent.
- The budget and resources needed have been reduced by 50 percent or more.
- The functionality, features, or other performance or technical requirements are twice what they should be under typical circumstances.

On the other hand, top-down estimating can be a very effective approach to cost and schedule analysis (8). More specifically, a top-down approach may force the project manager to examine the project's risks more closely so that a specific budget or schedule target can be achieved. By understanding the risks, trade-offs, and sensitivities objectively, the various project stakeholders can develop a mutual understanding that leads to better estimation. This outcome, however, requires that all stakeholders be willing to communicate and make trade-offs.

BOTTOM-UP ESTIMATING   Most real-world estimating is made using bottom-up estimating (8). Bottom-up estimating involves dividing the project into smaller modules and then directly estimating the time and effort in terms of person-hours, person-weeks, or person-months for each module. The work breakdown structure provides the basis for bottom-up estimating because all of the project phases and activities are defined.

The project manager, or better yet the project team, can provide reasonable time estimates for each activity. In short, bottom-up estimating starts with a list of all required tasks or activities and then an estimate for the amount of effort is made. The total time and associated cost for each activity provides the basis for the project's target schedule and budget. Although bottom-up estimating is straightforward, confusing effort with progress can be problematic (9).

Continuing with our earlier example, let's assume that after meeting with our software testers, the following durations were estimated for each of the following activities:

6.2.0	Test results report	
6.2.1	Review test plan with client	1 day
6.2.2	Carry out test plan	5 days
6.2.3	Analyze results	2 days
6.2.4	Prepare test results report and presentation	3 days
6.2.5	Present test results to client	1 day
6.2.6	Address any software issues or problems	5 days

How did we come up with these estimates? Did we guesstimate them? Hopefully not! These estimates could be based on experience. The testers may have done these activities so many times in the past that they know what activities have to be done and how long each activity will take. Or, these estimates could be based on similar or analogous projects. **Analogous estimation** refers to developing estimates based on one's opinion that there is a significant similarity between the current project and others (10).

POKER PLANNING   When it comes to estimating, many people tend either underestimate up to 50 percent or add buffers to every task because they lack confidence or are pessimistic (11). A new Agile estimation technique that is gaining in popularity is called poker planning. **Poker planning** is a variation of the Delphi technique that was refined by James Grenning (12) and later made popular by Mike Cohn (13).

Poker planning begins with a deck of cards that represent an estimate in days. One popular sequence is 0, 1/2, 1, 2, 3, 5, 8, 13, 20, 40, 100, while another is based on the Fibonacci numbers that create the sequence 1, 2, 3, 5, 8, 13, 21, 34, 55, . . . The Fibonacci set is created where each subsequent number is the sum of the previous two. Regardless, the idea is to create a set of possible estimates that have some distance between them. Often a deck will include an "unsure" card or an "I need a break" card. Teams can make up their own sets of cards or purchase them commercially.

Playing poker planning is straightforward and includes a moderator and the team of developers (i.e., programmers, database administrators, business or systems analysts, quality assurance testers, etc.). The idea is to have the people who will be actually doing the work participate. Anecdotal evidence suggests that up to ten poker planning players works best. While managers, customers, users, or product owners can participate in any discussions, raise questions, or answer questions, they cannot estimate.

The moderator can be the project manager, product owner, or an analyst, but the moderator's main role is to describe a particular task, feature, deliverable, or user story to be estimated. A **user story** is a sentence or two that captures a specific feature or piece of functionality that the user wants. A common structure is "*As a (role), I want (goal/desire)*." An example would be, "*As a marketing manager, I want to be able to track sales by geographical region*." The moderator or product owner can answer any questions that the estimators may have.

Each player has a set of poker planning cards. After all the questions are answered, each player privately chooses a card that best represents his or her estimate. No cards are shown until each estimator has had a chance to choose his or her card. Then, similar to real poker, all players turn over or show their cards simultaneously with the other players. This forces everyone to think independently and not be influence by the others.

Very often the estimates will differ significantly. This actually is considered a good thing because it gives the team a chance to engage in a valuable dialog. If the estimates differ, the estimators who played the highest and lowest cards explain the reasoning behind their estimates. For example, a player who makes the highest estimate may have certain knowledge or experience from a previous project that leads him or her to believe the task or user story will take longer. On the other hand, the player with the lowest estimate may know of a way to expedite the work. In any case, the team is usually given a minute or two to discuss the estimates before beginning a second round of estimation. It is important that the discussion not come across as an attack. Instead, the team should understand what everyone is thinking, especially if one person thinks a task is a 3 and another thinks it is a 13. This helps the team better understand the nature of the work and learn from those with more experience.

The goal is to arrive at a realistic estimate in a short amount of time. If a consensus is not reached after the first round, the team repeats the process. Most times a consensus is reached after the second or third round. Estimates should be based on reasonableness rather than on precision. For example, if after the third round the estimates are 8,8,8,8 and 5, the moderator may ask the low estimator if she or he is willing to go with 8. Moreover, if the estimates are split between say 3 and 5, the moderator may suggest that the higher of the two estimates (i.e., 5) be used. Anyone at any time can play the "I need a break" card if a time out is needed.

Many project teams have come to embrace this new technique. Many people believe it works because:

- It brings the people who will be doing the work together to do the estimates. In many cases, people with different disciplines will gain a fresh perspective and appreciation for a particular task or deliverable.

- People who are asked to justify their estimates may be forced to think more critically about the task at hand. This may help uncover missing information or understand the risks involved.

- Group discussions may help foster collaboration by engaging the entire team rather than relying on the estimates of a single person.

- While poker planning takes advantage of knowledge of the more experienced members of the team, the technique empowers everyone and ensures full team participation. This ensures that no one just sits back and defers to the opinion of someone else.

- Poker planning can make estimating more interesting while keeping the planning meeting focused and people motivated.

- The team can compare its estimates to its actual progress to see how accurate they were. This can provide a set of historical data that can be used for future poker planning sessions.

Keep in mind that estimates are a function of the activity itself, the resources, and the support provided. More specifically, the estimated duration of an activity will first depend on the nature of the activity in terms of its complexity and degree of structure. In general, highly complex and unstructured activities will take longer to complete than simple, well-structured activities. Unfortunately, no single method or tool is best for accurately estimating projects. It may be a good idea to use more than one technique for estimating. You will, however, very likely have two different estimates.

The resources assigned to a particular activity will also influence an estimate. For example, assigning an experienced and well-trained individual to a particular task should mean less time is required to complete it than if a novice were assigned. However, experience and expertise are only part of the equation. We also have to consider such things as a person's level of motivation and enthusiasm. Finally, the support we provide also influences our estimates. Support may include technology, tools, training, and the physical work environment. Once again, the project's infrastructure plays an important role in planning the project.

CHAPTER SUMMARY

- **Scope** defines the work boundaries and deliverables of the project so what needs to get done, gets done—and only what needs to get done, gets done. In other words, any work assigned to the project team comes at a cost in terms of time and budget.

- The triple constraint (Figure 5.1) provides a conceptual understanding of the relationship among scope, schedule, and budget. A project is "in balance" if these project objectives support the MOV, are realistic, and are agreed upon by the project stakeholders. A project can become "imbalanced" if scope increases without adjusting the schedule and budget accordingly.

- The scope management processes include:
  - Plan Scope Management
  - Collect Requirements
  - Define Scope
  - Create the Work Breakdown Structure (WBS)
  - Validate Scope
  - Control Scope

- A statement of work (SOW) is a narrative description of the product, service, or system.

- A **deliverable** is a tangible and verifiable work product. Deliverables can be divided into project-oriented deliverables and product-oriented deliverables.

- Project-oriented deliverables, or scope, support the project management processes as defined by the project life cycle (PLC) and the chosen project methodology. Project scope includes such things as the business case, project charter, and project plan and defines the work products of the various PLC phases. Project-oriented deliverables may also include specific deliverables such as a current systems study, requirements definition, and the documented design of the product or system.

- A useful tool to define the project-oriented deliverables is to create a **deliverable structure chart (DSC)**. Figure 5.4 provides an example of a DSC that maps all of the project deliverables of the project life cycle (PLC) and systems development life cycle (SDLC) phases.

- **Product scope** focuses on identifying the features and functionality of the product or system to be developed.

- A useful tool for refining the scope boundary and defining what the system must do is a modeling tool called the **use case diagram** (Figure 5.5). It provides a high-level model for defining, verifying, and reaching agreement on the product scope.

- Once the project's scope has been defined, it must be verified, validated, and formally accepted by the project sponsor and other appropriate stakeholders. This includes:
  - Verification of the MOV
  - Documentation of all Deliverables
  - Specification of Quality Standards
  - Identification of Milestones
  - Review and Acceptance

- Controlling scope is concerned with managing actual changes to the project's scope, as and when they occur, to ensure that any changes to the project's scope will be beneficial. In short, it is about understanding and managing the triple constraint. Scope control is also concerned with:
  - Scope Grope
  - Scope Creep
  - Scope Leap

- A scope change procedure should be in place before the actual work on the project commences. Scope change requests can be made, and each request's impact on the project can be assessed. Then, a decision whether to accept or reject the scope change can be made.

- The **work breakdown structure (WBS)** is a useful tool for developing the project plan and links the project's scope to the schedule and budget. The WBS provides a framework for developing a tactical plan to structure the project work.

- The WBS decomposes, or subdivides, the project into smaller components and more manageable units of work called **work packages**. Work packages provide a logical basis for defining the project activities and assigning resources to those activities so that all of the project work is identified.

- A **milestone** is a significant event or achievement that provides evidence that the deliverable has been completed or that a phase is formally over.

- When developing a WBS, things to keep in mind include:
  - The WBS should support the project's MOV
  - The WBS should be deliverable oriented
  - The level of detail should support planning and control
  - Developing the WBS should involve the people who will be doing the work

- Once the project deliverables and activities have been defined, the next step in developing the project schedule and budget is to estimate each activity's duration. The techniques discussed in this chapter include:
  - Guesstimating
  - The Delphi Technique
  - Time Boxing
  - Top-Down Estimating
  - Bottom-Up Estimating
  - Poker Planning

- The resources assigned to a particular activity will also influence an estimate. Things such as experience, training, motivation, and enthusiasm can influence estimates and should be considered.

REVIEW QUESTIONS

1. What is the triple constraint?
2. Describe the relationship among scope, schedule, and budget.
3. What is meant by project scope?
4. Briefly describe the six scope management processes.
5. Briefly describe the plan scope management process.
6. Briefly describe the collect requirements process.
7. Briefly describe the define scope process.
8. Briefly describe the purpose of a work breakdown structure (WBS).
9. Briefly describe the validate scope process.
10. Briefly describe the control scope process.
11. Why is it important to define the project's scope accurately and completely?
12. What is a scope boundary? What purpose does it serve?
13. What is the difference between product-oriented deliverables and project-oriented deliverables?
14. How does a project's scope support the MOV concept?
15. What is a statement of work? What purpose does it serve?
16. What is a scope statement? What purpose does it serve?
17. How does a use case diagram help to define the project's scope?
18. What is a deliverable structure chart (DSC)? What is its purpose?
19. What is a work breakdown structure (WBS)? How does it map to the deliverable structure chart (DSC)?
20. What is the purpose of validating and verifying a project's scope?
21. What is the purpose of scope change control procedures?
22. Briefly describe scope grope.
23. Briefly describe scope creep.
24. Briefly describe scope leap.
25. What are the benefits of having scope control procedures?
26. Briefly describe what should be included on a scope change request form.
27. What is the purpose of a scope change request log?
28. Discuss why a project's scope must be tied to the WBS.
29. What is a work package?
30. What is the difference between a deliverable and a milestone? Give an example of each.
31. What purpose do milestones serve?

32. What are some advantages of including milestones in the WBS?

33. What is a crux? Why should the project manager and project team identify the cruxes of a project?

34. What is the proper level of detail for a WBS?

35. Why should the WBS be deliverable oriented?

36. Explain why people who do the work on a project should be involved in developing the project plan.

37. How does the concept of knowledge management support the development of the project plan?

38. What is guesstimating? Why should a project manager not rely on this technique for estimating a project?

39. Describe the potential problems associated with providing an off-the-record estimate?

40. What is the Delphi technique? When would it be an appropriate estimating technique for a project?

41. What is time boxing? What are some advantages of using time boxing?

42. Describe top-down estimating. What are some advantages and disadvantages of top-down estimating?

43. Describe bottom-up estimating. What are some advantages and disadvantages of bottom-up estimating?

44. Describe poker planning. What are some advantages of poker planning?

45. What is a "death march" project? What situations in project planning can lead to a "death march" project?

■ HUSKY AIR ASSIGNMENT—PILOT ANGELS

NOTE: This case assignment will require you to use Microsoft Project®, a popular project management software tool. You should work through the Microsoft Project® Tutorial 1: Creating the Work Breakdown Structure (WBS) at www.wiley.com/go/marchewka/msprojecttutorial **before beginning this case assignment.**

This would also be a good chance for you and your team to do another learning cycle. Read through this assignment first and then meet as a team to develop a Project Team Record and an Action Plan. This will help to improve team learning and to assign responsibilities to complete the assignment.

The Scope Management Plan and WBS

Your client, Husky Air, has given your team the authority to develop the project's scope. The project's scope defines the project work. It includes the work boundaries and deliverables that you will deliver to your client. In addition, you will create a work breakdown structure (WBS) that will be used to create your project's schedule and budget in your next assignment.

Please provide a professional-looking document that includes the following:

1. **Project name, project team name, and the names of the members of your project team**

2. **A brief project description.**

3. **The project's MOV**—This should be revised or refined if necessary.

4. **A deliverable structure chart (DSC)**—This should be based on the project life cycle and the systems development life cycle. You should begin by creating a hierarchical chart that defines all of the project and system development phases. The system development phases will depend largely on the development approach you use (Waterfall or Agile). After you have identified all project phases, the next step in developing a DSC is to identify at least one project or product deliverable for each phase.

5. **A use case diagram (UCD)**—A UCD defines the high-level features and functionality that the application system should include. Although Figure 5.5 provides an example of a use case, you can build one:

    a. *Draw a box to represent the system boundary.*

    b. *Draw stick figures to represent the actors of the system.* Actors can be users, managers, customers, or even other systems that will interact with or use the application system. Actors should be drawn on the outside of the system boundary. Be sure to label each actor with a descriptive name to describe the actor's role.

    c. *Draw an oval inside the system boundary for each function and label the oval with a descriptive name.* A use case is a particular function that the application system will perform. Examples of use cases are: update customer information, print employee overtime report, create new vendor record, and so forth. This important step during your project necessitates a great deal of interaction with your client. Unfortunately, you will not have access to a real client, so you can be creative. Keep in mind, however, that additional (and often unused) functionality will require more time and resources to build the system, thus adding to the project's schedule and budget. You and your team need to be aware that any features and functionality of the system should help the organization achieve its MOV.

   d. *Draw a connecting line to identify the actors who will make use of a particular use case.*

6. **Convert your deliverable structure chart (DSC) to a WBS.** Using Microsoft Project®, create a work breakdown structure (WBS) by listing all of the project life cycle and systems development life cycle phases and the associated deliverables that you defined in the DSC. Be sure to work through the MPS tutorial first. Also, be sure to follow the work package concept shown in Figures 5.8 and 5.9. Your WBS should include:

   a. Milestones for each phase and deliverable—Achieving a milestone will tell everyone associated with the project that the phase or deliverable was completed satisfactorily.

   b. Activities/Tasks—Define a set of activities or tasks that must be completed to produce each deliverable.

   c. Resource Assignments—Assign people and other appropriate resources to each activity. This will be based on the people and resources that you identified when you completed the project infrastructure assignment from the previous chapter. Keep in mind that adding resources to an activity may allow the activity to be completed in a shorter amount of time; however, it may increase the cost of completing that task or activity.

   d. Estimates for Each Activity/Task—Based on the tasks or activities and the resources assigned, develop a time estimate for each task or activity to be completed. For the purposes of this assignment, you should use a combination of estimation techniques such as time-boxing and bottom-up estimation.

THE MARTIAL ARTS ACADEMY (MAA)—SCHOOL MANAGEMENT SYSTEM

NOTE: This case assignment will require you to use Microsoft Project®, a popular project management software tool. You should work through the Microsoft Project® Tutorial 1: Creating the Work Breakdown Structure (WBS) at www.wiley.com/go/marchewka/msprojecttutorial before beginning this case assignment.

This would also be a good opportunity for you and your team to do another learning cycle. Read through this assignment first and then meet as a team to develop a Project Team Record and an Action Plan. This will help to improve team learning and to assign responsibilities to complete the assignment.

The Scope Management Plan and WBS

Your client, MAA, has given your team the authority to develop the project's scope. The project's scope defines the project work. It includes the work boundaries and deliverables that you will deliver to your client. In addition, you will create a work breakdown structure (WBS) that will be used to create your project's schedule and budget in your next assignment.

Please provide a professional-looking document that includes the following:

1. **Project name, project team name, and the names of the members of your project team.**

2. **A brief project description.**

3. **The project's MOV**—This should be revised or refined if necessary.

4. **A deliverable structure chart (DSC)**—This should be based on the project life cycle and the systems development life cycle. You should begin by creating a hierarchical chart that defines all of the project and system development phases. The system development phases will depend largely on the development approach you use (Waterfall or Agile). After you have identified all project phases, the next step in developing a DSC is to

identify at least one project or product deliverable for each phase.

5. **A use case diagram (UCD)**—A UCD defines the high-level features and functionality that the application system should include. Although Figure 5.5 provides an example of a use case, you can build one:

   a. *Draw a box to represent the system boundary.*

   b. *Draw stick figures to represent the actors of the system.* Actors can be users, managers, customers, or even other systems that will interact with or use the application system. Actors should be drawn on the outside of the system boundary. Be sure to label each actor with a descriptive name to describe the actor's role.

   c. *Draw an oval inside the system boundary for each function and label the oval with a descriptive name.* A use case is a particular function that the application system will perform. Examples of use cases are: update customer information, print employee overtime report, create new vendor record, and so forth. This important step during your project necessitates a great deal of interaction with your client. Unfortunately, you will not have access to a real client, so you can be creative. Keep in mind, however, that additional (and often unused) functionality will require more time and resources to build the system, thus adding to the project's schedule and budget. You and your team need to be aware that any features and functionality of the system should help the organization achieve its MOV.

   d. *Draw a connecting line to identify the actors who will make use of a particular use case.*

6. **Convert your deliverable structure chart (DSC) to a WBS.** Using Microsoft Project®, create a work breakdown structure (WBS) by listing all of the project life cycle and systems development life cycle phases and the associated deliverables that you defined in the DSC. Be sure to work through the MPS tutorial first. Also, be sure to follow the work package concept shown in Figures 5.8 and 5.9. Your WBS should include:

   a. **Milestones for each phase and deliverable**—Achieving a milestone will tell everyone associated with the project that the phase or deliverable was completed satisfactorily.

   b. **Activities/Tasks**—Define a set of activities or tasks that must be completed to produce each deliverable.

   c. **Resource Assignments**—Assign people and other appropriate resources to each activity. This will be based on the people and resources that you identified when you completed the project infrastructure assignment from the previous chapter. Keep in mind that adding resources to an activity may allow the activity to be completed in a shorter amount of time; however, it may increase the cost of completing that task or activity.

   d. **Estimates for Each Activity/Task**—Based on the tasks or activities and the resources assigned, develop a time estimate for each task or activity to be completed. For the purposes of this assignment, you should use a combination of estimation techniques such as time-boxing and bottom-up estimation.

QUICK THINKING—SINKING A PROJECT

The trade magazine *Computerworld* contains a section called *Sharkbait* that allows people to submit real stories about their professional experiences. An anonymous writer described a situation where an IT manager decided to add a "cool new feature" to the next release of an internal software application. The new feature was added to the scope of the project, and the developers developed it and tested it at an additional cost of about $50,000. When the application was given to the users for acceptance testing, they were surprised to find the new functionality. Immediately, they sent the application back to the developers and informed them that they would not pay for something they did not ask for or need. The IT manager was soon transferred to another position.

1. Were the users justified in rejecting the application even though it contained a "cool new feature"?
2. What lessons can we learn from this experience?

SOURCE: "Scope Creep?." *Computerworld*. October 29, 2007. Accessed at http://shark bait.computerworld.com/node/1774.

QUICK THINKING—MORE PEOPLE = MORE PROBLEMS

The classic book, *The Mythical Man-Month*, by Fredrick P. Brooks was first published in 1975 with an anniversary edition published 20 years later (due to the fact that some things have not changed). Brooks worked at IBM as the manager of a large project that developed the OS/360 operating system. Although the OS/360 operating system was eventually a successful product for IBM, the system was late and cost several times more than originally estimated. In fact, the product did not perform well until after several releases. Based on his experience, Brooks wrote a number of essays that were embodied in his book. One timeless insight became known as:

Brooks' Law: Adding manpower to a late software project makes it later.

More recently, a study conducted by Quantitative Software Management (QSM) reports having a larger team on a software project can add millions of dollars to the cost of the project while only reducing the schedule by a few days. The study suggests that larger teams tend to create more defects or "bugs," and the additional rework detracts from any potential schedule benefits that may arise from having more people.

1. Why would adding more people to an alrcady late IT project make it even later?
2. Many projects tend to be overstaffed during the planning and requirements gathering stages of the project. Why would having a smaller or leaner project team be a better approach?

SOURCES:
Brooks, F. P. *The Mythical Man-Month: Essays on Software Engineering*, 2nd ed., 1975.
"More People, More Bugs." *Projects@Work*. October 6, 2005.

QUICK THINKING—POLITICS AND ESTIMATES

Very often project estimates are political. A project manager must not only come up with project estimates that are reasonable, but also acceptable to the project client or sponsor. Subsequently, political games ensue when the project manager attempts to "sell the right estimate." One game, for example, is to pad or inflate an estimate when one believes that it will be cut in some way. Therefore, the project manager may try to make an estimate high enough so that whatever is left over after the cut is adequate to carry out the project. Similarly, one may inflate an estimate with the idea that it is better to deliver ahead of schedule or below budget than to go over. Here, the project manager will try to make him- or herself look better by consistently beating the estimates. On the other hand, a strategy of low-balling or basing an estimate on what we feel others want to hear is rooted in human psychology. We often go to great lengths to tell people in power what they want to hear—not necessarily what they should hear.

1. Why would the project manager and project sponsor/client have different political interests in project estimates?
2. Why is either padding or low-balling project estimates a reasonable strategy?
3. As a project manager, how could you ensure that your project estimates do not put you and the project client/sponsor at political odds?

CASE STUDIES

The Vasa

The Vasa was a Swedish warship built in 1628 for King Gustavus Adolphus. On her maiden voyage, the ship floundered and keeled over in a light wind after sailing less than a nautical mile. Wives and children of the 125 crew were invited to take part in the maiden voyage; however, around 50 perished in the tragedy.

In the seventeenth century, Sweden rose to become one of the most powerful states in the Balkan Sea. Gustavus Adolphus became Sweden's king at the age of 17 in 1611 and was considered a born leader of great intellect and bravery. A decade later, Sweden was involved in a war with Poland and looking at the possibility of war with Germany. This required a strong navy, but several setbacks during the 1620s weakened Sweden's military dominance: a Swedish squadron of ten ships ran aground in 1625 and was wrecked by a bitter storm while two large warships were outmaneuvered by the Polish navy and defeated in 1627. In 1628, three more ships were lost within a month.

In January 1625, the king ordered Admiral Fleming to sign a contract with Henrik Hybertson and his brother Arend to build four ships, two smaller ones with keels of 108 feet (33m) and two larger ones of 135 feet (41 m). After losing the ten ships in a storm, the king sent a concerned letter to Admiral Fleming instructing him to tell Henrik Hybertson that the schedule for the two smaller ships must be expedited. The king also requested that these ships have 120 foot (37m) keels and include two enclosed gun decks so that they could carry more armament. This presented a dilemma for Hybertson because the timber had already been cut for the specifications outlined in the contract for one smaller ship and one larger ship. Moreover, no one had built a ship with two gun decks before. Hybertson tried to convince the king to follow the original specifications, but the king demanded that the ships be built according to his new measurements. Master Shipwright Hybertson soon became ill in 1625 and died in the spring of 1627, never seeing the Vasa completed. The project was handed over to Hybertson's assistant, Hein Jacobsson, who had very little management experience and no detailed records or plans from which to work.

In 1628, Admiral Fleming ordered a test of the Vasa's stability. This consisted of having thirty sailors running from one side of the ship to the other to assess how the ship would rock. The test was aborted only after three runs; otherwise, the ship would have keeled over. The two shipbuilders—Jacobsson and his assistant Johan Isbrandsson—were not present for the test. A member of the crew was heard to make a remark about the ship's instability, but the admiral replied that "The master shipbuilder surely has built ships before, so there is no need to have worries of that kind." No doubt the admiral, captain, and crew had wished the king were present, but he was fighting in Poland and sending a stream of messages instructing that the ship be launched immediately.

During the stability test, the ship's armament was being produced and artists were working feverishly to complete the decorations. The number and types of armaments to be carried by the redesigned Vasa went through a number of revisions as well. The original design called for thirty-two 24-pound guns, but the 135-foot version was to carry thirty-six 24-pound guns, twenty-four 12-pound guns, eight 48-pound mortars, and ten smaller guns. After further revisions, the king finally ordered the Vasa to carry sixty-four 24-pound guns (thirty-two on each deck) and as many as sixty 24-pound guns. The idea was to arm the Vasa with powerful guns and a high stern that could act as a firing platform in boarding actions for the 300 soldiers the ship was to carry.

Moreover, it was customary for warships to be decorated ornately with hundreds of gilded and painted sculptures of biblical, mythical, and historical themes to glorify the authority and power of the king and to frighten or taunt the enemy. The 500 sculptures added considerably to the effort and cost of the ship as well as to raising the ship's center of gravity and contributing to its instability. During this period, no methods for calculating the ship's center of gravity, heeling characteristics, and stability existed, so shipbuilders and captains had to design and learn how a ship handled through trial and error.

On August 10, 1628, Captain Sofring Hansson ordered the Vasa to set sail on its maiden voyage. The wind was relatively calm with only a light breeze from the southwest. The gun ports were open so that a salute could be fired as the ship left her shipyard in Stockholm. Suddenly, a gust of wind filled her sails and the ship heeled to port. The ship slowly righted herself, but another gust pushed the ship again to her port side where water began to flow through her open gun ports. The Vasa heeled even further, until she sank in about 100 feet of water not far from shore. The ship sank in front of hundreds of people who had come to see the ship sail on her first voyage. Survivors clung to debris while many boats rushed to their aid. Despite heroics and the short distance to shore, records indicate that as many as 50 people perished with the ship.

The king was notified of the Vasa's fate by letter. He wrote a reply that "imprudence and negligence" must have been the cause and that the guilty parties would be punished. Captain Hansson survived and was imprisoned immediately to await trial. The captain and crew were interrogated regarding the handling of the ship as well as the sobriety of the captain and crew. Crew members and contractors blamed each other and everyone swore that they had done their job without fault. When asked why the ship was built to be so narrow and so unstable, the shipwright Jacobsson said that he had simply followed orders as directed by the long dead and buried Henrik Hybertsson, who had followed the king's orders. In the end, no one was sent to prison or found guilty of negligence. The disaster was explained as an act of God, but the sinking of the Vasa ended up being a major economic disaster for a small country.

1. What were some of the major problems associated with this project?

2. What lessons can we learn from the sinking of Vasa that can be applied to modern-day projects?

SOURCES:

Vasa (ship) Wikipedia.com.

Fairley, R. E. and M. J. Willshire. "Why the Vasa Sank: 10 Problems and Some Antidotes for Software Projects." *IEEE Software*, March/April 2003, 18–25.

The Roles of the Business Analyst

The work of a business analyst has been labeled using various job titles. Although the roles and responsibilities may be similar, business analysts are often called business system analysts, systems analysts, business technology analysts, or requirements analysts. According to Thomas Wailgum, "Anyone who has ever worked on a complex and lengthy software development project knows that the involvement of a business analyst can mean the difference between success and failure. And that involvement starts at the very beginning of the project."

Business analysts are important to project success and the position is ranked consistently as one of the top jobs in demand. As Katherine Walsh contends, "The business analyst is a hot commodity right now due to

business reliance on technology and the global reach of technology creates a challenge to bridge the gap between IT and the business." While some business analyst positions lean more toward business functions like finance, operations, or marketing, others tend to be more IT-oriented; however, that distinction seems to be blurring.

This idea is reinforced as the demand for IT people with business knowledge increases. This is due to organizations investing more in the areas of relationship management, business analysis, and project management. Enterprise systems such as enterprise resource planning (ERP) or customer relationship management (CRM) tend to blur traditional lines between IT and the business as they cross functional boundaries and even different companies.

In addition, a growing number of organizations require a solid business case before investing in an IT project. A good business analyst must be able to work with the business people to solve business problems while also working closely with the technologists to implement the solution.

Thomas Wailgum defines eight roles or responsibilities for today's business analyst:

1. **Scope the system**—Business analysts must work closely with key business stakeholders to define and communicate the business vision for the project.

2. **Interpret business needs**—The business analyst must translate the stakeholders' requirements for the developers, as well as translate any questions or concerns the developers have back to the business stakeholders.

3. **Translate technical issues**—A good business analyst has the ability to explain complex technical issues in a way the business stakeholders can appreciate and understand them.

4. **Spell out the project details and requirements**—The business analyst will work with the various project stakeholders to identify and model business processes, business rules, data requirements, write use cases, as well as document system or technical specifications.

5. **Put the development team in touch with the right people**—Acting as a liaison, business analysts should have excellent connections within the organization and can therefore help the project team members find the right people to help or work with them.

6. **Political guide**—The business analyst can help the project team and other stakeholders avoid political issues and conflicts.

7. **Test and validation**—Having a good understanding of the business stakeholder needs, business analysts should be able to validate their requirements while working closely with the quality assurance group.

8. **Represent project stakeholders throughout the process**—Often, the business analyst can act as a surrogate for stakeholders if the developers don't have direct access to key individuals. The business analyst can play the role of the "customer" so that requirements, domain information, or business priorities can be defined.

One important role business analysts play today is to act as a liaison between the project team and the business stakeholders. The best business analysts have the ability to define the real business problem and then find an appropriate solution. Moreover, a business analyst should have a substantial knowledge of the business in order to provide solutions that work and provide value to the organization.

As Thomas Wailgum sums it up, "The 21st-century business analyst is a liaison, bridge, and diplomat who balances the oftentimes incongruous supply of IT resources and demands of the business." Forrester's research found that those business analysts who were the most successful were the ones who could "communicate, facilitate, and analyze."

1. You are the project manager of a customer relationship management project for a local bank. You will need to hire a business analyst to act as a liaison between the developers on your project team and the sales people who will use the system to recommend financial products and banking services to their customers. Using careerbuilder.com or monster.com, research the roles, responsibilities, skills, and salary ranges for a business analyst. Then, write a job description that you would use to attract potential candidates for the position.

SOURCES:
Wailgum, T. "What Do Business Analysts Actually Do for Software Implementation Projects?" *CIO Magazine*. April 28, 2008.
Cherubin, S. and K. Terribile. "Business Analysts: A Key to Companies, Success." *CIO Magazine*. August 12, 2008.

Overby, S. "The New IT Department: The Top Three Positions You Need." *CIO Magazine*. January 01, 2006.
Wailgum, T. "Why Business Analysts Are So Important for IT and CIOs." April 16, 2008.
Walsh, K. "Hot Jobs: Business Analyst." *CIO Magazine*. June 19, 2007.
Wailgum, T. "Six Secrets of Top-Notch Business Analysts." *CIO Magazine*. May 23, 2008.
Wailgum, T. "Why You Need to Break Down the Wall Between Business Analyst and QA Teams." *CIO Magazine*. September 29, 2010.

eXtreme Programming at Sabre

eXtreme programming (XP) was first introduced by Kent Beck when he was the project leader on a large, long-term project whose objective was to rewrite Chrysler Corporation's payroll system. He later outlined this development methodology in a book titled *Extreme Programming Explained: Embrace Change*. Some of the main concepts of XP include using small teams, using simple code, reviewing it frequently, testing it early and often, and working no more than a 40-hour work week. XP is often referred to as a lightweight methodology because it does not emphasize lengthy requirements definition and extensive documentation.

Instead, XP focuses on having the end user or customer develop user stories that describe what the new system must do. Beck suggests that project teams have no more than twelve developers working in pairs that work side by side on a single assignment. He believes that this approach leads to better quality code that takes less time to test and debug. Close communication between the developers and users/customers is key, as the user stories provide a basis for prioritizing the applications' most important functionality and estimating code releases that are tested and shared among the development team.

For many years, Sabre Airline Solutions relied on a large modeling and forecasting software package called AirFlite Profit Manager to make flight schedules more profitable. Release 8 of the software system contained approximately 500,000 lines of code and was four months late, with 300 known bugs or defects identified in final system testing. Moreover, a Sabre customer found 26 bugs in the first three days of acceptance testing, with an additional 200 bugs uncovered after the system was joint tested by Sabre and the customer.

Since then, the company has adopted XP and claims that XP has dramatically improved the quality and productivity of its 300 developers. More specifically, only 100 bugs were found 16 months after Release 10 of Air-Flite Profit Manager was shipped to its airline customers. Even more impressive was that Release 10 required just three developers to support thirteen customers, while Release 8 required thirteen people to support twelve customers. On another project, Sabre converted the user interface of its AirServ airline cabin provisioning optimization system from C++ to a web-based Java application over a two-year period that required rewriting about 100 GUI programs. After the development team changed over to XP halfway through the project, Sabre reported that programmer productivity—as measured by the number of labor hours required for each screen—still increased by 42 percent.

Other success stories include a Host Access Tool project that provides a common application programming interface for accessing legacy host systems. This system had more than 15,000 lines of code and was developed from the outset using the XP methodology. Twenty months after its ship date, the software has remained defect free. In addition, only four bugs have shown up after fifteen months in another software system called Peripheral Manager, a system that manages interactions between host systems and peripheral devices, and contains about 28,000 lines of code.

With XP as its new approach to development, Sabre Airline Solutions customers defined features in terms of user stories that are expressed in user terms and are simple enough to be coded, tested, and integrated in two weeks or less. Developers define criteria for automated test units, while customers define a broader set of criteria for acceptance testing. Both unit and acceptance testing are written before a feature or user story is coded. An inability to write a test usually means that the feature is not well defined or understood.

The coding is accomplished in an open lab in pairs by teams of developers to promote collective ownership of the code. The developers can sign up for the tasks they want to work on and/or the person they want to work with. Each team also has an "XP coach" and an "XP customer" who is a subject matter expert and prioritizes product features, writes user stories, and signs off on the test results. Developers are encouraged to refactor code, that is, to rewrite code not just to fix bugs or add features, but also to make it more efficient and easier to maintain. Customers see new releases in one to three months.

Suppose you have been hired as a consultant by a company that is interested in exploring XP as a development methodology. In the past, the company has developed systems using more traditional project management and development approaches, so the current IT staff has little or no knowledge of XP. The CIO has asked you to provide some insight into the following questions:

1. How should the company introduce XP? More specifically, should the company just jump right into it and attempt to use XP on a large, upcoming project that is mission critical to the company? Or, should it experiment with a smaller, less critical project?

2. Can traditional project management tools such as a work breakdown structure (WBS) be used in XP?

3. What methods for estimation would be most appropriate when following an XP approach?

4. If the company's developers have always followed a more traditional approach to IT projects, what impacts might introducing XP have on them?

SOURCES:

Beck, K. *Extreme Programming Explained*, 2nd Ed. Boston, MA: Addison-Wesley, 2005.

Copeland, L. "Extreme Programming." *Computerworld*. December 3, 2001.

Anthes, G. "Sabre Takes Extreme Measures." *Computerworld*. March 29, 2004.

BIBLIOGRAPHY

1. Project Management Institute (PMI). *A Guide to the Project Management Body of Knowledge (PMBOK Guide)*. Newton Square, PA: PMI Publishing, 2013.

2. Jacobson, I. *Object-Oriented Software Engineering: A Use Case Driven Approach*. Reading, MA: Addison-Wesley, 1992.

3. Fowler, M. and K. Scott. *UML Distilled: Applying the Standard Object Modeling Language*. Reading, MA: Addison-Wesley, 1997.

4. Haugan, G. T. *Effective Work Breakdown Structures*. Vienna, VA: Management Concepts, Inc., 2002.

5. Jones, T. C. *Estimating Software Costs*. New York: McGraw-Hill, 1998.

6. Roetzheim, W. H. and R. A. Beasley. *Software Project Cost and Schedule Estimating:*

Best Practices. Upper Saddle River, NJ: Prentice Hall, 1998.

7. Yourdon, E. *Death March*. Upper Saddle River, NJ: Prentice Hall, 1999.

8. Royce, W. *Software Project Management: A Unified Framework*. Reading, MA: Addison Wesley, 1998.

9. Brooks, F. P. *The Mythical Man-Month*. Reading, MA: Addison Wesley, 1995.

10. Rad, P. F. *Project Estimating and Cost Management*. Vienna, VA: Management Concepts, Inc., 2002.

11. Rothman, J. "The Team Estimate." *Projects @Works*. September 18, 2007.

12. Grenning, J. "Planning Poker." *Renaissance Software Computing* (2002). renaissancesoftware.net/papers/14-papers/44-planing-poker.html.

13. Cohn, M. "Agile Estimating and Planning." *Mountain Goat Software* (2005). www.mountaingoatsoftware.com/books/agile-estimating-and-planning.

6

Project Planning: The Schedule and Budget

CHAPTER OBJECTIVES

Chapter 6 focuses on developing the project schedule and budget and introduces a number of project management tools for developing the project plan. After studying this chapter, you should be able to:

- Develop a Gantt chart.
- Develop a project network diagram using a technique called activity on the node (AON).
- Identify a project's critical path and explain why it must be controlled and managed.
- Develop a PERT diagram.
- Describe the concept of precedence diagramming and identify finish-to-start, start-to-start, finish-to-finish, and start-to-finish activity relationships.
- Describe the concept of critical chain project management (CCPM).
- Describe the various types of costs that make up the project's budget.
- Define what is meant by the baseline project plan.

INTRODUCTION

The last several chapters have been leading up to the development of the project plan, which contains all of the details of the project's schedule and budget. This plan along with the project charter will be used to guide the project team and monitor the project's progress throughout the project life cycle.

In the last chapter, you learned about defining and managing the project's scope, as well as the development of the work breakdown structure (WBS) where resources and activities were identified to complete the scope deliverables. In this chapter, you will see how the project schedule and budget builds upon the WBS by identifying the sequence of activities as well as the interdependencies and relationships.

This relationship is represented in Figure 6.1, which illustrates the project planning framework that will serve as a guide for developing and assessing the project plan. It outlines the steps and processes to develop a detailed project plan that supports the project's MOV. Therefore, the MOV must be set at this point in the project so it aligns the project with the organization's strategy and objectives, and so it provides a link to the project's scope and to the project plan. In addition, the MOV can then be used to guide many of the decisions related to scope, schedule, budget, and resources throughout the project's life cycle.

Recall that scope includes all of the project deliverables needed to support the MOV. It is important to define the work boundaries and deliverables of the project so what needs to get done, gets done—and only what needs to get done, gets done because additional work assigned to the project team comes at a cost in terms of schedule and budget.

Once the project's scope is defined and validated to support the MOV, the project work is subdivided logically into phases and subphases to reduce risk and complexity. Each phase of the project should

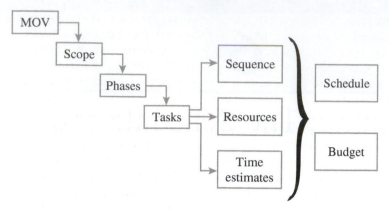

Figure 6.1 The Project Planning Framework

focus on providing at least one deliverable from the project's total scope requirements so that the project team can concentrate on each piece of the project while keeping an eye on the whole picture. Phases are largely determined by the project methodology and the approach chosen for carrying out the systems development life cycle (SDLC). As discussed in an earlier chapter, the SDLC can be implemented by using a more structured approach, such as the Waterfall method, or by using a more Agile approach.

The selection of an approach to implement the SDLC is an important decision that will affect not only how the product or system will be developed, but also will define the phases, deliverables, and tasks defined in the project plan. The appropriate decision depends on how quickly the product or system needs to be delivered as well as how well defined and stable the requirements of the system will remain throughout the project life cycle. For example, the Waterfall model would be more appropriate for a project where the requirements are well understood and complex, while an Agile would be more appropriate for a project characterized by uncertainty, change, and tight deadlines (1).

Once the project is divided in to phases, activities, or tasks, define the actions needed to complete each deliverable. The terms **activity** and **task** are often used interchangeably and may be thought of as specific actions or units of work to be completed. Examples of some project activities include interviewing a particular stakeholder, writing a program, testing links in a Web page, or preparing a presentation.

When identifying tasks to complete a specific project deliverable, it is important to consider sequences, resources, and time. Some tasks may be linear—that is, they have to be completed in a particular sequence—while others can be completed in parallel—that is, at the same time. Performing parallel tasks often provides an opportunity to shorten the overall length of the project. For example, assume that a project has two tasks: A and B. Task A will require only one day to complete; Task B requires two days. If these tasks are completed one after the other, the project will finish in three days. On the other hand, if these tasks are performed in parallel, the length of the project will be two days. In this case, the length of the project is determined by the time it takes to complete the longest task (i.e., Task B). This simple example illustrates that a project is constrained by the longest tasks, and that any opportunity to perform tasks in parallel can shorten the project schedule.

Tasks require resources, and there is a cost associated with using a resource. Resources on a project may include such things as technology, facilities (e.g., meeting rooms), and people. The use of a resource may be accounted for by using a per-use charge or on a prorated basis—that is, a charge for the time that resource is used. For example, a consultant is paid $104,000 a year and is assigned to work on a task that takes one day to complete. The cost of completing that particular task would be prorated as $400 (assuming an eight-hour day, five-day work week: ($104,000/52)/5).

However, the longer it takes a resource to complete a specific task, the longer the project will take to finish and the more it will cost. For example, if we plan on assigning our consultant who earns $104,000 a year to a task that takes two days, then we would estimate the cost of completing that task to be $800. If the consultant completes the task in one day instead of two, then the actual cost of doing that task will be $400. Moreover, if the consultant were then free to start another task, then our schedule would then be ahead by one day. Unfortunately, the reverse is true. If we thought the task would take two days to complete and it took the consultant three days to complete, then the cost of completing that task would be $1,200 and the project would be one day behind schedule and $400 over budget.

On the other hand, if the two tasks could be performed in parallel, with our consultant working on Task A (one day) and another similarly paid consultant working on Task B (two days), then even if Task A takes two days, our project schedule would not be impacted—as long as the consultant working on Task B completes the task within the estimated two days. While this parallel work may save our schedule, our budget will still be $400 over budget if Task A takes two days instead of one day to complete. Understanding this relationship among tasks, resources, and time will be important when developing the project plan and even more important later if it is necessary to adjust the project plan in order to meet schedule or budget constraints.

The detailed project plan is an output of the project planning framework. Once the tasks and their sequence are identified, including the resources required, estimated time to complete, and any indirect costs and reserves, it is a relatively straightforward step to determine the project's schedule and budget. All of this information can be entered into a project management software package that can determine the start and end dates for the project, as well as the final cost.

Once completed, the project plan should be reviewed by the project manager, the project sponsor, and the governance committee to make sure it is complete, accurate, and, most important, able to achieve the project's MOV. Generally, the project plan will go through several iterations as new information becomes known or if there are compromises with respect to scope, schedule, and budget until the triple constraint meets the project stakeholders' expectations. Once the project plan is approved, the plan becomes the **baseline project plan**. This milestone is an important achievement that marks the completion of the second phase of the project and gives the project manager and team the authority to begin carrying out the activities outlined in the plan. The project's actual progress is then compared to the baseline plan in order to gauge whether the project is ahead, behind, or on track.

DEVELOPING THE PROJECT SCHEDULE

The WBS identifies the activities and tasks that must be completed in order to provide the project scope deliverables. Estimates provide a forecasted duration for each of these activities and are based on the characteristics of the activity, the resources assigned, and the support provided to carry out the activity. Project networks, on the other hand, support the development of the project schedule by identifying dependencies and the sequencing of the activities defined in the WBS. The project network also serves as a key tool for monitoring and controlling the project activities once the project work begins.

In this section, several project management tools and techniques will be introduced to create a project network plan that defines the sequence of activities and their dependencies throughout the project. These tools include Gantt charts, activity on the node (AON), critical path analysis, PERT, and the precedence diagramming method (PDM). Many of these tools are integrated into most project management software packages; however, it is important to have a fundamental understanding of how these various project management tools work in order to make the most of an automated tool.

Gantt Charts

Working with the U.S. Army during World War I, Henry L. Gantt developed a visual representation that compares a project's planned activities with actual progress over time. Although Gantt charts have been around for a long time, they are still one of the most useful and widely used project management tools.

Tasks

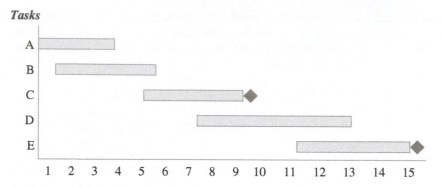

Figure 6.2 Gantt Chart for Planning

Figure 6.2 shows how a basic Gantt chart can be used for planning. Estimates for the tasks or activities defined in the WBS are represented using a bar across a horizontal time axis. Other symbols, for example, diamonds, can represent milestones to make the Gantt chart more useful.

The Gantt chart in Figure 6.2 depicts the general sequence of activities or work tasks. In this project example, there are five tasks of varying durations, and the project should be completed in 15 time periods (e.g., days). In addition, the two shaded diamonds following Tasks C and E indicate milestone events.

Gantt charts can also be useful for tracking and monitoring the progress of a project. As shown in Figure 6.3, completed tasks can be shaded or filled in, and one can get some idea of where the project stands for a given status or reporting date. In Figure 6.3, Tasks A, B, and C have been completed, but it looks like Task D is somewhat behind schedule.

Although Gantt charts are simple, straightforward, and useful for communicating the project's status, they do not show the explicit relationships among tasks or activities. For example, we can see from Figure 6.3 that Task D is somewhat behind schedule; however, the Gantt chart does not tell us whether there will be an impact on Task E and whether this impact will push back the project's original deadline. The Gantt chart introduced in this section follows a more traditional form. As you will see, the Gantt chart used in most project management software packages today integrates several techniques to overcome these limitations.

Tasks

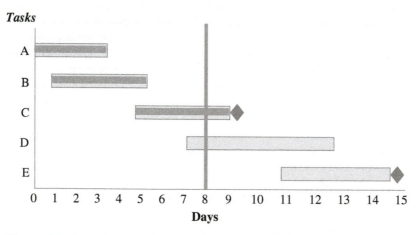

Figure 6.3 Gantt Chart Reporting Project's Progress

Project Network Diagrams

Project network diagrams include several useful tools for planning, scheduling, and monitoring the project's progress. Similar to Gantt charts, project network diagrams use the WBS as a basis to provide a visual representation of the workflow of activities and tasks. However, project network diagrams also provide valuable information about the logical sequence and dependencies among the various activities or tasks. Subsequently, a completion date or project deadline should be developed based on a sound estimating process rather than guesstimating a target date or a date set arbitrarily by upper management or the client.

In addition, project network diagrams provide information concerning when specific tasks must start and finish and what activities may be delayed without affecting the deadline target date. In addition, the project manager can make decisions regarding scheduling and resource assignments to shorten the time required for those critical activities that will impact the project deadline.

Activity on the Node (AON)—An activity or a task focuses on producing a specific project deliverable, generally takes a specific amount of time to complete, and requires resources. **Activity on the node (AON)** is a project network diagramming tool that graphically represents all of the project activities and tasks as well as their logical sequence and dependencies. Using AON, activities are represented as boxes (nodes) and arrows indicate precedence and flow.

To construct an AON network diagram, one begins with the activities and tasks that were defined in the WBS. Estimates for each activity or task defined in the WBS should have an associated time estimate. The next step is to determine which activities are **predecessors**, **successors**, or **parallel**. Predecessor activities are those activities that must be completed *before* another activity can be started; for example, a computer's operating system must be installed before loading an application package. On the other hand, successor activities are activities that must follow a particular activity in some type of sequence. For example, a program must be tested after it is written. A parallel activity is an activity or a task that can be worked on at the same time as another activity. Parallel activities may be thought of as an opportunity to shorten the project schedule; however, they also can be a trade-off since doing more than one thing at the same time can have a critical impact on project resources.

The activities, time estimates, and relationships for developing a simple corporate intranet can be summarized in a table similar to Table 6.1. Once the relationships and time estimates for each activity or task in the WBS have been developed, an AON project network diagram can be created, as in Figure 6.4.

Table 6.1 Activities for AON

Activity	Description	Estimated Duration (Days)	Predecessor
A	Evaluate current technology platform	2	None
B	Define user requirements	5	A
C	Design Web page layouts	4	B
D	Set up server	3	B
E	Estimate Web traffic	1	B
F	Test Web pages and links	4	C, D
G	Move Web pages to production environment	3	D, E
H	Write announcement of intranet for corporate newsletter	2	F, G
I	Train users	5	G
J	Write report to management	1	H, I

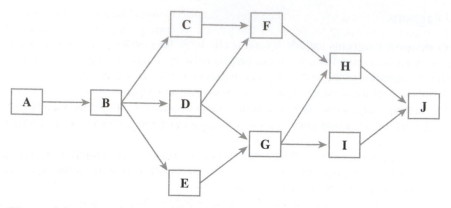

Figure 6.4 Activity on the Node (AON) Network Diagram

The work in an AON flows from left to right. An activity cannot begin until all of its predecessor activities have been completed. For example, Activity F (Test Web pages and links) cannot begin until Activities C (Design Web page layouts) and D (Set up Server) have been completed.

Critical Path Analysis—At this point, we have a visual road map of our project. Moreover, the time estimates for each of the activities determines the project schedule and tells us how long our project will take to complete. This is determined by looking at each of the possible paths and computing the total duration for each path, as shown in Table 6.2.

As can be seen in Table 6.2, the longest path in the AON network diagram is 19 days. This number is significant for two reasons. First, this tells us that our project is estimated to take 19 days (i.e., the project deadline will be 19 days after the project starts). Second, and perhaps more importantly, Path 4 is also our critical path. The **critical path** is the longest path in the project network and is also the shortest time in which the project can be completed.

Identifying the critical path is a major concern to the project manager because any change in the duration of the activities or tasks on the critical path will affect the project's schedule. In other words, the critical path has zero slack (or float). **Slack**, which is sometimes called **float**, is the amount of time an activity can be delayed, that is, take longer than expected, before it delays the project. For example, Activity E (Estimate Web traffic) is not on the critical path. In fact, the only path that includes Activity E is Path 5. Subsequently, the start of Activity E could be delayed for two days or take up to three days to complete before the project schedule is affected. On the other hand, Activities A, B, D, G, I, and J have no float because delaying their start or taking longer to complete than we estimated will increase the total duration of the project by the same amount.

Table 6.2 Possible Paths Through the Network Diagram

Possible Paths	Path	Total
Path 1	A + B + C + F + H + J	18
	2 + 5 + 4 + 4 + 2 + 1	
Path 2	A + B + D + F + H + J	17
	2 + 5 + 3 + 4 + 2 + 1	
Path 3	A + B + D + G + H + J	16
	2 + 5 + 3 + 3 + 2 + 1	
Path 4	A + B + D + G + I + J	19*
	2 + 5 + 3 + 3 + 5 + 1	
Path 5	A + B + E + G + I + J	17
	2 + 5 + 1 + 3 + 5 + 1	

*Critical Path

As a result, knowing the critical path can influence a project manager's decisions. For example, a project manager can **expedite**, or **crash**, the project by adding resources to an activity on the critical path to shorten its duration. The project manager may even be able to divert resources from certain activities, for example, Activity E because this activity has some slack or float. Diverting resources can reduce the overall project schedule, but keep in mind that there may be a trade-off—shortening the schedule by adding more resources may inflate the project's budget.

Another way to shorten the project schedule is to look for parallel activity opportunities. Doing two, or several, activities that were originally planned to be completed at the same time can shorten the critical path. It is known as **fast tracking** the project.

Can the critical path change? The answer is yes. As a result, it is imperative that the project manager not only identify the critical path, but monitor and manage it appropriately. In fact, it is very possible for a project to have more than one critical path.

Program Evaluation and Review Technique (PERT)—This tool was developed in the late 1950s to help manage the Polaris submarine project. At about the same time, the critical path method (CPM) was developed. The two methods are often combined and called PERT/CPM.

PERT uses the project network diagramming technique to create a visual representation of the scheduled activities that expresses both their logical sequence and interrelationships. PERT also uses a statistical distribution that provides probability for estimating when the project and its associated activities will be completed. This probabilistic estimate is derived by using three estimates for each activity: optimistic, most likely, and pessimistic.

An optimistic estimate is the minimum time in which an activity or a task can or is expected to be completed. This is a best-case scenario where everything goes well and there is little or no chance of finishing earlier. A most likely estimate, as the name implies, is the normally expected time required to complete the task or activity. A pessimistic estimate is a worst-case scenario and is viewed as the maximum time in which an activity can or should be completed.

One can use the following equation to compute a mean or weighted average for each individual activity that will be the PERT estimate:

$$\text{Activity Estimate} = \frac{\text{Optimistic Time} + (4 \times \text{Most Likely Time}) + \text{Pessimistic Time}}{6}$$

The total expected time to complete the project can be easily found by summing each of the individual activity estimates. For example, using the network diagram in Figure 6.4, a project manager and team came up with the estimates presented in Table 6.3.

Analyzing the various paths using PERT provides the critical paths presented in Table 6.4. As can be seen in Table 6.4, the critical path is still Path 4 and the expected completion date of the project is 20.5 days. In this case, the deadline increased from 19 days using the AON method to 21 days using the statistical technique associated with PERT.

In the first case, the most likely estimates were used, while PERT took into account not only the most likely estimates, but optimistic and pessimistic estimates as well. PERT is well suited for developing simulations whereby the project manager can conduct a sensitivity analysis for schedule planning and risk analysis. But, like any planning and scheduling tool, its usefulness is highly correlated to the quality of the estimates used.

Precedence Diagramming Method (PDM)—Another tool that is useful for understanding the relationships among project activities is the **precedence diagramming method (PDM)**. This tool is similar to the AON project diagram technique and is based on four fundamental relationships shown in Figure 6.5.

- *Finish-to-start (FS)*—A finish-to-start relationship is the most common relationship between activities and implies a logical sequence. Here, activity or Task B cannot begin until Task A is completed. For example, a program is tested after it is written. Or, in other words, the

Table 6.3 Activities for PERT

Activity	Predecessor	Optimistic Estimates (Days) (o)	Most Likely Estimates (Days) (m)	Pessimistic Estimates (Days) (p)	Expected Duration $\frac{o + 4m + p}{6}$
A	None	1	2	4	2.2
B	A	3	5	8	5.2
C	B	2	4	5	3.8
D	B	2	3	6	3.3
E	B	1	1	1	1.0
F	C,D	2	4	6	4.0
G	D,E	2	3	4	3.0
H	F,G	1	2	5	2.3
I	G	4	5	9	5.5
J	H,I	.5	1	3	1.3

program is written and then tested. This relationship is similar to the successor and predecessor relationships used in the AON method.

- *Start-to-start (SS)*—A start-to-start relationship between tasks or activities occurs when two tasks can or must start at the same time. Although the tasks start at the same time, they do not have to finish together—that is, the tasks can have different durations. A start-to-start relationship would be one type of parallel activity that can shorten a project schedule.

- *Finish-to-finish (FF)*—Another type of parallel activity is the finish-to-finish relationship. Here, two activities can start at different times, have different durations, but are planned to be competed at the same time. Once both of the FF activities are completed, the next activity or set of activities can be started, or if no more activities follow, the project is complete.

- *Start-to-finish (SF)*—The start-to-finish relationship is probably the least common and can be easily confused with the finish-to-start relationship. A SF relationship, as illustrated in Figure 6.5, is exactly the opposite of an FS relationship. In addition, an SF relationship means that Task A cannot end until Task B starts. An example of an SF relationship in real life might be a nurse working at a hospital. This person may have to work until relieved by another nurse who arrives to start the next shift.

Table 6.4 Possible PERT Activity Paths

Possible Paths	Path	Total
Path 1	A + B + C + F + H + J	18.8
	2.2 + 5.2 + 3.8 + 4.0 + 2.3 + 1.3	
Path 2	A + B + D + F + H + J	18.3
	2.2 + 5.2 + 3.3 + 4.0 + 2.3 + 1.3	
Path 3	A + B + D + G + H + J	18.6
	2.2 + 5.2 + 3.3 + 3.0 + 2.3 + 1.3	
Path 4	A + B + D + G + I + J	20.5*
	2.2 + 5.2 + 3.3 + 3.0 + 5.5 + 1.3	
Path 5	A + B + E + G + I + J	18.2
	2.2 + 5.2 + 1.0 + 3.0 + 5.5 + 1.3	

*The Critical Path

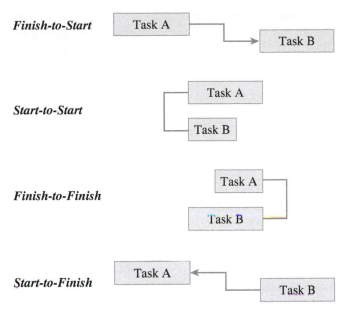

Figure 6.5 Precedence Diagramming Relationships

An advantage of using PDM is that the project manager can specify **lead** and **lag** times for various activities. More specifically, lead time allows for the overlapping of activities. For example, a project plan may have two activities or tasks that have been identified as a finish-to-start relationship. These two activities may be the setup of computers in a lab followed by the installation of an operating system on those computers. If we had two people, one to set up the computers and one to install the operating systems on each computer, the project plan might specify a finish-to-start relationship where the installation of the operating systems cannot begin until all of the computers have been set up in the lab. Based on this project plan, the person who installs the operating system must wait and watch while the other person works.

Let's assume, however, that it takes about half the time to install an operating system as it does to set up a computer. Furthermore, there is no reason why the software person cannot begin installing the operating system when the hardware person has about half of the computers set up. In this case, both tasks will finish about the same time, and we have created an opportunity to shorten the project schedule. By scheduling the task of installing the operating systems when the task of setting up the computers is 50 percent complete, we have used the concept of lead time to our advantage.

On the other hand, let's suppose further that before our hardware person starts setting up the computers in the lab, we want the lab walls to be painted. This would be another finish-to-start relationship because we would like to schedule the painting of the lab before we start installing the computers. Using lead time in this case, however, would not make sense because we do not want the hardware person and painters getting in each other's way. In this case, we may even want to give the freshly painted walls a chance to dry before we allow any work to be done in the lab. Therefore, we would like to schedule a lag of one day before our hardware person starts setting up the computers. Another way of looking at this is to say we are going to schedule a negative lead day in our project schedule.

Critical Chain Project Management (CCPM)

Critical chain project management (CCPM) is a relatively recent development in modern project management. CCPM was introduced in a book called *Critical Chain* by Eliyahu Goldratt (2).

CCPM is based on the idea that people often inflate or add cushioning to their time estimates in order to give themselves a form of "safety" to compensate for uncertainty. People may build safety into each task for three basic reasons. First, you may inflate an estimate if your work is dependent upon the work of someone else. For example, you may add a cushion to your time estimates if you believe there's a good chance your work will be delayed if the person you are depending on will not finish his or her task or work on time. Second, you may increase an estimate of an activity because of pessimism arising from a previous experience where things did not go as planned. Third, the project sponsor or customer may not be happy with a proposed schedule and therefore decides to cut the schedule globally by, say, 20 percent. If you know this is going to happen, you may inflate your estimates by 25 percent just to guard against the cut.

If people tend to build safety into each task, then why do projects still finish late? The answer is mainly human nature. More specifically, many people tend to wait until the last minute before they begin to work on a task. This is often referred to as **student's syndrome**, as many students procrastinate and then begin working on an assignment right before it's due—regardless of how much time is available. If things don't go exactly as planned, the task or assignment ends up being late.

The second reason why projects are still late has to do with **Parkinson's law**. This law states that work expands to fill the time available. For example, an individual or a team assigned to complete a particular task will rarely report finishing early because there is no incentive to do so. They may be afraid that management will cut their estimates next time or the individual or team waiting for them to complete their task won't be ready. As a result, the safety built into an estimate disappears. Any time saved by completing a task early is wasted while any overruns get passed along.

A third reason why added safety does not ensure that projects are completed on time has to do with the multitasking of resources. Goldratt calls this **resource contention**, whereby a project team member often is assigned to more than one project. In addition, this person may be required to attend meetings, training, or be pulled off one project task to work on another. As a result, this person can become a constraint to the project because he or she is no longer able to devote time and energy to tasks on the critical path. Subsequently, the task takes longer, and so does the project.

CCPM follows a completely different assumption: Instead of adding safety to each task, put that safety in the form of **buffers** where needed the most. This would be in the form of feeder buffers, resource buffers, and a buffer at the end of the project. Figure 6.6 provides a comparison of a traditional project network schedule and a CCPM schedule. The top diagram illustrates a project schedule that would have safety built into each estimate. The project has five tasks, with each task estimated to be completed in 10 days. The critical path would be Tasks A, B, C, and E, so the project schedule is 40 days.

However, CCPM begins by asking each person or team assigned to a task to provide an estimate that would have a 50 percent chance of being completed. For our example, let's say that each task will have a 50 percent chance of being completed in five days. Instead of adding safety to each task, we place buffers where needed. More specifically, we add a buffer to the end of the project by taking one-half of the time saved from the individual tasks. In this example, we saved a total of 20 days from our critical path Tasks A, B, C, and E. Therefore, one-half of 20 equals 10 days, and that becomes our project buffer. In addition, Task D requires a "feeder" buffer, since the work completed in Task D will be an input to Task C. This is important because a bottleneck can occur when a task acts as a feeder to any task on the critical path.

If Task D is delayed or takes longer than planned, it will impact when Task C can either start or finish.

As a result, this will have an impact on the critical path of the project. To minimize the chance of this happening, a feeder buffer is added to Task D that is one-half of the time saved (i.e., 2.5 days).

However, the critical chain is different from the critical path in that it also takes into account resource contention. Continuing with our example, let's say that each project task is to be completed by a different resource (i.e., person or team). Task C is on the critical path but is also part of the critical chain because of its potential to become a bottleneck if the resource assigned to this task must multitask by working on different projects. If this is the case, the CCPM approach takes a more project portfolio view and would suggest that other projects begin or start so that the person or team working on Task C can be dedicated to work solely on this particular task for this project.

Project Schedule with Safety in Each Task

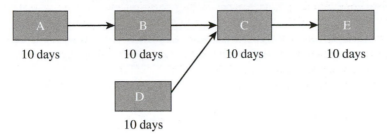

Critical Chain Project Schedule

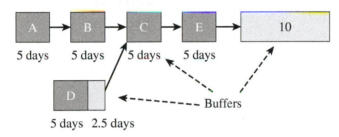

Figure 6.6 The Critical Chain Project Schedule

Therefore, CCPM proposes that a resource buffer for Task C be created so that the resource working on this task can dedicate time and effort to complete the task with a 50 percent probability in five days. In this case, the critical path and critical chain are the same; however, our project under the CCPM approach is expected to be completed in 30 days.

The CCPM approach requires that everyone understand that since each project task has a 50 percent chance of being completed as scheduled, approximately half of the tasks will be late. This is fine because this is the reason for having the project buffer. Instead of tracking each task individually, we become more concerned with the project buffer. In other words, the project will be late only if it uses more than the ten days allotted in the project buffer. Instead of penalties for being late, the organization may have to provide bonuses or other incentives for completing tasks early.

PROJECT MANAGEMENT SOFTWARE TOOLS

A number of software tools are available to make project planning and tracking much easier. In fact, it would be almost unthinkable to plan and manage even a small project without the aid of such a tool. In this section, you will see some examples of how these software tools incorporate and integrate the project management tools and concepts described in the previous section. The overview is intended to show you what these tools do, rather than tell you how to use them.

As you can see in Figure 6.7, the Gantt chart view integrates not only the Gantt chart, but also the project network diagram and PDM techniques. Most of the tasks show a finish-to-start relationship, while tasks *Develop Product* and *Test Product* have a start-to-start relationship. In addition, Daily Scrum Meeting provides an example of a reoccurring task to represent a daily one-hour meeting for the project stakeholders. Milestones have a duration of zero and are represented with a diamond-shaped icon. The Network Diagram View in Figure 6.8 then highlights the project's critical path. As can be seen in the Network view, the project has one critical path.

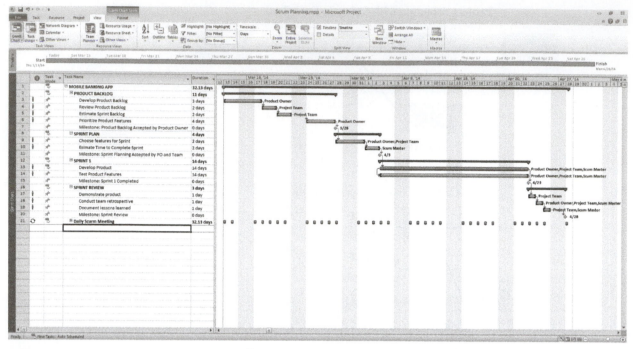

Figure 6.7 Gantt Chart in Microsoft Project®

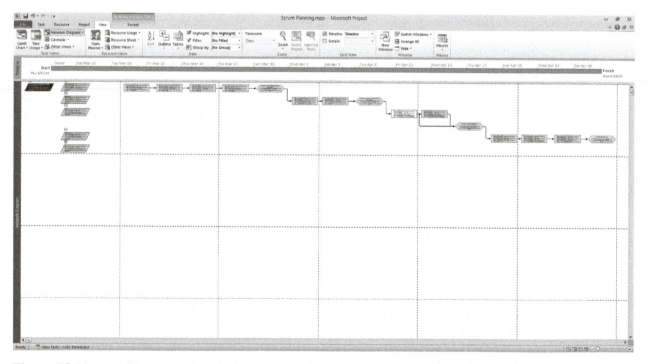

Figure 6.8 Network Diagram and Critical Path

Developing the project schedule and budget is an important planning process that requires that we sometimes define and estimate a large number of activities several months into the future. But, of course, predicting the future is difficult, and detailed project plans will have to be changed frequently to be useful. A technique called **rolling wave** planning is becoming common to help deal efficiently with project planning. Instead of developing a large, detailed project plan requiring frequent updates, the project manager can prepare an overall summary plan, or master schedule, and then develop detailed schedules for only a few weeks or a few months at a time (3).

DEVELOPING THE PROJECT BUDGET

The project's budget is a function of the project's tasks or activities, the duration of those tasks and activities, their sequence, and the resources required. In general, resources used on a project will have a cost, and the cost of using a particular task or activity must be included in the overall project budget. Unless these costs are accounted for, the project manager and the organization will not know the true cost of the project.

Cost Estimation—Estimating the cost of a particular activity or task with an estimated duration involves five steps:

1. Defining what resources will be needed to perform the work.
2. Determining the quantity of resources that are needed.
3. Defining the cost of using each resource.
4. Calculating the cost of the task or activity.
5. Ensuring that the resources are leveled—that is, not over allocated. An example of an over-allocated resource would be assigning a project team member to two tasks scheduled at the same time.

For example, let's suppose that we have identified a particular task and estimated that it will take one day to complete and requires one project team member. Let's also assume, for simplicity, that no other resources are needed.

This estimate may require that we define a cost for using this particular resource. For example, if our team member earns $20 an hour, that sum is what our employee sees on his or her paycheck (before taxes and other deductions). The organization, however, may also provide certain benefits to the employee (health care, life insurance, and so forth) that should be included in the cost for using this particular resource. Since these costs are going to vary from organization to organization, let's assume that our friends in the accounting department have conducted a cost accounting analysis for us and that the true cost of using this particular employee (i.e., hourly wage plus benefits) is $25 an hour. Subsequently, if we pay our employee for one day's work (i.e., an eight-hour day), the cost of completing this particular task is:

$$\text{Cost of Task} = \text{Estimated Duration} \times \text{True Cost of the Resource}$$
$$= 8 \text{ hours} \times \$25/\text{hour}$$
$$= \$200$$

We can even estimate the cost of a salaried employee by **prorating** her or his salary. This just means that we assign a portion of that salary to the task at hand. For example, let's say that the fully loaded, or true annual, cost to the organization is $65,000. If this employee works a five-day work week, the associated true cost to the organization would be for $5 \times 52 = 260$ days a year. Therefore, the prorated cost per day would be $65,000 \div 260$ workdays $= \$250$ a day.

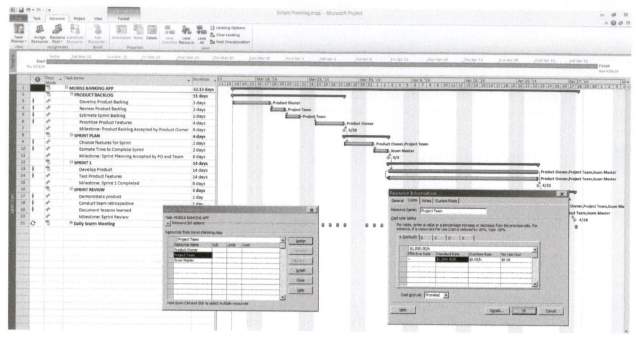

Figure 6.9 Project Resources Assigned to Project Tasks

However, this whole process can be greatly simplified if we use a project management software tool. We still have to identify the tasks and accurately estimate their durations, but determining the costs of a particular task and for the whole project becomes painless. Figure 6.9 shows how resources can be assigned to specific tasks on a project.

The project's total budget is computed using a bottom-up approach by summing the individual costs for each task or activity. As shown in Figure 6.10, the cost of the project owner, project team, and scrum master for this project is $487,000.

Other Costs—It is important to keep in mind that our example has only considered **direct costs**, or the cost of labor for using this resource directly. In addition to direct labor, resource costs include indirect labor, materials, supplies, and reserves (4). To determine the total project's budget, we need to include other costs as well. These costs include:

- *Indirect costs*—These costs include such things as rent, utilities, insurance, and other administrative costs. For example, a consulting firm may charge a client $150 an hour per consultant. Included in that hourly fee would be the salary and benefits of the consultant and enough margin to help cover the administrative and operation costs needed to support the consulting office.

- *Sunk costs*—Sunk costs are costs that have been incurred prior to the current project. For example, a previous attempt to build an application system may have ended in failure after three months and $250,000. This $250,000 would be considered a sunk cost, regardless of whether any work from the previous project is salvageable or of use to the current project.

- *Costs associated with a Learning curve*—Often we have to "build one and throw it away" in order to understand a problem or use a new technology effectively. In addition, inexperienced people will make mistakes and new technology will usually require a steep learning curve in the beginning. As a result, time and effort can be wasted. This time to learn should be considered in either the project schedule or budget.

- *Reserves*—Reserves provide a cushion when unexpected situations arise. Contingency reserves are based on risk and provide the project manager with a degree of flexibility. On the other

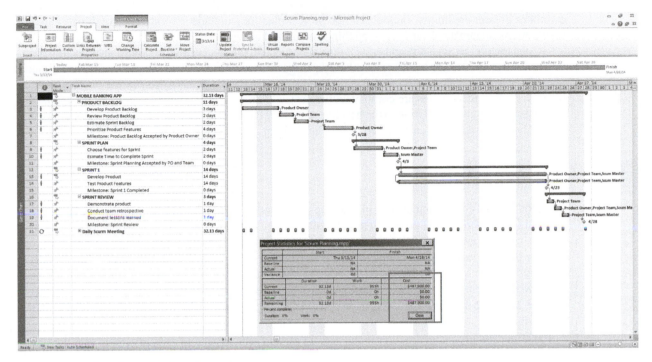

Figure 6.10 The Cost of Labor for the Project

hand, a project budget should have some management contingencies built in as well. Of course, reserves are a trade-off. Upper management or the client will view these as fat that can be trimmed from the project budget; however, the wise project manager will ensure that a comfortable reserve is included in the project's budget. For example, it would be sad to think that the project's budget would not allow the project manager to buy pizza or dinner for the team once in a while as a reward for working late to meet an important milestone.

Resource Allocation—Once the resources have been assigned to the project, it is important that the project manager review the project plan to ensure that the resources are level. In other words, resources cannot be over allocated; that is, most resources cannot be assigned to more than one task at the same time. Although the project manager may catch these mistakes early on, it is important that the level of resources be reviewed once the project schedule and resource assignments have been made. Not catching these mistakes early can have a demoralizing effect on the team and lead to unplanned (i.e., unbudgeted) costs.

THE BASELINE PLAN

The project schedule and budget may require several iterations before it is acceptable to the sponsor, the project manager, and the project team. In addition, it is important that the project manager document any and all assumptions used to come up with duration and cost estimates.

For example, this documentation may include estimating the salary of a database administrator (DBA) who will be hired at a future date. Instead of allocating a cost of what the project manager *thinks* a DBA will cost (or worse yet, what upper management would like to pay), the project manager could use salary surveys or salary information advertised in classified advertisements as a base cost estimate. So, the project manager should document the source of this cost in order to give the cost estimates greater credibility. In addition, the project plan may include several working drafts. Having assumptions documented can help keep things organized as well.

Once the project schedule and project plan are accepted, the project plan becomes the **baseline plan** that will be used as a yardstick, or benchmark, to track the project's actual progress with the original plan. Once accepted, the project manager and project team have the authority to execute or carry out the plan. As tasks and activities are completed, the project plan must be updated in order to communicate the project's progress in relation to the baseline plan. Any changes or revisions to the project's estimates should be approved and then reflected in the plan to keep it updated and realistic.

THE KICK-OFF MEETING

Once the project charter and project plan are approved, many organizations have a kick-off meeting to officially start work on the project. The kick-off meeting is useful for several reasons. First, it brings closure to the planning phase of the project and signals the initiation of the execution phase of the project. Second, it is a way of communicating to everyone what the project is all about. Many kick-off meetings take on a festive atmosphere in order to energize the stakeholders and get them enthusiastic about working on the project. It is important that everyone start working on the project with a positive attitude. How the project is managed from here on will largely determine whether that positive attitude carries through.

CHAPTER SUMMARY

- The project planning framework serves as a guide for developing and assessing the project plan. It outlines the steps and processes to develop a detailed project plan that supports the project's MOV. Therefore, the MOV must be set at this point in the project so it aligns the project with the organization's strategy and objectives, and so it provides a link to the project's scope and to the project plan. In addition, the MOV can then be used to guide many of the decisions related to scope, schedule, budget, and resources throughout the project's life cycle.

- Scope includes all of the project deliverables needed to support the MOV. It is important to define the work boundaries and deliverables of the project so what needs to get done, gets done—and only what needs to get done, gets done because additional work assigned to the project team comes at a cost in terms of time and budget.

- Once the project's scope is defined and validated to support the MOV, the project work is subdivided logically into phases and subphases to reduce risk and complexity. Each phase of the project should focus on providing at least one deliverable from the project's total scope requirements.

- The selection of an approach to implement the SDLC is an important decision that will affect not only how the product or system will be developed, but also will define the phases, deliverables, and tasks defined in the project plan.

- Once the project is divided in to phases, activities, or tasks, define the actions needed to complete each deliverable. The terms **activity** and **task** are often used interchangeably and may be thought of as specific actions or units of work to be completed.

- When identifying tasks to complete a specific project deliverable, it is important to consider sequences, resources, and time. Some tasks may be linear—that is, they have to be completed in a particular sequence—while others can be completed in parallel—that is, at the same time.

- Tasks require resources, and there is a cost associated with using a resource. Resources on a project may include such things as technology, facilities (e.g., meeting rooms), and people. The use of a resource may be accounted for by using a per-use charge or on a prorated basis—that is, a charge for the time that resource is used.

- The longer it takes a resource to complete a specific task, the longer the project will take to finish and the more it will cost.

- Once the tasks and their sequence are identified, including the resources required, estimated time to complete, and any indirect costs and reserves, a project management software package can determine the project's schedule and budget.

- Once the project plan is approved, the plan becomes the **baseline project plan**. This milestone is an important achievement that marks the completion of the second phase of the project and gives the project manager and team the authority to begin carrying out the activities outlined in the plan. The project's actual progress is then compared to the baseline plan in order to gauge whether the project is ahead, behind, or on track.

- The Gantt chart in Figure 6.2 depicts the general sequence of activities or work tasks. Gantt charts can also be useful for tracking and monitoring the progress of a project. As shown in Figure 6.3, completed tasks can be shaded or filled in, and one can get an accurate picture of where the project stands for a given status or reporting date.

- Project network diagrams use the WBS as a basis to provide a visual representation of the workflow of activities and tasks.

- *Activity on the Node (AON)* is a project network diagramming tool that graphically represents all of the project activities and tasks as well as their logical sequence and dependencies. Using AON, activities are represented as boxes (nodes) and arrows indicate precedence and flow.

- **Predecessor** activities are those activities that must be completed *before* another activity can be started. **Successor** activities are activities that must follow a particular activity in some type of sequence. A **parallel** activity is an activity or task that can be worked on at the same time as another activity.

- The **critical path** is the longest path in the project network and is also the shortest time in which the project can be completed.

- Identifying the critical path is a major concern to the project manager because any change in the duration of the activities or tasks on the critical path will affect the project's schedule. In other words, the critical path has zero slack (or float).

Slack, which is sometimes called **float**, is the amount of time an activity can be delayed, that is, take longer than expected, before it delays the project.

- *Program Evaluation and Review Technique (PERT)* was developed in the late 1950s to help manage the Polaris submarine project. At about the same time, the critical path method (CPM) was developed. The two methods are often combined and called PERT/CPM.

- *Precedence Diagramming Method (PDM)* is useful for understanding the relationships among project activities. This tool is similar to the AON project diagram technique and is based on four fundamental relationships:
  - *Finish-to-Start (FS)*
  - *Start-to-Start (SS)*
  - *Finish-to-Finish (FF)*
  - *Start-to-Finish (SF)*

- An advantage of using PDM is that the project manager can specify **lead** and **lag** times for various activities. More specifically, lead time allows for the overlapping of activities.

- **Critical Chain Project Management (CCPM)**—is based on the idea that people often inflate or add cushioning to their time estimates in order to give themselves a form of "safety" to compensate for uncertainty.

- CCPM follows a completely different assumption: Instead of adding safety to each task, this method puts that safety in the form of **buffers** where needed the most. This would be in the form of feeder buffers, resource buffers, and a buffer at the end of the project.

- The project's budget is a function of the project's tasks or activities, the duration of those tasks and activities, their sequence, and the resources required. The project's total budget can be computed using a bottom-up approach by summing the individual costs for each task or activity.

- In addition to direct labor, resource costs include indirect labor, materials, supplies, and reserves as well as:
  - Indirect costs
  - Sunk costs
  - Costs associated with a learning curve
  - Reserves

- Once the project schedule and project plan are accepted, the project plan becomes the **baseline plan** that will be used as a yardstick, or benchmark, to track the project's actual progress with the original plan. Once accepted, the project manager and project team have the authority to execute or carry out the plan.

- Many organizations have a kick-off meeting to officially start work on the project. The kick-off meeting brings closure to the planning phase of the project and signals the initiation of the execution phase of the project. The kick-off meeting is a way of communicating to everyone what the project is all about.

REVIEW QUESTIONS

1. Describe the project planning framework introduced in this chapter.
2. What is the purpose of a Gantt chart?
3. What are some advantages project network diagrams have over traditional Gantt charts?
4. Define predecessor, successor, and parallel activities. Give a real-world example of each.
5. How can parallel activities help shorten the project schedule? Are there any trade-offs?
6. What is meant by slack (or float)?
7. What is the difference between *crashing* and *fast tracking* a project's schedule?
8. What is the difference between AON and PERT?
9. Define the following and give a real-world example of each (other than the ones described in this chapter): finish-to-start; start-to-start; finish-to-finish; start-to-finish.
10. What is the difference between *lead* and *lag*? Give real-world examples (other than the ones used in this chapter) of how a project manager may use lead and lag in a project schedule.
11. Why do many people inflate their estimates?
12. Does adding safety, in terms of an inflated estimate, to each task or activity ensure that the project will be completed as scheduled? Why or why not?

13. In the context of critical chain project management (CCPM), what is resource contention?
14. In the context of CCPM, what is the purpose of buffers?
15. What is the critical chain? How is it different from the concept of a critical path?
16. What does prorating the cost of a resource mean? Give an example.
17. Why should the project manager ensure that the project resources are leveled?
18. When does the project manager or team have the authority to begin executing the project plan?
19. What is a task? Provide three examples of some typical tasks in a project.
20. What impact can the sequence of tasks have on a project's schedule?
21. How can resources impact the schedule of a project?
22. What is a baseline plan? What purpose does it serve once the project team begins to execute the project plan?
23. Why do many organizations have a "kick-off meeting?"

HUSKY AIR ASSIGNMENT—PILOT ANGELS

The Project Schedule and Budget

NOTE: This case assignment will require you to use Microsoft Project®, a popular project management software tool. You should work through the Microsoft Project® Tutorial 2 before beginning this case assignment.

www.wiley.com/go/marchewka/msprojecttutorial

You will also be working with the work breakdown structure (WBS) that you developed in the previous case

assignment; so before you begin, be sure to make a backup copy of your original WBS.

Now that you developed the work breakdown structure, it's time to start the process of determining how the work will be accomplished. This will require that you draw upon work you did in several previous assignments.

This would also be a good opportunity for you and your team to do another learning cycle. Read through this assignment first and then meet as a team to develop a Project Team Record and an Action Plan. This will help to improve team learning and to assign responsibilities to complete the assignment.

Please provide a professional-looking document that includes the following:

1. **Project name, project team name, and the names of the members of your project team**.
2. **A brief project description**.
3. **The project's MOV**. (This should be revised or refined if necessary.)
4. **A detailed project plan.**
   a. Using the work breakdown structure that you created in the previous assignment, assign a cost for each resource based on the project infrastructure that you developed in the assignment Chapter 4.
   b. Link the tasks. Look for opportunities to shorten the project schedule by performing tasks in parallel (i.e., start-to-start or finish-to-finish).
5. Answer the following questions:
   a. What are the beginning and end dates for your project? How many days will it take to complete the project?
   b. Does your project have a single critical path or multiple critical paths? What is the importance of the critical path?
   c. Does your project have any over-allocated resources? If so, be sure to level your resources.
6. Depending on what your instructor tells you, submit your project plan electronically or in printed form.

THE MARTIAL ARTS ACADEMY (MAA)—SCHOOL MANAGEMENT SYSTEM

The Project Schedule and Budget

NOTE: This case assignment will require you to use Microsoft Project®, a popular project management software tool. You should work through the Microsoft Project® Tutorial 2 before beginning this case assignment.

www.wiley.com/go/marchewka/msprojecttutorial

You will also be working with the work breakdown structure (WBS) that you developed in the previous case assignment; so before you begin, be sure to make a backup copy of your original WBS.

This would also be a good opportunity for you and your team to do another learning cycle. Read through this assignment first and then meet as a team to develop a Project Team Record and an Action Plan. This will help to improve team learning and to assign responsibilities to complete the assignment.

Now that you developed the work breakdown structure, it's time to start the process of determining how the work will be accomplished. This will require that you draw upon work you did in several previous assignments.

Please provide a professional-looking document that includes the following:

1. **Project name, project team name, and the names of the members of your project team**.
2. **A brief project description**.
3. **The project's MOV**. (This should be revised or refined if necessary.)
4. **A detailed project plan.**
   a. Using the work breakdown structure that you created in the previous assignment, assign a cost for each resource based on the project infrastructure that you developed in the assignment Chapter 4.
   b. Link the tasks. Look for opportunities to shorten the project schedule by performing tasks in parallel (i.e., start-to-start or finish-to-finish).
5. Answer the following questions:
   a. What are the beginning and end dates for your project? How many days will it take to complete the project?
   b. Does your project have a single critical path or multiple critical paths? What is the importance of the critical path?
   c. Does your project have any over-allocated resources? If so, be sure to level your resources.
6. Depending on what your instructor tells you, submit your project plan electronically or in printed form.

QUICK THINKING—PLANNING VERSUS THE PLAN

William Duncan believes that many projects suffer from inadequate planning. In his experience, many project managers offer the following excuses for not developing a project plan:

- "We didn't have enough time to plan because we needed to get started on the 'real work.'"
- "This project is just like the one we did before, so we know what has to be done."
- "It was a small project so why bother planning?"

However, Duncan says that these reasons are just symptoms of the real problem. He contends that poor project" planning is due to the following:

- *Trying to plan without information is futile.* Too often the project manager and teams will try to plan based on the systems development or product life cycle. It is difficult to plan a project based on requirements before they are defined. Duncan suggests that planning should be based on the project life cycle or management phases of the project. The plan can also change as more information becomes available.
- *People view changes to the plan as a poor job of planning.* Unfortunately, many project managers and team members need to overcome the psychological hurdle that they did not do a good job of planning if the plan needs to change. Project planners need to understand that change is inevitable and does not reflect poorly on their work.
- *Team members should learn to have fun planning.* Duncan believes that this is another psychological barrier that people need to overcome. He suggests having a prize for team members who most closely predict tasks that start or end on time, using sticky notes to develop the work breakdown structure, or having lunch or fun snacks available during the planning process. The idea is to make it fun and to find out what works best for a particular project.

1. Dwight D. Eisenhower once said, "I have always found that plans are useless, but planning is indispensable." Do you agree or disagree with this quote?

SOURCES:
Duncan, W. "Why Teams Won't Plan." *Projectsatwork.* December 10, 2009.
Carlson, J. "Dwight Was Right: Plans Are Useless." *Projectsatwork.* May 10, 2011.

QUICK THINKING—THE MAP IS NOT THE TERRITORY

Project planning is a critical activity regardless of whether one follows an Agile or a traditional approach to project management. Too often projects deviate from plans, and the project manager simply assumes that the project needs to be brought back on track. Unfortunately, this may be the result of a poor initial plan or because software is intangible and requirements can be difficult to specify.

Traditional approaches to project management tend to emphasize planning early in the project life cycle when not enough is known about the problem, business environment, or team dynamics. On the other hand, Agile methods tend to embrace the realities of IT projects and focus on making planning a more visible and iterative component of the project life cycle. However, a project sponsor will require some indication of how long a project will take and how much it will cost, so some sort of schedule and budget will be needed at the beginning of a project. This will require planning the entire project at a high level that outlines an overall timeline and iteration boundaries, but none of the details about individual features should be included in each iteration. Detailed iteration plans that include use cases or user stories are developed from meetings between the developers and customers for each iteration.

The high-level plan is then updated to include new details and velocity. Instead of trying to develop large, detailed plans that quickly deviate from reality and become difficult to maintain, Mike Griffiths suggests, "There is a reassurance and efficiency in knowing exactly where you are going before you set off on a trip. Proper planning creates that knowledge of how to get to the destination and avoid backtracking. However, many of today's projects are trips into uncharted territory for our organizations and no good maps exist to guide our way."

1. Alfred Korzybski is credited with the quote, "The map is not the territory." How does this quote reflect the realities of project planning?

2. Is an Agile approach to project planning better than a traditional approach to project planning where the project manager tries to develop a detailed project plan early in the project life cycle? When would one approach be a better choice than the other?

Sources:

Griffiths, M. "Extreme Planning." *ProjectManagement.com.* January 22, 2007.

Griffiths, M. "Why Planning Can Be Bad." *ProjectManagement.com.* June 20, 2013.

CASE STUDIES

Planning for Success

According to Eric Shoeniger, a number of major IT projects at Agere were in trouble. While many people were using Microsoft Project®, good project management decisions were not being made. Project plans ended up being more like historical records than like future projections. Moreover, there was no clear way to see interdependencies among projects.

Based in Allentown, Pennsylvania, Agere is a leading manufacturer of integrated chips for wireless devices, disk drives, and network equipment. The company has approximately 7,000 employees and about $2 billion in revenues. The company was spun off from Lucent Technologies in 2001 as the technology industry encountered major challenges and drastic belt tightening. Not surprisingly, Agere's IT budget was slashed from $270 million in 2001 to about $94 million in 2003.

However, before the spinoff from Lucent, Agere made the decision to implement Oracle's enterprise resource planning (ERP) system. With almost 550 business applications to support, the company decided that an integrated package was needed. Agere chose a project management software package called Primavera®, established a dedicated project management office, and endeavored to apply lessons learned and methodologies to every IT project. However, the company wasn't taking full advantage of this project management software tool.

More specifically, project teams weren't creating project plans that provided accurate schedules and budgets. Even worse, IT was trying to support every project requested by the business units. The high-risk ERP project was in trouble due to divisional conflicts, disjointed planning, and poor resource control. Even after a year, the project was at a standstill and the project plan provided little guidance for completing the project.

Even today, most ERP software projects continue to experience significant budget and schedule problems. Chris Kanaracus reports the findings of a study of 192 companies conducted by Panorama Consulting. It appears that 66 percent of the respondents said that their projects failed to realize more than half of the benefits envisioned, and 54 percent claimed that their projects were over budget. Moreover, about 72 percent of the respondents reported that their projects fell behind schedule.

Bart Perkins contends that project plans often "go off the rails" because the project manager does not consider basic constraints. For example, projects require team members with specialized skills. Too often a project manager will assume that key people will be available only to find that they are committed to other projects or available on a part-time basis. Many times the IT department is under pressure to take on more projects that it can support. A project can be doomed from the beginning if it doesn't have the staff and resources to support the entire project portfolio because even the best project plan won't be feasible. Therefore, project plans must be grounded in reality.

A project's network schedule provides a forecast of the project's future. As Jan Birkelbach points out, the accuracy of the work breakdown schedule's estimates can be improved by involving the "appropriately-skilled" team members. This provides a clearer picture of who does what and how and leads to a schedule that is reasonably accurate and stable even in an uncertain environment.

In addition, a project manager must manage and monitor the project's budget. Jason Westland provides four strategies to prevent major schedule and cost overruns:

- A project plan should be reviewed frequently and updated as required. This prevents the schedule and budget from getting out of control too quickly as a small overruns are easier to correct than substantially larger ones.

- A major cost to most projects is people. A project manager should continually review the project's usage of its resources to ensure that the right resources are in place and that they are being utilized efficiently and effectively.

- An informed team is an empowered team. A project team should take ownership of the project plan so that the team is more likely to be sensitive to the time and money charged against the project.

- The triple constraint should be managed closely. Scope creep is a major reason for schedule and budget overruns, so a scope change process must be in place to authorize additional funding and/or schedule adjustments.

Fortunately, Agere was able to jumpstart the ERP project by changing how projects were managed. The project team began by conducting a thorough understanding of Primavera®'s features and functions so that it could have a better idea of how the software tool could be better utilized. The team was able to better understand what Primavera® could do and, therefore, was able to turn the project around and get it back on track before Agere was spun off from Lucent.

In addition, two factors were critical for Agere's ability to transform its approach to project management. The first was unwavering support of multiple senior managers. The second was an effective project management solution. Primavera® provided the functionality needed and allowed multiple users to work simultaneously on a project plan. Most importantly, Agere was able to reduce its total budget from a $270 million to a $94 million budget in 18 months by better understanding the project load and utilization of resources. A subsequent analysis of the 11 largest projects indicated that all were on time and within budget.

1. How is managing projects from a project portfolio view different from a single-project view? What are the advantages? What are some challenges?

2. With a tightening of budgets for projects, what is the significance of using project management software to better understand the utilization of resources among projects?

3. Should all projects be planned using a project management software tool?

SOURCES:
Shoeniger, E. "From Chaos to Competency." *Projectsatwork*. June 17, 2004.
Kanaracus, C. "Majority of ERP Software Projects Still Over Time and Budget, Survey Finds." *CIO Magazine*. March 4, 2014.
Birkelbach, J. "Scheduling 101: Credibility." *Projectsatwork*. August 22, 2011.
Westland, J. "Project Management: 4 Ways to Manage Your Budget." *CIO Magazine*. June 23, 2011.

Poor Baseline Plans Lead to Federal Waste of IT

According to a survey of 104 U.S. government IT executives, an estimated $12 billion was wasted on IT projects in 2007. The study, called *A Cracked Foundation*, was conducted by Price Systems, a provider of program affordability management solutions.

The study suggests that 46 percent of the failed (cancelled, over-budget) projects could have been avoided if project baseline plans were more realistic, thus saving an estimated $5.5 billion annually. According to Larry Reagan, a vice president at Price Systems, "Agencies require stronger foundations upon which to base government IT program structures in order to avoid the continued rate of collapse. Better baselines can help fill in these structural cracks - arming agency personnel with the tools, training, and historical data necessary to build projects on solid rock." The study found that only 18 percent of the government IT executives expressed confidence in their IT budgets, with about 69 percent reporting that they usually begin to notice problems about halfway through their projects.

In addition, the study also reports:

- 78 percent believe they have inadequate cost estimating training.

- 77 percent believe they have inadequate risk identification and management training.

- 73 percent believe they have inadequate initial baseline development training.

- 67 percent believe they have inadequate project management training.

- 60 percent believe they do not have the necessary methodologies to collect historical data to produce realistic estimates when a baseline changes.

- 58 percent believe they do not have the necessary historical data to produce realistic estimates.

- 54 percent believe that they have inadequate tools to manage the cost estimating, control, and reporting processes for IT programs.

The respondents contend that the main reasons why projects are over budget include poor project management, scope creep, lack of proper baselines, and late understanding of risk. Moreover, the IT executives surveyed reported that the most important tool for ensuring that IT projects are on budget is a fully coordinated baseline followed by training, project management tools, and defined risk management.

Similarly, the IT executives identified schedule management, cost management, and risk management as being the most challenging baseline elements for their organizations. The study also reports why project managers fail to establish effective baselines. More specifically, 64 percent attributed this to a lack of personnel to perform the functions effectively, 47 percent stated a lack of training, 47 percent stated that timelines were too short, and 34 percent claimed that projects teams were not given appropriate tools and data for establishing accurate baseline plans up front.

Reagan claims, "In these days of heightened federal fiscal accountability, our government is not in a position to waste billions of dollars that could be redirected toward any number of programs. Supported by stronger structural foundations—including assigning responsibility for program affordability management; integrating cost estimating, project control, and knowledge management into a single team; providing effective training and certification; implementing a methodology for regularly scheduled, independent baseline reviews; and establishing the consistent use of a reusable knowledge-based framework—better baselines can empower agencies to achieve project and program objectives, effectively enabling them to better deliver upon their missions."

1. Do you agree that improving IT project baseline plans will help avoid failed projects?

2. Consider Larry Reagan's statement in the last paragraph. Do you agree with his assessment? Is there anything you would add that could be done to improve project success, not only for the federal government but also for any type of organization?

Sources: Reagan, L. "A Cracked Foundation: A Critical Look at the Role of Baselining in Government IT Project Management." 2006. Accessed from www.pricesystems.com.

Young, R.W. "Price Systems, Poor Baselines Cause of Federal IT Waste, Study Finds." *Projectsatwork*. November 30, 2006.
Smith, A. "A Cracked Foundation." *Projectsatwork*. January 25, 2007.

Project Runway (10–28)

Atlanta's Hartsfield-Jackson International Airport is one of the world's busiest, with an average of 2,500 daily departures and arrivals. In 2003, Dwight Pullen, a civil engineer for H. J. Russel & Company in Atlanta, Georgia, was named project manager for a $1.28 billion construction project to build a fifth runway. With only 13 years' experience, a friend joked that Pullen was the youngest person in the country to manage a billion-dollar project.

The 9,000 foot expansion runway project was built over a two-lane highway, Interstate 285, which loops around the city of Atlanta. This included building a 1,264-foot tunnel for the highway and building the runway on top of the tunnel to accommodate large planes like the Boeing 747 and Airbus A-380 that can weigh up to 1 million pounds. The project was expected to provide a financial boom that would save the airline industry an estimated $5 million a week in delay costs and was considered a project of national significance. Pullen asserted that completing the project on time and on budget was key for all stakeholders associated with the project. The project was completed 11 days ahead of schedule at $100 million under budget.

One of the biggest challenge of the project was dealing with the various stakeholders, which included Atlanta city council members, airport executives, the Federal Aviation Administration, the Georgia Department of Transportation, environmental groups, contractors, engineers, and architects. This required building and maintaining strong relationships with all of them. Although Pullen said that he didn't have to make best friends or go golfing with these people, he relied on these relationships to help with negotiations and to keep his team focused on milestones.

The project plan entailed about as much time in the planning phase as it did in the construction phase. Moreover, the design phase was the shortest phase in the master project schedule and included more than 15,000 scheduled activities. These activities were input into a project management software tool called Primavera®. Pullen contends that the work breakdown structure was critical to this project because it served as a "common language" for everyone working on the project and a best practice that allowed him to be successful in analyzing, forecasting, scheduling, and base-lining.

Pullen believes one of his keys to success was the idea of project celebrations to keep morale up and mark the completion of milestones along the way. For example, he instituted cake and ice cream parties for "employee of the quarter," project team awards, groundbreakings, and safety records. At the end of the successful project, the project team had dinner at the end of the runway while the lights were on. In addition, the team rode in the company's trucks and raced down the two-mile runway similar to a plane taking off. The project team also got to take a ten-minute flight around the city on a 767 that took off and landed on the new runway.

1. What is the importance of using project management software for managing a large-scale project?
2. A project will not fail because of a project manager's inability to use a particular project management software tool. What is the significance of relationships among the various project stakeholders and the project's schedule and budget?

SOURCES:

Klein, K. "A Runway Success." *Projectsatwork*. April 5, 2007.

Credeur, J. "New Runway Expected to Cut Hartsfield Delays in Half." *Atlanta Business Chronicle*. May 23, 2005.

Primavera Systems, Inc. "Primavera® Helps Atlanta Airport Deliver First Milestone of 15 Year Program Early and Under Budget." *PR Newswire*. March 7, 2007.

Hoffman, T. "Midproject Handoff at Hartsfield-Jackson Airport." *Computerworld*. August 13, 2007.

BIBLIOGRAPHY

1. DeCarlo, D. *eXtreme Project Management: Using Leadership, Principles, and Tools to Deliver Value in the Face of Volatility*. San Franciso, CA: Jossey-Bass, 2004.
2. Goldratt, E. M. *Critical Chain*. Barrington, MA: The North River Press, 1997.
3. Haugan, G. T. *Project Planning and Scheduling*. Vienna, VA: Management Concepts, Inc., 2002.
4. Kinsella, S. M. "Activity-Based Costing: Does it Warrant Inclusion in a Guide to the Project Management Body of Knowledge (PMBOK Guide)?" *Project Management Journal*, 2002, Vol. 3, 49–55.

Managing Project Risk

CHAPTER OBJECTIVES

Chapter 7 focuses on project risk management. After studying this chapter, you should be able to:

- Describe the project risk management planning framework introduced in this chapter.
- Apply risk identification tools and understand the causes, effects, and the integrative nature of project risks.
- Apply several qualitative and quantitative analysis techniques that can be used to prioritize and analyze various project risks.
- Describe the various risk strategies, such as insurance, avoidance, or mitigation.
- Describe risk monitoring and control.
- Describe risk evaluation in terms of how the entire risk management process should be evaluated in order to learn from experience and to identify best practices.

INTRODUCTION

In the previous chapter you learned how to develop a baseline project plan. This project plan is grounded upon a number of estimates that reflect our understanding of the current situation, the information available, and the assumptions we must make. The fact that we must estimate implies a degree of uncertainty in predicting the outcome of future events. Although no one can predict the future with 100 percent accuracy, having a solid foundation, in terms of processes, tools, and techniques, can increase our confidence in these estimates.

Unfortunately, things seldom go according to plan because the project must adapt to a dynamic environment. Project risk management focuses on identifying, analyzing, and developing strategies for responding to project risk efficiently and effectively (1). However, keep in mind that the goal of risk management is not to avoid risks at all costs, but to make well-informed decisions as to what risks are worth taking and to respond to those risks in an appropriate manner.

Project risk management also provides an early warning system for impending problems that need to be addressed or resolved. Although risk has a certain negative connotation, project stakeholders should be vigilant in identifying opportunities.

It is unfortunate that many projects do not follow a formal risk management approach (1). Because of their failure to plan for the unexpected, many organizations find themselves in a state of perpetual crisis characterized by an inability to make effective and timely decisions. Many people call this approach *crisis management* or *firefighting* because the project stakeholders take a reactive approach or only address the project risks after they have become problems. Several common mistakes in managing project risk include:

- *Not understanding the benefits of risk management*—Often the project sponsor or client demands results. Sponsors or clients may not care how the project team achieves its goal and objectives—just as long as it does. The project manager and project team may rely on aggressive risk taking with little understanding of the impact of their decisions. Therefore, it is important to create a risk-aware culture committed to managing risk (2). Conversely, project risks may also be optimistically ignored when, in reality, these risks may become real and significant threats to the success of the project. Unfortunately, risks are often schedule delays, quality issues, and budget overruns just waiting to happen (3).

- *Not providing adequate time for risk management*—Risk management and the ensuing processes should not be viewed as an add-on to the project planning process, but should grow as a capable and mature process integrated throughout all projects (4). The best time to assess and plan for project risk, in fact, is at the earliest stages of the project when uncertainty for a project is the highest. Catastrophic problems or surprises may arise that require more resources to correct than would have been spent earlier avoiding them (5). It is better to reduce the likelihood of a risk or be capable of responding to a particular risk as soon as possible in order to limit the risk's impact on the project's schedule and budget.

- *Not identifying and assessing risk using a standardized approach*—Not having a standardized approach to risk management can overlook both threats and opportunities. Consequently, more time and resources will be expended on problems that could have been avoided; opportunities will be missed; decisions will be made without complete understanding or information; the overall likelihood of success is reduced; and catastrophic problems or surprises may occur without advanced warning. Moreover, the project team may find itself in a perpetual crisis mode (6). Over time, crisis situations can have a detrimental effect on team morale and productivity.

Therefore, effective and successful project risk management requires (1):

- *Commitment by all stakeholders*—To be successful, project risk management requires a commitment by all project stakeholders. In particular, the project sponsor or client, senior management, the governance committee, the project manager, and the project team must all be committed. For many organizations, a new environment and commitment to following organizational and project processes may be required. For many managers, the first impulse may be to shortcut or sidestep many of these processes at the first sign that the project is in trouble. A firm commitment to a risk management approach will not allow these impulses to override the project management and risk management processes that the organization has in place.

- *Stakeholder responsibility*—It is important that each risk have an owner. This owner should be someone who will be involved in the project, who will take the responsibility to monitor the project in order to identify any new or increasing risks, and who will make regular reports to the project sponsor, client, or governance committee. The position may also require the risk owner to ensure that adequate resources be available for managing and responding to a particular project risk. Ultimately, however, the project manager is responsible for ensuring that appropriate risk processes and plans are in place.

- *Different risks for different types of projects*—A study that looked at IT project risks found that patterns of risk are different across different types of projects (1). The implication is that each project has its own unique risk considerations. To attempt to manage all projects and risks the same way may spell disaster.

The PMBOK® Guide (7) defines project risk as:

an uncertain event or condition that, if it occurs, has a positive or negative effect on one or more project objectives such as scope, schedule, cost, and quality. (p. 310)

The *PMBOK® Guide* definition provides an important starting point for understanding risk. First, project risk arises from uncertainty. This uncertainty comes from our attempt to predict the future based on estimates, assumptions, and limited information. Although project risk has a downside resulting from unexpected problems or threats, project risk management must also focus on positive events or opportunities. Therefore, it is important that we understand what those events are and how they may impact the project beyond its objectives. It is also important that we understand not only the nature of project risks but also how those risks interact and impact other aspects of the project throughout the life of a project.

Effective risk management requires a systematic process and a commitment to follow that process by the project's stakeholders. Figure 7.1 provides a framework that outlines six steps for managing project risk. Each of these steps will be discussed in more detail throughout the chapter; however, the six steps include:

1. Create a Risk Plan
2. Identify Risks
3. Analyze Risks
4. Develop Risk Strategies
5. Monitor and Control Risks
6. Respond and Evaluate Risk

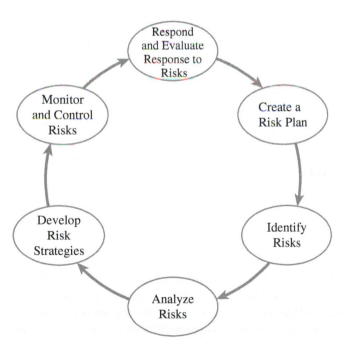

Figure 7.1 Project Risk Management Processes

CREATE A RISK PLAN

Creating a risk plan is the first step and begins with having a firm commitment to the entire risk management approach from all project stakeholders. In addition, risk management should align throughout the organization by including all projects, the entire project portfolio, and, where one exists, the project management office (PMO) (8). This commitment ensures that adequate resources will be in place to plan properly for and manage the various risks of the project.

Resources may include time, people, and technology. Stakeholders also must be committed to the process of identifying, analyzing, and responding to threats and opportunities. Too often plans are disregarded at the first sign of trouble, and instinctive reactions to situations can lead to perpetual crisis management. In addition to commitment, risk planning also focuses on preparation. It is important that resources, processes, and tools be in place to adequately plan the activities for project risk management. Systematic preparation and planning can help minimize adverse effects on the project while taking advantage of opportunities as they arise.

For example, Mozilla abruptly announced the cancellation of a touchscreen browser for Windows 8 just four days before its planned release. The version of its popular Web browser, Firefox, was called Metro and was a two year project that began in March 2012. The company tests the viability and quality of new products by allowing people to download prerelease versions. While millions of people have downloaded the desktop version, only thousands downloaded the touchscreen version. Without sufficient testing, Mozilla became concerned that too many problems, issues, or bugs would be discovered by its customers. Aside from the low demand for the product, too much time and money would be needed to redesign and test the browser to make the investment worthwhile (9).

IDENTIFY RISKS

Once commitment has been obtained and preparations have been made, the next step entails identifying the various risks to the project. Both threats and opportunities must be identified. When identifying threats to a project, they must be identified clearly so that the true problem, not just a symptom, is addressed. Moreover, the causes and effects of each risk must be understood so that effective strategies and responses can be made.

Risk identification deals with identifying and creating a list of threats and opportunities that may impact the project's measurable organizational value (MOV) and/or project objectives. Each risk and its characteristics should be documented to provide a basis for the overall risk management plan.

A Project Risk Identification Framework

Identifying and understanding the risks that will impact a project is not always a straightforward task. Many risks can affect a project in different ways and during different phases of the project life cycle. Therefore, the process and techniques used to identify risks must include a broad view of the project and attempt to understand a particular risk's cause and impact among the various project components.

Figure 7.2 provides a framework for identifying and understanding the sources and impacts of project risks. At the core of the project risk framework is the project's MOV. The next layer of the framework includes the project objectives in terms of scope, quality, schedule, and budget. Although these objectives are not by themselves sufficient conditions for success, together they do play a critical role in supporting the MOV.

The third layer focuses on the sources of project risk. Risks can arise as a result of the various people or stakeholders associated with a project, legal considerations, the processes (project and product), the environment, the technology, the organization, the product, and a catchall category called *other*.

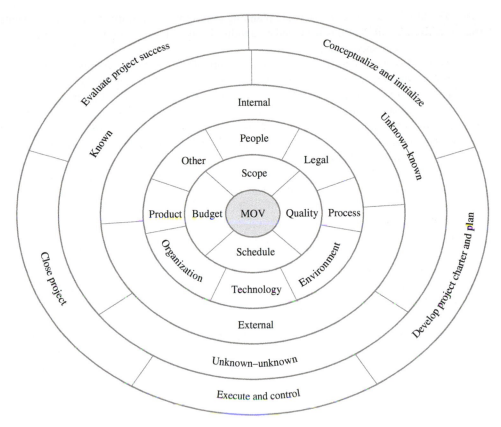

Figure 7.2 The Project Risk Identification Framework

The next layer focuses on whether the sources of risk are internal or external to the project. It is important to make this distinction because a project manager is responsible and accountable for all project risks internal to the project. For example, if a project team member is not adequately trained to use a particular methodology, then the project's objectives—scope, schedule, budget, and quality—may be impacted. In turn, this lack of training may inhibit the project from achieving its MOV. Once this project risk has been identified along with its impact, the project manager can devise a strategy to avoid or mitigate the risk by sending this particular project team member to training or by assigning certain critical tasks to a more experienced or skillful team member.

On the other hand, a project manager may not be responsible for external risks. For example, a consultant leading a project would not be responsible or accountable if the project were cancelled because the client organization went bankrupt. However, this would still be a critical risk to the project.

The distinction between internal and external risks is not always clear. For example, even though a particular hardware or software vendor may be external to the project, the project manager may still be responsible if that vendor is unable to deliver required technology resources. If the project manager chose that particular vendor, he or she would then be responsible or accountable for that risk. In short, a project manager will (or should) have control over internal risks, but not external risks. That distinction does not mean the project manager can ignore external risks. These risks can have a significant impact on the project, as well as on the project manager's employment.

The fifth layer of the project risk management framework includes three different types of risks: **known risks, known–unknown risks, and unknown–unknown risks** (3). *Known risks* are events that are going to occur. In short, these events are like death and taxes—they will happen and there is no uncertainty about it. However, because we know that they will occur, we can do something about it like take out life insurance or do estate planning to minimize the impact when these events happen. In this case, the *known* (death) is followed by another *known* (the amount of money your heirs will receive from your life insurance policy).

On the other hand, *known–unknowns* are identifiable uncertainty. For example, if you own a home or rent an apartment, you know that you will receive a bill next month for the electricity you use. If you have received bills in the past, you have an idea of what to expect based on whether you feel that your usage was consistent with how much electricity you used in previous months. Although you know the past amount for these bills, the precise amount you will owe the utility company will be unknown until you receive the actual bill. In this case, the *known* is that you will receive a utility bill, and the *unknown* is for the amount you will have to pay.

Lastly, *unknown–unknown* risks are residual risks that reflect what we don't know. For example, the possibility of a natural disaster like a snowstorm, earthquake, and so forth can have a major impact on the project's schedule and budget if the project team members are unable to do their jobs. In this case, the *unknown* is whether a natural disaster will occur (it may or may not) and is then followed by another *unknown,* which is the impact on the project (minor or major). Will the project's work be interrupted for a day? A week? Or a month? Unknown–unknown risks are really just a way to remind us that there may be a few risks remaining even after we think we have identified them all. In general, these are the risks that are easier to identify after they occur. For risks associated with natural or human-made disasters, a *disaster recovery* and *project continuity plan* could be created and communicated to all of the project stakeholders.

The outer layer provides a time element in terms of the project life cycle. It may help us determine or identify when risks may occur, but remind us that they may change over the life of the project. Although risk management is an important concern at the beginning of a project, the project risk management framework reminds us that we must be vigilant for opportunities and problems throughout the project life cycle.

APPLYING THE PROJECT RISK IDENTIFICATION FRAMEWORK To better understand how to apply the project risk identification framework summarized in Figure 7.2, let's use an example. A consulting firm has been hired by a client to develop a data warehouse that will include a business intelligence component to identify and better serve its more loyal customers. The project is still in the early stages, with the baseline project plan and charter almost finalized. Unfortunately, the client has been hit hard by a lawsuit and is ordered to pay significant legal fees and fines. The client is now strapped and must cut costs to survive. Not surprisingly, a number of the client's managers are suggesting that the data warehouse project be cancelled. However, due to the expected value the project can bring to this organization, it is decided that the product's scope will be cut in half in order to create two projects—one that will provide minimum functionality and another project that will add the remaining features and functions once the company becomes more financially stable. The contract between the consulting firm and the client will be renegotiated. The project's new scope will be reduced in order to reduce the budget and schedule as well. The risk faced by this team could be defined as:

- A threat that occurred in the *planning phase* of the project.
- It was an *unknown–unknown* risk because it was identified after it occurred and, therefore, caught the project team off guard.
- It was an *external risk*, and the project manager and project team should not be held responsible for the economic downturn experienced by the client.
- The sources of risk to the project include *environment* (economic), *organizational* (the client), and *people* (if you would like to argue that management was responsible for this problematic event).
- The impact on the project is significant because it affects the project's *scope, schedule,* and *budget.* Since the consulting firm should renegotiate the contract based on a trimmed scope,

we can assume that *quality* may not be an issue. But if the client's management insisted on maintaining the original scope, schedule, and budget, chances are good that quality would become an issue, especially if, for example, the scheduled testing time had to be shortened in order to meet the scheduled deadline.

■ It is likely that the project's *MOV* would change as well because the project team would not complete the scope as originally planned. A revised MOV would determine the revised scope, schedule, and budget for the project.

This example shows how a risk can be understood *after* it occurs. The framework can also be used to proactively identify project risks. For example, a project team could begin with the project phases defined in the outer core of the framework. Using the project's work breakdown structure (WBS) and the individual work packages, the team could identify the risks for each of the work packages under the various project phases. Again, it is important that both threats and opportunities be identified. These risks could be classified as either *known* risks or *known–unknown* risks. The category of unknown–unknown risks should serve as a reminder to keep asking the question, what other threats or opportunities have we not thought about? Hopefully, the project team will do a more thorough job of identifying risks early in the project and reduce the likelihood of being surprised later.

The risks identified by the team can then be categorized as *external* or *internal* to the project. The internal risks are the direct responsibility of the project manager or team, while external risks may be outside their control. Regardless, both external and internal risks must be monitored and responses should be formulated.

The next step involves identifying the various sources of risk. Instead of trying to neatly categorize a particular risk, it may be more important to understand how the sources of risk are interrelated with each other. In addition, it may be a situation where precise definitions get in the way of progress. Instead of arguing or worrying about the exact source of a particular risk, it is more important that the stakeholders understand the complex nature of a risk. Each risk-source category may mean different things to different stakeholders. Depending on the project, the stakeholders should be free to develop their own definitions and interpretations for each risk-source category. They should also feel free to add categories, as needed.

After identifying the nature and characteristics of a particular risk, the project team can assess how a particular risk will impact the project. At this point, the team should focus on the project objectives that would be impacted if a particular risk occurred and, in turn, whether the project's MOV would be impacted. Later on, these risks can be assessed to determine how the objectives will be impacted.

The example shows how, working from the outside and then inward toward the center of the model, risks can be identified using the project risk framework. This procedure works well as a first pass and when using the project plan or WBS as a source of input. Many threats and opportunities may, however, be overlooked when relying only on the WBS.

The project team could start with the inner core of the risk framework and work outward. For example, the project team could identify how the MOV may be affected in terms of threats or opportunities that impact the project's scope, schedule, budget, or quality. Working away from the center, the team could identify possible sources of risk and then categorize whether the risk is internal or external, known, known–unknown, or unknown–unknown (i.e., did we miss something?), and when during the project life cycle this particular risk might occur.

Other Tools and Techniques

Identifying risks is not always easy. Risks tend to be interrelated, and identifying each and every risk may not be possible or economically feasible. People may not want to admit that potential problems are possible for fear of appearing incompetent. As a result, stakeholders may deny or downplay a particular risk. Still, people and organizations have different tolerances for risk, and what may be considered a normal risk for one stakeholder or organization may be a real concern for another. So, the stakeholders may concentrate on a particular risk (that may or may not occur) at the expense of other risks that could have the same impact on the project.

It is, therefore, important that the project manager and team guide the risk management process. Risk identification should include the project team and other stakeholders who are familiar with the project's MOV and project objectives. Using one or more of the following tools, the project risk framework introduced earlier in this section can provide direction for identifying the threats and opportunities associated with the project:

- *Learning cycles*—The concept of learning cycles was introduced in an earlier chapter. The project team and stakeholders can use this technique, whereby they identify facts (what they know), assumptions (what they think they know), and question to be answered (things to find out), to identify various risks. Using these three categories, the group can create an action plan to test assumptions and conduct research about various risks. Based on the team's findings, both risks and lessons learned can then be documented.

- *Brainstorming*—Brainstorming is a less structured activity than learning cycles. Here, the team could use the project risk framework and the WBS to identify risks (i.e., threats and opportunities) starting with the phases of the project life cycle and working toward the framework's core or MOV or working from the MOV outward toward the project phases. The key to brainstorming is encouraging contributions from everyone in the group. Ideas must be generated without being evaluated. Once ideas are generated by the group as a whole, only then should they can be discussed and evaluated by the group.

- *Nominal group technique (NGT)*—The NGT is a structured technique for identifying risks that attempts to balance and increase participation (10).

    The NGT Process:

    1. Each individual silently writes her or his ideas on a piece of paper.
    2. Each idea is then written on a board or flip chart one at a time in a round-robin fashion until each individual has listed all of his or her ideas.
    3. The group then discusses and clarifies each of the ideas.
    4. Each individual then silently ranks and prioritizes the ideas.
    5. The group then discusses the rankings and priorities of the ideas.
    6. Each individual ranks and prioritizes the ideas again.
    7. The rankings and prioritizations are then summarized for the group.

- *Delphi technique*—If the time and resources are available, a group of experts can be assembled without ever having to meet face to face. Using the Delphi technique, a group of experts are asked to identify potential risks or to discuss the impact of a particular risk. Initially, in order to reduce the potential for bias, the experts are not known to each other. Their responses are collected and made available anonymously to each other. The experts are then asked to provide another response based on the previous round of responses. The process continues until a consensus exists. The advantage of using the Delphi technique is the potential for getting an insightful view into a threat or opportunity; but, the process takes time and may consume a good portion of the project resources.

- *Interviewing*—Another useful technique for identifying and understanding the nature of project risks is to interview various project stakeholders. This technique can prove useful for determining alternative points of view; but, the quality of the information derived depends heavily on the skills of the interviewer and the interviewees, as well as on the interview process itself.

- *Checklists*—Checklists provide a structured tool for identifying risks that have occurred in the past. They allow the current project team to learn from past mistakes or to identify risks that

Table 7.1 Example of a Project Checklist

Risk Checklist

✓ Funding for the project has been secured.

✓ Funding for the project is sufficient.

✓ Funding for the project has been approved by senior management.

✓ The project team has the requisite skills to complete the project.

✓ The project has adequate manpower to complete the project.

✓ The project charter and project plan have been approved by senior management or the project sponsor.

✓ The project's goal is realistic and achievable.

✓ The project's schedule is realistic and achievable.

✓ The project's scope has been clearly defined.

✓ Processes for scope changes have been clearly defined.

---

are known to a particular organization or industry. One problem with checklists is that they can lead to a false sense of security—that is, if we check off each of the risks on the list, then we will have covered everything. Table 7.1 provides an example of items that may be included in a project risk checklist.

Figure 7.3 SWOT Analysis—Strengths, Weaknesses, Opportunities, and Threats

- *SWOT analysis*—SWOT stands for Strengths, Weaknesses, Opportunities, and Threats. Brainstorming, NGT, or the Delphi technique could be used to identify and understand the nature of project risks by categorizing risks using the framework illustrated in Figure 7.3. The usefulness of using SWOT analysis is that it allows the project team to identify threats and opportunities as well as their nature in terms of the project or organizational strengths and weaknesses.

- *Cause-and-effect diagrams*—The most widely known and used cause-and-effect diagram is the fishbone, or Ishikawa, diagram developed by Kaoru Ishikawa to analyze the causes of poor quality in manufacturing systems. The diagram can also be used for understanding the causes or factors of a particular risk as well as its effects. An example of an Ishikawa diagram is illustrated in Figure 7.4. The diagram shows the possible causes and effects of a key member of the team leaving the project. This technique itself can be used individually or in groups by taking the following steps:

1. Identify the risk in terms of a threat or an opportunity.
2. Identify the main factors that can cause the risk to occur.
3. Identify detailed factors for each of the main factors.
4. Continue refining the diagram until satisfied that the diagram is complete.

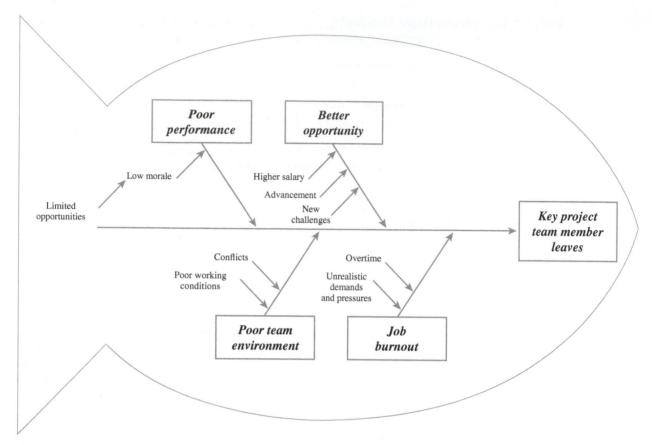

Figure 7.4 A Fishbone or Cause-and-Effect Diagram

- *Past projects*—One of the themes in this text has been the integration of knowledge management to support the project management processes. Lessons learned from past projects can provide insight and best practices for identifying and understanding the nature of project risks. The usefulness of these lessons takes time and a commitment by the organization and project team to develop a base of knowledge from past projects. The value of this knowledge base will increase as the base does, allowing project teams to learn from the mistakes and successes of others.

ANALYZE RISK

The framework and tools introduced in the previous section provide a beginning for identifying and understanding the nature of project risk. The next step requires that those risks be analyzed to determine what threats or opportunities require attention or a response. This provides a systematic approach for evaluating the risks that the project stakeholders identify. The purpose of this is to determine each identified risk's probability and impact on the project and then to prioritize risks so that an effective risk strategy can be formulated. In short, which risks require a response? To a great degree, this will be determined by the project stakeholders' tolerances to risk.

There are two basic approaches to analyzing and assessing project risk. The first approach is more qualitative in nature because it includes subjective assessments based on experience or intuition. Quantitative analysis, on the other hand, is based on statistical techniques. Each approach has its own strengths and weaknesses when dealing with uncertainty, so a combination of qualitative and quantitative methods provides valuable insight when analyzing project risk.

Qualitative Approaches

Qualitative risk analysis focuses on a subjective analysis of risks based on a project stakeholder's experience or judgment. Although the techniques for analyzing project risk qualitatively can be conducted by individual stakeholders, it may be more effective if done by a group. This group process allows each stakeholder to hear other points of view and supports open communication among the various stakeholders. As a result, a broader view of the threats, opportunities, issues, and points of view can be discussed and understood.

■ *Expected Value*—The concept of **expected value** provides the basis for both qualitative and quantitative risk analysis. Expected value is really an average, or mean, that takes into account both the probability and impact of various events or outcome. For example, let's assume that a project manager of a consulting firm would like to determine the expected return or payoff associated with several possible outcomes or events. These outcomes or events, in terms of possible schedule scenarios, determine the return or profit the project will provide to the consulting firm. The project manager believes each outcome has a probability of occurring and an associated payoff. The project manager's subjective beliefs are summarized in a **payoff table** in Table 7.2.

As you can see from Table 7.2, the project manager believes that the project has a relatively small chance of finishing 20 days early or 20 days late. The payoff for finishing the project early is quite high, but there appears to be a penalty for completing the project late. As a result, the expected value or return to the consulting firm is $88,000. Since each event is mutually exclusive (i.e., only one of the five events can occur), the probabilities must sum to 100 percent.

■ *Decision Trees*—Similar to a payoff table, a **decision tree** provides a visual, or graphical, view of various decisions and outcomes. Similar to a flowchart, each branch represents an option and outcome. To create a decision tree:

1. Start with a decision that needs to made.

2. From this decision, branch out toward the right with an option (decision) and a result (outcome).

3. Continue doing this until you have drawn out as many of the possible decisions and outcomes as you can.

4. Multiply the probability of each decision by the financial cost or benefit of the outcome.

5. Add together the probability multiplied by the financial outcome in the previous step for each branch of the decision tree.

Table 7.2 Expected Value of a Payoff Table

Schedule Risk	A Probability	B Payoff (in thousands)	A · B Prob · Payoff (in thousands)
Project completed 20 days early	5%	$ 200	$ 10
Project completed 10 days early	20%	$ 150	$ 30
Project completed on schedule	50%	$ 100	$ 50
Project completed 10 days late	20%	$ —	$ —
Project completed 20 days late	5%	$ (40)	$ (2)
	100%		$ 88

Let's see how this works using an example. Assume that a project is going to overrun its schedule and budget. The project manager is contemplating reducing the time allocated to testing the application system as a way of bringing the project back within its original schedule and budget objectives.

The project manager, then, is faced with a decision about whether the project team should conduct a full systems test as planned or shorten the time originally allocated to testing. The cost of a full test will be $10,000; but, the project manager believes that there is a 95 percent chance the project will meet the quality standards set forth by the client. In this case, no additional rework will be required and no additional costs will be incurred. Since there is only a 5 percent chance the system will not meet the standards, the project manager believes that it would only require a small amount of rework to meet the quality standards. In this case, it will cost about $2,000 in resources to bring the system within standards.

On the other hand, the shortened test will cost less than the full test and may be an opportunity to bring the project back on track. However, if the project team limits the testing of the system, it will very likely lower the probability of the system meeting the quality standards. Moreover, a failure will require more rework and cost more to fix than if these problems were addressed during a full testing of the system. As you can see from Figure 7.5, a limited testing of the system will cost only $8,000, but the chances of the system failing to meet the quality standards increase. Moreover, the time and cost to complete the rework will be higher.

Even though the project manager still has a difficult decision to make, it now becomes a more informed decision. If the project team continues with the testing activities as planned, there is a very good chance that the system will not require a great deal of rework. On the other hand, reducing the time to test the system is more of a gamble. Although there is a 30 percent

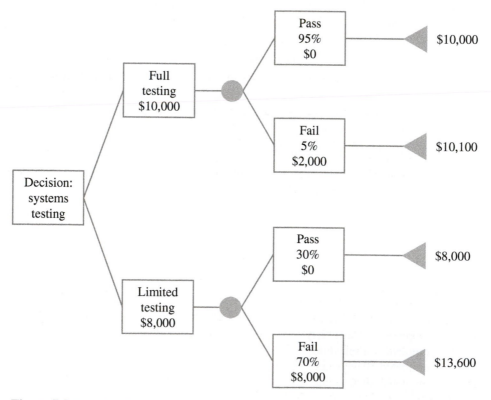

Figure 7.5 Decision Tree Analysis

Table 7.3 Project Risk Impact Table

Risk (Threats)	0–100% Probability	0–10 Impact	P · I Score
Key project team member leaves project	40%	4	1.6
Client unable to define scope and requirements	50%	6	3.0
Client experiences financial problems	10%	9	0.9
Response time not acceptable to users/client	80%	6	4.8
Technology does not integrate with existing application	60%	7	4.2
Functional manager deflects resources away from project	20%	3	0.6
Client unable to obtain licensing agreements	5%	7	0.4

chance the limited testing will save both time and money, there is a high probability that the system will not pass or meet the quality standards. As a result, the required rework will make the project even later and more over its budget. Which is the correct decision? That depends on the risk tolerances of the stakeholders, but at least now they have a better understanding of the probabilities and effects of the risk to make a better informed decision.

- *Risk Impact Table*—A **risk impact table** is a useful tool for analyzing and prioritizing various project risks. Let's use another example. Suppose a project manager has identified seven risks that could impact a particular project. The left-hand column of Table 7.3 lists the possible risks that were identified using the project risk framework illustrated in Figure 7.2. For simplicity, we will focus only on risks in terms of threats, but opportunities could be analyzed and assessed using the same technique.

    The second column lists the subjective probabilities for each of the risks. In this case, the probabilities do not sum to 100 percent because the risks are not mutually exclusive. In other words, none, some, or all of the risk events could occur. A probability of zero indicates that a probability has absolutely no chance of occurring, while a probability of 100 percent indicates an absolute certainty that the event will occur. The next column provides the potential impact associated with the risk event occurring. This also is a subjective estimate based on a score from 0 to 10, with zero being no impact and ten having a very high or significant impact on the project.

    Once a probability and an impact are assigned to each risk event, they are multiplied together to come up with a risk score. Although this score is based on the subjective opinions of the project stakeholders, it does provide a mechanism for determining which risks should be monitored and which risks may require a response. Once a risk score is computed for each risk, the risks can be ranked or prioritized as in Table 7.4.

Table 7.4 Risk Rankings

Risk (Threats)	Score	Ranking
Response time not acceptable to users/client	4.8	1
Technology does not integrate with existing application	4.2	2
Client unable to define scope and requirements	3.0	3
Key project team member leaves project	1.6	4
Client experiences financial problems	0.9	5
Functional manager deflects resources away from project	0.6	6
Client unable to obtain licensing agreements	0.4	7

Quantitative Approaches

Quantitative approaches to project risk analysis include mathematical or statistical techniques that allow us to model a particular risk situation. At the heart of many of these models is the probability distribution. Probability distributions can be *discrete* or *continuous*.

DISCRETE PROBABILITY DISTRIBUTIONS   *Discrete probability distributions* use only integer or whole numbers where fractional values are not allowed or do not make sense. For example, flipping a coin would allow for only two outcomes—heads or tails. If you wanted to find the probability of flipping a fair coin into the air and having the outcome of the coin landing with the heads side up, just divide the number of favorable events (heads) by the number of total outcomes (heads or tails). This results in a one-half, or 50 percent, probability of the coin coming up heads. Because these events (heads or tails) are mutually exclusive and exhaustive (one and only one of these events will occur), the probability of tails is 50 percent (i.e., 100 percent − 50 percent = 50 percent). Probabilities must be positive and the sum of all of the event probabilities must sum to one.

If you were to flip a coin repeatedly a few hundred times and then record the outcomes, you would end up with a distribution similar to Figure 7.6.

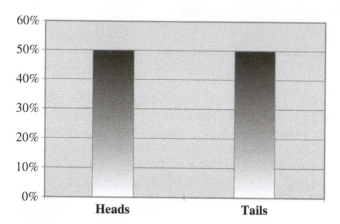

Figure 7.6 Binomial Probability Distribution

CONTINUOUS PROBABILITY DISTRIBUTIONS   **Continuous probability distributions** are useful for developing risk analysis models when an event has an infinite number of possible values within a stated range. Although in theory there are an infinite number of probability distributions, we will discuss three of the more common continuous probability distributions used in modeling risk. These include the **normal distribution**, the **PERT distribution**, and the **triangular (TRIANG) distribution**. A quick overview shows how these distributions may be used in the WBS or to develop models for simulation or sensitivity analysis.

Normal Distribution—One of the most common continuous probability distributions is the normal distribution, or bell curve. Figure 7.7 provides an example of a normal distribution.

The normal distribution has the following properties:

- The distribution's shape is determined by its mean (μ) and standard deviation (σ). In Figure 7.7, this particular distribution has a mean of 0 and a standard deviation of 1. Other combinations of means and standard deviations will result in normal distributions with shapes that are either flatter or taller.

- Probability is associated with the area under the curve. Therefore, the total area under the curve and the baseline that extends from negative infinity (−∞) to positive infinity (+∞) is 100 percent. Subsequently, to find the probability of an event occurring between any two points on the baseline, just find the area between those two points under the curve. This is done by standardizing a given value for X using the formula: $z = (X - \mu) \div \sigma$ to obtain a z score. A table with the various z scores is then used to compute the probability for the area between any two z scores.

- Since the normal distribution is symmetrical around the mean, an outcome that falls between −∞ and the mean, μ, would have the same probability of falling between the mean, μ, and +∞ (i.e., 50 percent).

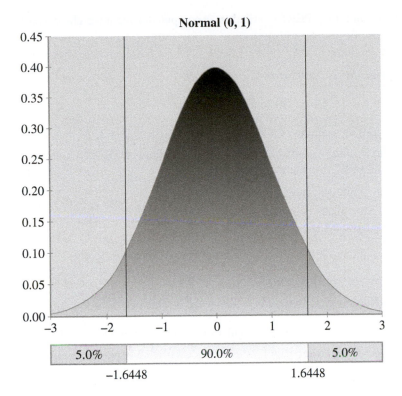

Figure 7.7 A Normal Distribution with a Mean = 0 and a Standard Deviation = 1

- Because the distribution is symmetrical, the following probability rules of thumb apply:
  - About 68 percent of all the values will fall between $\pm 1\sigma$ of the mean.
  - About 95 percent of all the values will fall between $\pm 2\sigma$ of the mean.
  - About 99 percent of all the values will fall between $\pm 3\sigma$ of the mean.

Therefore, if we know or assume that the probability of a risk event follows a normal distribution, we can predict an outcome with some confidence. For example, let's say that a particular project task has a mean duration of ten days. Moreover, over time we have been able to determine that this particular task has a standard deviation of two days. The mean tells us that if we were to complete this particular task over and over again, we would expect to complete this task, on average, in ten days. If we always completed the task in ten days, there would be no variability and the standard deviation would be zero. If, however, the task sometimes took anywhere between six and fifteen days to complete, we would have some variability, and the standard deviation would be a value greater than zero. The more variability we have, the larger the computed standard deviation, and the greater the inherent risk of the task being completed if the mean or average is used as an estimate.

Using the rules of thumb described above, we could estimate, for example, that we would be about 95 percent certain that the project's task would be complete within six to fourteen days ($\mu \pm 2\sigma = 10 \pm 2 \times 2$). In addition, we could also say that we would be about 99 percent confident that the task would be completed between four and sixteen days ($\mu \pm 3\sigma = 10 \pm 3 \times 2$).

PERT Distribution—Using the PERT distribution, one can find a probability by calculating the area under the curve. However, the PERT distribution uses a three-point estimate where:

- **O** denotes an Optimistic estimate.
- **M** denotes a Most likely estimate.
- **P** denotes a Pessimistic estimate.

Therefore, the mean for the PERT distribution is computed using a weighted average as follows:

$$\text{PERT Mean} = (O + 4M + P) \div 6$$

The standard deviation is computed:

$$\text{PERT Standard Deviation} = (P - O) \div 6$$

Figure 7.8 provides an example of a PERT distribution where O = 2, M = 4, and P = 8.

Triangular Distribution—Lastly, the triangular distribution, or TRIANG, also uses a three-point estimate similar to the PERT distribution where:

- O denotes an <u>O</u>ptimistic estimate.
- M denotes a <u>M</u>ost likely estimate.
- P denotes a <u>P</u>essimistic estimate.

However, the weighting for the mean and standard deviation are different.

$$\text{TRIANG Mean} = (O + M + P) \div 3$$
$$\text{TRIANG Standard Deviation} = [((P - O)^2 + (M - O)(M - P)) \div 18]^{1/2}$$

Figure 7.9 provides an example of a triangular distribution where O = 4, M = 6, and P = 10.

Simulations—In general, when people want to study a particular phenomenon, they pick a random sample. For example, if you wanted to know more about customer satisfaction or consumer tastes, you could survey a certain number of randomly selected customers and then analyze their responses.

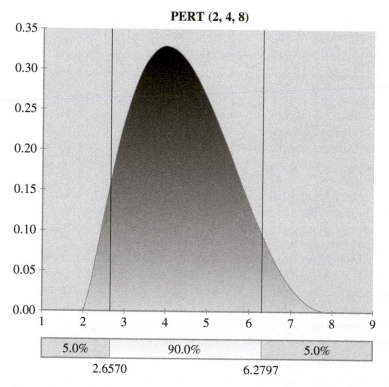

Figure 7.8 A PERT Distribution where <u>O</u>ptimistic = 2, <u>M</u>ost Likely = 4, and <u>P</u>essimistic = 8

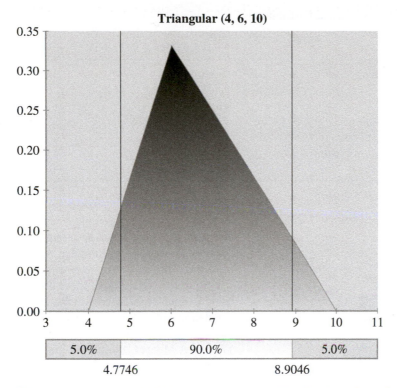

Figure 7.9 Example of a Triangular (TRIANG) Distribution where Optimistic = 4, Most Likely = 6, and Pessimistic = 10

On the other hand, if you wanted to study projects, you might randomly select a certain number of projects and then collect data about certain attributes in order to make comparisons. This same approach can be used to analyze and understand how different input variables (e.g., task durations) can impact some output variable (e.g., project completion date).

Monte Carlo simulation is a technique that randomly generates specific values for a variable with a specific probability distribution. The simulation goes through a specific number of iterations or trials and records the outcome. For example, instead of flipping a coin 500 times and then recording the outcome to see whether we get about the same number of heads as we do tails, a Monte Carlo simulation can literally flip the coin 500 times and record the outcome for us. We can perform a similar simulation using almost any continuous or discrete probability distribution.

If we would like to apply our knowledge of probability distributions to risk analysis, there are a number of software tools available that are add-ons to Microsoft Project®. These add-on tools are available from a number of software companies and can be used to analyze risk of the project plan by allowing us to develop a simulation. As an example of a Monte Carlo simulation, let's say that we are interested in modeling a section of the work breakdown structure (WBS) that includes six tasks to complete a deliverable called a test results report. The WBS, time estimates, and assumed probability distributions are illustrated in Table 7.5.

As you can see, the six tasks are expected to take 17 days. All of these estimates would be entered, for example, in Microsoft Project® as single-point estimates and do not take into consideration any variability or risk. However, the right column of Table 7.5 includes probability distributions that each task is assumed to follow. A probability distribution for a particular task could be an assumption that the project manager or team is willing to make or be based on data collected from past projects. In our example, we'll make an assumption that the "Review test plan with client" follows a PERT distribution

Table 7.5 WBS, Estimates, and Distributions for Simulation

Tasks	Estimates	Distributions
Review test plan with client	1 day	PERT(.5,1,4)
Carry out test plan	5 days	NORMAL(5,1)
Analyze results	2 days	TRIANG(1,2,4)
Prepare test results report	3 days	PERT(1,3,5)
Present test results to client	1 day	BINOMIAL(.5, 2)
Address any issues or problems	5 days	NORMAL(5,2)
Total	17 days	

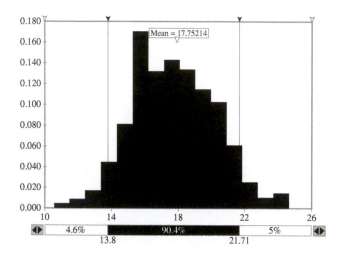

Figure 7.10 Output from the Monte Carlo Simulation

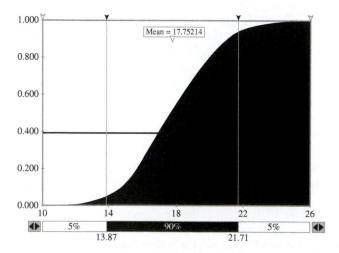

Figure 7.11 Cumulative Probability Distribution from the Monte Carlo Simulation

with an optimistic estimate of .5 days, a most likely estimate of 1 day, and a pessimistic estimate of 2 days. On the other hand, we make an assumption that the task "Carry out test plan" follows a normal distribution and has a mean of 5 and a standard deviation of 1.

Since the variability of these tasks can be modeled using various probability distributions, a Monte Carlo simulation will allow us to assess the probability of the test results report deliverable being completed in 17 days. A Monte Carlo simulation, for example, could be set to run 500 iterations, or trials. In short, instead of flipping a coin 500 times, the software will simulate the running of our project 500 times, according to the probability distributions we defined for each of the tasks, and record the results. A histogram for the tasks associated with the test results report deliverable is shown in Figure 7.10. As can be seen, the mean time to complete this deliverable is about 17.75214 days, with a 90.4 percent chance that the project will be completed between 13.8 and 21.71 days.

Figure 7.11 provides an alternative view for assessing the likelihood that the test results report will be finished in 17 days. A cumulative probability distribution shows that the deliverable has approximately a 40 percent chance of being completed in 17 days.

In addition, the project manager can conduct a sensitivity analysis to determine the tasks that entail the most risk. Figure 7.12 illustrates a tornado graph, which summarizes the tasks, with the most significant risks at the top. As the risks are ranked from highest to lowest, the bars of the graph sometimes resemble a tornado. The tornado graph allows us to compare the magnitudes of impact for each of the tasks by comparing the size of each bar. As you can see in Figure 7.12 the task "Address any issues or problems" has the greatest potential for impacting the project's schedule because of risk or uncertainty. Although this example used one component of the WBS, the same risk analysis could be conducted for each component as well as for the entire project.

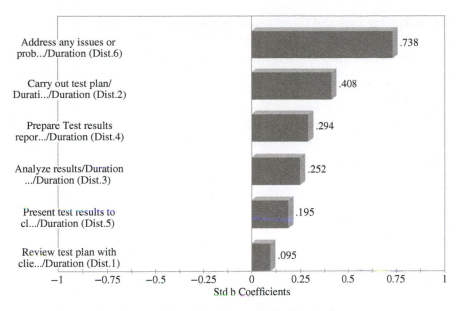

Figure 7.12 Tornado Graph from the Monte Carlo Simulation

DEVELOP RISK STRATEGIES

The purpose of risk analysis and assessment is to determine what opportunities and threats should be addressed. It is not feasible or advisable to respond to each and every threat or opportunity identified because avoiding all threats or chasing after every opportunity requires resources to be diverted from the real project work. Therefore, the risk strategy or response to a particular risk depends on:

- *The nature of the risk itself*—Is this really a threat to or an opportunity for the project? How will the project be affected? At what points during the project life cycle will the project be affected? What are the triggers that would determine if a particular risk is occurring? Why should the risk be taken?

- *The impact of the risk on the project's MOV and objectives*—A risk has a probability and an impact on the project if it occurs. What is the likelihood of this occurring? And if this risk occurs, how will the project be affected? What can be gained? What could be lost? What are the chances of success or failure?

- *The project's constraints in terms of scope, schedule, budget, and quality requirements*—Can a response to a particular threat or opportunity be made within the available resources and constraints of the project? Will additional resources be made available if a particular risk occurs? Can certain contractual obligations be waived or modified? What will happen if the desired result is not achieved?

- *Risk tolerances or preferences of the various project stakeholders*—Is a risk for one stakeholder a risk for another? How much risk is each stakeholder willing to tolerate? How committed is each stakeholder to the risk management process? Is the potential reward worth the effort?

In addition, a project manager may face opportunities that can have a positive impact on the project goal and objectives. In this case, one of the following strategies may be appropriate:

- *Exploitation*—This strategy attempts to take advantage of the situation to ensure that the opportunity is realized. For example, a project team may take advantage of a new systems development methodology or tool to reduce development time or costs, or to improve the overall quality of the system, product, or service.

- *Sharing of Ownership*—In this case, an opportunity may be shared with another party who can better capture the benefit of the positive event. This could include partnerships or joint ventures with vendors or customers so that all involved can gain from this joint ownership.

- *Enhancement*—This strategy attempts to increase the probability and/or impact of the opportunity. For example, more skilled or knowledgeable resources might be assigned to specific activities or tasks in order to improve quality or to complete the tasks earlier than planned.

- *Acceptance*—This implies that the project manager and team have an open mind so that they can take advantage of an opportunity should it arise without actively pursuing it.

A response to a particular risk in terms of a threat may follow one of the following strategies:

- *Accept or ignore*—Choosing to accept or ignore a particular risk is a more passive approach to risk response. The project stakeholders can either be hopeful that the risk will not occur or just not worry about it unless it does. This can make sense for risks that have a low probability of occurring or a low impact. However, reserves and contingency plans can be active approaches for risks that may have a low probability of occurring but with a high impact.

- *Management reserves*—These are reserves that are controlled and released by senior management at its discretion. These reserves are not usually included in the project's budget but provide a cushion for dealing with the unexpected.

- *Contingency reserves*—A contingency reserve is usually controlled and released within specific guidelines by the project manager when a particular risk occurs. This reserve is usually included in the project's budget.

- *Contingency plans*—Sometimes called an alternative plan, or plan "B," this plan can be initiated in the event that a particular risk occurs. Although these types of plans are viewed as plans of last resort, they can be useful in a variety of ways. For example, a project team should have a disaster recovery plan in place should a natural disaster, such as a snowstorm, hurricane, or earthquake, occur. This plan may have procedures and processes in place that would allow the project team to continue to work should its present workplace become unusable or unavailable. This type of disaster recovery plan is only useful if it is up-to-date and communicated to the various project stakeholders.

- *Avoidance*—The avoidance strategy focuses on taking steps to avoid the risk altogether. In this case, an active approach is made to eliminate or prevent the possibility of the threat occurring.

- *Mitigate*—The term mitigate means to lessen. Therefore, a mitigation risk strategy focuses on lessening the probability and/or the impact of threat if it does occur.

- *Transfer*—A transfer strategy focuses on transferring ownership of the risk to someone else. This transfer could be in the form of purchasing insurance against a particular risk or subcontracting a portion of the project work to someone who may have more knowledge or expertise in the particular area. As a result, this strategy may result in a premium, or added cost, to managing and responding to the risk.

Once the project risks and strategies are identified, they can be documented as part of the risk response plan. This plan should include the following:

- The project risk
- The trigger that flags whether the risk has occurred
- The owner of the risk (i.e., the person or group responsible for monitoring the risk and ensuring that the appropriate risk response is carried out)

- The risk response based on one of the four basic risk strategies
- The resources available to the owner of the risk

MONITOR AND CONTROL RISK

Once the risk response plan is created, the various risk triggers must be monitored continually to keep track of the various project risks. In addition, new threats and opportunities may present themselves over the course of the project, so it is important that the project stakeholders be vigilant.

Risk monitoring and control should be part of the overall monitoring and control of the project. Monitoring and control focus on metrics to help identify when a risk occurs and also on communication. The next chapter addresses how important it is to have a good monitoring and control system that supports communication among the various stakeholders and provides information essential to making timely and effective decisions.

Various tools exist for monitoring and controlling project risk. These include:

- *Risk audits*—A knowledgeable manager can be useful for auditing the project team from time to time. The audit should focus on ensuring that the project manager and team have done a good job of identifying and analyzing project risks and on ensuring that proper procedures and processes are in place. Risk audits should be conducted by people outside the project team. Using outsiders provides a fresh perspective; the project team may be too close to the project and miss significant threats or opportunities.

- *Risk reviews*—Risk audits should be conducted by individuals outside the project team; but, risk reviews can be conducted internally. Throughout the project life cycle, the project stakeholders should hold scheduled, periodic risk reviews. These reviews should be part of each team meeting and can be part of the project team's learning cycles.

- *Risk status meetings and reports*—Similar to risk reviews, a monitoring and control system should provide a formal communication system for monitoring and controlling project risks.

RESPOND AND EVALUATE RESPONSE TO RISK

The risk triggers defined in the risk response plan provide risk metrics for determining whether a particular threat or opportunity has occurred. A system for monitoring and controlling risk provides a mechanism for monitoring these triggers and for supporting communication among the various risk owners. The risk owners must be vigilant in watching for these triggers.

When a trigger occurs, the project risk owner must take appropriate action. In general, the action is responding to the risk as outlined in the risk response plan. Adequate resources must be available and used to respond to the risk.

The outcome of the risk response will either be favorable or unfavorable. Therefore, a great deal can be learned about the entire process of risk management (i.e., the preparedness of risk planning, identifying risks, analyzing and assessing risks, risk responses, and so forth). Lessons learned can lead to the identification of best practices that can be shared throughout the project organization. In summary, lessons learned and best practices help us to:

- Increase our understanding of project risk in general
- Understand what information was available to managing risks and for making risk-related decisions
- Understand how and why a particular decision was made
- Understand the implications not only of the risks but also of the decisions that were made
- Learn from our experience so that others may not have to repeat our mistakes

CHAPTER SUMMARY

- Project risk management also provides an early warning system for impending problems that need to be addressed or resolved. Although risk has a certain negative connotation, project stakeholders should be vigilant in identifying opportunities.

- Because of their failure to plan for the unexpected, many organizations find themselves in a state of perpetual crisis characterized by an inability to make effective and timely decisions.

- Several common mistakes in managing project risk include:
  - *Not understanding the benefits of risk management*
  - *Not providing adequate time for risk management*
  - *Not identifying and assessing risk using a standardized approach*

- Successful project risk management requires:
  - *Commitment by all stakeholders*
  - *Stakeholder responsibility*
  - *Different risks for different types of projects*

- The PMBOK® Guide defines project risk as: "an uncertain event or condition that, if it occurs, has a positive or negative effect on one or more project objectives such as scope, schedule, cost, and quality" (p. 310).

- Effective risk management requires a systematic process and a commitment to follow that process by the project's stakeholders. Figure 7.1 provides a framework that outlines six steps for managing project risk that include:
  1. Create a Risk Plan
  2. Identify Risks
  3. Analyze Risks
  4. Develop Risk Strategies
  5. Monitor and Control Risks
  6. Respond and Evaluate Risk

- Creating a risk plan is the first step and begins with having a firm commitment to the entire risk management approach from all project stakeholders.

- Once commitment has been obtained and preparations have been made, the next step entails identifying the various risks to the project. Both threats and opportunities should be identified.

- Identifying risks is not always easy. Risks tend to be interrelated and identifying each and every risk may not be possible or economically feasible.

- Risk identification should include the project team and other stakeholders who are familiar with the project's MOV and project objectives. The following are some tools that can be used along with the project risk framework for identifying threats and opportunities:
  - Learning Cycles
  - Brainstorming
  - Nominal Group Technique (NGT)
  - Delphi Technique
  - Interviewing
  - Checklists
  - Strengths, Weaknesses, Opportunities, and Threats (SWOT) Analysis
  - Cause-and-Effect Diagrams
  - Past Project Experiences

- The process of analyzing risk helps to determine what threats or opportunities require attention or a response. This provides a systematic approach for evaluating the risks that the project stakeholders identify. The purpose of this is to determine each identified risk's probability and impact on the project and then to prioritize risks so that an effective risk strategy can be formulated.

- Qualitative risk analysis focuses on a subjective analysis of risks based on a project stakeholder's experience or judgment. Some tools include:
  - Expected Value
  - Payoff Tables
  - Decision Trees
  - Risk Impact Tables

- Quantitative approaches to project risk analysis include mathematical or statistical techniques that allow us to model a particular risk situation.

- *Discrete probability distributions use only integer or whole numbers* where fractional values are not allowed or do not make sense. For example, flipping a coin would allow for only two outcomes—heads or tails. If you wanted to find the probability of flipping a fair coin into the air and having the outcome of the coin landing with the heads side up, just divide the number of favorable events (heads) by the number of total outcomes (heads or tails).

- *Continuous probability distributions* are useful for developing risk analysis models when an event has an infinite number of possible values within a stated range.

- Although in theory there are an infinite number of probability distributions, we discuss three of the more common continuous probability distributions used in modeling risk. These include the **normal distribution**, the **PERT distribution**, and the **triangular distribution**.

- If we know or assume that the probability of a risk event follows a normal distribution, we can predict an outcome with some confidence because the following probability rules of thumb apply:

  - About 68 percent of all the values will fall between $\pm 1\sigma$ of the mean.
  - About 95 percent of all the values will fall between $\pm 2\sigma$ of the mean.
  - About 99 percent of all the values will fall between $\pm 3\sigma$ of the mean.

- The mean for the PERT distribution is computed using a weighted average as follows:

$$PERT\ Mean = (O + 4M + P) \div 6$$

- The mean for the Triangular or TRIANG distribution is:

$$TRIANG\ Mean = (O + M + P) \div 3$$

- **Monte Carlo** simulation is a technique that randomly generates specific values for a variable with a specific probability distribution. The simulation goes through a specific number of iterations, or trials, and records the outcome.

- The purpose of risk analysis and assessment is to determine what opportunities and threats should be addressed. It is not feasible or advisable to respond to each and every threat or opportunity

identified because avoiding all threats or chasing after every opportunity requires resources to be diverted from the real project work. Therefore, the risk strategy or response to a particular risk depends on:

- The nature of the risk itself
- The impact of the risk on the project's MOV and objectives
- The project's constraints in terms of scope, schedule, budget, and quality requirements
- Risk tolerances or preferences of the various project stakeholders

- A project manager may face opportunities that can have a positive effect on the project goal and objectives. In this case, one of the following strategies may be appropriate:

  - Exploitation
  - Sharing of Ownership
  - Enhancement
  - Acceptance

- A response to a particular risk in terms of a threat may follow one of the following strategies:

  - Accept or Ignore
  - Management Reserves
  - Contingency Reserves
  - Contingency Plans
  - Avoidance
  - Mitigate
  - Transfer

- Once the risk response plan is created, the various risk triggers must be continually monitored to keep track of the various project risks.

- Tools for monitoring and controlling project risk include:

  - Risk Audits
  - Risk Reviews
  - Risk Status Meetings and Reports

- When a trigger occurs, the project risk owner must take appropriate action. In general, the action is responding to the risk as outlined in the risk response plan. Adequate resources must be available and used to respond to the risk.

- The outcome of the risk response will either be favorable or unfavorable. Therefore, a great deal can be learned about the entire process of risk management (i.e., the preparedness of risk planning, identifying risks, analyzing and assessing risks, risk responses, and so forth). Lessons learned can lead to the identification of best practices that can be shared throughout the project organization.

REVIEW QUESTIONS

1. What leads to uncertainty in a project?
2. How does a project risk management approach provide an early warning signal for impending problems or issues?
3. What is meant by crisis management? And why do many organizations find themselves in this mode?
4. Describe some of the common mistakes in project risk management.
5. Briefly describe what is required for effective and successful project risk management.
6. What is project risk?
7. What is project risk management?
8. What are the six project risk management processes?
9. What types of commitment are necessary for risk planning?
10. Why can identifying project risks be difficult?
11. What is a "known" risk? Give an example of one.
12. What is a "known–unknown" risk? Give an example of one.
13. What is an "unknown–unknown" risk? Give an example of one.
14. What is the difference between an internal and external risk? Give an example of each.
15. Describe some of the tools and techniques that can be used to identify project risks.
16. Describe the nominal group technique and how it can be applied to identifying project risks.
17. Describe how learning cycles can be used to identify project risks.
18. What is the Delphi technique? How can this technique be used to identify project risks?
19. How can interviewing be used as a technique for identifying IT project risks? What are some of the advantages and disadvantages of using this technique?
20. How do checklists help in identifying project risk? Discuss the pros and cons of using this technique.
21. What is SWOT analysis? How can this technique be used to identify project risks?
22. What is a fishbone (Ishikawa) diagram? How can this tool be used to identify project risks?
23. What is the purpose of the analyze risk process?
24. What is the difference between qualitative and quantitative risk analysis?
25. Describe the concept of expected value.
26. What is the purpose of a decision tree? What are the advantages and disadvantages of using a decision tree?
27. What is the purpose of a risk impact table?
28. What is the difference between a discrete probability distribution and a continuous probability distribution?
29. What are the rules of thumb that can be applied to a normal distribution?
30. Compare and contrast the normal distribution, the PERT distribution, and the triangular (TRIANG) distribution.
31. What is a simulation? What value do simulations provide when analyzing and assessing project risks?
32. What is a Monte Carlo simulation? Describe a situation (other than the one used in this chapter) that could make good use of a Monte Carlo simulation.
33. Define and discuss the four risk strategies described in this chapter.
34. What is the difference between a management reserve and a contingency reserve?
35. What is a contingency plan?
36. Why can't a project team respond to all project risks?
37. What is a risk response plan? What should be included?
38. What are risk triggers or flags?
39. Why is having a risk owner a good idea? What role does a risk owner play?
40. What is risk monitoring and control?
41. Describe the three risk monitoring tools that were discussed in this chapter.
42. What is the purpose of evaluating a response to a particular risk?

HUSKY AIR ASSIGNMENT—PILOT ANGELS

The Risk Management Plan

After reviewing your project plan, Husky Air's management has decided that the project's schedule needs to be cut by 10 percent and the project budget must be reduced by 20 percent. For example, if your original project plan estimated that the project would be completed in 100 days, you need to revise your plan so that the project will now be completed within 90 days. If the project budget was estimated to be $50,000, it now has to be revised so that the project does not cost more than $40,000.

NOTE: This case assignment will require you to use Microsoft Project®. To complete this assignment, you should be proficient with the skills outlined in Microsoft Project® Tutorial 1 and Tutorial 2 from the two previous chapters.

You will also be working with the project plan that you developed in the previous case assignment so, be sure to make a backup copy of your original plan before you begin.

This would also be a good opportunity for you and your team to do another learning cycle. Read through this assignment first and then meet as a team to develop a Project Team Record and an Action Plan. This will help to improve team learning and to assign responsibilities to complete the assignment.

Please provide a professional-looking document that includes the following:

1. **Project name, project team name, and the names of the members of your project team.**

2. **A brief project description.**

3. **The project's MOV.** (This should be revised or refined if necessary.)

4. **A printout of the Project Summary Report (original project plan)**—Include a copy of your original project schedule and budget. This is a canned Microsoft Project® Report. (See MSP Tutorial 2). This will provide a baseline for revising your project plan.

5. **A printout of the Project Summary Report (revised project plan)**—Modify your project plan so that your project schedule is reduced by 10 percent and the project budget is reduced by 20 percent. Provide a printout of the Project Summary report to show that the project schedule and budget now meet your client's needs. Provide an explanation of how you reduced the schedule and budget and logically support why you feel this strategy will not create a serious risk to your project. If your logic suggests that your original estimates were padded (i.e., you were overly "conservative"), then you can expect that Husky Air's management will ask you to revise your project schedule and budget even further.

6. **A project risk analysis and plan.**

   a. Using the Risk Identification Framework in Figure 7.2 as a basis, identify a total of five risks to your project. More specifically, identify one risk for each of the five phases of the project methodology depicted in the outer ring of the framework. Then, use the framework for analyzing each risk by moving from the outer ring to the center.

   b. For each of the five risks identified, assign an owner to each risk and describe a strategy for managing each particular risk.

 THE MARTIAL ARTS ACADEMY (MAA)—SCHOOL MANAGEMENT SYSTEM

Deliverable: The Risk Management Plan

After reviewing your project plan, MAA has decided that the project's schedule needs to be cut by 10 percent and the project budget must be reduced by 20 percent. For example, if your original project plan estimated that the project would be completed in 30 days, you need to revise your plan so that the project will now be completed within 27 days. If the project budget was estimated to be $5,000, it now has to be revised so that the project does not cost more than $4,000.

NOTE: This case assignment will require you to use Microsoft Project®. To complete this assignment, you should be proficient with the skills outlined in Microsoft Project® Tutorial 1 and Tutorial 2 from the two previous chapters.

You will also be working with the project plan that you developed in the previous case assignment so, be sure to make a backup copy of your original plan before you begin.

This would also be a good opportunity for you and your team to do another learning cycle. Read through this assignment first and then meet as a team to develop a Project Team Record and an Action Plan. This will help to improve team learning and to assign responsibilities to complete the assignment.

Please provide a professional-looking document that includes the following:

1. **Project name, project team name, and the names of the members of your project team.**
2. **A brief project description.**
3. **The project's MOV. (This should be revised or refined if necessary.)**
4. **A printout of the Project Summary Report (original project plan)**—Include a copy of your original project schedule and budget. This is a canned Microsoft Project® Report. (See MSP Tutorial 2). This will provide a baseline for revising your project plan.
5. **A printout of the Project Summary Report (revised project plan)**—Modify your project plan so that your project schedule is reduced by 10 percent and the project budget is reduced by 20 percent. Provide a printout of the Project Summary report to show that the project schedule and budget now meet your client's needs. Provide an explanation of how you reduced the schedule and budget and logically support why you feel this strategy will not create a serious risk to your project. If your logic suggests that your original estimates were padded (i.e., you were overly "conservative"), then you can expect that Geoff and Julie will ask you to revise your project schedule and budget even further.
6. **A project risk analysis and plan**.
   a. Using the Risk Identification Framework in Figure 7.2 as a basis, identify a total of five risks to your project. More specifically, identify one risk for each of the five phases of the project methodology depicted in the outer ring of the framework. Then, use the framework for analyzing each risk by moving from the outer ring to the center.
   b. For each of the five risks identified, assign an owner to each risk and describe a strategy for managing each particular risk.

QUICK THINKING—SEND IN THE RESERVES

The project's baseline budget should be based on realistic time and cost estimates as well as a reserve amount set aside for contingencies such as "unknown–unknowns." Once the project plan is executed, the cost of each individual task and the cumulative cost of the project should be monitored regularly to ensure that the project is kept under control. However, flawed estimates, anomalies, and permanent or minor variances can create budget issues.

a. *Flawed estimates*—Original estimates can present a budget risk because they simply can be wrong. As a result, new estimates should identify how much more money will be needed to complete the project as well as how much has been spent to date. It may be useful to note any lessons learned so that these errors can be avoided in the future.

b. *Anomalies*—These are risks that can come out of nowhere and take everyone by surprise because they are often one-time events that can significantly impact the project's budget. This type of risk is difficult to plan for ahead of time so you end up dealing with them after the fact. A large anomaly can be a project killer, while smaller anomalies can usually be absorbed by the reserve.

c. *Permanent variances*—These are variances that are expected to be typical for the rest of the project. For example, a project team member assigned to a number of tasks may not be as competent or skilled as expected. As a result, the budgeted amount for these tasks will increase if this team member requires more time to complete the work than originally estimated. As a project manager, you may accept these variances for the duration of the project, provide additional training, or bring in other people or contractors to help. Regardless, the project reserve will be consumed.

d. *Minor variances*—These normally occur in projects and are the reason for having a reserve in the first place. A reserve can be created for each project phase or deliverable. Since minor variances are expected, a threshold for "minor" can be determined so that everyone is clear as to what minor means in terms of a budget variance. For example, a variance would be considered minor if a task does not exceed its budgeted amount by more than 5 percent. However, the reserve must be closely monitored because it can become quickly consumed if several tasks exceed their budgeted amount by 5 percent.

1. How does having a reserve help manage project risks?

2. Can a project reserve become a risk if funds are too low or even too high?

3. Suppose you are a project manager and you've ordered ten new servers. The servers arrive one at a time and your team unpacks each one and begins to install them. After five of the servers are set up and installed, each one begins to fail because of a manufacturing problem. The vendor agrees to replace them immediately and assures you that it won't happen again, but you've spent half of your budget setting up and installing defective servers. You have a choice of reinstalling the new servers whereby your project will be late and use up your entire project's reserve, or subcontracting with another consulting firm that will ensure that the project is delivered on time but will exceed your reserve by 100 percent. How would you handle this situation?

SOURCES:

Snedaker, S. "Changes to Your Budget." *Projectsatwork*. June 1, 2006.

Vaughan, J. "How Project Managers Need to Deal with Risk Reserves." *CIO Blogs*. February 8, 2011.

Jordan, A. "What Do You Have in Reserve?" *Projectsatwork*. January 27, 2014.

QUICK THINKING—RISKY MANAGEMENT

Many project managers are uncomfortable with the probabilistic and speculative nature of risk management and therefore tend to avoid it. On the other hand, a project manager and team may sit down and identify project risks with sticky notes on the wall, estimate their probability and impact, and then log them into an Excel® spreadsheet with strategies for dealing with these risks. A reserve is then created by arbitrarily tacking on a percentage markup to the project's budget for contingencies. Unfortunately, the project plan, risk spreadsheet log, and reserve have little to do with each other. Too often the risk plans become forgotten or ineffective. Moreover, management or the project sponsor can easily cut the project's reserve when it becomes isolated from the project plan or just gets added as a line item to the project's budget.

Tom Westcott suggests that a risk plan should be integrated into the project plan so that a risk budget or reserve becomes part of the project's schedule and budget. For example, let's say that you are the project manager for a project to build a custom application for the human resources department. Upon reviewing the WBS, you and the team identify the task "load data" as a major risk. More specifically, the HR department is responsible for providing your team with the data but in the past this department has often given your team corrupt, improperly formatted, and incomplete data. Since "bad data" is viewed as a risk, you and your team look for ways to mitigate this risk.

A team member suggests holding a meeting with the HR department to discuss data requirements, responsibilities, and processes for ensuring that the data is usable, but this does not ensure that the risk will not occur on the day the data is scheduled to be loaded. Therefore, it is decided that a member of your team will be assigned the task of extracting, cleaning, formatting, and validating the data. This will require additional time and cost, but only in the event that the HR department does not provide good data. The main point is that instead of logging this risk into a spreadsheet and then adding a percentage markup to the schedule and budget as a contingency, you can actually build these actions into your project plan.

To incorporate this risk, your project plan would have three additional tasks: (a) hold data meeting with HR, (b) validate the data, and (c) clean the data. The first two tasks are tasks that would actually be done, so 100 percent of their time and cost would be included in the plan. However, the third task, clean the data, would be performed only if the risk occurs. Since this risk may or may not occur, we can assign a percentage of the estimated schedule and budget based on the probability of the risk occurring that we estimated during our risk management process. We can then multiply the impact of this contingency task (i.e., its cost, effort, and duration) by the probability of the risk's occurrence to get an expected monetary value (EMV). The risk reserve or contingency budget then becomes the sum of all the EMV's for all the contingency tasks in the project plan. Although the EMV for a particular contingency task may not be enough to cover a particular risk when it occurs, it is unlikely that all of the risks on the project will occur.

1. Contingency plans are not executed until after a risk occurs and often involve cleanup, rework, added resources, waste, and damage. Is an investment made in prevention less expensive than executing a contingency strategy?

2. Will incorporating prevention and risk management into a project plan lessen the chances of management or the project sponsor arbitrarily slashing the project's budget?

3. What other advantages can you see in having a more holistic project plan?

SOURCES:

Westcott, T. R. "The Risk in Risk Management." *Projectsatwork*. March 9, 2006.

Alleman, G. B. "Risk/Opportunity." *Projectsatwork*. September 22, 2005.

CASE STUDIES

Probabilities—Not Ones and Zeros

Montserrat is an island in the Caribbean West Indies that covers just 39 square miles. Its air and water temperatures rarely fall below 78 degrees Fahrenheit. With beautiful mountains, lush rain forests, and groves of mangoes, bananas, and coconuts, it is easy to call Montserrat a paradise. Unfortunately, Montserrat also is home to the Soufriere Hills Volcano, which first erupted in 1995 and continues to be a threat today. Approximately two-thirds of the island is now uninhabitable, and Montserrat's population has fallen to 4,000 from 11,000 since 1995. In 1997, twenty people perished and the island's economy, which relies mainly on tourism, has suffered. A recording studio owned by former Beatles producer George Martin that allowed rock stars, such as Sting, the Rolling Stones, and Paul McCartney, to record their music is now buried by volcanic ash.

Montserrat is now a dichotomy where one side of the island is paradise and the other uninhabitable part is called the Exclusion Zone. However, the island has become an excellent laboratory for conducting risk analysis. Based on probabilities, scientists know that there's only a 3 percent chance that the volcano will become dormant in the next six months. Moreover, they also know that there's a 10 percent chance that someone will be injured from the volcano on the border of the Exclusion Zone. Scientists are able to draw an imaginary line across the island where the risk from the volcano is the same as the risk from hurricanes and earthquakes. While a powerful computer was needed to do this type of statistical analysis 30 years ago, the same risk analysis can be accomplished using a laptop and spreadsheet software package.

As Scott Berinato explains, " ... this type of risk analysis ... ought to be good enough for CIOs, especially now that they're working in an economic environment looming ominously over their businesses as Soufriere Hills looms over Montserrat. For the most part, though, CIOs have not adopted statistical analysis tools to analyze and mitigate risk for software project management."

Many experts agree that statistical risk analysis is an important tool in managing individual projects as well as the project portfolio. One challenge to fully utilizing such tools as the Monte Carlo simulation and decision tree analysis may be common sense. For example, simple tasks like choosing a route when driving to work or school may involve a risk assessment that can be easily done in your head. Although the cost of being late may be high, the risk of encountering a new construction zone can be low and easily mitigated by tuning into a local radio station to get a traffic report. For example, common sense dictates that a company should have an offsite facility for backup if it is located near a fault line where earthquakes are common.

Authors Tom DeMarco and Timothy Lister believe that this type of common sense can impede doing real risk analysis. As Lister points out, "It's been very frustrating to see a best practice like statistical analysis shunned in IT. It seems there's this enormously strong cultural pull in IT to avoid looking at the downside." Many others are also perplexed by IT's laissez-faire attitude toward risk management because IT people need to start thinking in terms of probabilities, not ones and zeros. In addition, the best way to start is to have a formalized risk process that starts with identifying and managing risks. Research or brainstorming sessions are common techniques for identifying risks. Once project risks are identified, statistical tools can be applied.

Berinato believes that it is important that CIOs and IT project managers become familiar with two statistical tools that are becoming the workhorses of risk analysis: Monte Carlo simulation and decision tree analysis. As he points out, "Probabilities figure heavily into both, which means risk has to be quantified. CIOs must draw their own line between the Exclusion Zone, where it's too risky to venture, and the beaches, rain forests, and coconut groves, where the living is easy and the threats are manageable."

Monte Carlo simulation was a technique developed in the 1940s for the Manhattan Project and is used today for myriad applications, like oil-well drilling or compacting garbage at a waste treatment facility. It is based on the idea that if you roll a die (hence the name) 100 times and record the results, each face will come up about one-sixth of the time. This may not happen exactly due to randomness, but the results will come closer the more times you roll the die.

Each side of the die can represent a risk that is predictable and evenly distributed. So, for example, the probability of rolling a two has a one-sixth probability of occurring and a five-sixth probability of not occurring. A die could then represent a project risk and each side could represent a possible outcome of that risk. So, for example, rolling a die could represent a key member of the project team leaving the project, while rolling a one could represent that the project will be one week late, rolling a two could represent two weeks late, and so on. On the other hand, a project manager may believe that a particular program being written will have a 50 percent chance of passing a quality test and a 50 percent chance that it won't, resulting in a one-week delay of the project. A die could be rolled whereby an even number represents the program passing the quality test and an odd number represents the week's delay.

A Monte Carlo simulator allows for "rolling the dice" according to predefined probability distribution and then recording the results. This can help determine a project's risk profile so that additional resources or attention can help mitigate a particular risk.

Decision tree analysis is the other risk analysis tool that can be applied to IT projects. While Monte Carlo is excellent for understanding what happens to a project when many risks can come to play at once, a decision tree is most useful for mapping either-or situations and the sequential risks that can follow. For example, an application can either pass a quality test or it doesn't. Either

decision or action is a branch with a probability. Each branch can then lead to other branches that represent the risks associated with the original branch. A main advantage of a decision tree is that it shows that probabilities compound.

It often takes time to get used to risk analysis. For example, a weather forecast may indicate there's a 90 percent chance of sunshine tomorrow, but it rains. The analysis may have been correct—there was a 10 percent chance of rain and it rained. Therefore, risk analysis does not provide solid answers. It won't tell a CIO which project to do, and it won't tell a project manager whether a key employee will leave the project team. It will, however, tell you which risks have a certain level of threat and payoff.

1. Why do you think risk analysis tools like Monte Carlo simulation and decision tree analysis are not more common in analyzing project risks?

2. What could be done so that CIOs and IT project managers would be more apt to use these tools?

3. Suppose you are the project manager for an ERP project. Provide an example of a situation where Monte Carlo simulation would be appropriate. Also, provide an example of a situation where decision tree analysis would be appropriate.

Sources:

Berinato, S. "The Role of Risk Analysis in Project Portfolio Management." *Computerworld*. July 1, 2003. Accessed from http://wikitravel.org/en/Montserrat.

Hillson, D. "7 Steps to Monte Carlo." *Projectsatwork*. April 12, 2011.

Schmaltz, D. "You Can't Predict the Future –Or Projects." *Projectsatwork*. October 10, 2003.

Outsourcing—Big Savings, Big Risks

The top reason why organizations outsource services is to save money. However, many organizations are not saving as much money as they had hoped. According to Technology Partners International (TPI), the average savings from outsourcing is just less than 15 percent. Interestingly, a quarterly status report on outsourcing produced by TPI also stated that while the savings from outsourcing may not be what many organizations expect, outsourcing is still growing at a steady rate. The reason may not be the money an organization can save to reinvest into something else, but rather a shortage of experienced and skilled IT staff that can be hired. On the other hand, outsourcing has increasingly morphed from a cost savings strategy to a business strategy that can allow a company to enter new markets or consolidate several internal services to one provider. More organizations are finding out that saving money is only a small part of the overall picture.

However, outsourcing is not without risk. It's Tuesday morning at 8:30 a.m. and five members of a project team at Ondeo Nalco—a water treatment, chemical services company located in Naperville, Illinois—are gathered around a conference table while their project manager dials the speakerphone to call the company's counterparts in Manila. Meanwhile, it's 8:30 p.m. in Manila where three Filipino programmers from an outsourcing firm called Headstrong Corp. take the call after working a long day. Both teams know each other's faces behind the speakerphone because the three Filipino programmers spent two months in Naperville getting to know the Ondeo Nalco team. Although the programmers' English is excellent, a Filipino project manager takes part in the conference to make sure that all instructions are understood.

This outsourcing partnership has been running smoothly for almost a year. Ondeo Nalco entered into this project with Headstrong to develop jointly a business intelligence warehouse. While Ondeo Nalco believed it could save money by scaling back and letting offshore programmers make smaller enhancements to the system, it soon learned that the Philippines was a good place for outsourcing many of its IT needs. The popularity of the Philippines is due to its English proficiency, highly skilled workforce, developing telecommunications infrastructure, and low cost. For example, an experienced programmer in the Philippines earns between $6,000 and $12,000 a year.

The research firm Meta Group Inc. ranks the Philippines behind other Asia-Pacific countries because of its political instability and shortage of indigenous IT companies. The Philippines for the past decade has been dealing with militant Muslim insurgents. This can have a destabilizing effect for attracting and sustaining foreign capital investment. However, this threat is mainly limited to the southern islands and doesn't affect IT work in Manila. However, it is a good idea for companies that offshore work to the Philippines to have a solid business continuity and disaster recovery plan.

Moreover, there appears to be a shortage of experienced project managers in the Philippines to oversee projects, and more software developers are needed. Although the Philippines, with its large English-speaking population, is a logical choice for software development, there are only about 10,000 software programmers nationwide and only 30 companies that focus on writing software. In contrast, Ireland has a population

20 times smaller than the Philippines and has more than 800 indigenous software development firms.

Besides the time difference, Ondeo Nalco has found that a major challenge has been security. As a result, Ondeo Nalco and Headstrong spent a month determining which firewall ports should be open, what level of access people needed, and what work could be completed in Naperville, Illinois versus Manila.

1. Identify one technology risk and one nontechnology risk an organization may encounter when outsourcing a component of an IT project to a foreign country. Develop a risk management plan to manage these risks.

SOURCES:
Collett, S. "The Phillipines: Low Cost, but Higher Risk." *Computerworld*. September 15, 2003.
Ledford, J. "Outsourcing to Save Money? Think Again!" *Computerworld*. April 20, 2006.

Aviate, Navigate, and Communicate

According to Glen Alleman, managing project risks means dealing with the uncertainty of future events whose impacts are not well known. The outcomes of these events can be either favorable or unfavorable, and an effective, proactive risk management approach is definitely better than reacting to issues. As Alleman points out, "In the project management domain, the subject of risk management ranges from addressing the political risks of a project's outcome, to the risks of a supplier failing to deliver on time, to the technical failure of a product in the marketplace, to the nearly endless possibilities that could disrupt the path to success."

Even with a well-supported risk management process, projects can still fall into troubled waters. According to Gary Hamilton and colleagues, even experienced project managers may find themselves at the helm of a troubled project. As they suggest, "Projects can go off course for a variety of reasons, and some are outside your span of control."

Elizabeth Harrin believes that doing nothing can be an acceptable and appropriate response to some risks that are deemed insignificant or unlikely to occur. However, she asks, "But what happens on a project when you've done no risk mitigation and then the risk materializes?" For example, London's mayor, Boris Johnson, was criticized harshly for failing to keep the city's public services operating when the worst snowstorm in twenty years hit. The reason why the city was not prepared was simple: any risk mitigation strategy to prepare for this unlikely amount of snow seemed inappropriate.

Often, projects encounter their own "snowstorms" when a project sponsor leaves, a supplier goes out of business, or when flood, fire, other natural disasters occur. When a project falls into trouble, Barry Otterholt says it is important that a project manager "sees how it is" and has the courage to "call it like you see it" because these situations often change the rules by which the project is managed. He also contends that project sponsors and other stakeholders may become frustrated as the project fails to progress. Moreover, slipping schedules and budgets may cause tensions to increase as the potential for political embarrassment looms.

Pilots are trained to deal with unexpected events or emergencies in terms of aviate, navigate, and communicate. Aviate focuses on flying the plane. It may seem simple, but many pilots have crashed planes because they fixated on the problem at hand and forgot that they were flying a plane. Therefore, the first rule when dealing with a problem or crisis in the cockpit is to fly the plane and then assess the situation.

Navigate ensures that the pilot has options. This may include slowing the plane to its best glide speed, looking for a place to land, and maintaining or changing altitude or direction, and knowing their location. Communicate is the third step for a pilot faced with a crisis or emergency situation, even though using the radio to let everyone know he or she is in trouble is a strong impulse. Unlike the movies, no one on the ground is going to be able to help the pilot directly. When a pilot declares an emergency, an aircraft controller will ask, "What are your intentions?" Therefore, the pilot needs to understand the problem, his or her alternatives, and make a decision before communicating an answer to that question. As the PIC (pilot in command), pilots need to communicate who they are, where they are, the problem or situation, and what they plan to do.

Similarly, when faced with a crisis, a project manager first needs aviate by understanding and assessing the situation, but not to a point where he or she loses control over parts of the project that are not in trouble. According to Lisa Anderson, president of LMA Consulting Group, "When you know *what* you are dealing with you then need to swing into action. First, it starts with people. Immediately bring the project team together to understand the situation in order to brainstorm and develop plans."

For a project manager, navigate, may center on reviewing how the project schedule and budget may be impacted. As Anderson asks, "Will the unexpected circumstances affect the critical path? If not, rework a solution and remain steadfastly focused on the critical path. If yes, utilize the team to brainstorm and develop alternative critical path options."

Just like a pilot flying a plane, the project manager should communicate his or her intentions. For projects, it is critical that proper communication channels are in place so that everyone knows what is going on. As Anderson points out, "Ensure that critical changes to the project plan are communicated with clear next steps, project milestones, and with accountabilities assigned. The only time it is too soon to communicate with the organization or relevant sponsors is before the project team is in the loop." Moreover, she adds, "You need to recognize that you can't fix the problem by yourself. Your team is going to be key to sorting it out. However, the team won't respond well to a panicky project manager. The most critical elements of communicating successfully include a brief description of the obstacle, immediately followed by a clear plan and/or options being evaluated to correct the situation. In essence, when you convey confidence backed with specific steps, it typically eliminates chaos."

1. Suppose you are a project manager who has contracted with a consulting firm to implement SAP as your enterprise resource planning (ERP) system. The work that the firm is doing is about 50 percent complete. The cost to complete the remaining work by the consulting firm is about $250,000. You just learned that this consulting firm has been sued for breach of contract by another client. The settlement will put this consulting firm into bankruptcy and can impact your project's schedule and budget. How would you aviate, navigate, and communicate this situation to senior management?

2. After communicating your assessment of the situation and your intentions, the vice president of marketing makes a snide remark that this situation could have been avoided if you had done a better job of risk management. How would you respond?

SOURCES:
Alleman, G. B. "Risk/Opportunity." *Projectsatwork*. September 22, 2005.
Alleman, G. B. "Risk Rules." *Projectsatwork*. April 2, 2008.
Harrin, E. "A Guy Named Murphy." *Projectsatwork*. July 9, 2009.
Otterholt, B. "Are You a Troubled-Projects Manager?" *Projectsatwork*. October 27, 2010.
Hamilton, G. J. Hodgkinson, G. Byatt, and B. Monrow, "Rescuing Troubled Projects." *Projectsatwork*, December 8, 2010.

BIBLIOGRAPHY

1. Jones, T. C. *Assessment and Control of Software Risks.* Upper Saddle River: NJ: Yourdon Press/Prentice Hall, 1994.

2. Hillson, D. "Risk Management Building Blocks." *Projectsatwork.* February 2013.

3. Wideman, R. M. *Project and Program Risk Management: A Guide to Managing Project Risks and Opportunities.* Newton Square: PA: Project Management Institute, 1992.

4. Hillson, D. "How Mature is Your Risk Capability?" *Projectsatwork.* February 2011.

5. Alleman, G. "Risk Rules." *Projectsatwork.* April 2008.

6. Wrona, V. "Risk Management: A Seven Step Process." *Projectsatwork.* February 2008.

7. Project Management Institute (PMI). *A Guide to the Project Management Body of Knowledge (PMBOK Guide).* Newton Square, PA: PMI Publishing, 2013.

8. Jordan, A. "A Risk Management Partnership." *Projectsatwork.* February 2014.

9. Keizer, G. "Mozilla Shelves Metro Firefox, Cites User Apathy Toward Windows 8." *Computerworld.* March 2014.

10. Delbec, A., and A. H. Van de Van. "A Group Process Model for Identification and Program Planning," *Journal of Applied Behavioral Sciences*, 1971, Vol. 7, 466–492.

8

Managing Project Stakeholders and Communication

CHAPTER OBJECTIVES

Chapter 8 focuses on managing project stakeholders and communication. This includes developing a stakeholder analysis as well as a communications plan for tracking, monitoring, and reporting the project's progress. After studying this chapter, you should understand and be able to:

- Describe the informal organization.
- Develop a stakeholder analysis.
- Develop a project communications plan that includes tracking the project's progress to the baseline plan and the distribution of this information to the stakeholders.
- Apply several types of reporting tools that support the communications plan.
- Apply the concept of earned value and understand how earned value provides a means of monitoring and forecasting a project's progress.
- Describe how information may be distributed to the project stakeholders and the role information technology plays to support project communication.

INTRODUCTION

In Chapter 4, *The Project Infrastructure*, three primary organizational structures—the **functional**, **project**, and **matrix** were discussed. As a project manager, it is important to understand an organization's formal structure because organizational structure can influence the availability of resources, as well as define reporting relationships, project roles, and responsibilities.

While the formal organization, in terms of an organizational or a hierarchical chart, defines the official lines of authority and communication, the informal organization develops over time as a result of the inevitable relationships and internetworking of people within the organization. Conducting a stakeholder analysis is an important tool for understanding the informal organization because it can help the project manager and team better understand the politics and culture of the organization, as well as provide greater insight as to who makes the important decisions and why a particular decision was made. Moreover, a stakeholder analysis provides a basis for developing the project communications plan.

Developing a realistic and an effective baseline project plan is important, but is only part of the solution. The project manager must also have a clear picture of how the actual progress or work compares to the original baseline plan. Seldom do things go according to plan, so the project manager must have the means to monitor and manage the project. This will allow him or her to make well-informed decisions, take appropriate actions when necessary, or make adjustments to the project plan.

In addition, the project's progress must be communicated to the various stakeholders who may have different roles, interests, and information requirements. A project communications plan should include not only the information content for each stakeholder, but also the delivery of this information. Although a great deal of information can be obtained or distributed informally, the communications plan should detail the way data will be collected and the form in which information will be provided. Although opportunities for capturing and disseminating data and information exist, an IT-based solution may not be practical or effective in all situations. For example, email is a powerful tool for communication; however, richer forms of communication, such as face-to-face meetings, may be more appropriate or effective in certain situations.

When it comes to projects, no one likes surprises. Nothing can diminish a project manager's credibility faster than the surfacing of unexpected situations that should have been identified some time before. The unexpected does, however, happen, and no one can anticipate every conceivable contingency in a project plan. Senior management, the client, or governance committee will feel much more comfortable with a project manager who communicates unexpected problems, challenges, or issues early on and then suggests various alternatives. The project manager's credibility will rise if the project sponsor is confident that someone knows what the problem is and knows how to fix it. Conversely, confidence will diminish if problems surface that should have been communicated earlier.

 ## STAKEHOLDER ANALYSIS

The Informal Organization

The **formal organization** is the published structure that defines the official lines of authority, responsibilities, and reporting relationships. While the formal structure tells us how individuals or groups within an organization *should* relate to one another, it does not tell us how they *actually* relate (1). In many cases, the **informal organization** bypasses the formal lines of communication and authority because of the inevitable relationships that become established over time in any organization. While communication in the formal organization is supposed to flow through published channels, it can flow in any direction and at a much faster pace through the network of informal relationships—the famous grapevine. Power in an organization, therefore, is not only determined by one's place in the hierarchy, but also by how well one is connected in the informal network. A person's degree of connectedness in the informal organization largely determines what information is received or not received.

Stakeholders

Stakeholders are individuals, groups, or even organizations that have a stake, or claim, in the project's outcome. Often, we think of stakeholders as only those individuals or groups having an interest in the successful outcome of a project, but the sad truth is that there are many who can gain from a project's failure. While the formal organization tells us a little about the stakeholders and what their interests may be, the informal organization paints a much more interesting picture. Project managers must engage and involve people who may be affected by the project decisions and who may be involved with those decisions (2).

Stakeholder Analysis

A published organizational chart is usually fairly easy to acquire or create. The informal organization may be more difficult to understand or explain, even for those well-connected individuals. To help the project manager and project team understand the informal organization better, one can develop a stakeholder analysis as a means of determining who should be involved with the project and understanding the role that they must play. To develop a stakeholder analysis, one may start with the published organizational chart and then add to it as the complexities of the informal organization become known. Since the purpose of the stakeholder analysis is to understand the informal organization, it may be best to view this as an exercise rather than a formal document to be made public. The following steps provide a process for developing a stakeholder analysis:

1. Develop a list of stakeholders. Include individuals, groups, and organizations that must provide resources to the project or who have an interest in the successful or unsuccessful outcome of the project.

2. Next to each stakeholder, identify the stakeholder's interest in the project by giving the stakeholder a "+1" if they have a positive interest in the project's outcome or a "−1" if they have a negative interest. Neutral individuals or groups can be given a "0." If you are not sure, then give a stakeholder a "?."

3. Next, it may be useful to gauge the amount of influence each stakeholder has over the project. One can use a scale from 0 to 5, with 0 meaning no influence and 5 meaning extremely high influence—that is, this person or group could terminate the project.

4. After determining each stakeholder's degree of influence, the next step involves assessing whether potential conflict among the different stakeholders exists. A project is planned organizational change, and some stakeholders may act in their own self-interest. This self-interest can often be in conflict with the self-interest of other stakeholders. For example, an individual or a group may want to increase the functionality of a product or system. This increase in functionality will require more time and resources that may be in conflict with another individual or group that wants to limit the project's budget or shorten the project's schedule.

5. This step involves defining a role for each of the stakeholders. For example, every project should have a *champion* or someone prominent within the organization who will be a public supporter of the project. In addition, it is important to identify the owner of the project. This list may include an individual, group, or organization that will accept the transfer of the project's product. Other roles may include *consultant, decision maker, advocate, ally, rival, foe,* and so forth. Use adjectives or metaphors that provide a clear meaning and picture of the stakeholder.

6. Once you determine who has an interest in the project, what that interest is, and what influence they may have, it may be useful to identify an objective for each stakeholder. This may include such things as providing specific resources, expertise, or guidance navigating through the political waters of the organization. In the case of potential adversarial stakeholders, this may require getting their acceptance or approval concerning certain aspects of the project.

7. Lastly, it is important to identify various strategies for each stakeholder. These strategies may require building, maintaining, improving, or reestablishing relationships. This list should include a short description of how the objective could be attained.

The exercise for developing a stakeholder analysis can be conducted and summarized in a table as illustrated in Figure 8.1.

MONITORING AND CONTROLLING THE PROJECT

Let's begin with a story about a project manager. This particular project manager developed a detailed project plan and had several experienced and skillful members on the project team. The estimates were realistic and reasonably accurate. About two months into the project, one of the key team members left the project to play lead guitar in a country-western band. Although the team member/lead guitarist gave the usual two weeks' notice, the project manager could only recruit and hire a less experienced replacement. The learning curve was steep. The other team members were asked to help this new person (in addition to doing their own work). As a result, many of the tasks and activities defined in the project plan took longer than expected. The schedule was in trouble. With a deadline looming in the near distance, the team began to take shortcuts in an attempt to keep the project on track. The original project

Stakeholder	Interest	Influence	Potential Conflicts	Role	Objective	Strategy
Hirem N. Firem	(+1)	5	Competition for resources with other functional managers	Project sponsor and champion	Provide resources, approvals, and public support for the project	To maintain open communication so that political landmines can be avoided
Dee Manitger	+1	3	Resources not made available as promised by functional managers	Project Manager	Lead and manage the project so that it achieves its MOV	Work closely with project stakeholders and project team
Project Team	+1	2	This project will change a number of business processes. Affected users may resist change by withholding information	*Steve Turner-* Network Administrator *Shedelle Bivits-* Systems Analyst *Corean Jenkins-* Programmer/DBA *Myra Dickens-* Inventory Analyst	Provide expertise to complete the project work	Support project team with adequate resources while minimizing distractions
Will Sellit	−1	4	As the marketing manager, Sellit is not pleased that this project was chosen over his proposed project. May withhold promised resources.	Foe	Build and maintain best possible relationship to minimize attempts to divert resources	Maintain open communication, use project sponsor's influence as necessary

Figure 8.1 Example of a Stakeholder Analysis

plan, for example, called for one month of testing. That seemed like a lot of time, so maybe the product could be tested in two weeks. As more and more tasks began to slip, testing was cut to one week, and then two days—okay, maybe the team could test the programs as they write them. Then, they would just have to keep their fingers crossed and hope everything worked when the product was released.

On the day the product was supposed to be released, the project manager had to confess to senior management that the product was "not quite ready." Senior management then asked when the product *would* be ready. The project manager then sheepishly explained that there were a few *minor* setbacks due to unforeseen circumstances out of the project manager's control. Senior management once again asked when the product *would* be ready. After some hemming and hawing, the project manager explained that the project would take twice as long and cost twice as much to complete if the originally agreed-upon scope was maintained. Needless to say, the *new* project manager kept senior management informed about the project's progress.

The moral of this story is that project sponsors do not like surprises. Regardless of how well a project is planned, unexpected situations will arise. These unexpected events will require adjustments to the project schedule and budget. In fact, many cost overruns and schedule slippages can be attributed to poorly monitored projects (3). The project plan gets thrown out the window as slippage in one task or activity causes a chain reaction among the other interdependent tasks. If that task is on the critical path, the problem can be especially serious. You know you're in trouble if a project sponsor asks, why didn't you tell me about this earlier?

The problem may gain strength and momentum as the project manager attempts to react to these unexpected events. For example, resources may be reassigned to different tasks or processes and standards may be overlooked. The wiser project manager, on the other hand, will try to be more proactive and recognize the impact of these unexpected situations in order to plan and act in a definite and timely manner. As our story points out, many times things happen on projects that are out of our control. If the project manager had identified this problem earlier and analyzed its impact, he or she could have apprised senior management of the situation and then laid out several alternative courses of action and their estimated impact on the project's schedule and budget. Although senior management may not like the news, they probably would respect the project manager for providing an early warning. Moreover, having a feeling that someone is in control will project stakeholders a sense of security.

A project manager *will not* lose credibility because an unexpected event or a situation arises. He or she *will*, however, lose (or gain) credibility in terms of how a particular situation is handled. By addressing the problem early, the chain reaction and impact on other project activities can be minimized. There will be less impact on the project's schedule and budget.

Therefore, planning and estimating are not sufficient. A project needs an early warning system to keep things on track. This early warning system allows the project manager to control and monitor the project's progress, identify problems early, and take appropriate corrective action.

The baseline plan provides a benchmark, allowing the project manager to gauge the project's performance against planned expectations. Once the baseline plan is approved, actual progress can be compared to what was planned. This process is often referred to as comparing *actual to planned* performance, and the comparison is relatively easy and straightforward when using a project management software package.

Project control ensures that processes and resources are in place to help the project manager monitor the project. Although one might believe control has a negative connotation, it provides the capability to measure performance, alerts the project manager to problem situations, and holds people accountable. Controls also ensure that resources are being utilized efficiently and effectively while guiding the project toward its MOV. Controls can be either internal to the project (i.e., set by the project governance committee or methodology) or external (i.e., set by government or industry standards). The control and monitoring activities of a project must be clearly communicated to all stakeholders. Everyone must be clear as to what controls will be in place and how data will be collected and information distributed.

THE PROJECT COMMUNICATIONS PLAN

The project communications plan can be formal or informal, depending on the needs of the project stakeholders and the size of the project. Regardless, communication is vital for a successful project. It is important that all of the project stakeholders know how their interests stand in relation to the project's progress.

Developing a communications plan starts with identifying the various stakeholders of the project and their information needs. Recall that stakeholder analysis helps the project manager and project team determine the different interests and roles of each of the stakeholders. Although some of the information contained in the stakeholder analysis may not be suitable for general dissemination, it provides a starting point for identifying who needs what information and when. Keep in mind that even stakeholders who may have a vested interest in the project *not* succeeding must be kept informed. Otherwise, a lack of communication and information can result in an attitude that "no news must be bad news," or speculation and frivolous assumptions that the project is in trouble.

Figure 8.2 provides an example of a project communications plan. The idea behind this analysis is to determine:

- Who has specific information needs?
- What are those information needs?

Stakeholder	Reporting Requirements	Report/Metric	Reason
Sponsor or client	During periodic review meetings **Time Frame:** Considering projects with six months or more of duration, the project sponsor can be provided with this report monthly.	Project summary, budget, earned value	Sponsor or client will be concerned primarily with the strategic indicators including overall cost and value in the project. • Project summary report presents the overall cost that the project will incur. This report shows the baseline schedule and budget along with the actual schedule and budget and gives the project's overall status report. • The budget is also a top-of-view project summary of the cost for all tasks in the project. • Earned value report gives a top level summary of the project at a given status date. It also includes key metrics that monitor the health of the project.
Project manager	At periodic intervals or even online **Time Frame:** This report can be sent to the project manager once in every two weeks for a typical six month or more project.	Earned value, project summary, slipping tasks, critical tasks, milestone, current activities reports, over budget tasks and resources	The project manager will be concerned with making both operational and strategic decisions. Therefore, reports that are primarily involved in tracking the current status of the project and its health are of utmost importance. The project manager would be required to be informed of the work progress compared to the baseline plan.
Project team	At periodic intervals **Time Frame:** Receiving this report weekly would help the team members benefit from it. They also need to get an updated copy in case of any changes in the schedule.	"Who Does What When" and "To Do List" reports	The project team would be concerned with day-to-day execution of the project. Issues like who does what and when, what is assigned to a team member would be key needs. In case of interdependent tasks, the team members can also see who performs preceding or succeeding tasks.

Figure 8.2 Example of a Project Communications Plan

- How will a particular stakeholder's information needs be met?
- When can a stakeholder expect to receive this information?
- How will this information be received?

This format helps clarify what all of the stakeholders will need to know about the projects status and progress. The following describes each of the areas for developing the communications plan:

- *Stakeholders*—Communication requires a sender, a message, and a receiver; however, we often focus mainly on the first two (4). Stakeholders are individuals or groups who have a "stake" or claim in the project's outcome and, therefore, are the receivers of the project information we send. In general, this group would include the project sponsor or client, the governance committee, the project manager, and the project team because each would have a specific interest in the project's performance and progress. Other people, such as senior managers, business unit managers, customers, users, and vendors, may have a special interest in the project as well. Therefore, it is important that we keep these special interests informed.

- *Information requirements*—A diverse group of stakeholders will result in diverse information requirements. Identifying the information requirements of the various stakeholders allows the project manager and project team to better determine the information reporting mechanisms, timings, and delivery medium for each stakeholder. Instead of a single report that may or may not meet the needs of each stakeholder, a particular report or metric can be designed to meet an individual stakeholder's needs and, therefore, improve communication with that stakeholder. In general, these information requirements will focus on scope, schedule, budget, quality, and risk. Depending on the needs of the stakeholder, the requirements and level of detail may be different.

- *Type of report or metric*—Depending on the information needs of a particular stakeholder, a specific report or reporting mechanism can be identified. These may include specific reports that are provided by a project management software tool or a custom report with specific metrics. In addition, reporting mechanisms may include formal or informal reviews of deliverables, milestones, or phases. Other reporting mechanisms, such as newsletters and other public relations tools, can serve a general population of stakeholders.

- *Timings/Availabilities*—The timing and availability of the reports set expectations for the stakeholder. Some stakeholders may feel they need up-to-the-minute or real-time access to the project's performance and progress. Other stakeholders may have an almost casual interest. Set timing and availability to let people know when they will know. They also allow the project manager and team to stay focused by minimizing demands for ad hoc reports and status updates by powerful stakeholders.

- *Medium or format*—The medium or format defines how the information will be provided. Possible formats include paper reports, face-to-face, electronic files, email, or video conferencing. Defining the format also sets expectations and allows the project manager to plan the resources needed to support the communications plan.

PROJECT METRICS

The communications plan described in the previous section is the output of the communications planning process. However, a project metric system must be in place to support the information requirements for all of the stakeholders. In general, project metrics should focus on the following key areas:

- Scope
- Schedule
- Budget
- Resources
- Quality
- Risk

Data to support these metric categories can be collected in a number of ways. For example, project team members may be asked to submit periodic reports or even time cards that describe what tasks they worked on, the time spent working on those tasks, and any other resources that they may have used on those tasks. In addition, the project team could report deliverables, milestones, user stories, or even product features or functionality completed.

Collection of data from various sources allows the project manager to compile a set of metrics that can be used to create the various reports for the stakeholders defined in the communications plan. A **project metric** may be defined as a qualitative measurement of some attribute of the project. This metric should be obtained from observable, quantifiable data (5). In addition, these metrics can be useful for developing a measurement program that allows the team and other stakeholders to gauge the efficiency and effectiveness of the work being done. A good project metric must be:

- *Understandable*—A metric should be intuitive and easy to understand; otherwise, the metric will be of little value and will most likely not be used.

- *Quantifiable*—A quantifiable metric is objective. A metric should have very little bias as a result of personal influence or subjectivity.

- *Cost effective*—Data must be collected in order to produce a metric. Subsequently, a metric should be relatively easy and inexpensive to create and should not be viewed as a major disruption.

- *Proven*—A metric should be meaningful, accurate, and have a high degree of validity in order to be useful. The metric must measure exactly what one wants to manage.

- *High impact*—Although the efficiency of computing a metric is important, the metric must be effective. Why measure something that has little impact on the project?

Trying to manage a project team without a good measurement system is like trying to drive a car without a dashboard (6). Therefore, the following principles can act as a guide:

- *A measurement system should allow the team to gauge its progress*—The project metrics should let the team know when to take corrective action rather than waiting for the project manager to intervene. Instead of using a measurement system to control a team, it should be used to empower the team to solve problems on its own.

- *The team should design its own measurement system*—The people actually doing the work know what metrics are best suited. However, a team should not develop project metrics or a measurement system without the aid of the project manager or other members of the organization because independent action could result in inconsistencies and parochial interests being served.

- *Adopt only a handful of measures*—The old saying "What gets measured gets done" can be an opportunity if the right metrics and measurement system are in place. Adding more and more measures as a means of encouraging team members to work harder can have the opposite effect. Collecting data to support a measurement system takes time and can interfere with the planned work. Having a few key measures keeps the team focused and creates minimal interference. In addition, these measures create a common language among team members and the other project stakeholders.

- *Measures should track results and progress*—Using the metaphor of a car's dashboard, an array of graphic indicators and easy-to-read gauges can be useful in helping a project team measure and track its own progress and in letting it know when to take corrective action. For example, a relative measure could be used to track the remaining project budget. If money can be thought of as fuel for the project, Figure 8.3 vividly shows that the project may be in trouble of "running out of fuel" because it is consuming its budget faster than planned.

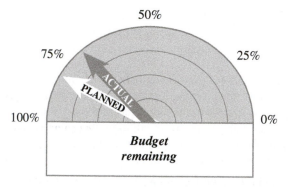

Figure 8.3 Example of a Project Dashboard Metric

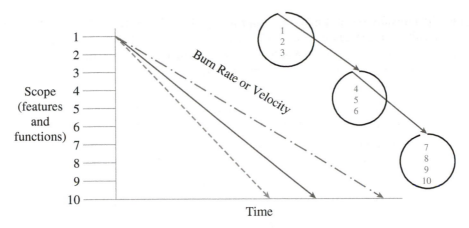

Figure 8.4 A Burn-Down Chart

Burn-Down Chart

Analogous to a dashboard gauge, a **burn-down chart** provides a useful tool for reporting a project's progress. Burn-down charts have become popular in the Agile software development methods like Scrum or XP and show how the scope, features or functionality, or work is being completed over time. For example, Figure 8.4 illustrates how a project's scope has been divided into three sprints starting with the three most important features and functionality. As the project team "burns" through the scope, the velocity or burn-down rate represents the amount of work that can be delivered in a single iteration. As a result, the completion of the project work can be predicted. The middle line, for example, would depict that the work would be completed on-time or as planned, while the steeper, dotted line would predict that the project would finish early. On the other hand, the line on the right shows that the project will take longer than expected.

A burn-down chart is simple to develop using a spreadsheet software package and a graphing function. A project team could predict a completion date based on the number of iterations or sprints and using time boxing as an estimation method. Once the project work begins, the team could then track its progress and use the work remaining to estimate the velocity or burn-down rate in order to predict a target completion date.

Earned Value

Suppose that we hired the infamous consulting firm Dewey, Cheatem, and Howe to develop an information system for your organization. The project is planned to cost $40,000 and take four months to complete. To keep things simple, let's also assume that the scope of this project includes twenty deliverables that are represented by twenty activities or tasks that are evenly divided over the four-month schedule. Since each task is expected to take the same amount of time, the expected cost per task is $2,000. This $2,000 is called the **planned value (PV)** because it is the planned or budgeted cost of work scheduled for an activity or component of the WBS. This information is summarized in Table 8.1.

However, the contract that we just signed stipulates that a payment of $10,000 must be made each month for four months. The total planned cost of our project is $40,000 and has a special name as well. It is called the **budget at completion (BAC)**. The BAC is also the total or cumulative **planned value (PV)** for the entire project. If we were to graph the planned expenditures for our project, the planned value for the cumulative cash flows would look like Figure 8.5.

Table 8.1 A Planned Project Schedule and Budget

Task	Month 1	Month 2	Month 3	Month 4
1	$2,000			
2	$2,000			
3	$2,000			
4	$2,000			
5	$2,000			
6		$2,000		
7		$2,000		
8		$2,000		
9		$2,000		
10		$2,000		
11			$2,000	
12			$2,000	
13			$2,000	
14			$2,000	
15			$2,000	
16				$2,000
17				$2,000
18				$2,000
19				$2,000
20				$2,000
Total	**$10,000**	**$10,000**	**$10,000**	**$10,000**

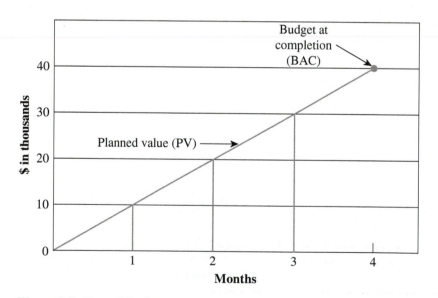

Figure 8.5 Planned Budget

At the end of the month, let's say that we receive the following invoice for $8,000:

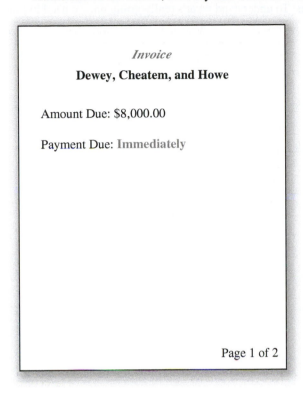

This actually sounds like good news. If you look at Figure 8.6, you will see that we planned to spend $10,000 at the end of the first month, but the invoice states that we only have to pay $8,000. It would appear that we are spending less money than planned. Since we will have to write a check to Dewey, Cheatem, and Howe for $8,000, we will call this the **actual cost (AC)**. It is the total cost incurred for completing a scheduled task or WBS component.

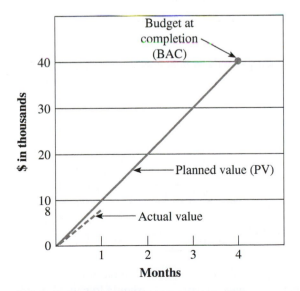

Figure 8.6 Planned Value versus Actual Cost

So, is our project really $2,000 ahead of budget? Actually, all we are doing is staying within the budgeted or planned expenditures. To understand what's really going on, we need to look at the second page of the invoice.

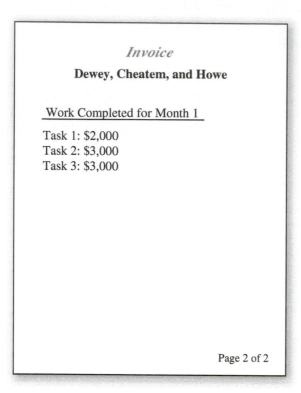

Invoice

Dewey, Cheatem, and Howe

 Work Completed for Month 1

Task 1: $2,000
Task 2: $3,000
Task 3: $3,000

Page 2 of 2

It looks like the consultants from Dewey, Cheatem, and Howe are only charging us $8,000, but they only completed three out of the five tasks that were expected to be completed by the end of the first month. As you can see in Table 8.2, we will have to pay $8,000 in actual costs for what we expected to achieve for $6,000. This $6,000 is called the **earned value (EV)**.

Analyzing Current Performance

EV provides a performance measurement that tells us how much of the budget we really should have spent for work completed so far. It provides a method that incorporates scope, schedule, and budget

Table 8.2 Planned, Actual, and Earned Values

Task	Planned Value	Actual Value	Earned Value
1	$2,000	$2,000	$2,000
2	$2,000	$3,000	$2,000
3	$2,000	$3,000	$2,000
4	$2,000		
5	$2,000		
Cumulative	$10,000	$8,000	$6,000
	↑	↑	↑
	What we *planned* to pay	What we *have* to pay	What we *should* to pay

to analyze project performance and progress (7). For example, we can determine the **cost variance (CV)**, which is the difference between a WBS component's planned or estimated cost and its actual cost. An earned value analysis of a project can be useful for understanding progress and refining the WBS estimates (8). The CV is computed by subtracting actual cost from earned value.

$$\text{Cost Variance (CV)} = \text{EV} - \text{AC}$$
$$= \$6,000 - \$8,000$$
$$= (\$2,000)$$

A CV can be a positive or a negative number. A negative $2,000 CV for our project is an important metric because it tells us that we have spent $8,000 in order to receive $6,000 worth of work. As you can see from our example, a negative CV indicates that the project is over budget. Unless appropriate action is taken to get the project back on track, we might have to increase the budget or reduce the project's scope. Conversely, a positive CV indicates that the project is under budget, while a CV of 0 would mean that the project is right on target.

In addition, we can also develop a performance metric for the project's schedule. The **schedule variance (SV)** shows the difference between the current progress of the project and its original or planned schedule. The SV is calculated by subtracting planned value from earned value.

$$\text{Schedule Variance (SV)} = \text{EV} - \text{PV}$$
$$= \$6,000 - \$10,000$$
$$= (\$4,000)$$

As you can see, a negative SV indicates that the project is behind schedule. Conversely, a positive SV indicates that the project is ahead of schedule, and a SV of 0 would mean that the project is right on schedule.

The CV and SV performance metrics can be converted to efficiency indicators to reflect the cost and schedule performance of a project and as a basis for predicting the outcome.

A **cost performance index (CPI)** can be computed by taking the ratio of earned value to actual cost.

$$\text{Cost Performance Index (CPI)} = \text{EV}/\text{AC}$$
$$= \$6,000/\$8,000$$
$$= .75$$

A CPI of .75 tells us that for every $1.00 we spent so far on this project, only $0.75 was really being completed. A CPI greater than 1.0 indicates that we are ahead of our planned budget, while a CPI of less than 1.0 means we are encountering a cost overrun. It follows, then, that a CPI equal to 1.0 indicates that we are right on our planned budget.

We can also develop a schedule efficiency metric called the **schedule performance index (SPI)**. This is calculated by dividing earned value by planned value.

$$\text{Schedule Performance Index (SPI)} = \text{EV}/\text{PV}$$
$$= \$6,000/\$10,000$$
$$= .60$$

The SPI provides a ratio of the work performed to the work planned or scheduled. Therefore, for every $1.00 of work that was expected to be completed, only $0.60 was accomplished. A SPI greater than 1.0 indicates that the project is ahead of schedule, while a SPI of less than 1.0 means we are behind schedule. A SPI equal to 1.0 indicates that the project is right on schedule.

Table 8.3 summarizes the earned value performance metrics for our example. This analysis can be made for each task or for a larger component of the WBS.

Table 8.3 Summary of Project Performance Metrics

Task	Planned Value (PV)	Actual Cost (AC)	Earned Value (EV)	Cost Variance (CV)	Schedule Variance (SV)	Cost Performance Index (CPI)	Schedule Performance Index (SPI)
1	$2,000	$2,000	$2,000	-0-	-0-	1.00	1.00
2	$2,000	$3,000	$2,000	($1,000)	-0-	0.67	1.00
3	$2,000	$3,000	$2,000	($1,000)	-0-	0.67	1.00
4	$2,000			-0-	($2,000)	—	0.00
5	$2,000			-0-	($2,000)	—	0.00
Cumulative	$10,000	$8,000	$6,000	($2,000)	($4,000)	0.75	0.60

Forecasting Project Performance

We planned on spending $40,000 on this project, but is this total cumulative planned value at completion (i.e., the BAC) still realistic? Often cost and schedule overruns do not correct themselves and may become worse as the project progresses (9). In fact, if things continue as they are in our example, we can get a better feel for how much our project will end up costing us by using these performance metrics to forecast the project's final performance. Earned value analysis can be used to predict or forecast the future resource or budget needs of the project based on the project's current performance (6).

The **estimate at completion (EAC)** provides a revised estimate for the total cost of the project based on the actual costs incurred so far plus the scheduled work that remains. The EAC can be just a revised schedule and budget if, for example, Dewey, Cheatem, and Howe informs us that the project work will take longer and cost more than we originally planned. On the other hand, we can calculate the EAC depending on whether the variances we encountered so far are expected to continue in the future.

If we believe the variances encountered so far will most likely continue for the remainder of the project, then EAC is calculated by subtracting the cumulative earned value to date from the budget at completion and then dividing by the cumulative cost performance index. Although this may sound complicated, the formula is just:

$$\text{EAC} = \text{Cumulative AC} + (\text{BAC} - \text{Cumulative EV})/\text{Cumulative CPI}$$
$$= \$8,000 + (\$40,000 - \$6,000)/.75$$
$$= \$53,333.33$$

Or

$$\text{EAC} = \text{BAC}/\text{CPI}$$
$$= \$40,000/.75$$
$$= \$53,333.33$$

As you can see, our total project budget will cost around $53,333 if things continue as they are. But what if these variances are influenced by issues or problems reflected in both the CPI and the SPI? Then, a more appropriate conservative approach would be to multiply the CPI and the SPI to take into account how the remaining work might be influenced. The formula to use becomes:

$$\text{EAC} = \text{Cumulative AC} + (\text{BAC} - \text{Cumulative EV})/(\text{SPI} * \text{CPI})$$
$$= \$8,000 + (\$40,000 - \$6,000)/(.75 * .60)$$
$$= \$65,500.00$$

Under this scenario, it appears that the final cost of our project could be somewhere between $53,333 and $65,500.

In addition, the **variance at completion (VAC)** and the **to complete performance index (TCPI)** offer two additional useful earned value metrics. The VAC compares the original planned budget or BAC with the EAC to determine whether a budget surplus or deficit exists. It is calculated as follows:

$$\text{VAC (CPI Only)} = \text{BAC} - \text{EAC}$$
$$= \$40,000 - \$53,333$$
$$= (\$13,333)$$

or if considering the effect of both the CPI and SPI:

$$\text{VAC (CPI and SPI)} = \text{BAC} - \text{EAC}$$
$$= \$40,000 - \$65,000$$
$$= (\$25,500)$$

A negative VAC reflects a budget deficit, while a positive VAC indicates a budget surplus. In our example, a VAC of ($13,333) considers the impact of only the CPI, while the VAC of ($25,500) considers the impact of both the SPI and CPI as a multiplier effect. In both cases, the VAC tells us that the project is operating way over budget. As a result, the BAC appears to be no longer realistic and the EAC should become the new budget.

A TCPI that is greater than 1 suggests that the project will be more difficult to complete based on the remaining resources, while a TCPI that is less than one suggests less difficulty. The TCPI can be calculated for the original BAC or the EAC. The formula is:

For the original BAC:

$$\text{TCPI} = (\text{BAC} - \text{EV})/(\text{BAC} - \text{AC})$$
$$= (\$40,000 - \$6,000)/(\$40,000 - \$8,000)$$
$$= 1.06$$

For the EAC:

$$\text{TCPI (CPI Only)} = (\text{BAC} - \text{EV})/(\text{EAC} - \text{AC})$$
$$= (\$40,000 - \$6,000)/(\$53,333 - \$8,000)$$
$$= .75$$

or if considering the effect of both the CPI and SPI:

$$\text{TCPI (CPI and SPI)} = (\text{BAC} - \text{EV})/(\text{EAC} - \text{AC})$$
$$= (\$40,000 - \$6,000)/(\$65,500 - \$8,000)$$
$$= .59$$

As you can see the project may have a more difficult time achieving its original budget of $40,000. Therefore, achieving an EAC of $53,333 or $65,500 would be much easier. Table 8.4 summarizes the earned value analysis for our example.

Earned value can also be calculated in terms of completion of the planned value. In this case, we just multiply the planned value of an activity, task, or WBS component by its percentage of completion. Table 8.5 provides an example of a project with five tasks. In this case, earned value is equal to planned value multiplied by its associated percent complete. An earned value analysis with the various project performance metrics described previously can then be used.

Table 8.4 Earned Value Analysis

Earned Value Metrics	Description	Amount/Formula	Value	Analysis
Actual Performance to Baseline Plan				
Budget At Completion (BAC)	Total Planned budget	Given	$40,000	
Planned Value (PV)	Amount authorized to spend	Given	$10,000	
Actual Cost (AC)	Actual cost of work performed	Given	$8,000	
Earned Value (EV)	Amount that should have been spent on the work completed	Given	$6,000	
Schedule Variance (SV)	Amount ahead or behind schedule	$SV = EV - PV$	$(4,000)	A negative SV indicates the project is behind schedule
Cost Variance (CV)	Budget surplus or deficit	$CV = EV - AC$	$(2,000)	A negative CV indicates the project is over budget
Schedule Performance Index (SPI)	Efficiency indicator of how well team is using the planned schedule	$SPI = EV/PV$	0.60	A SPI <1 indicates the project is behind schedule
Cost Performance Index (CPI)	Efficiency indicator of how well project resources are consuming the budget	$CPI = EV/AC$	0.75	A CPI <1 indicates the project is over budget
Projected Performance Based on Actual Performance				
Estimate at Completion (EAC) (CPI only)	The projected total cost of the project if CPI remains the same	$EAC = AC + (BAC - EV)/CPI$	$53,333	If the current CPI continues, the project will cost $53,333
Estimate at Completion (EAC) (CPI and SPI)	A worst case that considers the efficiency of both the schedule and budget	$EAC = AC + (BAC - EV)/(CPI * SPI)$	$65,500	If both the SPI and CPI continue to influence the project, the project will cost $65,500

(continued)

Table 8.4 (*continued*)

Earned Value Metrics	Description	Amount/Formula	Value	Analysis
Estimate to Complete (ETC)	The projected cost to complete the remaining work of the project. (CPI Only)	ETC = EAC − AC	$45,333	If the current CPI continues, $45,333 will be needed to complete the project
	(SPI and CPI)	ETC = EAC − AC	$57,500	If both the SPI and CPI continue to influence the project, $57,500 will be needed to complete the project
Variance at Completion (VAC)	The projected budget surplus or budget (CPI only)	VAC = BAC − EAC	$(13,333)	If the current CPI continues, the project will be $13,333 over budget
	The projected budget surplus or budget (CPI and SPI)	VAC = BAC − EAC	$(25,500)	If both the SPI and CPI continue, the project will be $25,500 over budget
To Complete Performance Index (TCPI)	An efficiency measure that compares the work remaining (BAC − EV) to the remaining funds (BAC − AC) based on the BAC	TCPI = (BAC − EV)/(BAC − AC)	1.06	TCPI >1 so the project will be more difficult to complete with remaining budget
	An efficiency measure that compares the work remaining (BAC − EV) to the remaining funds (EAC − AC) based on the EAC	TCPI = (BAC − EV)/(EAC − AC)	0.75	TCPI <1 so the project will be easier to complete with new EAC. (CPI Only)
			0.59	TCPI <1 so the project will be easier to complete with new EAC. (SPI and CPI)

Table 8.5 Earned Value = Planned Value (PV) × Percent Complete

Task	Planned Value	Percent Complete	Earned Value
A	$1,000	100%	$1,000
B	$1,500	100%	$1,500
C	$2,000	75%	$1,500
D	$800	50%	$400
E	$1,200	50%	$600
Cumulative	$6,500		$5,000

REPORTING PERFORMANCE AND PROGRESS

Once the project data have been collected, the project manager can use it to update the project plan. The project manager has a wide variety of software tools at his or her disposal.

In addition, project reporting tends to fall under one of the following categories:

- *Reviews*—Project reviews may be formal or informal meetings that include various project stakeholders. These reviews may focus on specific deliverables, milestones, or phases. The purpose of a review is to not only show evidence that the project work has been completed, but also that the work has been completed according to certain standards or agreed-upon requirements. In addition, review meetings provide a forum for surfacing issues, problems, and even opportunities that may require stakeholders to negotiate or make decisions.

- *Status reporting*—A status report describes the present state of the project. In general, a status report compares the project's actual progress to the baseline plan. Analogous to a balance sheet used by accountants, a status report may include, for example, a variance analysis that compares actual schedule and cost information to the baseline schedule and budget.

- *Progress reporting*—A progress report tells us what the project team has accomplished. This report may compare the activities or tasks that were completed to the activities or tasks outlined in the original project network.

- *Forecast reporting*—A forecast report focuses on predicting the future status or progress of the project. For example, it may include an earned value analysis that tells us how much funding will be needed to complete the project.

INFORMATION DISTRIBUTION

To complete the project communications plan, the project manager and team must determine how and when the required information will be provided to the various stakeholders. In addition, it is important that stakeholders are willing to share information (10). Although a variety of media exist, most communication will involve:

- *Face-to-face meetings*—A great deal can be learned from face-to-face meetings. Such meetings may range from informal conversations to more formal meetings and presentations (11). The advantage of face-to-face meetings is that one can see the expressions and body language of others. Sometimes the way people say something can be more expressive than what they say. On the other hand, face-to-face meetings require arranging of schedules and additional costs if travel is involved. Certain issues and problems, of course, require people to meet face to face. For example, firing a person should only be done face to face. There are a number of war

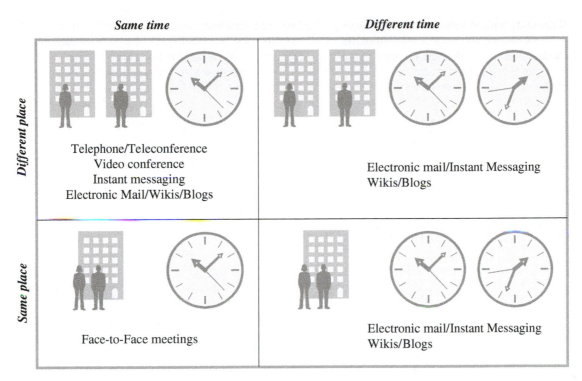

Figure 8.7 Communication and Collaboration Matrix

stories in the business world about people who found out they were let go by email. The general consensus is that this is an insensitive and tactless way to treat people.

■ *Telephone, electronic mail, and other wireless devices*—It appears that we are in the midst of a wireless and mobile revolution. Mobile phones, tablets, and other wireless devices are commonplace and have increased our mobility and accessibility. Although these communication devices are not as personal as face-to-face meetings, they certainly make communication possible when people cannot be at the same place at the same time. The communications plan (and project budget) should also include electronic means for the project team and other stakeholders to communicate.

■ *Collaboration technology*—There are a variety of information technology tools to support communication and collaboration. For example, a project team could use Internet or Web-based technologies to develop a project blog, wiki, or instant messaging. The project communications plan must focus on supporting communication for people working in different places and at different times. Figure 8.7 provides an example of how people communicate and interact today and some examples of how they may be supported.

CHAPTER SUMMARY

● While the formal organization, in terms of an organizational or hierarchical chart, defines the official line of authority and communication, the informal organization includes the informal relationships and internetworking of people within the organization that develops over time.

● Understanding the formal and informal sides of an organization is important because it will help the project manager and project team better understand the politics and culture of the organization and provide greater insight into the decision-making process.

- Project planning and estimation are critical processes. To be useful, the project plan must be accurate and realistic. But, even the best plans will fall short if the project manager and team do not follow the plan or know when to take corrective action.

- A project manager must be in control of the project and identify problems, issues, and situations that will impact the project schedule and budget.

- A measuring and reporting system allows the project manager to identify these situations early so that various alternative courses of action can be assessed and recommended. Although project sponsors may not like bad news, it is better for a project manager to deliver problematic news early than to have upper management unaware of the situation.

- A project communications plan may be formal or informal, depending on the size of the project and number of project stakeholders, but it must support an effective and efficient means of communication among the various project stakeholders.

- The development of a communications plan focuses on identifying the various stakeholders and their information requirements. In addition, the plan also sets expectations in terms of how and when this information will be made available.

- The project communications plan must include a variety of ways for project stakeholders to communicate. This may allow for communication to take place:
  - Same time–same place
  - Same time–different place
  - Different times–same place
  - Different times–different place

- Today, a number of IT-based tools and technologies are available to support the different needs of the project stakeholders; however, richer forms of communication, such as face-to-face meetings, are important and more appropriate in certain situations.

REVIEW QUESTIONS

1. Describe what is meant by the informal organization.

2. Why should the project manager or project team be concerned with understanding the informal organization?

3. What is a stakeholder?

4. How does conducting a stakeholder analysis help the project manager and project team understand the informal organization?

5. Why would the project manager and project team not want to make a stakeholder analysis public to the entire organization?

6. In conducting a stakeholder analysis, why is it important not only to identify those who will gain from the project's success, but also those who may gain from its failure?

7. What is the purpose of defining a role and objective for each stakeholder identified in the stakeholder analysis?

8. Why should a project manager be concerned with monitoring a project's progress?

9. What is the purpose of developing a project communication plan?

10. Compare the information requirements of a project sponsor to those of a project team member. How are they similar? How are they different?

11. Why is effective and efficient communication vital to a project?

12. What are project metrics?

13. Describe the qualities of a good project metric.

14. Why should a project have a good measurement system in place?

15. Discuss why a good measuring system should guide the progress of the project team rather than management alone.

16. What are the advantages of having the project team design its own metrics and measuring system?

17. If "what gets measured gets done," why should a project team not be accountable to numerous project metrics?

18. What is a burn-down chart? What purpose does it serve?

19. Describe the concept of earned value.

20. What is PV?

21. What is EV?

22. What is BAC?

23. Describe how the SPI and CPI can be used to forecast the final cost of a project.

24. What is a project review and what purpose does it serve?

25. What is a status report?

26. What is a progress report?

27. What is a forecast report?

28. When are face-to-face meetings more appropriate than phone calls or email?

29. Describe the role IT can play in supporting the project communications plan.

30. Give an example of how IT might support project stakeholders meeting:

   a. Same time–same place

   b. Same time–different place

   c. Different times–same place

   d. Different times–different place

HUSKY AIR ASSIGNMENT—PILOT ANGELS

Deliverable: Earned Value Analysis

NOTE: This case assignment will require you to use Microsoft Project®. You should work through the Microsoft Project® Tutorial 3 before beginning this case assignment. The tutorial can be found at www.wiley.com/go/marchewka/msprojecttutorial.

To save time and money, you have decided to outsource the testing of a software system to another organization called BugBusters. This company specializes in product testing and is located in another country. Moreover, you have signed a contract and sent them a copy of your software system to fulfill their end of the contract. However, you have asked BugBusters for a WBS and to update you on their progress during the testing phase.

This would also be a good chance for you and your team to do another learning cycle. Read through this assignment first and then meet as a team to develop a Project Team Record and an Action Plan. This will help to improve team learning and to assign responsibilities to complete the assignment.

1. *The following table was received from Bug-Busters. Using this information, create a WBS in Microsoft Project®. You can be creative (i.e., use your own style) in developing the WBS, just be sure that all of the information is entered accurately. The cost of Resource A is $30.00 an hour and the cost of Resource B is $35.00 an hour. All the task activities are sequential—that is, finish-to-start. Testing or the project start date will begin on the first Monday in January of next year regardless of any holidays.*

	Estimate (in days)	Resource Assigned
Phase 1: Test Planning		
Develop unit test plan	2	A
Develop integration test plan	3	A
Develop acceptance test plan	2	B
Phase 2: Unit Testing		
Code walk-through with team	3	A
Test software units	5	B
Identify programs that do not meet specifications	2	B
Modify code	4	A
Retest units	4	B
Verify code meets standards	2	B
Phase 3: Integration Testing		
Test integration of all modules	4	A
Identify components that do not meet specifications	1	B
Modify code	4	A
Retest integration of modules	4	B
Verify components meet standards	2	A
Phase 4: Acceptance Testing		
Business review with client	1	B
Identify units and components that do not meet specifications	2	B
Modify code	3	A
Retest units and components	4	B
Verify that system meets standards	2	A

2. Set baseline for the entire project. This would be a good time to save your work if you haven't already.

A few weeks have now passed, and you just received the following information from Bug-Busters. Update the project's progress.

	Estimate (in days)	Actual (in days)	Percent Complete
Phase 1: Test Planning			
Develop Unit test plan	2	3	100%
Develop integration test plan	3	4	100%
Develop acceptance test plan	2	2	100%
Phase 2: Unit Testing			
Code walk-through with team	3	3	100%
Test software units	5	8	100%
Identify programs that do not meet specifications	2	2	100%
Modify code	4	7	100%
Retest units	4	5	100%
Verify code meets standards	2	2	100%
Phase 3: Integration Testing			
Test integration of all modules	4	5	100%
Identify components that do not meet specifications	1	2	75%
Modify code	4	4	50%
Retest integration of modules	4	4	75%
Verify components meet standards	2	2	80%
Phase 4: Acceptance Testing			
Business review with client	1		0%
Identify units and components that do not meet specifications	2		0%

	Estimate (in days)	Actual (in days)	Percent Complete
Modify code	3		0%
Retest units and components	4		0%
Verify that system meets standards	2		0%

3. *Let's assume that the current date and project status day is the second Wednesday in March, so you'll need to set those dates accordingly.*

a. *Create and print an Earned Value Report. Conduct an earned value analysis to determine how BugBusters is doing. In addition, your analysis should include the Cost Variance, Schedule Variance, and Estimate at Completion as well as an assessment as to whether the original Budget at Completion is still reasonable.*

4. *In addition, run at least two Microsoft Project® standard reports to determine whether you think BugBusters can get the testing of this software back on track. If you think it can, provide a recommendation and solution. If you think Bug-Busters won't be able to get things back on track, remember, that it was your decision to outsource the testing phase to BugBusters and if the testing phase is late or over budget, your final project schedule and budget will be late and over budget. As a result, you'll need to prepare an explanation to your client who may not be all that happy to hear this news.*

5. *What to turn in:*

a. *A professional-grade report that provides an analysis of how BugBusters is doing and your recommendation or explanation to your client. This should include your earned value analysis and at least two other Microsoft Project® standard reports to support your analysis. Include these and any other reports in an appendix.*

b. ***Run and print a Project Summary Report.** Include this as an appendix.*

THE MARTIAL ARTS ACADEMY (MAA)—SCHOOL MANAGEMENT SYSTEM

Deliverable: Earned Value Analysis

NOTE: This case assignment will require you to use Microsoft Project®. You should work through the Microsoft Project® Tutorial 3 before beginning this case assignment. The tutorial can be found at www.wiley.com/go/marchewka/msprojecttutorial.

To save time and money, you have decided to outsource the testing of the MAA School Management System to another organization called TestIt4U. This company specializes in product testing and is located in another country. Moreover, you have signed a contract and sent the company a copy of your software system to fulfill its end of the contract. However, you have asked TestIt4U for a WBS and to update you on its progress during the testing phase.

This would also be a good chance for you and your team to do another learning cycle. Read through this assignment first and then meet as a team to develop a Project Team Record and an Action Plan. This will help to improve team learning and to assign responsibilities to complete the assignment.

1. *The following table was received from TestIt4U. Using this information, create a WBS in Microsoft Project®. You can be creative (i.e., use your own style) in developing the WBS, just be sure that all of the information is entered accurately. The cost of Resource A is $20.00 an hour and the cost of Resource B is $25.00 an hour. All the task activities are sequential—that is, finish-to-start. Testing or the project start date will begin on the first Monday in January of next year regardless of any holidays.*

	Estimate (in days)	Resource Assigned
Phase 1: Test Planning		
Develop unit test plan	2	A
Develop integration test plan	3	A
Develop acceptance test plan	2	B
Phase 2: Unit Testing		
Code walk-through with team	3	A
Test software units	5	B
Identify programs that do not meet specifications	2	B
Modify code	4	A

Retest units	4	B
Verify code meets standards	2	B
Phase 3: Integration Testing		
Test integration of all modules	4	A
Identify components that do not meet specifications	1	B
Modify code	4	A
Retest integration of modules	4	B
Verify components meet standards	2	A
Phase 4: Acceptance Testing		
Business review with client	1	B
Identify units and components that do not meet specifications	2	B
Modify code	3	A
Retest units and components	4	B
Verify that system meets standards	2	A

2. **Set baseline for the entire project. This would be a good time to save your work if you haven't already.**

A few weeks have now passed, and you just received the following information from TestIt4U. Update the project's progress.

	Estimate (in days)	Actual (in days)	Percent Complete
Phase 1: Test Planning			
Develop unit test plan	2	3	100%
Develop integration test plan	3	4	100%
Develop acceptance test plan	2	2	100%
Phase 2: Unit Testing			
Code walk-through with team	3	3	100%
Test software units	5	8	100%
Identify programs that do not meet specifications	2	2	100%
Modify code	4	7	100%

Retest units	4	5	100%
Verify code meets standards	2	2	100%
Phase 3: Integration Testing			
Test integration of all modules	4	5	100%
Identify components that do not meet specifications	1	2	75%
Modify code	4	4	50%
Retest integration of modules	4	4	75%
Verify components meet standards	2	2	80%
Phase 4: Acceptance Testing			
Business review with client	1		0%
Identify units and components that do not meet specifications	2		0%
Modify code	3		0%
Retest units and components	4		0%
Verify that system meets standards	2		0%

3. **Let's assume that the current date and project status day is the second Wednesday in March, so you'll need to set those dates accordingly.**

a. *Create and print an Earned Value Report. Conduct an earned value analysis to determine how TestIt4U is doing. In addition, your analysis should include the Cost Variance, Schedule Variance, and Estimate at Completion as well as an assessment as to whether the original Budget at Completion is still reasonable.*

4. **In addition, run at least two Microsoft Project® standard reports to determine whether you think TestIt4U can get the testing of this software back on track. If you think it can, provide a recommendation and a solution. If you think TestIt4U won't be able to get things back on track, remember, that it was your decision to outsource the testing phase to TestIt4U and if the testing phase is late or over budget, your final project schedule and budget will be late and over budget. As a result, you'll need to prepare an explanation to your client who may not be all that happy to hear this news.**

5. **What to turn in:**

a. **A professional-grade report that provides an analysis of how TestIt4U is doing and your recommendation or explanation to your client. This should include your earned value analysis and at least two other Microsoft Project® standard reports to support your analysis. Include these and any other reports in an appendix.**

b. **Run and print a Project Summary Report.** *Include this as an appendix.*

QUICK THINKING—PROJECTS AS SOCIAL NETWORKS

Simply storing and disseminating information will not encourage individuals assigned to a project to share ideas or become involved as a team. A project social network is an influential mapping of people and ideas.

Managing a project is more than just a set of project plans, tools, and assignment to activities. It's also about people. An effective project manager understands that people assigned to a project enter with a set of self-interests and expectations so it's important to know what makes them tick. For example, a newbie might try to over-achieve and impress, while a more seasoned veteran may believe that he or she has seen it all, and a negative neutron may find all kinds of reasons why nothing will work. As a result, a social network is created as each person shows

and communicates a strong set of self-interests that, in turn, inform and influence the people they work with. Command-and-control techniques or a one-size-fits-all approach will not get people to work together. The project manager must understand the signals each person is sending out and how interests and events can be aligned to create a basis for a successful project.

The available resource pool is an important input for acquiring a project team. Unfortunately, many project managers don't consider fully a person's previous experience, interests, and characteristics when negotiating for or assigning people to a project team. Project managers should not just staff a project, but staff the social network in their favor.

In addition to getting the right people, the project manager adds to the social network by creating a sense of belonging that goes beyond a celebratory project kick-off. This may include thanking people for being part of the project or by bringing them into the loop by asking them what they think about the project charter, scope, or plan.

The project manager can create an environment where people want to belong to the project. By meeting with each person individually, the project manager can get a realistic sense of each person's involvement and commitment.

The project manager should craft a shared vision that is a collection of the expectations and interests of each of the team members. A constancy of purpose should tie everyone together and make everyone feel as though they've been heard. However, one of the most important criteria for creating a social network is a candid, approachable, and likeable project manager.

1. Why is understanding project social networks important?

2. What other aspects should a project manager consider when developing a social network for the project?

SOURCES:

Nagarajan, S. "The Project Social Network." *Projectsatwork*. November 29, 2007.

Nagarajan, S. "The Project Social Network, Pt. II." *Projectsatwork*. December 6, 2007.

Whitepaper, T. "Social Project Management." *Projectsatwork*. September 20, 2012.

QUICK THINKING—COMMUNICATION AND MENTORING

Effective communication is one of the most important aspects of a project manager's job. Today, many project managers spend up to 90 percent of their time communicating with their project team, project sponsor, and other project stakeholders. However, up until about twenty years ago this wasn't the case. Back then, the cornerstone of project management was scheduling. This involved a meticulous and complex process that often involved plotting and hanging large Gantt charts on walls. Today, anyone with access to a personal computer and project management software can "do" projects. However, this won't guarantee success unless you have the right "soft skills" that allow you to communicate effectively with people.

If communication is so important, then why is it so difficult to do well? Often project managers have been in an organization for some time and their familiarity with people, processes, and technology may create a "comfort zone" that is difficult to leave. Second, many times project managers are functional experts who rise through the ranks because of their expertise. Unfortunately, they may have limited or undeveloped communication skills and knowledge about project management processes. Lastly, communication issues often are a result of a person's personality. This may influence how they deal with other people and comfort in using a particular communication style. For example, a person who does not like to deal with others face to face may prefer to rely on email as a primary way to communicate.

Since most project managers do not have a degree in project management or a PMP certification, mentoring can be a valuable means for teaching and learning project management. A project management mentor can play the role of advisor, coach, or teacher to work with a project manager in different ways.

1. How could a project mentor work with an inexperienced project manager in the following situations?

   a. A project manager who doesn't want to try a new approach because she is afraid that suggesting a change may be "rocking the boat"—that is, disruptive change.

   b. A project manager who was a star programmer and is now leading her first software development project.

   c. A project manager who often screams at his project team when he feels that the team is not going to make a scheduled milestone.

SOURCES:

Anich, B. "Talk to Me." *Projectsatwork*. February 16, 2006.

Bashrum, M. "When Experience Walks Out the Door." *Projectsatwork*. November 19, 2012.

Klein, K. E. "Give and Get." *Projectsatwork*. April 21, 2005.

CASE STUDIES

A Case of Collaborative Technologies and a Virtual Team

Jim Tisch, director of Knowledge Management Solutions for Robbins Gioia, LLC, describes a successful rollout of an enterprise content management system and portal platform to support an internal knowledge management initiative for more than 700 employees. The nine targeted outcomes of this project included:

- Improving the management of corporate knowledge
- Bringing together employee knowledge to create best practices for customer engagements
- Creating effective taxonomies and metadata to effectively search for knowledge artifacts
- Developing a rich online environment to promote employee community
- Integrating core business application systems to improve operational efficiencies
- Centralizing reporting to provide access to key business intelligence
- Reducing operating costs
- Replacing paper-based processes with online forms and workflow
- Sharing intellectual capital

Aside from these aggressive requirements, the core team members were geographically dispersed among five states across the United States. As the project neared completion, the project team met at the company's headquarters for a final face-to-face review and decision to launch. This virtual project team met all of its deadlines and goals and made the decision to go live.

Tisch reflected how this was possible without the team relying on face-to-face conference room meetings. As Tisch believes, "The team succeeded by leveraging the use of collaborative technologies, following some online rules of engagement, having a strong virtual work ethic, and demonstrating good communication behaviors. It also succeeded because of trust, empowerment, management, and dedication to the program."

The virtual team relied on collaborative online workspaces to capture issues, schedules, tasks, and other key project information. Other collaboration tools, such

as instant messaging, were useful for quick communication and discussion among team members. All of these online tools together provided an online virtual high performance team. However, some basic rules of engagement added to these technologies:

- Even though there were time zone differences, the team was online with presence technology at designated times during the day.
- Instant messaging tags such as "busy" or "on a call" were respected.
- Status reports were stored in a central workspace.
- Issues, risks, etc., were discussed during regularly scheduled conference calls.
- Documents and other files were tagged and stored in a central workspace.
- WebEx sessions allowed team members to share each other's desktops and allowed for program review sessions.

In addition, Tisch credits the success of the project to several additional factors. These include following a rapid applications development approach rather than a traditional "waterfall" approach and management's support in allowing the practice of telecommuting. As Tisch summarizes, "Businesses must embrace the Web as a platform and utilize its strengths for managing a geographically dispersed project team. If you have not looked at enterprise instant messaging, shared workspaces, Web conferencing, presence, etc., for how they can improve the collaboration and communication of your project teams, now is the time. The confinement of brick and mortar meetings has passed; today's workforce is more mobile and agile."

1. What is the importance of having rules of engagement to successfully support a virtual team when using collaborative technologies? Can you come up with any other rules that could be added?

2. Jim Tisch describes a number of advantages for using collaborative technologies. What resistance might be encountered if, for example, older workers were expected to use these technologies?

3. Using the Web as a resource, design a suite of available collaborative technologies that would

support a geographically dispersed project team located in New York City, San Francisco, and Beijing. What specific communication needs would each technology support?

SOURCES:

Tisch, J. "Know-Go." *Projectsatwork*. October 25, 2007.

Webber, C. "Making Collaboration Work." *Projectsatwork*. January 27, 2005.

Gerber, K. "Better Rapport with Virtual Teams." *Projectsatwork*. May 14, 2013.

Social Software for Project Management

Social software is an emerging technology that is being applied to a wide range of applications to support personal communication and relationships using an electronic network. Social networking Web sites such as Facebook® and Twitter® are examples of social software, as are blogs and wikis. Other types of social software such as virtual worlds—Second Life® or SimCity™—instant messaging, and email may fit into this category.

The term blog, short for Web log, focuses on a specific topic or interest. It is a Web site that allows people to post journal entries, with the most recent posting at the top. Many organizations are using blogs to communicate a corporate position or message to the public. People create and participate in blogs to chronicle their daily lives or to make their views and ideas public. Blogs can also include pictures or video clips that can be viewed by anyone on the Web or by a select few within an organization, if protected by a firewall. Readers can post comments that can evolve into a type of conversation.

Wiki is short for the Hawaiian term "wiki wiki," which means quick, and is a Web site that allows people to edit content collectively. The main difference between a blog and a wiki is that an author's post on a blog remains unaltered, while a wiki allows for shared authorship where people can add new content or change existing content without permission. Proponents of wikis believe that collaborative authorship provides a type of synergy that is greater than the sum of each individual author's contribution. Similar to blogs, a wiki can be open to the public or restricted within the organization. Blogs and wikis can also be combined into a hybrid technology that combines the best features of each tool. Articles, postings, or other content can be arranged in reverse chronological order on a main page like a blog but allows for the content to be edited like a wiki.

Today, blogs and wikis are viewed as new types of organizational collaboration tools. While many people still rely on email as a primary source of communication, they are finding that email makes it difficult to find what they need or to manage documents effectively. Often important information is buried in an inbox, and searching for this information can be inefficient. Moreover, sharing information via email can be disorganized and haphazard because this information can be passed along largely on the prerogative of the sender. This can be in terms of the "to" or "cc" (carbon copy), or "bc" (blind copy) fields. As Chris Alden, vice president with an enterprise blogging company called Six Apart, suggests "If there is information in a cc storm and you're not on it, then you don't have any idea about what's going on. With blogs, information about specific topics lives on the intranet, and critical information can be broadcast to all who want to see it and who have permission to see it." In addition, another disadvantage of email is that when individuals leave an organization their email account is deleted, along with any valuable information that was in their account. As Anil Dash, chief evangelist for Six Apart points out "It's forever lost. If it's a blog, it doesn't disappear when that person leaves."

Blogs and wikis are becoming more common in organizations because they are relatively inexpensive and easy to set up and maintain. Because these technologies are browser based, there is a short learning curve for the users. For example, Eugene Roman is a group president of systems and technology at Bell Canada and uses an enterprise blog as a forum where employees can discuss new product ideas, streamline processes, or even find new ways to cut energy costs. The blog effort was called "ID-ah" and first used by a few hundred employees. By the end two years, Bell Canada employees have submitted over 1,000 ideas with about 3,000 comments on those ideas. Of those 1,000 ideas, 27 have been culled for review and 12 have been implemented.

Interest in organizational wikis and blogs is growing as project teams are beginning to use them to improve communication, create a sense of community, and as a medium for collaboration and document management. They can provide a central location for meeting notes, files, calendars, ideas, and schedules.

1. Social software can provide a number of opportunities for managing projects. What are some

challenges or issues that should be considered before a project team implements a blog or a wiki?

2. Jonathan Edwards, an analyst with the Yankee Group, states, "Some people clutch to their corporate email boxes as if they were cigarettes. They're hopelessly addicted. We're all so accustomed to it. You can't change the way people work overnight." Blogs and wikis have a number of advantages over email. As a project manager, how could you reduce your project team's resistance to rely less on email and embrace the use of social software?

3. Come up with an application specific to project management that uses social software. This could include a blog, wiki, instant messaging, or even a virtual world simulator.

SOURCES:

Waters, J. K. "ABC: An Introduction to Blogs and Wikis in the Business World." *CIO Magazine*. July 6, 2007.

Lynch, C. G. "How to Use Enterprise Blogs to Streamline Project Management." *CIO Magazine*. December 7, 2007.

Lynch, C. G. "Seven Reasons for Your Company to Start an Internal Blog." *CIO Magazine*. June 20, 2007.

A Failure to Communicate

Communication is one of the most important project management core areas. For small projects, communication can be as informal and simple as telling a stakeholder when project work is going to start or when the work is completed. For larger projects, a formal communication plan that tells stakeholders of the project's current status, its progress since the last report, and forecasted outcomes is critical. In addition, communication should include outstanding issues, scope change requests, and risks so that stakeholder expectations are managed efficiently and effectively. An effective communication plan should be proactive and tailored to the project stakeholders.

However, many project managers become too involved with managing the project, problem solving, and acting as a leader for the project team. Unfortunately, many project managers are not proficient in communicating with the project stakeholders. As Tom Mochal suggests, "… when your manager or client asks how the project is going, you of course, reply 'oh fine.' My experience with project managers is that many of them try to communicate with the minimum possible effort and the fewest words. I know that part of this hesitancy is a lack of comfort with written and verbal

communication in general. I am also convinced that most project managers simply do not understand what proactive communication provides to a project."

According to Robert Anich, many times communication issues result from a project manager's personality and style of communication. More specifically, Anich contends, "If the project manager does not like social interaction and talking to people face to face—either because he or she is non-confrontational, reserved, or fearful of accountability or responsibility—the project may be heading for disaster."

Robert Scott also suggests, "Silence exists in organizations because people feel it's not safe to speak up about the problems they see. They shy away from discussions about behavior, expectations, or performance because they are afraid of a negative outcome—like making an enemy, enduring a miserable argument or getting canned."

This idea is supported by empirical evidence. A worldwide study called "Silence Fails: The Five Crucial Conversations for Flawless Execution" was conducted by The Concours Group and VitalSmarts LC and included 1,000 project managers and executives from major organizations analyzed more than 2,200 projects. The study reports that although 90 percent of the project managers surveyed said that they routinely encounter one or more critical problems during a project, the most detrimental is silence.

As Robert Scott points out, "Initiatives are derailed when people are unwilling or unable to have conversations about the problems they see." In addition, "… problems fester, work-arounds proliferate, politics prevail, and failure becomes almost inevitable."

There is good news. The study reports that projects can get back on course when project stakeholders are able and willing to talk about the project's issues. Lastly, Tom Mochal believes that no news is bad news. More specifically, "Remember, delivering bad news is not a communication problem. Not effectively managing expectations is a problem if clients or stakeholders end up being surprised. Lay it all out in the status report. Don't surprise people."

1. Why is having a proactive communications plan important for managing project stakeholder expectations?

2. Using Figure 8.7 (The Communication and Collaboration Matrix), what is the best way for a project manager to deliver bad news to a project sponsor or client? What would be the least effective? Be sure to support your answers.

3. Suppose you are the mentor for a relatively inexperienced project manager who is uncomfortable delivering news to a project sponsor. Based on the project manager's projections, it appears that the project is going to be six months late and 40 percent over budget. Aside from looking for a new job, what advice would you give this project manager to handle this situation effectively?

SOURCES:
Mochal, T. "Communication 101-Plus." *Projectsatwork*. June 17, 2004.
Anich, R. "Talk to Me!" *Projectsatwork*. February 16, 2006.
Scott, R. "For IT Projects, Silence Can Be Deadly." *ComputerWorld*. February 5, 2007.

BIBLIOGRAPHY

1. Nicholas, J. M. *Managing Business and Engineering Projects: Concepts and Implementation*. Upper Saddle River, NJ: Prentice-Hall, 1990.

2. Crews, N. "Stakeholder Management 101." *Projectsatwork*. October 16, 2013.

3. Van Genuchten, M. "Why is Software Late? An Empirical Study of Reasons for Delay in Software Development." *IEEE Transactions on Software Engineering*, 1991, Vol. 17, no. 6.

4. Neuendorf, S. *Project Measurement*. Vienna, VA: Management Concepts, 2002.

5. Edberg, D. T. "Creating a Balanced Measurement Program." *Information Systems Management*, Spring, 1997, Vol. 14, no. 2, 32–40.

6. Meyer, C. "How the Right Measures Help Teams Excel." *Harvard Business Review*, May–June, 1994, 95–103.

7. Project Management Institute (PMI). *A Guide to the Project Management Body of Knowledge (PMBOK Guide)*. Newton Square, PA: PMI Publishing, 2013.

8. McGevna, V. "The Fog of Earned Value." *Projectsatswork*. November 2, 2011.

9. Flemming, Q. W., and J. M. Koppelman. *Earned Value Project Management*. Newton Square, PA: Project Management Institute, 1996.

10. Lenoff Schiff, J. "15 Ways to Screw Up an IT Project." *CIO Magazine*. July 17, 2013.

11. Jordan, A. "Two Ears, One Mouth." *Projectsatwork*. July 12, 2011.

9

Managing Project Quality

CHAPTER OBJECTIVES

This chapter will focus on the philosophies, processes, and tools for project quality management to develop a project quality management plan. After studying this chapter, you should understand and be able to:

- Describe project quality management (PQM) in terms of planning for quality, quality assurance, and quality control to continuously improve the project's products and supporting processes.

- Identify several quality gurus, or founders of the quality movement, and their role in shaping quality philosophies that can be applied to project management.

- Define process capability and maturity defined under a quality management systems called the capability maturity model integrated (CMMI).

- Distinguish between verification and validation activities and how these activities support project quality management.

- Apply the quality concepts, methods, and tools introduced in this chapter to develop a project quality plan.

INTRODUCTION

What is quality? Before answering that question, keep in mind that quality can mean different things to different people. For example, if we were comparing the quality of two cars—an expensive luxury car with leather seats and every possible option to a lower priced economy car that basically gets you where you want to go—many people might be inclined to say that the more expensive car has higher quality. Although the more expensive car has more features, you might not consider it a bargain if you had to keep bringing it back to the shop for expensive repairs. The less expensive car might start looking much better to you if it were more dependable or met higher safety standards. On the other hand, why do car manufacturers build different models of cars with different price ranges? If everyone could afford luxury cars, then quality comparisons among different manufacturers' cars would be much easier. Although you might have your eyes on a luxury car, your current financial situation might be a constraint. You might have to buy a car you could afford. Therefore, it is important to distinguish between quality and grade. **Quality** focuses on fulfilling requirements, while **grade** centers on the intent of the design (1).

Therefore, it is important not to define quality only in terms of features or functionality. Other attributes such as dependability or safety may be just as important to the customer. Similarly, we can build products or systems that have a great deal of functionality (i.e., high grade), but that are considered "low quality" if they perform poorly. On the other hand, we can develop products or systems that have few features or limited functionality (i.e., low grade), but that are considered "high quality" if they have no defects. The project team and manager must work closely with the customer, user, or sponsor to determine the acceptable standards for quality and grade.

However, we still need a working definition of quality. The dictionary defines **quality** as "*an inherent or distinguishing characteristic; a property,*" or as something "*having a high degree of excellence.*" In business, quality has been defined in terms of "*fitness for use*" and "*conformance to requirements.*" "Fitness for use" concentrates on delivering a product or system that meets the customer's needs, while "conformance to requirements" centers more on meeting a predefined set of standards. Therefore, quality depends on the needs or expectations of the customer. It is up to the project manager and project team to define accurately those needs or expectations, while allowing the customer to remain within resource constraints (2).

Although the concepts and philosophies of quality have received a great deal of attention over the last 60 years in the manufacturing and service sectors, many of these same ideas have been integrated into a discipline called **project quality management (PQM)**. The PMBOK Guide® defines PQM (1) as:

> "*... the processes and activities of the performing organization that determine quality policies, objectives, and responsibilities so that the project will satisfy the needs for which it was undertaken.*" (p. 227)

Figure 9.1 provides a summary of the PQM concepts discussed in this chapter. PQM begins with defining the quality standards in terms of grade and tolerances for quality. Will the customer or user be willing to sacrifice quality in order to start using the product, service, or system more quickly?

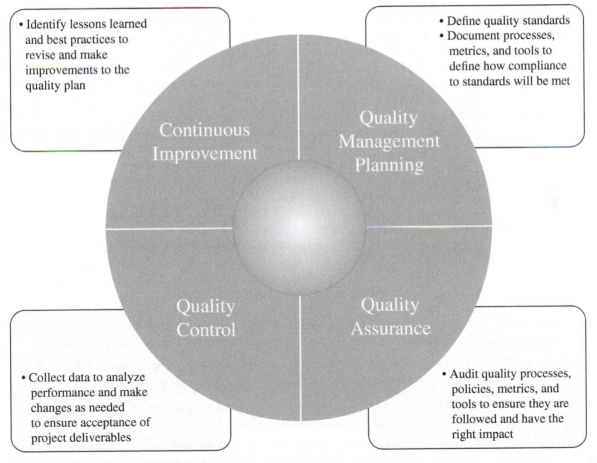

Figure 9.1 Project Quality Management

For example, if you were to build a new house, would you delay moving in if the paint on one of the walls had a small scratch? Probably not, because this could be easily fixed. On the other hand, a lack of plumbing or a roof may be a reason to delay the closing.

Quality management planning requires that adequate time and budget are allocated in the project plan for testing and other activities to ensure the project team is building the right product or system and building it the right way. In addition, all of the quality standards along with the processes, metrics, and tools to determine whether these standards are met are documented in a project quality plan.

Quality assurance, on the other hand, focuses on auditing or defining a set of checks and balances to ensure that the project team is following the processes outlined in the quality management plan and that metrics are being collected and analyzed as part of **quality control**. Following the quality assurance and quality control activities, the project stakeholders should reflect and document lessons learned. This can lead to **continuous improvement** by identifying best practices and improvements to the quality management planning processes.

The activities of PQM should focus on both the project's *deliverables* and *processes*. From our point of view, the project's most important deliverable is the product or system that the project team must deliver. The product or system must be "fit for use" and "conform to specified requirements" outlined in both the project's scope and requirements definition. More importantly, the product or system must add measurable value to the sponsoring organization while meeting the scope, schedule, and budget objectives.

Quality can, however, also be built into the project management and product development processes. We can also view these processes as part of a quality chain where outputs of one process serve as inputs to other project management processes and phases (3). By focusing on both the product and chain of project processes, the project organization can use its resources more efficiently and effectively, minimize errors, and meet project stakeholder expectations.

The cost of quality can be viewed as the cost of conforming to standards (i.e., building quality into the product and processes through training, testing, and so forth) as well as the cost of not conforming to the standards (i.e., rework, liabilities, downtime, maintenance, and so forth). Substandard levels of quality can be viewed as waste, errors, or the failure to meet the project sponsor's or client's needs, expectations, or requirements (4). Failing to meet the quality requirements or standards can have negative consequences for all project stakeholders and can impact the other project objectives. More specifically, adding additional work or repeating project activities will probably extend the project schedule and expand the project budget. According to Barry Boehm, a software defect that takes one hour to fix when the systems requirements are being defined will end up taking 100 hours to correct if not discovered until the system is in production (5).

Although the amount of rework may not be linear, Figure 9.2 provides an illustration of why finding a defect becomes more costly as the project progresses. For example, let's say that a project team is working with a key stakeholder to develop a new mobile app. Unfortunately, a key requirement is not included during the requirements definition. If this missing requirement is caught early, for example, during the requirements definition, the amount of rework is minimal because the missing requirement can just be added to the list. However, as the project progresses the amount of rework increases. Let's assume that the missing requirement is discovered during implementation or after the app is released. In this case, the requirement would have to be defined in terms of developing the user story, developed, tested, and then re-released. Therefore, the costs of a product or system defect may include (6):

- The time and effort spent by the project team investigating and diagnosing the defect.
- The time and effort of redesigning, developing, and retesting the defect.
- Any additional time and effort if retesting uncovers any new defects.
- The embarrassment and loss of good will if a defect is found by the customer.

The remainder of this chapter will focus on introducing and delving into several PQM concepts. It includes an overview of the quality philosophies and a brief history of the people who provided

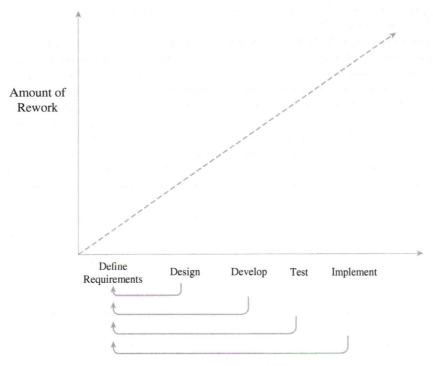

Figure 9.2 The Impact of Rework

the cornerstones for quality initiatives. Finally, a framework to support PQM will integrate these concepts to provide a foundation for quality management planning, quality assurance, quality control, and continuous improvement.

QUALITY PHILOSOPHIES

In this section, we will focus on the concepts associated with quality management with a brief history of the people who helped shape this important area. This knowledge may help in giving us a better understanding of how to apply the quality concepts and tools when developing a project quality plan.

Craftsmanship

Since the dawn of humankind, *quality* has been synonymous with *craftsmanship*. For the earliest Homo sapiens, the quality of their tools and weapons often determined survival. The idea of craftsmanship was formalized during the Middle Ages when the quality of products and the processes to produce those products were held in high esteem. Guilds were created by merchants and artisans for each trade or craft. These guilds regulated who could sell goods or practice a trade in a particular town. Members charged similar prices for products of similar quality and ensured that there never were more craftsmen of a particular trade in a town than could make a decent living. Guilds also ensured the quality of a particular product by regulating the forms of labor. Members of the guild were classified as masters, apprentices, and journeymen. The masters owned the shops and trained the apprentices. Training for apprentices required several years, and, upon completion, an apprentice could become a journeyman. Journeymen who wanted to become masters had to demonstrate the quality of their work to the guild.

Scientific Management

As a young man, **Frederic W. Taylor** (1856–1915) worked as an apprentice at the Enterprise Hydraulics Shop in Pennsylvania. Supposedly, he was told by the older workers how much he should produce each day—no more, no less (7). The workers were paid on a piece-rate basis, and if they worked harder or smarter, management would change the production rates and the amount a worker would be paid. These arbitrary rates, or *rules of thumb*, restricted output, and workers produced well below their potential.

Later, as an engineer, Taylor became one of the first to study systematically the relationships between people and tasks. He believed that the production process could become more efficient by increasing the specialization and the division of labor. Using an approach called **scientific management**, Taylor believed that a task could be broken down into smaller tasks and studied to identify the best and most efficient way of doing each subtask. In turn, a supervisor could then teach the worker and ensure that the worker did only those actions essential for completing the tasks, in order to remove human variability or errors. At that time, most workers in U.S. factories were immigrants, and language barriers created communication problems among the workers, their supervisors, and even with many coworkers. The use of a stopwatch as a basis for time-motion studies provided a more scientific approach. Workers could produce at their full potential, and arbitrary rates set by management would be removed.

Under the scientific management approach, quality, to a great degree, focused on improving the processes and machines (or technology), with less emphasis on the role people played. More specifically, although the scientific management approach became quite popular, it was not without controversy. Many so-called efficiency experts ignored the human factors and tended to believe that profits could be increased by speeding up the workers. Dehumanizing the workers led to conflict between labor and management and eventually laid the foundation for labor unions.

The Total Quality Management (TQM) Gurus

W. Edwards Deming (1900–1933) became aware of the extensive division of labor while working at the Western Electric Hawthorne plant in Chicago, Illinois, during the 1920s. Management tended to treat the workers as just another cog in the machinery. Moreover, the workers were not directly responsible for the quality of the products they produced. Final inspection was used as a means to control quality but did little to reduce the waste associated with scrap and rework.

As a trained statistician, Deming was interested in the application of statistical theory so that management could make decisions based on facts rather than on intuition. Deming also realized that costly inspections could be eliminated if workers were properly trained and empowered to monitor and control the quality of the items they produced.

Soon after World War II, Japan was a country faced with the challenge of rebuilding itself after devastation and military defeat. Moreover, Japan had few natural resources so the export of manufactured goods was essential to rebuilding its economy. Unfortunately, the goods that it produced were considered inferior in many world markets.

To help Japan rebuild, a group called the Union of Japanese Scientists and Engineers (JUSE) was formed to work with U.S. and allied experts to improve the quality of the products Japan produced. As part of this effort, in the 1950s, Deming was invited to provide a series of day-long lectures to Japanese managers. The focus of these lectures was statistical quality and control. The Japanese embraced these principles, and the quality movement acquired a strong foothold in Japan. In tribute to Deming, the Japanese even named their most prestigious quality award the Deming Prize.

Until the 1970s, Deming was virtually unknown in the West. In 1980, a television documentary entitled *If Japan Can, Why Can't We?* introduced him and his ideas to his own country and to the rest of the world. Many of Deming's philosophies and teachings are summarized in his famous 14 points for quality that are outlined and discussed in his book *Out of the Crisis* (pp. 22–23). The following summarizes some of Deming's main ideas:

- Organizations must have constancy of purpose to be competitive, stay in business, and provide jobs.
- Leadership is critical.
- Don't rely on mass inspection of the end project. Build quality into the processes and product along the way.
- Train and educate people, drive out fear, and let people take pride in their work.
- Always strive to improve the quality and productivity associated with the manufacturing process or services provided.
- Improve communication among departments and business units.
- Eliminate slogans, work quotas, and management by numbers.
- Quality is the responsibility of everyone in the organization.

While processes and machines (or technology) play an important role in quality, Deming's teachings (as well as the following TQM experts) emphasize the value and importance of people to a greater extent than the scientific method.

Joseph Juran (1904–2008)—Juran's philosophies and teachings have also had an important and significant impact on many organizations worldwide. Like Deming, Juran started out as an engineer in the 1920s. In 1951, he published the *Quality Control Handbook*, which viewed quality as "fitness for use" as perceived by the customer. Like Deming, Juran was invited to Japan by JUSE in the early 1950s to conduct seminars and lectures on quality.

Juran's message on quality focuses on his belief that quality does not happen by accident—it must be planned. In addition, Juran distinguishes external customers from internal customers. Juran's view of quality consists of a quality trilogy—*quality planning, quality improvement,* and *quality control.*

- *Quality Planning*
  - Identify the customer
  - Determine the customer's needs
  - Be sure to understand those needs
  - Develop a product that meets the customer's needs
  - Ensure that the product meets the customer's needs as well as the needs of the organization
- *Quality Improvement*
  - Design a process that can produce the product
  - Optimize the process
- *Quality Control*
  - Provide evidence that the process can produce the product
  - Operationalize the process

Phillip Crosby (1926–2001)—Similar to F.W. Taylor, Crosby developed many of his ideas from his experience working on an assembly line. After serving in the U.S. Navy during the Korean War, he worked his way up in a variety of quality control positions until he held the position of corporate vice president and director of quality for ITT. In 1979, he published a best-selling book, *Quality is Free*, and he eventually left ITT to start his own consulting firm that focused on teaching other organizations how to manage quality.

Crosby defined quality as conformance to requirements based on the customer's needs and advocated a top-down approach to quality in which it is management's responsibility to set a quality example for workers to follow. Crosby also advocated "doing it right the first time" and "zero defects," which translate into the idea that quality is free and that nonconformance to requirements costs money.

Based on the writings and teachings of such quality gurus as Deming, Juran, and Crosby, the core values of these quality programs have a central theme that includes a focus on the customer, leadership, incremental or continuous improvement, and the idea that prevention is less expensive than relying solely on inspection. While originally focused on manufacturing, the concepts of quality have been extended to other types of industries, as well as to project management.

PROCESS CAPABILITY AND MATURITY

In 1986, the Software Engineering Institute (SEI), a federally funded research development center at Carnegie Mellon University, set out to help organizations improve their software development processes. With the help of the Mitre Corporation and Watts Humphrey, a framework was developed to assess and evaluate the capability of software processes and their maturity. This work evolved into the capability maturity model (CMM) (8).

Since the original CMM initiative, organizations have used a number of CMMs for different disciplines or areas. Although helpful, using several different models can be problematic because a particular model may limit process improvements to a specific area or discipline within the organization. As a result, the CMMI project was initiated to sort out the problem of using a number of CMMs by combining several models into a single framework that could be used to improve processes across the organization. The CMMI framework was designed so that other disciplines could be integrated in the future (9). In this section, we will focus on how the CMMI can support project QA activities.

The CMMI provides a set of recommended practices that define key process areas specific to software development. The objective of the CMMI is to offer guidance on how an organization can best control its processes for developing and maintaining a product or system. In addition, the framework provides a path for helping organizations evolve their current software processes toward software engineering and management excellence (10). In fact, research has shown that organizations that increased their maturity by one level have seen significant improvements in productivity and customer satisfaction (11).

To understand how the CMMI may support project quality, several concepts must first be defined:

- *Process*—A set of activities, methods, or practices and transformations used by people to develop and maintain a product of system and the deliverables associated with the project. Included are such things as project plans, design documents, code, test cases, user manuals, and so forth.

- *Process capability*—The *expected* results that can be achieved by following a particular process. More specifically, the capability of an organization's processes provides a way of predicting the outcomes that can be expected if the same processes are used from one project to the next.

- *Process performance*—The *actual* results that are achieved by following a particular process. Therefore, the actual results achieved through process performance can be compared to the expected results achieved through process capability.

- *Process maturity*—The extent to which a particular process is explicitly and consistently defined, managed, measured, controlled, and effectively used throughout the organization.

One of the keys to the CMMI is using the idea of process maturity to describe the difference between immature and mature organizations. In an immature organization, processes are improvised or developed ad hoc. For example, a project team may be faced with the task of defining user requirements. When it comes time to complete this task, the various members of the team may have different ideas concerning how to accomplish it. Several of the members may approach the task differently and, subsequently, achieve different results. Even if a well-defined process that specifies the steps, tools, resources, and deliverables required is in place, the team may not follow the specified process very closely or at all.

Mature organizations, on the other hand, provide a stark contrast to the immature organization. More specifically, processes and the roles of individuals are defined explicitly and communicated throughout the organization. The processes are consistent throughout the organization and improved continually based on experimentation or experiences. The quality of each process is monitored so that the products and processes are predictable across different projects. Budgets and schedules are based on past projects so they are more realistic, and the project goals and objectives are more likely to be achieved. Mature organizations are proactive, and they are able to follow a set of disciplined processes throughout the project.

The CMMI defines five levels of process maturity, each requiring many small steps as a path of incremental and continuous process improvement. These stages are based on many of the quality concepts and philosophies of Deming, Juran, and Crosby (10). Figure 9.3 illustrates the CMMI framework for process maturity. Each level allows an organization to assess its current level of process maturity and then helps it prioritize the improvement efforts in terms of the key process area it needs to have in place to reach the level of maturity (12).

Maturity levels provide a well-defined evolutionary path for achieving a mature process organization. There are five levels of process maturity.

Level 1: Initial—The initial level generally provides a starting point for many organizations. This level is characterized by an immature organization in which the project process is ad hoc and often reactive to crises. Few, if any, processes for developing and maintaining the product or system are defined. The Level 1 organization does not have a stable environment for projects, and success of a project rests largely with the people on the project and not the processes that they follow. As a result, success is difficult to repeat across different projects throughout the organization.

Level 2: Repeatable—At this level, basic policies, processes, and controls for managing a project are in place. Project schedules and budgets are more realistic because planning and managing new projects are based upon past experiences with similar projects. Although processes between projects

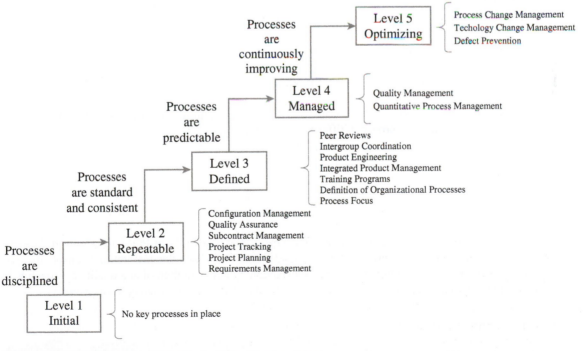

Figure 9.3 CMMI Process Maturity and Key Process Areas

may be different at this level, the process capability of Level 2 organizations is more disciplined because processes are more documented, enforced, and improving. As a result, many previous project successes can be repeated by other project teams on other projects.

Level 3: Defined—At Level 3, engineering and management processes are documented and standardized throughout the organization and become the organization's standard process. Also, a group is established to oversee the organization's processes, and an organization-wide training program to support the standard process is implemented. Subsequently, activities, roles, and responsibilities are well defined and understood throughout the organization. The process capability of this level is characterized as being standard, consistent, stable, and repeatable. However, this standard process may be tailored to suit the individual characteristics or needs of an individual project.

Level 4: Managed—At this level, quantitative metrics for measuring and assessing productivity and quality are established for both products and processes. This information is collected and stored in an organization-wide repository that can be used to analyze and evaluate processes and products. Control over projects is achieved by reducing the variability of project performance so that it falls within acceptable control boundaries. The processes of organizations at this level are characterized as being quantifiable and predictable because quantitative controls are in place to determine whether the process performs within operational limits. Moreover, these controls allow for predicting trends and identifying when assignable causes occur that require immediate attention.

Level 5: Optimizing—At the highest level of process maturity, the whole organization is focused on continuous process improvement. These improvements come about as a result of innovations using new technology and methods and incremental process improvement. Moreover, the organization has the ability to identify its areas of strengths and weaknesses. Innovations and best practices based on lessons learned are identified and disseminated throughout the organization.

As an organization's process maturity increases, the difference between expected results and actual results narrows. In addition, performance can be expected to improve when maturity levels increase because costs and development time will decrease, while quality and productivity increase. According to the SEI, skipping maturity levels is counterproductive. If an organization was evaluated at Level 1, for example, and wanted to skip to Level 3 or Level 4, it might be difficult because the CMMI identifies levels through which an organization must evolve in order to establish a culture based on experiences. The CMMI model can provide a repeatable method for continuous improvement and maturity that can lead to greater competitiveness and effectiveness (13).

THE PROJECT QUALITY MANAGEMENT PLAN

All project stakeholders want quality; unfortunately, there is no commonly accepted approach for PQM, so many project managers approach it differently (14). Therefore, a basic framework will be introduced here to guide and integrate quality planning, quality assurance, quality control, and quality improvement. This framework provides a basic foundation for developing a project quality plan to support the project's quality objectives.

This plan may be formal or informal, depending on the size of the project; however, the underlying philosophies, standards, and methods for defining and achieving quality should be well understood and communicated to all project stakeholders.

PQM also becomes a strategy for risk management. The objectives of PQM are achieved through a quality plan that outlines the goals, methods, standards, reviews, and documentation to ensure that all steps have been taken to guarantee customer satisfaction by assuring them that a quality approach has been taken (14). Figure 9.4 provides a framework for the project quality management plan.

Quality Philosophies and Principles

Before setting out to develop a project quality management plan, the project organization should define the direction and overall purpose for developing the plan. This purpose should be grounded upon the

Figure 9.4 A Framework for the Project Quality Management Plan

quality philosophies, teachings, and principles that have evolved over the years. Although several different quality gurus and their teachings were introduced earlier, several common themes can provide the backbone for any organization's plan for ensuring quality of the project's processes and product. These ideas include: focusing on customer satisfaction, preventing mistakes, improving the process to improve the product, making quality everyone's responsibility, and employing fact-based management.

Focus on Customer Satisfaction—Customer satisfaction is the foundation of quality philosophies and concepts. Customers have expectations, and meeting those expectations can lead to improved customer satisfaction. In addition, it is important to keep in mind that customers may be internal or external project stakeholders. The external customer is the ultimate customer—that is, the project sponsor, client, user, or paying customer.

However, internal customers are just as important and may be thought of as an individual or a group who are the receivers of specific project deliverables or an output from a process. For example, project team members may be assigned the task of defining the detailed features or requirements for a new product or application system. These features or requirements may be handed off to one or several engineers or systems analysts who will develop the design models and then hand these models off to the developers. The quality of the requirements specifications, in terms of accuracy, completeness, and understandability, for example, will have a direct bearing on the quality of the models developed by the engineers or systems analysts. In turn, the quality of the models will impact the quality of the product or application developed. Therefore, we can view the series of project and product development processes as a customer chain made up of both internal and external customers.

As you might expect, a chain is only as strong as its weakest link, and any quality problems that occur can impact the quality of the project's product downstream. The primary focus of the project team should be to meet the expectations and needs of the customers or stakeholders because they are the ultimate judge of quality (15).

Prevention, Not Inspection—One of Deming's most salient ideas is that quality cannot be inspected into a product. Quality is either built into the product or it is not. Therefore, the total cost of quality is equal to the sum of four components—prevention, inspection, internal failure, and external failure. The costs associated with prevention consist of all the actions a project team may take to prevent defects, mistakes, bugs, and so forth from occurring in the first place. The cost of inspection entails the costs associated with measuring, evaluating, and auditing the project processes and deliverables to ensure conformance to standards or requirement specifications.

Costs of internal failure can be attributed to rework or fixing a defective product before it is delivered to the customer. These types of problems are, hopefully, found before the product is released. External failure costs entail the costs to fix problems or defects discovered after the product has been released. External failure costs can create the most damage for an organization because the customer's views and attitudes toward the organization may keep the customer from doing repeat business with the organization in the future. Therefore, prevention is the least expensive cost and can reduce the likelihood of a defect or bug reaching the customer undetected. In turn, this will reduce the cost of development and improve the overall quality of the product or system (14).

Improve the Process to Improve the Product—Processes are needed to create all of the project's deliverables and the final product or system. Subsequently, improving the capability and maturity of a process will improve the quality of the product. Project processes must be activities that add value to the overall customer chain. In addition, processes can be broken down into subprocesses and must be repeatable and measurable so that they can be controlled and improved. Improving any process, however, takes time because process improvement is often incremental. Most importantly, improvement should be continuous.

Quality Is Everyone's Responsibility—Quality improvement requires time and resources. As many of the quality gurus point out, quality has to be more than just a slogan. It requires a commitment from management and the people who will do the work. Quality requires a team effort that requires quality-consciousness throughout the project (16). Management must not only provide resources, but must also remove organizational barriers and provide leadership. On the other hand, those individuals who perform the work usually know their job better than their managers. These people are often the ones who have direct contact with the end customer. Therefore, they should be responsible and empowered for ensuring quality and encouraged to take pride in their work. Quality improvement may not be all that easy to achieve because it may require an organization to change its culture and focus on long-term gains at the expense and pressure to deliver short-term results.

Fact-Based Management—It is also important that a quality program and project quality plan be based on hard evidence. Managing by facts requires that the organization capture data and analyze trends that determine what is actually true about its process performance. The organization must structure itself in such a way that it is more responsive to all stakeholders and collect and analyze data and trends that will provide a key foundation for evaluating and improving processes (17).

Quality Standards, Processes, and Metrics

Standards are agreed upon specifications or criteria to ensure that all of the project's deliverables meet their intended purpose. They must be meaningful and clearly defined in order to be relevant and useful. Standards also provide a basis for measurement because they provide a criterion, or basis, for comparison.

Figure 9.5 illustrates some examples of project's standards. These standards can be defined in terms of the project's scope or deliverables. For example, several dimensions can serve as quality standards for a software product. These include the application's reliability, usability, performance, response, security, aesthetics, and maintainability (18). Although these dimensions focus on an application system, other standards can be identified for each of the project deliverables (e.g., business case, project charter and baseline project plan, project reporting, user documentation, etc.). For example, standards could help ensure the quality of the business case by defining how research should be conducted or how alternatives should be analyzed. On the other hand, standards may be in place for collecting and documenting customer requirements or for estimating tasks or activities.

Metrics are vital for gauging quality by establishing tolerance limits and identifying defects. A **defect** is an undesirable behavior associated with the product or process (15). It is a failure to comply with a required standard (14). Defects are often referred to as *bugs*.

A set of metrics allows the project manager and team to monitor each of the project standards. There are two parts to a metric—the metric itself and an acceptable value or range of values for that metric (15). Metrics should focus on three categories (18):

- *Process*—The defects introduced by the processes required to develop or create the project deliverables should be controlled. Process metrics can be used to improve product development or maintenance processes. Process metrics should focus on the effectiveness of identifying and removing defects or bugs.

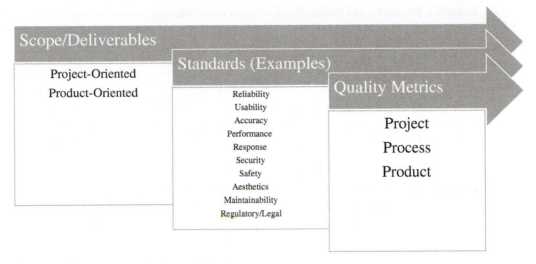

Figure 9.5 Project Standards and Metrics

- *Product*—The intrinsic quality of the deliverables and the satisfaction of the customer with these deliverables is important to measure. These metrics should attempt to describe the characteristics of the project's deliverables and final product. Examples of product metrics may focus on customer satisfaction, performance, reliability, security, and so forth.

- *Project*—The project management processes to ensure that the project meets its overall goal as well as its scope, schedule, and budget objectives must be managed effectively.

Metrics can be used to determine whether the product and project deliverables meet requirements for "fitness for use" and "conformance to requirements" as defined by the internal or external customers. Many technical people, however, often feel that standards are restricting and only serve to stifle creativity. Although too many standards that are rigidly followed can lend support to that argument, well-defined standards and procedures are necessary for ensuring quality. A quality approach can also decrease development costs because the sooner a defect or bug is found and corrected, the less costly it will be down the road (14). Table 9.1 provides a summary of some common process, product, and project metrics.

Quality Assurance

Quality assurance (QA) provides an auditing of the project to ensure that the documented standards, processes, and metrics defined in the quality management plan are being followed (1). Verification and validation (V&V) are important QA activities to continually prompt us to ask whether we will deliver a product or system that meets our project customer's needs and expectations (19).

The concept of **verification** emerged about thirty years ago in the aerospace industry, where it was important that software perform all of its intended functions correctly and reliably because any error in a software program could result in an expensive or a disastrous mission failure (14). Verification focuses on the process-related activities of the project to ensure that the product or deliverable meets its specified requirements before final testing of the system begins.

Verification requires that the standards and metrics be defined clearly. Moreover, verification activities focus on asking the question of whether we followed the right procedures and processes. In general, verification includes three types of reviews (15):

- *Technical reviews*—A technical review ensures that the product or system will conform to the specified requirements. This review may include conformance to graphical user interface (GUI)

Table 9.1 Examples of Process, Product, and Project Metrics

Type	Metric	Description
Process	Defect Arrival Rate	The number of defects found over a specific period of time.
	Defects by Phase	The number of defects found during each phase of the project.
	Defect Backlog	The number of defects waiting to be fixed.
	Fix Response Time	The average time it takes to fix a defect.
	Defective Fixes	The number of fixes that created new defects.
Product	Mean Time to Failure	Average or mean time elapsed until a product fails.
	Defect Density	The number of defects per lines of code (LOC) or function points.
	Customer Found Defects	The number of defects found by the customer.
	Customer Satisfaction	An index to measure customer satisfaction–e.g., scale from 1 (very unsatisfied) to 5 (very satisfied)
Project	Scope Change Requests	The number of scope changes requested by the client or sponsor.
	Scope Change Approvals	The number of scope changes that were approved.
	Over due tasks	The number of tasks that were started but not finished by the expected date or time.
	Tasks that should have started	The number of task that should have started but have been delayed.
	Over budgeted tasks	The number of tasks (and dollar amount) of tasks that have cost more to complete than expected
	Earned Value	SV, CV, SPI, CPI, ETC, EAC
	Over allocated Resources	The number of resources assigned to more than one task.
	Turnover	The number of project team members who quit or terminated.
	Training Hours	The number of training hours per project team member.

standards, programming and documentation standards, naming conventions, and so forth. Two common approaches to technical reviews include structured walk-throughs and inspections. A **walk-through** is a review process in which a developer leads the team or a group of his or her peers through a program or technical design. The participants may ask questions, make comments, or point out errors or violations of standards. Similarly, **inspections** are peer reviews in which the key feature is the use of a checklist to help identify errors. The checklists are updated after data is collected and may suggest that certain types of errors are occurring more or less frequently than in the past (14). Although walkthroughs and inspections have generally focused on the development of software, they can be used as a verification of all project deliverables throughout the project life cycle.

- *Business reviews*—A business review is designed to ensure that the product or system provides the required functionality specified in the project scope and requirements definition. However, business reviews can include all project deliverables to ensure that each deliverable is complete, provides the necessary information required for the next phase or process, meets predefined standards, and conforms to the project methodology.

- *Management reviews*—A management review basically compares the project's actual progress against the baseline project plan. In general, the project manager is responsible for presenting the project's progress to provide a clear idea of the project's current status. Issues may need to be resolved, resources adjusted, or decisions made either to stay or alter the project's course. In addition, management may review the project to determine if it meets scope, schedule, budget, and quality objectives.

Validation, on the other hand, is a product-oriented activity that attempts to determine if the system or project deliverable meets the customer or client's expectations and ensures that the system performs as specified. Unlike verification, validation activities occur toward the end of the project or after the product or system has been developed. Therefore, testing makes up the majority of validation activities. Volumes and courses can be devoted to product and software testing; however, understanding what needs to be tested, and how, is an important consideration for developing a quality strategy and project plan.

Testing provides a basis for ensuring that the product or system functions as intended and has all the capabilities and features that were defined in the project's scope and requirements. In addition, testing provides a formal, structured, and traceable process that gives management and the project sponsor confidence in the quality of the system. In addition, the following provides several suggestions for making testing more effective (14):

- Testing should be conducted by someone who does not have a personal stake in the project. For example, programmers should not test their own programs because it is difficult for people to be objective about their own work.

- Testing should be continuous and conducted throughout all the development phases.

- In order to determine whether the test met its objectives correctly, a test plan should outline what is to be tested, how it will be tested, when it will be tested, who will do the testing, and the expected results.

- A test plan should act as a service-level agreement among the various project stakeholders.

- A key to testing is having the right attitude. Testers should not be out to "break the code" or embarrass a project team member. A tester should evaluate a product with the intent of helping the developers meet the customer's requirements and make the product even better.

Quality Control

Quality control focuses on monitoring the activities and results of the project to ensure that the project complies with the quality standards. Once the project's standards are in place, it is important to monitor them to ensure that the project quality objective is achieved. Moreover, control is essential for identifying problems in order to take corrective action and also to make improvements once a process is under control. To support the quality control activities, several tools and techniques are now introduced.

Control Charts—In 1918, Walter Shewhart (1891–1967) went to work at the Western Electric Company, a manufacturer of telephone equipment for Bell Telephone. At the time, engineers were working to improve the reliability of telephone equipment because it was expensive to repair amplifiers and other equipment after they were buried underground. Shewhart believed that statistical theory could be used to help engineers and management control variation of processes. He also reasoned that the use of tolerance limits for judging quality was short sighted because it provided a method of judging quality for products only after they were produced (7). Shewhart introduced the control chart as a tool to better understand variation and to allow management to shift its focus away from inspection and more toward the prevention of problems and the improvement of processes.

A control chart provides a picture of how a particular process is behaving over time. All control charts have a center line and control limits on either side of the center line. The center line represents the observed average, while the control limits on either side provide a measure of variability. In general, control limits are set at $\pm 3\sigma$ (i.e., ± 3 sigma) or $\pm 3s$, where σ represents the population standard deviation and s represents the sample standard deviation. If a process is normally distributed, control limits based on three standard deviations provides .001 probability limits.

Variation attributed to **common causes** is considered normal variation and exists as a result of normal interactions among the various components of the process—that is, chance causes. These components include people, machines, material, environment, and methods. This type of variation will be random and will vary within predictable bounds.

If chance causes are only present, the probability of an observation falling above the upper control limit would be one out of a thousand, and the probability of an observation falling below the lower control limit would be one out of a thousand as well. Since the probability is so small that an observation would fall outside either of the control limits by chance, we may assume that any observation that does fall outside of the control limits could be attributed to an **assignable cause**. The left side of Figure 9.6 provides an example of a control chart where a process is said to be stable or in **statistical control**.

Variations attributed to assignable causes can create significant changes in the variation patterns because they are due to phenomena not considered part of the normal process. An example of assignable cause variation can be seen by the pattern on the right side of Figure 9.6. This type of variation can arise because of changes in raw materials, poorly trained people, changes to the work environment, machine failures, inadequate methods, and so forth. Therefore, if all assignable causes are removed, the process will be stable because only chance factors remain. Control charts are a valuable tool for monitoring quality; however, it is important to keep in mind that one can see patterns where patterns may not exist (20).

Cause and Effect of Diagrams—Kaoru Ishikawa (1915–1989) believed that quality improvement is a continuous process that depends heavily on all levels of the organization—from top management down to every worker performing the work. In Japan, this belief led to the use of quality circles that engaged all members of the organization. In addition to the use of statistical methods for

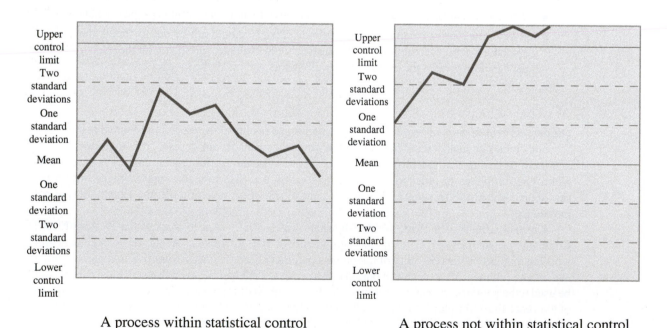

A process within statistical control   A process not within statistical control

Figure 9.6 Control Charts for Statistical Control

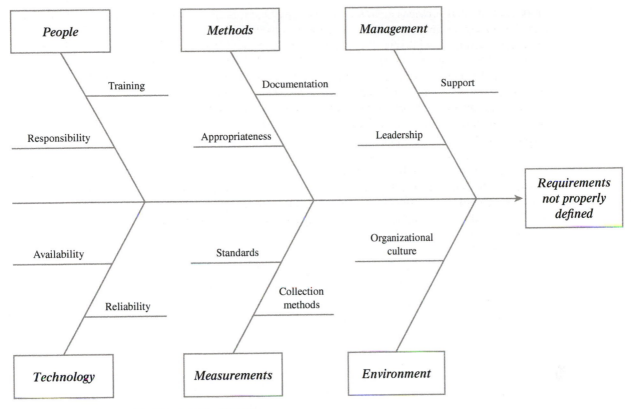

Figure 9.7 Ishikawa (aka Fishbone) Diagram

quality control, Ishikawa advocated the use of easy-to-use analytical tools that included cause-and-effect diagrams (called the Ishikawa diagram, or fishbone diagram, because it resembles the skeleton of a fish).

Although the Ishikawa, or fishbone, diagram was introduced in an earlier chapter, it can be used in a variety of situations to help understand various relationships between causes and effects. An example of an Ishikawa diagram is illustrated in Figure 9.7. The effect is the rightmost box and represents the problem or characteristic that requires improvement. A project team could begin by identifying the major causes, such as people, materials, management, equipment, measurements, and environment that may influence the problem or quality characteristic in question. Each major cause can then be subdivided in potential subcauses. For example, causes associated with people may be lack of training or responsibility in identifying and correcting a particular problem. Once the diagram is complete, the project team can investigate the possible causes and recommend solutions to correct the problems and improve the process.

Another useful tool is a **Pareto chart (or diagram)**, which was developed by **Vilfredo Federico Damaso Pareto** (1848–1923). Pareto studied the distribution of wealth in Europe and found that about 80 percent of the wealth was owned by 20 percent of the population. This idea has held in many different settings and has become known as the 80/20 rule. For example, 80 percent of the problems can be attributed to 20 percent of the causes.

A Pareto chart can be constructed by collecting and summarizing the quality-related data by rank order of the classifications from largest to smallest, from left to right (3). For example, let's say that we have tracked all the calls to a call center over a period of one week. If we were to classify the different types of problems and graph the frequency of each type of call, we would end up with a chart similar to Figure 9.8. As you can see, the most frequent type of problem had to do with documentation questions. In terms of quality improvement, it may suggest that the user documentation needs to be updated.

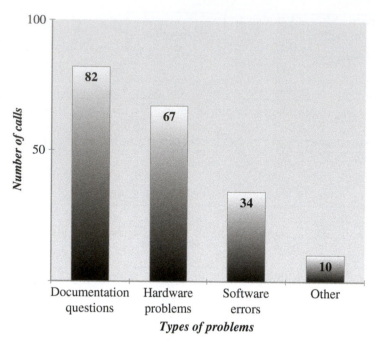

Figure 9.8 A Pareto Chart

In addition, a number of other tools are available to support quality control activities. Figure 9.9 summarizes some of these tools. Checklists can be used as an aid to ensure things are not forgotten. In addition, flowcharts or process maps can be useful for documenting a sequence of steps and decision points. This can be useful for understanding the complexity of a process in order to find opportunities to make processes more effective and efficient. Lastly, the collection of data can provide the basis for fact-based management and statistical analysis. Forecasting using regression or correlation analysis can help identify trends and hidden relationships.

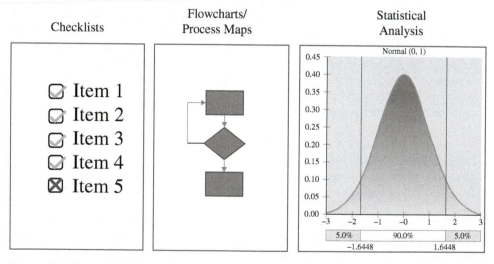

Figure 9.9 Some Additional Quality Control Tools

Continuous Improvement: Learn, Mature, and Improve

A central theme of this text has been the application of knowledge management as a tool for team learning and identifying best practices. Monitoring and controlling activities and tools can help point out problem areas, but the project team must solve these problems. Therefore, it is important that the lessons learned from a project team's experiences be documented so that best practices are identified and disseminated to other project teams. Continual, incremental improvements can make a process more efficient, effective, stable, mature, and adaptable (3). A project quality plan should be more than an attempt to build a product or system, it should also support the organization in searching for ways to build a *better* product or system (7).

CHAPTER SUMMARY

- **Quality** focuses on fulfilling requirements, while **grade** centers on the intent of the design.

- In business, quality has been defined in terms of "fitness for use" and "conformance to requirements." "Fitness for use" concentrates on delivering a system that meets the customer's needs, while "conformance to requirements" centers more on meeting some predefined set of standards.

- **Quality management planning** requires that adequate time and budget are allocated in the project plan for testing and other activities to ensure that the project team is building the right product or system and building it the right way.

- **Quality assurance** focuses on auditing or a set of checks and balances to ensure that the project team is following the processes outlined in the quality management plan and that metrics are being collected and analyzed as part of **quality control**.

- The cost of quality can be viewed as the cost of conforming to standards (i.e., building quality into the product and processes through training, testing, and so forth) as well as the cost of not conforming to the standards (i.e., rework, liabilities, downtime, maintenance, and so forth). Substandard levels of quality can be viewed as waste, errors, or the failure to meet the project sponsor's or client's needs, expectations, or requirements.

- Using an approach called **scientific management**, F.W. Taylor believed that a task could be broken down into smaller tasks and studied to identify the best and most efficient way of doing each subtask. Under the scientific management approach, quality focused mainly on improving the processes and machines (or technology), with less emphasis on people.

- While processes and machines (or technology) play an important role in quality, Deming's teachings (as well as the other TQM experts) emphasize the value of people to a greater extent than the scientific method.

- **Standards** are agreed upon specifications or criteria to ensure that all of the project's deliverables meet their intended purpose. They must be meaningful and clearly defined in order to be relevant and useful.

- The capability maturity model integrated (CMMI) provides a set of recommended practices that define key process areas specific to software development. The objective of the CMMI is to offer guidance on how an organization can best control its processes for developing and maintaining a product or system.

- The immature organization is characterized as being reactive; the project manager and project team spend a great deal of their time reacting to crises or find themselves in a perpetual state of *firefighting*. Schedules and budgets are usually exceeded.

- With mature organizations, processes and the roles of individuals are defined explicitly and communicated throughout the organization. The processes are consistent throughout the organization and improved continually based on experimentation or experiences.

- The CMMI defines five levels of process maturity, each requiring many small steps as a path of incremental and continuous process improvement:
  - Level 1: Initial
  - Level 2: Repeatable
  - Level 3: Defined
  - Level 4: Managed
  - Level 5: Optimizing
- **Metrics** are vital for gauging quality by establishing tolerance limits and identifying defects.
- A **defect** is an undesirable behavior associated with the product or process.
- **Verification** requires that the standards and metrics be defined clearly. Moreover, verification activities focus on asking the question of whether we followed the right procedures and processes.

- **Validation** is a product-oriented activity that attempts to determine if the system or project deliverable meets the customer or client's expectations and ensures that the system performs as specified.
- Testing provides a basis for ensuring that the product or system functions as intended and has all the capabilities and features that were defined in the project's scope and requirements.
- **Quality control** focuses on monitoring the activities and results of the project to ensure that the project complies with the quality standards.
- The lessons learned from a project team's experiences should be documented so that best practices are identified and disseminated to other project teams. Continual, incremental improvements can make a process more efficient, effective, stable, mature, and adaptable.

REVIEW QUESTIONS

1. Define quality in your own words. How would you define quality in a word processing, spreadsheet, or presentation software package?
2. Why is the number of features of a product or software system not necessarily the best measure of that system's quality?
3. How does "conformance to requirements" or "fitness for use" provide a definition of quality for a product or information system?
4. What is PQM?
5. Define the following: (a) Quality planning; (b) quality assurance; (c) quality control.
6. Why should quality management include both the products and processes of a project?
7. What is scientific management? Why was it so popular? Why was it so controversial?
8. Why did the teachings of Deming and Juran have such an important impact on Japan just after World War II?
9. What is a standard? What role do standards play in project quality management?
10. What is process capability?
11. What is process maturity?
12. Describe an immature organization.
13. Describe a mature software organization.
14. What is the relationship between standards and metrics?
15. What is a process metric? Give an example.
16. What is a product metric? Give an example.
17. What is a project metric? Give an example.
18. What is a defect? Give an example of a software defect.
19. Describe verification. What activities support verification?
20. Describe validation. What activities support validation?
21. Describe how technical, management, and business reviews are different.
22. What is a control chart? When is a process said to be in statistical control? How would you know if it was not?
23. What is an Ishikawa diagram? How can it be used as a quality control tool for projects?
24. What is a Pareto diagram? How can it be used as a quality control tool for projects?

25. What is a flow chart (or process map)? How can it be used as a quality control tool for projects?

26. What role do lessons learned and best practices play in continuous quality improvement?

 HUSKY AIR ASSIGNMENT—PILOT ANGELS

The Quality Management Plan

In this assignment, you and your team will develop a quality management plan to support your project with Husky Air.

This would also be a good chance for you and your team to do another learning cycle. Read through this assignment first and then meet as a team to develop a Project Team Record and an Action Plan. This will help to improve team learning and to assign responsibilities to complete the assignment.

Please provide a professional-looking document that includes the following:

1. Project name, project team name, and the names of the members of your project team.

2. A brief project description. (This helps your instructor if different teams are working on different projects in your class.)

3. The project's MOV. (This should be revised or refined if appropriate.)

4. A quality management plan—The plan should include the following:

   a. A short statement that reflects your team's philosophy or objective for ensuring that you deliver a quality system to your client.

   b. Other than the examples of quality-based metrics found in Table 9.1, develop and describe two process metrics, two product metrics, and two project metrics that can be used to monitor the quality of your project.

   c. Develop and describe a set of verification activities that your project team could implement to ensure quality.

   d. Develop and describe a set of validation activities that your project team could implement to ensure quality.

 THE MARTIAL ARTS ACADEMY (MAA)—SCHOOL MANAGEMENT SYSTEM

The Quality Management Plan

In this assignment, you and your team will develop a quality management plan to support your project with MAA.

This would also be a good chance for you and your team to do another learning cycle. Read through this assignment first and then meet as a team to develop a Project Team Record and an Action Plan. This will help to improve team learning and to assign responsibilities to complete the assignment.

Please provide a professional-looking document that includes the following:

1. Project name, project team name, and the names of the members of your project team.

2. A brief project description. (This helps your instructor if different teams are working on different projects in your class.)

3. The project's MOV. (This should be revised or refined if appropriate.)

4. A quality management plan—The plan should include the following:

   a. A short statement that reflects your team's philosophy or objective for ensuring that you deliver a quality system to your client.

   b. Other than the examples of quality based metrics found in Table 9.1, develop and describe two process metrics, two product metrics, and two project metrics that can be used to monitor the quality of your project.

   c. Develop and describe a set of verification activities that your project team could implement to ensure quality.

   d. Develop and describe a set of validation activities that your project team could implement to ensure quality.

QUICK THINKING—WHY DO WE ACCEPT LOW-QUALITY SOFTWARE?

Would you buy a car even if you had to agree to a contract not to hold the manufacturer liable for any damages or harm even if the car maker was negligent? Probably not, but many times that's exactly what you do when you mindlessly click the button to agree to an end user license agreement (EULA). Many EULAs today protect the software vendors from liability due to their negligence and only cover the cost of the media on which the software is delivered. This can have a major impact as many organizations purchase software that becomes the backbone of their infrastructure. Unfortunately, as many organizations are under pressure to do more with fewer resources, so are software vendors. Pressure to get software out the door as quickly as possible often compromises the due diligence of quality and testing. In fact, less than a third of all organizations test their mobile applications.

Another concern for users is security. For example, General Motors' EULA for OnStar® allows the company to gather information about your car and then sell that information "in order to improve the quality of their services and offerings." Moreover, the terms of service for Microsoft's Hotmail® allows Microsoft to "access, disclose, or preserve information associated with your use of the services, including (without limitation) your personal information and content, or information that Microsoft acquires about you through your use of the services . . . "

Many software users have a history of expecting, accepting, and putting up with poor-quality software. While no one wants to deliver low-quality software, why does it still happen? One reason is history. In addition, the "historical" or traditional model of software development centers on software development teams following a serial or waterfall model where each step in the development process depends on the completion of a previous step or process. For example, requirements definition leads to design, coding, testing, and implementation. These processes are primarily the domain of the software developers and any quality assurance teams become involved only later in the software development cycle. Subsequently, quality becomes an afterthought instead of being built in from the beginning. Deadlines and features or functionality take priority over quality. Lastly, the quality assurance team historically sits physically outside the development team and has less power or influence. That's too bad, because software vendors need to realize that proper software quality is critical and should not be undercut. Quality can be an important product feature and can be a powerful differentiator that can provide a competitive advantage.

1. Suppose an organization is considering the purchase of an enterprise software package that would be a mission-critical application for that organization. How could the project manager ensure that her company does not purchase a low-quality software solution?

2. Choose a software package and find the EULA (usually you can find this under Help). What is the software vendor's liability for a defect in the software?

SOURCES:

Svoia, A. "Click Here to Accept Poorly Tested, Low-Quality Software." *Computerworld*. February 10, 2006.

Olavsrud, T. "Are Mobile Apps Leaving Quality Assurance Behind?" *CIO Magazine*. October 22, 2012.

von Hoffman, C. "Is Your Car Spying on You?" *CIO Magazine*. September 22, 2011.

Gralla, P. "Microsoft Snoops on Blogger's Email Account. Is Yours Safe?" *Computerworld*. March 21, 2014.

QUICK THINKING—OPM3®

In 1998, the Project Management Institute (PMI) initiated a project to create the Project Management Maturity Model (OPM3®). While the traditional focus of the *Guide to the Project Management Body of Knowledge* (*PMBOK® Guide*) was the management of individual projects, the intent of OPM3® was to provide a global standard for managing projects across the organization. The OPM3® contains more than 500 best practices. In addition to the capability maturity model (CMM), twenty-six other maturity models were reviewed during the research phase of the OPM3® project. OPM3® was originally published in 2003 and includes three interlocking elements:

- *Knowledge*—Outlines project management and organizational maturity
- *Assessment*—Describes the methods, processes, and procedures needed to assess maturity
- *Improvement*—Presents a process for moving from a present maturity level to a higher maturity level

However, some critics believe that the OPM3® is a fad exulted over by academics, management gurus, and consultants. For example, Dhanu Kothari contends, "Ambiguities and uncertainties are part of project management. If a rational approach worked every time we wouldn't need project managers." Moreover, standard processes defined by maturity models can become overly bureaucratic, especially when strict adherence to a process is promoted over a simpler, more common sense approach. Organizations must also make a sizable commitment in terms of executive sponsorship, tools, training, and resources, so justifying the cost as well as the demonstrable progress can be tricky.

1. Why is it that a project team can follow a process and still fail?

2. Do maturity models neglect ambiguities and uncertainties of projects or do they do just the opposite?

SOURCES:

Sullivan, J.L. "Comparing CMMI® and OPM3®." *AllPM.Com.* Accessed from www.allpm.com.

Padgaonkar, A. "Assessing OPM3®." *Projectsatwork.* January 15, 2007.

Schlichter, J. "PMOs, OPM3 and Culture Transformation." *Projectsatwork.* June 22, 2009.

Unknown. "New Practice Guide on Complexity." *Projectsatwork.* February 12, 2014.

CASE STUDIES

Speed versus Quality

The mantra for many organizations today is "Do more with less." Often management is demanding that IT solutions be delivered within weeks instead of months, with key features and functions that are expected to provide immediate, bottom-line results. Unfortunately, this often means that quality and testing are sacrificed for speed.

The conflict between quality and speed becomes compounded when people are spread thin across several projects. Moreover, project managers must make sure that the project's scope is realistic and achievable, especially when the project's schedule is compressed. Too often management urges the project manager to "cut corners" in order to deliver an IT solution on time without reducing functionality. For example, an IT manager was pressured by senior managers to expedite an ERP implementation by bypassing several important business processes. However, it is important that project managers help executives understand the risks of taking shortcuts. Making mistakes that get publicized as a result of taking a shortcut can hurt the organization's public image.

1. Does there have to be a trade-off between the speed of delivery of an IT solution and quality?

2. If you were a project manager and senior management asked you to strongly consider taking a shortcut that could compromise quality, what argument could you make to convince management to not sacrifice quality over schedule?

SOURCE: Adapted from Hoffman, T. "IT Project Management: Balancing Speed and Quality." *Computerworld.* February 14, 2004.

Pay to Play?

The capability maturity model (CMM) was born in the 1980s out of U.S. Air Force and Department of Defense frustration with purchasing the right software. Carnegie Mellon University won the bid to create an organization called the Software Engineering Institute (SEI) to help improve the process of choosing the right software and vendor. In 1986, Watts Humphrey, a former software development chief at IBM, was brought in to lead this effort. As Humphrey explains, "We were focused on identifying competent people, but we saw that all of the projects the Air Force had were in trouble. It didn't matter who they had doing the work. So we said let's focus on improving the work rather than just the process."

The initial CMM developed in 1987 was a questionnaire designed to identify good software processes practiced by the software vendors bidding on the contracts. Unfortunately, many of these companies learned how to "work the system" in terms of filling out the questionnaire regardless of the quality of their software practices.

In 1991, the SEI refined the CMM to overcome these abuses. A more detailed model of software development best practices was created along with a group of lead appraisers trained and authorized by the SEI to audit and verify that the software vendors were following the practices that they said they were doing. The lead appraisers led a team within the organization being reviewed and attempted to verify that the vendor was implementing the policies, procedures, and practices outlined in the CMM across a "representative" subgroup (about 10 percent to 30 percent) of all of the company's software projects. Over a period of one to three weeks, a number of confidential interviews with project managers and developers were conducted to confirm what was really going on. Since the lead appraiser led a team of the software vendor's own employees, there often could be a conflict of interest for these people to tell the truth. As one anonymous lead appraiser recalled, "It can be very stressful for the internal team. They have conflicting objectives. They need to be objective, but the organization wants to be assessed at a certain level."

Another lead appraiser, David Constant, also recalls a situation where the software developers were coached by management to say the right things. According to Constant, "I had to stop the interviews and demand to see people on an ad hoc basis, telling the company who I wanted to speak to just before each interview began. And the sad part was that they didn't need to coach anybody. They would have easily gotten the level they were looking for anyway. They were very good."

As of 1994, the newer model became more difficult to exploit. Mark Martak of Westinghouse told his management that "This is a different ball game now. If you have a good lead appraiser, you can't fake it out." He was able to lead his group to a Level 4 assessment.

It is widely believed that moving up the CMM levels will allow an organization to better serve its customers. However, a higher CMM level does not guarantee the effectiveness of performance, only that the organization has processes in place for managing and monitoring software development that organizations on a lower level do not yet have. As Jay Douglas, director of business development at the SEI, points out "Having a higher maturity level significantly reduces the risk over hiring a company

with a lower level, but it does not guarantee anything. You can be a Level 5 organization that produces software that might be garbage."

CMM can be costly and time consuming for an organization. On average, it takes about seven years for an organization to move from Level 1 up to Level 5. The cost for a CMM assessment alone can be around $100,000, and this cost doesn't even include the expense and disruption of developing repeatable software processes and the training needed to disseminate them throughout the organization.

Therefore, it's not uncommon for organizations to make false claims. Ron Radice, a lead appraiser and former SEI official, recalls a Chicago-based company that was deceived by an offshore company that falsely claimed to have a CMM rating. Not wanting to name the guilty party, Radice said "They said they were Level 4, but in fact they had never been assessed." In addition, some appraisers may feel pressured in their assessment. For example, Frank Koch, a lead appraiser with a software services consulting firm called Process Strategies, Inc., said that some Chinese consulting firms he worked with promised their clients that they had a certain CMM level and then expected that he would just give it to them. According to Koch, "We don't do work with certain [consultancies in China] because their motives are a whole lot less than wholesome. They'd say we're certain [certain clients] are a Level 2 or 3 and that's unreasonable, to say nothing of unethical. The term is called selling a rating."

Given the investment in time and resources to achieve a CMM rating, it's not uncommon for organizations "pay to play" or bribe appraisers for a particular rating. Many government agencies in the United States require companies who bid for their business to obtain at least a Level 3 rating, while many CIOs use a CMM in choosing an offshore provider. Will Hayes, a quality manager at SEI, acknowledged one case where an appraiser had his license revoked for improperly awarding a Level 4 rating. The difficulty in knowing whether an organization's claim to a CMM rating is that the SEI does not monitor the organizations that claim to have a CMM rating, nor do they release any information regarding which organizations were assessed or the outcome of their assessment. As Hayes points out, "We weren't chartered to be policemen. We're a research and development group." Moreover, SEI does not have any intention of becoming a governing body like the American National Standards Institute (ANSI), which governs ISO certification in the United States. As Watts Humphrey contends, "No one has asked us to become a governing body, and that's not our mandate. And if we did, what would we solve? It wouldn't excuse anyone from doing their homework."

1. What is the value of having a CMM rating?
2. Do you think there should be a governing body to oversee CMM assessments?
3. As a project manager looking to outsource the programming of your project overseas to a software house claiming a Level 5 rating, what could you do as part of a due diligence to make sure that the claim is not false?

SOURCES:
Koch, C. "Software Quality: Bursting the CMM Hype." *CIO Magazine.* March 1, 2004.
Tarne, B. "A Practical Guide to Improving PM Maturity." *Projectsatwork.* December 17, 2007.
King, J. "The Pros and Cons of CMM." *Computerworld.* December 8, 2003.

How Many Hours Do You REALLY Work?

A recent online poll by Slashdot.com asked the question, "How many hours do you *REALLY* work?" More than 27,000 people participated in the survey and only 27 percent said that they work 7 or more hours during the standard workday. Surprisingly, 40 percent reported working fewer than 4 hours a day, while 24 percent claimed to work, on average, between 4 and 6 hours. Approximately 6 percent of the hard-charging work fanatics declared to work more than 11 hours a day.

Although one needs to be careful of the validity of online polls and how we define "work," an individual's personal productivity is an important consideration, especially when project team member's time working on a project is billed to a sponsor or client.

Many organizations have adopted surveillance software to monitor employee activities. Such software can go beyond productivity and notify management of security problems or inappropriate behaviors. According to Michael Cones, a director of IT who uses surveillance and monitoring software system from SpectorSoft, "It's like a video camera. You can record every snapshot of a screen and keystroke they've done." The SpectorSoft software can identify and notify a manager when an employee uses keywords or tries to access certain files.

For example, Ellen Messmer reports that the Hanley Center in Florida monitors every single keystroke each employee makes. The Hanely Center provides treatment for substance abuse, where a number of the patients are celebrities. The Center believes this is the best way to ensure privacy. Employees are well aware that their actions are being monitored and receive training as to what is deemed appropriate use of the computer. According to Counes, only a few employees have been dismissed because of poor judgment concerning sensitive information.

In addition, Tam Harbert believes that many organizations are becoming increasingly interested in monitoring employee activities in response to stricter regulatory and legal requirements. As Harbert points out, "As corporate functions, including voice and video, converge onto IP-based networks, more corporate infractions are happening online. Employees leak intellectual property or trade secrets, either on purpose or inadvertently; violate laws against sexual harassment or child pornography; and waste time while looking like they are hard at work."

It appears that organizations are not only interested in how many hours an employee works, but what they do during the day. This may be especially true for people who would like to work from home or telecommute. This trend is expected to increase, as many believe that working from home can be more productive mainly because of a person's ability to work during the time they would otherwise be commuting to and from the office. Some other benefits include the ability to hire more qualified staff, regardless of where they live, and the potential to reduce auto emissions. However, many managers are reluctant to allow telecommuting because they unable to monitor how employees spend their time during the workday.

Ann Bednarz describes a new breed of software that monitors what an employee does during the workday without being stealthy. One product called RescueTime can tell you how much you actually get done. As Joe Hruska, CEO and co-founder of RescueTime claims, "It's very surprising to people how little, on average, gets done that's productive during an eight-hour workday. If you're doing four to five hours of productive work on a computer, you're in the top percentile. It's pretty rare that we see anybody go over five hours a day of productive time on a computer."

The concept behind RescueTime is to provide productivity information automatically without any user effort. As Hruska also points out, "That was the key to our tenant: Understanding this info with no data entry. There's nothing more distracting than having to stop being productive and then go fill out a timesheet." RescueTime is particularly useful to those who are self-employed or entrepreneurs whose time is billed to a client. The individual can define a set of categories such as email, social networking, writing, software development, or shopping.

The user can then assign a value for different activities associated with the categories. For example, using a spreadsheet program could be considered a +2 (very productive), while visiting a social networking sight would be a −2 (very unproductive). On the other hand, using email could be a +1 (productive), and family time off line could be 0 (neutral). The software will then track what the user does on the computer and calculate a productivity score for a given time period (i.e., day, week, month, etc.). The user can also set productivity goals, and the software will provide a warning if those goals are not being met. The company's Web site claims that using Rescue-Time can recover an average of 9 percent in productive time per week in 6 weeks.

RescueTime comes in both individual and team versions. There is a free version, but the paid version provides more features and functionality. For example, while the free version will track whether a user is using word processing, the paid version will track which documents are used. In addition, the paid version also allows for the capability for people to see how they are doing compared to other members of their team. For example, a team member may notice that he or she is spending more time on a social networking site or other unproductive tasks than the team average. The team member may decide to scale back before it becomes an issue with other team member or the manager.

Another similar product is called RWave, which is a cloud-based system that monitors what users do and then compares their activity to what they are actually assigned to work on. More specifically, Tony Redmond, the CEO and founder of RWave Software, contends, "People can set tasks for themselves, or have their managers set their tasks. At the end of the day, you can see the tasks you've been assigned and the actual amount of time you've spent being productive on those tasks."

RWave can track work activity with a breakdown of how the workday is spent. This includes time spent offline in meetings or for personal time, on the phone, or working with specific applications on the computer. The software is intended to give managers a "bird's-eye view" of an individual or team that can automatically record a project's progress and generate time sheets automatically. Redmond hopes that a future version of RWave will allow people to import and export tasks to and from Microsoft Project and work on a smartphone.

A business and consulting firm in Ireland called The Purple Patch uses RWave to keep track of its employees. Damion Donion, who works for The Purple Patch, says, "We spend a large amount of time in front of clients, which was easily measurable, but we wanted a method of recording the amount of time we spent behind the scenes working for those clients to ensure that we were getting accurately compensated for our time. As I travel from meeting to meeting, I can see the exact status of projects and tasks for all clients without having to explicitly ask. I no longer have to rely on a third party telling me that something is done, when in fact it may not have been."

Although many people resent the idea of being spied upon, Ann Bednarz believes that products like Rescue-Time and RWave provide a benefit because the software allows employees to document how much they really are accomplishing. Moreover, neither product wants to be viewed as a sneaky spy tool. According to Redmond, "We would absolutely never want to have a stealth mode. (We) are very overt about what it's doing. It shows people exactly what statistics it sees. We make it very obvious."

Moreover, Hruska commented, "We don't like being compared to Big Brother that is absolutely not what RescueTime is trying to be. There was a time when Rescue-Time could be installed without employee's knowledge, but that capability has since been disabled."

1. In your opinion, would you find value in using a software tool that would track your personal productivity? Why or why not?

2. Suppose a project manager was interested in having her team adopt and use a product like RescueTime or RWave. However, she is concerned that the team would view using this software as a means to spy on them. What advice would you give her?

SOURCES:

Levinson, M. "Survey: Telecommuting Improves Productivity, Lowers Costs." *NetworkWorld*. October 8, 2008.

McNamera, P. "40% of Geeks Surveyed Really Work Fewer Than … Say What?." *NetworkWorld*. February 23, 2009.

Messmer, E. "Feel Like You're Being Watched at Work? You May be Right." *NetworkWorld*. March 31, 2010.

Harbert, T. "Employee Monitoring: When IT is Asked to Spy." *Computerworld*. June 16, 2010.

Bednarz, A. "Pay No Attention to that Widget Recording Your Every Move." *Computerworld*. February 28, 2011.

www.rescuetime.com.

www.rworks.com.

BIBLIOGRAPHY

1. Project Management Institute (PMI). *A Guide to the Project Management Body of Knowledge (PMBOK Guide)*. Newton Square, PA: PMI Publishing, 2013.

2. McGevna, V. "Do It Right." *Projectsatwork*. September 5, 2012.

3. Besterfield, D. H., C. Besterfield-Michna, G. H. Besterfield, and M. Besterfield-Sacre. *Total Quality Management*. Upper Saddle River, NJ: Prentice Hall, 1999.

4. Kloppenborg, T. J., and J. A. Petrick. *Managing Project Quality*. Vienna, VA: Management Concepts, 2002a.

5. Boehm, B. W. *Software Engineering Economics*. Englewood Cliffs, NJ: Prentice Hall, 1981.

6. Koch, A. "Cut Defects, Not Corners." *Projectsatwork*. June 2, 2005.

7. Woodall, J., D. Rebuck, and F. Voehl. *Total Quality in Information Systems and Technology*. Delray Beach, FL: St. Lucie Press, 1997.

8. Humphrey, W. "Characterizing the Software Process: A Maturity Framework." *IEEE Software*, 1988, Vol. 5, no. 3, 73–79.

9. Chrissis, M. B., M. Konrad, and S. Schrum. *CMMI Guidelines for Process Integration and Product Improvement*. Boston, MA: Addison-Wesley Professional Series: The SEI Series in Software Engineering, 2003.

10. Paulk, M. C., B. Curtis, C. V. Weber, and M. B. Chrissis. "The Capability Model for Software Engineering." *IEEE Software*, 1993, Vol. 10, no. 4.

11. Tarne, B. "A Practical Guide to Improving PM Maturity." *Projectsatwork*. December 17, 2007.

12. Caputo, K. *CMM Implementation Guide: Choreographing Software Process Development*. Reading, MA: Addison-Wesley, 1998.

13. McBride, P. "Turning Metrics into Maturity." *Projects At Work*. June 5, 2012.

14. Lewis, W. E. *Software Testing and Continuous Quality Improvement*. Boca Raton, FL: Auerbach, 2000.

15. Ginac, F. P. *Customer Oriented Software Quality Assurance*. Upper Saddle River, NJ: Prentice Hall, 1998.

16. McKay, J. "Quality Just Doesn't Happen." *CIO Magazine*. May 24, 2007.

17. Kloppenborg, T. J. and J. A. Petrick. *Managing Project Quality*. Vienna, VA: Management Concepts, 2002b.

18. Kan, S. H. *Metrics and Models in Software Quality Engineering*. Boston, MA: Addison-Wesley, 1995.

19. Jarvis, A., and V. Crandall. *Inroads to Software Quality: How to Guide and Toolkit*. Upper Saddle, NJ: Prentice Hall, 1997.

20. Florac, W. A., R. E. Park, and A. Carleton. *Practical Software Measurement: Measuring for Process Management and Improvement*. Pittsburg, CA: Software Engineering Institute, 1997.

21. Deming, W. E. *Out of the Crisis*. Cambridge, MA: The MIT Press, 1982.

10

Leading the Project Team

CHAPTER OBJECTIVES

Chapter 10 focuses on project leadership and two important related components—ethics and development of the project team. After studying this chapter, you should understand and be able to:

- Define leadership and understand its role and importance in successfully managing projects.
- Describe the five approaches to exemplary leadership.
- Describe six leadership styles.
- Define the concept of emotional intelligence and how it can help one to become a more effective leader.
- Define ethics and understand its importance in project leadership.
- Understand some of the ethical challenges that you may face as a project leader or project team member.
- Describe a process for making ethical decisions.
- Describe the difference between a work group and a team.
- Understand culture and diversity as well as some of the challenges of leading and managing a multicultural project.

INTRODUCTION

Up to this point, we have covered the important tools and processes needed to be an effective project manager. However, a successful project requires leadership (1). A project leader most certainly would be the project manager, but a project can also have other individuals who must assume leadership roles at different times over the course of the project life cycle. For example, a project team member may be called upon to provide leadership or guidance because of his or her experience, knowledge, or expertise in a particular area.

Although there is no dearth of books and articles on the topic of leadership, we will look at some commonsense approaches to leadership that can help you become an effective leader. In addition, we will discuss two important components of leadership. The first focuses on ethics, which has become an increasingly important topic for organizations as well as business programs in colleges and universities. The high-profile ethical meltdowns reported in the media are not limited to large organizations or senior managers. People at all levels in organizations of all sizes face ethical issues every day. No doubt you will encounter ethical dilemmas throughout your career. Since only an overview of ethics can be covered in such a limited space and time, we will therefore take a more practical view to help you prepare for some of the common ethical dilemmas you may face in a project setting. These approaches are also important to project leaders in developing a culture that supports an ethical environment.

Chapter 4 focused on the selection of the project manager and team. The roles, skills, and experience of these key project stakeholders are important components in terms of defining the project's infrastructure. One of the greatest responsibilities of the project manager is the selection and recruitment of the project team. However, once the project team is in place, the project manager must also ensure that the project team members work together to achieve the project's MOV. Therefore, the language and discipline of *real teams* versus *work groups* will be introduced. These concepts will provide the basis for understanding the dynamics of the project team.

In addition, a multicultural project could include an international project or a domestic organization that would like to benefit from having a diverse workforce. Regardless, multicultural projects require an understanding of culture and diversity. Today, a successful project leader must also be able to effectively manage and lead projects that deal with multicultural clients and project team members.

PROJECT LEADERSHIP

What is a leader? Are leaders born? Can one learn to become an effective leader? And how is leadership different from management? According to John Kotter (2), there is nothing mystical or mysterious about leadership. Leadership has less to do with being charismatic or having specific personality traits. In fact, leadership and management are different but complementary functions necessary for success in today's complex business environments.

Management focuses on policies and procedures that bring order and predictability to complex organizational situations. Traditionally, management is defined within such activities as planning, organizing, controlling, staffing, evaluating, and monitoring (3).

Although management and leadership tend to overlap, leadership centers on vision, change, and getting results. As Kouzes and Posner point out (4), leaders should inspire a shared vision that their constituents will want to follow. Moreover, leaders strive to change the status quo by creating something that has never been done before. Often, leaders live their lives backward by seeing the final destination or having a clear image of what the end result will look like before getting started. This is what pulls a leader forward and inspires people to follow as they accept the vision as their own. Commitment to a vision can only be inspired and never commanded.

Up to this point, we have concentrated on the planning activities and processes for *managing* projects. From earlier chapters, we defined project management as meeting stakeholder expectations by applying and integrating the various project management processes. However, successful projects also require *leadership* that involves setting direction and aligning and motivating people. This requires understanding several approaches to leadership and appropriate leadership styles.

Some Modern Approaches to Leadership

Often when we hear the term "leader," we think of famous and powerful people in history. Some believe that certain individuals are born with traits that make them natural leaders. Others, however, believe that leadership is a function of the environment. Although we are born with certain traits, a person can develop leadership potential by developing or nurturing these traits. Personality, motivation, and intelligence are important traits, yet leadership, to a great degree, is about having the courage to do the right thing and being open minded (2).

James Kouzes and Barry Posner conducted research for more than twenty years on effective leadership experiences (3). They found that leaders are often ordinary people who help guide others along pioneering journeys rather than follow well-worn paths. Based on this research, they defined five practices of exemplary leadership (see Figure 10.1) that can help you have a clearer direction to become a more effective and successful project leader:

1. *Model the way*—The most effective leaders lead by example. A leader's *behavior* wins respect, not his or her title or position within the organization. You must find your own voice based on your personal values and beliefs, but what you do in terms of your behavior and daily actions is

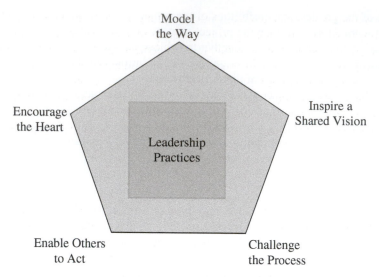

Figure 10.1 Kouzes and Posner's Model for Leadership

often more important than what you say. Your words and deeds must be consistent so that you convey the right message. Leaders set an example of what they expect from others by modeling the way they want others to behave. This provides the leader with the respect and the right to lead others. People follow the person first, not the plan.

2. *Inspire a shared vision*—An exemplary leader has an exciting vision or a dream that acts as a force for inventing the future. In turn, this vision should inspire people so they become committed to a purpose. This requires leaders to know their constituents so that they will believe the leader understands their needs, interests, and "speaks their language." A leader must engage in dialogue, not monologue, to understand the hopes and dreams of others and gain their support. A leader should try to ignite the passion in others through communication and enthusiasm of what the future *could be*.

3. *Challenge the process*—Exemplary leaders do not rely on fate or luck. They venture out and accept challenges. Leaders are pioneers who challenge the status quo by seeking out new opportunities to innovate, grow, and improve. However, most leaders do not create, develop, or come up with new products, services, or processes. Often leaders are good listeners who recognize good ideas, support those ideas, and then challenge the process to make these new ideas happen. Leaders are also early adopters of innovation, but innovation and change require experimentation, risk, and failure. Although leaders accept risk and failure, they minimize it by taking and encouraging others to make incremental steps. They strive for small wins to boost confidence, commitment, and learning. However, people must feel safe and comfortable in taking risks so that both leaders and constituents learn from their failures and their successes.

4. *Enable others to act*—Visions and dreams do not just happen because of one person's actions. This requires a team effort, so a leader's ability to get others to act is crucial. Exemplary leaders enable others to act by encouraging collaboration and building trust among all the project stakeholders. Leaders provide an environment that makes it possible for others to do good work. People should feel empowered and motivated to do their best, feel a sense of ownership, and take pride in what they do. A leader enables others to act by giving power away, not by hanging onto it. People should be made to feel strong and capable; otherwise, they will not give their best or stay around very long. In short, a leader must turn constituents into leaders themselves.

5. *Encourage the heart*—Often the project journey is long and difficult. People can become tired, disillusioned, frustrated, and willing to give up. Exemplary leaders rally others to carry on by encouraging the heart. Although this encouragement can be a simple gesture such as a thank-you note or something more dramatic like a marching band, the leader should show appreciation for people's contributions and create a culture of celebration that recognizes those accomplishments. Recognition and celebration should not be phony or lame. It is important to visibly link rewards with performance. Authentic rituals and celebrations that align with the team's values can build a strong collective identity and spirit that can carry the team through turbulent waters.

Leadership Styles

Although the five practices of exemplary leadership provide a model for effective leadership, research has also suggested that many effective leaders employ a collection of distinct leadership styles. Based on a sample of about 4,000 managers worldwide, Daniel Goleman identified six distinct leadership styles (5). More important, Goleman found that the best leaders do not rely on only one leadership style, but tend to use several or a combination style, depending on the situation. The following summary of the six styles will help you understand how a particular leadership style influences performance and results. It can also offer guidance as to when you should use or change to another style.

1. *The coercive style*—The coercive style can be summarized as a "do as I say" approach to leading others. This style can be effective in a crisis, to kick-start a turnaround situation, when dealing with a problem employee, or when the leader is attempting to achieve immediate compliance. Although effective in some situations, the coercive style can have a negative impact on the climate of the organization or project. For example, an extreme top-down approach to decision making and communication can often obstruct new ideas if people believe their ideas will be shot down or limit communication if people are apprehensive of being the bearer of bad news. Moreover, people will soon lose their initiative, motivation, commitment, and sense of ownership because the coercive style can make people resentful and disillusioned.

2. *The authoritative style*—The leader who follows the authoritative style takes a "come with me" approach in which the leader outlines a clearly defined goal but empowers people to choose their own means for achieving it. The authoritative leader provides vision and enthusiasm. He or she motivates people by making clear how their work fits into the larger picture. People know that what they are doing has meaning and purpose. Standards for success and performance are clear to everyone. The authoritative style works well in most organizational and project situations, but is best suited for situations when the organization or project team is adrift. However, this approach may not be best for inexperienced leaders who are working with experts or a more experienced team. In this case, the leader can undermine an effective team if he or she appear pompous, out of touch, or overbearing.

3. *The affiliative style*—This style follows the attitude that "people come first." The affiliative style centers on the value of the individual rather than goals and tasks and attempts to keep people happy by creating harmony among them. The leader who uses this style attempts to build strong emotional bonds that translate into strong loyalty. Moreover, people who like each other tend to communicate more, share ideas and inspiration, and take risks. Flexibility is higher because the leader does not impose unnecessary rules and structures that define how the work must get done—that's up to those who must do the work. The affiliative style works well in situations that require building team harmony, morale, trust, or communication. However, often situations occur in which people need some structure or advice to navigate through complex tasks, and having little or no direction can leave them feeling rudderless. In addition, an over-caring and over-nurturing approach that focuses exclusively on praise can create a perception that mediocrity is tolerated.

4. *The democratic style*—The democratic style attempts to develop consensus through participation by asking, "What do you think?" Using this style, the leader spends time getting other people's ideas, while building trust, respect, and commitment. People's flexibility and responsibility are increased because they have a greater say in the decisions that affect their goals and work. Subsequently, morale tends to be high, and everyone has a more realistic idea of what can or cannot be done. The democratic style works best when the leader needs to build buy-in or consensus, or to gain valuable input from others. For example, the leader may have a clear vision, but needs innovative ideas or guidance as to the best way to achieve that vision. However, this style can also lead to seemingly endless meetings in a vain attempt to gain group consensus. This can cause conflicts, confusion, and the perception that the group is leaderless. In addition, the democratic style would not be appropriate in a crisis or when the team does not have competence or experience to offer sound advice.

5. *The pacesetting style*—A leader who uses the pacesetting style sets high-performance standards and has a "do as I do, now" attitude. This style exemplifies an obsession with doing things better and faster for him or herself and everyone else. Poor performers are quickly identified and replaced if standards are not met. Although the leader may try to get better results by setting an example for high performance, morale can deteriorate if people feel overwhelmed by the pacesetter's demands for excellence and performance. Often goals and expectations may be clear to the leader, but are poorly communicated to the rest of the team. An "if I have to tell you what to do, then you're the wrong person for this job," can turn into a situation in which people try to second-guess what the leader wants. People lose energy and enthusiasm if the work becomes task-focused, routine, and boring. Subsequently, the pacesetting leader may micromanage by attempting to take over the work of others. As a result, people lose their direction or sense of how their work is part of a larger picture. Moreover, if the leader leaves, people will feel adrift since the pacesetting leader sets all direction. However, this style may be appropriate in situations that require quick results from a highly motivated, self-directed, and competent team. Given this situation, the pacesetter sets the pace for everyone else so that the work is completed on time or ahead of schedule.

6. *The coaching style*—The coaching style leader follows the "try this" approach to help people identify their unique strengths and weaknesses so that they can reach their personal and career goals. The leader who uses the coaching style encourages people to set long-term professional goals and then helps them develop a plan for achieving them. Coaching leaders are good at delegating and giving people challenging, but attainable, assignments. Even short-term or minor failures are acceptable and viewed as positive learning experiences. Goleman's research has found that the coaching style is the least often used, but can be a valuable and powerful tool for performance and for improving the climate of the organization or project. The coaching style works well in many situations, but is most effective when people are "up for it"—that is, when people want to be coached. Consequently, this style is least effective when people are resistant to change or when the leader does not have the knowledge, capability, or desire to be a coach. However, too often a leader will resort to micromanagement when the team goes off track or performs poorly (6).

Emotional Intelligence

Goleman's study also suggests that leaders who have mastered the authoritative, democratic, affiliative, and coaching styles tend to create the best climate and have the highest performance. Moreover, the most effective leaders have the flexibility to switch among the leadership styles as needed. Individuals can expand their repertoire by understanding their emotional intelligence competencies. Emotional intelligence can be defined as the ability to understand and manage our relationships and ourselves better. Although a person's intelligence quotient (IQ) is largely genetic, emotional intelligence can be learned at any age. Unfortunately, improving one's emotional intelligence is like changing a bad habit. It takes time, patience, and a great deal of effort. For example, as a leader you may follow a democratic style of leadership when things are going smoothly on a project, but may use a more coercive style when things don't go according to plan. As a result, you may tend to flare up and tune out other people's ideas and suggestions just when you need them the most.

Emotional intelligence includes four capabilities: self-awareness, self-management, social awareness, and social skills that comprise specific sets of competencies (5, 7, 8).

- *Self-awareness*—As a leader you should be aware of your emotions and understand how your emotions can affect people around you. This requires a self-assessment so that you understand your strengths and weaknesses in order to have greater confidence in yourself and a positive feeling of self-worth. In short, self-awareness is about managing your own emotions.

- *Self-management*—By having a greater self-awareness, you can begin to understand your impulses and negative emotions so that you can better keep them in check. This allows for maintaining a higher level of honesty and integrity, as well as the ability to adapt to new situations, overcoming challenges, and taking advantage of new opportunities.

- *Social awareness*—It is important that you become perceptive to others' emotions, customer's needs, as well as the day-to-day organizational politics. This requires empathy or the genuine concern for people's problems and interests. Therefore, social-awareness is about having an increased awareness of other people as well as how the project fits within a larger system like the organization or industry.

- *Social skills*—Ultimately, this requires a set of skills to inspire, influence, communicate, facilitate the resolution of conflicts, as well as develop cooperation and relationships with others.

Goleman, Boyatzis, and McKee suggest several ways to strengthen your emotional intelligence and emotional leadership (9). The first step entails asking two questions: "Who am I now?" and "Who do I want to be?" The idea is to make an honest assessment of how others view your leadership and how you would like to be viewed in the future. This may require gathering 360-degree feedback from your peers, subordinates, and superiors so that you can take stock of your strengths and weaknesses. The next step involves devising a plan for getting from where you are as a leader to where you want to be. This may mean having a trusted coach who can provide honest feedback and point out progress and relapses as you constantly rehearse new behaviors that lead you to improve specific emotional intelligence competencies. In time, this will allow you to learn new leadership styles.

ETHICS AND LEADERSHIP

Over the last several years, a great deal of attention has been given to organizations that have had ethical meltdowns. The questionable business dealings of Enron executives, for example, led to the largest corporate bankruptcy in U.S. history. This sinking ship also led to the demise of Arthur Andersen, LLP, which at one time was one of the Big Five international accounting firms. Although these are just two examples, the list of questionable ethical behaviors by organizational leaders is long and distinguished. Unfortunately, this list is getting longer.

As a result, many organizations are mandating and investing in ethical training for their employees. Over the last few years, many business programs in colleges and universities have added ethics courses or ethical components to courses to give students a sounder ethical foundation. In fact, ethics is becoming an important trend in project management (10). From a philosophical view, **ethics** can be defined as a set of moral principles and values. Ethical dilemmas arise when our personal values come into conflict. However, Trevino and Nelson take a more practical view that can help you understand and apply several principles of ethics in a project setting (11). More specifically, they define ethics as the principles, norms, and standards of conduct that guide individuals and groups. Just as an employer establishes rules, such as appropriate dress, working hours, and customer service, that employees are expected to follow, rules for expected ethical behavior is quite similar. As a result, ethics becomes an extension of strong leadership and good management where appropriate conduct is communicated and engrained in the organizational culture.

You may be wondering whether this reaction is worth the time and effort. The answer is that unethical business behaviors cost organizations money and jobs. For example, at the end of 2000, Enron's stock was trading at more than $80 a share. Less than a year later, it fell to less than a dollar a share. The dreams of many innocent investors went up in smoke. Even more disconcerting is the fact that more than 20,000 employees lost their jobs.

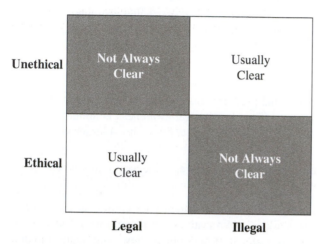

Figure 10.2 Ethics and Legality

In addition, acting unethically can also mean breaking a law. This can lead not only to financial penalties, but also jail time. Moreover, acting ethically is just the right thing to do. It's not only in your best interest; it's in the best interest of people who are part of organizations and society. People want to work for and do business with organizations they can trust. Credibility and reputation take a great deal of effort and time to build, but they can be ruined almost in an instant.

Unfortunately, ethical decisions are not always that clear-cut. For example, Figure 10.2 shows that while some decisions (i.e., legal and ethical or illegal and unethical) are usually clear to us, we often have to make decisions that fall in the gray area represented by the shaded quadrants. These types of decisions are more difficult because we may be torn by decisions or actions that may be legal but unethical, or illegal but ethical. To a large degree, legality and the ethicalness of certain actions are governed by society and culture.

A project manager is a leader who can create, maintain, or change the culture of the project organization. **Culture** can be defined as the shared beliefs, assumptions, and values that we learn from society or a group that guides or influences our behavior (6). More specifically, culture can be created, changed, or maintained in terms of formal systems that are in place. This would include such factors as the authoritative structure as well as policies and procedures for hiring, firing, rewarding performance, and training. However, culture can be influenced by informal systems such as the acceptable everyday norms and behaviors. These can be viewed in terms of how people associated with a particular group dress, as well as their heroes, myths or stories, rituals, and language. For example, Microsoft's culture is still largely influenced by the legend of a young and brash group of technical wizards led by Bill Gates.

Ethical Leadership

People who are brought into an organization learn its culture through a process called **socialization**. This process of "learning the ropes" can occur through formal means such as training and mentoring or through less formal ones such as interaction with peers and superiors. New people not only learn such things as how to dress appropriately, they also learn what behaviors are acceptable and unacceptable. Subsequently, socialization can encourage or discourage ethical behavior (6).

People look to their leaders for ethical guidance. If the leader does not provide this guidance, people may seek others who can. Often, this may allow them to be influenced by others who may intentionally or unintentionally lead them toward unethical behaviors. Therefore, a project manager must act as a moral individual and a moral leader. A moral individual is viewed as someone having certain personal traits such as integrity, honesty, and trustworthiness. A moral leader, on the other hand, is an individual who defines the right set of values and sends out the right message to shape an ethical culture. As Shriberg, Shriberg, and Kumari suggest, a leader can fall into one of the following categories (2):

- *Unethical leadership*—Unethical leaders are generally weak moral individuals and weak moral managers. For example, Al Dunlap was a senior executive who had a reputation for turning around struggling companies. His strategy usually included firing as many employees as possible to drastically reduce payroll. Dunlap was given the nickname "Chainsaw Al" for his slash-and-cut approach. Dunlap was successful, but he was also known for emotionally abusing his employees by being belligerent and condescending. Subordinates were expected to make the numbers at all costs. Those who did were rewarded. Those who didn't would suffer his wrath. Not surprisingly, people used questionable accounting and sales techniques, and, as CEO of Sunbeam, Chainsaw Al was caught lying and trying to cover up these questionable business practices. Sunbeam's board of directors fired Dunlap in 1998, but the company was near ruin. Dunlap paid $500,000 in a settlement with the SEC and agreed never to serve again as an officer of a publicly traded company.

- *Hypocritical leadership*—Probably the worst type of leader is the one who extols the virtues of integrity and ethical conduct, but then engages in unethical behavior, encourages others to do so, rewards bottom-line results by any means, or fails to discipline any wrongdoing. By standing on a pedestal of integrity and moral values, the leader may encourage people to place their trust in whatever the leader says or does. Sometimes they are led to believe that the ends justify the means and disregard ethical standards themselves or believe that it's fine for the leader to do so. On the other hand, many people can become cynical if they believe what the leader and his or her followers are doing is wrong. One example of a hypocritical leader is the reverend Jim Bakker. In the late 1970s and early 1980s, Bakker developed the PTL Ministries into the largest religious broadcasting empire. Bakker took in millions of dollars by convincing people to purchase a limited number of lifetime memberships for hotels that were part of a theme park. As part of the deal, only 25,000 memberships were to be made available and a membership would allow a family to stay free each year for four days and three nights. Unfortunately, over 66,000 memberships were sold, that would make it impossible for the hotels to support that many people. Moreover, a good portion of this money was diverted to supporting other PTL expenses such as large salaries and bonuses for Bakker and his wife Tammy Faye. Bakker resigned three months before the PTL filed for bankruptcy in 1987 and the IRS revoked the PTL's tax-exempt status. In 1989, Baker was convicted of fraud. He spent the next eight years in prison.

- *Ethically neutral leadership*—Many leaders tend to fall in a neutral zone where they are neither strong nor weak ethical leaders. As a result, they do not provide clear ethical guidance because people do not know what the leader's ethical beliefs are or whether the leader cares. Unfortunately, no message often sends a message whereby people interpret silence to mean that the leader doesn't care how business goals are met—just that they are met. For example, in 2002, *Fortune* magazine described Citigroup as a moneymaking machine, but one that engaged in a number of questionable business practices such as allegedly helping Enron hide debt. Sandy Weill, chairman of the board and former CEO of Citicorp, told Citicorp's board of directors that his most important task would be to ensure that Citicorp now operated at the highest level of ethics and integrity. Weill can be viewed as a neutral ethical leader since he often looked the other way and seemed to take notice only after these problems became public.

- *Ethical leadership*—An ethical leader, then, is someone who makes it clear that bottom-line results are important, but only if they can be achieved in an ethical manner. Moreover, research suggests that when a culture is viewed as being ethical, employees tend to engage in fewer unethical behaviors, are more committed to the organization, and are more willing to report problems to management (6).

Some Common Ethical Dilemmas in Projects

There is no doubt that you will encounter ethical dilemmas when your values will be in conflict. Your career can be enhanced or be damaged depending on how you handle the situation. However, many ethical situations are predictable, so you can be prepared in advance to deal with them. Some of the more common ethical situations you might encounter include (6):

- *Human resource situations*—Project leaders must ensure that qualified team members are recruited and retained. This entails creating a project environment in which people feel safe and appreciated so that they want to put forth their best work. Issues that can lead to ethical situations include discrimination, privacy, sexual, or other types of harassment, as well as appraisals, discipline, hiring, firing, and layoff policies and decisions. The key consideration should be fairness in terms of equity (only performance counts), reciprocity (expectations are understood and met), and impartiality (prejudice and bias are not factors).

- *Conflicts of interest*—Organizations and projects involve a number of relationships between people. These relationships can be professional and personal. Impartiality can come into question when these relationships overlap, and a conflict of interest can occur. For example, would a gift or favor from a vendor or a customer be viewed as having an influence on your judgment or on a project-related decision? Trust is a key ingredient for personal and business relationships, and conflicts of interest can weaken trust if special favors are extended only to special friends at the expense of others. Many organizations have policies that define situations that are and are not acceptable. Conflict of interest issues can include such things as overt or subtle bribes or kickbacks as well as relationships that could question your impartiality. Moreover, as a project team member, you will gain access to confidential and private information that could be of value to you or someone else. When in doubt, it's best to provide full disclosure to mitigate any risk of impropriety.

- *Confidence*—A project includes a number of stakeholders. Meeting project stakeholder expectations, especially the client's, requires maintaining a strong sense of confidence with respect to such issues as confidentiality, product safety or reliability, truth in advertising, and special fiduciary responsibilities that require special commitments or obligations to the client or other project stakeholders. Although confidence issues can include a wide variety of issues, they can create special ethical considerations that can affect your relationship with project stakeholders. Trust can erode when your fairness, honesty, or respect come into question.

- *Corporate resources*—As a project team member, you are a representation of both your team and your organization. This means that you are considered an agent of your organization and your actions can be considered the actions of your organization. For example, if you are a consultant working with a client, people will infer that you are representing and speaking on behalf of your company. In turn, your company may give you an email address with their domain, business cards, and stationery with the corporate letterhead. Therefore, your email and organizational stationery should only be used for business purposes. For example, writing a letter of recommendation for someone means that both you and your organization share the same opinion. Make sure that your personal opinion and corporate opinions are not in conflict. In addition, company equipment and services should only be used for business purposes. Often companies have policies about personal phone calls and email or the acceptable use of equipment. Another important issue concerns the truth. Many times people are asked to "fudge" the numbers by making things appear better than they are. Although many organizations now have procedures to follow if you're asked to engage in this type of behavior, you may want to consult with someone outside the chain of command, such as someone in the legal department or human resources department, if this type of situation arises and no policy exists. However, becoming a "whistleblower" can have its consequences—intended and unintended—and should be an option used with caution and as a last resort.

Making Sound Ethical Decisions

It appears that a single approach to dealing with ethical dilemmas does not exist. For example, let's say that you are working on a project and have just completed the testing of a product or system component. Let's also assume that the test results have shown that the system component does not meet certain performance and quality standards set by the client. The component will require rework that will make an already late and over-budget project even later and more over budget. A superior has asked you to change the results so that they will meet the client's specification. The supervisor reasons with you that the results are "really not all that bad and that the component of the system can be fixed before going live." Trevino and Nelson provide a prescriptive approach for making sound ethical decisions in business that can be applied to a number of ethical dilemmas you may encounter in a project setting (6):

1. *Gather the facts*—It is easy to assume that you have all the facts, but we often jump to a conclusion without having enough relevant information. Begin by focusing on the historical facts that led to this situation and then what has happened since. This can be difficult because the facts may not be that clear or readily available. However, you should also keep in mind that there are limitations if you do not have all the facts or information at hand. Given our example, the stress of dealing with a project that is going to be late and over budget may lead to situations in which people look to cut certain corners. Perhaps we are dealing with an inexperienced supervisor or a person who has gotten away with cutting corners in the past.

2. *Define the ethical issue*—Many people react impulsively to ethical dilemmas and jump to a conclusion without really understanding the underlying issues. We often stop at the first ethical issue we identify, but a number of related and interwoven issues may complicate things once we begin to realize them. Challenge yourself and others to see as many issues as you can so that you have a fuller understanding of the problem. The main ethical issue here deals with trust. The client expects to receive a product or system that meets or exceeds expectations. Is close enough good enough? Or, will the product or system component really be fixed so that it meets those standards later on?

3. *Identify the affected stakeholders*—The next step involves identifying those who will be affected by the decision as well as any benefits or harm that will come to them. It is important to see things through the eyes of the visibly affected stakeholders and then consider those who are more indirectly affected. Obviously, the client is impacted directly. But what about the client's customers? The shareholders? Also, how will you and the rest of your project team be affected? If you're a consultant, how will your organization be affected? What about your family? Your team's families? And the families of your clients?

4. *Identify the consequences*—Once you identify the affected stakeholders, the next step is to think about the potential consequences for each stakeholder. Although it may be impossible to identify every consequence, you can still get a good idea of whether the good of your decision or action outweighs the bad. In our example, the company's reputation and financial position could be damaged if the system component fails to perform as intended. In turn, this could have a negative impact on your project organization and your career. The idea is to think of your actions as having a number of impacts, much like the waves that are created when you toss a stone into still waters. The impact of your actions can be immediate and felt over time.

5. *Identify the obligations*—After you have identified the consequences of your action or decision, the next step involves identifying the obligations you have to the affected stakeholders. It may

help to think of obligations in terms of values, principles, character, and outcomes. For example, you may feel loyalty toward your supervisor because he or she hired you at a time when you were financially desperate or because you want to be viewed as a team player. On the other hand, you have an obligation to the client to tell the truth and report the results as they are.

6. *Consider your character and integrity*—Many people find the "sleep test" as a proxy for how the world would view their actions. Will your action or decision allow you to sleep restfully at night? Another way is to ask yourself, would you feel comfortable if your action or decision were to appear on the news? Moreover, what would someone close to you (and whose opinion really matters) say if you told that person about your action or decision? In short, do you want people to say that you were a person of integrity or not?

7. *Think creatively about potential actions*—In coming up with a potential solution to an ethical dilemma, it is important that you do not "force yourself into a corner" by framing your decision in terms of two choices. In our example, this may mean either changing the test results as the supervisor wants or bypassing the supervisor's authority and telling your boss's boss what your supervisor asked you to do. There may be a policy in your organization that outlines steps you could follow for blowing the whistle on your supervisor, but another option may be to talk with your supervisor and explain that you are uncomfortable with changing the results. Explaining the impact and consequences of the action may be enough to change the supervisor's mind. If that doesn't work, other options might include making sure that someone else knows what the original (and correct) test results report. Each situation is unique and therefore requires a unique and sometimes creative approach. Talking to someone outside the situation can be a great help.

8. *Check your intuition*—Although the previous steps tend to follow a rational approach, you still need to check your gut or intuition. Empathy should not be discarded over logic because it can raise a warning flag that someone might be harmed. If your intuition is troubling you, then it may be time for more thought on the issue or situation. However, making a decision based solely on emotion is probably not a good idea either. This should be a final stage of the process that provides you with confidence in your action or decision.

TEAMS AND LEADERSHIP

The project team has a direct influence on the outcome of the project. Therefore, it is important that the team's performance be of the utmost concern to the project manager. In *The Wisdom of Teams*, Jon R. Katzenbach and Douglas K. Smith provide an insightful and highly usable approach for understanding the language and discipline of teams (12). In refining the language of teams, they provide a distinction between work groups and several types of teams.

Work Groups—The work group is based on the traditional approach where a single leader is in control, makes most of the decisions, delegates to subordinates, and monitors the progress of the assigned tasks. Therefore, the performance of a work group depends greatly on the leader.

A work group can also include members who interact to share information, best practices, or ideas. Although the members may be interested in each other's success, work groups do not necessarily share the same performance goals, do not necessarily provide joint work products, and are not necessarily held mutually accountable. A study group is an example of a work group. You and several members of a class may find it mutually beneficial to study together for an exam, but each of you (hopefully) will work on the exam individually. The grade you receive on the exam is not a direct result of the work produced by the study group, but is rather of your individual performance on the exam. In an organizational context, managers may form work groups to share information and help decide direction or policy, but performance will ultimately be a reflection of each manager and not the group. Work groups or single leader groups are viable and useful in many situations.

Real Teams—In cases where several individuals must produce a joint work product, teams are a better idea. More specifically, Katzenbach and Smith define a team as (7):

a small number of people with complementary skills who are committed to a common purpose, performance goals, and approach for which they hold themselves mutually accountable. (p. 45)

Moreover, calling a group of people a team does not make it one nor does working together make a group a team. Teamwork focuses on performance, not on becoming a team. Subsequently, there are several *team basics* that define a real team:

- *A small number of people*—Ideally, a project team must be between two to twelve people. Although a large number of people can become a team, a large team can become a problem in terms of logistics and communication. As a result, a large team should break into subteams rather than try to function as one large unit.

- *Complementary skills*—For achieving the team's goal, a team must have or develop the right mix of skills that are complementary. These skills include:

  - Technical or functional expertise

  - Problem-solving or decision-making skills

  - Interpersonal skills—that is, people skills

- *Commitment to a common purpose and performance goals*—Katzenbach and Smith distinguish between activity goals (e.g., install a local area network) and performance goals (e.g., ship all orders within 24 hours of when they are received). The concept of a performance goal is similar to the concept of the MOV and sets the tone and aspirations of the team while providing a foundation for creating a common team purpose. As a result, the team develops direction, momentum, and commitment to its work. Moreover, a common performance goal and purpose inspires pride because people understand how their joint work product will impact the organization. A common goal also gives the team an identity that goes beyond the individuals involved.

- *Commitment to a common approach*—Although teams must have a common purpose and goal, they must also develop a common approach to how they will work together. Teams should spend as much time developing their approach as they do defining their goal and purpose. A common work approach should focus not only on economic and administrative issues and challenges, but also on the social issues and challenges that will shape how the team works together.

- *Mutual accountability*—A group can never become a team unless members hold themselves mutually accountable. The notion that "we hold ourselves accountable" is much more powerful than "the boss holds me accountable." Subsequently, no team can exist if everyone focuses on his or her individual accountability. Mutual accountability requires a sincere promise that each team member makes to herself or himself and to the other members of the team. This accountability requires both commitment and trust because it counters many cultures' emphasis on individualism. In short, it can be difficult for many people to put their careers and reputations in the hands of others. Unless a common approach and purpose has been forged as a team, individuals may have a difficult time holding themselves accountable as a team.

Based on their in-depth study of several teams, Katzenbach and Smith provide several common-sense findings:

- *Teams tend to flourish on a demanding performance challenge*—A clear performance goal is more important to team success than team-building exercises, special initiatives, or seeking team members with ideal profiles.

- *The team basics are often overlooked*—The weakest of all groups is the pseudo team, which is not focused on a common performance goal. If a team cannot shape a common purpose, it is doomed to achieving mediocre results. We cannot just tell a group of individuals to be a team.

- *Most organizations prefer individual accountability to team accountability*—Most job descriptions, compensation plans, and career paths emphasize individual accomplishments and, therefore, tend to make people uncomfortable trusting their careers to outcomes dependent on the performance of others.

Katzenbach and Smith provide some uncommon sense findings as well:

- *Strong performance goals tend to spawn more real teams*—A project team cannot become a real team just because we call them a team or require them to participate in team-building activities or exercises. However, their findings suggest that real teams tend to thrive as a result of clearly defined performance-based goals.

- *High-performance teams are rare*—In their study of teams, Katzenbach and Smith identified high-performance teams. These are real teams that outperform all other teams and even the expectations given. This special type of team requires an extremely high level of commitment to other team members and cannot be managed.

- *Real teams provide the basis of performance*—Real teams combine the skills, experiences, and judgments of the team members to create a synergy that cannot be achieved through the summation of individual performance. Teams are also the best way to create a shared vision and sense of direction throughout the organization.

- *Teams naturally integrate performance and learning*—Performance goals and common purposes translate into team members developing the skills needed to achieve those goals. As a result of open communication and trust, the members of a team are more apt to share their ideas and skills so that they may learn from one another. Moreover, successful teams have more fun, and their experiences are more memorable for both what the team accomplished and in terms of what each member learned as a result of the team process.

MULTICULTURAL PROJECTS

A common type of multicultural project would be an international one. However, domestic projects are becoming increasingly multicultural as many organizations attempt to diversify their workforce. Although ethics is an important component of leadership, the ability to lead and manage a multicultural team will become an increasingly more important skill for successful project leaders.

The Challenges of International Projects

The thought of being part of an international project can be exciting—travel, hotels, exotic food, and different customs. However, international projects also entail new challenges that can make or break your career depending on how well you handle these new and strange situations. International projects are more complex because geographical, cultural, and social differences must be taken into account (13). These complexities include:

- *Number of locations*—Often international projects are located in several different countries, cities, or regions. Travel time and costs must be taken into account as well as differences in time zones.

- *Currency exchange*—Most countries today still have their own unique currency. These currencies are subject to fluctuations in exchange rates and inflation. Moreover, some currencies are not valued outside the issuing country.

- *Regulations and laws*—Each country has its own regulations and laws, but laws can be local and interpreted differently.

- *Political instability*—Doing a project in a politically unstable country can create interesting challenges that can endanger the safety and welfare of the project team.

- *Attitude toward work and time*—Different cultures can have different attitudes toward work and time. For example, in some cultures work is perceived as something that is not that critical. People do what they have to do, and getting ahead is not important. On the other hand, work for some becomes an obsession and their job and title define who they are. For these individuals, competition to be the best is important because it can lead to promotion and more pay. In addition, people in some cultures feel less pressure to be regulated by a clock and may not even own one. As a result, a project leader who attempts to make people work harder or adhere to time pressure will meet resistance.

- *Religion*—Although religion has an important influence in all societies, some societies are more affected in terms of how they go about their daily life and their work. For example, in many Islamic countries the weekend is on Thursday and Friday, while in other countries the weekend is on Saturday and Sunday. In such cases, offices in two different countries may be able to communicate only on Mondays, Tuesdays, and Wednesdays (14).

- *Language*—Not everyone speaks the same language you do. Although English has become the international language of business, not everyone can speak it fluently and words can have different meanings. Careful selection of words and phrases is important to reduce the likelihood that they are misunderstood or misinterpreted.

- *Food*—Some people have different tastes and are more willing to try new things. Each country has its own cuisine that may seem strange, but don't forget that what seems normal to you can be strange or even disgusting to someone from somewhere else.

Understanding Diversity

Culture is a set of social lessons of behaviors that we learn over time. For example, these behaviors influence our language and customs in terms of how we eat, sleep, or conduct business. Often, we become emotionally attached to our cultural beliefs. We then try to preserve them rather than learn from other cultures. **Diversity** is defined as differences in culture as well as nationality, ethnicity, religion, gender, or generation. To a great degree, the ability to lead an international project successfully requires understanding diversity. As a project leader, you may encounter diversity in terms of your client or sponsor as well as within the project team. To be an effective leader, it is important that you develop an awareness of the different dimensions of culture that make up the various project stakeholder groups.

Diversity may be thought of as four different dimensions that represent each individual (2). The first dimension represents a person's personality—the internal aspects that define us (e.g., introvert versus extrovert, hard-charging Type A versus laidback Type B, etc.). The second dimension represents individual characteristics that are often visible to others, while the third dimension includes a set of social characteristics such as education, marital status, economic status, and religion that tend to shape our beliefs and behaviors. Lastly, the fourth dimension represents several organizational aspects that also help to shape our identity. These include such factors as seniority, formal position within the organization, and the physical location where we work. The value of understanding and thinking about team diversity is that it can remind us that even though some individuals may appear to look like us, they may represent a different culture even within our own country or region. As a result, we can then begin to understand how each dimension of diversity can influence attitudes, motivations, and behaviors as well as social and business customs. This may allow us to see not only how people are different, but also how we might be similar.

CHAPTER SUMMARY

- Although leadership and management are closely related and complementary, leadership focuses on the relationship between people. Leadership concentrates on inspiring a vision, creating change, and getting results. On the other hand, management emphasizes the processes and activities associated with planning, organizing, controlling, staffing, evaluating, and monitoring.

- Although some are born with certain traits that make them natural leaders, a person can still develop leadership potential by having the courage to do the right thing and by being an active learner.

- The five practices for exemplary leadership include:
  - model the way
  - inspire a shared vision
  - challenge the process
  - enable others to act
  - encourage the heart

- The six leadership styles discussed include:
  - the coercive style
  - the authoritative style
  - the affiliative style
  - the democratic style
  - the pacesetting style
  - the coaching style

- Each style has its own place when it is most effective as well as situations when it is least effective. Moreover, effective leaders have the flexibility to switch among the different styles as needed.

- The concept of emotional intelligence (i.e., the ability to understand our relationships and ourselves) is an important element for learning a new leadership style. Emotional intelligence is composed of four capabilities:
  - self-awareness
  - self-management
  - social awareness
  - social skills

- Ethics has received a great deal of attention in the media because of the ethical transgressions of a number of high-profile leaders. From a philosophical view, ethics can be seen as a set of moral principles and values.

- Ethical dilemmas arise when these values come into conflict. However, ethical decisions and actions are not always clear-cut, especially when some actions or decisions may be ethical but illegal, or unethical but legal.

- Culture is defined as the shared beliefs, assumptions, and values that we learn from society or a group. In a project setting, a project leader can create, change, or maintain a particular culture in terms of the formal and informal systems that are in place.

- People look to their leaders for ethical guidance. Leaders can be considered:
  - unethical
  - hypocritical
  - ethically neutral
  - ethical

- An ethical leader is someone who makes it clear that bottom-line results are important, but only if they can be achieved in an ethical manner.

- Some common ethical situations you may face in a project setting include those involving human resources, conflicts of interest, confidence issues, or corporate resources.

- A work group can follow a traditional approach where a single leader or boss is in control, makes most of the decisions, and delegates to subordinates who work independently of each other. Or, a work group can include several individuals who come together to share information or set policy, but work independently of one another and do not necessarily share the same performance goals or work products.

- Real teams are a special type of team, with a few individuals with complementary skills who focus on a performance-based goal and share a common purpose and approach.

- Multicultural projects can be international projects or domestic projects whereby an organization is attempting to diversify its workforce.

- Just as ethics is an important component of leadership, the ability to manage a multicultural team is becoming an increasingly important skill for successful project leaders.

- Diversity, is defined as the differences between cultures, nationality, ethnicity, religion, gender, or generation.

REVIEW QUESTIONS

1. Develop your own definition of leadership.
2. What is the relationship between leadership and management?
3. What role does leadership play in project management?
4. What does a leader do?
5. Describe the five practices for exemplary leadership.
6. Describe the coercive leadership style.
7. Describe the authoritative leadership style.
8. Describe the affiliative leadership style.
9. Describe the democratic leadership style.
10. Describe the pacesetting leadership style
11. Describe the coaching leadership style.
12. What is emotional intelligence?
13. Describe the emotional intelligence competency called self-awareness.
14. Describe the emotional intelligence competency called self-management.
15. Describe the emotional intelligence competency called social awareness.
16. Describe the emotional intelligence competency called social skills.
17. What is the definition of ethics?
18. Why is the application of ethics to business settings important?
19. What is the difference between ethical and legal? Can something be ethical but illegal? Unethical but legal?
20. Define culture.
21. How can a project leader change, maintain, or create culture?
22. What is the difference between a formal system and an informal system with respect to culture?
23. What is socialization?
24. Describe unethical leadership.
25. Describe hypocritical leadership.
26. Describe ethically neutral leadership.
27. Describe ethical leadership.
28. What is an ethical dilemma? Give an example.
29. Develop a hypothetical ethical dilemma for a human resource situation.
30. Develop a hypothetical ethical dilemma for a conflict-of-interest situation.
31. Develop a hypothetical ethical dilemma for a confidence situation.
32. Develop a hypothetical ethical dilemma for a corporate resource situation.
33. For a hypothetical ethical dilemma you develop, use the eight-stage process for making a sound ethical decision.
34. What is the difference between a work group and a real team?
35. What is the difference between a performance-based goal and an activity-based goal? Give an example of each.
36. Why is focusing on a performance-based goal, such as a project's MOV, more important than having the team go through a series of team-building exercises?
37. Why are international projects more complex than domestic projects?
38. What is diversity?
39. Why is understanding diversity important when managing a multicultural project?

HUSKY AIR—PILOT ANGELS

Deliverable: A Time for Leadership

For this case assignment you will face a hypothetical situation. This would also be a good chance for you and your team to do another learning cycle. Read through this assignment first and then meet as a team to develop a Project Team Record and an Action Plan. This will help to improve team learning and to assign responsibilities to complete the assignment.

Over the past few weeks you have talked to a number of hardware vendors and requested quotes to provide the needed equipment to support the Pilot Angels application system. The deadline for each vendor to submit a bid is next week. During a casual conversation with L.T. Scully's administrative assistant, you learn that a salesperson from one of the vendors who will be submitting a bid has invited L.T. to a professional hockey game tomorrow evening. The vendor has rented a private box where complementary food and drinks will be available while watching the game in comfort. If the home team wins tomorrow night, they clinch a chance to be in the playoffs. The game is sold out, making a ticket to this game very valuable and in high demand.

Please provide a professional-looking document that includes the following:

1. Project name, project team name, and the names of the members of your project team.
2. If this rumor is true, discuss why this may be an ethical dilemma for L.T. Scully and for you as a project manager?

3. Think about and answer the following questions:
   a. Who are the stakeholders involved?
   b. What are the consequences for each stakeholder?
   c. What are your obligations to each of the stakeholders?
4. Suppose that you walk into L.T.'s office and see an open, gift-wrapped box with a jersey of the home team. You know that the cost of the jersey is about $180 because you just purchased one for your nephew as a gift. L.T. confirms that he was invited to the game by the vendor and that he just received the jersey from that vendor's salesperson. How would you handle this situation?
5. As a leader, how could you help your project team avert ethical dilemmas or illegal situations in the future?

THE MARTIAL ARTS ACADEMY (MAA)—SCHOOL MANAGEMENT SYSTEM

Deliverable: A Time for Leadership

For this case assignment you will face a hypothetical situation. This would also be a good chance for you and your team to do another learning cycle. Read through this assignment first and then meet as a team to develop a Project Team Record and an Action Plan. This will help to improve team learning and to assign responsibilities to complete the assignment.

Suppose that a member of your project team includes a software developer named Denise who just joined your consulting firm a few months ago. She is a single parent in her mid-40s, and this job and the paycheck is really important to her. Denise has been tasked with installing and conducting the final testing of the school management system. You've had no reason to ever worry or concern yourself with Denise's job performance, but recently another team member has approached you with information that Denise has made an illegal copy of the software system and intends to sell it at a much discounted rate to another martial arts school.

Please provide a professional-looking document that includes the following:

1. Project name, project team name, and the names of the members of your project team.
2. If this rumor is true, discuss why this may be an ethical dilemma for Denise and for you as a project manager?
3. Think about and answer the following questions:
   a. Who are the stakeholders involved?
   b. What are the consequences for each stakeholder?
   c. What are your obligations to each of the stakeholders?
4. Suppose that you confront Denise and the rumor is true. As the project manager, what is your decision? How would you handle this situation?
5. As a leader, how could you help your project team avert ethical dilemmas or illegal situations in the future?

QUICK THINKING—LEADERSHIP AND LISTENING

Project managers and other IT leaders tend to focus on sharpening their technical skills, but effective leaders need to work on their soft skills; the ability to listen may be the most crucial soft skill for being an effective leader. Steven Covey, author of the bestselling book, *The 7 Habits of Highly Effective People*, writes "Seek first to understand, then to be understood." Moreover, former CEO of Chrysler Corporation Lee Iacocca once said "Business people need to listen at least as much as they talk. Too many people fail to realize that real communication goes in both directions." Being a good listener makes you a better leader and makes your direct reports feel appreciated. In fact, listening is one of the most important skills a project manager will use on a daily basis. Consider the following example:

You walk into your project manager's office with a problem that you hope he can help you work out. He invites you to take a seat and tell him about it, but as you begin to speak he turns his attention to his computer screen. He encourages you to tell him more about your problem as he reads and answers a list of new emails. Without turning your way, he nods and grunts a couple of "uh-huhs." After you finish explaining your problem,

he turns from the screen to face you and says, "I have the utmost faith that you'll handle this problem, and how you handle it is entirely up to you."

The phone rings and your manager says that he's expecting an important call, which is an indication for you to leave. As you walk out of his office, he tells you to stop by any time you have a problem and that he's happy to help.

1. We've all experienced the above situation in some way. What effect would this have on your morale? Sense of value to the organization? Or your motivation?

2. As a project leader, what are some things you could do to become a better listener?

SOURCES:

Daniel, D. "Soft Skills: Listening for Better Leadership." *CIO Magazine*. September 4, 2007.

Jordan, A. "Two Ears, One Mouth." *Projectsatwork*. July 12, 2011.

Burley-Allen, M. "The Power of Listening." *Projectsatwork*. November 19, 2013.

QUICK THINKING—SITTING DUCKS

According to Bart Perkins of *Computerworld*, "Every organization has some 'ducks.' Ducks are employees who have a detrimental effect on productivity. Their work is consistently substandard, they rarely meet deadlines, and their skills are out of date. They hate change, resist taking responsibility and blame their failures on their co-workers. They constantly complain about their projects, their teammates, their workloads, and their managers. They stifle innovation by shooting down new proposals, claiming that changes 'just can't be done.'"

A "duck" can be brought into an organization in any number of ways. Ducks can be hired in, or they can be acquired through mergers or acquisitions. It would make sense to limit the number of ducks in an organization by firing them, helping them gain new skills, by providing counseling, or by transferring them to a job that better meets their skills and experience.

Unfortunately, many ducks are not interested in change, and keeping them around can demotivate other employees. For example, high performers may become demoralized if their pay raises are only slightly higher than a nonperformer. It's important to keep in mind that employees pay more attention to what leaders do than to what they say. Too often organizational policies or culture makes it difficult to get rid of the ducks.

A large organization hired a CIO with a mandate to improve IT services across the business units. He soon learned that there were many ducks among his staff. He needed to change the IT unit, but corporate policy made it difficult just to fire these nonperformers. With the knowledge and understanding of the executive team, the CIO created a "duck pond" that was a special, low-priority project that included all of the nonperforming employees. Once the ducks were herded together, the project was cancelled and the nonperforming employees were let go.

1. Some may argue that an ineffective IT organization could be outsourced, so sacrificing the ducks to save the rest of the IT function was best for the better performing employees. Do you agree?

2. Was the action of the CIO ethical?

SOURCES:

Perkins, B. "IT Full of 'Ducks'? Declare Open Season." *Computerworld*. April 28, 2008.

Kendrick, T. "Bad Attitudes." *Projectsatwork*. April 13, 2011.

Miller, J. and B. Bedford. "As Above, So Below." *Projectsatwork*. December 13, 2013.

 CASE STUDIES

Don't Tell Anyone or You're Fired!

The CIO of your organization walks into your office one Friday afternoon. As she closes the door behind her she says that "If you say anything to anyone concerning what I'm about to tell you, you're fired." She then explains that the team of developers that you supervise will be "released to seek other options," and all of your project's development tasks will be outsourced to a country in Eastern Europe. Your job is to coordinate with this new outsource provider so that all development work can be scheduled and transferred over in less than three months. In addition, you're not to let on to any of the company's developers that they will soon be replaced. She instructs you to carry on as if nothing has changed. In fact, the company will give them a bonus if they can complete their current work assignment in three months rather than the scheduled four months.

As the project manager of this team, you've gotten to know each of the developers fairly well. For example, one of the developers has just signed a mortgage to purchase her first house. Another is a single mother with her oldest child just entering college, and another has confided in you that he has been experiencing some health problems lately.

1. What would you do?
   a. Follow your CIO's orders because that is what you're expected to do.
   b. Update your resume and start looking for a new job.
   c. Pretend to comply with the CIO's orders, but tell the developers anyway.
   d. Wait until Monday and then go talk with your CIO to try and convince her that telling them is the right thing to do. (What will you do if the CIO rejects your suggestion?)
   e. Do something else? If so, what?

SOURCES:

Based on Esther Schindler, a blog posted on *CIO Magazine*, Advice & Opinion: You're the Boss, November 13, 2006.

Hamm, J. "Have You Earned the Right to Lead?." *Projectsatwork*. March 14, 2011.

A Failed ERP Implementation Results in a Lawsuit

Waste Management provides trash and waste removal, recycling, and environmentally safe waste management services in the United States and Canada. Recently, Waste Management has filed a lawsuit against the SAP AG for a fraudulent sales scheme that resulted in a failed ERP project. The legal action is an attempt by Waste Management to recover more than $100 million in project costs as well as the savings and benefits that SAP promised to Waste Management.

About three years before, Waste Management was interested in a new revenue management system. According to a Waste Management statement, "SAP proposed its Waste and Recycling product and claimed it was a tested, working solution that had been developed with the needs of Waste Management in mind." In addition, the statement also states that SAP promised that the ERP system could be implemented throughout Waste Management within eighteen months.

Waste Management also claims that SAP made assurances from the outset that its system was an "out of the box" solution that would not require any customization or improvements. However, Waste Management soon discovered that these assertions were not true and that SAP conducted product demonstration in a contrived software environment that did not represent the actual ERP system. A court document filed by Waste Management states that the demos were "rigged and manipulated." The complaint also states SAP executives and engineers represented that the software was a mature solution and conducted a demonstration that turned out to be a "mockup" version intended to deceive Waste Management.

Waste Management signed a contract with SAP in October 2005, but the SAP implementation team quickly discovered gaps between the ERP system's functionality and Waste Management's business requirements. Waste Management contends that SAP's development team in Germany knew before the sales contract was signed that the software lacked the basic functionality to run Waste Management's business. On the other hand, SAP's implementation team countered and blamed Waste Management for the gap in business requirements and for submitting change requests.

The complaint also states that SAP promised that a pilot implementation would be completed in New Mexico by December 2006, but it appears that the implementation still had not been completed even after eighteen months past the promised date. SAP conducted a Solutions Review in the summer of 2007 and concluded that the ERP system was not an enterprise solution that would meet Waste Management's needs. Moreover, the complaint contends that SAP said Waste Management would have to start over and allow SAP to develop a new version of the system if it wanted to have the software implemented across the business. According to Waste Management, SAP's new proposal was exactly the kind of risky and costly project it wanted to stay away from when it reviewed proposals from other ERP vendors. The complaint states "Indeed, the development project that SAP proposed would drastically lengthen the implementation timetable from the original December 2007 end-date to an end-date sometime in 2010 without any assurance of success."

1. If you were the project manager at Waste Management, what would be your recommendation to senior management?
2. Why might this be an ethical issue?
3. Do you think the blame lies with SAP only? Should Waste Management share in the blame?
4. If you were a project manager of an ERP project, what are some things you could do to lessen the chances of a misunderstanding?

Sources:
Kanaracus, C. "Waste Management Sues SAP over ERP Implementation." *Computerworld*. March 27, 2008.
Kanaracus, C. "SAP: We've Spent Millions So Far on Waste Management Suit." *CIO Magazine*. April 09, 2009.
Kanaracus, C. "Waste Management Now Demanding $500 Million from SAP." *CIO Magazine*. February 12, 2010.
Kanaracus, C. "SAP, Waste Management Settle Lawsuit." *Computerworld*. May 3, 2010.
Kanaraus, C. "Biggest ERP Failures of 2010." *Computerworld*. December 17, 2010.

Ethical Behaviors, Policies, and Technology

Corporate ethics originally meant compliance with laws and regulations. However, in the 1990s, many business schools started to stress the notion of integrity-based ethics to encourage organizations to go beyond state and federal mandates and focus more on their own values and priorities. As Mary Pratt points out, "Motives range from pure altruism to the notion that ethics make for good business."

Unfortunately, only a few organizations follow their ethics statements, standards, and policies in their day-to-day business. As Mike Distelhorst, a law professor at Capital University Law School, contends, "You'd be hard-pressed to find any company that doesn't have a beautiful ethics and compliance program. They're talking about it, and they're working it all out in various strategic documents. But the question is whether they're actually living by it. Some are, and clearly some aren't."

Texas Health Resources, Inc. is one company that delivers more than technical functionality and business requirements. According to Pratt, Texas Health also meets organizational ethical standards. For example, Federal agencies mandate that health providers like Texas Health must ensure that patient records remain private. However, caregivers must have timely access to this information when appropriate. According to Texas Health's vice president and deputy CIO, Michael Alverson, the organization gives doctors and nurses with the right authorization easy access to patients under their direct care. However, additional authorization is needed to access information for patients when they aren't under their immediate care. The system also records who accesses what information so company officials can audit and review any possible unauthorized or inappropriate access to confidential information. In addition, corporate policies prohibit employees from taking gifts from vendors, and a Business and Ethics Council is available for guidance to help people navigate the gray areas.

Tam Harbert believes "IT professionals have privileged access to digital information, both personal and professional throughout the company, and they have the technical prowess to manipulate that information. That gives them the power and the responsibility to monitor and report employees who break company rules. IT professionals may also uncover evidence that a co-worker is, say, embezzling funds, or they could be tempted to peek at private salary information or personal emails. But there is little guidance on what to do in these uncomfortable situations."

In an ideal world, corporate ethics policies and standards should go beyond the law and replace personal judgment. According to John Reece, a consultant for John C. Reece and Associates, "having clear ethical guidelines also lets employees off the hook emotionally if the person they discover breaking the policy is a friend, a direct report, or a supervisor." Therefore, a policy should provide clear instructions as to what an employee should do when someone violates a policy, including how to bring it to the attention of senior management. Moreover, Reece believes a good policy should include a "whistle-blower" provision that protects employees from retaliation.

Unfortunately, ethical decisions are left up to the individual when policies are not clear or are nonexistent, and this will vary based on the person and the circumstances. For example, Pratt describes a situation where marketing employees of a large telecommunications company spent millions of dollars to compile a list of customers from the organization's databases who frequently placed calls to the Washington, DC area. The plan was to sell this customer list to other marketers, but senior management put a stop to this before the list was sold. Afterward, IT developed a system to monitor use and block any future unauthorized access to this type of information.

Harbert also describes a situation of an IT director who discovered an executive who used his company computer to visit dozens of pornographic Web sites. The IT director helped develop the corporate policy to prohibit such behaviors and was also responsible for monitoring Web sites and reporting any violations to senior management. The executive was popular within the company and came up with an outlandish explanation that the company accepted.

Another problem may be finding a law enforcement agency that will take action when a computer crime is committed. According to Harbert, " ... efforts to report cyber crime can become mired in a complex web of overlapping jurisdictions or might even be totally ignored. Who you call depends on many factors, including how much money is involved, the media used (Internet? U.S. mail? Telephone?) and whether the criminal activity originated domestically or overseas." Although many cybercrimes in the United States are reported to the Federal Bureau of Investigation (FBI), other local, state, and federal agencies may have jurisdiction.

Ethical meltdowns and illegal behaviors can cost organizations money and ruin their reputations. Most people by now know that Web browsing histories are stored on our computers. While these histories can be easily deleted, packet-capturing and forensic products can record this information if you are connected to a corporate network.

Moreover, many organizations are increasingly looking to IT to use cameras and artificial intelligence software to look for unacceptable behavior. Mike Elgan believes, "The machines are watching us, and they are making judgments about what we do. Another way at looking at these colliding trends is that we are beginning to offload the human capacity for ethics, morality, and good citizenship to computer systems. At the very least, these systems are replacing the traditional role of the nosy neighbor."

For example, Alabama's Troy University has about 11,000 online students worldwide and is concerned with students who cheat during online exams. As a result, the school is spending about $125 per student to implement a system developed by Software Secure, Inc. to include fingerprint authentication to ensure that the appropriate student takes the test. Then, the software enables the school to lock out the student's computer so searches cannot be made locally or even across a network. An additional device with a microphone and camera can provide a 360-degree view to ensure no other help is given. Even more interesting is that the software scans the audio and video and will flag any suspicious noises or movements. An instructor can then review the flags to determine if any cheating took place. But Elgan believes that while the anticheating technology can lead to new ways to help counter major crimes and prevent terrorism, it may lead to a slippery slope.

More specifically, Elgan posits, "On the one hand there's nothing wrong with people getting caught for being unkind, unethical, using profanity, chewing gum in class, littering, and other minor or unpleasant actions. On the other hand, do we want to live in a world where cameras and computers watch our every move and report every transgression? Are we heading toward a system where fines are issued on the spot for profanity, like the 1993 Sylvester Stallone movie Demolition Man? Each individual case can be justified, but there can be no justification for us to blindly slouch toward an Orwellian society in which computer software is employed to watch and judge everyone—and expose, record, and punish every minor transgression."

1. Discuss the statement: "When policies aren't clear, ethical decisions are left to the judgment of the person."

2. Let's assume that you are a project manager leading a team of three members who are working on a customer relationship management project for a bank. Your team will undoubtedly have access to the financial information of the bank's customers. Develop a policy to ensure that no customer's information will be accessed without authorization.

3. In the last paragraph of the case, Mike Elgan describes what could happen if information technology is used to monitor and ensure employees conform to strict ethical standards and behaviors. Discuss whether you believe it is ethical to use a system like Troy University's anticheating system to watch and judge an employee's behavior.

SOURCES:

Elgan, M. "Big Brother is Watching You … And He's a Computer." *Computerworld*. June 22, 2007.

Strom, D. "Your Boss is Spying On You Right Now. What Can You Do About it?." *Computerworld*. July 23, 2007.

Pratt, M.K. "Ethics: IT Should Help the Company Steer Clear of Corporate Scandals." *Computerworld*. August 24, 2009.

Harbert, T. "Ready to Blow the Whistle on a Cybercrime? Who Ya Gonna Call?." *Computerworld*. September 12, 2007.

Harbert, T. "Ethics in IT: Dark Secrets, Ugly Truths—And Little Guidance." *Computerworld*. October 29, 2007.

BIBLIOGRAPHY

1. Jordan, A. "You Are Not a Project Manager." *Projectsatwork*. March 9, 2011.

2. Kotter, J. P. "What Leaders Really Do." *Harvard Business Review*, December, 2001, 3–11.

3. Shriberg, A., D. L. Shriberg, and R. Kumari. *Practicing Leadership: Principles and Applications, 3rd edition.* Hoboken, NJ: John Wiley & Sons, 2005.

4. Kouzes, J., and B. Posner. *The Leadership Challenge, 3rd edition.* San Francisco, CA: Jossey-Bass, 2002.

5. Goleman, D. "Leadership That Gets Results." *Harvard Business Review*, March–April, 2000, 79–90.

6. Jamail, N. "Micromanaging vs. Coaching." *Projectsatwork*. October 21, 2012.

7. Christensen, K. "*Thought Interview: Daniel Goleman.*" *Rotman Management.* Winter 2014.

8. Goleman, D. "The Focused Leader." *Harvard Business Review*, December 2013.

9. Golemen, D., R. Boyatzis, and A. McKee. "Primal Leadership: The Hidden Driver of Great Performance." *Harvard Business Review*, December 2001, 42–51.

10. Reichel, C. "5 PM Trends to Jump On in 2014." *Projectsatwork*. January 22, 2014.

11. Trevino, L. K., and K. A. Nelson. *Managing Business Ethics.* Hoboken, NJ: John Wiley & Sons, 2004.

12. Katzenbach, J. R., and D. K. Smith. *The Wisdom of Teams.* New York: Harper-Collins Publishers, 1999.

13. Lientz, B. P., and K. P. Rea. *International Project Management.* San Diego, CA: Academic Press, 2003.

14. Murphy, O. J. *International Project Management.* Mason, OH: Thompson, 2005.

11

Managing Organizational Change, Resistance, and Conflict

CHAPTER OBJECTIVES

Projects are planned organizational change. Moreover, change can be difficult for many of the project's stakeholders, thereby increasing the potential for resistance and conflict. After studying this chapter, you should understand and be able to:

- Describe the discipline of organizational change management.
- Understand the impact of change.
- Describe how change can be viewed as a process and the emotional responses people might have when faced with change.
- Apply the concepts and ideas in this chapter in order to develop a change management plan. This plan should focus on assessing the organization's willingness and ability to change, developing a change strategy, implementing and tracking the progress toward achieving the change and then evaluating whether the change was successful and documenting the lessons learned from those experiences.
- Discuss the nature of resistance and conflict and apply several techniques for dealing with conflict and resistance in an efficient and effective way.

INTRODUCTION

Most technical people tend to enjoy the challenges of setting up a network, developing cool applications using the latest and hottest technology, or designing a solution to solve some organizational problem. After all, that is what they're trained to do, and most people who enter a profession enjoy new challenges and learning new things. Many professionals believe that given enough time, training, and resources just about any technical or organizational problem can be solved. Being stuck in a boring job with obsolete skills is not a condition for career longevity—people will often leave to find new challenges. It is important to keep pace with technological changes, and many of these changes are welcome.

As discussed earlier, projects are planned organizational change. Organizations are made up of people, and the implementation of the project's product can change the way people work, affect the way they share information, and alter their relationships. Whether you are an outside consultant or work for an internal department within the organization, your mere presence will often be met with suspicion and hostility because you will be viewed as a person who has the potential to disrupt stability. You are an agent of change. As an old saying goes, the only people who like change are wet babies.

It is easy to concentrate on the technical or engineering side of project management. Dealing with the people issues, or the soft side of technology, is an area that most technical people do not enjoy. It is human nature to focus on what we can accomplish with minimal conflict or on what we can control.

Implementing a network of computers that communicate with each other or getting a new mobile app to work properly may be much easier and less stressful than dealing with resistance and conflict during development.

In addition, many technical people and managers naively believe that the customers or users within the organization will gladly embrace a new product or system if it is built properly. Although a product or system may include the required features and functionality and perform as intended, this "build a better mousetrap and the world will beat a path to your door" mentality can still lead to a product or system that is a technical success but an organizational failure.

Implementation of the new product or system is a technical challenge. The product or system must be moved from the development environment to a production environment and properly tested before being released. The customer or stakeholders within the organization, however, must be prepared for the impact that the new product or system will have on them. Often times a project can create a change that transforms the organization. It is easy to underestimate this impact and, given human nature, downplay the response people will have. Managers and technical people may be given to false beliefs:

- "People want this change."
- "Monday morning we'll release the new product or system and they'll be thankful to have it."
- "A good training program will answer all of their questions and then they'll love it."
- "Our people have been through a lot of change—what's one more change going to matter?"
- "We see the need for helping our people adjust, but we had to cut something."
- "They have two choices: They can change or they can leave."

These statements reflect the view that it is easier to gain compliance than it is to gain acceptance. This supposition is faulty because it assumes that everyone will comply and that compliance will be long lasting. The results may be quite different:

- The change may not occur.
- People will comply for a time and then do things to get around the change.
- Users will accept only a portion of the change.
- Customers will not purchase your product or users will not use the system.

The full benefits of the project are never realized or are realized only after a great deal of time and resources have been expended.

The central theme of this text has been the concept of measurable organization value. The MOV is not only the overall goal of the project, but is also a measure of the project's success. It is how we define the value our project will bring to the organization after the product is released or the system is implemented as originally envisioned. It provides a means for determining which projects should be funded and drives many of the decisions associated with the project throughout its life cycle. If the project's MOV is not realized in its entirety, then only a portion of the project's value to the organization is realized. Organizations today cannot afford to mismanage change initiatives. Competitive pressures provide little room for error. There is also the potential for lawsuits arising from stress-related disabilities and wrongful discharge (1). Therefore, while it is important that we manage the development of our project well, we also need to ensure that the project's product is transferred successfully and accepted by the organization with minimal adverse impact.

Acceptance is much more powerful and longer lasting than compliance, which means we need to ensure that the people within the organization are prepared properly *before* the product is released or the system is implemented. The discipline called **change management** is the area of project management that helps smooth the transition and implementation of the new product or system. As Anderson and Anderson contend, leadership is an important component for successful change (2). More specifically, traditional change management approaches have focused primarily on solving two key problems—how to plan for a more successful implementation and how to overcome resistance. Unfortunately, true transformation change has been difficult to achieve because true change leadership is needed to develop effective strategies that go beyond implementation and resistance.

The remainder of this chapter will focus on how change may be viewed as a process and on the emotional aspects normally associated with change. A framework for developing a change management plan and several techniques for dealing with the resistance and conflict that are a natural part of the change initiative will be introduced. Although this chapter deals will the soft side of project management, it is an important foundation for planning the release or implementation of the project's product that will be discussed in the next chapter.

 ## THE NATURE OF CHANGE

In order to effectively plan and manage organizational change, it is important to understand the impact of change, how change may be viewed as a process, and the emotional behavioral patterns of change.

Change Has an Impact

At any given time we must deal with changes that affect us. These changes may result from world or local events, the organizations we are part of, or personal decisions and relationships (3). Think about the changes that are going on in your life right now. You may be graduating soon, seeking employment, moving to a new residence, or scheduling a root canal with your dentist the day after tomorrow. The point is that there are a number of changes going on in our lives at any given moment. We may view these changes as being either positive or negative.

Nearly all change in our lives entails some amount of anxiety. Anxiety combined with hope is anticipation, while anxiety combined with apprehension is dread. Whether we view change as positive (anticipation) or negative (dread), there is a certain amount of stress that accompanies each change (4). For example, let's say that you will graduate this semester and start a new job that requires you to move to a distant city. Although you may be looking forward to leaving school and starting your professional career, you may still feel some apprehension. After all, you will have to leave your circle of friends and/or family and the familiarity of your present environment. Once you arrive in your new city, you will need to find a new place to live, make new friends, and become familiar with your new job, the company, and your coworkers. Moving to a new city is relatively easy compared to the transition. The move itself is a change that will occur fairly quickly; the transition required to adjust to the change takes longer.

Individuals must deal with a variety of changes in life and must assimilate these changes over time (3). **Assimilation** is the process of adapting to change and determines our ability to handle current and future change (5). For example, you may be dreading that root canal work next Wednesday, but once it's over you won't have the same level of anxiety that you are feeling right now. Or, you may be in the midst of planning a wedding. Most people view weddings as happy occasions, but anyone who has planned and gone through a wedding knows it can be stressful. The stress and anxiety felt before the ceremony, however, become a distant memory once happy couples celebrate their first anniversary. It simply takes time to assimilate change because we must adjust to the transition. Major changes, whether positive or negative, will require more time to assimilate than small ones. But once change is assimilated, it no longer creates the same level of anxiety or stress.

Problems occur when we have to deal with too many changes or when we cannot assimilate change fast enough. More specifically, change can have a cumulative effect over time. Different people will assimilate change at a different pace, and this ability to assimilate change becomes our resiliency to handle change. When an individual passes a certain stress threshold, he or she may exhibit dysfunctional behaviors. The behaviors depend largely on the person and may range from mild irritability to depression or dependence on alcohol or drugs. Therefore, it is important to manage the assimilation of change to keep things below the change threshold. In order to do this, an individual may try various tactics, such as exercising more regularly or postponing major life changes so as to deal more effectively with the present changes.

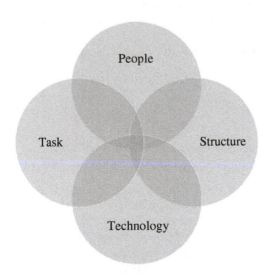

Figure 11.1 Change Has an Impact
SOURCE: Based on Leavitt, H. J., ed. "Applied Organizational Change in Industry: Structural, Technical and Human Approaches." In *New Perspectives in Organizational Research*. Chichester: John Wiley & Sons, 1964.

Organizations are made up of people, and these people have any number of personal changes going on in their lives. Changes proposed by an organization (e.g., reorganization, downsizing, implementing a new information system) will certainly affect the way people work and the relationships that have become established. Although these organizational changes will have to be assimilated by each person, the organization must assimilate change similar to an individual. After all, organizations are made up of people. Therefore, each change adopted by an organization must be assimilated and managed within the stress threshold. Just like people, organizations can exhibit dysfunctional behaviors. These behaviors may include an inability to take advantage of new opportunities or solve current problems. Eventually, an organization's inability to assimilate change will be reflected in the organization's ability to make a profit. Like an individual who cannot effectively deal with change and the associated stress, the long-term health and sustainability of the organization becomes questionable.

Change within an organization can affect different things in different ways. Leavitt's model, as illustrated in Figure 11.1, suggests that changes in people, technology, task, or organizational structure can influence or impact the other areas (6). These four components are interdependent, where a change in one can result in a change or an impact in the others. For example, a change in the organization's technology (e.g., implementing new information system) can impact the people within the organization (e.g., new roles, responsibilities) as well as the tasks the individual's perform, and the organization's structure (i.e., formal or informal). The key takeaway from Leavitt's model is that even a supposedly simple or minor change can affect other areas of the organization in ways that one might never envision. Hopefully, this can get us to think in broader terms to reduce the likelihood of surprise when resistance and conflicts arise.

Change Is a Process

Although a great deal has been written about change management, one model that has stood the test of time for understanding change was developed by Kurt Lewin (7). Lewin developed the **concept of force-field analysis** or **change theory** to help analyze and understand the forces for and against a particular plan or change initiative. A force-field analysis is a technique for developing a big picture that involves all the forces in favor of or against a particular change. Forces that are viewed as facilitating the change are viewed as **driving forces**, while the forces that act as barriers or that work against the change are called **resisting forces**. By understanding all of the forces that act as aids or barriers to the change, one may enact strategies or decisions that take into account all of the various interests.

Lewin's basic model includes three concepts: **unfreezing, changing,** and **refreezing** as illustrated in Figure 11.2. The present state represents an equilibrium or a status quo. To change from the current state, there must be driving forces both to initiate and to motivate the change. This requires an unfreezing, or an altering of the current state's habits, perceptions, and stability.

Figure 11.2 also depicts a transition from the present state to the desired state. This state is sometimes referred to as the neutral zone and can be a limbo or emotional wilderness for many individuals (8). Problems arise when managers do not understand, expect, or acknowledge the neutral zone. Those

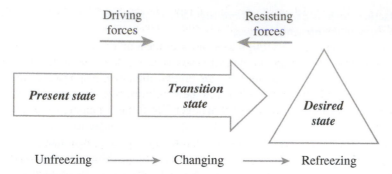

Figure 11.2 Change Process
SOURCE: Based on Lewin, K. *Field Theory in Social Science*. New York: Harper and Row, 1951.

in the organization who act on and support the driving forces for the change may be likely to rush individuals through the transition. This rushing often results in confusion on the part of those in the neutral zone, and the resisting forces (i.e., the emotional and psychological barriers) tend to push those individuals back to their present state. People do not like being caught in the neutral zone. They may try to revert to the original status quo or escape. Escape may mean leaving the organization or resistance to the change initiative altogether. In addition, individuals who find themselves in the neutral zone too long may attempt to create a compromise in which only a portion of the change is implemented. This compromise will only result in missed opportunities and sets a bad precedence for the next change initiative—if this one did not work, why should anyone believe the next one will?

People do not necessarily resist change; they resist losses and endings. Unfreezing, or moving from the current state, means letting go of something. Therefore, viewing change from Lewin's model suggests that beginning a change starts with an ending of the present state. Transition through the neutral zone also means a loss of equilibrium until an individual or organization moves to the desired state. Once there, it is important that the attitudes, behaviors, and perceptions be refrozen so that the desired state becomes the new status quo and equilibrium for the individuals involved.

Change Can Be Emotional

Until now, we have looked at change as a process and how change affects different areas of the organization. Change can also bring about emotional responses. An individual may have an emotional response to a change when the change is perceived as a significant loss or upsets a familiar or well-established equilibrium. In her book *On Death and Dying*, Elizabeth Kübler-Ross (1926–2004) provides insight into the range of emotions one may experience from the loss of a loved one (9). These same emotional responses have been applied to managing change whenever people experience the loss of something that matters to them.

The original model included five stages that we go through as part of a grieving process that leads to eventual healing. If people are not allowed to grieve and go through the first four stages, it becomes difficult to reach the last stage—acceptance. A person may have a number of emotions, such as sorrow, loneliness, guilt, and so forth, but the inability to work through these five stages can create more stress and difficulties than working through the stages. Although Kübler-Ross's model has been widely accepted, it has also been criticized as being oversimplified. However, it still provides some valuable insight for understanding how people may react to significant changes that affect their lives. The five stages include:

- *Denial*—The first stage is characterized by shock and denial. It is a common reaction when a person is given first notice of a change that will have significant impact. For example, when a person is informed that he or she is being fired by an organization, the initial response may be, are you serious? This can't be true! The reality may be too overwhelming. Disbelief may be the immediate defense mechanism. The initial news, however, provides a beginning for understanding the full impact of the change that is about to take place.

- *Anger*—Once a person gets over the initial shock of the announcement, he or she may become angry toward others, or even the messenger. The reaction is to blame someone responsible for creating the change. Although anger is a more active emotional response, it can be a cathartic expression when people are allowed to vent their emotions. Keep in mind that there is a difference between feeling anger and acting out in anger. While having feelings is always acceptable, the latter never is.

- *Bargaining*—In the third stage, the person is no longer angry. In fact, he or she may be quite cooperative and may try to make deals in order to avoid the change. For example, the person who lost her job may begin making promises to "double my productivity" or "take a cut in pay" in order to avoid being let go. A person may look for ways to extend the status quo, or the present equilibrium, by trying to "work things out."

- *Depression*—Once a person realizes that the change is inevitable, he or she may understand the full impact of the change and may enter the fourth stage—depression. This stage generally occurs when there is an overwhelming sense of the loss of the status quo. Although losing a job involves losing income, most people become depressed because they also lose the identity associated with their job.

- *Acceptance*—The last stage is when a person comes to grips with the change. A person does not have to like the change in order to accept it. This fifth stage has more to do with one's resolve that the change is inevitable and must be dealt with. Acceptance is an important part of ending the status quo and getting on with a new state. These emotional responses can help us understand why people react the way they do when faced with organizational change. Because of these emotions, people may be drained and productivity in the organization will suffer. It is also important to understand that people will have different perceptions of change. But their perception is their reality. Often management and the project team will have known about and had time to prepare for an upcoming change. While they may be impatient for the change to occur, others in the organization will lag. Management and the project team may want to "get on with it," while others are still dealing with their emotions during the transition. Instead of trying to suppress these individuals and their emotions, the leaders of change should accept them as a normal part of the change process and address them in the change management plan (4).

THE CHANGE MANAGEMENT PLAN

The key to successful organizational change is to plan for and manage the change and the associated transition effectively. This entails developing a change management plan that addresses the human side of change. The mere existence of such a plan can send an important message throughout the organization that management cares about the people in the organization and will listen and take their needs and issues seriously (8). Depending on the size and impact of the change initiative, the change management plan can be an informal or a formal document; however, the project team and sponsor should address and be clear on several important areas. These areas are summarized in Figure 11.3, and provide a framework for developing a change management plan discussed in this section.

Assess Willingness, Readiness, and Ability to Change

The first step to developing a change management plan is to assess peoples' willingness, readiness, and ability to change. A stakeholder analysis can provide a useful starting point for defining who the players or stakeholders involved in the change will be, their roles, and how they will interact with each other (1). Each stakeholder in a change initiative may play the role of the sponsor, change agent, or target (3).

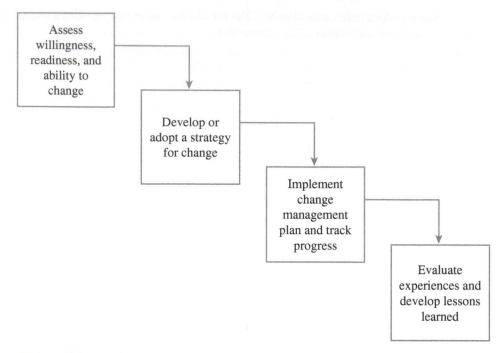

Figure 11.3 Change Management Plan

Sponsor—The sponsor can be an individual or a group that has the willingness and power, in terms of authority and making resources available, to support the project. Although this person or group is often the project sponsor, an **initiating sponsor** may hand off the project to a **sustaining sponsor**. More specifically, after making the decision to fund and support the project, the initiating sponsor may become completely removed from the project. Without the support of a sustaining sponsor, the project will eventually lose steam and direction. Therefore, the sustaining sponsor must become the primary sponsor for the project. A major portion of peoples' ability and willingness to support the change rests with the sponsor's commitment to the project and the associated change that will impact the organization. This commitment may be in terms of how they communicate with the rest of the organization, how they deal with challenges and issues, and the amount and quality of resources made available. In addition, sponsors must be effective leaders. If the project fails because people cannot adapt to the change, the project's envisioned value to the organization is lost and the sponsor's credibility is diminished.

Change Agents—In the most basic terms, the change agents will be the project manager and team; however, others from inside or outside the organization may be involved as well. An agent may be an individual or group responsible for making the change happen in order to achieve the project's goal and objectives. Change agents often report directly to the sponsor and must be able to diagnose problems, deal with these issues and challenges effectively, and act as a conduit of communication between the sponsor and the targets of change. The ability to sustain the change associated with the project rests largely with the change agents. They must be ready and properly prepared to meet the challenges they face.

Targets—The target is the individual or group that must change. In general, they may include customers or those who will use or be directly involved with final product or system. The term "target" is used because these are the people who are the focus of the change effort and who play a critical role in the ultimate success of the project (3). Although the project sponsors and change agents play important roles in supporting and carrying out the change effort, the dynamics associated with the targets of change become the most critical. Therefore, the willingness, ability, and readiness to change also rest largely with the change targets. This may require clarifying the real impacts of the change, understanding the breadth of change, defining what's over and what's not, and determining whether the rules for success have changed.

The project team and sponsor often do not think about how the planned change and transition will really affect people within the organization. As described in the previous section, change often brings about endings and a sense of loss of control. The project team and sponsor should take the time to think about what various individuals or groups stand to lose. For example, perceptions of loss may include power, relationships with other people, stability, or even control. As a result, people may become confused, disoriented, and resistant.

People also become confused and resistant when the rules for success change or are no longer clearly defined. Let's say that you have been working at a company for several years. Over that time, you have come to understand and become part of that culture. You know from your own experience and from those around you that promotion is based solely on seniority. As long as you meet the minimum performance requirements of your job, you know that promotions and the pay raises that follow will come after working a specific amount of time in a particular job. If the company ever has to lay off employees, layoffs will begin with the employees with the least seniority. But what if the company you work for has been acquired by a larger organization? The acquiring company has decided to "make a few changes" and starts by downsizing the workforce in your company. But now each employee's performance will be reviewed and only the top performers will be invited to stay. You can only begin to imagine peoples' reactions. The rules for success have changed.

Develop or Adopt a Strategy for Change

Once the organization's capability to change is assessed, the next step involves developing or adopting a strategy for change. The following are four strategies for change management (5).

RATIONAL-EMPIRICAL APPROACH   The rational-empirical approach to change management is based on the idea that people follow predictable patterns of behavior and that people will follow their own self-interests. Therefore, a change agent must be persuasive in convincing, explaining, and demonstrating how a particular change will benefit a particular person or group identified as a target of the change.

It is important that the individuals affected by the change be provided with consistent and timely information. Consistent information means that the project team and sponsor send the same message to all individuals and groups throughout the organization. Mixed messages can lead to confusion and suspicion. Credibility should not become suspect. In addition, each message must be accurate and timely. Often the excuse is, "It may be better to wait until we have all the details." But, saying nothing at all can send the wrong message.

When people are not given enough information, they tend to seek information from other sources. Often, these sources rely on innuendos, misinformation, and opinions, which become gossip that spreads through the informal organization. Stress levels rise until a point is reached where the organization becomes dysfunctional. It is better to be honest and tell people that there is no news before the rumor mill goes into warp drive.

Many managers believe that it is better to spare people bad news until the very last moment. However, it may be better to give people enough advanced warning to allow them to prepare for any upcoming changes. Then, they can deal effectively with the gamut of emotions that will be brought on by the change.

The change management plan based on this strategy should provide each individual with the purpose, a picture, and a part to play. Purpose is the reason for the change. Often individuals within the organization have a narrow view of their job and its relationship to the rest of the organization. It may be useful to provide people with a chance to see or experience the problem or opportunity first hand. For example, a person may be given the chance to witness how the current level of poor service is affecting the organization's customers. Then, it should be clear to that person that unless the organization does something (i.e., implement a new process or information system), it will continue losing customers to its competition. In time, the company will have to reduce its workforce or inevitably face bankruptcy.

A picture, on the other hand, provides a vision or a picture in the individual's mind as to how the organization will look or operate in the future. However, sometimes people need to be prepared to see things at their worst before they can get better (10). If done effectively, this procedure can help the individual buy into the proposed change.

A part to play can be very effective in helping the individual become involved in the proposed change. Although purpose and a picture of the proposed change are important, it is also important for the individual to understand and visualize the part he or she will play once the change is instituted. Having a part may provide the needed WIIFM (or, what's in it for me?) to help them through the transition.

NORMATIVE-REEDUCATION APPROACH   This approach takes the basic view that people are social beings and that human behavior can be changed by changing the social norms of a group. Instead of trying to change an individual, one must focus on the core values, beliefs, and established relationships that make up the culture of the group. For example, you may hear, "That's the way things are done around here." The targets of change may band together as a group and be highly resistant to new ideas or new ways of doing things.

This approach can be very difficult and time consuming because the change agents and sponsor must study the existing values and beliefs of a group. It requires unfreezing the current norms so that the change can take place and so that a new set of norms can be refrozen in order to solidify the acceptance of the new way of doing things by the group. As a result, change becomes more effective when each person adopts the beliefs and values of the group. The focus for managing change under this strategy becomes helping people redefine their existing social norms into a new set that supports the change effort. Some key principles include:

- Capacity for change is directly related to a person's participation in a group. When we become part of a group, our views and beliefs and those of the group become interwoven with each other.

- Effective change requires changing something not only about the individual's values and beliefs, but also the values and beliefs that make up the existing group's culture.

- Bias and prejudice toward guarding one's closely held beliefs and values diminishes one's ability to think rationally. Even when presented with the facts, many people may not act upon them in a rational way.

POWER-COERCIVE APPROACH   The power-coercive approach to change management attempts to gain compliance from the change targets through the exercise of power, authority, rewards, or threat of punishment for nonconformance. Many managers may be lured into using this deceptively easy and straightforward approach, but there is a real risk when used in the wrong situation. People may comply (or at least go through the motions of compliance), but an approach based solely on rewards or punishment may have only a short-term effect. For example, people may comply for the time being, until they can find new employment. On the other hand, a person may view the change as temporary and just "wait out the storm" until it is convenient or safe to go back to the old way of doing things.

There are, however, situations where the power-coercive approach is useful and effective. In such cases, the targets of change recognize the legitimate power or expertise of the change agent. For example, a person may not change his indolent lifestyle until the doctor admonishes him that certain health problems will get worse unless he changes his diet and begins an exercise program. Similarly, an organization may be faced with a situation that requires immediate attention—that is, any inaction or time lost trying to get everyone "on board" would spell disaster for the company. In this case, the use of rewards and threats would be a rational approach. As Davidson observes (5), the effectiveness of sanctions used under the power-coercive approach depends upon how dependent a person is on the organizations. More specifically, if a person lives paycheck to paycheck and has employment alternatives, then the power-coercive approach may be effective if used judiciously. On the other hand, Davidson believes it may be less effective if a person is financially, mentally, or emotionally able to leave the organization.

The objective is to change the behaviors of the targets so that their new behavior supports the change effort. Sanctions should be imposed on an individual level and should focus on what individuals value and what they dread losing—perhaps a bonus, a paycheck, or a position within the organization. Moreover, sanctions can be imposed in ascending order to demonstrate a point in the beginning and to keep any target's losses at a minimum. A change agent or sponsor can lose credibility, however, if they issue a warning or sanction that they do not fully intend to carry out. Finally, the change agent or sponsor should never be abrasive or disrespectful and should not impose sanctions in a cruel or vindictive manner.

ENVIRONMENTAL-ADAPTIVE APPROACH   Like a pair of old, comfortable shoes, people often become attached to and comfortable with a certain way of doing things, perhaps an older system or established processes that have become part of the group's culture and norms. The premise of the environmental-adaptive approach is that although people avoid disruption and loss, they can still adapt to change.

Following this approach, the change agent attempts to make the change permanent by abolishing the old ways and instituting the new structure as soon as possible. Cortez, the explorer, probably displayed the most drastic form of this approach. After landing in the New World, many of his men began to grumble about the conditions and what lay ahead. In response, Cortez burned the boats so that there was no option other than to press on. A much less drastic example would be upgrading everyone's operating system over the weekend so that when everyone returned to work on Monday morning, they would have no choice but to use the new software. In both examples, the targets of change were given no choice but to change.

Although this approach may be effective in certain situations, it is still important that the targets of change assimilate the change as quickly as possible in order to adapt to the change as soon as possible. Some ways may include helping the targets of change see the benefits and showing them how the new way is similar to their old, familiar way of doing things.

The change management strategies introduced here are typical for many change initiatives. A single strategy or approach, however, may not be effective in every situation. A more useful approach may be to combine the different strategies, depending on the impact of the change and the organization. Transformational change is a process of stages, not a single event (11).

Implement the Change Management Plan and Track Progress

Once the players and the strategy for the change management plan have been defined, the next step entails implementing the change management plan and tracking its progress. Although tracking progress should be integrated into the overall project plan and monitored using the various project tools, such as the Gantt chart, PERT chart, and so forth, introduced in an earlier chapter, milestones and other significant events should be identified and used to gauge how well the organization is adapting to the change.

In addition, one of the most critical issues for ensuring that the change takes place as planned is the establishment of effective lines of communication. At the very outset of any change initiative, gossip, rumors, and people's perceptions will find their way in both the formal and informal organizations. It is important that the project team and project sponsor create and open channels of communication.

The communication media can be important, especially when delivering certain types of news. For example, a richer media, such as face-to-face communication, is generally preferable when delivering important or bad news. There are a number of stories about people who realized that they were being let go when they found their phone line and network connections disconnected and security guards standing by their desk waiting to escort them out of the building. Delivering bad news is something that no one really enjoys, but it must be done nonetheless. The point is that management can handle difficult situations with class or with very little class.

Finally, open channels of communication should be both ways. The project team and sponsor must communicate effectively with the various groups within the organization affected by the change, and these groups, in turn, must be able to communicate effectively with the project team and sponsor. In addition, Web sites, emails, memos, and newsletters can all be mediums for effective communication.

Evaluate Experience and Develop Lessons Learned

As the project team members carry out the change management plan, they will, no doubt, learn from their experiences. These experiences should be documented and made available to other team members and other projects so that experiences can be shared and best practices can be identified. At the end of the project, it is important that the overall success of the change management plan be evaluated. This evaluation may help determine the effectiveness of the different players or a particular change management strategy. The important thing is to learn from experience and to share those experiences with others while adding new form and functionality to the organization's project methodology.

 ## DEALING WITH RESISTANCE AND CONFLICT

Resistance and conflict are a natural part of change (5). In this section, we will look at the nature of resistance and conflict and several approaches for dealing with these two issues. Keep in mind that the concept of conflict presented in this section can be applied to conflicts within the project team as well as external conflicts brought about by the change effort.

Resistance

Resistance should be anticipated from the outset of the project. Rumors and gossip will add fuel to the fire, and the change effort can easily run out of steam if those affected by the change begin to resist. Resistance can be either overt, in the form of memos, meetings, and so on, or covert, in the form of sabotage, foot dragging, politicking, and so forth. Once the change is compromised, management and the project team will lose credibility, and the organization may become resistant to all future changes.

Resistance can arise for many valid reasons. For example, someone may resist an information system because the response time is too slow or because a product does not provide the features or functionality that were originally specified as part of the requirements. On the other hand, resistance due to cultural or behavioral reasons is harder to rationalize, but still can keep a project from reaching its intended goal. People may resist change even though they understand that the change will be beneficial (5). For example:

- Some people perceive the change as requiring more time and energy than they are willing to invest.

- Sometimes people feel that a change will mean giving up something that is familiar, comfortable, and predictable.

- People may be annoyed with the disruption caused by the change, even if they know that it will be beneficial in the long run.

- People may believe that the change is being imposed on them externally, and their egos will not tolerate being told what to do.

- In addition, people may resist because of the way the decision to change was announced or because it was forced on them.

Resistance is human nature and a natural part of any change process. Understanding what an individual or a group perceives as a loss is the first step to dealing with resistance effectively. Because the project team and sponsor are the agents of change, it is easy to see those who resist as overreacting or not being logical. As the proponents of change, the project team and sponsor have had the luxury of knowing about the change early and, therefore, have had the time to become used to it. The rest of the organization, however, may learn about the change much later and, therefore, may not be at the same place for digesting the change. Subsequently, it is important that the project team and sponsor listen to what the rest of the organization is saying. Instead of arguing and trying to reason, it is better to allow people to vent their anger and frustration. Again, having defined a boundary of what is and what is not part of the change can help deal with stressful conflict situations. Keep in mind that empathizing or sympathizing with an individual is not the same as agreeing with them.

Conflict

Closely associated with resistance is the concept of conflict. Conflict arises when people perceive that their interests and values are challenged or are not being met. Conflict management focuses on preventing, managing, or resolving conflicts. Therefore, it is important to identify potential conflicts as early as possible so that the conflict can be addressed. Although conflict can be positive and help form new ideas and establish commitment, negative conflict left unresolved can lead to damaged relationships, mistrust, unresolved issues, continued stress, dysfunctional behavior, and low productivity and low morale (5). As Verma suggests (12), most people dislike conflict. As a result many people will attempt to avoid conflicts with the hope that it will just go away. Unfortunately, many conflicts that we avoid or ignore tend to reappear and often escalate later on. Therefore, Verma believes that the best way to handle conflict is to confront it.

There are three different views of conflict that have evolved from the late nineteenth century to today. These views include the traditional view (mid-nineteenth century to mid-1940s), the contemporary view (mid-1940s to 1970s), and the interactionist view (1970s to present) (12):

- *Traditional view*—the traditional view considers conflict in a negative light and suggests that conflict should be avoided. Conflict, according to this view, leads to poor performance, aggression, and devastation if left to escalate. Therefore, it is important to manage conflict by suppressing it before it occurs or eliminating it as soon as possible. Harmony can be achieved through authoritarian means, but the root causes of the conflict may not be adequately addressed.

- *Contemporary view*—The contemporary view, on the other hand, suggests that conflict is inevitable and natural. Depending on how conflict is handled, conflict can be either positive or negative. Positive conflict among people can stimulate ideas and creativity; however, negative conflict can have damaging effects if left unresolved. Therefore, positive conflict should be encouraged, while keeping negative conflict in check.

- *Interactionist view*—Today, the interactionist view holds that conflict is an important and necessary ingredient for performance. Although the contemporary view accepts conflict, the interactionist view embraces it because teams can become stagnant and complacent if too harmonious or tranquil. Subsequently, the project manager should occasionally "stir the pot" in order to encourage conflict to an appropriate level so that people engage in positive conflict. This may, however, be a fine line to walk for many project managers. Although someone who plays the role of the "devil's advocate" can be effective in many situations, people may become annoyed when it is used in every situation or used ineffectively.

Subsequently, conflict within projects can fit one, or a combination, of three following categories (10):

- Conflicts associated with the goals, objectives, or specifications of the project.

- Conflicts associated with the administration, management structures, or underlying philosophies of the project.

- Conflicts associated with the interpersonal relationships among people based on work ethics, styles, egos, or personalities.

For the project manager and project team, the seeds of resistance can easily lead to negative conflicts. Subsequently, it is important to understand how to deal with conflict. The following provides five approaches for dealing with conflict. A project team member or project manager should choose an appropriate approach for managing conflict based on the situation (12, 13).

- *Avoidance*—Avoiding conflict focuses on retreating, withdrawing or ignoring conflict. Sometimes, a cooling-off period may be a wise choice, especially when emotions and tempers are high. Avoidance may be appropriate when you can't win, the stakes are low, or gaining time is important. However, it may not be useful when the immediate, successful resolution of an issue is required.

- *Accommodation*—Accommodation, or smoothing, is an approach for appeasing the various parties in conflict. This approach may be useful when trying to reach an overall goal when the goal is more important than the personal interests of the parties involved. Smoothing may also be effective when dealing with an issue that has low risk and low return or when in a no-win situation. Because accommodation tends to work only in the short run, conflict may reappear in another form later on.

- *Forcing*—When using this approach, a person uses his or her dominant authority to resolve the conflict. This approach often results in a one-sided or win–lose situation in which one party gains at the other's expense. This approach may be effective when no common ground exists, when you are sure you are right, when an emergency situation exists, or when time is of the essence. Forcing resolution may, however, cause the conflict to redevelop later because people dislike having a decision or someone else's views imposed on them.

- *Compromise*—Compromise includes aspects of both forcing and accommodation; it gives up more than forcing and less than accommodation. Compromise is essentially bargaining—one person or group gives up something in exchange for gaining something else. In this case, no party actually wins and none actually loses, so that some satisfaction is gained from resolution of the conflict. This approach may be useful when attempting to resolve complex problems that must be settled in a short time and when the risks and rewards are moderately high. Unfortunately, important aspects of a project may be compromised as a means of achieving short-term results—for example, quality standards may be compromised in order to meet the project's schedule.

- *Collaboration*—When the risks and benefits are high, collaboration may be the best approach for dealing with conflict. This approach requires confronting and attempting to solve the problem by incorporating different ideas, viewpoints, and perspectives. The focus of collaboration is learning from others and gaining commitment, trust, respect, and confidence from the various parties involved. Collaboration takes time and requires a sincere desire to work out a mutually acceptable solution. In addition, it requires a willingness to engage in a good-faith problem-solving process that facilitates open and honest communication.

Each conflict situation is unique and the choice of an approach to resolve conflict depends on:

- Type of conflict and its relative importance to the project.

- Time pressure to resolve the conflict.

- Position of power or authority of the parties involved.

- Whether the emphasis is on maintaining the goals or objectives of the project or maintaining relationships.

CHAPTER SUMMARY

- Understanding organizational change is an important area for project management. Otherwise, this can result in the development of a product or system that is a technical success but an organizational failure.

- The project manager and the project team help prepare the users, or targets, of the intended change before the product or system is implemented. Preparation requires that we first understand the nature of change when a change is introduced into the organization.

- People and organizations can only assimilate or process change at a given rate, the cumulative effect of change can result in stress and dysfunctional behavior if an individual's or organization's threshold for change is exceeded.

- Kurt Lewin introduced the concept of force-field analysis, in which we try first to understand the driving and resisting forces that push and repel the change. In addition, Lewin's model of change helps us to understand that we must unfreeze the current state, or status quo, and then move through a transitional state until the new or desired state is reached. Then, these new behaviors must be refrozen so that they become ingrained as the new status quo.

- Initiating a change begins with an ending of the current equilibrium and may bring out a number of emotional responses as a result of a perceived loss.

- Understanding the effects of change on the organization allows us to develop a change management plan. This plan should first focus on assessing the organization's willingness, readiness, and ability to change.

- The next step of the change management plan should focus on adopting a strategy to support the change. Four approaches were outlined in the chapter:

  - rational-empirical approach
  - normative-reeducation
  - power-coercive approach
  - environmental-adaptive approach

- A change management plan could include one or a combination of approaches, depending on the situation.

- The third component of the change management plan should center on implementing the plan and tracking its progress.

- The change management plan should also include the evaluation and documentation of lessons learned. It is important that the effectiveness of a given strategy be assessed and experiences be documented so that they may be shared and so that best practices can be identified.

- Resistance and conflict are a natural part of the change process and should be anticipated from the outset of the project. Resistance can arise for many reasons and take many forms. Although the traditional view of conflict suggests that all conflict is bad and should be avoided or resolved as soon as possible, the contemporary and interactionist views of conflict support the idea that positive conflict can stimulate new ideas and improve creativity.

- Several approaches to managing or dealing with conflict were introduced:

  - avoidance
  - accommodation
  - forcing
  - compromise
  - collaboration

- Each approach has its advantages and disadvantages, and a project stakeholder should choose an appropriate approach based on the situation.

REVIEW QUESTIONS

1. As a member of a project team, why does your mere existence in an organization suggest change?

2. Why is it just as important to deal with the people issues of a project as it is to deal with the technical issues?

3. Why do many technical people shy away from dealing with the people issues?

4. How can a system be a technical success but an organizational failure?

5. How does change management fit with project management?

6. What is wrong with the idea of just expecting people to adapt to a new system by compliance?

7. Why is acceptance more powerful than compliance?

8. What are some down sides if an organization does not accept the project's final product as originally envisioned?

9. In your own words, define change management.

10. What is the difference between positive change and negative change? Do positive changes create stress for an individual? Why or why not?

11. Define assimilation and its importance to understanding how people deal with change.

12. What happens when an individual cannot assimilate change fast enough?

13. What happens when an organization cannot assimilate change fast enough?

14. Describe force-field analysis.

15. Describe the three stages of Lewin's model for change.

16. Why is the transition state often referred to as the neutral zone?

17. What might happen if the project manager and sponsor do not understand, expect, or acknowledge the neutral zone?

18. What is the difference between a change and a transition? Give an example of each.

19. Why would a person have emotional responses when faced with doing her or his job differently or being forced to use and learn new technology?

20. Describe the emotional responses a person might go through when given the news that her job has been eliminated as a result of a merger.

21. Why is having a change management plan important?

22. Why should the project manager assess the willingness, readiness, and ability of the organization to change?

23. What is a change sponsor? What is the difference between an initiating sponsor and a sustaining sponsor?

24. What important criteria should be used to determine whether a sponsor can help the organization through the planned change?

25. What is a change agent? What role does a change agent play?

26. What is a target? Why are targets important to a change initiative?

27. Why should the real impacts of change be clarified in the change management plan?

28. Using Leavitt's model, provide an example of how a new point of sale (POS) application might affect a restaurant's people, technology, task, and structure.

29. Why should the project team and sponsor be clear on defining what is over and what is not before a new system is implemented?

30. What are rules for success? Why is it important to determine whether the rules for success have changed in an organization before a new system is implemented?

31. Describe the rational-empirical approach to change. What things might a change management plan address under this approach?

32. Describe the normative-reeducation approach to change. What things might a change management plan address under this approach?

33. Describe the power-coercive approach to change. What things might a change management plan address under this approach?

34. Describe the environmental-adaptive approach to change. What things might a change management plan address under this approach?

35. How can you track the progress of your change management plan?

36. Why is it important to evaluate your change management experiences and document them as lessons learned?

37. What is resistance? How might an individual or group resist the implementation of a new information system?

38. Why would people resist change even if it were beneficial to them?

39. Why would a manager think that an individual or group is overreacting to a planned change?

40. What is conflict? Why should you anticipate conflict over the course of your project?

41. In your own words, define conflict management.

42. Why is it worse to try to ignore conflict than to deal with it?

43. Describe the traditional view of conflict.

44. Describe the contemporary view of conflict.

45. Describe the interactionist view of conflict.

46. What is the avoidance approach to dealing with conflict? When is it most useful? When is it not appropriate?

47. What is the accommodation approach to dealing with conflict? When is it most useful? When is it not appropriate?

48. What is the forcing approach to dealing with conflict? When is it most useful? When is it not appropriate?

49. What is the compromise approach to dealing with conflict? When is it most useful? When is it not appropriate?

50. What is the collaboration approach to dealing with conflict? When is it most useful? When is it not appropriate?

HUSKY AIR ASSIGNMENT—PILOT ANGELS

The Change Management Plan

In this assignment, you and your team will develop a change management plan to support your project with Husky Air. This would also be a good chance for you and your team to do another learning cycle. Read through this assignment first and then meet as a team to develop a Project Team Record and an Action Plan. This will help to improve team learning and to assign responsibilities to complete the assignment.

You and your team arrive on time for your meeting with Richard Woodjack, vice president of operations for Husky Air. The conference room has a finely polished oak table that can comfortably sit everyone. On the walls are pictures of older airplanes that epitomize a long-ago period. Richard greets you and the members of your team and then asks if anyone would care for a beverage before getting started.

As Richard takes a seat at the conference table, he smiles and says, "I want to thank you for coming in on such short notice. I know that the project has been progressing as planned, but I wanted to make all of you aware of a situation that may cause some problems going forward. We have two employees who have voiced several concerns with the new system that you will be implementing. One of the employees is Betty, who has been with the company for many years. Betty is close to retirement, but she knows more about the internal operations of this company than anyone else on my staff. In fact, most people around here say that if you have a question, go ask Betty. She's also well-liked and respected by just about everyone. Some of the pilots and mechanics even call her Mom because she tends to look out for their best interests. The problem is that Betty does not like change. As a matter of fact, she came into my office yesterday and told me that the idea of learning how to use a computer system frightens her. She's thinking of taking an early retirement before the system is implemented so that she won't have to deal with all the stress. I was counting on her being here for a few more years, or at least until I could find someone to replace her. Betty leaving before someone could transition into her job would have a major impact on company operations. Moreover, she is so popular that I think we would have a morale problem around here for a while. If at all possible, I would like to have Betty stay on and get someone up to speed to take over her job in the next couple of years."

Richard paused for a moment and then drew a deep breath before continuing. "And then there's Junior. Junior has been with Husky Air for about three years. He has an uncle who is on the airport's planning and control commission. Quite frankly, Junior is not one of our favorite employees, but every time we've tried to get rid of him, he threatens that he will sue for wrongful termination or use his uncle's connections to create all kinds of problems for us. Even though we have nothing to hide, the time and money to fight these little problems are a disruption we can do without. Although he can be a troublemaker, it's been easier for us to keep him around and let him do things that won't impact safety or quality. However, Junior has been spreading rumors about the new system to just about anyone who will listen. The latest rumor is that the new system will allow the company to lay off half of our employees. That's totally untrue, as you know. In fact, our management team is predicting significant growth and planning on adding more planes, pilots, instructors, mechanics, and staff to support that growth."

A secretary knocks on the conference room door and tells Richard that he is needed in the hangar. Richard asks if you and your team have any questions. He then excuses himself and leaves the room.

Based on your conversation with Richard Woodjack, develop a change management plan to support the implementation of the new system.

Please provide a professional-looking document that includes the following:

1. **Project name, project team name, and the names of the members of your project team.**

2. **A brief project description**. (This helps your instructor if different teams are working on different projects in your class.)

3. **The project's MOV**. (This should be revised or refined if appropriate.)

4. **A list that identifies the change sponsor(s), target(s), and agent(s) of change**.

5. **A change assessment**—Assess the two employees' willingness, readiness, and ability to change.

6. **A change strategy**—Develop and discuss a strategy for change. Your strategy should be based on one or a combination of the following approaches:
   a. Rational-empirical
   b. Normative-reeducation
   c. Power-coercive
   d. Environmental-adaptive

7. **Develop and describe a process for tracking the progress of your change management plan**.

THE MARTIAL ARTS ACADEMY (MAA)—SCHOOL MANAGEMENT SYSTEM

Deliverable: The Change Management Plan

In this assignment, you will develop a change management plan to support your project with the MAA. This would also be a good chance for you and your team to do another learning cycle. Read through this assignment first and then meet as a team to develop a Project Team Record and an Action Plan. This will help to improve team learning and to assign responsibilities to complete the assignment.

You arrive at MAA for your 10:00 a.m. meeting with Geoff and Julie. After giving them an update of how the project is progressing, you notice that Julie looks worried, and you ask her if she is concerned with the project work so far. Julie responds that she has some concerns, but not with the work that you and your team are doing. It seems that the senior black belt instructor, Tracy, is worried that the new system will be too complicated for him to use. He told Julie that he is not "technology savvy," and that learning to use a new computer system will be difficult. Moreover, he's been overheard complaining to some of the other instructors and students that he wishes MAA would stick to its current system because "that's the way we've always done things here." In fact, Tracy has hinted that it may be time for him to move on and start his own school "that would be more traditional in how it is run and how the curriculum is taught." Both Geoff and Julie said that Tracy is a good friend and an excellent instructor who is valued at MAA.

Geoff also tells you that they are having issues with Rod, one of the student's parents who is spreading rumors that MAA is wasting money on a new computer system. As a result, MAA will have to increase the price of its classes. Geoff and Julie have had several experiences with this particular parent over the past several years. For example, Rod told many of the other students' parents

that MAA would close its doors when Grandmaster Taylor announced his retirement. This caused a number of problems as several students, who believed this rumor, left to join another martial arts school. Geoff also tells you that Rod does Web development and hosting part time and was hired to develop a Web site for MAA. Geoff and Julie decided to have their Web site developed and hosted by another local company after paying Rod $3,000 for a Web site that never materialized.

Please provide a professional-looking document that includes the following:

1. **Project name, project team name, and the names of the members of your project team**.

2. **A brief project description**.

3. **The project's MOV**. (This should be revised or refined if appropriate.)

4. **A list that identifies the change sponsor(s), target(s), and agent(s) of change**.

5. **A change assessment**. Assess Tracy's and Rod's willingness, readiness, and ability to change.

6. **A change strategy**. Develop and discuss a strategy for change. In particular, how should Geoff and Julie deal with Tracy and Rod. Your strategy should be based on one or a combination of the following approaches:
   a. Rational-empirical
   b. Normative-reeducation
   c. Power-coercive
   d. Environmental-adaptive

7. **Develop and describe a process for tracking the progress of your change management plan**.

QUICK THINKING—IT'S NOT EASY GOING GREEN

Sustainability and social responsibility are increasingly becoming strategic goals for many organizations. Well-Point, a health benefits company in Indianapolis, Indiana is greening its IT users. The company was a founding partner in Dell's "Plant a Forest for Me" program where it pays an additional $40 when it purchases a server from Dell. Dell then gives the money to a conservation group to offset the carbon emissions produced by the server.

In addition to recycling and using recycled paper, Well-Point has tried to become a better citizen by substituting videoconferencing for travel. In fact, employees will spend 25,000 hours videoconferencing a year that will save 4,500 tons of carbon dioxide emissions from cars and planes. Dave McDonald, vice president of infrastructure support services, says that WellPoint will also replace 900 older, inefficient computers with server consolidations, as well as most of its old CRTs with more energy efficient LCD monitors.

However, there has been some resistance to Well-Point's green initiative. With respect to videoconferencing, a number of people were intimidated by the technology until they became used to it. Sometimes a senior sponsor is needed to remove entitlements like a printer in every office or travelling to meetings.

1. Some people may believe that a green initiative would be an easy sell within an organization. Why would people be resistant to such a seemingly beneficial change?

2. Why is senior sponsorship so necessary for such a change initiative? What are some ways in which senior management could show implicit and explicit support for a green initiative?

SOURCES:

Anthes, G. "Top 12 Green-IT Users: No. 8 WellPoint Inc." *Computerworld*. February 15, 2008.

Smith, A. "A Sustainable Future." *Projectsatwork*. January 29, 2014.

QUICK THINKING—CROSS-FUNCTIONAL AND MULTICULTURAL TEAMS

Cross-functional projects are common in many organizations. Too often these project teams are composed of people who do not work together or even know one another. They may believe that they've been thrown together and are expected to produce something right away. Moreover, many projects may also be multicultural, either because of the organization's global reach or because many workers today have emigrated from another country.

Unfortunately, cross-functional and multicultural projects almost always entail conflict because people often have different ideas of leadership, cultural backgrounds, language, or attitudes such as the importance of deadlines or the flexibility of rules. Cultural differences impeded the credit rating agency Moody's Investors Service's ability to conduct software testing and process audits. The organization's culture could be described as "a largely homogeneous American development environment" that encouraged independent thought and an open acknowledgment of defects. The quality assurance methodology depended upon democratic social discourse that supported freedom to express opinions, challenge others, and brainstorm solutions. Lastly, the organizational culture also encouraged a "tell it like it is" where everyone could express criticism without embarrassment or fear of reprisal. Many of these values and behaviors collided when the technical employees at Moody's became more multicultural. For some, a caste system or hierarchy established rules for social interaction, while others observed a strict obedience to authority. It became increasingly difficult to resolve conflict, as open disagreement and criticism could be viewed as a personal loss of face.

More specifically, developers were perceived to have a higher level of status than the testers. Developers became less willing to collaborate with the testers, and the testers became less willing to criticize and potentially shame their betters. Since intellectual give-and-take might be perceived as a challenge to the developers, the testers began to show their productivity and worth by running a large series of easy, superficial tests that generated a mountain of documentation. While productivity appeared to be high, quality assurance in terms of testing and process audits were declining.

1. Often cross-cultural conflicts can be mistaken for personality or job performance issues. What signs might you look for to identify conflicts that result from cultural differences?

2. As a project manager, what would you do to reduce conflict and bridge the communication differences between the testers and the developers?

SOURCES:

Barry, D. "The People Side." *Projectsatwork*. January 24, 2008.

Barry, D. "One on Ones." *Projectsatwork*. January 15, 2008.

Ensworth, P. "Patricia Ensworth on Managing Multicultural Project Teams at Moody's." *Computerworld*. October 1, 2003.

Ward, L. "The 6 Sins of Project Leadership." *Projectsatwork*. October 8, 2013.

 # CASE STUDIES

ERP and Change Management at Nestlé

A year after signing a $200 million contract with SAP and more than $80 million for consulting services and maintenance, HSBC securities in London, downgraded their recommendation on Nestlé SA stock. Although the Enterprise Resource Planning (ERP) project will probably provide long-term benefits, the concern was what short-term effect the project will have on the company.

Nestlé Company's goal is to build a business as the world's leading nutrition, health, and wellness company. The company was founded in 1867 when Henri Nestlé developed the first milk food for infants and saved the life of a neighbor's child. Nestlé is headquartered in Vevey, Switzerland with offices worldwide. Aside from chocolate and confectionaries, the company is widely known by its major brands, which include Purina®, Kit Kat®, Stouffer's®, and Poland Spring®. Revenues reported in 2007 were 107,552 million Swiss francs with a net profit of 10,649 Swiss francs.

In the early 1990s, Nestlé was a decentralized company where each of its brands, such as Carnation® and Friskies®, operated independently. The brands were unified and reorganized under Nestlé USA, but the divisions still had geographically dispersed headquarters and made their own business decisions autonomously. Moreover, a team charged with examining the various systems and processes throughout the company found many problematic redundancies. For example, Nestlé USA brands were paying twenty-nine different prices for vanilla to the same vendor. Jeri Dunn, vice president and CIO of Nestlé USA, said "Every plant would buy vanilla from the vendor, and the vendor would just get whatever it thought it could get. And the reason we couldn't check is because every division and every factory got to name vanilla whatever it wanted to. So you could call it 1234,

and it might have a whole specification behind it, and I might call it 7778. We had no way of comparing." Dunn and her team recommended technology standards and common systems for each brand to follow that would provide for cost savings and group buying power. Dunn then went to Switzerland to facilitate the implementation of a common methodology for Nestlé projects worldwide, but when she returned stateside two years later as a CIO she found that only a few of her recommendations were being followed. As Dunn recalls, "My team could name the standards, but the implementation rollout was at the whim of the businesses."

Dunn's return to the states followed USA chairman and CEO Joe Weller's vision for uniting all of the individual brands into one tightly integrated company. Reflecting on the company's condition, Dunn said "I don't think they knew how ugly it was. We had nine different general ledgers and twenty-eight points of customer entry. We had multiple purchasing systems. We had no clue how much volume we were doing with a particular vendor because every factory set up their oven vendor masters and purchased on their own." Dunn and a group of managers from finance, supply chain, distribution, and purchasing formed a key stakeholder team to study what Nestlé did right and what could be improved upon. They were given about two hours to present their findings to Joe Weller and other top executives, but the meeting ended up taking the whole day.

The blueprint from the stakeholder team included SAP as a cornerstone project that would take three to five years to implement. As Dunn points out, "We made it very clear that this would be a business process reorganization and that you couldn't do it without changing the way you did business. There was going to be pain involved. It was going to be a slow process, and this was not a software project." Unfortunately, senior management did not take the key stakeholder team's recommendation to heart, nor did they understand the pain it would create. As Dunn said, "They still thought it was just about software."

In October, a team of fifty senior business managers and ten senior IT managers formed a team to carry out the SAP implementation. The team was responsible for defining a set of common processes for every division. More specifically, each divisional function, such as purchasing, manufacturing, inventory, accounting, and sales, would have to give up their old ways and start doing things the new Nestlé way.

Another team spent eighteen months reviewing each piece of data in all the divisions in order to come up with a common data design across the entire business. For example, vanilla would now be coded as 1234 in every division so that the SAP system could be customized with uniform business processes and data. However, the team decided against using SAP's supply-chain module, Advanced Planner and Optimizer (APO), because it was recently released and therefore viewed as too risky. Instead, the team recommended a supply-chain module called Manugistics that was developed by an SAP partner.

By March, the team had a project plan in place where Nestlé would implement five SAP modules: purchasing, financials, sales and distribution, accounts payable and receivable, and the Manugistics supply-chain module across every Nestlé division. Implementation began in July with a deadline of approximately eighteen months. The deadline was met, but just as many problems were created as were solved.

Before all of the modules were rolled out, there was a great deal employee resistance. It appears that the problem was that none of the groups affected by the new system and processes were represented on the key stakeholder team. Dunn recalls her near fatal mistake. "We were always surprising [the heads of sales and the divisions] because we would bring something up to the executive steering committee that they weren't privy to."

By the time of the expected rollout, the project had collapsed into chaos. Workers did not understand how to use the new system or the new processes. The divisional managers were just as confused as their employees and probably even a bit angrier. Dunn's help desk took 300 calls a day, and she admits "We were really naive in the respect that these changes had to be managed."

Subsequently, morale deteriorated and nobody took an interest in doing things a new way. Turnover reached a new high of 77 percent. Supply-chain planners were unable and unwilling to abandon their familiar spreadsheets in favor of the complex Manugistics system. Other technical problems began to arise due to the rush to make the project's deadline. Integration points between modules were overlooked. For example, although the purchasing departments now used common data conventions and followed the same processes, their systems could not integrate with the financial or sales groups.

The project was stopped in June. A co-project manager was reassigned and Dunn was given full responsibility. In October, Dunn invited nineteen key stakeholders and business managers to a three-day offsite retreat. While the retreat started off as a gripe session, the members eventually made the decision that the project would have to be started over. The project team had lost sight of the big picture of how the various components would fit together. It was decided that the project would begin again with defining the business requirements before trying to fit the business into a mold that had to be completed by a predetermined deadline. Perhaps more importantly, they concluded that they required support from key divisional managers and that better communication was needed to tell all the employees when changes were taking place, when, why, and how.

By the following April, the project team had a well-defined plan to follow. By May, Tom James was hired as director of process change and was responsible for acting as a liaison between the project team and the various divisions. James was shocked by the still poor relationships between the project team and divisions, so he and Dunn began meeting face to face with the division managers and started conducting regular surveys better to understand how the employees were affected by the new systems and how they were coping with the changes.

One difference was Dunn and the project team would act on what they found. For example, a rollout of a new co-manufacturing package was delayed six months because feedback from the users suggested that they would not be prepared to make the process changes in time.

Although this project took much longer than expected, Dunn is not ashamed of the schedule overrun or the numerous dead ends. She believes that slow and steady wins the race, and that the project has already achieved a significant return on investment, especially in terms of better demand forecasting. According to Dunn, "The old process involved a sales guy giving a number to the demand planner, who says 'Those guys don't know what the hell they are talking about; I'm going to give them this number.' The demand planner turns [that number] over to factory, and the factory says the demand planner doesn't know what the hell he's talking about. Then the factory changes that number again."

Now, SAP provides common databases and processes that allow for demand forecasts to be more accurate. Since all of Nestlé USA is using the same data, it can forecast down to the distribution center level. Subsequently, inventory levels and redistribution expenses can be reduced. The company reports that improvements in the supply chain alone have accounted for a major piece of the $325 million Nestlé has saved by implementing SAP.

Dunn reflects that if she had to do it over again, she would focus on changing the business processes, getting universal buy-in, and then and only then installing SAP. As she said, "If you try to do it with a system first, you will have an installation, not an implementation. And there is a big difference between installing software and implementing a solution."

1. What could Nestlé have done better in implementing SAP?

2. What did it do right?

3. What would have been the value of having a change management plan from the beginning?

4. The primary lesson that Dunn says she gained from this project is "No major software implementation is really about the software. It's about change management." Do you agree with her statement?

SOURCES:
Worthen, B. "Nestlé's Enterprise Resource Planning (ERP) Odyssey." *Computerworld*. May 15, 2002. Accessed from www.nestle.com.
Lemos, R. "Open Source ERP Grows Up." *CIO Magazine*. April, 2008.
Weiss, M. and J. Drewry. "How to Overcome Resistance to Global IT Standardization." *Computerworld*. September 27, 2013.

From Ballpoints to Bits

An organization can develop or purchase an IT solution with the intent of adding value, but even the best solutions can fall short if the users do not accept the system. Projects are planned organizational change, so preparing the people within an organization is important to the success of the project.

Pfizer

Kolette is an epidemiologist at Pfizer who manages clinical trials for the treatment of metabolic diseases. She helped develop a data capture system called Investigator Net (I-Net) that automates data collection and analysis for drug development studies.

Pfizer recruited a university hospital to take part in a new study. Kolette met with the hospital's nursing coordinator to go over the program, but upon seeing the new computer being removed from the box the nursing coordinator exclaimed that computers were the "foot soldiers of the devil!"

Chicago Police Department

The Chicago Police Department is one of the largest police forces in the United States. The department began development of a relational database system called Citizen Law Enforcement Analysis and Reporting (CLEAR) to help the police sift through massive amounts of data to fight crime.

Joe is a 50-year-old veteran cop who has been working the streets of Chicago for decades. For his entire career he has filled out five-ply carbon forms to process his arrests and casework. On his first day of training on a PC, he picks up the mouse, points it at the screen, and starts clicking away. He then asks why the darn thing isn't working when nothing happens on the screen. Even the detectives who are computer literate grumble about the system. They claim that it isn't user friendly and getting approval from supervisors is cumbersome.

Procter & Gamble

Procter & Gamble encountered user resistance when it rolled out its Corporate Standards System (CSS)—a global, centralized system that manages all of the technical standards for each of the company's products to its 8,200 users. These technical standards are important in managing each product's life cycle and provide a communication link that connects R&D through the entire supply chain. For example, the beauty care group has an average of 125 standards for information regarding formulas, regulatory requirements, and packaging. Before CSS, people kept information about the technology standards in three-ring binders or on various computers.

Most complaints from the users were that the system was too slow, but it was discovered that the real reason wasn't the technology but the process. For example, an employee may have been used to documenting last-minute change requests from a vendor on the back of an envelope, but now documenting those changes in CSS required more rigor and thus was more cumbersome for the employee.

1. Which change management strategy do you think would be the best approach for each of the above situations?

2. If you were a project manager, how would you implement your chosen strategy?

SOURCES:

Datz, T. "Change Management: Planning Is Crucial." *CIO Magazine*. February 15, 2004.

Pastore, R. "Chicago Police Department Uses TI to Fight Crime, Wins Grand CIO Enterprise Value Award 2004." *CIO Magazine. February* 15, 2004.

Waxer, C. "From Computers to Crime Busting." *CIO Magazine*. April 28, 2009.

Koch, C. "IT's Role in Collaboration and Innovation at Proctor & Gamble." *CIO Magazine*. February 1, 2007.

Transformation and Project Management

The Importance of Change Management

A recent study by the Executive Program on Leading Organizational Change at the University of Pennsylvania's Wharton School reports that only about 20 to 50 percent of major corporate reengineering projects at Fortune 1000 companies have been successful. Moreover, another research study conducted by *CIO Magazine* revealed similar findings. More specifically, Dan Cohen wrote, "Our research, based on interviews with hundreds of executives in Fortune 1000-type companies around the world, revealed that it is not the complexity of the technology, a lack of buy-in from top management, high cost, or the failure to create shareholder value that derails new projects. Instead, the single biggest challenge in any transformation project is simply getting people to change their behavior." Another report, *Best Practices in Change Management*, by a company called Prosci, suggests a connection between change management and meeting project objectives. The study includes 10 years of research and almost 600 participants from various industries. For example, the study reports that "95 percent of participants with excellent change management had met or exceeded objectives, while only 16 percent with poor change management met or exceeded project objectives. In short, projects with excellent change management were six times more likely to meet objectives than those with poor change management."

Unfortunately, many project managers do not see the importance of an effective change management plan. As Creasey contends, "Some of the pushback by project managers is their sense that change management will slow them down and cost more. But the data show a strong correlation between the more effectively you manage the people side of change, the more likely you are to stay on schedule and budget. Correlation data also show that mismanaging change will result in delays and greater expenditures in rework as you react to the fact that the people side of change was ignored."

So, why is change management so important to achieving project objectives? Creasey adds, "We view the individual as the unit of change. It's an individual reaching his or her own future state who actually delivers value." He also draws the analogy, "When a mutual fund turns in a strong financial performance, it's the individual stocks inside the mutual fund that perform. A project works the same way. It's the individual contributors inside the company who change the way they do their work that makes for a return on investment."

A Life Cycle Approach

Jonathan Gilbert explains that people, processes, and technology drive organizational change and are affected by the change. Processes are defined by process maps and include policies, procedures, and business rules that define how work is done. Processes need to change when necessary in order to make the organization more efficient or to better serve its internal or external customers. In turn, this drives the adoption of new technology. Therefore, technology provides a means for the organization to become more efficient by processing data with more accuracy, dependability, or speed.

Gilbert also suggests, "Generally, organizations excel at designing new or improving existing processes. They also do well at identifying or developing technology to realize the power of new processes. However, most organizations fail to focus sufficient attention on the role people play in the processes and technology used to accomplish that desired organizational change. The overwhelming percentage of organizational change efforts fail because people are not sufficiently considered at the outset of the initiative."

Gilbert provides a life cycle approach to change management that focuses on identifying the change, engaging the people, and implementing the change. The first step, identifying the change, usually begins with a senior executive who initiates or spearheads the change by establishing a need for the change and by creating a vision for the transformation. This message must be communicated in a way that the need for change is heard, understood, and accepted by everyone regardless of his or her level in the organization. Unfortunately, many senior managers do not understand how even the rumor of change can have an intellectual, an emotional, and a neurological impact on people. A message such as "we need to cut our operating expenses by 20 percent" can create fear, skepticism, or apathy if people believe that management is really saying staffing levels will be reduced.

Dan Cohen agrees, "We also discovered that when people really do change their behavior, it's rarely because they are offered a logical analysis that shifts their thinking but because they are shown a compelling truth that influences their feelings. Emotions are what trigger action—impelling people to behave in the often radically different and difficult ways that substantial change demands."

During the identify stage, Gilbert recommends aligning people's disturbances. As he explains, "Neurologically speaking a disturbance is a conflict between a person's current mental model (the way they think about something) and the mental map they need to operate in the changed state. To align disturbances means to create a common disturbance among the minds of the people in the organization to create agreement between the gap that people have between their current mental model and the mental model needed to operate in the changed state. When these gaps aren't in alignment, everybody will respond to the change differently, and won't be able to agree on the direction and intent of the change. Leaders can reduce the disturbance and distraction of change by getting people's attention."

A carefully crafted message that helps people understand the vision for what the future will look like once the change is implemented can help align these disturbances. For example, Gilbert proposes removing people from their daily routine by meeting at an off-site location may help create a sense of urgency and allow people to concentrate the change message. In addition, Cohen suggests that the most effective leaders use simple, candid, and heartfelt messages using multiple channels to secure support for their visions.

The second phase, engaging the people, centers on including the people in the planning of the organizational change. As Gilbert points out, "People within the organization must be allowed the opportunity for intellectual, emotional, and psychological reaction to the desired change. Providing this opportunity enables people to become accustomed to the idea of change and to align their thinking in ways that will help both identify potential problem areas and contribute substantively to the process improvement."

For example, Cohen describes how a CIO at a major food company showed how a new ERP system could integrate with the different units within the organization. He went beyond just talking to the employees by giving teams of people from the different departments colored string that represented different modules of the ERP system. The teams then connected their strings to other team's strings where they would integrate. This resulted in a multicolored web that showed how the business was interconnected. As Cohen explains, "In this way, the CIO established a clear vision of an efficient enterprise-wide system, while simultaneously communicating why collaboration and integration were so critical."

Implementing the change is the third phase and translates the *identify* and *engage* stage into tactics or actions for achieving the transformation. However, Gilbert warns that many change initiatives fail because not enough time was devoted to the first two stages. As he contends, "During the implementation, employees throughout the organization need to remember why they are working so hard on implementing change. Therefore, change leaders should continually remind people, using multiple media (formal emails, progress celebrations, informal conversations) what the change is and why it is so important."

As Cohen suggests, this may include removing barriers to change. Such barriers may include removing a disempowering supervisor, improving information flow or systems, or boosting someone's self-confidence. Moreover, Cohen adds, "In the best cases, change leaders don't let up; they monitor, measure, and reinforce behavioral change until the transformation becomes a reality."

Gilbert believes that if organizations are successful in the first two phases, the implementation phase becomes a monitoring activity to ensure that the activities are completed as planned, energy and enthusiasm remain high, and alignment continues to exist among the stakeholders.

Change Management and e-Health Records

Although two combined surveys suggest the number of doctors using e-health records (EHR) in the United States is increasing, only about 10 percent use a fully functional system. In an attempt to encourage more physicians and hospitals to deploy EHRs, Lucas Mearian reports that the U.S. government is using a "carrot and stick approach." More specifically, a physician may receive about $44,000 under Medicare and almost $64,000 under Medicaid, while hospitals can receive millions of dollars for implementing and using a certified EHR under both Medicare and Medicaid. However, physicians and hospitals that don't implement EHRs by 2016 will be penalized by receiving cuts in Medicare payments.

According to Dr. Tom Handler of Gartner, "One of the main barriers to adoption, valid or not, are concerns about the productivity and usability of EHR systems. Many physicians also believe that the data collected by the government through EHR reporting criteria will be used to decrease Medicare and Medicaid reimbursements."

In addition, Handler also said, "Ultimately, what I hear doctors saying is, 'Let me get this straight. You want me to spend money to put in a system that will be harder to use and slow me down, so I will earn less money, and that the end result is that someone else makes more money. If you phrase it that way, it's not illogical to see why they don't want to do it."

Handler also believes that current EHR systems do not address what physicians consider to be some of the most important health-care reforms needed today. For example, an electronic patient record system can flag duplicate patient test orders, but physicians are not penalized for ordering duplicate tests. Unfortunately, the patient, insurance company, and ultimately society pays for the duplicate tests, while the physician only has to pay for the system.

Moreover, Dr. Harry Greenspun, a chief medical information officer at Dell, believes that resistance to adopting EHR can be as simple as a doctor not wanting to change a process that he or she has done for years. As Greenspun suggests, "It's really easy to write a prescription; you just jot it down on note paper. On a computer screen it can take a lot longer. If you have to go through a checklist or menu driven program, it can be clunky, and a barrier to adoption. On the other hand, if I can share [radiological] images, pull data from other systems, write a prescription all from one screen … and get valid prescription alerts and find out about public health threats, then the value is obvious."

1. Suppose you are managing a project that will implement an EHR for a private clinic that employs ten doctors. During a meeting where the features and functionality of an e-prescription module are being discussed, one doctor remarks before storming out, "*I didn't go to medical school to become a data entry clerk so that the pharmacy could hire one less tech to enter information into the system.*" What could you do to change this doctor's perception and behavior so that she would accept this transformation to EHR?

SOURCES:

Cohen, D. S. "Change Management: Emotions Count." *CIO Magazine*. December 1, 2005.

Gilbert, J. "The Change Management Lifecycle." *Projectsatwork*. January 20, 2009.

Rizzuto, J. "Change Management Changes Results." *Projectsatwork*. February 24, 2010.

Mearian, L. "Only 10% of Doctors Using Complete e-Health Record Systems, Surveys Find." *ComputerWorld*. January 18, 2011.

BIBLIOGRAPHY

1. Bridges, W. *Managing Transitions: Making the Most of Change*. Cambridge, MA: Perseus Books, 1991.

2. Anderson, D. and L. A. Anderson. *Beyond Change Management: How to Achieve Breakthrough Results Through Conscious Leadership*. Hoboken, NJ: John Wiley & Sons, 2010.

3. Connor, D. *Managing at the Speed of Change: How Resilient Managers Succeed and Prosper Where Others Fail*. New York: Ramdom House, 2006.

4. Duck, J. *The Change Monster: The Human Forces That Fuel or Foil Corporate Transformational Change*. New York: Crown Business, 2001.

5. Davidson, J. *Change Management*. Indianapolis, IN: Alpha, 2002.

6. Leavitt, H. J. ed. "Applied Organizational Change in Industry: Structural, Technical, and Human Approaches." In *New Perspectives in Organizational Research*. Chichester: John Wiley & Sons, 1964.

7. Lewin, K. *Field Theory in Social Science*. New York: Harper and Row, 1951.

8. Bridges, W. *Managing Transitions: Making the Most of Change*. Cambridge, MA: Perseus Books, 1991.

9. Kubler-Ross, E. *On Death and Dying*. New York: MacMillian, 1969.

10. McComb, W. L. "Transformation Is An Era, Not an Event." *Harvard Business Review*, April 2014, 1–2.

11. Kotter, J. P. "Leading Change: Why Transformation Efforts Fail." *Harvard Business Review*, January 2007, 1–10.

12. Verma, V. K. "Conflict Management." In *Project Management Handbook*, edited by J. K. Pinto. San Francisco, CA: Jossey-Bass, 1998.

13. Blake, R. R. and J. S. Mouton. *The Managerial Grid*. Houston, TX: Gulf Publishing, 1964.

12

Project Completion

CHAPTER OBJECTIVES

In this chapter, we will focus on three important areas necessary for project completion: project implementation, closure, and evaluation. After studying this chapter, you should understand and be able to:

- Describe the three tactical approaches to product release or system installation, as well as compare the advantages and disadvantages of each approach:
  - direct cutover
  - parallel
  - phased
- Describe the processes associated with project closure to ensure that the project is closed in an orderly manner.
- Identify four different types of project evaluations or reviews that include:
  - individual performance review
  - team close-out meeting
  - project audit
  - evaluation of the project's MOV

INTRODUCTION

The topic of change management was introduced in Chapter 11 and focused on preparing the people within the organization for the upcoming change and, more importantly, the transition that will occur as a result of the change. Understanding the human element or the "soft side" of project management is critical for ensuring that customers embrace the release of a new product or the individuals or groups within the organization accept a new information system implemented by the project team.

In this final chapter, we will concentrate on project completion. This includes project implementation, closure, and evaluation. **Project implementation** focuses on installing or releasing the project's major deliverable in the organization—namely, the product or system that was built or installing the software package purchased. This release or implementation requires a tactical plan that allows the project team to move the project's product from a development and test environment to the day-to-day operations of the organization or in the hands of the customer.

In general, release or installation can follow one of three approaches. These approaches are direct cutover, parallel, or phased. Each approach has unique advantages and disadvantages that make a particular approach appropriate for a given situation. Subsequently, understanding and choosing an appropriate approach can have a profound impact on the success or failure of the project.

As discussed in Chapter 1, a project is a temporary endeavor undertaken to accomplish a unique purpose. This means that a project has a definite beginning and a definite end. Once the product is released or the system is installed, the project manager and team must prepare for closing the project. Closing a project includes organizing and archiving project documents and deliverables, performing an audit and assessment of the project, evaluating the performance of the project manager and team, releasing project resources, and closing all project-related accounts.

For a project to be closed successfully, the product of the project must be formally accepted by the project stakeholders or customer. Not all projects, of course, are successful; however, a number of administrative tasks must still be completed. In such cases, it is necessary to assess whether any salvage value exists, and, more importantly, to understand the reasons why the project was not successful.

Once the project is closed, the project manager should evaluate each project team member individually in order to assess and provide feedback to the individual about his or her performance on the project. In addition, the project manager and project team should meet to conduct a **postmortem review** or **close-out meeting** of the project. The outcome of this review should be a final set of documented lessons learned and best practices that can be shared throughout the organization.

The project should also be reviewed by an impartial outside party. An audit or outside review can provide valuable insight on how well the project was managed and on how well the project members functioned as a team. The auditor or audit team should also determine whether the project manager and team acted professionally and ethically.

The project's real success will be determined by the project sponsor or customer. In this text, the project's overall goal was defined as the MOV, or measurable organizational value. The MOV must be clearly defined and agreed upon in the early stages of the project. Unfortunately, the project's true value to the organization may not be discernible immediately following the release of a product or implementation of a new system. It may take weeks or even months after a product or system is released before a valid evaluation can be made to determine whether the project was successful, as defined by its MOV.

PRODUCT RELEASE OR SYSTEM IMPLEMENTATION

At some point, testing is complete and the project team and project manager then become responsible for ensuring that the product or system is transferred successfully from the development and test environment to the operational environment of the customer or organization.

This transfer requires a tactical approach that is defined during the planning stages of the project, but the actual implementation activities can be a stressful time for all the stakeholders involved. Choosing an inappropriate implementation approach can negatively impact the project's remaining schedule and budget. In general, the project team can take one of three implementation approaches: (a) direct cutover, (b) parallel, and (c) phased.

Direct Cutover

The direct cutover approach, as illustrated in Figure 12.1, can be used to replace an existing product or system. In short, the old product or system is shut down and the new product or system is released or turned on. In general, a target, or *release,* date is agreed upon, and the new product or system simply replaces the old.

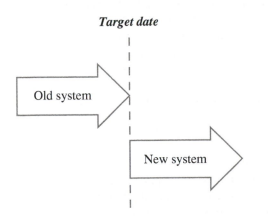

Figure 12.1 Direct Cutover

This approach is also appropriate when releasing a new product or system, when quick delivery is critical, or when the existing product or system is so poor that it must be replaced as soon as possible. Direct cutover may also be appropriate when a system is not mission critical—that is, the system's failure will not have a major impact on the organization. It is important, however, that the new product or system be thoroughly tested so everyone is confident that few, if any, major problems will arise.

Although there are some advantages to using the direct cutover approach, there are also a number of risks involved that generally make this the least favored approach except in a few, carefully planned situations. Although the direct cutover approach can be quick, it may not always be painless. You might think of this approach as walking a tightrope without a safety net. You may get from one end of the tightrope to other quickly, but not without a great deal of risk. Subsequently, there may be no going back once an old system is turned off and a new system is turned on. As a result, the organization could experience major delays, frustrated users and customers, lost revenues, and missed deadlines. The pressure of ensuring that everything is right or having to deal with problems and irate customers or project stakeholders can create a great deal of stress for the project team.

Parallel

As Figure 12.2 illustrates, the parallel approach to implementation allows the old and the new product or system to run concurrently for a time. At some point, the organization switches entirely from the old to the new. The parallel approach is appropriate when problems or the failure of the product or system can have a major impact on the organization. For example, an organization may be implementing a new accounts receivable package. Before switching over completely to the new system, the organization may run both systems concurrently in order to compare the outputs of both systems. This approach provides confidence that the new system is functioning and performing properly before relying on it entirely.

Although the parallel approach may not be as stressful for the project team as the direct cutover approach, it can create more stress for the customers or users of the system. For example, the users of accounts receivable system will probably have to enter data into both the old and the new systems and even be responsible for comparing the outputs. If the new system performs as expected, they may be willing to put up with the extra workload until the scheduled target date when the new system stands alone. If, however, unexpected problems are encountered, the target date for switching from the old to the new system may be pushed back. The extra workload and overtime hours may begin to take their toll and pressure for the project team to "get on with it" may create a stressful environment for everyone involved.

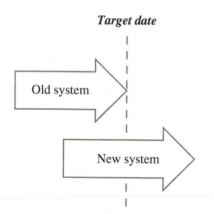

Target date

Old system

New system

Figure 12.2 Parallel

On the other hand, many organizations have two versions of a product that are available to their customers. For example, a company that develops and sells an operating system may support several versions for some time until the older version is finally phased out. Subsequently, this can result in significant support, maintenance, and selling costs as both products are available to its customers.

Phased

Following the phased approach, the product or system is released in modules or in different parts of the organization incrementally as illustrated in Figure 12.3. For example, an organization may implement an enterprise resource planning (ERP) system by first purchasing and installing the general ledger component, then accounts payable and accounts receivable, and so forth.

The phased approach may be appropriate when introducing a software system to different areas of the organization. When upgrading an operating system, for example, the IT department may perform the

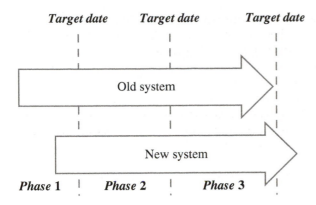

Figure 12.3 Phased

upgrade on a department-by-department basis according to a published schedule. In this case, a target date for each department would be set to allow each department to plan for the upgrade accordingly. A phased approach may also allow the project team to learn from its experiences during the initial implementation so that later implementations run more smoothly. Similarly, a project team developing a product using Agile, may plan for several product releases where increasing features and functionality are added to each subsequent product release.

Although the phased approach may take more time than the direct cutover approach, it may be less risky and much more manageable. Also, overly optimistic target dates or problems experienced during the early phases of implementation may create a chain reaction that pushes back the scheduled dates of the remaining planned implementations.

Table 12.1 provides a summary of each of the three implementation approaches discussed. As the end of the project draws near, everyone may become anxious to finish the project and move on to other things. Unfortunately, there is often a great deal of work that still needs to be completed. Delays or unanticipated problems may require additional time and unbudgeted resources, leading to cost and schedule overruns or extra unpaid effort, especially if an implied warranty exists (1).

During the final stages of the project, the project team may be faced with both time and performance pressures as the project's deadline looms in the near future. On the other hand, the sponsor or customer may become more concerned about whether the time and money spent on the project will reap the envisioned benefits. The project manager is often caught in the middle attempting to keep the project team happy and on track, while assuring the project sponsor that all is well.

Table 12.1 Comparison of Implementation Approaches

Direct Cutover	Parallel	Phased
Implementation can be quick	Provides a safety net or backup in case problems are encountered with the implementation of the new product or system	Allows for an organized and managed approach for implementing product or system modules in different departments or geographical locations
Can be risky if product or system is not fully tested	Can increase confidence in the new product or system when output of old system and new system is compared	Experience with early implementation can guide and make later implementations go more smoothly
Places more pressure on the project team	Takes longer and may cost more than direct cutover approach	Takes longer and may cost more than the direct cutover approach
	Places more pressure on the customers or users of the product or system	Problems encountered during early phases can impact the overall project schedule and budget

PROJECT CLOSURE

Although all projects must come to an end, a project can be terminated for any number of reasons. There are five circumstances for ending a project: normal, premature, perpetual, failed, and changed priorities (2).

- *Normal*—A project that ends normally is one that is completed as planned. The project's scope is achieved within the cost, quality, and schedule objectives, although there probably was some variation and modification along the way. The project is transferred to the project sponsor or released to the customers, and the end of the project is marked with a celebration, awards, and recognition for a job well done by those involved. As you might suspect, this is an ideal situation.

- *Premature*—Occasionally, a project team may be pushed to complete a project early even though the product or system may not include all of the envisioned features or functionality. For example, an organization may need to have a new system operational—with only a core set of original requirements—to respond to a competitor's actions, to enter a new market early, or as a result of a legal or governmental requirement. Although there is pressure to finish the project early, the risks of this decision should be carefully thought through by all of the project stakeholders.

- *Perpetual*—Some projects seem to take on a "life of their own" and are known as runaway, or perpetual, projects. These projects never seem to end. Perpetual projects may result from delays or a scope or an MOV that was never clearly defined or agreed upon. Then, the project sponsor (or even the team) may attempt to add on various features or functionality to the product or system, which results in added time and resources that increase the project schedule and drain the project budget. Some runaway projects result from an organization not making the appropriate decision to "pull the plug" on an unsuccessful project. The decision to terminate a project is not an easy one if egos and perhaps even careers or jobs are on the line. This phenomenon may also occur when the project has a high payoff to the organization and when admitting to failure is strongly against the corporate culture (3). No matter what the cause, project resources are eventually drained to a point where a potentially successful project becomes unsuccessful (4). Attention to defining and agreeing to the project's MOV, the project scope processes, and timely project reviews can reduce the risk of perpetual projects.

- *Failed*—Sometimes projects are just unsuccessful. In general, a project fails if insufficient attention is paid to the people, processes, or technology. Even though the project's MOV may define the project's value to the organization, cost and schedule overruns may drain the project's value to a point where the costs of completing the project outweigh the benefits.

- *Changed priorities*—In some circumstances, a project may be terminated as a result of a change in priorities. Financial or economic reasons may dictate that resources are no longer available to the project. Or, management may decide to divert resources to higher priority projects. This change can happen when the original importance or value of the project was misjudged or misrepresented or when organizational needs or technology change over the course of a long-term project. Some projects are "terminated by starvation," whereby successive budget cuts over time can slowly starve a project budget to the point where it is ended but the termination is masked (5). Senior management may not want to admit that it had championed a failed project or that a project will be unsuccessful in meeting its goals. The project budget receives a large cut or a series of smaller cuts. The result is that the project will die eventually and the project resources will be reassigned, even though the project is never officially closed.

Ideally, a project is closed or terminated under normal circumstances. The project achieves its desired goal and objectives. The project sponsor is delighted with the project's product and shows his or her delight by paying for the invoiced project work on time and contracts for more work in the future. Unfortunately, closing a project does not often happen this way. Many times the project team is exhausted as the project nears completion and may leave in haste without completing all of the deliverables (6). It is important that the project manager and team be prepared to deal with the following realities (7):

- *Team members are concerned about future employment*—Often the members of the project team are borrowed from different departments or functional areas of the organization. Once the project is finished, they will return to their previous jobs. For consulting firms, the project team members will move from one project to the next as part of their career path. Regardless, as the project nears its end, these project team members may begin to wonder what they will do next. For some, there will be a rewarding life after the project—for others it may mean looking for new jobs. For many it may mean disrupting a close-knit relationship with other members of the project team (5). Therefore, project team members may become preoccupied with moving on with their lives, and the project at hand may become a lesser priority. As a result, the project team members may not focus on what has to be done to close the project, and wrapping up the project may be a challenge.

- *Bugs still exist*—Testing the product or system is an important process. However, testing may not find all the defects, and certain bugs may not become known until after the product has been released or system has been implemented. The appearance of these problems can be frustrating and stressful to all the project stakeholders. Unless these defects and bugs are promptly addressed and fixed, the project sponsor's or customers' satisfaction with the product or system may become an issue.

- *Resources are running out*—Resources and the project schedule are consumed from the project's earliest inception. At the end of the project, both resources and time remaining are usually depleted. As unanticipated issues, problems, or challenges arise, the project manager may find that adequate resources to deal with these events effectively are not available. The project manager may find his or her situation aggravated if management decides to cut or control the project's budget.

- *Documentation attains paramount importance*—Most projects have a great deal of documentation requirements. They require project, system, training, and user documentation. Under ideal circumstances, the time to write documentation is built into the project plan and completed throughout the project. Many times, however, documentation is put off until the end of the project. As the end draws near, documentation becomes increasingly important. As a result, documentation may require more time and resources to complete, or shortcuts are taken to remain within the current project constraints.

- *Promised delivery dates may not be met*—Most projects experience schedule slippage. This slippage may be due to poor project management, implementation risks, competitive requirements, or overly optimistic estimates. A project will require a certain amount of resources and a certain amount of time to complete. Any misjudgment concerning what has to be done, what is needed to complete the job, and how long it will take will result in a variance between the planned and actual schedule and budget.

- *The players may possess a sense of panic*—As schedules begin to slip and project resources become depleted, various project stakeholders may experience a sense of alarm. The managers or partners of a consulting firm may worry that the project will not be profitable or satisfactory to the customer. The sponsor or customer may worry that the product or system will not be delivered on time and within budget or provide the expected value to the organization. Moreover, the project manager and team may also be worried that the project will not be successful and the blame will rest squarely on their shoulders. As the sense of panic increases, the chances for an orderly completion grow dim.

Regardless of whether a project ends normally or prematurely, it is important that an orderly set of processes be followed in order to bring it to closure. A good closeout allows the team to wrap up the project in a neat, logical manner. From an administrative view, this procedure allows for all loose ends to be tied up. From a psychological perspective, it provides all of the project stakeholders with a sense that the project was under control from the beginning through to its end (6).

Project Sponsor Acceptance

The most important requirement for closure under normal circumstances is obtaining the project sponsor's acceptance of the project. Delivery, installation, and release of the product or system do not necessarily mean that the project sponsor or customer will accept the project's product. Since acceptance depends heavily on the fulfillment of the project's scope and quality objectives, the project manager becomes responsible for demonstrating that all project deliverables have been completed according to specifications (8). Ancillary items, such as documentation, training, and ongoing support, should not be afterthoughts. These items should have been included in the original scope of the project. Any attempt to renegotiate what is and what is not part of the project work at this late stage of the project can create ill feelings or hold up payment by the client (1).

Project sponsors may be shortsighted or knowledgeable. **Shortsighted sponsors** tend to view the project as a short-term buyer–seller relationship in which getting the most for their money is the most important criteria for accepting the project. This view often leads to an adversarial relationship if the sponsor attempts to renegotiate the project scope or price at the end of the project.

Knowledgeable sponsors, on the other hand, realize that they have an important stake in the outcome of the project. As a result, they will be actively involved throughout the project in a constructive manner. Knowledgeable sponsors may ask tough questions during project reviews, but their objective is not to embarrass the project team or manager, but to ensure the success of the project.

Instead of an adversary trying to get the most in a "win–lose" situation, the knowledgeable sponsor will negotiate intelligently and in good faith. Regardless of whether the sponsor is shortsighted or knowledgeable, the project manager and team can improve the likelihood that the project will be accepted if they clearly define the acceptance criteria for the project at the early stages of the project, and document the completion of all project deliverables and milestones.

A clear definition of the project deliverables is an important concern for project scope management. Yet, defining and verifying that the project scope and system requirements are accurate and complete is only one component. Having scope change procedures in place that are understood by all the project stakeholders also ensures that everyone has the same expectations concerning what will and what won't be delivered at the end of the project.

The project approach incorporated in this text also focused on managing the project based on phases that focus on specific deliverables. Project milestones provide a quality check to ensure that the deliverables are not only complete but completed right. Documenting each deliverable and milestone throughout the project provides confidence to the project sponsor that the project has been completed fully.

The Final Project Report

In general, the project manager and team should develop a final report and presentation for the project sponsor and other key stakeholders. The objective of the report and presentation should be to give the project sponsor confidence that the project has been completed as outlined in the business case, project charter, and project plan. By gaining this confidence, the sponsor or customer will be more likely to formally accept the project that will allow for a smooth termination of the project.

The report may be circulated to key stakeholders before the presentation in order to get feedback and to identify any open or unfinished items that need to be scheduled for completion (1, 9). Once finalized, the final project report provides a background and history of the project. The report should include and discuss the following areas at a minimum:

- Project summary
- Project description
- Project MOV
- Scope, schedule, budget, and quality objectives
- Comparison of planned versus actual
- Original scope and history of any approved changes
- Original scheduled deadline versus actual completion date
- Original budget versus actual cost of completing the project
- Test plans and test results
- Outstanding issues
- Itemized list and expected completion
- Any ongoing support required and duration
- Project documentation list
- Product or Systems documentation
- User manuals
- Training materials
- Maintenance documentation

The Final Meeting and Presentation

If the project manager has been diligent in gaining the confidence of the project sponsor, the final meeting and presentation should be a simple, straightforward affair. The final meeting is useful for (9):

- *Communicating that the project is over*—By inviting key stakeholders to the meeting, the project manager is formally announcing that the project is over. This action not only provides a sense of closure for those close to the project, but also for the organization.
- *Transference of the product or system*—Although the product or system may have been implemented and is being used by the organization or the customer, the final meeting provides a formal exchange of the project's product from the project team to the organization. Unless some type of ongoing support is part of the contractual agreement, this transfer signals that the project team will not be at the customer or sponsor's site much longer.
- *Acknowledging contributions*—The meeting provides a forum for the project manager to acknowledge the hard work and contributions of the project team and other key stakeholders.
- *Getting formal signoff*—Finally, the meeting can provide a ceremony for the sponsor or customer to formally accept the product or system by signing off on the project. A space for signatures could be part of the final project report or part of some other contractual document.

Administrative Closure

Once the project is accepted by the sponsor or customer, a number of administrative closure processes remain. These last items can be difficult because the project manager or team may view these administrative items as boring or because they are already looking forward to and thinking about their next assignment (2). Unfortunately, administrative closure is a necessity because once the project manager and team are officially released from the current project, getting the sponsor or customer to wrap up the last of the details will be difficult. The requirements for administrative closure include:

- Verifying that all deliverables and open items are complete
- Verifying the project sponsor or customer's formal acceptance of the project
- Organizing and archiving all project deliverables and documentation
- Planning for the release of all project resources (i.e., project team members, technology, equipment, facilities)
- Planning for the evaluations and reviews of the project team members and the project itself
- Closing of all project accounts
- Planning a celebration to mark the end of a (successful) project

PROJECT EVALUATION

The question on everyone's mind throughout the project is, "Will this project be successful?" Different stakeholders will have different views of success. For the project team members, it may be gaining valuable experience and feeling that their work will have a positive impact on the organization. For the project manager, it may be leading a project that will be profitable to the firm or a promotion to a larger and more visible project. On the other hand, the client or sponsor may view project success in terms of organizational value received after the project is implemented. Evaluating the project at its completion provides an opportunity for retrospection that can improve the capabilities of both the project team members and the organization and satisfies the human need for closure (10).

Therefore, four types of project evaluations should be conducted. There should be:

1. An individual review of each team member's performance by the project manager
2. A project close-out review (sometimes called a postmortem review) by the project manager and project team
3. An audit of the project by an objective and respected outside party
4. An evaluation sometime after the product is released or the system is implemented to determine whether the project achieved its envisioned MOV.

Individual Performance Review

The project manager should conduct an individual performance review with each project team member. Although the project organization may have its own process and procedure for conducting reviews, the project manager should focus on the following points:

- *Begin with the individual evaluating his/her performance*—Evaluating someone's performance can be an emotional experience. Even with the best intentions, being critical of someone can put her or him on the defensive. Instead of beginning an evaluation with a critique of the individual's performance, it is usually more effective to begin by asking how that person would evaluate her or his performance. Surprisingly, most people are more critical of themselves. This opening provides an opportunity for the person doing the evaluation either to agree or to disagree with the individual's self-evaluation and to point out several positive aspects of the person's performance. This system creates a useful dialog that provides the individual with more useful feedback.
- *Avoid "why can't you be more like ... ?"*—It's easy to compare individuals. Unfortunately, comparisons can have a counter effect. First, the person you exalt may not be the shining star

you think. Second, others may become jealous and look for ways to discredit or disparage the individual. Keep in mind that people are different and should be evaluated as individuals.

■ *Focus on specific behaviors, not the individual*—When discussing opportunities for improvement with a person, it is important to focus on specific behaviors. For example, if a project team member has a habit of consistently showing up late and disrupting team meetings, it is important not to focus on the individual (i.e., Why are you so lazy and disrespectful?), but on how showing up late to team meetings is disruptive. Often people do not realize how their behaviors affect others.

■ *Be consistent and fair*—Being consistent and fair to everyone is easier said than done. The person conducting the evaluation should be aware of how decisions concerning one person may affect the entire group. Also, be aware that people talk to one another and often compare notes. Therefore, making a decision concerning one person may set a precedent for others. Having policies and procedures in place and sticking to them can mitigate the potential for inconsistency and the perception that the evaluator is not fair with everyone.

■ *Reviews should provide a consensus on improving performance*—The purpose of conducting a review or evaluation with each project team member is to provide constructive feedback for individuals. No one is perfect, so understanding where individuals can improve and how they might go about improving is important. The individual and the evaluator should agree on what areas the individual needs to improve upon and how the organization can support this endeavor. For example, the individual and the evaluator may agree that the team member should improve his or her communication skills. The evaluator may then recommend and provide support for the person to attend a particular training class.

The meeting can serve to help prepare the individual to move on and accept the psychological fact that the project will end (2). And, in most cases, the project manager could use this meeting to discuss the project team member's next assignment.

Project Close-Out (Postmortem) Review

Shortly after the final project report and presentation are completed, the project manager and project team should conduct a close-out meeting or postmortem review of the project. This should be done before the project team is released from the current project. It is more difficult to get people to participate once they are busy working on other projects or if they no longer work for the project organization.

Moreover, memories tend to become clouded as time passes. Thoroughness and clarity are critical (4). The formal project summary report should focus on the project's MOV and the project management knowledge areas. The focus of this review should include the following:

■ *Review the initial project's MOV*—Was the project's MOV clearly defined and agreed upon? Did it change over the course of the project? What is the probability that it will be achieved?

■ *Review the project scope, schedule, budget, and quality objectives*—How well was the scope defined? Did it change? How effective were the scope management processes? How close were the project schedule and budget estimates to the actual deadline and cost of the project? Were the quality objectives met? How well did the quality management processes and standards support the project processes?

■ *Review each of the project deliverables*—How effective were the business case, the project charter, the project plan, and so forth? How could these deliverables be improved?

■ *Review the various project plans and the project and product methodologies*—The team should review its effectiveness in the following areas:

  ■ Product/systems development
  ■ Project scope management

- Project time management
- Project cost management
- Project quality management
- Project team and resource acquisition
- Project stakeholder and communications management
- Project risk management
- Organizational change management
- Product release or system implementation

- *How well did the project team perform?*—Were conflicts handled effectively? Did the team suffer any morale problems? What main challenges did the team face? How well did they handle these challenges? How well did the members function as a cohesive team? This is also a good opportunity to celebrate the end of the project as well as announcing any promotions. Tying rewards to a successful project can be a great morale builder (11).

The discussion and recommendations from the close-out/postmortem review should be documented. In particular, the project manager and team should identify what they did right and what they could have done better. Although lessons learned should be documented throughout the project when they occur, this final meeting provides a last chance to review past experiences and document any new lessons learned so that they can be shared with others in the organization (12). Moreover, best practices should be identified and become part of the project and product methodologies.

Project Audit

The individual performance and postmortem reviews provide an important view of the internal workings of the project. In general, these reviews are conducted between the project manager and the project team. To provide a more objective view of the project, an audit or review by an outside party may be beneficial for uncovering problems, issues, or opportunities for improvement.

Similar to the close-out/postmortem review, the auditor or audit team should focus on how well the project was managed and executed. This may include the project plans, processes, and methodologies. In addition, the auditor or audit team should assess whether the project manager and team acted in a professional and ethical manner.

The depth of the audit depends on the organization's size, the importance and size of the project, the risks involved, and the problems encountered (2). The audit may involve the project manager and the project team, as well as the project sponsor and other key project stakeholders. In addition, the third-party auditor or audit team should:

- Have no direct involvement or interest in the project
- Be respected and viewed as impartial and fair
- Be willing to listen
- Present no fear of recrimination from special interests
- Act in the organization's best interest
- Have a broad base of project and/or industry experience

The findings or results of the project audit should be documented as well as any new lessons learned and best practices.

Evaluating Project Success—The MOV

The MOV, or measurable organization value, was defined at the beginning of the project. It provided the basis for taking on the project and supported many of the decision points throughout the project life cycle. Often, the MOV cannot be readily determined at the close of the project. Many of the benefits envisioned by the implemented system may require weeks or even months before they are realized.

Although the different project stakeholders and players may have different views as to whether the project was a success, it is important to assess the value that the project provides the organization. This review may be conducted by several people from both the project sponsor or client's organization and the organization or area responsible for carrying out the project. In particular, this review should focus on two questions: Did the project achieve its MOV? And is the sponsor/customer satisfied?

Before conducting this evaluation, the consulting firm or individuals representing the project should be sure that the product or system delivered has not been changed. Often, when a product or system is handed over to the project sponsor, the users or support staff may make changes. It is not uncommon for these changes to have unintended adverse effects. Care should be taken to ensure that the product or system being evaluated is the product or system that was delivered (4).

The evaluation of the project's MOV may be intimidating—it can be the moment of truth as to whether the project was really a success. However, a successful project that brings measurable value to an organization provides a foundation for organizational success.

CHAPTER SUMMARY

- The release of a product or implementation of a system requires a tactical approach for ensuring that it is transferred efficiently and effectively from the project environment to the customer or day-to-day operations of the organization.

- Three approaches to implementation were discussed in this chapter. The first approach, called direct cutover, provides the quickest means for implementation. In general, the new product is released or the old system is turned off and the new system is turned on. This approach can be risky if the system has not been thoroughly tested. As a result, it can put a great deal of pressure on the project team to "get it right" the first time, especially if the system supports a mission-critical function of the organization.

- The parallel and phased approaches are less risky alternatives, although implementation may take longer. The parallel approach requires that both the old product or system and new product or system run concurrently for a time until there is enough confidence that everything is working properly. At some point, a switch is made from the old to the new. The parallel approach can be stressful for the users of the system because they may be required to provide input for both systems and then compare the outputs.

- The phased approach may be appropriate when implementing an upgrade product or a modular system in different departments or at different geographical locations. Under this approach,

implementation takes place over phases according to a published schedule. Experience gained from early implementations can make later implementations go more smoothly; on the other hand, any unanticipated problems can create a chain reaction that pushes back the entire implementation schedule.

- Choosing and implementing the correct implementation approach can have a significant impact on the project schedule and budget.

- Once the product has been released or the system has been implemented, the project manager and team must plan for an orderly end to the project.

- Projects can be terminated for a variety of reasons, but a project must be properly closed, regardless of whether the project ends successfully or unsuccessfully.

- Ideally, the project is closed under normal conditions—that is, the project scope is completed within reasonable modifications to the original schedule, budget, and quality objectives.

- Delivery of the product or installation of the system does not necessarily mean that the project's sponsor or customer will accept the project. Therefore, closure must focus on providing both proof and confidence that the project team has delivered everything according to the original business case, project charter, and project plan.

- Several processes for closing a project were discussed in this chapter. They include closing the project accounts, releasing or transferring project resources, documenting lessons learned, and archiving all project documents and deliverables.

- Before a project is completed, it is important that several reviews or evaluations be conducted. These evaluations include a performance review between the project manager and each project team member. A closeout or postmortem review with the project manager and the entire team should include all of the project deliverables, project plans, and, in general, the various project management body of knowledge areas.

- Although lessons learned should be documented and best practices identified throughout the project, the completion of the project provides one last chance to identify any lessons learned and best practices.

- The performance reviews and postmortem should provide preparation for the project audit. In this case, a respected and objective third party should review all of the project deliverables and processes to assess how well the project was managed.

- The auditor or audit team should also focus on the specific challenges the project manager and team faced and how well they addressed these challenges. The professional and ethical behavior of the project manager and project team should be examined as well.

- Although different stakeholders may have different views of project success, the overall guiding mechanism for determining whether the project was a success is the project's MOV. Unfortunately, the organizational value that a project provides may not be readily discernible immediately after the information system is implemented. Even if it takes place weeks or months after the project is officially closed, an evaluation as to whether the project has met its MOV must still be conducted.

REVIEW QUESTIONS

1. What is implementation?
2. Describe the three approaches to releasing a product or implementing a system.
3. What are the advantages and disadvantages of the direct cutover approach?
4. What are the advantages and disadvantages of the parallel approach?
5. What are the advantages and disadvantages of the phased approach?
6. Describe the various scenarios for project termination.
7. Why might an organization terminate a project prematurely? What are the risks?
8. What is a perpetual project? Why might an organization be reluctant to terminate a project that many would consider unsuccessful?
9. Why would senior management cut a project's budget without officially terminating the project?
10. Why might some project team members be reluctant to see the end of a project?
11. Why can the end of a project be stressful for many of the project stakeholders?
12. Why is the sponsor's acceptance of the project important to project closure?
13. How can the project manager and project team facilitate the project sponsor's acceptance of the project?
14. What is the difference between a *shortsighted* and a *knowledgeable* project sponsor? How can making this distinction help the project manager during project closure?
15. What is the purpose of the final project report?
16. What is the purpose of the final meeting and presentation?
17. Describe some of the steps for administrative closure.
18. What is the purpose of the project manager conducting a performance review with each member of the project team?
19. What is the purpose of conducting a close-out or postmortem review?
20. What is the purpose of a project audit?
21. What criteria should be used to choose a project auditor or auditing team?
22. What is the purpose of evaluating the project's MOV?

23. Why would it be difficult to evaluate whether or not a project achieved its MOV shortly after the product is released or the system is implemented?

24. Why should any lessons learned from project evaluations be documented?

25. Why would evaluating whether a project achieved its MOV make many project managers and teams anxious? Why should it still be done?

HUSKY AIR ASSIGNMENT—PILOT ANGELS

The Implementation and Project Closure Plan

The testing of the application system is now close to being complete. In this assignment, you and your team will develop an implementation and project closure plan to support your project with Husky Air.

This would also be a good chance for you and your team to do another learning cycle. Read through this assignment first and then meet as a team to develop a Project Team Record and an Action Plan. This will help to improve team learning and to assign responsibilities to complete the assignment.

Please provide a professional-looking document that includes the following:

1. **Project name, project team name, and the names of the members of your project team**.

2. **A brief project description**. (This helps your instructor if different teams are working on different projects in your class.)

3. **The project's MOV**. (This should be revised or refined if appropriate.)

4. **A conversion strategy**—Develop a strategy for converting Husky Air's current system to the new application system your consulting firm has developed.

    Be sure to explain why you have chosen one of the following conversion strategies as well as why you didn't select one of the other two strategies:

    a. Direct cutover

    b. Parallel

    c. Phased

5. **A closure checklist**—Develop a checklist that the project team will use to ensure that the project has been closed properly.

6. **A project evaluation**—Prepare an outline and discussion of how your project's MOV will be evaluated.

THE MARTIAL ARTS ACADEMY (MAA)—SCHOOL MANAGEMENT SYSTEM

Deliverable: Project Implementation and Closure

The testing of the school management application system is now nearing completion. In this assignment, you will develop an implementation and project closure plan.

This would also be a good chance for you and your team to do another learning cycle. Read through this assignment first and then meet as a team to develop a Project Team Record and an Action Plan. This will help to improve team learning and to assign responsibilities to complete the assignment.

Please provide a professional-looking document that includes the following:

1. **Project name, project team name, and the names of the members of your project team.**

2. **A brief project description.**

3. **The project's MOV.** (This should be revised or refined if appropriate.)

4. **A conversion strategy.** Develop a strategy for converting MMA's current system to the new application system. Be sure to explain why you have chosen one of the following conversion strategies as well as why you didn't select one of the other two strategies:

    a. Direct cutover

    b. Parallel

    c. Phased

5. **A closure checklist.** Develop a checklist that you will use to ensure that the project has been closed properly.

6. **A project evaluation.** Prepare an outline and discussion of how your project's MOV will be evaluated.

QUICK THINKING—KILLING A PROJECT

The decision to cancel a project that has little or no chance of meeting its envisioned benefits or meeting its objectives can be a difficult and complex decision. Many people are afraid to face the truth when it comes to a failed project. According to Bart Perkins, euthanizing these projects is important to the health of the organization. However, before "pulling the plug," it's important to understand and plan for a number of important issues. For example, large projects can have political ramifications, especially if powerful stakeholders have a vested interest in the project. This can lead to finger pointing and looking for someone to blame for the project's failure. Moreover, a cancelled project can be expensive if cancelling a project includes severance packages, contractual agreements (i.e., early termination penalties), litigation, writing off sunk costs, or missed business opportunities. Failed projects can also impact relationships. This may include damaged working relationships with suppliers who may refuse to work with your organization in the future. Lastly, killing a project can also affect the project team. Project team members' morale may suffer if they have an emotional attachment to the project's failure. Disillusioned employees may become unproductive or those with highly marketable skills may leave, often making it difficult to attract or retain other valuable project team members.

1. What criteria should be used to cancel a project?
2. Who should make the decision to kill a project?
3. How can an organization ensure that a doomed project is euthanized as early as possible?
4. As a project manager of a doomed project, what would be your top three priorities for planning the cancellation of the project?

SOURCES: Adapted from Perkins, B. "Opinion: Before You Kill That Project. ... " *Computerworld*. March 10, 2008.
Glen, P. "Five Signs a Project is Headed for Trouble." *CIO Magazine*. May 4, 2009.
Mersino, A. "Project Fear and Denial." *Projectsatwork*. February 2, 2011.

QUICK THINKING—THE POST-IMPLEMENTATION AUDIT

Once an off-the-shelf Web-based procurement system was implemented, the CIO of a $405 million engineering and construction company, Michael Baker Corp., was inundated by questions regarding the system's effectiveness. Unfortunately, the CIO didn't have any concrete proof that the system improved efficiency. As a result, he decided to conduct the company's first post-implementation audit that included a thorough evaluation of the system's benefits, security, and project management processes. Although the CIO found out that the system's return on investment was lower than originally envisioned due to a miscalculation of the number of user licenses needed, the audit uncovered that the company was saving more than $150,000 a year. He also learned several valuable lessons on what not to do on future projects. While postimplementation audits are a useful tool to show the value of projects, it is estimated that only 20 percent of organizations conduct one. Many organizations are reluctant to make a post-implementation audit a standard process for three main reasons. First, they may take too much time, which adds to a project's cost and schedule. Second, post-implementation audits often require massive amounts of documentation to validate results. Lastly, uncovering unfavorable results may lead to a fear that someone will be blamed. However, post-implementation audits serve an important role, especially during challenging economic times as organizations feel increased pressure to spend money efficiently and effectively.

1. As a consultant, how could you convince your client that conducting a post-implementation audit is worth the added time and cost?

SOURCES: Adapted from Levinson, M. "How to Conduct Post-Implementation Audits." *CIO Magazine*. October 1, 2003.
Smith, C. "Advice for Project Audits." *Projectsatwork*. January 10, 2008.
Kothari, D. "Roadmap for Project Recovery." *Projectsatwork*. April 12, 2012.

CASE STUDIES

Kaiser e-Health Records Management System Implementation

Kaiser Foundation Health Plan/Hospitals' implementation of HealthConnect, a $4 billion electronic health records management system from Epic Systems Corp., received media attention as another IT project in serious trouble. As the project drew public attention, Kaiser's CIO, Cliff Dodd, resigned while another Kaiser employee, Justen Deal, sent a memo to all fellow employees detailing the project's financial and technological problems. Deal, a publication project supervisor in the Health Education and Training Department, stated that he also made his concerns known to Kaiser management, but company officials reported that Deal's concerns were looked into and that the HealthConnect project's implementation was not a failure. One of Kaiser's attorneys replied in a letter to Deal that "in the implementation of a new, large and complex system such as KP HealthConnect, various technical problems are likely to arise, but none that you mention are unknown to KP-IT nor were as insurmountable as you imply."

Kaiser did not offer any details regarding Cliff Dodd's departure, and Justen Deal was placed on administrative leave.

The HealthConnect system was expected to provide more than 100,000 of Kaiser's doctors and employees with immediate access to almost nine million patient medical records. In addition, the system would provide e-messaging, online order entry and filling of prescriptions that would also integrate with appointment scheduling, registration and billing, as well as other functionality that would be available to Kaiser members through its Web site.

However, a 722-page internal report obtained by *Computerworld* listed hundreds of technical problems, some that impacted patient care. Deal's memo stated that reliability and scalability were the main issues because the Citrix Application Delivery infrastructure implemented by Kaiser could not handle the load of the Epic system. According to Deal, "We're the largest Citrix deployment in the world. We're using it in a way that's quite different from the way most organizations are using it. A lot of users use it to allow remote users to connect to the network. But we actually use it from inside the network. For every user who connects to HealthConnect, they connect via Citrix, and we're running into monumental problems in scaling the Citrix servers. Epic simply cannot scale to meet the size and needs of Kaiser Permanente. And we're wasting billions of dollars trying to make it. The issues for me are the financial repercussions of trying to launch such an ineffective and inefficient and unreliable system across the organization. Using Citrix is something that defies common sense. It would be like trying to use a dial-up modem for thousands of users. It's just not going to work, and it's not something anyone would tell you a dial-up modem should work for." Deal also stated that Kaiser is wasting more than $1.5 billion a year on HealthConnect as well as other troubled IT projects.

Scott Herren, a group vice president and general manager at Citrix Systems Inc., believes the problem isn't scalability but the overall architecture that is being used to support loads this large. Moreover, he states that HealthConnect's problems do not have anything to do with the Citrix product: "In fact, we have many very large successful Epic deployments around the world. However, in order to support large deployments, the Citrix implementation must be architected accordingly."

Matthew Schiffgens, a spokesperson for Kaiser, said "As you move out with a very large deployment like this, you encounter challenges along the way, and we have a process to systematically address challenges as they arise. The problem at the Corona data center was a good one. It came up, we addressed it, and we feel confident that we made the proper infrastructure to manage that. That is a fundamental practice of running a good business. Does that mean there are systematic and ongoing problems? No. You identify issues and address them as they go along."

However, a number of Kaiser employees are still concerned. As one Kaiser IT employee, who wished to remain anonymous, stated: "People out in the field are frustrated, and the people in IT are just as frustrated because this was a solution forced upon us and was not an IT solution. I know in conversations I've had with my superiors there was a big push back in selecting Epic, and it was not a choice made by IT simply because of the large infrastructure needed to support it."

1. In your opinion, do you think that by "blowing the whistle" Justen Deal was a troublemaker, or a concerned employee who did the right thing by detailing the project's problems to all employees across the organization?

2. Compare the views of Justen Deal, Scott Herren, and Matthew Schiffgens. Why would these

individuals have such different views of this project's implementation?

3. Should Kaiser terminate this project? Or should it continue with the implementation? What are the ramifications for terminating the project, or continuing?

SOURCES: Adapted from Rosencrance, L. "Problems Abound for Kaiser e-Health Records Management System." *Computerworld*. November 13, 2006.

Chen, C., T. Garrido, D. Chock, G. Okawa, and L. Liang. "The Kaiser Permanente Electronic Health Record: Transforming and Streamlining Modalities of Care." *Healthaffairs*. March/April 2009, Vol. 28, no 2, 323–333.

Kolbasuk McGee, M. "Kaiser Permanente Finishes EMR Rollout." *Informationweek*. March 10, 2010.

Snyder, B. "How Kaiser Bet $4 Billion on Electronic Health Records—and Won." *Infoworld*. May 2, 2013.

Project Ocean—Part 2[1]

Project Ocean was a new water billing system that the city of Philadelphia initiated in 2002. By 2006, the city had spent more than $18 million (twice what it expected to spend), the project was two years late, and the system still had not been deployed. The project suffered from a number of problems that included software vendor problems, turnover of key employees, poor project management, and weak governance. However, when Michael Nutter was sworn in as mayor in January 2008, the city had a new and functional water billing system.[1]

Although Oracle was the original software provider, the final implementation of the system was provided by a new off-the-shelf billing system from Prophecy International PTY in Adelaide, Australia. According to the city's CIO, Terry Phillis, the Prophecy billing system was implemented one month ahead of schedule and 25 percent under budget. The Prophecy system was chosen after Phillis and the city of Philadelphia decided to scrap most of the original Oracle applications chosen by Dianah Neff, Phillis' predecessor. The new system replaces a 30-year-old mainframe legacy system that still relied on punch cards. Changes to the old system required writing new Cobol programs, which could take up to a year. The new system now allows the city to make changes in a matter of days and allows customers to track their water conservation efforts. According to Phillis, "Converting this thing over was a huge effort. We had to deal with 30 years of garbage data in the old system." After taking over as the city's new CIO, Phillis led an implementation team of managers from three city agencies.

The implementation of the project comes with the hefty price tag of $47 million. However, according to Phillis, this estimate includes many years of costs associated with changing the system prior to starting Project Ocean in 2002. Phillis believes that the biggest lesson learned from this experience is that "technology is not the prime concern in being successful in a project of this size. Instead success is a matter of process, collaboration, and leadership, although the technology has to work and it has to match your skill sets. We had to spend a lot of time upfront deciding how to run this and how to collaborate between three departments."

1. Although Philadelphia's new water billing system was implemented, would you consider this project a success?

SOURCES: Adapted from Hamblen, M. "Philadelphia Buoyant after Completing Water Billing System." *Computerworld*. January 18, 2008.

Gelbart, M. "Water-bill Changes Finally Flowing Philadelphia's Project Ocean, Begun in 2002, is Working At Last. Total Cost: about $25 million." *Philly.com.*, January 18, 2008.

The Many Impacts of Implementation Failure

Enterprise software applications include enterprise resource planning (ERP), customer relationship management (CRM), business intelligence (BI), and supply-chain management (SCM). However, according to Thomas Wailgum, the implementation of these multi-million dollar applications have produced "spectacular failures and huge spending nightmares; vendor marketing bravado that breeds cut-throat competition and contempt; and embarrassing and costly lawsuits over botched implementations and intellectual property breaches."

Over the years, a number of enterprise system failures have received public attention. For example, Hershey Foods' implementation of SAP, CRM, and supply-chain applications resulted in a spectacular failure when the company was unable to deliver $100 million with of chocolate candy in time for Halloween. On the other hand, Waste Management is involved in a $100 million lawsuit with SAP over an implementation of its ERP software. The legal battle focuses on fraudulent claims that SAP promised that its software would be an "out of the box solution for Waste Management's business processes," while SAP claims Waste Management breached its side of the contract by failing to "timely and accurately define its business requirements" and failing to provide "sufficient, knowledgeable, decision-empowered users and managers to work on the project."

---

[1]*A description of Project Ocean can be found in Chapter 1.*

Failed enterprise system implementations can also put a company into bankruptcy. For example, a Colorado-based jewelry chain called Shane Co. filed for Chapter 11 bankruptcy and attributed this move due to rampant cost overruns on an SAP implementation. According to a court filing, Shane Co. entered into a contract with SAP for a "highly sophisticated point of sale and inventory management system at an originally projected cost of $8 million to $10 million and a one year project schedule." Unfortunately, the company found that the software "did not yet provide accurate inventory count numbers, causing it to be substantially overstocked with inventory, and with the wrong mix of inventory." The court document also cites that while the system became stable it still does not include all that functionality detailed in the contract.

These failures not only impact the organization but the careers of senior managers as well. As Thomas Wailgum states, "Your department—information technology—has just played a starring role in blowing a multimillion dollar enterprise software project. The intense glare from the CEO, CFO, and other business leaders is squarely focused on the CIO, VP of applications, project managers, and business analysts charged with making sure that this didn't happen." However, Wailgum is also quick to point out that IT is never 100 percent at fault for these types of project failures, but "the unfortunate and unfair fact is that because these initiatives are considered 'technology projects,' the business will most always look in IT's direction when there's blame to be tossed around."

An IT governance study included more than 250 interviews with senior managers reported that about 50 percent of the respondents believe that IT is "very important to the enterprise" and about 75 percent said that they align IT with their business strategies. In addition, about 70 percent identified "executive management" as the group that should be held accountable to IT governance and IT project accountability.

Chris Curran is a consulting partner at Diamond Management & Technology Consultants and its Chief Technology Officer (CTO). Curran contends, "Business investments need to have business accountability, but when a project goes south, especially high-profile ERP implementations, IT gets blamed—but it's not an IT project." Moreover, Curran has seen his share of problematic projects and observes, "I've never seen any cases where a CIO just moved along like, 'Everything's fine.' Often, they're eventually demoted or pushed off into some operational role. Once you have a high-profile

project that has your name on it and it fails, I don't know if you can recover."

Failed implementations can have a different kind of impact for those working directly on the project. As Michael Fitzgerald believes, "It's not hard to get emotional when lengthy, high-profile projects are unfairly killed, mercifully euthanized, or launched with flaws." Moreover, Ken Corless, an executive director of enterprise applications management at Accenture, explains, "A lot of your job satisfaction comes out of seeing your product go live, being used by your business and customers. If you've been on something for 19 months, working 80-hour weeks for six months, and you're supposed to go live in six weeks and the rug gets pulled out, you feel pretty bad."

Bill Hagerup is a senior consultant at Ouelette & Associates Consulting, Inc. in Bedford, NH, and was a lead analyst who worked long hours on a project at a health insurer. Despite the extra effort, the project's scope was too large for the scheduled deadline, and he and his team delivered about 60 percent of what the company expected. According to Hagerup, "There was not joy in IT-ville, not even an 'attaboy' for the effort. Some negative feelings about the poor outcome were probably inevitable, but it would have helped if there had been some empathy for the IT team."

Hagerup believes that some simple words of appreciation for their effort from senior management would have helped with the feelings of anger at the unreasonable deadline and lack of support. Hagerup and his team of about ten people went through several weeks in a depression where productivity and morale were at an all-time low. As Hagerup explains, "By talking informally at lunch and commiserating over beers on Friday nights, we gradually came out of it. We circled the wagons a little bit, took strength from each other and reminded ourselves it wasn't our fault." He also adds that while the team eventually continued to work on the project and eventually met most of its initial goals, it never received any credit. Hagerup also believes that he and his team members would have come out of their depression more quickly had management talked to them about the situation and allowed them to have a dialog regarding whether the project was a failure.

On the other hand, a project team may be less emotional when a project is cancelled because the business needs change since it's no one's fault. However, this may not always be the case. As John F. Fisher, a former CIO and current chief value officer at a software contracts advisor called NET (net) Inc., "People take it pretty hard when a project that's going well is killed, anyhow. They feel like, 'Could I have done something better? How could we make it work for the business? Well, you can't. And that frustrates a lot of IT people."

Fisher was involved in cancelling a two-year project to develop an international banking platform to enable a bank to update its European operations. As the European systems manager, Fisher was brought into the project after it had started. It became clear to him that the platform was missing several important features, and there was no cost-effective solution to fix those problems. It was a difficult decision, but Fisher had to lay off about a dozen contractors in London and scrap a data center. As Fisher explains, "I felt good at the time." After all, he was saving time and money for the bank. However, he soon realized that he and the remaining members of his team were tainted. They were not included on the team assigned to work on the new system, even though they had gained valued experience. Despite no difference in the bank's overall financial performance from the previous year, Fisher received a much lower end-of-year bonus and some of his original team were assigned to less interesting, lower profile projects for a time.

Ken Corless believes that management can best help people by dealing with troubled projects quickly and directly. As Corless advises, "Rip the Band-Aid off—tell people live and in person. Don't shift the blame by saying something like, 'I wouldn't have canceled it, but this is what the COO wants to do'. That says you're not part of the leadership team. Such managers lose a chance to build credibility and rapport with their teams."

Most importantly, Corless believes managers need to keep in mind what motivates IT people: the chance to learn new things and develop new skills. With that in mind, Corless contends, "To that end, the best way to help employees grieving over a dead project is to quickly get them into [another] meaty and interesting role. Project failures may not be fun at the time, but it doesn't have to keep a good IT person down."

1. In your opinion, do you think IT receives more than its share of blame when the implementation of an enterprise project fails?

2. What steps could senior management take to help lessen the feelings of frustration and anger that could lead to lower morale and productivity when a project is canceled?

SOURCES: Adapted from Fitzgerald, M. "Project Management: When Good IT Projects Go Bad." *CIO Magazine*. July 26, 2010.
Kanaracus, C. "SAP Project Costs Cited in Jeweler's Bankruptcy Filing." *CIO Magazine*. January 14, 2009.
Kanaracus, C. "SAP: We've Spent Millions So Far on Waste Management Suit." *CIO Magazine*. April 9, 2009.
Wailgum, T. "10 Famous ERP Disasters, Dustups, and Disappointments." *CIO Magazine*. March 24, 2009.
Wailgum, T. "After a Massive Tech Project Failure: What IT Can Expect." *CIO Magazine*. August 5, 2009.

BIBLIOGRAPHY

1. Rosenau, M. D. *Successful Project Management*. New York: John Wiley & Sons, 1998.

2. Gray, C. F. and E. W. Larson. *Project Management: The Managerial Process*. Boston, MA: Irwin McGraw-Hill, 2000.

3. Keil, M. "Pulling the Plug: Software Project Management and the Problem of Project Escalation." *MIS Quarterly*, December 1995, 421–447.

4. Nicholas, J. M. *Managing Business and Engineering Projects: Concepts and Implementation*. Upper Saddle River, NJ: Prentice Hall, 1990.

5. Meredith, J. R. and S. J. Mantel. *Project Management: A Managerial Approach*. New York: John Wiley & Sons, 2000.

6. Oltmann, J. "Finish Strong." *Projectsatwork*. September 20, 2011.

7. Frame, J. D. "Closing Out the Project." In *Project Management Handbook, edited by* J. K. Pinto. San Francisco, CA: Jossey-Bass, 1998.

8. Wysocki, R. K., R. Beck Jr., and D.B. Crane. *Effective Project Management*. New York: John Wiley & Sons, 1995.

9. Buttrick, R. *The Interactive Project Workout*. London: Prentice Hall/Financial Times, 2000.

10. Oltmann, J. "Let That be a Lesson Learned." *Projectsatwork*. March 10, 2010.

11. Rizzuto, J. "Happy Endings." *Projectsatwork*. December 1, 2002.

12. Reich, B. "Lessons Not Learned." *Projectsatwork*. October 9, 2008.

INDEX

A

AC, *See* Actual cost (AC)
Acceptance, 283
  in organizational change, 287
  project charter, 109
  strategies, risk, 192
  validate scope, 128
Accommodation, 294
Accountability
  governance, project, 94
  mutual, 271
  PRINCE2®, 34
Activity
  for AON, 153
  definition, 150, 164
  estimates for, 141, 142
  for PERT, 156
Activity on the node (AON)
  activities for, 153
  definition, 165
  network diagram, 153–154
Actors, 126
Actual cost (AC), 215–217, 220
Administration, project, 108–109
Administrative closure, *See also*
  Closing project
  description, 313–314
  requirements for, 314
Affiliative leadership style, 263
Agents, 288
Agile, 38–41, 48
  approach, 150
  core beliefs and values, 38–40
  definition, 38
  doing/being, 54–55
  manifesto for, 38–40
  methods of, 40–41
  principles, 40
  projects, 135
  themes/categories, 40
  waterfall model and, 41–42,
    56–57
Agreement, 69
Alleman, Glen, 202

Allocation, resource, 163
American National Standards
  Institute (ANSI), 256
Analogous estimation, 136
Analysis of risk, 181–191
Analysis phase, SDLC, 34
Anamolies, budget, 198
Anger, in organizational change,
  287
Anich, Robert, 232
Anti-terrorism, 84–85
Anxiety, 284
AON, *See* Activity on the node
  (AON)
Approval of project, 109
Areas of impact for IT projects, 63
  customer, 63
  financial, 63
  identifying, 63
  operational, 63
  social, 63
  strategic, 63
ARPANET project, 6
Assessment
  capability maturity model, 256
  OPM3®, 255
  of risk, 70
Assignable cause, in quality
  management, 248
Assimilation, 284
Assumptions
  project charter, 108
  and risks, 3
Assurance, quality, *See* Quality
  assurance (QA)
Attributes, project
  interdependent tasks, 3
  manager, 95
  organizational change, 3–4
  organizational environment, 4
  ownership, 2
  project roles, 3
  purpose, 2
  resources, 2

  risks and assumptions, 3
  time frame, 2
Audit, project
  description, 316
  post-implementation, 320
Authoritative leadership style, 263
Authority
  functional organization and, 98
  project organization and, 99
Authorization, project governance,
  94
Avoidance
  conflict managing, 294
  risk strategies, 192

B

Bargaining, in organizational
  change, 287
Baseline plan, 151, 165
  actual performance to, 220–221
  definition, 164
  lead to federal waste of IT,
    170–171
  project schedule and budget,
    163–164
BearingPoint Inc., 22
Beck, Kent, 40
Bednarz, Ann, 257, 258
Benchmarking, 64
Berinato, Scott, 56, 200, 201
*Best Practices in Change
  Management,* 303
Binomial probability distribution,
  186
Bird's-eye view, 258
Birkelbach, Jan, 169
Blogs, 231–232
Boehm, Barry, 236
Bottom-up estimating, 136
Boundary, scope, 123–124
Boyatzis, R., 265
Brainstorming, 180
Breadth, of learning, 46
Breakeven cash flow model, 71

Bridge building, 69
Brodkin, Jon, 118
Brooks, Fredrick P., 143
Brooks' Law, 143
Budget, project, 108, 165
  baseline plan, 151, 165
    actual performance to,
      220–221
    definition, 164
    lead to federal waste of IT,
      170–171
    project schedule and budget,
      163–164
  budget at completion, 213, 220
  contingency reserves, 162
  cost estimation, 161–162
  cost of task, 161
  developing, 161–163
  indirect costs, 162
  labor cost for project, 163
  learning curve, 162
  planned, 214
  reserves, 162–163
  resource allocation, 163
  sunk costs, 162
Buffers, 158, 165
BugBusters, 225–226
Bugs, 146–147, 244, 311
Burn-down chart, 213
Business analyst, roles of,
  145–146
Business case
  cross-functional teams
    business case formation,
      68–69
    and multicultural teams,
      299–300
  definition, 59–60, 67–68, 77
  development
    defining MOV, 68
    defining total benefits of
      ownership, 70
    defining total cost of
      ownership, 70
    feasibility, 69–70
    financial models, 71–73
    identifying alternatives, 69
    proposed recommendation
      support, 75
    risk, 69–70
    scoring models, 73–75

status quo, 69
template, 75
good, 68
MOV, *See* Measurable
  organizational value (MOV)
objective of, 77
PRINCE2®, 32, 34, 67
realistic, 75
Business process outsourcing, 101
Business reviews, 246–247
Business strategy, 1
Business/organization knowledge,
  96

C
Capability maturity model
  (CMM), 240, 255–257
Capability maturity model
  integration (CMMI), 251
  objectives of, 240
  process maturity levels
    initial (Level 1), 241
    managed (Level 4), 242
    optimizing (Level 5), 242
    repeatable (Level 2),
      241–242
  project quality, 240
Capability, process, 240
CAPPS II, 84–85
Cash flow models
  breakeven, 71
  definition, 71
  net present value, 72–73
  payback, 71
  return on investment, 71–72
Cause-and-effect diagrams, 181,
  182, 248
CCPM, *See* Critical chain project
  management (CCPM)
Challenged project, 8
Change management
  assimilation, 284
  definition, 283
  and e-Health Records, 304–305
  importance of, 303
  Leavitt's model of
    organizational change, 285
  life cycle approach, 303–304
  nature of change, 284–287
    acceptance, 287
    anger, 287

bargaining, 287
change can be emotional,
  286–287
change is a process,
  285–286
denial, 286–287
depression, 287
impact of change, 284–285
at Nestlé, 301–302
planning, 287–292
  ability to change, assessing,
    287–289
  change agents, 288
  developing lessons learned,
    292
  developing/adapting a
    strategy for, 288–291
  environmental-adaptive
    approach, 291
  evaluating experience, 292
  normative-reeducation
    approach, 290
  power-coercive approach,
    290–291
  rational-empirical approach,
    289–290
  readiness, assessing,
    287–289
  sponsor, 288
  targets, 288–289
  and track progress, 291–292
  willingness, assessing,
    287–289
PRINCE2® themes, 33
Change request, 129–130
Change theory, 285
CHAOS study
  definition, 7–8
  involving the user, 19
  MOV statements, 66
  project-management approach,
    10
Charter, project, 92, 111
  acceptance and approval, 109
  assumptions and risks, 108
  measurable organizational
    value, 107
  project administration,
    108–109
  project budget, 108
  project description, 107

project identification, 106–107
project schedule, 107
project scope, 107
project stakeholders, 107
purpose of, 105–106
quality standards, 108
references, 109
resources, 108
template, 109
terminology, 109
Checklists, 180–181, 250
Chicago Police Department, 302
Chief executive officer (CEO), 5
Chief information officer (CIO), 5
Citizen Law Enforcement Analysis
and Reporting (CLEAR), 302
Citrix Systems Inc., 321
Class diagram, 41
Close-out review of project,
315–316
Closing project, 26, 310–314
administrative closure,
313–314
changed priorities, 310
definition, 307
failed, 310
final meeting and presentation,
313
acknowledging
contributions, 313
communicating that project
is over, 313
getting formal signoff, 313
transference of
product/system, 313
final project report, 312–313
normal, 310
perpetual, 310
premature, 310
PRINCE2®, 32
project sponsor acceptance, 312
knowledgeable sponsors,
312
shortsighted sponsors, 312
realities in, dealing with,
311–312
bugs, 311
delivery dates, 311
documentation, 311
future jobs, 311
resources, 311

sense of panic, 311
Cloud computing
arguments for, 118
basic types of, 118
description, 117
infrastructure as service, 118
platform as service, 118
software as a service, 118
CMM, See Capability maturity
model (CMM)
CMMI, See Capability maturity
model integration (CMMI)
Coaching leadership style, 264
Coercive leadership style, 263
Cohen, Dan, 303, 304
Collaboration
conflict, 294
customer collaboration over
negotiation contract, 39–40
technology, 223, 230–231
tools, 105, 230
Collect requirements, 123
Committee
governance, project, 92, 110
steering, 93
Common causes, 248
Communications, project
email, 206
face-to-face, 291
in formal organization, 206
improved, 99, 100
management, 28
and mentoring, 229
plan, 108, 205–206, 209–211,
224
information requirements,
210–211
medium/format, 211
stakeholders, 210
timings/availabilities, 211
type of report/metric, 211
project plan, 205–206, 209–211
small and larger projects, 232
Competition in IT projects, 11
Competitive forces model, 60
Complementary skills, 271
Complex process, 229
Compromise, 294
Computer technology, 5, 121
Computerworld, 142–143, 277,
321

Cones, Michael, 257
Confidence, ethics and, 268
Conflict
accommodation, 294
avoidance, 294
collaboration, 294
compromise, 294
contemporary view, 293
dealing with, 293–294
forcing, 294
higher potential for, 100–101
interactionist view, 293
interest and ethics, 268
between quality and speed, 255
traditional view, 293
Constant, David, 256
Contemporary view of conflict,
293
Contingency plans, 192
Contingency reserves, 162, 192
Continuous improvement, 236
Continuous probability
distributions, 186–191, 195
Monte Carlo simulation,
189–191
normal distribution, 186–187
PERT distribution, 187–188
simulations, 188–189
triangular distribution, 188, 189
Contracts, 111
closure of, 104
cost-reimbursable, 103–104
cost-plus-fee, 104
cost-plus-fixed-fee, 104
cost-plus-incentive-fee, 104
cost-plus-percentage-of-cost,
104
customer collaboration over
negotiation, 39–40
definition, 103
fixed-price, 103
lump-sum, 103
between sellers and buyers,
103–104
time and materials, 103
Control charts, for quality
management, 247–248
assignable cause, 248
common causes, 248
process not within statistical
control, 248

process within statistical control, 248
statistical control, 248
Control of project, 207–209
    plan, 26
    procedure, 129–130
    quality, 239, 247–251
    risk, 174
    scope, 128–130
Corless, Ken, 323, 324
Corporate resources, ethics and, 268–269
Corporate Standards System (CSS), 302
Corrective actions, 30, 94, 209, 212, 247
Cost estimation, 161–162
Cost management, 27
Cost of task, 161
Cost performance index (CPI), 217, 220
Cost variance (CV), 217, 220
Cost-plus-fee (CPF), 104
Cost-plus-fixed-fee (CPFF), 104
Cost-plus-incentive-fee (CPIF), 104
Cost-plus-percentage-of-cost (CPPC), 104
Cost-reimbursable contracts, 103–104
    cost-plus-fee, 104
    cost-plus-fixed-fee, 104
    cost-plus-incentive-fee, 104
    cost-plus-percentage-of-cost, 104
Covey, Steven, 277
CPI, See Cost performance index (CPI)
Craftsmanship, quality philosophies, 237
Crash, project, 155
Credibility
    cross-functional team, 68
    project managers and, 209
Crisis management, 173
Critical chain, 157
Critical chain project management (CCPM), 157–159, 165
Critical path
    analysis, 154–155
    definition, 154, 165

Critical path method (CPM), 155
Crosby, Phillip, 239–240
Cross-functional teams
    business case formation
        access to real costs, 68
        agreement, 69
        bridge building, 69
        credibility, 68
        organizational goal alignment, 68
        ownership, 68
    and multicultural teams, 299–300
Cruxes, 131–132
Culture
    definition, 266, 274
    project environment, 105
Cumulative probability distribution, 190
Curran, Chris, 323
Currency exchange, in international projects, 272
Customer, 31
    Agile Manifesto principles, 40
    satisfaction, 243
Customer relationship management (CRM), 124, 322
Cutoff rate, 72
CV, See Cost variance (CV)

D

Daily Scrum, 41
Dashboard metric, 212
Data center, 116–118
Data mining, 84–85
    pattern-based, 84
    subject-based, 84
Data processing (DP) manager, 5
Database administrator (DBA), 163
Davidson, J., 290–291
Death march project, 135
Decision making
    ethical, 92
    governance, project, 94
    improving, 70
Decision trees, 183–185, 200–201
Defect
    costs of product/system, 236
    definition, 244, 252
    prevention, 243–244

Deliverable structure chart (DSC)
    definition, 125, 126
    developing WBS, 132
    professional-looking document, 141–142
    to WBS, 141, 142
Deliverables, 125
    documentation of, 128
    and milestones, 131–132
    project-oriented, 125
    types, 125
Delivery dates, meeting, 311
Dell, 299
Delphi technique, 134–136, 180
DeMarco, Tom, 200
Deming Prize, 238
Deming, W. Edwards, 238–239
Democratic leadership style, 264
Denial, in organizational change, 286–287
Depression, in organizational change, 287
Depth, of learning, 46
Description, project, 107
Design phase, SDLC, 34–35
Dewey, John, 42
Diagrams
    cause-and-effect, 181, 182, 248
    fishbone, 182, 249–250
    Ishikawa diagram, 181, 249–250
    project network, 153–157
        activity on the node, 153–154
        critical path analysis, 154–155, 160
        definition, 153
        precedence diagramming method, 155–157
        program evaluation and review technique, 155, 156
Digital convergence, 6
Dilemmas, ethical, 268–269
Direct costs, 162
Direct cutover approach to implementation, 307–309, 317
Direct project, PRINCE2®, 32
Direct/up-front costs, 70
Discount rate, 72
Discrete probability distributions, 186, 194–195

Distelhorst, Mike, 279
Distributions
    binomial probability, 186
    cumulative probability, 190
    information, 222–223
    normal, 186–187
    PERT, 187–188
    triangular, 188, 189
Diversity
    definition, 273, 274
    understanding, 273
Documentation
    closing project, 311
    of deliverables, 128
    working software over
        comprehensive, 39
Driving forces, 285–286
DSC, *See* Deliverable structure
    chart (DSC)
Duncan, William, 168
Dunn, Jeri, 300–302
Duplication
    of effort, 100
    functional structures, 98

E

EAC, *See* Estimate at completion
    (EAC)
Earned value (EV), 213–216,
    220–221
Economic feasibility, 69
Edelman, Russ, 87
Effectiveness, 11
Efficiency, in IT projects, 11
EHRs, *See* Electronic health
    records (EHRs)
Electronic commerce (EC), 35
Electronic data processing (EDP),
    5
Electronic health records (EHRs),
    304–305
Electronic mail, for information
    distribution, 223
Elevator pitch, 83–84
Elevator speech, 83–84
Elgan, Mike, 280, 281
Emotional intelligence, 264–265
    self-awareness, 265
    self-management, 265
    social awareness, 265
    social skills, 265

Emotions in organizational
    change, 286–287
End user license agreement
    (EULA), 254
Enterprise resource planning
    (ERP), 169
    and change management at
        Nestlé, 301–302
    impacts of implementation
        failure, 322–323
    implementation, 278–279
    phased approach, 308
Environment, project, 111
    culture, 105
    office supplies, 105
    place to call home, 105
    technology, 105
Environmental-adaptive approach,
    291
Epic Systems Corp., 321
ERP, *See* Enterprise resource
    planning (ERP)
Estimate at completion (EAC),
    218, 220
Estimate to Complete (ETC), 221
Estimation, 134–138, *See also*
    Project estimation
    analogous estimation, 136
    bottom-up estimating, 136
    cost estimation, 161
    Delphi technique, 134–135
    estimate at completion, 218
    guesstimating, 134
    poker planning, 136–138
    and politics, 143
    time boxing, 135
    top-down estimating, 135
Ethical leadership, 266–268
Ethically neutral leadership, 267
Ethics in projects, 265–270
    behaviors, policies, and
        technology, 279–281
    common ethical dilemmas,
        268–269
        conficts of interest, 268
        confidence, 268
        corporate resources,
            268–269
        human resource situations,
            268
    culture, 266

definition, 265
    ethical decisions making,
        269–270
        check your intuition, 270
        consider your character and
            integrity, 270
        define the ethical issue, 269
        gather the facts, 269
        identify the affected
            stakeholders, 269
        identify the consequences,
            269
        identify the obligations,
            269–270
        think creatively about
            potential actions, 270
    ethics and legality, 266
EV, *See* Earned value (EV)
Evaluation, project, 26
    individual performance review,
        314–315
    postmortem review, 315–316
    project audit, 316
    project close-out review,
        315–316
    success of project, 316–317
    types of, 314–317
Execution
    phase PMBOK® Guide, 30
    project plan, 26
Expectations for IT projects, 11
Expected monetary value (EMV),
    200
Expected value
    concept of, 183
    of payoff table, 183
Expedite, 155
Expeditionary Combat Support
    System, 7
Exploitation, risk strategies,
    191–192
External risks, 3
eXtreme programming (XP),
    40–41, 48, 146–147
*Extreme Programming Explained:
    Embrace Change,* 145

F

FAA NextGen Air Traffic Control
    Project, 20
Face-to-face meetings, 222–223

Fact-based management, 244
Failed closure, 310
Failed project, 8, *See also* Project failure, reasons for
Fast tracking, 25, 155
Feasibility
    economic feasibility, 69
    ethical feasibility, 70
    legal feasibility, 70
    organizational feasibility, 69–70
    technical feasibility, 69
FedEx, 56
Final project report, 312–313
Financial models
    breakeven, 71
    definition, 71
    net present value, 72–73
    payback, 71
    return on investment, 71–72
Finish-to-finish (FF), 156
Finish-to-start (FS), 155–156
Firefighting, 173
Fishbone diagrams, 182, 249–250
Fisher, John F., 323–324
Fixed-price contracts, 103
Flawed estimates, budget, 198
Flexibility
    affiliative leadership style, 263
    in organizations, 98
Flight Reservation System, 107
Float, 154, 165
Focus
    on customer satisfaction, 243
    improving, 100
    on specific behaviors, not the individual, 315
Food, international projects and, 273
Force-field analysis, 285
Forcing, conflict, 294
Forecast reporting, 222
Formal organization, 205, 206, 223
Fortune magazine, 267
Friedman, Thomas L., 6
Full-insourcing approach, 101–102
Full-outsourcing approach, 102
Functional matrix, 96
Functional organization, 96–99
    advantages, 98

    breadth and depth of knowledge and experience, 98
    increased flexibility, 98
    less duplication, 98
    disadvantages, 98–99
    determining authority and responsibility, 98
    poor integration, 99
    poor response time, 98–99
    structure, 96–99
Funding of IT projects, 6–7

G

Gantt charts, 151–152, 165, *See also* Project network diagrams
    in Microsoft Project®, 160
    for planning, 152
    reporting project's progress, 152
Gantt, Henry L., 151
Gilbert, Jonathan, 303–304
Glass, Robert, 8
Global positioning system (GPS) technology, 20
Globalization, 6, 13
Goals, project, 25–26
Goldratt, Eliyahu, 157–158
Goleman, Daniel, 264, 265
Governance, project, 92, 110
    accountability, 94
    authorization, 94
    committee, 92, 110
    decision making, 94
    framework, 93
    oversight, 94
    purpose of project charter, 106
    resources, 94
    structure, 92–94
Grade, 234, 251
Greenspun, Harry, 305
Greiner, Lynn, 116–117
Groups
    project management process, 29–31
    work, 270
Guantanamo system, 85
Guesstimating, 134
Guide to the Project Management Body of Knowledge (PMBOK© Guide), 2

H

Hagerup, Bill, 323
Handler, Tom, 304–305
Hanley Center in Florida, 257
Harbert, Tam, 257, 279, 280
Harrin, Elizabeth, 202
Hartsfield-Jackson International Airport, 171–172
Hayes, Will, 256
Headstrong Corp., 202
HealthConnect system, 321–322
Herren, Scott, 321
Hruska, Joe, 257, 258
Hubbard, Douglas, 83
Hugos, Michael, 53
Human resources
    management, 27
    plan, 109
    situations, 268
Human side of project management
    functional organization, 96–99
    matrix organization, 100–101
    project organization, 99–100
Humphrey, Watts, 240, 255–257
Hurdle rate, 72
Husky Air Assignment—Pilot Angels
    change management plan, 297–298
    earned value analysis, 225–226
    getting started with learning cycles, 50–51
    implementation and project closure plan, 319
    MOV and business case, 78–80
    nature of IT projects, 14–16
    project infrastructure, 112–113
    project schedule and budget, 166–167
    quality management plan, 253
    risk management plan, 197
    scope management plan and WBS, 140–141
    time for leadership, 275–276
Hybrid organization, 96
Hypocritical leadership, 267

I

Identification, project, 106–107

If Japan Can, Why Can't We
    documentary, 238
Immeasurability, as illusion, 83
Implementation of project,
    307–309
    definition, 306
    direct cutover approach,
        307–309, 317
    parallel approach, 308, 309, 317
    phased approach, 308–309, 317
Improvement, quality, 239
Indirect costs, 70, 162
Individual performance review in
    project evaluation, 314–315
Informal organization, 205, 206
Information distribution, 222–223
    collaboration technology, 223
    electronic mail, 223
    face-to-face meetings, 222–223
    telephone in, 223
    wireless devices, 223
Information technology project
    management (ITPM), *See also*
    Project management
    competition, 11
    efficiency and effectiveness, 11
    expectations, 11
    funding, 6–7
    resources, 11
    value measure problem, 83
Infrastructure
    hardware and, 88
    project, 92, 105–106, 110
        component, 93
        purpose of, 105–106
Initiate project, PRINCE2®, 32
Initiating sponsor, 288
Inspections, 246
Intangible benefits, 70
Integration
    functional organization, 99
    high level of, 99, 100
    management, 27
Interactionist view of conflict, 293
Interdependent tasks, 3
Internal risks, 3
International projects, challenges
    of, 272–273
    attitude toward work and time,
        273
    currency exchange, 272

food, 273
language, 273
number of locations, 272
political instability, 273
regulations and laws, 273
religion, 273
Interpersonal skills, 96
Interviewing, 180
Intranets, 70, 153, 231
Ishikawa diagram, 181, 249–250
Ishikawa, Kaoru, 248–249
Isolation, project, 99

J
James, Tom, 301
Johnson, Boris, 202
Jones, T. Capers, 134
Juran, Joseph, 239

K
Kaiser e-Health records
    management system
    implementation, 321–322
Kaiser Foundation Health Plan,
    321–322
Kanaracus, Chris, 169
Katzenbach, Jon R., 271, 272
Kerzner, Harold, 76
Kick-off meeting, 164
Kill points, 25
Killing a project, 320
Knowledge management
    OPM3®, 255
    project environment, 105
    for project success, 11
Knowledgeable sponsors, 312
Known risks, 177–179
Known–unknown risks,
    177–179
Koch, Frank, 256
Kotter, John, 261
Kouzes, J., 261–262
Kübler-Ross, Elizabeth, 286
Kumari, R., 267

L
Lag times, 157, 165
Language, international projects
    and, 273
Lawsuit

failed ERP implementation
    results in, 278
IT project management, 7
Lead times, 157, 165
Leadership, 261
    emotional intelligence,
        264–265
    ethical leadership, 266–268
    ethically neutral leadership, 267
    hypocritical leadership, 267
    and listening, 277
    modern approaches to, 261–263
        challenge the process, 262
        enable others to act, 262
        encourage the heart, 263
        inspire a shared vision, 262
        model the way, 261–262
    practices for, 274
    styles, 263–264
        affiliative style, 263
        authoritative style, 263
        coaching style, 264
        coercive style, 263
        democratic style, 264
        pacesetting style, 264
    teams and, 270–272
        commitment to a common
            approach, 271
        complementary skills, 271
        mutual accountability, 271
        real teams, 271–272
        small number of people, 271
        work group, 270
    unethical leadership, 267
Learning curve, 162
Learning cycles, 48, 105, 180
    action plan example, 44
    and lessons learned, 42–46
    over project life cycle, 45
    phases
        act, 43–44
        plan, 43
        reflect and learn, 44–45
        understand and frame
            problem, 42–43
    record, 44
    team learning
        breadth, 46
        depth, 46
        speed, 46
    theory, 42

Leavitt's model of organizational change, 285
Lessons learned
    from experiences on project, 53–54
    learning cycles and, 42–46
    PRINCE2®, 34
Lewin, Kurt, 285, 295
Life cycle approach, change management, 303–304
Linear task, 150
Lines of code (LOC), 146, 147
Listening, leadership and, 277
Lister, Timothy, 200
Low-quality software, acceptance of, 254
Lump-sum contracts, 103

M

Maintenance, SDLC, 35
Management information system (MIS), 5
Management plan
    change management plan, 109, 287–292
        ability to change, assessing, 287–289
        change agents, 288
        developing lessons learned, 292
        developing/adapting a strategy for, 288–291
        environmental-adaptive approach, 291
        evaluating experience, 292
        normative-reeducation approach, 290
        power-coercive approach, 290–291
        rational-empirical approach, 289–290
        readiness, assessing, 287–289
        sponsor, 288
        targets, 288–289
        and track progress, 291–292
        willingness, assessing, 287–289
    quality, 109
    scope, 108, 123
Management reserves, 192

Management reviews, 247
Managers, project, 94–95
Managing project risk, 199–200, *See also* Project management
    analysis, 181–191
        Monte Carlo simulation, 189–191
        qualitative approaches, 183–185
        quantitative approaches, 186–191
    aviate, navigate, and communicate, 202–203
    creating risk plan, 176
    effective, 174, 175
    identifying risks, 176–182
        applying framework, 178–179
        brainstorming, 180
        cause-and-effect diagrams, 181, 182
        checklists, 180–181
        Delphi technique, 180
        framework, 176–179
        interviewing, 180
        known risks, 177–178
        known–unknown risks, 177, 178
        learning cycles, 180
        nominal group technique, 180
        past projects, 182
        SWOT analysis, 181
        unknown–unknown risks, 177, 178
    mistakes in, 174
    outsourcing, 201–202
    PMBOK® Guide, 175, 194
    probabilities, 200–201
    processes, 175
    requirement
        commitment by all stakeholders, 174
        different risks for different types of projects, 174
        stakeholder responsibility, 174
    risk monitoring and control, 193
        risk audits, 193
        risk reviews, 193

        risk status meetings and reports, 193
        risk response and evaluation, 193
        risk strategies, 191–193
            acceptance, 192
            accept/ignore, 192
            avoidance, 192
            contingency plans, 192
            contingency reserves, 192
            enhancement, 192
            exploitation, 191–192
            management reserves, 192
            mitigate, 192
            sharing of ownership, 192
            transfer, 192
    successful, 174
Martial Arts Academy (MAA)—School Management System
    change management plan, 298
    earned value analysis, 227–228
    getting started with learning cycles, 51–53
    implementation and project closure plan, 319
    MOV and business case, 80–82
    nature of IT projects, 16–19
    project infrastructure, 113–114
    project schedule and budget, 167
    quality management plan, 253
    risk management plan, 197–198
    scope management plan and WBS, 141–142
    time for leadership, 276
Matrix organization, 100–101
    advantages, 100
        high level of integration, 100
        improved communication, 100
        increased project focus, 100
    disadvantages, 100–101
        higher potential for conflict, 100–101
        poorer response time, 101
McDonald, Dave, 299
McKee, A., 265
Measurable organizational value (MOV), 107, 120, 149

appropriate metric, developing, 64–65
  money, 64
  numeric value, 64
  percentage, 64
be agreed upon, 61
be measurable, 61
be verifiable, 61
business case, 59–60
change management, 283
clear/concise statement/table, summarizing, 65–66
closing project, 307
competitive forces model, 60
definition, 59
desired areas of project impact, identifying, 63
desired value of IT project, identifying
  better, 63–64
  cheaper, 63–64
  do more, 63–64
  faster, 63–64
evaluating project success, 316–317
healthy living awareness, process summary, 66, 67
mission statement, 60
project alignment, 60
project goal, 61
and project objectives, 61–62
project stakeholders agreement, verifying, 65
project's scope, 121, 122, 124
provide value, 61
purpose of project charter, 105
statements examples, 66
table format examples, 66
time frame setup for achieving, 65
verification of, 128
vision statement, 60
Meetings
  face-to-face, 222–223
  final, 313
  team, 50
Mentoring, communication and, 229
Messmer, Ellen, 257
Meta Group Inc., 202
Methodology, project, 10, 24, 46

advantages, 25
PMBOK® Guide, 27–28
  communications management, 28
  cost management, 27
  human resource management, 27
  integration management, 27
  procurement management, 28
  quality management, 27
  risk management, 28
  stakeholder management, 28
  time management, 27
PRINCE2®
  principles, 33
  processes, 31–32
  themes, 32–33
Metrics, 252
  project, 211–222
    burn-down chart, 213
    cost effective, 212
    definition, 211
    earned value, 213–216
    forecasting performance, 218–222
    high impact, 212
    performance, 216–218
    proven, 212
    quantifiable, 212
    team's role, 212
    understandable, 211
  quality, 244–246
    process category, 244–245
    product category, 245
    project category, 245
Meyer, Dean, 117
Michael Baker Corp., 320
Micro era projects, 5, 13
Microsoft's SharePoint®
  change management, 88
  communities, 87
  community participation, 88
  composites, 87
  consulting costs, 88
  content, 87
  governance, 88
  hard savings, 89
  hardware and infrastructure, 88
  insights, 87
  IT staff, 88

Microsoft SQL Server® Licenses, 88
product licenses, 87
quality assurance, 88
risk mitigation, 89
search, 87
sites, 87
soft savings, 89
third-party vendors, 88
training, 88
virus protection and backup, 88
Windows Server®, 88
Milestones
  deliverables and, 131
  identification of, 128
  for phase/deliverable, 141, 142
  work breakdown structure, 131–132
Minor variances, in budget, 198–199
Mission statement, 60
Mochal, Tom, 232
Moczar, Lajos, 54
Monitoring project, 207–209
Monte Carlo simulation, 195
  cumulative probability distribution from, 190
  and decision tree analysis, 200–201
  description, 189–191
  Tornado Graph from, 191
Moody's Investors Service's, 299
MOV, See Measurable organizational value (MOV)
Mueller, John, 57
Multicultural projects, 272–274
  diversity, understanding, 273
  international projects, challenges of, 272–273
    attitude toward work and time, 273
    currency exchange, 272
    food, 273
    language, 273
    number of locations, 272
    political instability, 273
    regulations and laws, 273
    religion, 273
Multicultural teams, 299–300
Mythical Man-Month, The (Brooks), 143

N

Nature of IT projects
early 1970s, 6
early 1980s, 5
EDP era, 5, 13
globalization, 6, 13
in late 1960s, 6
micro era, 5, 13
network era, 6, 13
Nelson, K. A., 265, 269
Net cash flow, 72–73
NET (net) Inc., 323
Net present value (NPV), 72–73
Network era project, 6, 13
Nolan, Richard, 5
Nominal group technique (NGT), 180
Nonaka, Ikujiro, 38
Normal closure, 310
Normal distribution, 186–187
Normative-reeducation approach, 290

O

Objectives, project, 61–62
Offshoring, 101
On Death and Dying (Kübler-Ross), 286
Ongoing costs, 70
OPM3®, 254–255
Organization
functional organization, 96–99
advantages, 98
disadvantages, 98–99
structure, 96–99
matrix organization, 100–101
advantages, 100
disadvantages, 100–101
project, 99–100
advantages, 99
disadvantages, 99–100
pure project organization, 99
Organizational change, 3–4
managing, 283, *See also* Change management
Organizational environment, 4
Organizational feasibility, 69–70
Organizational goal, 68
Organizational governance, 92, 93
Organizational infrastructure, 11, 35

Organizational structure
functional, 96–99
matrix, 100–101
project, 99–100
Otterholt, Barry, 203
Ouelette & Associates Consulting, Inc., 323
Out of the Crisis (Deming), 239
Outsourcing
business process outsourcing, 101
definition, 101
full-insourcing approach, 101
full-outsourcing approach, 102
managing project risk, 201–202
project model, 102
Oversight, project governance, 94
Ownership, 68
attributes, project, 2
cross-functional teams, 68
sharing of, 192
total benefits of ownership, 70
accuracy and efficiency, 70
customer service improvement, 70
decision making, 70
high-value work, 70
total cost of ownership, 70
direct or up-front costs, 70
indirect costs, 70
ongoing costs, 70

P

Pacesetting leadership style, 264
Parallel activity, 153, 165
Parallel approach to implementation, 308, 309, 317
Parallel task, 150, 151
Pareto charts, 249–251
Parkinson's law, 158
Past projects, 182
Pattern-based data mining, 84
Paul, Lauren Gibbons, 116–117
Payback cash flow model, 71
Payoff table, 183
PDM, *See* Precedence diagramming method (PDM)
Peer reviews, 246
Percent complete, 39, 135, 157, 219, 222
Performance

Agile Manifesto principles, 40
analyzing current, 216–218
forecasting, 218–222
index
cost, 217
schedule, 217
process, 240
reporting, 222
team, 270–272
real teams, 271–272
work group, 270
Perkins, Bart, 169, 277
Permanent variances, in budget, 198
Perpetual closure, 310
Personal computer (PC), 13
PERT, *See* Program evaluation and review technique (PERT)
Pfizer, 302
Phases
approach to implementation, 308–309, 317
definition, 149–150
exits, 25
Phillis, Terry, 322
Philosophies
craftsmanship, 237
quality, 237–240
scientific management, 238
TQM gurus, 238–240
Plan procurements, 102–103
Planned budget, 214, 217, 219
Planned value (PV), 213, 215, 216, 220
Planning phase
definition, 91, 110
SDLC, 34
Planning, project, 26, 96–101, 106, 168–169, *See also* Project communications; Project planning framework
Gantt charts for, 152
for success, 169–172
PLC, *See* Project life cycle (PLC)
PMBOK® Guide, *See* Project Management Body of Knowledge (PMBOK®) Guide
PMI®, *See* Project Management Institute (PMI®)
PMO, *See* Project management office (PMO)

PMP®, *See* Project Management Professional (PMP®)
Poker planning, 136–138
Polaris missile project, 5, 13
Political instability, international projects and, 273
Politics, project estimation and, 143
Porter, Michael, 60
Portfolio of projects, 4
Posner, B., 261–262
Post-implementation audit, 320
Postmortem review, 315–316
Power-coercive approach, 290–291
Pratt, Mary, 279, 280
Precedence diagramming method (PDM), 155–157, 165
    advantage, 157
    finish-to-finish, 156
    finish-to-start, 155–156
    start-to-finish, 156
    start-to-start, 156
Predecessors activity, 153, 165
Premature closure, 310
Presentation, of project, 313
Price Systems, 170
Price-Waterhouse Coopers (PWC), 55
Primavera®, 169–171
PRINCE2®, *See* PRojects IN Controled Environments (PRINCE2®)
Probability distributions
    binomial, 186
    continuous, 186–191, 195
        Monte Carlo simulation, 189–191
        normal distribution, 186–187
        PERT distribution, 187–188
        simulations, 188–189
        triangular distribution, 188, 189
    cumulative, 190
    discrete, 186
Process
    change, 285–286
    definition, 236
    PMBOK® Guide, 28
    product-oriented, 29

project management, 29
    closing process, 30–31
    executing, 30
    initiating process group, 29
    monitoring and controlling, 30
    planning process group, 29–30
    procurement, 101–104
    subdivision, 28–29
Process Strategies, Inc., 256
Procter & Gamble, 302–303
Procurements, *See also* Project procurement management
    external project resources, 101–104
    management, 28
    plan, 102–103
Product
    Agile Manifesto principles, 40
    backlog, 41
    owner, scrum roles, 41
    scope, 125
Product release, 307–309
    definition, 306
    direct cutover approach, 307–309, 317
    parallel approach, 308, 309, 317
    phased approach, 308–309, 317
Product-oriented processes, 29, 35
Product-oriented scope, 125–128
Program evaluation and review technique (PERT), 165
    activities for, 156
    distribution, 187–188, 195
    estimation, 155
    project network diagrams, 155
Progress reporting, 222
Project
    alignment, 60
    attributes of
        interdependent tasks, 3
        organizational change, 3–4
        organizational environment, 4
        ownership, 2
        project roles, 3
        purpose, 2
        resources, 2
        risks and assumptions, 3
        time frame, 2

audit
    description, 316
    post-implementation, 320
board, 31, 93
cost management, 461
definition, 2, 12
imbalanced, 121
integration management, 27
MOV, *See* Measurable organizational value (MOV)
objectives, MOV, 61–62
organization, 99–100
plan, 151
portfolio, 4
    approval, 76
    selection, 76
resource, use of, 121
roles
    project manager/leader, 2, 3
    project sponsor, 3
    subject matter experts, 3
    technical experts, 3
selection, 59
    and approval decision, 76
    and funding process, 76
    PRINCE2®, 76
show explicit commitment to, 106
sponsor, 3
time management, 27
Project charter, 92, 111
    acceptance and approval, 109
    assumptions and risks, 108
    measurable organizational value, 107
    project administration, 108–109
    project budget, 108
    project description, 107
    project identification, 106–107
    project schedule, 107
    project scope, 107
    project stakeholders, 107
    purpose of, 105–106
    quality standards, 108
    references, 109
    resources, 108
    template, 109
    terminology, 109
Project communications
    email, 206

Project communications
    (continued)
    face-to-face, 291
    in formal organization, 206
    improved, 99, 100
    management, 28
    and mentoring, 229
    plan, 108, 224
        information requirements,
            210–211
        medium/format, 211
        stakeholders, 210
        timings/availabilities, 211
        type of report/metric, 211
    project plan, 205–206, 209–211
    small and larger projects, 232
Project environment, 105, 111
    culture, 105
    office supplies, 105
    place to call home, 105
    technology, 105
Project estimation, 134–138
    analogous estimation, 136
    bottom-up estimating, 136
    Delphi technique, 134–135
    guesstimating, 134
    poker planning, 136–138
    and politics, 143
    time boxing, 135
    top-down estimating, 135
Project failure, reasons for
    organization, 9–10
    people, 8–9
    processes, 9
    technology, 9
Project governance, 92, 110
    accountability, 94
    authorization, 94
    committee, 92, 110
    decision making, 94
    framework, 93
    oversight, 94
    purpose of project charter, 106
    resources, 94
    structure, 92–94
Project infrastructure, 92, 110
    component, 93
    purpose of, 105–106
Project life cycle (PLC), 25–27,
    46, 91, 125, See also Systems
    development life cycle (SDLC)

characteristics, 27
closing project, 26
development, 25–27
evaluation, project, 26
executing plan, 26
goal, defining, 25–26
learning cycles over, 45
planning phase, 26
and SDLC, 35, 36
Project management, 12, See also
    Managing project risk
    data processing manager, 5
    definition, 4
    modern-day project
        management, 5, 13
    processes, 29
    program, 4, 12
    project portfolio, 4
    social software for, 231–232
    software packages, 120
    software tools, 159–161
    state of
        challenged project, 8
        CHAOS study, 7
        Expeditionary Combat
            Support System, 7
        failure, reasons for, 8–10
        project success, 8
        software crisis, 7
        success, approaches for,
            10–11
    success, 120
    supporting IT projects, reasons
        for
        competition, 11
        efficiency and effectiveness,
            11
        expectations, 11
        resources, 11
    time-honored tradition, 122
    tool, 120
    user involvement, 19
Project Management Body of
    Knowledge (PMBOK®) Guide,
    27–28, 46–47, 122
    communications management,
        28
    cost management, 27
    definition, 175
    human resource management,
        27

integration management, 27
managing project risk, 175, 194
procurement management, 28
quality management, 27, 235
    perform quality assurance,
        236
    perform quality control, 236
    plan quality, 236
risk management, 28
stakeholder management, 28
time management, 27
Project Management Institute
    (PMI®), 2, 27, 55
Project management office (PMO),
    93, 99, 110
Project Management Professional
    (PMP®), 55–56
Project manager/leader, 2, 3, 12,
    94–95, 205, 210, See also Project
    estimation
    attributes, 95
    credibility, 206
Project methodologies, 24, 46
    advantages, 25
    PMBOK® Guide, 27–28
        communications
            management, 28
        cost management, 27
        human resource
            management, 27
        integration management, 27
        procurement management,
            28
        quality management, 27
        risk management, 28
        stakeholder management, 28
        time management, 27
    PRINCE2®
        principles, 33
        processes, 31–32
        themes, 32–33
Project metrics, 211–222
    burn-down chart, 213
    cost effective, 212
    definition, 211
    earned value, 213–216
    high impact, 212
    performance
        analyzing current, 216–218
        forecasting, 218–222
    proven, 212

quantifiable, 212
team's role
  adopt only a handful of
    measures, 212
  design its own measurement
    system, 212
  to gauge its progress, 212
  tracking results and
    progress, 212
understandable, 211
Project network diagrams,
  153–157
  activity on the node, 153–154
  critical path analysis, 154–155,
    160
  definition, 153
  precedence diagramming
    method, 155–157
  program evaluation and review
    technique, 155, 156
Project Ocean, 20–21, 322
Project planning framework, 149,
  150, 164
  kick-off meeting, 164
  MOV, 149
  schedule and budget, baseline
    plan, 163–164
  subdividing the project into
    phases, 149–151
  tasks, 150–151
    resources, 150
    sequence, 150
    time estimates, 150–151
Project procurement management,
  101–104
  contracts between sellers and
    buyers, 103–104
  procurement planning, 102–103
Project quality management
  (PQM), 235–236, See also
  Quality management
Project schedule, 107
  critical chain project
    management, 157–159
  developing, 151–159
  Gantt charts, 151–152
  planned, 214
  project network diagrams,
    153–157
    activity on the node,
      153–154

critical path analysis,
  154–155
precedence diagramming
  method, 155–157
program evaluation and
  review technique, 155
schedule performance index,
  217
schedule variance, 217
Project scope, 107, 122
  change procedure, 129–130
    request form, 130
    request log, 130
  collect requirements, 123
  management plan, 123
  managing and defining, 122
  scope creep, 129
  scope definition
    product-oriented scope,
      125–128
    project-oriented scope, 125
    scope boundary, 123–124
    scope statement, 124–125
    statement of work, 124
  scope grope, 128–129
  scope leap, 129
  scope management plan, 108
Project stakeholders, 107, 121, 210
  analysis, 205
    description, 206–207
    example of, 208
    informal organization, 206
    process for developing, 207
  commitment by, 174
  communications plan, 210
  definition, 206
  managing, 210
  responsibility, 174
Project success, 8
  approaches for
    knowledge-management
      approach, 11
    project-management
      approach, 10–11
    socio-technical approach, 10
    value-driven approach, 10
  measure of, MOV, 62
Project team(s), 120, 210
  Agile Manifesto principles, 40
  implementation approaches,
    307–309

definition, 306
direct cutover, 307–309
parallel, 308
phased, 308–309
project manager, 94–95
  ability to communicate with
    people, 95
  ability to create and sustain
    relationships, 95
  ability to deal with people,
    95
  ability to organize, 95
  roles of, 94–95
skills, 95–96
team selection and acquisition
  business/organization
    knowledge, 96
  interpersonal skills, 96
  technology skills, 95
Project-based matrix, 96
Project-management success
  approach, 10–11
Project-oriented deliverables, 125
Project-oriented scope, 125
PRojects IN Controled
  Environments (PRINCE2®), 47
  business case, 67
  principles, 33
    accountability, 34
    adapt to the project, 34
    business case driven, 34
    lessons learned, 34
    manage by exception, 34
    manage the stage, 34
    product focus, 34
  processes, 31–32
    close project, 32
    control stage, 32
    direct project, 32
    initiate project, 32
    manage product delivery, 32
    manage stage boundaries, 32
    start project, 31
  themes, 32–33
    business case, 32
    change, 33
    organization, 33
    planning, 33
    progress, 33
    quality, 33
    risk, 33

Prosci, 303
Pure project organization, 99
PV, *See* Planned value (PV)

Q

QA, *See* Quality assurance (QA)
Qualitative approaches, for risk
  analysis, 183–185
    decision trees, 183–185
    expected value, 183
    risk impact table, 185
Quality
  conflict between speed and, 255
  PRINCE2® themes, 33
Quality assurance (QA), 236,
  245–247, 251, 252
    testing, 247
    validation, 247
    verification
      business reviews, 246–247
      management reviews, 247
      technical reviews, 245–246
Quality control, 239, 251
  cause and effect of diagrams,
    248–249
  control charts, 247–248
    assignable cause, 248
    common causes, 248
    process not within statistical
      control, 248
    process within statistical
      control, 248
    statistical control, 248
  definition, 247–251
  fourteen points for, 239
  improvement, 239
  Pareto charts, 249–251
  planning, 239
Quality Control Handbook (Juran),
  239
Quality management, 27, 109
Quality plan, IT project
  continuous improvement, 251
  control charts, 247–248
    assignable cause, 248
    common causes, 248
    process not within statistical
      control, 248
    process within statistical
      control, 248
    statistical control, 248
  diagrams, 248–251

Ishikawa diagram, 249
Pareto charts, 249–251
pay to play, 255–257
philosophies, 237–240,
  242–244
  fact-based management, 244
  focus on customer
    satisfaction, 243
  improve process to product,
    244
  prevention, not inspection,
    243–244
  quality is everyone's
    responsibility, 244
planning, 236
PMBOK® definition, 235
  perform quality assurance,
    236
  perform quality control, 236
  plan quality, 236
quality control, 239
quality improvement, 239
quality standards, processes,
  and metrics, 244–246
scientific management, 238
speed and, 255
total quality movement,
  238–240
Quality standards, 108, 117, 128
Quantitative approaches, for risk
  analysis
    continuous probability
      distributions, 186–191
    discrete probability
      distributions, 186
    Monte Carlo simulation,
      189–191
    simulations, 188–189
    triangular distribution, 188, 189

R

Radice, Ron, 256
Rational-empirical approach,
  289–290
Reagan, Larry, 170–171
Real teams, 271–272, 274
Redding, John, 42–46
Redmond, Tony, 258
Reece, John, 280
References, project charter, 109
Regulations, in international
  projects, 273

Religion, international projects
  and, 273
Reporting performance and
  progress, 222
    forecast reporting, 222
    progress reporting, 222
    reviews, 222
    status reporting, 222
Request for bid (RFB), 124
Request for information (RFI), 124
Request for proposal (RFP), 102,
  111, 117, 124
RescueTime, 257–258
Reserves
  budget, project, 162–163
  contingency, 162, 192
  management, 192
  send in, 198–199
Resistance, dealing with, 292–293
Resisting forces, 285–286
Resources
  allocation, 163
  assignments, 141, 142
  contention, 158
  corporate, 268–269
  end of, 311
  governance, project, 94
  in IT projects, 11
  over allocation, example of, 163
  plan project, 26
  project charter and, 108
  task, 150–151, 164
  use of, 150
Response time
  functional organization, 98–99
  matrix organization, 101
Responsibility
  functional organization and, 98
  project organization and, 99
Return on investment (ROI),
  71–72
Reverse scoring, 75
Reviews
  business, 246–247
  management, 247
  postmortem, 315–316
  reporting performance and
    progress, 222
  technical, 245–246
  validate scope, 128
  walk-through, 246
RFID supply chain, 85–86

Risks, 69, *See also* Managing
 project risk
  assessment, 70
  and assumptions, 3
  identification, 70
  impact table, 185
  known risks, 177–179
  known–unknown risks,
   177–179
  management, 28
  mitigation, 89
  PRINCE2® themes, 33
  project charter, 108
  rankings, 185
  response, 70, 191
  scores, 74
  strategies, 191–193
   accept or ignore, 192
   acceptance, 192
   avoidance, 192
   contingency plans, 192
   contingency reserves, 192
   enhancement, 192
   exploitation, 191–192
   management reserves, 192
   mitigate, 192
   sharing of ownership, 192
   transfer, 192
  unknown–unknown risks, 177,
   178
Rolling wave planning, 161
Roman, Eugene, 231
Royce, Winston, 36–37
Rules of thumb, 187, 238
RWave Software, 258

S

Sarbanes-Oxley Act of2002, 92
Schedule performance index (SPI),
 217, 220
Schedule, project, 107
 critical chain project
  management, 157–159
 developing, 151–159
 Gantt charts, 151–152
 planned, 214
 project network diagrams,
  153–157
  activity on the node,
   153–154
  critical path analysis,
   154–155

precedence diagramming
 method, 155–157
program evaluation and
 review technique, 155
schedule performance index,
 217
schedule variance, 217
Schedule variance (SV), 217, 220
Scientific management of quality,
 238, 251
Scope creep, 129
Scope grope, 128–129
Scope leap, 129
Scope management processes,
 123, 138
 collect requirements, 123
 control scope, 128–130
 define scope
  product-oriented scope,
   125–128
  project-oriented scope, 125
  scope boundary, 123–124
  scope statement, 124–125
  statement of work, 124
 plan scope management, 123
 validate scope, 128
 work breakdown structure, *See*
  Work breakdown structure
  (WBS)
Scope, project, 107, 122
 change procedure, 129–130
  request form, 130
  request log, 130
 collect requirements, 123
 definition, 120, 138
 management plan, 123
 managing and defining, 122
 scope creep, 129
 scope definition
  product-oriented scope,
   125–128
  project-oriented scope, 125
  scope boundary, 123–124
  scope statement, 124–125
  statement of work, 124
 scope grope, 128–129
 scope leap, 129
 scope management plan, 108
Scoring models
 bias of financial models, 74
 comparison of project
  alternatives, 73–74

definition, 73
qualitative and quantitative
 criterions, 73
realistic business case, 75
reverse scoring, 75
risk scores, 74
subjective weights and scores,
 73–74
Scott, Robert, 232
Scrum, 48
 daily, 41
 definition, 40
 master, 41
 roles
  development team, 41
  product owner, 41
  Scrum master, 41
SDLC, *See* Systems development
 life cycle (SDLC)
SEI, *See* Software Engineering
 Institute (SEI)
Self-awareness, in leadership,
 265
Self-management, in leadership,
 265
Sellers
 contracts, 103–104
 selection, 103
Semi-Automated Business
 Research Environment
 (SABRE), 107
Senior supplier, 31
Senior user, 31
Service level agreements (SLAs),
 116–119
Sharkbait, 142–143
Shewhart, Walter, 247
Shoeniger, Eric, 169
Shortsighted sponsors, 312
Shriberg, A., 267
Shriberg, D. L., 267
Signoff, formal, 313
"Silence Fails: The Five Crucial
 Conversations for Flawless
 Execution,"232
Simulations, 188–189, *See also*
 Monte Carlo simulation
Slack, 154, 165
SLAs, *See* Service level
 agreements (SLAs)
Smith, Douglas K., 271, 272
Social awareness, 265

Social networks, 114–115, 228–229
Social responsibility, sustainability and, 299
Social skills, in leadership, 265
Social software, for project management, 231–232
Socialization, 266
Socio-technical success approach, 10
Software capability maturity, model for, *See also* Software process maturity
    low-quality software, acceptance of, 254
    process, 240
    process capability, 240
    process maturity, 240
    process performance, 240
Software crisis, 7
Software Engineering Institute (SEI), 240, 255–256
Software process capability, 240–241
Software process maturity
    defined (Level 3), 242
    initial (Level 1), 241
    managed (Level 4), 242
    optimizing (Level 5), 242
    repeatable (Level 2), 241–242
Software Secure, Inc., 280
Software tools, project management, 159–161
Speed, 255
    conflict between quality and, 255
    of learning, 46
SPI, *See* Schedule performance index (SPI)
Sponsor(s)/client(s), 114, 210
    acceptance of closure, 312
        knowledgeable sponsors, 312
        shortsighted sponsors, 312
    initiating sponsor, 288
    sustaining sponsor, 288
Sprint, 41
Stage gates, 25
Stakeholders, project, 107, 121, 210
    analysis, 205
        description, 206–207

example of, 208
    informal organization, 206
    process for developing, 207
    commitment by, 174
    communications plan, 210
    definition, 206
    managing, 210
    responsibility, 174
Standards, quality, 244–245
Start-to-finish (SF), 156
Start-to-start (SS), 156
Statement of scope, 124–125
Statement of work (SOW), 124
Statistical control, 248
Status quo, 69
Status reporting, 222
Steering committee, 93
7 Habits of Highly Effective People, The (Covey), 277
Strategies, risk, 191–193
    accept or ignore, 192
    acceptance, 192
    avoidance, 192
    contingency plans, 192
    contingency reserves, 192
    enhancement, 192
    exploitation, 191–192
    management reserves, 192
    mitigate, 192
    sharing of ownership, 192
    transfer, 192
Structure, project governance, 92–94
Student's syndrome, 158
Subcontractors, 101
Subject matter experts (SME), 3
Subject-based data mining, 84
Success
    planning for, 169–172
    project management, 120
Successors activity, 153, 165
Sunk costs, 162
Sustainability and social responsibility, 299
Sustaining sponsor, 288
SV, *See* Schedule variance (SV)
SWOT analysis, 181
Systems development life cycle (SDLC), 25, 34–42, 47, 123, 125
    Agile systems development, 38–41

core beliefs and values, 38–40
    definition, 38
    manifesto for, 38–40
    methods of, 40–41
    principles, 40
    themes/categories, 40
    waterfall model and, 41–42
    analysis phase, 34
    design phase, 34–35
    implementation, 35
    maintenance and support, 35
    planning phase, 34
    PLC and, 35, 36
    waterfall model, 36–37

T

Tabor, David, 54–55
Takeuchi, Hirotaka, 38
Tangible benefits, 70
Targets, 288–289
Tasks
    definition, 141, 142, 150, 164
    description, 150
    estimates for, 141, 142
    linear, 150
    parallel, 150, 151
    resource, 150–151, 164
Tata Consultancy Services, 8
Taylor, Frederic W., 238, 239
TCPI, *See* To complete performance index (TCPI)
Team formation, cross-functional business case
    access to real costs, 68
    agreement, 69
    bridge building, 69
    credibility, 68
    organizational goal alignment, 68
    ownership, 68
Teams
    choosing, 115–119
    development, Scrum roles, 41
    learning cycles
        act, 43–44
        action plan example, 44
        breadth of learning, 46
        depth of learning, 46
        and lessons learned, 42–46
        over project life cycle, 45
        plan, 43

record, 44
reflect and learn, 44–45
speed of learning, 46
understand and frame the problem, 42–43
meetings, 50
performance, *See also* Project team(s)
and leadership, 270–272
real teams, 271–272
work group, 270
virtual, 230–231
Technical experts (TE), 3
Technical feasibility, 69
Technical infrastructure, 69
Technical reviews, 245–246
Techniques, for risk, 179–182
Technology Partners International (TPI), 201
Technology skills, 95
Telephone, for information distribution, 223
Template, business case, 75
Terminology, project charter and, 109
Terrorism prevention, 84–85
Testing, quality assurance, 247
Texas Health Resources, Inc., 279
Thibodeau, Patrick, 118
Time and materials (T&M) contracts, 104
Time boxing, 135
Time management, 27
Time-honored project management tradition, 122
Tisch, Jim, 230
T&M contracts, *See* Time and materials (T&M) contracts
To complete performance index (TCPI), 219, 220
Top-down estimating, 135
Tornado graph, 190–191
Total benefits of ownership (TBO), 70
accuracy and efficiency, 70
customer service improvement, 70
decision making, 70
high-value work, 70
Total cost of ownership (TCO), 70
direct or up-front costs, 70
indirect costs, 70

ongoing costs, 70
Total quality movement (TQM), 238–240
Tracking, 291–292
Traditional view of conflict, 293
Trevino, L. K., 265, 269
Triangular distribution, 188, 189
Triple constraint
definition, 121, 138
relationship among scope, schedule, and budget, 121–122

U

Unethical leadership, 267
Unified Modeling Language (UML), 126
Union of Japanese scientists and engineers (JUSE), 238
Unity of command, 99, 100
Unknown–unknown risks, 177, 178
Up-front costs, 70
Use case diagram, 140–142
definition, 125–126
development of, 126
use cases and actors, 126
User friendliness, 83
User story, 40–41, 136

V

VAC, *See* Variance at completion (VAC)
Validate scope, 128
Validation, 252
activities, 247
definition, 247
quality assurance, 247
test and, 146
Value actual, 215–217
earned, 213–216
planned, 213, 215, 216
Value-driven success approach, 10
Variance at completion (VAC), 219, 220
Vasa, 144–147
Verification, 252
concept of, 245
of MOV, 128
quality assurance
business reviews, 246–247
management reviews, 247

technical reviews, 245–246
scope, 128
Verma, V. K., 293
Virtual team, 230–231
Vision statement, 60

W

Wailgum, Thomas, 146, 322, 323
Walk-through review, 246
Wal-Mart's RFID supply chain, 85–86
Walsh, Katherine, 145
Waste Management, 278, 279, 322
Waterfall model, 47, 150
advantage of, 36
and Agile systems development, 41–42, 56–57
disadvantages, 47
SDLC, 36–37
U.S. Department of Defense, 56
WBS, *See* Work breakdown structure (WBS)
WellPoint, 299
Westcott, Tom, 199
Westland, Jason, 170
Whistle blower, 269, 280
Wiki, 231–232
Wireless devices, for information distribution, 223
Wisdom of Teams, The, 270
Work breakdown structure (WBS), 120, 130–133
definition, 130
deliverables, 131–132
development, 132–133, 149
DSC to, 141, 142
milestones, 131–132
project schedule, *See* Schedule, project
scope management plan and, 140–141
work packages, 131, 133
Work group, 270, 274
Work packages, 131, 133

X

XP, *See* eXtreme programming (XP)

Y

Yourdon, Ed, 135